W0227664

Hands-On Network Machine Learning with Python

Bridging theory and practice in network data analysis, this guide offers an intuitive approach to understanding and analyzing complex networks. It covers foundational concepts, practical tools, and real-world applications using Python frameworks including NumPy, SciPy, scikit-learn, graspologic, and NetworkX.

Readers will learn to apply network machine learning techniques to real-world problems, transform complex network structures into meaningful representations, leverage Python libraries for efficient network analysis, and interpret network data and results. The book explores methods for extracting valuable insights across various domains such as social networks, ecological systems, and brain connectivity. Hands-on tutorials and concrete examples develop intuition through visualization and mathematical reasoning. The book will equip data scientists, students, and researchers in applications using network data with the skills to confidently tackle network machine learning projects, providing a robust toolkit for data science applications involving network-structured data.

Eric W. Bridgeford is a postdoctoral scholar in the Department of Psychology at Stanford University. Eric's background includes Computer Science, Bioengineering, and Biostatistics, and he develops methods for veridical data science. Eric is interested in biases presenting inferential obstacles to neuroscience, and how these limitations challenge analytical approaches and clinical adoption of neuroimaging methods.

Alexander R. Loftus is a doctoral student in David Bau's group in the Department of Computer Science at Northeastern University, studying interpretability in deep neural networks. He has worked on implementing network algorithms in Python. He won first place in a $100,000 Kaggle competition and has published work in top AI/ML conferences.

Joshua T. Vogelstein is Associate Professor of Biomedical Engineering at Johns Hopkins University. His research intersects natural and artificial intelligence, applying machine learning to biomedical challenges. He has published extensively in top scientific and AI venues, received numerous grants, and cofounded successful startups in quantitative finance and software development.

"Networks are everywhere these days. The exponential growth of network datasets demands ever more sophisticated, flexible and scalable modeling techniques. This book provides a concise introduction to basic concepts, mathematical foundations, and algorithmic approaches in network analysis. Highly recommended to all practitioners, students, and professionals alike."

Olaf Sporns, *Distinguished Professor, Indiana University Bloomington*

Hands-On Network Machine Learning with Python

ERIC W. BRIDGEFORD
Stanford University

ALEXANDER R. LOFTUS
Northeastern University

JOSHUA T. VOGELSTEIN
The Johns Hopkins University

CAMBRIDGE
UNIVERSITY PRESS

Shaftesbury Road, Cambridge CB2 8EA, United Kingdom

One Liberty Plaza, 20th Floor, New York, NY 10006, USA

477 Williamstown Road, Port Melbourne, VIC 3207, Australia

314–321, 3rd Floor, Plot 3, Splendor Forum, Jasola District Centre, New Delhi – 110025, India

103 Penang Road, #05–06/07, Visioncrest Commercial, Singapore 238467

Cambridge University Press is part of Cambridge University Press & Assessment, a department of the University of Cambridge.

We share the University's mission to contribute to society through the pursuit of education, learning and research at the highest international levels of excellence.

www.cambridge.org
Information on this title: www.cambridge.org/9781009405393

DOI: 10.1017/9781009405379

First published 2025

Cover image: Courtesy of Ben Pedigo

A catalogue record for this publication is available from the British Library

A Cataloging-in-Publication data record for this book is available from the Library of Congress

ISBN 978-1-009-40539-3 Paperback

Contents

Preface

The Network Machine Learning Earthquake

In the early 1990s, a Stanford University Computer Science PhD student named Larry Page turned his attention to the the world wide web.

With colleague Sergey Brin, Page conceptualized the complex web of document links on the web as a large *network*, where a link from one page allows navigation to another. Page and Brin theorized that the number of incoming links to a document indicated its "popularity," which they called the *page rank*. The pair developed a query system to parse sentences into keywords and an indexing system mapping keywords to high-ranking pages. After publishing with other computer scientists, Page and Brin developed the Google search Engine prototype in 1998 and founded Google, Inc. shortly after.

Networks have since become a dominant data structure for understanding many everyday concepts. Social networks ushered in a new era of human interconnectedness, led by multibillion dollar corporations such as Meta (Facebook), X (Twitter), LinkedIn, Instagram, Douyin (TikTok), and WeChat. The global economy forms an interconnected network of companies and countries engaged in daily trade. The Earth's food chain constitutes an ecological network where plants and animals compete for survival. Neurons of the brain form a web of axons and synapses, uniquely producing an individual identity.

Network Machine Learning in your Projects

Network science has advanced rapidly, providing new strategies for deriving insights about the world. Its researchers can expose shadowy financial networks and corporate fraud, or create frameworks for measuring healthcare teamwork. Ecologists can model relationships between animal species, while neuroscientists can map neuronal communities in the brain. Data scientists can view diverse company data – from user logs to financial records to sensor data – as networks, revealing hidden insights.

Whatever your motivation, exploring and exploiting networks for analysis is a worthy endeavor.

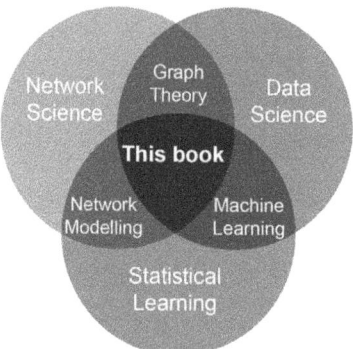

Figure 0.0.1 Broadly, we think that the techniques developed and described in this book fall somewhere in the middle of this Venn diagram.

Objective and Approach

This book assumes minimal prior knowledge of network analysis. Its goal is to equip readers with the concepts, the intuitions, and tools needed to apply statistical learning and data science techniques to network data, as illustrated in Figure 0.0.1.

We will cover the fundamentals of network machine learning, focusing on developing intuition through both theory and relevant `python` code. By the end of this book, readers will be able to utilize efficient, easy-to-use tools for network anlaysis. The text introduces a range of new techniques, including representations, theory, and algorithms for networks.

We will demonstrate these concepts using production-ready `python` frameworks:

1. `numpy` [1] and `scipy` [2] provide scientific computing capabilities, including array objects for computational network representation and linear algebra techniques.
2. `scikit-learn` [3] offers efficient implementations of many machine learning algorithms, serving as an excellent starting point for network analysis.
3. `graspologic` [4] and `networkx` [5] are open-source Python packages that provide utilities and algorithms for network-valued data analysis.

Our approach emphasizes intuitive understanding of networks through concrete working examples and foundational theory. While the book can be read without a computer, we strongly encourage readers to experiment with the code examples.

Many languages and software packages support network analysis, but time constraints prevent us from covering all of them: `matlab` offers numerous built-in utilities, while R's `igraph` package [6] provides functionality complementary to the techniques we discuss.

Readers unfamiliar with `python` versed in other languages should not find this a significant obstacle. Working through the examples provides ample opportunity to acquire new programming skills.

Prerequisites

Network science is fundamentally rooted in linear algebra. We expect readers to have some familiarity with vectors, matrices, and basic operations on these objects such as vector/matrix multiplication and addition.

A background in machine learning will enhance understanding of the book's concepts. Much of the content relates to *statistical learning*, which integrates statistics with machine learning. We assume basic familiarity with probability and statistics, such as coin flip models (Bernoulli trials) and expected values of random quantities (means). The main content of the book uses formal mathematics as a supplementary tool to develop intuition (rather than rigorous proofing).

Some programming experience is beneficial, as we use `python`. Those with limited Python or math background need not worry – we provide resources to get started.

We also employ `jupyter`, a useful and easy-to-learn tool. We offer resources for those unfamiliar with Python's scientific libraries, and provide a preconfigured programming environment via `docker` which is version controlled for all packages in the text [7].

For readers interested in the underlying mechanics, appendices cover the theoretical foundations of the techniques discussed. These sections assume college-level understanding of calculus, linear algebra, probability, and statistics.

Roadmap

This book is organized into four parts.

Part I Foundations introduces network machine learning and demonstrates solving a complete problem. It covers:
- What a network is and sources of data,
- Motivations for studying networks,
- Examples of ways you could apply network machine learning to your own projects,
- An overview of the types of problems network machine learning is good at dealing with, and
- Exploring a real network machine learning dataset.

Part II Representations explores network conceptualization and representation methods. Topics include:
- Properties of different network types,
- Preparation of network data for analysis,
- How to conceptualize networks with statistical models, and the utility of this point of view,
- Network representation methods and their utility,
- Transforming networks into tabular forms, both individual networks and groups of networks, and
- How to incorporate additional information (attributions) to networks.

Part III Applications is about exploiting the representations from Part II for downstream learning tasks. It covers the following topics:

- Figuring out if communities in networks are different from each other,
- Selecting reasonable statistical models to represent the data,
- Finding interesting nodes, edges, or communities,
- Finding anomolous time points in networks which are evolving over time,
- Handling new data after model training,
- How hypothesis testing works with networks,
- Figuring out which nodes are the most similar in a pair of networks, and
- Diffusion methods and graph neural networks.

The appendices provide mathematical background for curious readers; these sections present technical details omitted from the main text.

Other Resources

Numerous resources compliment the content of this book.

For readers new to machine learning, we recommend Aurélian Géron's excellent work [8] as a starting point. Key ideas to familiarize oneself with include types of machine learning problems, common algorithms and techniques (e.g., K-Means, testing, validation), and basic machine learning data structures.

To our knowledge, this is the first book to explicitly focus on network machine learning for single and multiple network problems with a programming component. For broader exposure to networks, we recommend:

1. "Network Science" [9], an accessible introduction to network science.
2. "Networks" [10], an overview of the mathematics of networks and network models.
3. "Python for Graph and Network Analysis" [11], network analysis techniques in Python.
4. "Network Analysis" [12], network data structures and summary statistics.
5. "A User's Guide to Network Analysis in R" [13], hands-on network analytics in R.
6. "Statistical Analysis of Network Data" [14], statistical models and methods for network science.

Readers needing a linear algebra refresher may find the first two lectures of "Numerical Linear Algebra" [15] helpful for later chapters of the book. Basic statistics and statistical inference knowledge is also beneficial; the ability to understand the top portion of the Wikipedia summaries of "random variable," "normal distribution," and "Bernoulli distribution" should suffice.

For a more comprehensive statistical overview, we recommend "Statistical Inference" [16] or "Mathematical Statistics" [17]. An explicit introduction to statistical learning, such as "An Introduction to Statistical Learning" [18], may also prove valuable.

Conventions Used in this Book

This book employs the following conventions:

- *Italics* denote definitions of terms or concepts.
- `Unicode block`: indicates algorithm names, function names, package names, programmatic text elements, and related concepts.

Box 0.0.1 Remarks

These boxes contain ideas directly relevant or supplementary to the main content, though not essential for understanding core concepts of a section or paragraph.

Code Examples

All code for simulations and algorithms appears within the book. Python code blocks and their expected output follow this format:

```
def howdy_world():
    # A function to print informative text.
    print("Howdy world!")
howdy_world()
# Howdy world!
```

When discussing initial environment setup, we occasionally demonstrate `bash` commands for direct use in a terminal session. Mac and Linux users can access these via the preinstalled `terminal` utility. Windows users should refer to instructions in Chapter 2.

Bash code blocks, identified by a leading $, appear as follows:

```
$ echo "this is a bash demo"
this is a bash demo
```

The book emphasizes visualizations and plotting. We provide explicit code for generating all figures initially, and assume that readers will become familiar with the basic plotting utilities as we use them more frequently and be able to reproduce the plots themselves in later sections. All plotting code and detailed information for configuring your environment to reproduce our plots is available online at `www.cambridge.org/9781009405393`. Readers can locate specific plots by navigating to the appropriate book section.

How to Read this Book

As with all quantitative books, we recommend taking the time to carefully think through the equations and math. The new information content contained in a single equation can be much higher than that contained in a paragraph of text, and should be treated accordingly.

We refer to other chapters or sections of the book regularly, referring them by their number designation (e.g., "Section 4.7"). This is to help readers build their mental network: Concepts should always be understood through their connection to each other rather than in isolation. For this reason, we also recommend that readers pay careful attention to chapter and section numbers.

A Note on Randomness

Most examples in this book employ simulations and approaches involving inherent randomness. Executing the same code twice will likely yield different results. We sometimes use simulations without fixed seeds for three reasons:

1. Real-world networks tend to be large, with potentially slow analysis algorithms. This presents a trade-off: Using real-world examples may better demonstrate certain properties but can be computationally intensive. Simulations allow readers to develop intuition more quickly, with examples running in seconds rather than minutes.
2. Simulations enable readers to modify and experiment with algorithms and approaches, fostering insight by altering simulation parameters. We encourage hands-on exploration to challenge and refine intuition. This approach means that each run will produce slightly different results, and plots may not exactly match those in the book.
3. Many network algorithms incorporate randomness to achieve faster or numerically superior solutions. To familiarize readers with relevant field techniques, we cannot ignore these methods. Running the same algorithm on an identical network may produce slightly different numerical results, even if conclusions remain similar.

While specific outputs may differ, the broad implications of each code segment should lead to similar conclusions as those presented in our plots. Readers should expect qualitatively similar but quantitatively different results. This adds another dimension to the learning process, requiring readers to identify important aspects of figures and solidify their intuition about whether they have reproduced the intended conclusion.

Situationally, we will use hard-coded seeds to ensure reproducibility. However, readers should generally anticipate that their outputs will match ours qualitatively (exhibiting the same phenomena) but not necessarily quantitatively (specific numerical values may differ).

Using Code Examples, Citations, and Feedback

This book aims to teach network machine learning code development. We provide this code for readers to borrow and repurpose in their programs and documentation. Brief snippets may be used with proper attribution to our citation (provided below). Programs borrowing code may be written without permission. However, permission is required for selling or financially profiting directly from code provided in this book.

To cite this textbook, you can use the following MLA citation:

Bridgeford, Eric W. et al. *Network Machine Learning*. Cambridge University Press, 2025.

For permission requests, feedback, or discussion, please contact the authors directly using the information provided on our website at www.cambridge.org/ 9781009405393.

Acknowledgements

We first want to acknowledge the scientific contributions that made this book possible. Our work builds on numerous collaborators within the broader scientific community; academic books are as much a product of their authors as of the researchers whose work they synthesize. Each chapter's bibliography lists key papers that informed our insights. Readers can use these references, along with the appendix where applicable, to find more detailed technical descriptions of the algorithms and techniques we discuss.

We want to offer special thanks to all who have been reading the book and giving feedback as we write. This list includes our wonderful editor Lauren Cowles for her comprehensive feedback in helping us to distill these concepts to you all. We are grateful for feedback from Jesús Arroyo, Carey Priebe, Dax Pryce, Jaewon Chung, Ben Pedigo, Ross Lawrence, Geoff Loftus, Alexandra McCoy, Olivia Taylor, Peter Brown, Harris Abdul Majid, Ted Kyi, Can Rager, Jaden Fiotto-Kaufman, Eric Todd, Chris White, and Nick Voorsanger. Writing a large textbook is challenging, and we deeply appreciate the thoughtful feedback offered throughout this process.

Bibliography

[1] Harris CR, Millman KJ, van der Walt SJ, Gommers R, Virtanen P, Cournapeau D, et al. Array programming with NumPy. Nature. 2020 Sep.;585(7825):357–362.

[2] Virtanen P, Gommers R, Oliphant TE, Haberland M, Reddy T, Cournapeau D, et al. SciPy 1.0: Fundamental algorithms for scientific computing in Python. Nature Meth. 2020;17:261–272.

[3] Pedregosa F, Varoquaux G, Gramfort A, Michel V, Thirion B, Grisel O, et al. Scikit-learn: Machine learning in Python. J. Mach. Learn. Res. 2011;12:2825–2830.

[4] Chung J, Pedigo BD, Bridgeford EW, Varjavand BK, Helm HS, Vogelstein JT. GraSPy: Graph statistics in Python. J. Mach. Learn. Res. 2019;20(158):1–7.

[5] Hagberg A, Swart P, S Chult D. Exploring network structure, dynamics, and function using NetworkX. Los Alamos National Lab.(LANL), Los Alamos, NM (United States); 2008.

[6] Csardi G, Nepusz T. The igraph software package for complex network research. InterJournal. 2006;Complex Systems:1695.

[7] Merkel D. Docker: Lightweight linux containers for consistent development and deployment. Linux J. 2014;2014(239):2.

[8] Géron A. Hands-On Machine Learning with Scikit-Learn and TensorFlow. Sebastopol, CA, USA: O'Reilly Media, Inc.; 2017.

[9] Barabási AL, Pósfai M. Network Science. Cambridge, England, UK: Cambridge University Press; 2016.

[10] Newman M. Networks. Oxford, England, UK: Oxford University Press; 2018.

[11] Al-Taie MZ, Kadry S. Python for Graph and Network Analysis. Cham, Switzerland: Springer International Publishing; 2017.

[12] Brandes U, Erlebach T. Network Analysis. Berlin, Germany: Springer; 2005.

[13] Luke D. A User's Guide to Network Analysis in R. Cham, Switzerland: Springer International Publishing; 2015.

[14] Kolaczyk ED. Statistical Analysis of Network Data. New York, NY, USA: Springer; 2009.

[15] Trefethen LN, Bau D. Numerical Linear Algebra. Society for Industrial and Applied Mathematics; 1997.

[16] Casella G, Berger RL. Statistical Inference. Boston, MA, USA: Cengage Learning; 2001.

[17] Bickel PJ, Doksum KA. Mathematical Statistics: Basic Ideas And Selected Topics: 1. London, England, UK: Pearson; 2006.

[18] James G, Witten D, Hastie T, Tibshirani R. An Introduction to Statistical Learning: with Applications in R (Springer Texts in Statistics). New York, NY, USA: Springer; 2021.

Terminology

In this section, we define the mathematical terminology, notation, and operations used throughout the book.

Mathematical Concepts

Symbol	Definition	Description/Example
x	A scalar number	$x = 5$
$\vec{x}$	A column vector	$\vec{x} = \begin{bmatrix} 5 \\ 2 \\ 6 \end{bmatrix}$
x_i	the ith element of a column vector	$x_2 = 2$
$\mathcal{X}$	A set	$\mathcal{I} = \{1, 2\}$
$\sum_{i \in \mathcal{N}} x_i$	A sum indexed by a set $\mathcal{N}$	$\sum_{i \in \mathcal{I}} x_i \equiv \sum_{i=1}^{2} x_i = 7$
$\prod_{i \in \mathcal{N}} x_i$	A product indexed by a set $\mathcal{N}$	$\prod_{i \in \mathcal{I}} x_i \equiv \prod_{i=1}^{2} x_i = 10$
Y	A matrix	$Y = \begin{bmatrix} 1 & 2 \\ 3 & 4 \end{bmatrix}$
y_{ij}	The (i, j)th element of a matrix	$y_{22} = 4$

Mathematical Operations

Operation	Name	Definition
$\vec{x}^\top \vec{y}$	The Euclidean inner product	$\sum_{i=1}^{n} x_i y_i = |\vec{x}||\vec{y}| \cos \theta$
$C = AB$	Matrix multiplication	$c_{ij} = \sum_{k=1}^{n} a_{ik} b_{kl}$
$||\vec{x}||_k$	The k-norm of $\vec{x}$	$\left(\sum_{i=1}^{n} |x_i|^k \right)^{\frac{1}{k}}$
$||\vec{x} - \vec{y}||_2$	The Euclidean distance between $\vec{x}$ and $\vec{y}$	$\sqrt{\sum_{i=1}^{n} (x_i - y_i)^2}$
$||X||_F$	The Frobenius norm of X	$\sqrt{\sum_{i=1}^{r} \sum_{j=1}^{c} x_{ij}^2}$

Probability and Statistics Concepts

We assume an undergraduate-level background in probability and statistics. Readers should have a grounded concept of randomness, and know what a random variable is (e.g., a normal or Gaussian random variable, or a Bernoulli "coin flip" random variable). Unprepared readers can educate themselves by exploring the pages for "random variable," "normal distribution," and "Bernoulli distribution" on Wikipedia. The notation that we will use in this book is:

Symbol	Explanation	Example
$\mathbf{x}$	A random variable	$\mathbf{x}$ takes the value 0 or 1 with probability 0.5
$\vec{\mathbf{y}}$	A random vector	$\vec{\mathbf{y}} = \begin{bmatrix} \mathbf{y}_1 \\ \mathbf{y}_2 \end{bmatrix}$
$\mathbf{Z}$	A random matrix	$\mathbf{Z} = \begin{bmatrix} \mathbf{z}_{11} & \mathbf{z}_{12} \\ \mathbf{z}_{21} & \mathbf{z}_{22} \end{bmatrix}$
$Pr(A)$	Probability that an event A happens	$Pr(\mathbf{x} = 1) = 0.5$
$Bern(p)$	The Bernoulli distribution with probability p	If $\mathbf{x}$ is a $Bern(p)$ random variable, then $Pr(\mathbf{x} = 1) = p$, and $Pr(\mathbf{x} = 0) = 1 - p$

Part I

Foundations

1   The Network Machine Learning Landscape

We begin by exploring the network machine learning landscape. We start with high-level concepts about networks, introducing basic terminology required to understand network data. This will make Chapter 3 more digestible when we formally introduce network data structures and how to manipulate them.

We also describe the different types of problems in network machine learning, and how network data fit into the types of problems practitioners need to address.

This chapter covers the following:

1. How do networks fit into the world of machine learning, and why are they important?
2. What does it mean to learn from a network, and what kinds of things should we try to learn?
3. How can we use network-valued data to understand the world better?
4. What challenges might we encounter when we analyze network-valued data?

This high-level understanding provides the context necessary for understanding the practical significance of the methods that we will develop throughout the book.

1.1   What Is Network Machine Learning?

Machine learning is a field of inquiry devoted to understanding and building methods that learn; that is, methods that leverage data to improve predictive performance on some set of tasks [1].

Machine learning has grown enormously over the past few decades, and its use-cases are rapidly pervading modern life. For instance, a photo editor working in pattern recognition might want to automatically segment an object so that they can blur the background (see Figure 1.1.1). An audio engineer might want to identify and separate unique instruments in a song. A student might have software draft an essay. All of these examples use data to learn a pattern that can be leveraged to accomplish some task.

1.1.1   Traditional Machine Learning Leverages Tabular Data Structures

In traditional machine learning, data follow a *tabular format*. The data are arranged in a table or array, where each row represents a single observation or data point, and each column represents a feature or dimension. This tabular structure is convenient

Before　　　　　　　　　　After

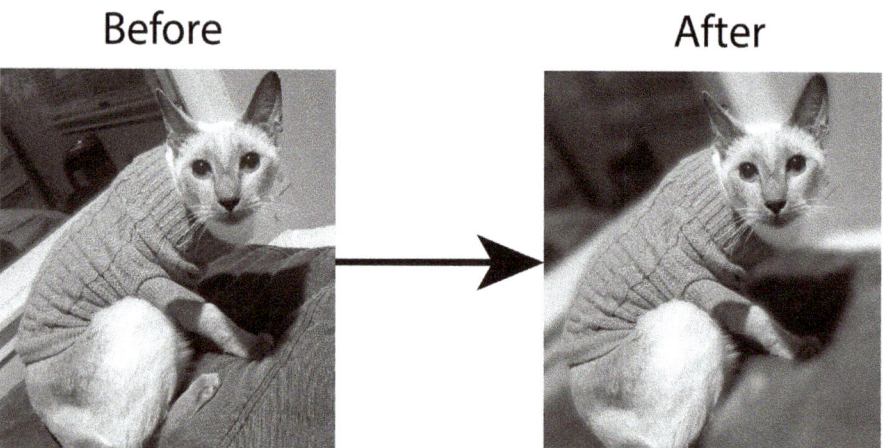

Figure 1.1.1 Learning how to segment an image to blur the background. A machine learning system is trained using numerous images with the foreground segmented out. This trained system is then used to segment out the foreground on new images, and then the background is blurred.

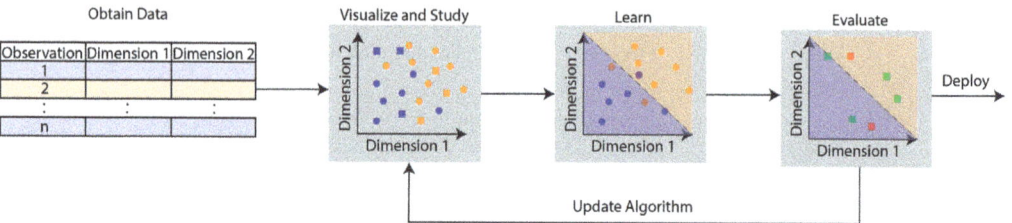

Figure 1.1.2 Machine learning systems start by obtaining inputs as tabular data, where the rows are observations and the columns are features, i.e., *dimensions* of each observation.

because it allows techniques developed in one domain of machine learning to be modified or applied to problems in another domain without reinventing the wheel. For example, given a tabular dataset where each row represents a particular lobster with columns representing its length and sex, we might try to predict the lobster's claw size. We could accomplish this by fitting a linear regression model for the claw size of other lobsters depending on their length and biological sex. For a more detailed discussion of tabular data structures, we recommend the pandas tutorial on tabular data [2].

In Figure 1.1.2, we explore how tabular data are used in a machine learning system using a basic classification task. Each observation is either blue or orange. Some of the data (the training set, circles) are used to train a machine learning algorithm (learning, the transparent blue and orange cells above and below the diagonal), and the remainder of the data are used to test the trained algorithm on new data (evaluating, the new colored red and green squares). The trained model can then be further refined (updated), or deployed for an intended use-case.

1.1.2   What Is a Network?

Many people have some notion of a "network" as describing a system like the internet, or cell phone towers transmitting data. Networks have a specific definition in machine learning and data science. In a network:

1. We have a group of items (e.g., people in a social network), and
2. These items are interconnected through clearly defined relationships (e.g., which people are friends with one another).

Unlike tabular data where each row represents an independent observation, networks capture relationships between nodes. These connections cannot be easily represented in the tabular format without losing crucial structural information. This necessitates specialized approaches in network science for analysis and learning.

Networks can also be referred to as graphs. In this book, we primarily use the term "network" rather than "graph" to avoid confusion with the other use of the word graph (plots on x/y coordinate axes). However, we may encounter the word "graph" in some algorithm or tool names.

Each object in a network is called a *node*, or a vertex (for consistency we'll stick to "node" in this book). A connection between two nodes is called an *edge*. Figure 1.1.3(A) illustrates a simple network of business with eight nodes, with edges indicating transactions. We observe that some nodes are well-connected with other nodes – for example, the node in the center has edges with four other nodes – and we also have nodes which are not connected to anything, like the disconnected business.

Networks might also contain extra information. For example, each node might be associated with a feature vector. For instance, in the business transaction network shown in Figure 1.1.3, we might have information about the company size. We could reasonably assume that larger companies tend to have more business transactions with other companies. Figure 1.1.3(B) illustrates this scenario, where the network includes company size information represented by the size of each node. In this case, each node is associated with a scalar value (the company size), which can be thought of as a length-one vector.

(A) A simple 8-node network of businesses   (B) Business network with business size metadata

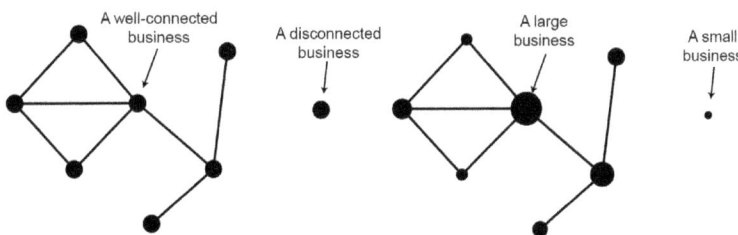

Figure 1.1.3 Panel (**A**) indicates a simple network, where nodes are businesses, and edges exist if a given pair of businesses transact with one another. Panel (**B**) indicates the same simple network, but each node also has a piece of information attached to it, the number of employees (indicated by the node size).

1.1.3   Why Do We Study Networks?

Networks are ubiquitous and can be used to model almost any scenario involving objects interacting with each other. Some examples include:

- Social networks, where nodes represent people and edges represent friendships.
- Computer networks, where nodes represent computers and edges represent data transmission.
- Air traffic networks, where nodes represent cities and edges represent flights between them.
- Infection networks, where nodes represent people and edges represent disease transmissions.
- Brain networks in neuroscience, where nodes represent neurons and edges represent their white matter connections.

More examples include ecological networks, electrical networks, and gene networks. We frequently use networks to represent mathematical relationships:

- In Bayesian networks, nodes represent variables and edges represent conditional dependencies.
- Correlation networks can be created from data, where nodes represent variables and edges represent their correlations.
- We can create semantic networks in natural language processing, where nodes represent concepts and edges represent their semantic distance from one another.
- Neural networks in computer science, where nodes are artificial neurons and edges are weights between them.
- Attention networks in large language models like ChatGPT, where nodes are tokens (parts of words), and edges define the information that should be transferred between them.
- More generally, we can create Euclidean networks from any tabular dataset by representing data points as nodes and defining a distance or similarity metric between pairs of data points to create edges.

Our own daily cognitive processes can be viewed as movement through a vast semantic network, with nodes as concepts or ideas and edges as mental associations between them. To see this directly, visualize a concept or object. Perhaps the food you had for breakfast this morning, or the city you live in. Now, think about the connections between those concepts and others. Maybe you had eggs and toast for breakfast. Eggs and toast are connected with a multitude of other concepts in your mind: forks and silverware, kitchens, hunger, protein, carbohydrates, your morning routine, chickens, wheat, other breakfast foods, and so forth. Exploring these mental relationships is equivalent to walking along a small subset of your personal cognitive network.

For business-minded readers, this is an opportune time to learn about networks. Language models have become ubiquitous in the startup environment, but they hallucinate and need to be well-grounded. Using networks as their backbone is an excellent way to accomplish this goal. The application section of the book provides many tools useful for tackling real-world network problems. Some examples include analyzing social networks, optimizing supply chains, detecting fraud, developing recommendation systems, and using graph neural networks to develop new medical treatments.

The development of network machine learning follows a typical pattern in scientific advancement:

1. **Academic phase:** Researchers spend 10–20 years publishing proof-of-concept papers, exploring problem-solving approaches, and developing fundamental tools. This work is often done informally, with code existing primarily in Jupyter notebooks.
2. **Industry adoption:** As the field matures, companies begin to recognize the potential of these academic tools. They adapt them to enhance their products or services and develop user-friendly packages (like `networkx` or `graspologic`) to make the tools accessible to a broader audience.

Network machine learning is currently at a critical juncture. Its academic foundations have been established over the past two decades, and we are now seeing the transition of its tools from academia to industry. This presents a unique opportunity for early adoption of application-focused network machine learning tools in business contexts.

1.1.3.1　Why Do We Need Special Machine Learning Approaches for Networks?

In the wild, networks primarily exist as nodes and edges rather than in a tabular format. This presents a challenge, since techniques that were developed over decades for tabular data cannot be directly applied for network-valued data. However, we can adapt networks to traditional tabular formats using network representation tools. Once we transform these networks into more conventional structures, we can apply techniques from other domains of machine learning to analyze our networks.

Figure 1.1.4 illustrates the high-level process of network machine learning. By *network machine learning*, we refer to machine learning techniques applied to network-valued data (data which are a network, not a tabular structure). This process typically involves the following steps:

1. Obtain a network dataset,
2. Select a suitable representation for the network, based on the questions we wish to address,

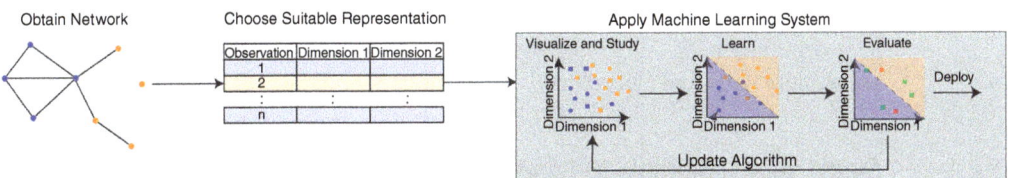

Figure 1.1.4 The network machine learning pipeline: We start with a network, choose a suitable representation, apply appropriate machine learning techniques, and interpret the results in the context of the original network.

3. Apply appropriate machine learning techniques to our representation, and
4. Interpret the results in the context of the original network structure.

We will now explore the types of problems we might encounter in network machine learning. Then, in Chapter 2, we will walk through a simple end-to-end network analysis project.

1.2   Types of Network Machine Learning Problems

There are many different types of network machine learning systems. We broadly group them into the following categories:

- whether they involve one or multiple networks (single or multiple network learning systems),
- whether they require additional information in the form of network attributes (attributed or nonattributed network learning systems),
- whether they ask questions about an edge, a node, a group of edges/nodes, or about the network itself, and
- whether the approach can be used in isolation from a statistical model (nonmodel-based or model-based network learning systems).

To illustrate these criteria, we will use two running examples:

Example 1.2.1 Brain networks for musicians and nonmusicians
Brain networks have been acquired from a large group of people. The nodes represent areas of the brain, and the edges represent whether a pair of areas can communicate using neurons. Each network is either from a musician or a nonmusician.

Example 1.2.2 A pair of social networks for students at a school
We will also use social networks for students at two schools. Nodes represent students, and edges represent whether the students are connected on social media. Networks exist from two social media sites: Facebook and Instagram.

These categories are not mutually exclusive, and a network machine learning system will pull elements from several categories simultaneously. For instance, a system might be single network, node-attributed, and nonmodel-based like a community detection algorithm.

1.2.1   Single versus Multiple Network Learning Systems

1.2.1.1   Single Network Learning Systems
In many network learning scenarios, there is only a single sample: the network itself. A *single network learning system* derives insight from a single network, which is a

single collection of nodes and edges. This differs from traditional machine learning frameworks, in which having a single sample would be disastrous: In that case, insight would be impossible, because we need multiple observations to identify trends or patterns.

However, in network learning, a single sample is not necessarily limiting. While there may be only one network, it is defined by a collection of many nodes and edges. Thus, it is still possible to learn about relationships that exist among the nodes, edges, or both. The caveat is that the conclusions drawn are limited by the specific network under study, which may not be representative of the global population of networks. This limitation is often not significant, depending on what the network represents. Most of the tools in this book are for single network learning systems.

1.2.1.2 Multiple Network Learning Systems

A *multiple network learning system* derives insight from multiple networks, each consisting of collections of nodes and edges. Unlike a single network learning system where conclusions can only be drawn based on characteristics of that particular network, a multiple network learning system can generate insights both within and across the networks.

The following are examples of multiple network learning systems:

- multiple network representation learning in Section 5.5,
- anomaly detection in Section 8.1,
- signal subnetworks in Section 8.2, and
- graph neural networks in Section 9.1.

1.2.2 Nonattributed versus Richly Attributed Network Learning Systems

While machine learning typically distinguishes between unsupervised and supervised learning, network learning employs more specific terminology for these concepts.

1.2.2.1 Nonattributed Network Learning Systems

The concept of a nonattributed network learning system is analogous to fully unsupervised machine learning. *Unsupervised learning* can be defined as a learning problem where the data provided to the algorithm do not include the desired solutions, known as *labels*. A network learning system is considered *nonattributed* if the data given to the system include only the nodes and edges at the time of the analysis.

For instance, consider the Facebook network from Example 1.2.2. Suppose that the information about which students attend which school has been lost. We hypothesize that there might be two groups of students in the network, called communities, and that if a student is in a particular community, they tend to be better friends with other students in the same community. We want to see if we can identify these communities programmatically, and perhaps recover the school information for each student. Figure 1.2.1 illustrates a nonattributed network learning problem. The groups of nodes that are heavily connected (indicated by the gray circles) correspond to the schools that each student attends.

Examples of nonattributed network learning systems include:

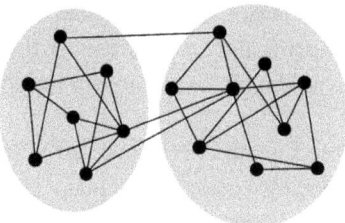

Figure 1.2.1 A school network. Nodes represent students, and edges indicate friendships. The gray circles indicate guesses as to which school each student belongs to.

- network embeddings in Section 5,
- community detection in Section 6.1,
- latent position comparisons in Section 7.1, and
- anomaly detection in Section 8.1.

1.2.2.2   Attributed Network Learning Systems

Similarly, the concept of an attributed network learning system is analogous to supervised or semisupervised machine learning. *Supervised learning* can be loosely defined as a learning problem where data provided to the algorithm include labels, and *semisupervised learning* can be loosely defined as a learning problem in which the data provided to the algorithm include some of the labels. A network is an *attributed network learning system* if, at the time of analysis, the network(s) include attributes in addition to nodes and edges. These attributes do not necessarily have to be scalar-valued labels: they can be vectors as well. There are four main types of attributed network learning systems. They are:

- Networks with node attributes,
- Networks with edge attributes,
- Networks with network attributes, and
- Networks with multiple-network attributes.

Networks with Node Attributes
When networks have *node attributes*, each node has an additional piece of information describing it. Returning to the school example, consider a scenario where, for each student, there is an additional piece of information: their school. The goal is to investigate whether the probability of two students being friends is higher in school one or in school two. A problem for networks with node attributes is shown in Figure 1.2.2(A).
    Examples of problems that deal with node attributes include:

- joint representation learning in Section 5.6,
- model selection in Section 6.4,
- testing for differences in block matrices in Section 7.2, and
- testing for differences between groups of edges in Section 6.3.

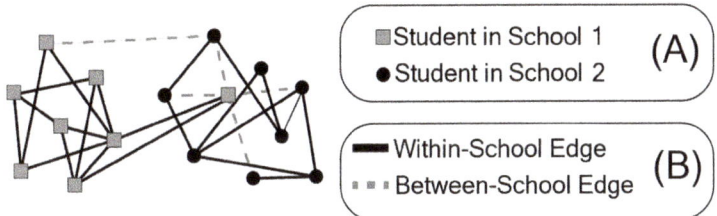

Figure 1.2.2 **(A)** The school network for Facebook, analyzed using node attributes. **(B)** The school network for Facebook, analyzed using edge attributes.

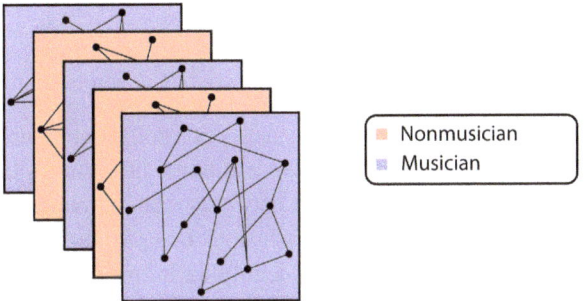

Figure 1.2.3 A collection of brain networks, where the nodes represent areas of the brain and the edges indicate which brain areas can communicate. The color of the box around each network indicates whether it comes from a musician or a nonmusician.

Networks with Edge Attributes

When networks have *edge attributes*, each edge has an additional piece of information describing it. For example, in the school network, we could entirely ignore the school assignments, and simply focus on whether the students have more friends within schools (solid edges) or between schools (dashed edges). This example is illustrated in Figure 1.2.2(B). Rather than focusing on the school assignments of the nodes, we focus on two groups of edges (the within-school edges, and the between-school edges).

An example of a problem with edge attributes is testing for differences between groups of edges in Section 6.3.

Networks with Network Attributes

When networks have *network attributes*, each network has an additional piece of information describing it. Referring back to Example 1.2.1, each brain network was from either a musician or a nonmusician. This piece of information characterizes each of the networks as either from a musician or a nonmusician individual, and applies to the entire collection of nodes and edges for a given network. Figure 1.2.3 illustrates a network with network attributes.

Examples of problems that leverage network attributes are signal subgraph estimation in Section 8.2, and graph neural networks in Section 9.1.

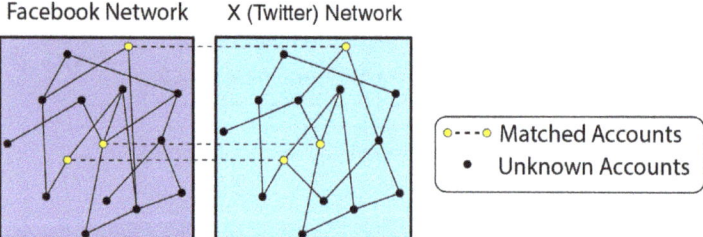

Facebook Network   X (Twitter) Network

○---○ Matched Accounts
•   Unknown Accounts

Figure 1.2.4 Two social networks from different social media sites. The nodes are people's accounts on the social media sites (they are the same for both sites) and the edges indicate which pairs of accounts follow one another for that particular site. For three people, we know a matching across the two networks (yellow nodes, dashed edges).

Networks with Multiple-Network Attributes
A network with *multiple-network attributes* consists of a collection of networks (each of which has nodes and edges) where we have additional information that describes how the nodes (or the edges) of the different networks relate to one another. Returning to Example 1.2.2, let's add another dimension. Imagine the accounts are, for all intents and purposes, anonymous, since identifying information is not shared by default on Facebook or Instagram accounts. However, we know that a particular Facebook account corresponds to the same person's Instagram account for three people. We want to see if we can use this cross-network attribute (the matched accounts) to discover suitable matchings for the remaining accounts in the network. A problem with multiple-network attributes is shown in Figure 1.2.4.

An example of a problem which leverages cross-network attributes is seeded graph matching, in Section 7.3.

1.2.3   Scope of Network Analysis

Network machine learning often tempts researchers to explore entire networks, even when questions are more focused. Consider a transportation network with stations as nodes and rush-hour ridership counts between stations as edges. A different network might exist for each week of the year. The following examples demonstrate questions about different network components.

1. Studying a single edge: Determining whether a particular route needs an additional train due to rush hour popularity might require examining this route across many networks to estimate passenger numbers.
2. Studying a single node: Deciding on station expansion could involve analyzing passenger throughput at a specific station.
3. Studying groups of nodes or edges: Evaluating the impact of canceling an entire line would require considering effects on other stations (groups of nodes) and passenger numbers on other lines (groups of edges).
4. Studying the entire network: Assessing the need for increased public transportation funding might entail analyzing the city's weekly cost across the entire transportation network.

1.2.4 Model-Based versus Nonmodel-Based Network Learning Systems

Statistics forms a core component of network learning systems. This is because network learning problems inherently involve randomness, whether in the sampled networks, the set of acquired networks, the collected data, or other factors.

In statistics, we often sample observations from a population, and then use what we learn from the sample to extrapolate to the population. We often build statistical models in service of this.

Consider a statistical model as a conceptual framework that explicitly accounts for variation, randomness, or error in the networks we obtain compared to the entire population. The balance between model-based and nonmodel-based network learning is a core aim of this book, so we will explain the difference without reference to networks.

1.2.4.1 Model-Based Learning Systems

A *model-based learning system* requires a statistical model to derive meaning from an analysis.

Consider two coins, each flipped twenty times. To determine if the probability of heads is the same or different for these coins, we use a hypothesis test. We have two hypotheses: that we have the same (first hypothesis) or different (second hypothesis) probability of landing on heads. A *hypothesis test* determines whether or not the data provide evidence against the first hypothesis.

This question requires a statistical model because "probability" has a specific statistical interpretation. To answer this question, several factors about the experiment require clarification:

- Are heads and tails the only possible outcomes for each coin? For example, could a thicker coin have a nonzero probability of landing on its edge?
- Is the probability of heads consistent across all twenty flips for each coin? Could different flipping techniques in the first and last ten flips affect the frequency of heads?
- Are the outcomes of coin flips independent? For instance, would saying a prayer after two tails influence the probability of getting heads on the next flip?
- Is the sample size sufficient to detect differences between the coins? Many statistical tests, including this one, can be interpreted in various ways. With small sample sizes, assumptions must be carefully considered, as certain testing approaches (like the chi-squared test) may only be meaningful with larger datasets.

In order to make a conclusion based on our hypothesis test, we need to be specific about the assumptions we make about these details of the our data sample, since the answer to our question depends on these assumptions. Therefore, we need to understand the assumptions that we made, so that we can make a decision based on the outcome of the hypothesis test that we performed.

1.2.4.2 Nonmodel-Based Learning Systems

Many questions can be addressed using either model-based or nonmodel-based techniques. While models can provide intuition, they are not always necessary to answer

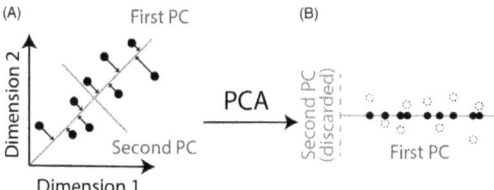

Figure 1.2.5 (**A**) Two-dimensional data shown in a scatter plot. The first principal component (PC) represents the axis of maximum variation, while the second PC is orthogonal to the first and captures the next highest variation. Arrows show data projection onto the first PC. (**B**) PCA projects data onto the first PC by reorienting the dataset along the first and second PCs (dashed circles and lines), then removing the second PC (solid circles). This reduces dimensionality from two to one, discarding the direction of less variation.

questions. A *nonmodel-based learning system* does not require a statistical model to derive meaning from an analysis.

To illustrate this concept, consider principal components analysis (pca), a nonmodel-based machine learning technique. pca reduces high-dimensional data to a more manageable number of dimensions, allowing for downstream analysis with other strategies. Figure 1.2.5 provides a visual illustration of pca, showing data reduction from two dimensions to one along the first principal component (PC).

pca can be executed without additional knowledge about the data, simply as an algorithm to make data more manageable for other machine learning techniques. However, understanding pca through the lens of a statistical model (assuming normally distributed observations) provides additional insight. In this context, principal components represent directions of maximum variation in the data.

In Figure 1.2.5(A), the black points spread more along the first PC than the second PC. The degree of variation preserved by each PC is indicated by its score. This interpretation is useful for machine learning tasks like K-means clustering, where distinguishable classes require variability between observations.

1.3   Challenges of Network Machine Learning

Like other branches of science, network machine learning is not without its challenges. The networks we analyze often contain random imperfections. Rather than collecting exhaustive data, we typically examine reasonably sized subsets. This may mean studying a social network with 1000 nodes instead of 100 million, or 200 brain networks rather than one from every person in the world.

Because our data are not perfect, we often use tools from *statistical learning*, a machine learning framework that uses statistics to refine problems, quantify the reasonableness of conclusions, and make rigorous inferences about networks. In this section, we will discuss several of the challenges that may arise as a result of random imperfections in network data. The remainder of the book will be dedicated to developing models and techniques that allow us to overcome some of these limitations.

1.3.1 We Might Imperfectly Observe the Network

In many branches of science, collecting network data can be an imperfect and noisy process. Only recently did we acquire a detailed map of the connectome of a complex organism, the fruit fly larva [3]. Even though fruit fly larvae are small, this was a substantial undertaking: The fruit fly brain is comprised of several thousand neurons (nodes), and hundreds of thousands of neuronal connections (edges), all of which fit into a volume smaller than a cubic millimeter. To study the brain at the neuron-scale, researchers sliced it into thousands of tiny pieces smaller than a human hair, and then examined each piece individually with a microscope. From there, algorithms and manual tracing were performed to reconstruct, slice-by-slice, which neurons were connected with which other neurons. To complicate matters further, all of this work was derived from a single organism. This means that each step allowed minimal room for error. The neuron-by-neuron map was used to construct a network (called the *connectome* of the organism) of connections between neurons.

With so many areas for potential error, it is almost impossible that the fruit fly connectome is absolutely perfect. We may have missed some neurons, overlooked connections, or made small mistakes anywhere in this complicated process. Figure 1.3.1 explores what it means for a network to be imperfectly observed. In Figure 1.3.1(A), we see the underlying network we are trying to obtain. In Figure 1.3.1(B), we see the actual network we obtained: we might be missing some of the nodes (gray dashed nodes), we might be missing some of the edges (gray dashed edges), or we might see edges which should not really be present (nonfaithful edges, gray solid edges). While a portion of the network might faithfully represent the underlying system (solid black nodes and edges), we do not actually know what part of our sample is faithful or unfaithful with respect to the true underlying network. The key is that when we build network machine learning systems, we desire insights that are robust to these imperfect observations. This is because in some cases, it might be impossible to ever obtain the data that we need otherwise.

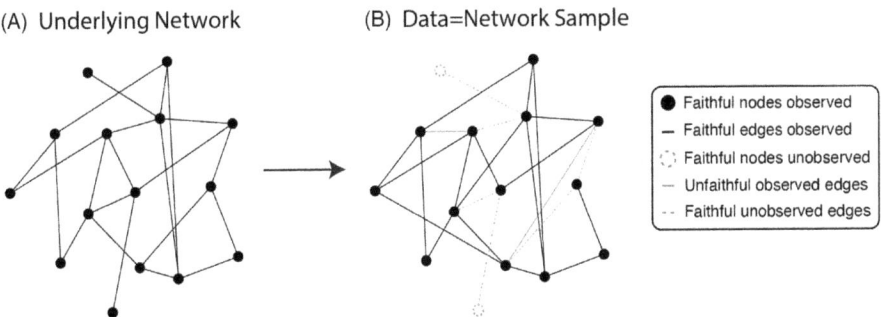

Figure 1.3.1 The true underlying network contains a lot of information that we did not measure properly in the course of observing or sampling the network.

1.3.2   We Might Not See the Whole Network

When studying a network, we rarely observe the entire system perfectly. For instance, consider a social network, in which the nodes are people within the network, and edges represent friendships. If we wanted to study the network in its rawest form, we might need to collect data from millions, or billions, of accounts to construct a network that might take an infeasible amount of space just to store. Actually analyzing the network represents another huge hurdle; we would need to be able to devise techniques which could efficiently churn through terabytes worth of data. However, focusing our attention on a subset of the network involving a few thousand or hundred thousand people may allow us to ask richer questions. On this reduced subset of people, we are less limited by computational constraints and so we can apply a wider range of analytical techniques.

The fruit fly larva (*Drosophila*) connectome example illustrates how researchers have approaches studying large networks over time. While the complete connectome was mapped only recently, brain networks have been studied for decades. Previously, owing to economic, computational, and analytical challenges, investigations focused on subsets of the brain rather than the whole. Despite only collecting bits and pieces of the network, major insights were learned which directly informed the effort to collect the entire network.

In both of these cases, we can learn a lot of valuable information by reducing the size of a network, learning from it, and then applying what we learned to the entire network. Figure 1.3.2 illustrates sampling a subset of nodes from a network. Figure 1.3.2(A) depicts shows the true underlying network with both solid and dashed edges and nodes. Figure 1.3.2(B) depicts the sampled network, which only includes a subset of the nodes and edges.

1.3.3   We Might Only See a Subset of the Networks

Consider again Example 1.2.1 of musician and nonmusician brain networks. A team of psychologists might hypothesize that the brains of musicians tend to be better connected in areas responsible for fine motor coordination and hearing, which are

(A) Network Population   (B) Data = Network Sample

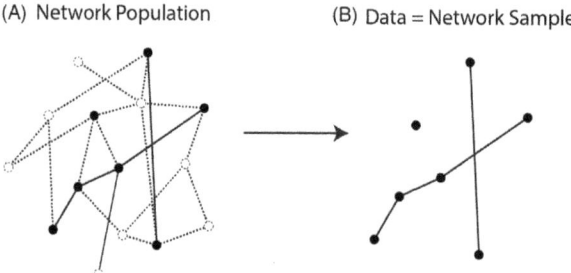

Figure 1.3.2 The true underlying network has both solid and dashed edges and nodes, shown in (**A**). However, when we sample the network in (**B**), our sample only includes the subset of nodes and edges that are solid.

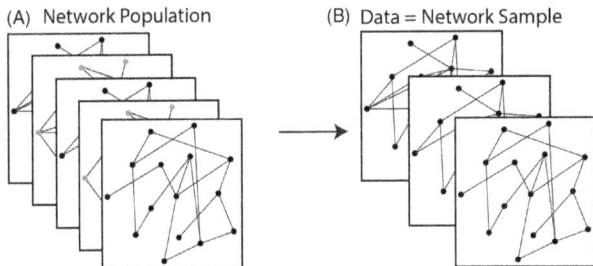

(A) Network Population   (B) Data = Network Sample

Figure 1.3.3 The true underlying population contains many more networks than we are able to actually sample. In (**A**), we have black and gray networks, but in the sample in (**B**), we only get to see the gray networks.

crucial skills for many instruments. To test this hypothesis, the psychologists could take one of two approaches. They could collect brain networks from every individual, or they could collect a subset of brain networks from groups of musicians and nonmusicians in their area. Figure 1.3.3 demonstrates sampling a subset of networks from a population. Despite the fact that the psychologists only studied a subset of musicians and nonmusicians, with some statistical assumptions they can derive conclusions that will apply more broadly than just to the group of people they analyzed.

1.3.4   Statistics Allows Us to Generalize to the Unseen from the Seen

If we collect a set of brain networks, we have collected a *sample*, a subset of objects from the larger population. Statistical analysis of the sample allows us to draw broader conclusions. Rather than limiting our findings to the specific group or network we sample, statistics enables us to rigorously extend conclusions to a more general population. Figure 1.3.4 summarizes this concept. Note that "network population" may have different interpretations depending on the specific question. It might refer to a population of many networks, from which we observe a sample with some level of uncertainty, or to a "true" single network, which we can only observe with some level of randomness because of how the nodes or edges were obtained.

We can learn many things about our network data without leveraging statistics at all. However, using statistical learning gives us a quantitative framework to generalize our findings. Conclusions can then be applied more broadly to the general population rather than being limited to our specific network data.

1.3.5   Other Challenges

Section 1.2 introduced several types of network machine learning problems. The field is rapidly evolving, with new problem formulations continually emerging. Researchers face numerous challenges, including:

1. Categorizing problems appropriately,
2. Reformulating research questions to align with existing techniques,

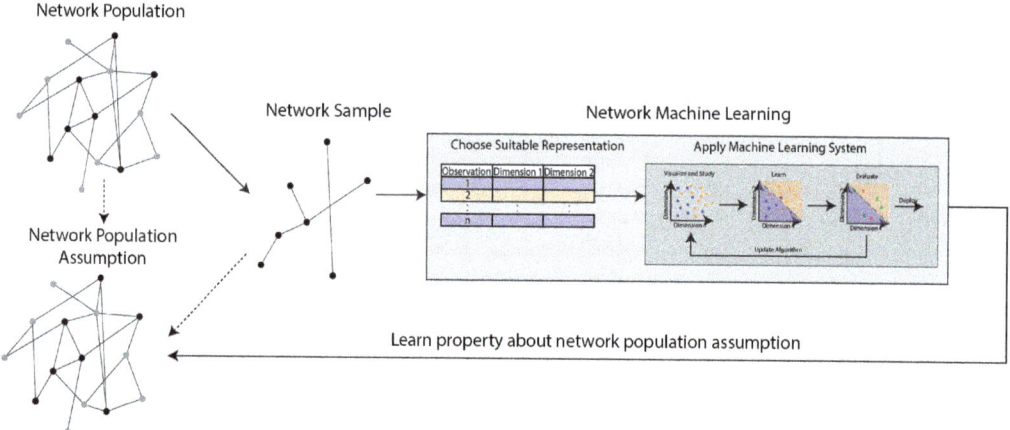

Figure 1.3.4 We have a network population, which in this case means a large network that we cannot properly observe. We obtain a sample of this network, and then use analyses on this sample and knowledge of how it was taken from the population to derive assumptions about our system. Ideally, this will reasonably represent the network population itself. Using network machine learning, we try to understand the properties of this network population.

3. Selecting suitable analytical strategies, and
4. Developing entirely new methods when necessary.

These challenges often require significant effort and resources to address. Chapter 2 presents an example data analysis in network machine learning, illustrating how researchers approach these problems in practice.

Bibliography

[1] Contributors to Wikimedia projects. Machine learning – Wikipedia; 2023. [Online; accessed Jan. 11, 2023.]
[2] What kind of data does pandas handle?; 2022. https://pandas.pydata.org/docs/getting_started/intro_tutorials/01_table_oriented.html [Online; accessed Jan. 11, 2023.]
[3] Winding M, Pedigo BD, Barnes CL, Patsolic HG, Park Y, Kazimiers T, et al. The connectome of an insect brain. Science. 2023 Mar.;379(6636):eadd9330.

2 End-to-End Biology Network Machine Learning Project

This chapter provides a practical introduction to network machine learning, offering a behind-the-scenes look at the complete process of working through a project.

This chapter covers the following:

1. Section 2.1 discusses how to approach a network machine learning problem.
2. Section 2.2 guides readers through setting up a local environment for running the code in this textbook and obtaining example data.
3. Section 2.3 prepares the data for downstream analysis.
4. Section 2.4 covers the algorithm selection process for network data.
5. Section 2.5 demonstrates a learning algorithm for network data.
6. Section 2.6 illustrates how network machine learning can reveal new insights about network data.

While some of the material in this section may feel opaque, we choose to begin by emphasizing the big picture rather than minute details, giving the reader a "global view" before diving into detail in Chapter 3. This approach also ensures a proper setup of code and dependencies from the outset, which generally leads to a smoother workflow. Readers are strongly recommended to follow along in code, diverging and exploring as they go.

2.1   Looking at the Big Picture

Welcome to the Neurobiology Institute! A colleague has come to you with an interesting problem. Brains consist of neurons. Neuronal connection patterns produce the brain's unique functions: breathing, moving, hearing, seeing, and higher-level thought.

When they are electrically stimulated, neurons can transmit that electrical signal to other neurons. This process consumes a lot of energy; while the brain is only about 2 percent of the body's weight, it consumes about 20 percent of its daily energy. To keep the neurons replenished with energy (and to remove waste that the cells produce when they work), the brain has a complicated network of blood vessels. When a brain area is in use, the body dedicates blood supply to the area that will need it most.

Neurobiologists have come up with a clever way to decipher brain activity in humans by looking at this blood flow. Using MRI, they can follow blood movement towards particular areas. Because blood movement correlates with neuron activity,

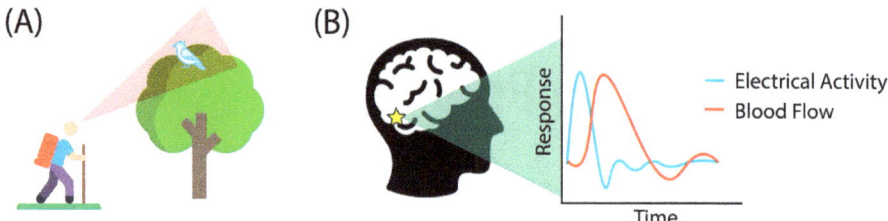

Figure 2.1.1 (**A**) A hiker on a trail sees a bird perched in a tree in his field of view (faint red triangle). (**B**) The occipital lobe, which is responsible for sight, sits in the back of the brain (star). The presence of the bird in the field of view causes neurons to be electrically stimulated (blue line). The activity of the neurons causes the brain to send blood to the area as the neurons are stimulated (red line). While individual neurons are too small to see, the blood flow caused by many neurons firing at once can be picked up by an fMRI scanner.

following blood movement can tell scientists about that activity. Experiments have been performed that empirically demonstrate this strong correlation.

This imaging technology, known as functional MRI (fMRI), has proven to be useful for neuroscientists [1]. By measuring pairs of brain areas, researchers can see whether the two areas tend to be active together. The idea is that, perhaps, different combinations of brain areas tend to work together as a unit, allowing the complicated thought patterns that humans are capable of. By viewing the different areas of the brain as nodes of a network, and the blood flow correlations as its edges, scientists can use network machine learning to study the brain. This area of study, called connectomics, is an active and network-centric subdomain of neuroscience research [2].

Your colleague has come to you with a set of networks from fMRI sessions, and wants to know whether there are any groups of brain areas that tend to have similar activity. Can you, as a network scientist, take this network of nodes and edges, and figure out a way to break the nodes into functionally similar groups?

2.1.1   Framing the Problem

The first question to ask your colleague is: What exactly is the objective here? In network machine learning, the choice of the model used is *everything*. The model determines what sorts of questions we are capable of asking, and what sorts of *answers* we are capable of learning. Asking about the objectives will directly shape which models and approaches you use.

Your colleague wants to know whether there are any subgroups of areas that tend to behave similarly. By "behave similarly," what your colleague means is, are there subgroups of brain areas that tend to work together in conjunction with other subgroups of brain areas?

The next task is to determine what type of network machine learning problem you have. What type of data exist? Are there covariates associated with those data? Do you need to change your question based on this information? Do you want to test a hypothesis, or make predictions? What characteristics will your model need to be able to answer the question appropriately? Before you progress further, you should answer these questions for yourself.

Once you have gotten a sense of the question and the data, you need to determine what other researchers have already tried. This will prevent you from repeating work, help you understand where to start approaching the problem, and give you a reference for how well your techniques are performing. This step will likely involve reading literature and having conversations with colleagues about what work has already been done.

You emerge from this process with new information. The data are a set of fMRI scans taken from patients doing nothing, lying in a scanner. Remembering back to the types of network machine learning problems in Section 1.2, you conclude that this is a multiple network learning problem. Your networks are nonattributed, since you only know their nodes and edges. You want to understand relationships between groups of nodes and edges. You are going to need to come up with a definition of what it means for pairs of areas to be similar, and you are going to want to be able to group areas in a way that is meaningful for your colleague.

2.1.2   Check the Assumptions

Throughout the course of this book, we will try to keep the assumptions being made by our techniques in mind. We want to choose the simplest set of assumptions that can reasonably reflect the data, which means using the simplest statistical model that can properly answer the questions we ask. In this case, we don't care about individual brain area-to-brain area connections at all: We only care about how groups of brain areas behave in relation to other groups of brain areas. This means that we want to choose models which will allow us to learn about pairs of brain area groups, which is a very different problem from learning about individual brain areas themselves.

After talking over your understanding of the problem with your colleague, you are confident that he wants a way to be able to group brain areas together based on how similar they are, and you have the freedom to define that however you choose. You have the green light to begin coding.

2.2   Getting the Data and Configuring Your Environment

In this section, we will start to get our hands dirty with some real network datasets. We recommend walking through these examples with your laptop in a Jupyter notebook. To ease your ability to interact directly with the code of this book, we've developed a standalone `docker` container that you can use.

2.2.1   Interacting with the Book via `docker`

Getting software to run across multiple operating systems, particularly software with lots of dependencies, can range from difficult to impossible. While most of the packages required to run the contents of this book can be installed relatively easily via a combination of git, pip, and virtual environments, the easiest and fastest way to get to coding and interacting with real `python` code is `docker`.

`docker` allows you to run standalone software in a separate area of your computer called a *docker container* to allow software to operate without conflicting with your local operating system. This means that you can, with a very small number of button clicks, create deployable software that thousands of people can use.

To install `docker`, see their installation guide at [3].

2.2.1.1   Obtaining the Docker Container for the Textbook

Once you have `docker` installed on your computer, you can obtain the docker container for the book relatively easily. If you have a ubuntu/mac operating system and the docker daemon running on your computer, you can open up a terminal session and type the following command:

```
$ docker pull neurodata/graph-stats-book
```

which will fetch the docker container for the book from [4].

This docker container contains all of the dependencies needed to run the code within this book, and will allow you to use the book in conjunction with `jupyter`, a lightweight, web-based interactive computing platform that you can access through your web browser at `localhost:<port>`, where `<port>` is the port you provide to the container for execution. We will use port `8888` by default. You can start the docker container like this:

```
$ docker run -ti -v <path/to/local/working/directory>:/home/book -p
    <port>:8888 neurodata/graph-stats-book \
    jupyter-lab --ip=0.0.0.0 --port=8888 /home/book/ \
    --NotebookApp.token="graphbook"
```

This will launch a `jupyter-lab` session, and should automatically log you into the session in your browser. If it does not, open up a browser of your choice, and go to `localhost:<port>`, where you will be prompted to enter the log-in password for your session. That log-in password is `graphbook`, generated from `-NotebookApp.token` in the command above. The port is so that your browser can communicate with the Jupyter session inside the docker container (which runs Jupyter internally on port `8888`).

If you don't want to use the docker container, that's fine too: You can install the dependencies as they arise manually in an environment of your choice. Detailed information for configuring your environment, working with the docker container, and viewing section-by-section preprepared Jupyter notebooks can be found via links on our companion website `www.cambridge.org/9781009405393`.

2.2.2   Downloading the Data

When we work with network data, it is rarely the case that the raw data that we will use are already a network. The *raw data* are the least processed version of the data for a project, and is the information upon which the rest of the data are derived. A *derivative* is a piece of information that is derived from the raw data. For us, the raw data are the brain scans. These brain scans were preprocessed by breaking the scans into brain regions, and then finding blood-flow correlation between those regions.

We have access to that preprocessed data. You could navigate over to the neurodata website and download these data directly, but it tends to be useful to do this programmatically, because if the data change, you might want your analysis to automatically use the latest and best version of the data at the time you execute your function. Further, if you intend your code to be reproducible, having a function which downloads and prepares the data in a way which the computer can use will simplify the process of disseminating your work.

To begin, we will start with a code snippet which fetches the required data for our analysis:

```python
import os
import urllib
import boto3
from botocore import UNSIGNED
from botocore.client import Config
from graspologic.utils import import_edgelist
import numpy as np
import glob
from tqdm import tqdm


# the AWS bucket the data is stored in
BUCKET_ROOT = "open-neurodata"
parcellation = "Schaefer400"
FMRI_PREFIX = "m2g/Functional/BNU1-11-12-20-m2g-func/Connectomes/" + \
    parcellation + "_space-MNI152NLin6_res-2x2x2.nii.gz/"
FMRI_PATH = os.path.join("datasets", "fmri") # the output folder
DS_KEY = "abs_edgelist" # correlation matrices for the networks to
    exclude


def fetch_fmri_data(bucket=BUCKET_ROOT, fmri_prefix=FMRI_PREFIX,
                    output=FMRI_PATH, name=DS_KEY):
    """
    A function to fetch fMRI connectomes from AWS S3.
    """
    # check that output directory exists
    if not os.path.isdir(FMRI_PATH):
        os.makedirs(FMRI_PATH)
    # start boto3 session anonymously
    s3 = boto3.client('s3', config=Config(signature_version=UNSIGNED))
    # obtain the filenames
    bucket_conts = s3.list_objects(Bucket=bucket,
                Prefix=fmri_prefix)["Contents"]
    for s3_key in tqdm(bucket_conts):
        # get the filename
        s3_object = s3_key['Key']
        # verify that we are grabbing the right file
        if name not in s3_object:
            op_fname = os.path.join(FMRI_PATH,
                str(s3_object.split('/')[-1]))
            if not os.path.exists(op_fname):
```

```
                     s3.download_file(bucket, s3_object, op_fname)

def read_fmri_data(path=FMRI_PATH):
    """
    A function which loads the connectomes as adjacency matrices.
    """
    fnames = glob.glob(os.path.join(path, "*.csv"))
    # sort for consistency
    fnames.sort()
    # import edgelists with graspologic
    # edgelists will be all of the files that end in a csv
    networks = [import_edgelist(fname) for fname in tqdm(fnames)]
    return np.stack(networks, axis=0)
```

Now when you call `fetch_fmri_data()`, it creates a new directory called `datasets/fmri` in your workspace, and downloads the adjacency matrices, the standard way to represent a network as a mathematical object (see Section 3.4), into your local directory `datasets/fmri`.

Throughout this book, we will also use the `graspologic` package, built for statistical analysis on networks. We load the dataset using the `graspologic` utility `import_edgelist()`:

```
fetch_fmri_data()
As = read_fmri_data()
```

2.2.3   Visualizing the Data

Next, let's take an in-depth look at one of the adjacency matrices. In network machine learning, when dealing with a new dataset, our recommendation is to always start with visualization. We typically visualize network data using a heatmap. The resulting plot is shown in Figure 2.2.1(A).

```
from graphbook_code import heatmap

A = As[0]
ax = heatmap(A, vmin=-1, vmax=1, title="Heatmap of Functional
    Connectome")
```

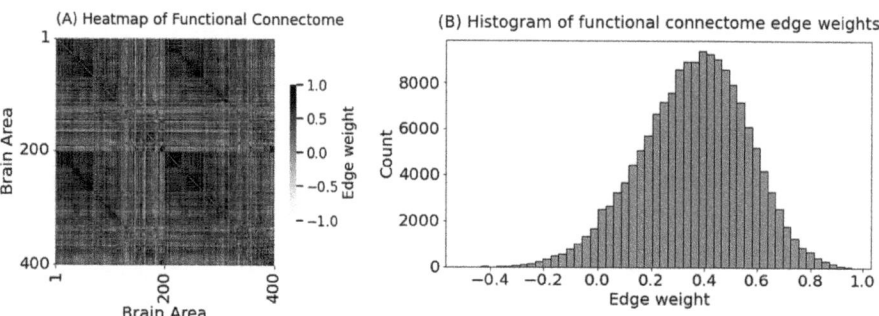

Figure 2.2.1 **(A)** A raw connectome, and **(B)** the raw connectome edge-weight histogram.

This plots the adjacency matrix for the functional connectome of a human, illustrated in Figure 2.2.1(A). The nodes of this network are numbered sequentially. A heatmap is a network visualization in which the x and y coordinates of a given entry in the matrix indicate the pair of nodes an edge is connected to, and the color for the (x, y) point in the figure indicates the weight of the edge between nodes x and y. The edge weight is stronger if the pair of brain areas are active together more, and lower if the pair of brain areas are less active together. These are real data, generated from actual fMRI scans.

One thing that we can notice from this plot is that a lot of the edges have tiny weights. Let's explore this a little bit further.

A useful summary of the network is to look at a histogram for the edge weights. A histogram shows the number of edges (on the vertical axis) which have a given edge-weight range (indicated by the width of a particular bar on the horizontal axis). You can call this directly on the adjacency matrix (albeit flattened), and it will plot a histogram of the edge weights. We will do this using seaborn's `histplot()`:

```
import seaborn as sns
import matplotlib.pyplot as plt

ax = sns.histplot(A.flatten(), bins=50)
ax.set_xlabel("Edge weight")
ax.set_title("Histogram of functional connectome edge-weights")
```

A plot of the adjacency matrix's edge weights is shown in Figure 2.2.1(B). A lot of the edge weight tend to be right around the 0.2 to 0.6 range, which tells us that, in general, the pairs of fMRI regions have slightly correlated activations. This is because the correlation metric used for fMRI data is between -1 and 1, where higher values indicate higher correlations. When some node tends to be active, other nodes also tend to be active. If this were not the case, the histogram would be a bit more centered around 0.0.

2.3   Preparing the Data

Next, it's time for us to prepare our networks for analysis. When we implement code, we will try to be modular and functional. This is because:

1. Functions will make the useful data preparation code that we write usable on new networks,
2. We can gradually build libraries of utility functions,
3. We can modularize functions into other parts of our analysis pipeline to keep a lean module-oriented design, and
4. We can easily try different transformations of the data and evaluate which ones tend to work best.

2.3.1   Data Cleaning

Many network machine learning algorithms cannot work with a node that is *isolated*, meaning that the node has no edges. Let's start with fixing this. We can remove isolated nodes from the network as follows:

1. Compute the number of nodes each node connects to. This consists of summing the matrix along the rows (or columns). The network is undirected, which means that if a node can communicate with another node, the other node can communicate back.
2. Identify any nodes which are connected to zero nodes along either the rows or columns. These are the isolated nodes.
3. Remove the isolated nodes from the adjacency matrix.

Let's see how this works in practice. We begin by first taking the row sums of each node, which tells us how many nodes each node is connected to. Next, we remove all nodes which are not connected to any other nodes (the row and column sum are both zero) from both the adjacency matrix and the labels:

```python
def remove_isolates(A):
    """
    A function which removes isolated nodes from the
    adjacency matrix A.
    """
    degree = A.sum(axis=0) # sum along the rows to obtain the node
        degree
    out_degree = A.sum(axis=1)
    A_purged = A[~(degree == 0),:]
    A_purged = A_purged[:,~(degree == 0)]
    print("Purging {:d} nodes...".format((degree == 0).sum()))
    return A_purged

A = remove_isolates(A)
# Purging 0 nodes...
```

So no isolated nodes were found, and consequently no nodes were purged. Great! What else can we do?

With functional MRI connectomes, we often want to look at absolute correlations rather than the original correlations. The intuition is that, if one node is less active when another node is active, that kind of indicates that they are still operating together. Let's see how to compute absolute correlations:

```python
import matplotlib.pyplot as plt
from graphbook_code import heatmap

A_abs = np.abs(A)
fig, axs = plt.subplots(1,3, figsize=(21, 6))
heatmap(A, ax=axs[0], title="Human Connectome, Raw", vmin=np.min(A),
    vmax=1)
heatmap(A_abs, ax=axs[1], title="Human Connectome, Absolute",
    vmin=np.min(A), vmax=1)
heatmap(A_abs - A, ax=axs[2], title="Difference (Absolute - Raw)",
    vmin=0, vmax=1)
```

Several of the values will change (the faint bands), which is indicated by larger differences from the raw to the absolute data. We can use this `heatmap` function to plot the adjacency matrix as we manipulate it later on in this section.

To streamline the process of cleaning up the raw data, we often need to write custom data cleaners. We will want our cleaners to work seamlessly with `sklearn`'s functions, since we will be using that package regularly. This requires us to implement three class methods: `fit()`, `transform()`, and `fit_transform()`. By adding `TransformerMixin` as a base class, we do not even have to implement the third method. If we use `BaseEstimator` as a base class, we will also obtain `get_params()` and `set_params()` methods, which may be useful for hyperparameter tuning steps later.

Here is an example cleaner class which purges the adjacency matrix of isolates and remaps the categorical labels to numbers. A key step to implementing this all as cleanly as possible is that the inputs, an adjacency matrix and a vector of node labels, are passed in as a *single* tuple object. This is because `sklearn` anticipates that the return arguments from calls of `transform()` can be passed sequentially to one another.

```python
from sklearn.base import TransformerMixin, BaseEstimator

class CleanData(BaseEstimator, TransformerMixin):

    def fit(self, X):
        return self

    def transform(self, X):
        print("Cleaning data...")
        Acleaned = remove_isolates(X)
        A_abs_cl = np.abs(Acleaned)
        self.A_ = A_abs_cl
        return self.A_

data_cleaner = CleanData()
A_clean = data_cleaner.transform(A)
# Cleaning data...
# Purging 0 nodes...
```

2.3.2 Edge-Weight Transformations

One of the most important transformations that we will come across in network machine learning is called an *edge-weight transformation*. Many networks, such as the human functional connectome, will have edge weights which do not just take values of 1 or 0 (edge or no edge, a *binary* network); rather, many networks may have discrete-weighted edges (the edges take nonnegative intervalues, such as 0, 1, 2, 3, ...), or decimal-weight edges (the edges take values like 0, 0.1234, 0.234, 2.4234, ...). For a number of reasons discussed in Section 3.6, this is often not a desirable characteristic. The edges in a network might be error prone, and it might be desirable to capture only one (or a few) properties about the edge weights, rather than complicating things by leaving them in their raw values. Further, a lot of the techniques we explore throughout this book might not work on nonbinary networks. For this reason, we should get accustomed to transforming edge weights to take new sets of values.

There are two common approaches to transform edge weights: The first is called binarization (set all of the edges to take a value of 0 or 1), and the second is called an ordinal transformation.

2.3.2.1   Binarization of Edges

Binarization is quite simple. It means the edges in the raw network take nonbinary values (values other than just 0s and 1s), and we need them to be 0s and 1s for some reason; often, so that an algorithm can work properly. How should we do this rigorously?

The simplest thing to do is usually to just choose a threshold, and set edges with weights less than the threshold to 0, and edges with weights greater than the threshold to 1. Let's take a look at how we can implement this using `graspologic`. We first look at the network before binarization, and then after:

```
from graspologic.utils import binarize

threshold = 0.4
A_bin = binarize(A_clean > threshold)
```

When we plot the cleaned adjacency matrix and the binarized adjacency matrix in Figure 2.3.1(B), we see that it retains a lot of the "general idea" of the weighted adjacency matrix, but is a lot simpler. Whereas the edge weights in Figure 2.3.1(A) were *continuous*, we've now *binarized* the edges of the network to only take two possible values (0 or 1). This has the effect of potentially reducing the variance (since we no longer will need as complicated of descriptions to summarize the edge weights), but potentially increasing the bias (since we have simplified our data and have therefore potentially "thrown away" information that might be important).

We also could have normalized these edge weights using a *pass to ranks*. The rank of an edge is its index if all nonzero edges are ordered by their magnitude. Through pass to ranks, nonzero edges are replaced with a function of their ordinal rank, from smallest to largest, with the largest item having a rank of one, and the smallest item having a rank of 1/(number of nonzero edges). This is called an *ordinal transformation*, in that it preserves the *orders* of the edge weights, but discards all other information. The adjacency matrix of the ranked connectome is shown in Figure 2.3.1(C).

```
from graspologic.utils import pass_to_ranks

A_ptr = pass_to_ranks(A_clean)
```

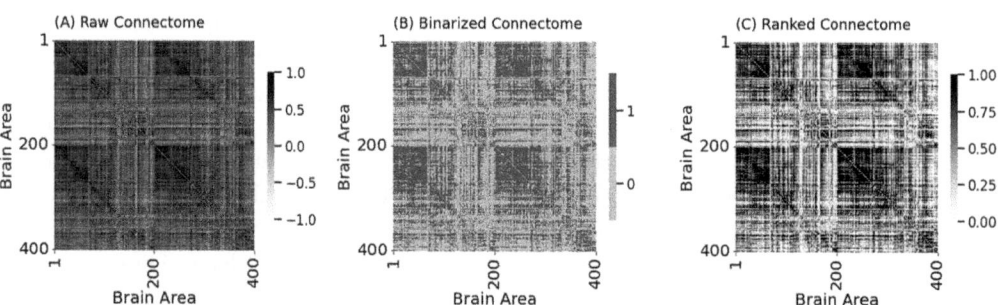

Figure 2.3.1 (**A**) The cleaned connectome, before reweighting. (**B**) The binarized connectome. (**C**) The ranked connectome.

This has shifted the histogram of edge weights, as we can see by plotting a histogram:

```python
import seaborn as sns

fig, axs = plt.subplots(2, 1, figsize=(10, 10))
sns.histplot(A_clean[A_clean > 0].flatten(), ax=axs[0], color="gray")
axs[0].set_xlabel("Edge weight")
axs[0].set_title("Histogram of human connectome, non-zero edge
    weights")
sns.histplot(A_ptr[A_ptr > 0].flatten(), ax=axs[1], color="gray")
axs[1].set_xlabel("ptr(Edge weight)")
axs[1].set_title("Histogram of human connectome, passed-to-ranks")

plt.tight_layout()
```

The histograms before and after passing the adjacency matrix to ranks are shown in Figure 2.3.2.

Passing to ranks has the desirable property that it bounds the network's edge weights to be between 0 and 1, as we can see above. This is often crucial if we seek to compare two or more networks and the edge weights between the networks differ in magnitude (an edge's weight might mean something in relation to another edge's weight in that same network, but an edge's weight means nothing in relation

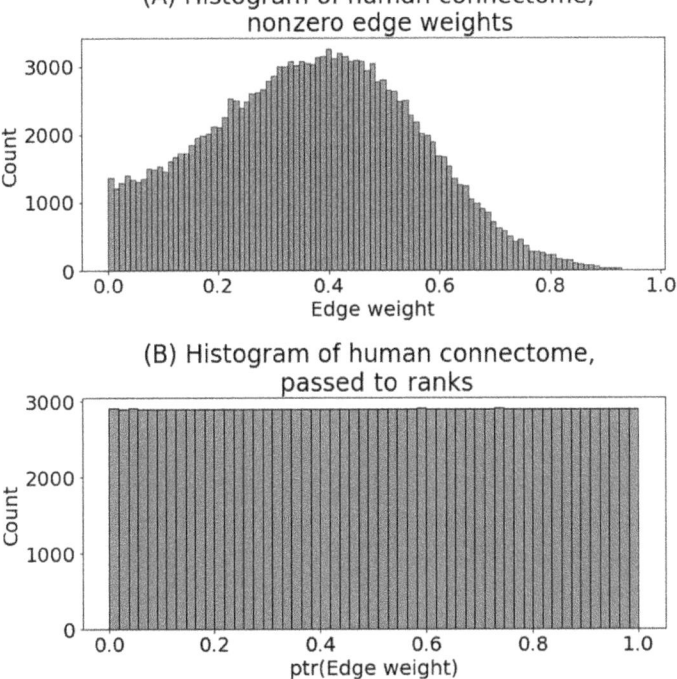

Figure 2.3.2 (**A**) Histogram of the edge weights in the adjacency matrix before normalization. (**B**) Histogram of the edge weights in the adjacency matrix after `ptr`.

to another edge's weight in a separate network). Further, passing to ranks allows us to lower our susceptibility to outliers, as we will see in later chapters.

Again, we will turn the edge-weight transformation step into its own `sklearn`-compatible class:

```
class FeatureScaler(BaseEstimator, TransformerMixin):

    def fit(self, X):
        return self

    def transform(self, X):
        print("Scaling edge-weights...")
        A_scaled = pass_to_ranks(X)
        return (A_scaled)

feature_scaler = FeatureScaler()
A_cleaned_scaled = feature_scaler.transform(A_clean)
# Scaling edge-weights...
```

2.3.2.2   Transformation Pipelines

As you can see, there are a number of data transformations that need to be executed to prepare network data for machine learning algorithms. For this reason, it may be desirable to develop a pipeline which automates the data preparation process. We can create this using the `Pipeline` class from `sklearn`, which can apply sequences of transformations to data inputs. Here is a simple pipeline for doing all of the steps we have performed so far:

```
from sklearn.pipeline import Pipeline

num_pipeline = Pipeline([
    ('cleaner', CleanData()),
    ('scaler', FeatureScaler()),
])

A_xfm = num_pipeline.fit_transform(A)
# Cleaning data...
# Purging 0 nodes...
# Scaling edge-weights..
```

The pipeline class takes a list of name/estimator pairs defining a sequence of steps. All but the last estimator must be transformers, which implement the `fit_transform()` method. In our case, this is handled directly by the `TransformerMixin` base class.

When you call the `fit_transform()` method of the numerical pipeline, it calls the `fit_transform()` method on each of the transformers, and passes the output of each call as the parameter to the next call, until it reaches the final estimator, for which it just calls the `fit()` method.

Next, we see the real usefulness of the `Pipeline` module. The reason we went to lengths to define a pipeline was that we wanted to have an easily reproducible procedure that we could efficiently apply to new connectomes. This is easy to apply to the second subject in our dataset:

```
A_xfm2 = num_pipeline.fit_transform(As[1])
# Cleaning data...
# Purging 0 nodes...
# Scaling edge-weights...
```

2.4 Selecting and Training a Network Machine Learning Model

You've got your data loaded and preprocessed. Now comes the fun part: modeling your data. To do this, you first want to think about the generative process that made it: What probabilistic model should you assume?

When you've made a decision, you should use that probabilistic model to create a representation for your data, often by moving from network space, with nodes and edges, to Euclidean space, with points on a coordinate axis. Moving to Euclidean space is equivalent to converting to tabular data; we usually think about geometry when we say "Euclidean," and about data tables when we say "tabular data." The rows of the data table are equivalent to points in Euclidean space, with the columns corresponding to the axes of that space.

Finally, you want to implement some downstream analysis method which helps answer whatever question you set out to answer. For your case, you want to use models and representations amenable to finding groups of correlated nodes.

2.4.1 Generating New Representations from Your Data

As we briefly mentioned in Section 1.1, a major problem with learning from network data is that networks in their rawest form are not tabular datasets. To apply techniques from general machine learning (typically designed for tabular datasets), we need to adapt the network to be compatible with tabular approaches, or adapt our general machine learning architecture for network layouts such as adjacency matrices, which properly convey the dependencies in network data. This is called *representation learning*, and is an important field of study across machine learning.

We will use a representation learning technique called a spectral embedding, which you will learn about in Chapter 5. Spectral embedding will appear many times, whether you are studying one network, pairs of networks, or multiple networks. Let's use it to create representations for our connectomes, also called *embedding* them:

```
from graspologic.embed import AdjacencySpectralEmbed

embedding = AdjacencySpectralEmbed(n_components=3,
    svd_seed=0).fit_transform(A_xfm)
```

An embedding takes the adjacency matrix, which is a matrix representation of the entire network, and turns it into a tabular array. Each row of the array is called an *estimated latent position* for a given node, and each column is called an *estimated latent dimension* of the network. If there are *n* nodes, there are *n* rows of the spectral embedding array, and if there are *d* estimated latent dimensions of the network, there are *d* columns. The spectral embedding has taken the $n \times n$ adjacency matrix, which we can't use traditional machine learning algorithms on, and transformed it into a $n \times d$ tabular array, which we can use machine learning algorithms on. We'll visualize this embedding using a *pairs plot*, which is a scatter plot where each node is a single point in the plot, and the *x*- and *y*-axes are different *pairs* of latent dimensions:

```
from graspologic.plot import pairplot

_ = pairplot(embedding, title="Spectral Embedding for connectome")
```

This pairs plot is shown in Figure 2.4.1(A).

The representation of the adjacency matrix we chose, which uses the spectral embedding, can be tied to a statistical model with some assumptions. In particular, it ties to the stochastic block model described in Section 4.3. In a stochastic block model, each node is a member of a subgroup, called a *community*, and its connectivity probability to other nodes in the network is dictated by which community it is a member of, and which community the other node is a member of. This sounds a *lot* like the question that your colleague wanted you to explore, since it gives a way to take the nodes of the network and form "functionally similar" subgroups from them.

2.4.2   Using the Representations to Learn New Features from the Network

Now that we have a tabular representation of the data, we can use the intuition and assumptions of the stochastic block model to cluster our nodes. Let's see what happens when we apply KMeans to our data:

```
from sklearn.cluster import KMeans

labels = KMeans(n_clusters=2, random_state=0).fit_predict(embedding)
_ = pairplot(embedding, labels=labels, legend_name="Predicter
    Clusters",
                title="KMeans clustering")
```

The results of this pairs plot are shown in Figure 2.4.1(B). So, it looks like the *K*-means was able to learn two clusters of brain regions from our dataset. These clusters are indicated by the "blobs" of points that are red or blue, respectively.

If we're careful, we will notice we did something a little weird here. Why did we choose two? Why not five? Why not eight? We chose two somewhat arbitrarily. In general, when you don't know what to expect from your data (we didn't know what to expect here, other than that we wanted a modestly sized way to group the nodes up), it's a good idea to use quantitative means to make these determinations for you.

With KMeans, we can use a metric called the silhouette score to do this for us. You choose the optimal number of clusters as the clustering with the highest silhouette score (this is covered in Section 6.1 when you learn about community detection). graspologic makes this process pretty straightforward with a KMeansCluster

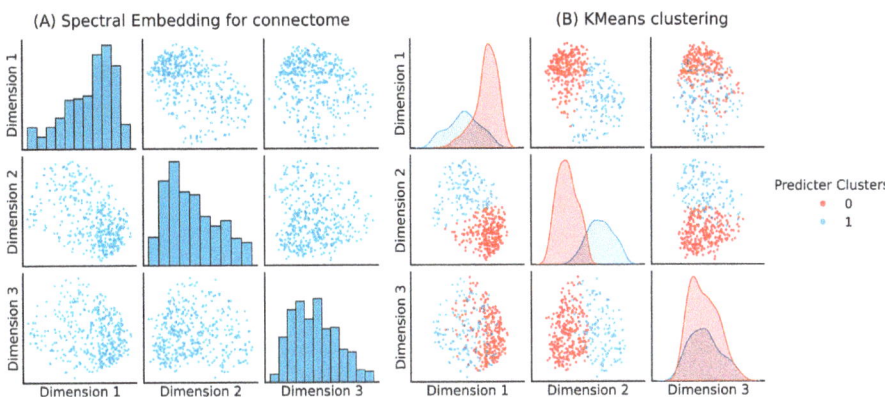

Figure 2.4.1 (**A**) The pairs plot for the estimated latent dimensions. (**B**) The pairs plot with predicted communities of nodes via KMeans with two clusters.

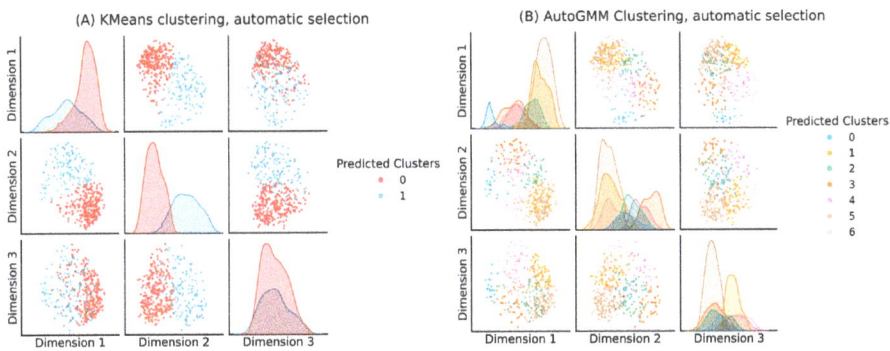

Figure 2.4.2 (**A**) The pairs plot for the embedded data, with node communities estimated by KMeans. (**B**) The pairs plot for the embedded data, with node communities estimated by AutoGMM.

class, which uses the silhouette score under the hood to predict the number of clusters:

```
from graspologic.cluster import KMeansCluster

labels = KMeansCluster(max_clusters=10,
    random_state=0).fit_predict(embedding)
_ = pairplot(embedding, labels=labels, title="KMeans clustering,
    automatic selection",
            legend_name="Predicted Clusters")
```

Dynamically identifying an ideal number of clusters might not necessarily get you the same number when you repeat it multiple times: Clustering algorithms tend to include some randomization. Here, we got three predicted clusters. The pairs plot for the embedded data with the new labels is in Figure 2.4.2(A). Note that you might get a different number of estimated clusters than we did, because there is some randomness in the unsupervised learning procedure that we used.

So, what about other possible approaches? Unless you are pretty confident that the clusters you are looking for have "blobs" that are totally spherically symmetric (basically, they look like "balls" in the dataset), K-means can be a bad idea. Another strategy called the Gaussian mixture model, or GMM, handles this slightly more elegantly, allowing the cluster blobs to be any ellipse-like shape. We can use GMM and automatically select the number of clusters using the Bayesian information criterion, or BIC, with `AutoGMMCluster`:

```
from graspologic.cluster import AutoGMMCluster

labels = AutoGMMCluster(max_components=10,
    random_state=0).fit_predict(embedding)
_ = pairplot(embedding, labels=labels, title="AutoGMM Clustering,
    automatic selection",
            legend_name="Predicted Clusters")
```

The pairs plot for the embedded data with the labels determined by GMM is in Figure 2.4.2(B). You might get a different number of clusters when you run it than us (again, due to randomness); here, we got seven.

2.5   Fine Tuning a Network Machine Learning Model

In Section 2.4 we took one of the fMRI networks, created a representation for it with spectral decomposition, and used various clustering techniques to learn about latent structure between the brain regions.

However, there is a big caveat: Your colleague sent you over a hundred networks, and you ignored all but one of them. Surely, there's something that you can learn from all of them.

Fortunately, when you have a multiple network problem, there are plenty of approaches that you can use to learn from all of them simultaneously. Let's break down how we can approach this.

We want to produce a representation of all of our networks. The corresponding nodes of all of these networks represent the same areas of the brain. For all intents and purposes, we can assume that these different nodes mean the same thing across all of the different people, even if the networks vary for each individual. We want to learn whether there is some shared group structure across all of the different networks, so that we can find groups of related brain regions. To do this, we will want to take all of our networks, and combine them to produce a single embedding in which we can look at brain regions separately from individuals. Does anything exist to help us?

A particular representation called MASE from Section 5.5.3 does just this. It allows us to take many networks, and learn a single representation for the nodes across all of the networks. This representation will use information from all of the networks, so we will not have to worry about ignoring informative networks like we did before.

```
from graspologic.embed import MultipleASE

# transform all the networks with pipeline utility
As_xfm = [num_pipeline.fit_transform(A) for A in As]
```

```
# and embed them
embedding = MultipleASE(n_components=5,
    svd_seed=0).fit_transform(As_xfm)
_ = pairplot(embedding, title="Multiple spectral embedding of all
    connectomes")
```

The MASE embedding used all of the networks to produce a single latent embedding called embedding. It is an array with rows corresponding to nodes (brain regions), and columns corresponding to dimension. Let's see what happens when we apply our clustering method to this embedding:

```
labels = AutoGMMCluster(max_components=10,
    random_state=0).fit_predict(embedding)
_ = pairplot(embedding, labels=labels,
            title="Multiple spectral embedding of all connectomes",
            legend_name="Predicted Clusters")
```

The pairs plot of the MASE embedding with labels estimated by GMM is shown in Figure 2.5.1. Again, AutoGMMCluster, the clustering algorithm, has some element of randomness to it. Don't be concerned if you don't get the exact same number of predicted clusters as we did, or if your clusters look a little different.

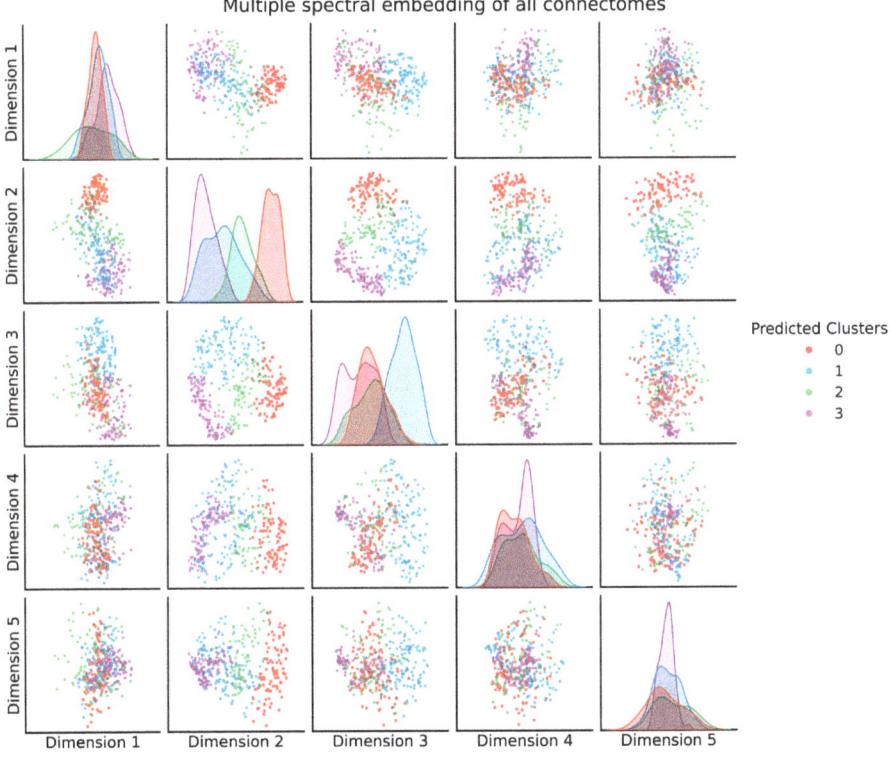

Figure 2.5.1 The MASE embedding, with labels learned by GMM.

2.6   Discover and Visualize the System to Gain Insights

We now have a codebase built to read in the input data, get them cleaned up, embed them using information from all networks, and predict brain region clusters.

We now arrive at the most important part of any computational analysis: making sense of whatever it is that we did.

How could we visualize node clusters (formally called *communities*)? We already known about the pairs plot, which we saw in Figure 2.5.1(B).

The nodes in this analysis correspond to areas of the brain, and our goal is to figure out if there are groups of brain regions that are related to each other. We can therefore gain insight by visualizing how the clusters we found really look in the brain's natural space.

We picked a set of networks such that the nodes correspond to known three-dimensional (3D) points in the brain. This means that, with some minor work, we can figure out the coordinates of the individual nodes for the brain. You don't need to worry too much about how this code works; at a high level, it just obtains 3D coordinates for the nodes of the network in a json file, and then parses them into a pandas dataframe:

```python
from urllib import request
import json
import pandas as pd
from pathlib import Path

coord_dest = os.path.join(FMRI_PATH, "coordinates.json")
with open(coord_dest) as coord_f:
    coords = []
    for roiname, contents in json.load(coord_f)["rois"].items():
        try:
            if roiname != "0":
                coord_roi = {"x" : contents["center"][0], "y" :
                    contents["center"][1], "z" : contents["center"][2]}
                coords.append(coord_roi)
        except:
            continue

coords_df = pd.DataFrame(coords)
```

Now that we have the coordinates, let's try plotting the nodes, but in their native spatial position. Here, the color will indicate the predicted label, from our clustering. The slices we show will be a saggital slice through the brain. A saggital slice shows the brain nodes oriented from back (left of the plot) of the brain to front (right of the plot), and from bottom (bottom of the plot) to top (top of the plot). On the left, we show the brain with the lobe annotations, and on the right, the predicted labels of each node in color, where each node is shown in its true physical location:

```python
import matplotlib.image as mpimg

coords_df["Community"] = labels
coords_df['Community'] = coords_df['Community'].astype('category')
```

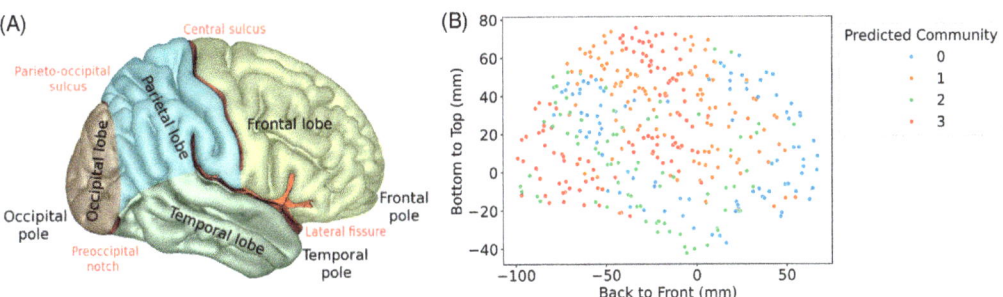

Figure 2.6.1 (**A**) Brain lobe annotations for different areas of the brain (created by [5]), and (**B**) predicted node communities oriented by spatial position of each node in the brain.

```
fig, axs = plt.subplots(1, 2, figsize=(18, 6))
axs[0].imshow(mpimg.imread('./Images/lobes.png'))
axs[0].set_axis_off()
sns.scatterplot(x="y", y="z", data=coords_df, hue="Community",
    ax=axs[1])
```

The resulting plot is shown in Figure 2.6.1. So, the estimated communities of each node don't quite perfectly align with the brain lobe that the node is in. However, nodes tend to be spatially close to other nodes in the same estimated community. Notice, for instance, that a lot of nodes in the left side of the brain, the part marked "occipital lobe" in the plot, are the same color. In our plot, these nodes are red; in your plot, they might be a different color.

In neuroimaging, there tend to be "groups" of brain areas that are organized together, which are delineated in files called "parcellations." The idea is that they "parcellate" (segment) different areas of the brain based on two factors: whether the areas of the brain work together, and whether they are located near each other in the brain. This is a generalization of the concept of "brain lobes" that we briefly went over above.

Let's see how well the labels we obtained align with one of these parcellations, known as the "Yeo7" parcellation. We will begin by finding which "Yeo7" parcels the nodes of our network are positioned in. We will do this using some code borrowed from the `neuroparc` repository [6]. The code below will first grab the mapping of image pixels to Yeo7 parcels, and then grab the mapping of image pixels to nodes in our network (Schaefer400 parcels). These are stored in the files with the extensions `.nii.gz` below. Once we have those files, we will compare the parcels of nodes in our network to figure out which Yeo7 parcels they fall within spatially:

```
import datasets.dice as dice

# obtain the Yeo7 parcellation
group_dest = os.path.join("./datasets/",
    "Yeo-7_space-MNI152NLin6_res-2x2x2.nii.gz")
request.urlretrieve("https://github.com/neurodata/neuroparc/" +
    "blob/master/atlases/label/Human/" +
```

```
                        "Yeo-7_space-MNI152NLin6_res-2x2x2.nii.gz?raw=true",
                          group_dest);
# obtain the Shaefer parcellation
roi_dest = os.path.join("./datasets/", parcellation +
    "_space-MNI152NLin6_res-2x2x2.nii.gz")
request.urlretrieve("https://github.com/neurodata/neuroparc/" +
    "blob/master/atlases/label/Human/" +
                    parcellation +
                        "_space-MNI152NLin6_res-2x2x2.nii.gz?raw=true",
                    roi_dest);

# decipher which Schaefer labels fall within Yeo7 regions
dicemap, _, _ = dice.dice_roi("./datasets/", "./datasets",
                        "Yeo-7_space-MNI152NLin6_res-2x2x2.nii.gz",
                        parcellation +
                            "_space-MNI152NLin6_res-2x2x2.nii.gz",
                        verbose=False)
actual_cluster = np.argmax(dicemap, axis=0)[1:] - 1
```

So, to be clear, we have now produced two mappings:

1. For each node, we have an estimated (predicted) community for the node. This is a delineation on the basis of functional similarity of the nodes from the data that we observed across the networks.
2. For each node, we have a Yeo7 region for the node. This will serve as the "True parcel" for the nodes.

Next, we will try to figure out whether our predicted communities and the true communities align with a confusion matrix. Its rows are each of the true parcels in the reference (Yeo7 region), and its columns are the predicted communities that we found earlier. The entries of the matrix are the counts of nodes in the network that are assigned to a given predicted community and a given parcel:

```
import contextlib
from sklearn.metrics import confusion_matrix
from graphbook_code import cmaps

# make confusion matrix
cf_matrix = confusion_matrix(actual_cluster, labels)

# and plot it
ax = sns.heatmap(cf_matrix, cmap=cmaps["sequential"])
ax.set_title("Confusion matrix")
ax.set_ylabel("True Parcel")
ax.set_xlabel("Predicted Community")
```

The resulting plot is shown in Figure 2.6.2. The MASE embedding followed by clustering tends to find groups of nodes that have similar connectivity patterns in the connectomes (it will do a good job at finding the nodes that work together). The nodes in the same community tend to behave "as a unit," in that they tend to be active/inactive together. What the plot above shows is that nodes that have similar connectivity patterns (from the networks) tend also to be in the same true parcel, which makes sense since the parcels are based on connectivity profiles from brains.

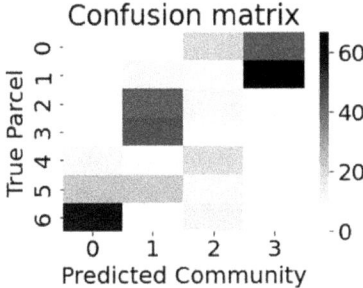

Figure 2.6.2 The confusion matrix of the estimated clusters for each node in the networks, compared to the parcel that each node is in.

The clustering is not perfect, in that it is never the case that a single predicted label corresponds to exactly one true label. If that were the case, we would expect nodes assigned to each column in the "confusion matrix" to only have one possible true label assigned to them (which is not quite what we saw here).

Taking these conclusions together, we find that some areas of the brain (such as the occipital and parietal areas) feature nodes which are both functionally and spatially similar: They tend to show similar connectivity patterns with respect to other groups of nodes in the network, and are in similar spatial positions in the brain. On the other hand, for other areas of the brain, while the nodes may be functionally similar, they might not necessarily be spatially similar. This is where the domain expertise kicks in: We don't know how to interpret this particular aspect of our finding, but maybe our colleagues do.

Further, while this analysis only really ended up looking at whether different groups of regions worked together, there's no reason we couldn't also incorporate spatial information about the nodes into our analysis. In Section 5.6, we will learn techniques for incorporating both the network data and other information about the nodes through a technique called covariate-assisted spectral embedding (CASE).

And this is where the fun of network machine learning comes into play: Network machine learning is a tool not only to apply algorithms to data, but to facilitate learning new things about the data as well. We might get some predictable conclusions (such as some of the nodes being both functionally and spatially similar), and we might get some unpredictable conclusions (such as some of the nodes being functionally, but not spatially, similar). Your ability to understand network machine learning, while crucial, is going to go hand in hand with your ability to understand the intricacies of the domain you want to apply network machine learning to. We hope that we can help with the former part; we will leave the latter to you.

2.6.1   Try It Out

This chapter gave a small scale peek at what a network machine learning project looks like, and a brief introduction to some tools we can use to gain novel insights from our network data. The process from obtaining data to choosing appropriate network machine learning problems can often be extremely arduous. In fact, as a network machine learning scientist, you might find that just obtaining data in a useful form (a network) and cleaning the data to be usable takes an enormous chunk of your time.

If you haven't already done so, now is a fantastic time to grab your laptop, select a network dataset you are interested in, and start trying to work through the whole process from A to Z. If you need some pointers, the `graspologic` package makes several datasets available [7]. We recommend working through the contents of this book by first using the example data presented in the chapter, and then trying to apply the techniques to your own new data.

Bibliography

[1] Poldrack RA, Mumford JA, Nichols TE. Handbook of Functional MRI Data Analysis. Cambridge, England, UK: Cambridge University Press; 2011.

[2] Munsell BC, Wu G, Bonilha L, Laurienti P. Connectomics: Applications to Neuroimaging (The MICCAI Society book Series). Cambridge, MA, USA: Academic Press; 2018.

[3] Docker Engine installation overview; 2023. [Online; accessed Jan. 19, 2023.]

[4] Bridgeford EW. neurodata/graph-stats-book – Docker Image; 2023. [Online; accessed Jan. 19, 2023.]

[5] Sebastian023. File:LobesCaptsLateral.png – Wikimedia Commons; 2012. Image made available for unaltered reuse under CC BY-SA 3.0 License.

[6] Lawrence RM, Bridgeford EW, Myers PE, Arvapalli GC, Ramachandran SC, Pisner DA, et al. Standardizing human brain parcellations. Sci Data. 2021 Mar.;8(78):1–9.

[7] Microsoft. Datasets – graspologic 2.0.1 documentation; 2023. [Online; accessed Feb. 4, 2023.]

Part II

Representations

3 Characterizing and Preparing Network Data

In Section 1.3, we introduced Figure 1.3.4, which will recur throughout this book to contextualize the process of learning from networks. Figure 3.0.1 dives into the first step after obtaining our data: describing our network sample. Chapter 3 takes a careful look at this step: We explore basic properties, relationships, statistics, representations, and preprocessing methods for samples of network-valued data.

We cover the following:

1. Section 3.1 introduces the basic properties and representations of networks, including a formal description of the adjacency matrix.
2. Section 3.2 covers descriptive properties of nodes and relationships between nodes in a network.
3. Section 3.3 explains key network summary statistics like density, clustering coefficient, and average path length.
4. Section 3.4 discusses matrix representations of networks beyond adjacency matrices, including degree and Laplacian matrices.
5. Section 3.5 covers subnetworks and connected components within larger networks.
6. Sections 3.6 and 3.7 explain regularization techniques for networks, including node pruning and edge thresholding.
7. Section 3.8 describes methods for rescaling edge weights in weighted networks.

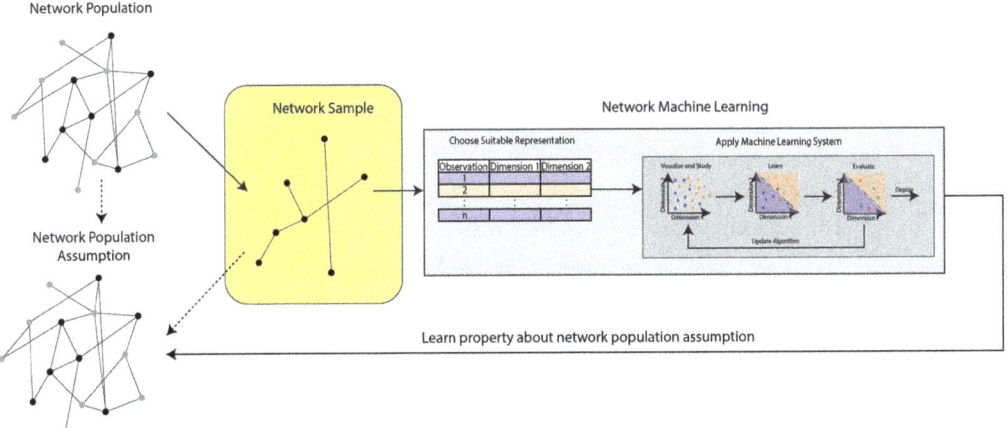

Figure 3.0.1 The statistical learning pipeline.

We will often use the term "observed network" or "network sample." As described in Section 1.3, we call it this because the sample of network data that we observe constitutes only a noisy observation of the population of network data that we actually want to study. In Chapter 4, we will explore how we can use random network models to account for the imperfections in our observed network sample.

3.1   The Basics of Networks

In Section 1.1, we introduced the concept of networks as collections of nodes and edges. Together, the nodes and edges are known as the *topology of the network*. This section expands on that foundation, developing a framework in which to understand network properties and representations.

We begin with adjacency matrices, the primary mathematical representation for network data. The adjacency matrix encodes the nodes and edges of a network in matrix form, providing a foundation for network analysis.

We then explore key properties of networks, including:

1. Edge directionality,
2. Node loops, and
3. Edge weightedness.

We use a running example of New York City boroughs connected by major bridges to illustrate these concepts concretely. Later, Section 3.4 explores the degree matrix and the Laplacian. Sections 3.6, 3.7, and 3.8 build on concepts from this section to develop preprocessing techniques.

The fundamental object we use to describe networks is called the *adjacency matrix* [1], which is a large square matrix whose (i, j)th entry is 0 if an edge does not exist between nodes i and j, and nonzero if an edge does exist. Many ways to represent networks can be directly derived from the adjacency matrix.

3.1.1   Adjacency Matrices for Simple Networks

Let's say we have a network with n nodes. We give each node an index (usually some value between 1 and n, with one value per node) and then we create an $n \times n$ matrix. If there is an edge between node i and node j, we fill the (i, j)th and (j, i)th values of the matrix with a value of 1, and we say that nodes i and j are *adjacent*. We leave it as 0 otherwise.

The adjacency matrix looks like this:

$$A = \begin{bmatrix} a_{11} & \cdots & a_{1n} \\ \vdots & \ddots & \vdots \\ a_{n1} & \cdots & a_{nn} \end{bmatrix}.$$

Let's see this in action. We will make a small, simple network with only three nodes, and then see what it looks like as an adjacency matrix. To visualize this network, we use a layout plot, provided by `nx.draw_network()`.

```python
import numpy as np
import networkx as nx

G = nx.DiGraph()
# add nodes to the network
G.add_node("1", pos=(1,1))
G.add_node("2", pos=(4,4))
G.add_node("3", pos=(4,2))
# add edges to the network
G.add_edge("1", "2")
G.add_edge("2", "1")
G.add_edge("1", "3")
G.add_edge("3", "1")

# the coordinates in space to use for plotting the nodes
# in the layout plot
pos = {"1": (0, 0), "2": (1, 0), "3": (.5, .5)}

nx.draw_networkx(G, with_labels=True, node_color="white", pos=pos,
            font_size=10, font_color="black", arrows=False,
                edge_color="black",
            width=1)
```

The resulting plot of the network is shown in Figure 3.1.1(A). Our network has three nodes, labeled 1, 2, and 3. Each of these three nodes is either adjacent or not adjacent to the other nodes. We'll make a square matrix A, with three rows and three columns, so that each node has its own row and column associated to it.

So, let's fill out the matrix. We start with the first row, which corresponds to the first node, and move along the columns. If there is an edge between the first node and the node whose index matches the current column, we put a 1 in the current location. If the two nodes aren't adjacent, we add a 0. When we're done with the first row, we move on to the second. We keep going until the whole matrix is filled with 0s and 1s.

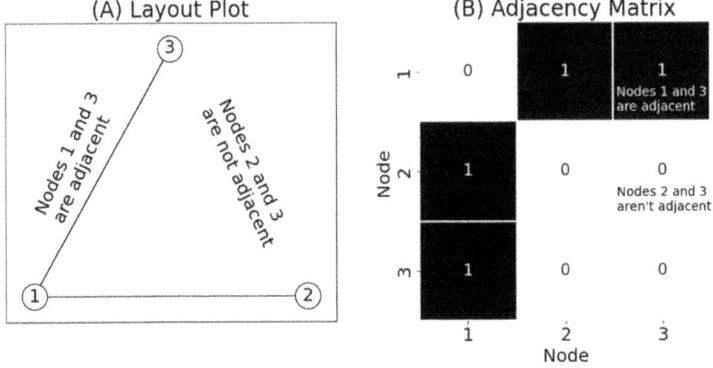

Figure 3.1.1 (**A**) A layout plot of the network, where nodes are circles and edges are the lines connecting them. (**B**) The network, visualized as an adjacency matrix.

Since the second and third nodes aren't adjacent, there is a 0 in locations $a_{2,1}$ and $a_{1,2}$. There are also zeros along the diagonals, since nodes don't have edges with themselves. Here we plotted the adjacency matrix using heatmap(); we won't always show this plot in the future.

```
from graphbook_code import heatmap
import matplotlib.pyplot as plt
import seaborn as sns

# convert the networkx graph to a numpy array
A = np.asarray(nx.to_numpy_array(G))

heatmap(A, annot=True, linewidths=.1, cbar=False,
        title="Adjacency matrix", xticklabels=[1,2,3], xtitle="Node",
        yticklabels=[1,2,3], ytitle="Node"
        )
```

The resulting adjacency matrix is shown in Figure 3.1.1(B).

3.1.2   A Running Example for the Sections Ahead

Now that we understand the basics of the adjacency matrix, we are ready for a running example that we will use for the next few sections.

Let's say we have a network representing the five boroughs of New York (Staten Island SI, Brooklyn BK, Queens Q, the Bronx BX, and Manhattan MH). The nodes in our network are the five boroughs. An edge (i, j) of our network exists if one can travel from borough i to borough j along a bridge. Let's start by defining a network with networkx's DiGraph() function:

```
import networkx as nx
from graphbook_code import heatmap

# create an undirected network G
G = nx.Graph()
# add the nodes like before
G.add_node("SI", pos=(2,1))
G.add_node("MH", pos=(4,4))
G.add_node("BK", pos=(4,1.7))
G.add_node("Q", pos=(6,3))
G.add_node("BX", pos=(6,6))

# specify boroughs that are adjacent to one another
pos = nx.get_node_attributes(G, 'pos')
G.add_edge("SI", "BK")
G.add_edge("MH", "BK")
G.add_edge("BK", "Q")
G.add_edge("MH", "Q")
G.add_edge("MH", "BX")
G.add_edge("Q", "BX")

A = nx.to_numpy_array(G)
```

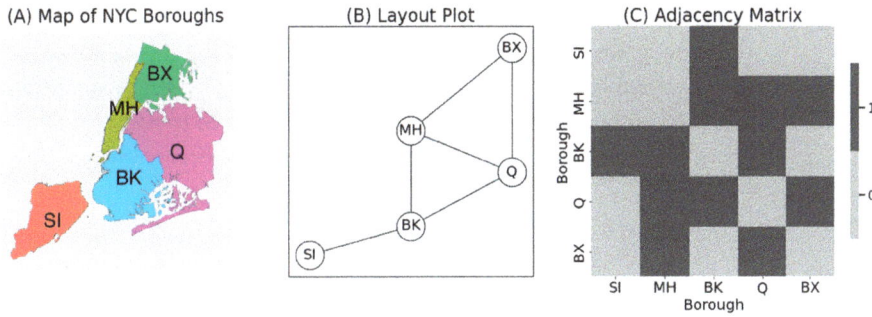

Figure 3.1.2 (**A**) A map of New York. We use this to construct a network of New York, where the nodes are boroughs of New York and the edges are bridges between different boroughs. (**B**) Visualized as a layout plot. (**C**) Visualized as a heatmap.

```
# plotting
nx.draw_networkx(G, with_labels=True, node_color="black", pos=pos,
         font_color="white", edge_color="black")

# pass in the xticklabels and yticklabels corresponding to the
# appropriately ordered boroughs (in the order we constructed them)
heatmap(A.astype(int), xticklabels=["SI", "MH", "BK", "Q", "BX"],
     yticklabels=["SI", "MH", "BK", "Q", "BX"],
     xtitle="Borough", ytitle="Borough"
     )
```

Figure 3.1.2 shows a map of New York City, a layout plot representation of a network derived from the the boroughs of New York, and an adjacency matrix as a heatmap of this network.

3.1.3   Directionality and Networks

There is a concept of directedness in edges. We have two nodes i and j. In an undirected network, if there is an edge from node i to node j, there is also an edge from j to i; the two nodes are simply adjacent. In a directed network, this is not necessarily the case: An edge from j to i doesn't imply an edge from i to j. We will primarily deal with undirected networks in this book, but it is useful to know that directed networks exist.

Let's explore this idea with the New York City borough example. When we decide to travel from borough i to borough j, we care about whether we can actually drive in that direction. The directedness of the bridge network describes whether we need to worry about one-way bridges and bridge closures. If our network contains one-way bridges, then a bridge from borough i to borough j doesn't necessarily imply that a path along that bridge from borough j to borough i exists. If, for instance, the bridges in the Brooklyn (BK) to Staten Island (SI) direction are closed, this would appear as a directed edge in our network.

We typically show directionality using arrows in the layout plot. Note that there is no arrow going from Brooklyn to Staten Island along this edge, so we cannot drive directly from BK to SI via a bridge. We can do this by removing the arrowhead from BK to SI, although there is still an arrowhead from SI to BK:

```
from copy import deepcopy

G_dir = G.to_directed()

# remove the edge from BK to SI
G_dir.remove_edge("BK", "SI")

nx.draw_networkx(G_dir, with_labels=True, node_color="black", pos=pos,
                 font_color="white", arrows=True, edge_color="black")
```

Note that we passed the `arrows=True` argument, which tells `networkx` to include the arrows in our plot. A plot of this network is shown in Figure 3.1.3(B). There are bidirectional arrows (arrows from one node to the other, as well as the reverse) for all pairs of nodes except Brooklyn and Staten Island. When we see a layout plot without any arrows like in Figure 3.1.2(B), this typically indicates that the network is undirected.

A plot of the undirected network is shown in Figure 3.1.3(A). For the adjacency matrix A, remember that an edge between nodes i and j is represented by the adjacency value a_{ij}. This means that if the network is undirected, $a_{ij} = a_{ji}$ for all pairs of nodes i and j. By definition, this tells us that the adjacency matrix A is *symmetric*, so $A = A^\top$. We can verify this condition with `graspologic`:

```
from graspologic.utils import is_symmetric

A = nx.to_numpy_array(G)
is_symmetric(A)
# True
A_dir = nx.to_numpy_array(G_dir)
is_symmetric(A_dir)
# False
```

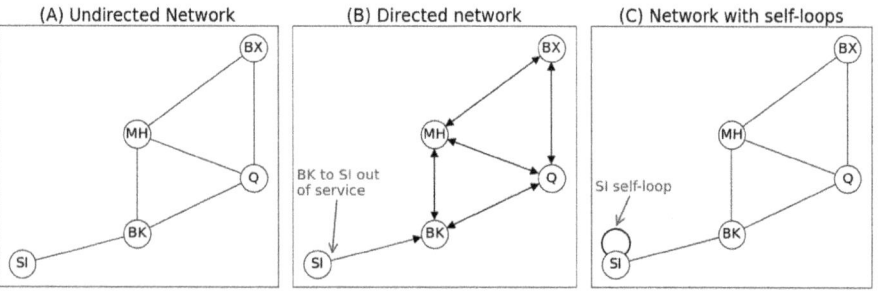

Figure 3.1.3 (**A**) The undirected network. (**B**) A plot of the network with the bridge from BK to SI out of service. (**C**) A plot of the network with a self-loop.

3.1.4   Loops and Networks

If we are already in a borough, why would we want to take a bridge to that same borough? This logic relates to the concept of self-loops in a network. A *self-loop* in a network describes whether nodes can connect back to themselves. For instance, consider the following loop on Staten Island. This would have the interpretation of a bridge which connects Staten Island back to itself:

```
G_loopy = deepcopy(G)
# add edge from SI to itself
G_loopy.add_edge("SI", "SI")
nx.draw_networkx(G_loopy, with_labels=True, node_color="black",
    pos=pos,
              font_color="white", edge_color="black")
```

A plot of this network is shown in Figure 3.1.3(C). A network is *loopless* if self-loops are not possible. It is also important to note that both directed and undirected network can have self-loops; we only show the undirected case.

For the adjacency matrix A, a self-loop would be represented by the adjacencies a_{ii} for all nodes i, the diagonal entries of A. Therefore, for a loopless network, all adjacencies a_{ii} on the diagonal do not exist. Mathematically, we represent this by defining the diagonal entries to be 0, which means that the matrix is *hollow*. This property is often abbreviated by stating that the diagonal of the adjacency matrix is 0, or $diag(A) = 0$. It is important to understand that if a network is loopless, there is a theoretical distinction between 0 and does not exist. Denoting the diagonal in an adjacency matrix of a loopless network with 0 is a convenience and a convention for the field.

We can verify this condition using:

```
from graspologic.utils import is_loopless
is_loopless(A)
# True
A_loopy = nx.to_numpy_array(G_loopy)
is_loopless(A_loopy)
# False
```

3.1.5   Weightedness and Networks

For most examples in this book, we will discuss unweighted or binary networks. A network is *unweighted* or *binary* if we only care about whether edges are present or absent. In an unweighted network, a potential edge a_{ij} takes the value 1 if there is an edge from node i to node j, and takes the value 0 if there is not an edge from node i to node j.

In our borough example, we could use edge weights $w(i, j)$ to describe the average speed of traffic on the bridge. The network is undirected, so we do not have to worry about directionality differences. The edge weight is indicated by the number along the corresponding edge.

```
G_weight = nx.Graph()

G_weight.add_node("SI", pos=(2,1))
G_weight.add_node("MH", pos=(4,4))
G_weight.add_node("BK", pos=(4,1.7))
G_weight.add_node("Q", pos=(6,3))
G_weight.add_node("BX", pos=(6,6))

# this time, we add weights to the edges
pos = nx.get_node_attributes(G, 'pos')
G_weight.add_edge("SI", "BK", weight=20)
G_weight.add_edge("MH", "BK", weight=15)
G_weight.add_edge("BK", "Q", weight=5)
G_weight.add_edge("MH", "Q", weight=15)
G_weight.add_edge("MH", "BX", weight=5)
G_weight.add_edge("Q", "BX", weight=15)

edge_wts = nx.get_edge_attributes(G_weight, "weight")
nx.draw_networkx(G_weight, with_labels=True, node_color="black",
    pos=pos,
               font_color="white", edge_color="black")
nx.draw_networkx_edge_labels(G_weight, pos, edge_wts)
```

We can identify whether a network is unweighted using `is_unweighted()`:

```
from graspologic.utils import is_unweighted

A_weight = nx.to_numpy_array(G_weight)
is_unweighted(A)
# True
is_unweighted(A_weight)
# False
```

In a lot of your data analyses, you will come across weighted networks, so we give you an example of what they will look like in Figure 3.1.4(B).

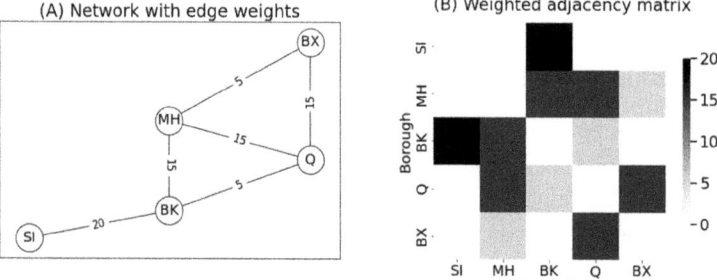

Figure 3.1.4 The New York City borough network, where weights indicate the average speed of traffic. (**A**) A layout plot for the weighted network, and (**B**) a heatmap of an adjacency matrix for the weighted network.

The Weighted Adjacency Matrix

In most situations, it is favorable to organize these weights $w(i, j)$ in a weighted adjacency matrix W. The weighted adjacency matrix is simply the $n \times n$ matrix whose entries (for adjacent pairs of nodes) w_{ij} are the weights $w(i, j)$ between all pairs of nodes i and j.

We will need to be careful to choose an appropriate way to represent the idea that no edge exists between a pair of nodes in the weighted adjacency matrix. In our example, traffic moving at 0 mph is approximately similar to two boroughs having no bridge between them (e.g., traffic at a standstill still means we cannot move between a pair of nodes), and therefore we could just set w_{ij} to 0 for nodes not linked by a bridge and the weight of 0 would make sense for both adjacent and nonadjacent nodes alike.

Consider, for instance, if the edge weights instead represent the travel time between a pair of nodes i and j. In this case, a travel time of zero would indicate that in no time we can get from node i to j. In this situation, it might instead make more sense to use a value other than 0 for nonadjacent pairs of nodes (such as infinity, since you can never travel from one node to the other along a nonexistent bridge).

For this reason, the utility for converting a `networkx` network to a weighted adjacency matrix has an argument `nonedge` which indicates the default weight for nonadjacent nodes. In our example where edge weight represents average speed of traffic, we can simply specify `nonedge=0`:

```
A_weight = nx.to_numpy_array(G_weight, nonedge=0).astype(float)

heatmap(A_weight, xticklabels=["SI", "MH", "BK", "Q", "BX"],
    yticklabels=["SI", "MH", "BK", "Q", "BX"], title="Weighted
        adjacency matrix",
    xtitle="Borough", ytitle="Borough")
```

The heatmap for the borough network weighted adjacency matrix is shown in Figure 3.1.4(B).

Box 3.1.1 This book considers simple networks

A *simple network* is loopless, undirected, and unweighted. We develop most of the examples and techniques in this book for simple networks. Fortunately, focusing on simple networks is not usually a significant limitation, because the techniques and packages we describe extend naturally to directed networks and networks with weights or loops. Most approaches discussed in this book apply to these more complex network types.

Software package like `networkx`, `graspologic`, or `igraph` typically warn or raise errors if a technique is incompatible with a given network type. When implementing network analysis methods independently, we recommend reviewing documentation to ensure the method is compatible with the network structure.

3.2   Node Properties and Relationships

In Section 3.1, we explored the general properties of networks and their edges. Just as networks have properties, so too do individual nodes or groups of nodes. We explore several of these node properties here. We will cover:

1. Node neighbors and incidences, which describe how nodes are linked to each other,
2. Node degree, which quantifies the number of edges incident to a node, and
3. Path length, which describes how far apart two nodes are in the network.

Exploring these node properties often provides quick intuition on the overall network. In Section 3.3, we will build on these concepts and the concepts discussed in Section 3.1 to explore statistics that summarize network and node properties. The degree matrix in Section 3.4 will then solidify the idea of a node degree into its own matrix representation.

3.2.1   Node Neighbors and Incidences

The simplest property of a network is adjacency. A pair of nodes i and j in an undirected network are *neighbors* (or, *adjacent*) if an edge exists between them. In the adjacency matrix, two nodes i and j are neighbors if their potential edge a_{ij} is nonzero. A node is *incident* to an edge if it is one of the two nodes linked by that edge.

In the bridge example in Figure 3.1.2(B), we might say that MH and BK are neighbors because there is a bridge between them (the Brooklyn Bridge, amongst other bridges). Alternatively, we could say that both MH and BK are incident to the Brooklyn Bridge.

3.2.2   Node Degree Quantifies the Number of Edges

The simplest summary statistic for a node is known as the node degree. The *node degree* of a node i in a simple network is the number of nodes with which it is a neighbor. Remember that if two nodes are not neighbors, the adjacency matrix entry corresponding to this potential edge takes a value of zero. This means that we can just count the potential edges a_{ij} for a node i to get its degree. We do this by just summing the ith row (or equivalently, if the network is undirected, its ith column):

$$d_i = degree(i) \triangleq \sum_{j=1}^{n} a_{ij} = \sum_{j=1}^{n} a_{ji}. \tag{3.1}$$

The reason for the equality of these expressions is that for an undirected network, the adjacency matrix is symmetric, so $a_{ij} = a_{ji}$. This is not just counting edges which exist, since it counts every potential edge for node i. If an edge exists, a_{ij} takes a value of 1, whereas if an edge does not exist, a_{ij} takes a value of 0. This means that every a_{ij} is either zero or one:

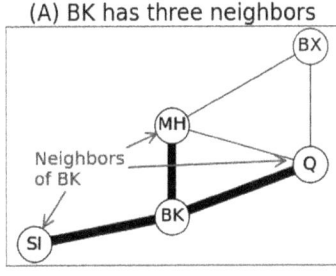 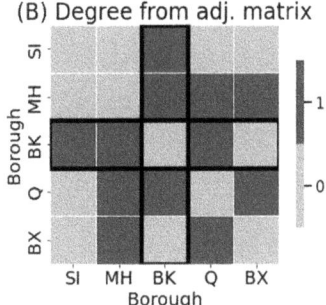

Figure 3.2.1 A case study of the BK borough. Panel (**A**) shows that BK has three neighbors, SI, MH, and Q (edges to SI/MH/Q are bold-faced). Panel (**B**) shows the axes of the adjacency matrix which could also be summed to derive this fact. Note the row/column corresponding to BK (black boxes) has a sum value of three.

$$d_i = \sum_{j=1}^{n} a_{ij}$$

$$= \sum_{j:a_{ij}=1} a_{ij} + \sum_{j:a_{ij}=0} a_{ij}$$

$$= \sum_{j:a_{ij}=1} 1 + 0.$$

In the left sum in the middle line, since every a_{ij} is defined to be 1, this is just the number of times that node i neighbors another node. The right sum has every a_{ij} defined to be zero, so this is just zero.

For instance, the node BK in our example touches three edges, indicated in bold in Figure 3.2.1(A), so $degree(BK) = 3$. In the corresponding adjacency matrix, summing the entries for node BK along its row outputs three. The entries which would be summed row-wise or column-wise for BK are shown in black boxes, in Figure 3.2.1(B).

Further, if the network is loopless, we can explicitly exclude the diagonal from our computation, because for a node i, $a_{ii} = 0$. So Equation (3.1) can equivalently be written:

$$d_i = degree(i) = \sum_{j \neq i} a_{ij} = \sum_{j \neq i} a_{ji}. \qquad (3.2)$$

This expression will be useful when computing properties of random networks.

3.2.2.1 Degrees for Directed Networks

In directed networks, we distinguish between the in-degree and out-degree of a node.

The *out-degree* of a node i in a directed network is its number of outgoing connections, which we obtain by summing node i's outgoing connections along its row i of the adjacency matrix:

$$d_i^{out} = \sum_{j=1}^{n} a_{ij},$$

whereas the *in-degree* of a node i is its number of incoming connections, which we obtain by summing node i's incoming connections along its column i:

$$d_i^{in} = \sum_{j=1}^{n} a_{ji}.$$

Here, a_{ji} is 1 if there is a directed edge from node j to node i, and 0 otherwise. Note that the expression in Equation (3.1) has defined the in-degrees and out-degrees to be equal for undirected networks.

We can use the following code to calculate the in-degrees and the out-degrees for a network, given its adjacency matrix.

```
def in_degrees(A):
    """
    A function to compute the in-degrees for the nodes of an adjacency
        matrix.
    """
    return A.sum(axis=1)

def out_degrees(A):
    """
    A function to compute the out-degrees for the nodes of an adjacency
        matrix.
    """
    return A.sum(axis=0)

# get the degree for node BK, which is node 2 in our network,
# using either the in- or out-degree
print(in_degrees(A)[2])
# 3.0
```

3.2.2.2   Degrees for Weighted Networks

If the network is weighted, then all of the logic we've learned so far applies directly both for directed and undirected networks. The adjacency matrix A has entries $a_{ij} = w(i, j)$ if the edge exists between nodes i and j and usually 0 otherwise. This means that when we compute the degrees (either the undirected node degree, the in-degree, or the out-degree), we instead sum edge weights when the edge exists, and usually 0s otherwise. Note that the defining and interpreting node degrees in weighted networks may change based on the properties of the edge weights. For instance, a 0 place-holder for "nonexistent" edges could be substituted for other values depending on the edge weight interpretations.

3.2.3   The Path Length Describes How Far Two Nodes Are

How many bridges would you need to cross to get from Staten Island to the Bronx? This is an example of a path in a network. A *path* between two nodes i and j is a sequence of edges which starts at node i, and traverses through other nodes in the network until reaching node j. By convention, paths do not traverse the same node or set of nodes multiple times. Two nodes are described as *connected* if a path exists

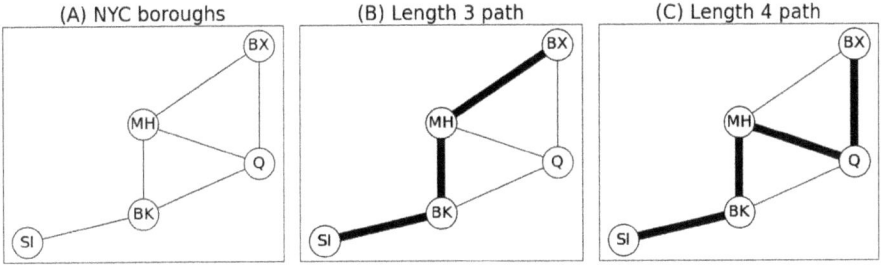

Figure 3.2.2 (**A**) The New York boroughs. (**B**) A length-three path from SI to BX. (**C**) A length-four path from SI to BX.

between them. The *path length* is the number of edges in the path. In the New York example, one could travel from Staten Island to the Bronx in four possible ways, two of which are indicated in (B) and (C) in Figure 3.2.2.

In this case, there are only four paths from SI to BX which do not visit the same node more than once, but in a larger network, there may be many possible paths from one node to another. We will usually be interested in one particular path, the shortest path. The *shortest path length* or *distance* between nodes i and j is the path with the smallest path length that connects nodes i and j. In our example, a shortest path is indicated by Figure 3.2.2(B), in which the shortest path length is three. There are multiple shortest paths of length three in this example. If it is not possible to get from node i to node j using edges of the network, the shortest path length is defined to be infinite.

A common statistic is the distance matrix for the network D, which is the $n \times n$ matrix whose entries d_{ij} are the shortest path lengths between all pairs of nodes in the network. For the New York example, we can compute and visualize the distance matrix using:

```
D = nx.floyd_warshall_numpy(G)
heatmap(D, title="Distance matrix", xticklabels=["SI", "MH", "BK",
    "Q", "BX"],
    yticklabels=["SI", "MH", "BK", "Q", "BX"], xtitle="Borough",
        ytitle="Borough")
```

Paths in Directed Networks
If the network is directed, the interpretation of a path is the same, except we have to be careful to account for the directionality when finding paths from one node to the next. For instance, in Figure 3.1.3(B), there is a path from the node SI to BK, MH, Q, or BX, but there are no paths from BK, MH, Q, nor BX to SI (since the bridge from BK to SI is out of service).

Paths in Weighted Networks
If the network is weighted, path lengths typically are instead the sum of edge weights along the path. For instance, in Figure 3.1.4(A), the path from SI to MH via BK would have a path length of 35.

3.3   Network Summary Statistics

We have now explored the basic properties and representations of networks in Section 3.1, as well as descriptive properties of nodes and relationships between nodes in Section 3.2.

Building on this foundation, we now turn our attention to network summary statistics, which provide concise quantitative measures of network structure and characteristics.

In this section, we will learn several network summary statistics, including:

1. The network density, which quantifies how many edges are present relative to the total possible edges,
2. The clustering coefficient, which measures the tendency of nodes to form tightly connected groups, and
3. The average shortest path length, which captures the typical distance between pairs of nodes in the network.

These summary statistics complement the network representations we will explore in Chapter 5. They provide a "bird's-eye" understanding of the relationships within and between networks, though they should be complimented by direct examination of the full network structure. Section 4.6.3.1 extends the concept of network density to random networks, and Section 6.2 explores how sparsity impacts computational efficiency in large-scale network analysis.

Box 3.3.1 Shorthands in network science

There are a number of shorthands to be familiar with in network science. The most common ones are:

1. Double sums $\sum_{i=1}^{n} \sum_{j=1}^{n} x_{ij}$ will often be abbreviated as $\sum_{i,j=1}^{n} x_{ij}$. Here, i and j are both summing over the same indexing set $\{1, \ldots, n\}$, and therefore it is redundant to write it twice.
2. Likewise, triple sums $\sum_{i=1}^{n} \sum_{j=1}^{n} \sum_{k=1}^{n} x_{ijk}$ will often be abbreviated as $\sum_{i,j,k=1}^{n} x_{ijk}$.
3. There may be ambiguous sums, such as $\sum_{i,j} x_{ij}$. This would sum over all possible values i and j could take that would make sense when considered with the summand (e.g., the x_{ij} term). For example, if x_{ij} are the entries of an $n \times m$ matrix X, this sum would be $\sum_{i=1}^{n} \sum_{j=1}^{m} x_{ij}$.
4. Sums may index inequalities, such as $\sum_{i \neq j} x_{ij}$. This means to consider all possible pairs (i, j) where $i \neq j$. Two of these appear frequently for square adjacency matrices A:
   - $\sum_{i \neq j} a_{ij}$, which means $\sum_{i=1}^{n} \sum_{j \neq i} a_{ij}$.
   - $\sum_{j > i} a_{ij}$, which means $\sum_{i=1}^{n} \sum_{j=i+1}^{n} a_{ij}$.

3.3.1   The Network Density

Given the adjacency matrix A of a simple network, what fraction of the possible edges actually exist?

To understand this quantity, first we must understand how many edges are possible in a network. This is where the "caveat" about loopless networks come in: We need to count in such a way that we don't accidentally assume that self-loops are potential edges; since the self-loops are simply not possible, we need to ignore them.

There are n total nodes in a network, so A is an $n \times n$ matrix. Therefore, A has n^2 total entries. However, over half of these entries are redundant for simple networks. Since we assume the network is simple, it is by definition loopless. This means that every entry is by default 0 along the diagonal. Since each node i has a corresponding diagonal entry a_{ii}, this comes to n entries that we do not need to count. This leaves n^2 total possible edges (the total number of entries in the matrix A) minus n (the total number of entries which are automatically 0), or $n^2 - n = n(n - 1)$. This quantity represents the total number of possible edges not in the diagonal.

If the network is undirected, every node that is not in the diagonal is also being double counted. This is because in the adjacency matrix of an undirected network, for every pair of nodes i and j, $a_{ij} = a_{ji}$. So we are overcounting the number of possible edges not in the diagonal by a factor of two. This leaves the total number of possible edges in the network as $\frac{1}{2}n(n - 1)$: the total number of possible edges not in the diagonal reduced by a factor of two. This quantity is notated by $\binom{n}{2}$, which is read as "n choose 2." In the network in Figure 3.3.1(B), we see all of the possible edges indicated. If you were to count them up, there are $\frac{1}{2} \cdot 5 \cdot (5 - 1) = 10$ possible edges.

Now, how many edges actually exist in the network? The sum of all of the entries of A can be represented by the quantity $\sum_{i,j=1}^{n} a_{ij}$. For each node i, we sum all of the a_{ij}, and then we add these across all of the nodes. Since A is loopless, we don't need to count the diagonal entries. This brings the quantity to $\sum_{i \neq j} a_{ij}$, since we don't need to count any edges along the diagonal of A. Next, owing to the undirected property, if an edge in A exists between nodes i and j, both a_{ij} and a_{ji} take the value of 1. To obtain the edge count of A, we only need to count either a_{ij} or a_{ji}. By convention

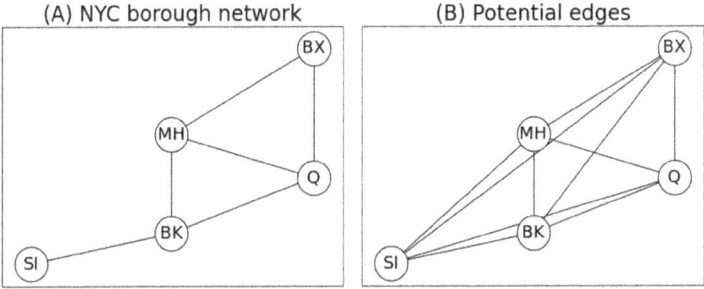

Figure 3.3.1   (**A**) The New York borough network. The actual edges are shown. (**B**) The New York borough network with all possible potential edges.

we will always count the entries a_{ij} in the upper triangle of A, which are the entries where $j > i$. This brings the quantity to $\sum_{j>i} a_{ij}$.

The six total edges in the network are indicated in Figure 3.3.1(A).

To put it all together, the *network density* indicates the density of edges which are present in the network. For a simple network, the network density can be defined as the ratio between the total number of edges in A and the total number of edges possible in A:

$$density(A) = \frac{\sum_{j>i} a_{ij}}{\binom{n}{2}} = \frac{2\sum_{j>i} a_{ij}}{n(n-1)}. \tag{3.3}$$

In our example, this is simply the ratio of edges which actually exist to edges which could possibly exist, which is $\frac{6}{10} = 0.6$. We can use `networkx` to compute the network density using the function `density()`:

```
nx.density(G)
# 0.6
```

In a simple network, there are additional ways this equation can be written. Notice the following inequality, by definition of a simple network:

$$\sum_{i,j=1}^{n} a_{ij} = \sum_{j>i} a_{ij} + \sum_{i>j} a_{ij} + \sum_{i=1}^{n} a_{ii}$$

$$= \sum_{j>i} a_{ij} + \sum_{i>j} a_{ij} + 0,$$

because the network is loopless (so the diagonal is 0). Further, since $a_{ij} = a_{ji}$, the first term is exactly equal to the second term, so:

$$\sum_{i,j=1}^{n} a_{ij} = \sum_{j>i} a_{ij} + \sum_{i>j} a_{ij}$$

$$= \sum_{j>i} a_{ij} + \sum_{j>i} a_{ij} = 2\sum_{j>i} a_{ij}$$

$$\Rightarrow \sum_{j>i} a_{ij} = \frac{1}{2} \sum_{i,j=1}^{n} a_{ij}.$$

This gives us the useful relationship that we can plug into Equation (3.3):

$$density(A) = \frac{\frac{1}{2}\sum_{i=1}^{n}\sum_{j=1}^{n} a_{ij}}{\binom{n}{2}} = \frac{\sum_{i=1}^{n}\sum_{j=1}^{n} a_{ij}}{n(n-1)}.$$

We wrote out the double sum to point out a key relationship. Notice that the innermost sum is just computing the degree d_i of each node i, because $d_i = \sum_{j=1}^{n} a_{ij}$ in an undirected network. This means that:

$$density(A) = \frac{\frac{1}{2}\sum_{i=1}^{n} d_i}{\binom{n}{2}} = \frac{\sum_{i=1}^{n} d_i}{n(n-1)}. \tag{3.4}$$

Finally, notice that $\frac{1}{n} \sum_{i=1}^{n} d_i$ is the *average degree* over all of the n nodes in the network. We will typically abbreviate this quantity using the symbol d. Using this fact with the right-most equality in Equation (3.4), we see that:

$$density(A) = \frac{d}{n-1}.$$

The density can therefore be conceptualized as the average degree of each node in the network, divided by the maximum possible degree each node could have (which, in a simple network, is $n-1$, since a node could at most have an edge to the other $n-1$ nodes in the network). This concept will become useful when we discuss sparsity in Section 6.2.

3.3.2 The Clustering Coefficient Indicates How Much Nodes Tend to Cluster Together

A *triplet* is an ordered tuple of three nodes which are connected by two or three edges. For a tuple of three nodes to be a triplet, there must be a contiguous path from one end of the triplet to the other. The triplets are *closed* if there are three edges, and *open* if there are only two edges.

The clustering coefficient indicates the fraction of closed triplets. In the New York example, we look at only Brooklyn, Manhattan, Queens, and the Bronx, and temporarily ignore Staten Island:

```
G_clus = nx.Graph()

G_clus.add_node("MH", pos=(4,4))
G_clus.add_node("BK", pos=(4,1.7))
G_clus.add_node("Q", pos=(6,3))
G_clus.add_node("BX", pos=(6,6))


pos = nx.get_node_attributes(G, 'pos')
G_clus.add_edge("MH", "BX")
G_clus.add_edge("MH", "BK")
G_clus.add_edge("BK", "Q")
G_clus.add_edge("MH", "Q")
G_clus.add_edge("Q", "BX")

nx.draw_networkx(G_clus, with_labels=True, node_color="black", pos=pos,
                font_color="white", edge_color="black")
```

The plotted result is shown in Figure 3.5.1(B). We have the following triplets:

1. Open triplets between Bronx, Manhattan, and Brooklyn: (BX, MH, BK), (BK, MH, BX).
2. Open triplets between Brooklyn, Queens, and Bronx: (BX, Q, BK), (BK, Q, BX).
3. Closed triplets between Brooklyn, Manhattan, and Queens: (BK, MH, Q), (BK, Q, MH), (MH, BK, Q), (MH, Q, BK), (Q, BK, MH), (Q, MH, BK).
4. Closed triplets between Bronx, Manhattan, and Queens: (BX, MH, Q), (BX, Q, MH), (MH, BX, Q), (MH, Q, BX), (Q, BX, MH), (Q, MH, BX).

To clarify a fine technical point of open triplets, we do not count (BK, Q, MH) as a triplet because there is no edge from BK to Q. We must be able to go from the first node to the second to the third along edges that exist in the network in order for three nodes to count as a triplet. In our example, there are 12 closed triplets amongst the nodes (delineated in numbers 3. and 4. above), and there are four open triplets (delineated in numbers 1. and 2. above). The global clustering coefficient (or transitivity) is defined as:

$$C = \frac{\text{number of closed triplets}}{\text{number of closed triplets} + \text{number of open triplets}}.$$

In our example, this comes to $C = \frac{12}{2 \cdot 6 + 2 \cdot 2} = 0.75$. This equation can also be understood in terms of the adjacency matrix. If a triplet between nodes i, j, and k is closed, then all three of the potential edges a_{ij}, a_{jk}, and a_{ki} have a value of 1. Therefore, the number of times that $a_{ij}a_{jk}a_{ki} = 1$, is the number of closed triplets. This means that the number of closed triplets can be expressed as $\sum_{i,j,k=1}^{n} a_{ij}a_{jk}a_{ki}$.

For a given node i, we can find an arbitrary triplet (either open or closed) with the following procedure.

1. Pick a single neighbor j for node i. The node i has a number of neighbors equal to $degree(i) = d_i$, so there are d_i possible neighbors to choose from.
2. Pick a different neighbor k for node i. Since node i had d_i neighbors, it has $d_i - 1$ neighbors that are not node j.
3. Since nodes j and k are both neighbors of node i, we know that a_{ij} and a_{ik} both have values of one, and therefore the edges (i, j) and (i, k) exist. Therefore, the tuple of nodes (i, j, k) is a triplet, because at least two edges exist amongst the three nodes. This tuple is closed if the edge (j, k) exists, and open if the edge (j, k) does not exist.
4. Therefore, there are $d_i(d_i - 1)$ triplets in which node i is the leading node of the triplet.

Since triplets are ordered tuples, we can repeat this procedure for all nodes, which counts the total number of triplets for the entire network. Therefore, the number of open and closed triplets in the network is the quantity $\sum_i d_i(d_i - 1)$. Then we can express the clustering coefficient in terms of the adjacency matrix as:

$$C = \frac{\sum_{i,j,k=1}^{n} a_{ij}a_{jk}a_{ki}}{\sum_{i=1}^{n} d_i(d_i - 1)},$$

which gives us an expression to implement programmatically. The clustering coefficient can be computed via `networkx` using:

```
nx.transitivity(G_clus)
# 0.75
```

3.3.3   The Average Shortest Path Length

Another common statistic computed using the distance matrix from Section 3.2.3 is the average shortest path length. Conceptually, the distance matrix D can be thought of as capturing the "accessibility" of the network, in that if it tends to have larger values, nodes tend to be separated by longer paths, and vice versa.

The average shortest path length $\bar{d}$ of a simple network is the average of all of the shortest paths between two distinct nodes i and j of the distance matrix:

$$\bar{d} = \frac{1}{n(n-1)} \sum_{i \neq j} d_{ij}.$$

The normalizing factor is $n(n-1)$ because the sum $\sum_{i \neq j}$ is short-hand for the double-sum $\sum_{i=1}^{n} \sum_{j \neq i}$. In a network with self-loops, the average shortest path length does not exclude the diagonal, and therefore we should be careful with which expression we use. The left-most sum has n terms, and for each node i, there are $n - 1$ other possible values that j can take where $j \neq i$. This means that we are summing $n - 1$ terms n times (which is $n(n-1)$). This can be computed using networkx:

```
dbar = nx.average_shortest_path_length(G)
# 1.5
```

3.4 Degree Matrices and Laplacians

In Section 3.1, we introduced adjacency matrices as the primary mathematical representation for network data. This section explores additional matrices derived from the adjacency matrix.

We cover the following matrix representations for networks:

1. The degree matrix, which encodes node degrees on its diagonal, and
2. The network Laplacian and its variations, including the normalized Laplacian, the DAD Laplacian, and the regularized Laplacian (used to address issues with low-degree nodes).

The Laplacian and its properties in particular are fundamental to several of the spectral methods we will learn about in Chapter 5. Further, many of the spectral methods we develop in Chapters 6, 7, and 8 can be equivalently applied to the Laplacian, with unique advantages over other spectral methods. In Section 4.6.4, we will extend the Laplacian to random networks, and then use the Laplacian to build an embedding technique in Section 5.4. Section 5.6 creates a joint representation using the regularized Laplacian, and Section 6.2 explores how the sparsity of the DAD Laplacian impacts computational efficiency in network analysis.

In general, we will represent networks with matrices. In addition to being computationally convenient, using matrices to represent networks lets us use tools from linear algebra and statistics. Using matrices also lets us use common python tools for array manipulation like numpy or pytorch.

3.4.1 The Degree Matrix

In Section 3.2.2, we defined the *degree* of a node i in a simple network as the number of nodes that i is connected to.

> **Remark 3.4.1** Overloading notation
>
> In Section 3.2, we used the same letter, D, for the distance matrix as we do for the degree matrix. From now on in the book, D will refer to the degree matrix, unless stated otherwise.

The degree matrix takes this a step further, representing the degree of every node in the network. The degree matrix appears relatively often as a step in creating other matrix representations of networks. It is a diagonal matrix with the values along the diagonal corresponding to the degree of each node:

$$D = \begin{bmatrix} d_1 & 0 & \cdots & 0 \\ 0 & \ddots & \ddots & \vdots \\ \vdots & \ddots & \ddots & 0 \\ 0 & \cdots & 0 & d_n \end{bmatrix}, \quad d_i = degree(i).$$

D is called *diagonal* because all of the entries $d_{ij} = 0$ unless $i = j$. The diagonal entries d_{ii} of the degree matrix are the node degrees $degree(i)$ for each node i. Using the counting procedure described in Section 3.2.2, we see that the node SI has degree one, the node BK has degree three, the node MH has degree three, the node Q has degree three, and the node BX has degree two. We can compute the degree matrix for an unweighted, undirected network by using either of the following commands:

```
# in-degree matrix
D_in = np.diag(in_degrees(A))
# out-degree matrix
D_out = np.diag(out_degrees(A))
# the network is undirected, so in and out degrees are same
print(np.all(D_in == D_out))
# True
```

These two methods are identical when the network is undirected because the in-degrees and out-degrees for undirected networks are the same.

```
# arbitrarily set degree matrix to in-degree matrix
D = D_in
```

Figure 3.4.1 plots the degree matrix using the `heatmap` utility that developed for the adjacency matrix.

3.4.2   The Laplacian Matrix

The standard Laplacian matrix $L = D - A$ [2] is a direct derivative of the adjacency matrix A, since the degree matrix D can be calculated from A. It is used in practice because it has a number of interesting mathematical properties which are useful for analysis. For instance, the magnitude of its second-smallest eigenvalue, called the Fiedler eigenvalue, tells us how well connected our network is, and the number of

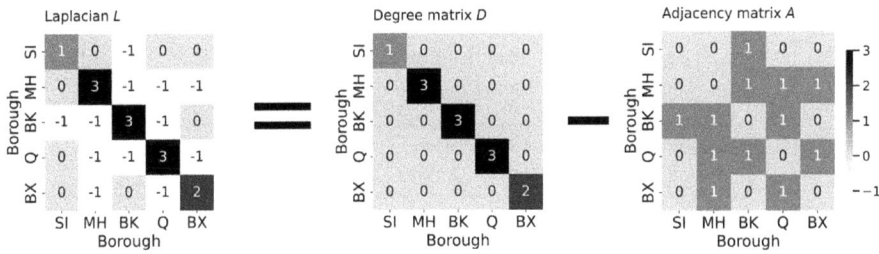

Figure 3.4.1 The Laplacian matrix, along with the components that are used to compute it (the degree matrix and the adjacency matrix).

eigenvalues equal to zero is the number of "islands" or connected components our network has (a concept introduced in Section 3.5.1). Incidentally, this means that the smallest eigenvalue of the Laplacian will always be 0, since any simple network always has at least one connected component (itself).

Another interesting property of the Laplacian is that the sum of its diagonals is twice the number of edges in the network. This is because the ith diagonal, L_{ii}, is the degree of node i, and $a_{ij} = a_{ji}$ causes us to over-count. Because the sum of the diagonal of a matrix is the trace, and the trace is also equal to the sum of the eigenvalues, this means that the sum of the eigenvalues of the Laplacian is equal to twice the number of edges in the network.

Since the only nonzero values of the degree matrix is along its diagonals, and because the diagonals of an adjacency matrix never contain zeros if its network doesn't have nodes connected to themselves, the diagonals of the Laplacian are just the degree of each node. The values on the nondiagonals work similarly to the adjacency matrix: They contain a -1 if there is an edge between the two nodes, and a 0 if there is no edge.

The Laplacian for a simple network looks like the degree matrix, but with -1s in all the locations where an edge exists between nodes i and j. We compute it in Python below.

```
L = D - A
```

Figure 3.4.1 shows a plot of the Laplacian matrix as a heatmap, along with the degree and adjacency matrices.

3.4.3 The Normalized Laplacian

There are a few variations on the standard $D - A$ version of the Laplacian which are widely used in practice, and which (confusingly) are often also called the Laplacian. They tend to have similar properties. The normalized Laplacian, $L^{norm.}$ is one such variation. The normalized Laplacian [2] is defined as:

$$L^{norm.} = D^{-1/2} L D^{-1/2} = I - D^{-1/2} A D^{-1/2},$$

where I is the identity matrix.

Below we can see the normalized Laplacian in code. We use graspologic's `to_laplacian()` function, with the form set to I - DAD, which computes $L^{norm.}$ above.

```
from graspologic.utils import to_laplacian
L_sym = to_laplacian(A, form="I-DAD")
```

A heatmap of the normalized Laplacian is shown in Figure 3.4.2(A).

We can understand the normalized Laplacian from the name: We can think of it as the Laplacian normalized by the degrees of the nodes associated with a given entry.

Here is what the operation is doing:

$$L^{norm.} = D^{-\frac{1}{2}} L D^{-\frac{1}{2}}$$

$$= \begin{bmatrix} d_1 & & \\ & \ddots & \\ & & d_n \end{bmatrix}^{-\frac{1}{2}} \begin{bmatrix} l_{11} & \cdots & l_{1n} \\ \vdots & \ddots & \vdots \\ l_{n1} & \cdots & l_{nn} \end{bmatrix} \begin{bmatrix} d_1 & & \\ & \ddots & \\ & & d_n \end{bmatrix}^{-\frac{1}{2}}$$

$$= \begin{bmatrix} \frac{1}{\sqrt{d_1}} & & \\ & \ddots & \\ & & \frac{1}{\sqrt{d_n}} \end{bmatrix} \begin{bmatrix} l_{11} & \cdots & l_{1n} \\ \vdots & \ddots & \vdots \\ l_{n1} & \cdots & l_{nn} \end{bmatrix} \begin{bmatrix} \frac{1}{\sqrt{d_1}} & & \\ & \ddots & \\ & & \frac{1}{\sqrt{d_n}} \end{bmatrix}$$

$$= \begin{bmatrix} \frac{l_{11}}{d_1} & \cdots & \frac{l_{1n}}{\sqrt{d_1}\sqrt{d_n}} \\ \vdots & \ddots & \vdots \\ \frac{l_{n1}}{\sqrt{d_n}\sqrt{d_1}} & \cdots & \frac{l_{nn}}{d_n} \end{bmatrix}. \qquad (3.5)$$

So the normalized Laplacian has entries $l_{ij}^{norm.} = \frac{l_{ij}}{\sqrt{d_i}\sqrt{d_j}}$.

We can plug in the value of L to obtain a similar relationship with the adjacency matrix A:

$$L^{norm.} = D^{-\frac{1}{2}} L D^{-\frac{1}{2}}$$
$$= D^{-\frac{1}{2}}(D - A)D^{-\frac{1}{2}}$$
$$= D^{-\frac{1}{2}} D D^{-\frac{1}{2}} - D^{-\frac{1}{2}} A D^{-\frac{1}{2}}$$
$$= D^{\frac{1}{2}} D^{-\frac{1}{2}} - D^{-\frac{1}{2}} A D^{-\frac{1}{2}}$$
$$= I_{n \times n} - D^{-\frac{1}{2}} A D^{-\frac{1}{2}}.$$

The $D^{-1/2}DD^{-1/2}$ term can be thought of as spiritually the same as what we would think of as $\frac{D}{D}$ (if that were not undefined!), since it just works out to be the identity matrix. The $D^{-1/2}AD^{-1/2}$ is just doing the same thing to A that we did to L. So we're normalizing the entries of the adjacency matrix by the degrees of the nodes a given entry is concerned with; that is, $\frac{a_{ij}}{\sqrt{d_i}\sqrt{d_j}}$.

The eigenvalues of the normalized Laplacian are bounded between 0 and 2, and so the Laplacian is a *positive semidefinite matrix*, which means that it is a matrix with nonnegative eigenvalues. This means that a suite of linear algebra techniques, which may not run successfully on the adjacency matrix (which is not positive semidefinite in its most raw form for simple networks, as we will learn in Section 4.5), can be executed on the network Laplacian. For more details about the properties of the Laplacian, see [3].

3.4.4 The DAD Laplacian

We will often use the *spectral embedding* of the Laplacian (see Section 5.4). To understand the spectral embedding, we will need a related Laplacian, called the DAD Laplacian:

$$L^{DAD} = D^{-\frac{1}{2}} A D^{-\frac{1}{2}}.$$

L^{DAD} and $L^{norm.}$ share major similarities. Performing the same manipulations as in Equation (3.5), we find that $l_{ij}^{DAD} = \frac{a_{ij}}{\sqrt{d_i}\sqrt{d_j}}$. We can therefore understand the DAD Laplacian to be the adjacency matrix, but with entries a_{ij} normalized by the square root of the degrees of the nodes i and j.

In Section 5.4, we will learn about the importance of the singular value decomposition for spectral embedding of Laplacians. The singular value decomposition will allow us to look at the Laplacian as a sum of simpler matrices. "Simple," in this context, means a rank-one matrix created from the outer product of two vectors. By looking only at a few of these "simple" matrices, we can learn about the Laplacian and reduce noise in the Laplacian itself. The properties of the DAD Laplacian are discussed at length in [4] and [5].

The most important connection is that these "simple" matrices will be identical for $L^{norm.}$ and L^{DAD}, except for one important fact: They will be in reverse order from one another. In $L^{norm.}$, the matrices we will want to use will be the last few, and in L^{DAD}, the matrices we will want to use will be the first few. When we compute the singular value decomposition, there are ways to only compute the first few matrices without having to go through the trouble of computing all of them, whereas the reverse is not true. To get the last few simple matrices, we would have to compute all of the preceding ones first. This means that to get the simple matrices we want, we can get much better computational performance using L^{DAD} instead of $L^{norm.}$.

We can compute the L^{DAD} in graspologic similarly to above, but with form="DAD":

```
L_dad = to_laplacian(A, form="DAD")
```

Figure 3.4.2(B) shows a heatmap of the DAD Laplacian.

3.4.5 The Regularized Laplacian

The regularized Laplacian is an adaptation of the DAD Laplacian. When networks have degree matrices where some of the degrees are extremely small, the spectral clustering approach we will learn about in Section 6.1 will not perform well: The spectral clusterings will be influenced by the small-degree nodes. To overcome this

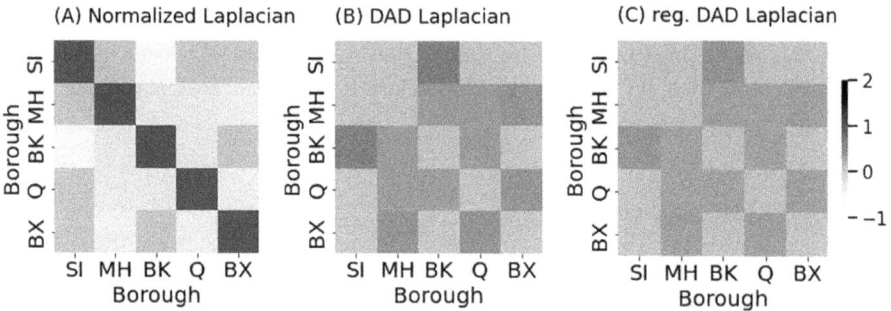

Figure 3.4.2 Different variations of Laplacians for the same underlying network.

hurdle, instead of using the DAD Laplacian, we can use the regularized Laplacian, defined similarly to the DAD Laplacian, as:

$$L^{rDAD}(\tau) = D_\tau^{-\frac{1}{2}} A D_\tau^{-\frac{1}{2}},$$

where τ is a regularization constant which is greater than or equal to zero, and $D_\tau = D + \tau I$. This τ term "inflates" the diagonal elements of the degree matrix by increasing the small degrees by τ. This is make the nodes with small degrees less impactful on our results. If $\tau = 0$, then $L^{rDAD}(\tau) = L^{DAD}$. The regularized Laplacian is discussed at length in [6].

Let's see what $L^{rDAD}(\tau)$ and L^{DAD} look like when we pick τ to be 1. We can do this in graspologic using form="R-DAD", and then setting regularizer appropriately:

```
tau = 1
L_rdad = to_laplacian(A, form="R-DAD", regularizer=tau)
```

The R-DAD Laplacian is shown in Figure 3.4.2(C).

We will learn about some other ways to handle nodes with very low degrees in Section 3.6.

3.5   Subnetworks and Connected Components

In Sections 3.1, we introduced the basic representation of networks, the adjacency matrix. We built some understanding of network and node properties in Sections 3.2 and 3.3. Building on this foundation, we now turn our attention to subnetworks and connected components within larger networks.

This section covers:

1. The concept of subnetworks, including induced subnetworks,
2. Connected components and their properties, and
3. The largest connected component (LCC) and its significance in network analysis.

Understanding subnetworks and connected components allows us to focus on specific regions of interest or to decompose large networks into manageable parts. These concepts are particularly important during preprocessing, where we often choose to operate only on the largest connected component. Section 4.10 uses the concept of subnetworks to define a statistical model. Sections 8.3 and 8.2 demonstrate how identifying specific subnetworks can reveal important signals in applied settings. Using relevant substructure rather than full networks often leads to more computationally tractable solutions in applied settings.

It is often useful to break a large network into smaller bits. For instance, when we were looking at the clustering coefficient in Section 3.3.2, we found it useful to break out the nodes BK, Q, BX, MH and their edges so that we could count triplets.

A subset of nodes and their edges pulled from a network is called a *subnetwork*. In this case, the network topology of the New York example is $(V, \mathcal{E})$ defined by the sets:

1. The nodes V: $\{SI, BK, Q, MH, BX\}$, and
2. The edges E: $\{(SI, BK), (BK, MH), (MH, Q), (MH, BX), (Q, BX)\}$;

and the subnetwork which removed Staten Island, SI is the network:

1. The nodes V_s: $\{BK, Q, MH, BX\}$, and
2. The edges E_s: $\{(BK, MH), (MH, Q), (BK, Q), (MH, BX), (Q, BX)\}$.

In the subnetwork with nodes and edges (V_s, E_s), every element in V_s is an element of V, the nodes of the complete network, and every element in E_s is an element of E, the edges of the complete network. So (V_s, E_s) is a subnetwork of (V, E). This particular subnetwork is also induced. A subnetwork is *induced* by a set of nodes if the following conditions hold:

1. The nodes V_s are a subset of the nodes of the network V, and
2. The edges E_s consist of all of the edges from the original network where both of the corresponding nodes are in V_s.

An example of our induced subnetwork is shown in Figure 3.5.1(B). Figure 3.5.1(C) shows an example of a subnetwork which is not an induced subnetwork. We can create an induced subnetwork (in this case, from BK, MH, Q, and BX) using `networkx`:

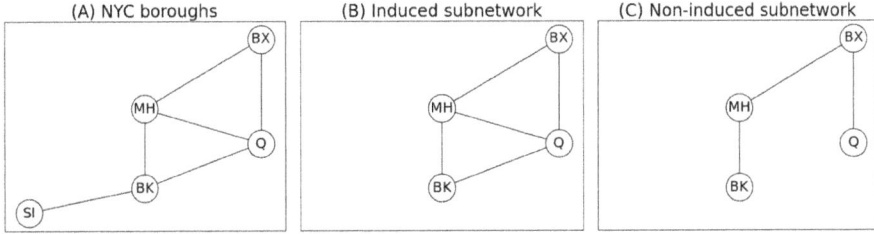

Figure 3.5.1 (**A**) The New York borough example. (**B**) The subnetwork induced by the node set {BX, MH, Q, BX}. This is also the example that we used to study clustering. (**C**) A noninduced subnetwork.

Box 3.5.1 A caveat with the adjacency matrix of subnetworks

Conceptualizing an induced subnetwork as a mere deletion of rows and columns, without regard for network structure, complicates later analysis. This approach obscures node identities, making it difficult to associate retained nodes with their original properties or metadata. For example, a vector containing useful node information becomes challenging to interpret if we lose track of which nodes remain in the subnetwork. To avoid confusion, we recommend recording the indices of the nodes from the initial network when computing a subnetwork.

```
G_induced = G.subgraph(["BK", "MH", "Q", "BX"]).copy()
nx.draw_networkx(G_induced, with_labels=True, node_color="black",
    pos=pos,
            font_color="white", edge_color="black")
```

3.5.0.1   Representing Subnetworks

A subnetwork is a collection of nodes and edges defined on these nodes. Therefore, a subnetwork is itself also a network. This means that we could still represent a subnetwork using an adjacency matrix, with the caveat that its size might change (since the nodes of a subnetwork are a subset of the nodes of the network) and the density might change (since the edges of a subnetwork are a subset of the edges of the network).

3.5.1   The Largest Connected Component

A particular induced subnetwork that we will often be concerned with is known as the largest connected component (LCC). To define the largest connected component, we will need to modify our example slightly. Let's say the bridge network also includes the Boston area, and we have two new nodes, Boston (BO) and Cambridge (CA). Boston and Cambridge have several bridges between one another, so an edge exists between them. However, there are no bridges between boroughs of New York and the Boston area, so there are no edges from nodes in the Boston area to nodes in the New York area.

```
G_withbos = deepcopy(G)
G_withbos.add_node("BO", pos=(8, 6))
G_withbos.add_node("CA", pos=(8, 8))
G_withbos.add_edge("BO", "CA")
# fetch positions with boston and cambridge added
pos = nx.get_node_attributes(G_withbos, 'pos')
# plot
nx.draw_networkx(G_withbos, with_labels=True, node_color="black",
    pos=pos,
            font_color="white", edge_color="black")
```

We visualize the network with Boston and Cambridge in Figure 3.5.2(A). The entire network can be described by the sets:

1. $\mathcal{V} = \{SI, MH, BK, BX, Q, CA, BO\}$, and
2. $\mathcal{E} = \{(SI, BK), (MH, BK), (MH, Q), (BK, Q), (MH, BX), (MX, Q), (CA, BO)\}$.

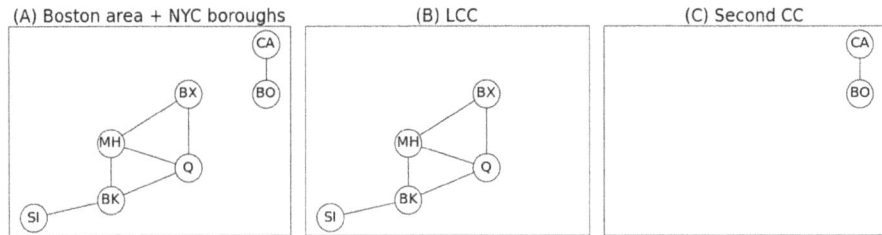

Figure 3.5.2 Panel (**A**) shows the New York boroughs with the added nodes for Boston and Cambridge. Panel (**B**) shows the connected component induced by the boroughs of New York, which is also the LCC. Panel (**C**) shows the connected component induced by Boston and Cambridge.

We have two distinct sets of nodes, those of New York and those of Boston, which are only connected amongst one another. These two sets of nodes induce connected components of the network topology $(\mathcal{V}, \mathcal{E})$. A *connected component* is an induced subnetwork in which any two nodes are connected to each other by a path through the network. The *largest connected component* (LCC) of a network is the connected component with the most nodes.

The two connected components are the New York induced subnetwork:

1. The nodes $\mathcal{V}_N$: $\{SI, BK, Q, MH, BX\}$, and
2. The edges $\mathcal{E}_N$: $\{(SI, BK), (BK, MH), (MH, Q), (BK, Q), (MH, BX), (Q, BX)\}$;

and the Boston induced subnetwork:

1. The nodes $\mathcal{V}_B$: $\{CA, BO\}$, and
2. The edges $\mathcal{E}_B$: $\{(CA, BO)\}$.

We plot each individually in Figure 3.5.2(B) and Figure 3.5.2(C). If the network and the largest connected component are equivalent, we can omit the term component, and just say that the network is *connected*.

In our example, the New York connected component has five nodes, whereas the Boston connected component has two nodes. Therefore, the New York connected component is the LCC of this simple network. We can compute the connected components and plot the largest connected component using `networkx` like this:

```
# returns a list of connected components, ordered
# by decreasing size (#nodes)
cc_withbos = nx.connected_components(G_withbos)
# return the connected components, as networks
CC_nets = [G_withbos.subgraph(cc).copy() for cc in cc_withbos]

# plot the LCC
nx.draw_networkx(CC_nets[0], with_labels=True, node_color="black",
    pos=pos,
            font_color="white", edge_color="black")
```

Often our networks will already be in the form of adjacency matrices. We can pass adjacency matrices directly into `graspologic` to obtain a LCC using:

```
from graspologic.utils import
    largest_connected_component as lcc

A_withbos = nx.to_numpy_array(G_withbos)
A_lcc, retained_nodes = lcc(A_withbos, return_inds=True)
```

This is one of the most common instances in which our warning about retaining subnetwork indices arises. The `return_inds` argument returns the rows/columns of `A_withbos` that were retained for the LCC. The default functionality is to not return these indices, so proceed with caution.

3.5.2   Connected Components in Directed Networks

Connected components for directed networks need to be defined differently than for undirected networks. A directed subnetwork is *strongly connected* if directed paths exist between every pair of nodes in the subnetwork.

A directed subnetwork is *weakly connected* if the underlying directionalities are ignored, and the resulting undirected subnetwork is a connected component. Figure 3.1.3(C) shows an example of a strongly connected network, because we can travel along a path from each node to every other node in the network. On the other hand, Figure 3.1.3(B) shows an example of a weakly connected component when the bridge from MH to BK is out of service. This is because there is no longer a way to follow a path from SI or BK to MH, Q, and BX. When we ignore the arrows entirely, the resulting undirected network is still connected, as shown in Figure 3.1.3(A).

3.6   Regularization and Node Pruning

In Sections 3.1 through 3.5, we built techniques to understand the properties of simple network observations. However, real-world observations of networks are often noisy and biased. To build predictive models, we usually preprocess and regularize our data. We now turn our attention to techniques which do this to help mitigate overfitting and improve generalization.

This section covers:

1. The concept of regularization in network machine learning,
2. Node pruning as a regularization technique, and
3. Methods for removing nodes based on degree and other properties.

Regularization is crucial for reducing noise and improving the robustness of network analyses. Node pruning, in particular, allows us to focus on the most relevant parts of a network by removing nodes that may introduce noise or instability.

Real world networks are often noisy, and so the analysis of one real world network might not generalize very well to a similar real world network. *Regularization* is the process by which we either:

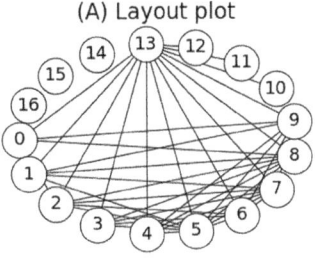
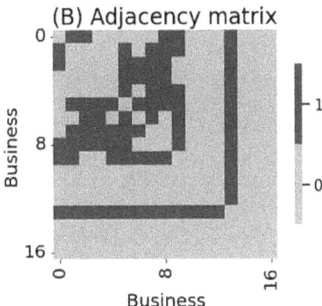

Figure 3.6.1 The business network, where nodes are businesses and edges are whether the pairs of businesses have a business relationship.

1. Modify data for the purpose of mitigating overfitting due to idiosyncrasies of the observed data, and/or
2. Modify the function we are estimating due to its fragility to the idiosyncracies of the observed data.

We first focus our attention on *node pruning*, a regularization technique in which we remove nodes for one reason or another. Typically, we will remove nodes due to some property about their degrees, or other properties (such as their connectedness with other nodes). These strategies are covered loosely in the book [7], and can be found in more computation-heavy network papers.

For each section covering regularization, we will give an example, a simulation, and code for how to implement the desired regularization approach. We might use several of these techniques simultaneously in practice, or we might use techniques that go outside of our working examples.

For node regularization, we will introduce a business network working example, discussed in Example 3.6.1, and visualized in Figure 3.6.1.

Example 3.6.1 Business network

There are 17 nodes in a network corresponding to local businesses. An edge exists between a pair of businesses if they have business dealings with one another (they buy or sell products from/with the company). Three of these businesses operate in total exclusion and do not have any edges. Three of these businesses only work with one other business. One businesses works with all of the nonexcluded businesses.

```
from graphbook_code import heatmap
from matplotlib import pyplot as plt
from graspologic.simulations import er_np
import networkx as nx

n = 10
A_bus = er_np(n, 0.6)
```

```
# add pendants
n_pend = 3
A_bus = np.column_stack([np.row_stack([A_bus, np.zeros((n_pend, n))]),
                         np.zeros((n + n_pend, n_pend))])
n = n + n_pend

# add pizza hut node
n_pizza = 1
A_bus = np.column_stack([np.row_stack([A_bus, np.ones((n_pizza, n))]),
                         np.ones((n + n_pizza, n_pizza))])
n = n + n_pizza

# add isolates
n_iso = 3
A_bus = np.column_stack([np.row_stack([A_bus, np.zeros((n_iso, n))]),
                         np.zeros((n + n_iso, n_iso))])
A_bus = A_bus - np.diag(np.diag(A_bus))
n = n + n_iso

# as a heatmap
node_names = [i for i in range(0, n)]
heatmap(A_bus.astype(int), title="Business Network Adjacency Matrix",
        xticklabels=node_names, yticklabels=node_names)

# as a layout plot
G_bus = nx.from_numpy_array(A_bus)
node_pos = nx.shell_layout(G_bus)

plt.figure()
nx.draw(G_bus, pos=node_pos, node_color='white', edgecolors='black',
    with_labels=True, node_size=1500)
```

3.6.1   Degree Trimming Removes Nodes with Unfavorable Degrees

In our business network, there are several low-degree nodes which will impart "strange" properties undesirable for downstream analysis. They may generate numerical instability when we apply machine learning algorithms to them, for instance. For this reason, it may be advantageous to remove nodes whose degrees are very different from the other nodes in the network, sometimes called *outlier nodes*.

One special case of degree trimming is removing isolates. An *isolated node* has a degree of 0, meaning that it is not connected to any other nodes in the network. See if you can spot the isolates in Figure 3.6.1.

Another special case of degree trimming is called the removal of pendants. A *pendant node* has a degree of 1, meaning that it is only connected to one other node in the network. Try spotting the pendants in Figure 3.6.1.

We can easily remove isolates or pendants. We simply need to compute the degree of each node in the network, and then retain the nodes with a degree above our chosen threshold. To remove isolates, we would pick this threshold to be 0 (retain nodes with nonzero degree), and to remove both pendants and isolates, we would pick this threshold to be 1 (retain nodes with a degree exceeding 1). We can do this as follows:

```
def compute_degrees(A):
    # compute the degrees of the network A
    # since A is undirected, we can just sum
    # along an axis.
    return A.sum(axis=1)

def prune_low_degree(A, return_inds=True, threshold=1):
    # remove nodes which have a degree under a given
    # threshold. For a simple network, threshold=0 removes isolates,
    # and threshold=1 removes pendants
    degrees = compute_degrees(A)
    non_prunes = degrees > threshold
    robj = A[np.where(non_prunes)[0],:][:,np.where(non_prunes)[0]]
    if return_inds:
        robj = (robj, np.where(non_prunes)[0])
    return robj

A_bus_lowpruned, nonpruned_nodes = prune_low_degree(A_bus)
```

Next, we'll plot the network as a layout plot. In Section 3.5, we discussed that if we just "threw away" nodes without retaining their indices we would run into trouble. Here is an example. If we had just pruned the low-degree nodes, we would have no idea which nodes were originally plotted where in the initial layout plot. Fortunately, since we included this information, we can easily recover the spatial position of each node, and replot the network with the nodes that were not pruned in the same place that they were before:

```
# relabel the nodes from 0:10 to their original identifier names
node_names_lowpruned = {i: nodeidx for i, nodeidx in
    enumerate(nonpruned_nodes)}

G_bus_lowpruned = nx.from_numpy_array(A_bus_lowpruned)
G_bus_lowpruned = nx.relabel_nodes(G_bus_lowpruned,
    node_names_lowpruned)

nx.draw(G_bus_lowpruned, pos=node_pos, with_labels=True,
    node_color='white', edgecolors='black', node_size=1500)
```

The resulting layout plot is shown in Figure 3.6.2(A).

A useful way to determine whether we have isolates or pendants is to look at the *degree distribution histogram* of the network, which indicates the number of nodes (y-axis) within a given range of degrees (x-axis, individual "buckets" for the histograms). When the values we want a histogram for can only take a limited number of possible values, we may choose to make each possible value its own bucket. Sometimes, when there are a large number of possible values, this might not be possible. We might have to *bin* similar values together to make the plot appreciable. The degree distribution, before and after removing pendants/isolates, looks like this:

```
degrees_before = compute_degrees(A_bus)
degrees_after = compute_degrees(A_bus_lowpruned)
```

(A) Pruned degree ≤ 1   (B) Pruned degree ≤ 1 and pizza hut:

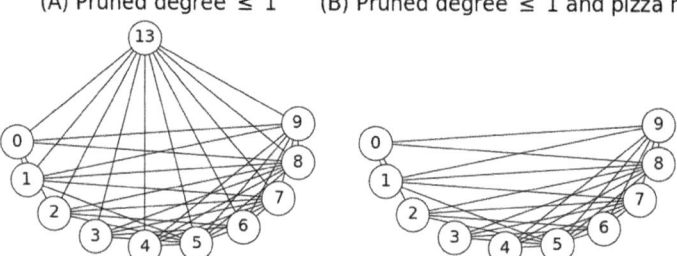

Figure 3.6.2 **(A)** The business network after pruning nodes with a degree less than or equal to 1, which consists of isolates and pendants. **(B)** The business network after pruning isolates and pendants followed by pizza hut nodes.

and can be plotted like this:

```
from seaborn import histplot
fig, axs = plt.subplots(1,2, figsize=(15, 4))

ax = histplot(degrees_before, ax=axs[0], binwidth=1, binrange=(0, 14))
ax.set_xlabel("Node degree");
ax.set_ylabel("Number of Nodes");
ax.set_title("Business Network, before pruning");
ax = histplot(degrees_after, ax=axs[1], binwidth=1, binrange=(0, 14))
ax.set_xlabel("Node degree");
ax.set_title("Business Network, after pruning")
```

3.6.1.1   Removing Pizza Hut Nodes

On the other end of the spectrum, it is often useful to remove nodes which tell us nothing about the network because they are connected to everything. We call these *pizza hut nodes*, because pizza hut can be delivered anywhere. After pruning, we actually created a pizza hut node, which we can see from the low-degree pruned network in Figure 3.6.2(A).

We can prune these nodes just as easily as before. This time, note that our pruning threshold is simply set as the maximum possible node degree. Further, since we pruned the pizza hut node from the low-pruned network, we again need to recover which nodes from the original network were retained.

```
def prune_high_degree(A, return_inds=True, threshold=0):
    # remove nodes which have a degree over a given
    # threshold. For a simple network, threshold=A.shape[0] - 1
    # removes any pizza hut node
    degrees = compute_degrees(A)
    non_prunes = degrees < threshold
    robj = A[np.where(non_prunes)[0],:][:,np.where(non_prunes)[0]]
    if return_inds:
        robj = (robj, np.where(non_prunes)[0])
    return robj
```

```
# pruning nodes
A_bus_pruned, highpruned_nodes = prune_high_degree(A_bus_lowpruned,
    threshold=A_bus_lowpruned.shape[0] - 1)

# relabel the nodes from 0:9 to their original identifier names,
# using the previous filters from node_names_lowpruned
node_names_highpruned = {i: node_names_lowpruned[lowpruned_idx] for
                i, lowpruned_idx in enumerate(highpruned_nodes)}

G_bus_pruned = nx.from_numpy_array(A_bus_pruned)
G_bus_pruned = nx.relabel_nodes(G_bus_pruned, node_names_highpruned)
nx.draw(G_bus_pruned, pos=node_pos, with_labels=True,
    node_color='white', edgecolors='black', node_size=1500)
```

The result of both low-degree pruning (for isolates and pendants) and high-degree pruning (for pizza hut nodes) is shown in Figure 3.6.2(B).

Again, we might want to visualize the degree distribution histogram to decide whether we want to prune nodes with high degrees.

3.6.2 The Largest Connected Component Is the Largest Subnetwork of Connected Nodes

Section 3.5.1 explored the largest connected component. This is a node pruning technique, because it "throws out" all of the nodes other than the ones which are in the largest connected component.

3.7 Edge Regularization

In Section 3.6, we introduced regularization techniques for networks, focusing on node pruning. This section extends those concepts to edge regularization, which involves modifying the edges of a network to improve its properties for analysis.

We cover the following edge regularization techniques:

1. Diagonalization methods to deal with loops,
2. Sparsification methods to reduce network density,
3. Thresholding approaches to convert weighted networks to unweighted networks, and
4. Edge-weight transformations to adjust the distribution of edge weights.

We use a hobby network and a friendship network as reference throughout this section. Edge regularization is crucial for reducing noise, improving computational efficiency, and enhancing the interpretability of network analyses. These techniques are particularly important for weighted and dense networks where the number of edges can overwhelm traditional analysis methods. The concepts introduced here build upon earlier discussions of network density (Section 3.3.1) and compliment other regularization approaches like the regularized Laplacian (Section 3.4.4).

3.7.1   Running Examples for Regularization

To explore edge regularization, we will introduce some new examples from the preceding business network. We have two nonsimple networks, covered in Example 3.7.1 and Example 3.7.2.

Example 3.7.1 Activity/hobby network

The nodes of this network are a group of 50 school students, the first 25 of whom are athletes, and the second 25 are in marching band. To collect the first network, we ask each student to select from a list of 50 school activities and outside hobbies that they enjoy. For a pair of students i and j, the weight of their interest alignment will be a score between 0 and 50 indicating how many activities or hobbies that they have in common.

We will refer to this as the activity/hobby network. This network is undirected, since if student i shares x activities or hobbies with student j, then student j also shares x activities or hobbies with student i. It is also weighted, since the score is between 0 and 50. Finally, this network is loopless, because it would not make sense to look at the activity/hobby alignment of students with themselves, since every student would have perfect alignment of activities and hobbies with him or herself.

Because the network is undirected, the researchers have only saved the portion of the adjacency matrix that includes the entries a_{ij} where $j > i$.

Example 3.7.2 Friendship network

This network is collected using the same 50 students as the activity/hobby network. To collect the second network, we ask each student to rate how good of friends they are with other students, on a scale from 0 to 1. A score of 0 means they are not friends with the student or do not know the student, and a score of 1 means the student is their best friend. We will refer to this network as the friendship network. This network is directed, since two students may differ on their understanding of how good of friends they are. It is also weighted, since the score is between 0 and 1. Finally, this network is also loopless, because it would not make sense to ask students how good of friends they are with themselves.

Our scientific question of interest is how well activities and hobbies align with perceived notions of friendship. We want to use the networks of Examples 3.7.1 and 3.7.2 to learn about a hypothetical third network, whose nodes are identical to these two networks, but whose edges are whether the two individuals are friends (or not) on Facebook. To answer this question, we have to do to some work to make our networks better suited to the task. We will simulate some example networks, with plots illustrated in Figure 3.7.1.

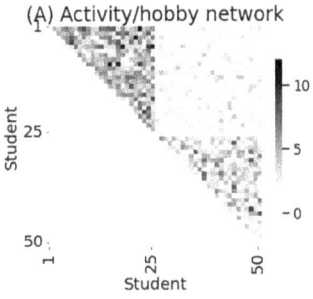
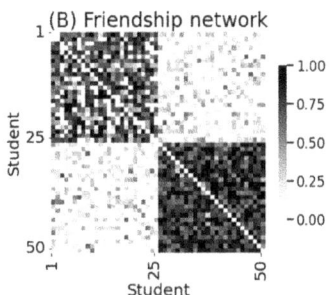

Figure 3.7.1 A comparison of the two networks that we sampled to use in this section. The activity/hobby network is shown in (**A**), and the friendship network is shown in (**B**).

```
from graspologic.simulations import sbm
import numpy as np

wtargsa = [[dict(n=50, p=.09), dict(n=50, p=.02)],
           [dict(n=50, p=.02), dict(n=50, p=.06)]]
# activity network as upper triangle matrix
A_activity_uppertri = sbm(n=[25, 25], p=[[1,1], [1,1]],
    wt=np.random.binomial, wtargs=wtargsa, loops=False,
    directed=False)
A_activity_uppertri = np.triu(A_activity_uppertri)

# friend network
wtargsf = [[dict(a=4, b=2), dict(a=2, b=5)],
           [dict(a=2, b=5), dict(a=6, b=2)]]
A_friend = sbm(n=[25, 25], p=[[.8, .4], [.4, 1]], wt=np.random.beta,
    wtargs=wtargsf, directed=True)
```

3.7.2   Symmetrizing Adjacency Matrices

If we wanted to learn from the friendship network about whether two people shared similar hobbies/activities, a reasonable first place to start might be to symmetrize the friendship adjacency matrix. The activity/hobby network is undirected, which means that if a student i shares hobbies with student j, then student j also shares hobbies with student i. On the other hand, the friendship network is directed. Since our question of interest is about an undirected network but the network we have is directed, it might be useful to take the directed friendship network and build an undirected network from it.

We also might seek to symmetrize the friendship adjacency matrix because we think that asymmetries that exist in the adjacency matrix are just noise. We might assume that the adjacency entries a_{ij} and a_{ji} relate to one another, so together they might be able to produce a single summary number that better summarizes their relationship all together.

As a final reason, we might think that the asymmetries are meaningful, but that they are not feasible to consider. Many statistical models for networks, and many techniques developed to analyze networks, might only have interpretations for undirected networks. This means that if we want to use these techniques, we might have to settle for using undirected networks, even if our data are not undirected.

Remember that in a symmetric matrix (for an undirected network), $a_{ij} = a_{ji}$, so in an *asymmetric* adjacency matrix (for a directed network), $a_{ij} \neq a_{ji}$ for at least one pair of nodes i and j. To symmetrize the friendship network, we want a new adjacency value, which we will call w_{ij}, which will be a function of a_{ij} and a_{ji}. Then, we will construct a new adjacency matrix A', where each entry a'_{ij} and a'_{ji} are set equal to w_{ij}. The little "prime" just signifies that this is a potentially different value than either a_{ij} or a_{ji}. Note that by construction, A' is in fact symmetric, because $a'_{ij} = a'_{ji}$ due to how we built A'. For this matrix, we will look at a generic adjacency matrix that looks like this:

$$A = \begin{bmatrix} a_{11} & a_{12} & \cdots & & a_{1n} \\ a_{21} & \ddots & & \ddots & \vdots \\ \vdots & \ddots & & \ddots & a_{n-1,n} \\ a_{n1} & \cdots & & a_{n,n-1} & a_{nn} \end{bmatrix}.$$

3.7.2.1 Ignoring a "Triangle" of the Adjacency Matrix

The easiest way to symmetrize a network A is to just ignore part of it entirely. In the adjacency matrix A, we have an upper and a lower triangular part of the matrix. The upper triangle looks like this:

$$\Delta = \begin{bmatrix} a_{11} & a_{12} & \cdots & & a_{1n} \\ 0 & \ddots & \ddots & & \vdots \\ \vdots & \ddots & & \ddots & a_{n-1,n} \\ 0 & \cdots & & 0 & a_{nn} \end{bmatrix}.$$

This is called the *upper triangle* because if we look at the nonzero entries, they form a triangular shape in the matrix when the matrix is in its row/column orientation like this. Note this matrix is identical to A for any row i and column j where $j \geq i$, but is equal to 0 for any entries where $j < i$. The transpose of this matrix is:

$$\Delta^{\top} = \begin{bmatrix} a_{11} & 0 & \cdots & & 0 \\ a_{12} & \ddots & & \ddots & \vdots \\ \vdots & \ddots & & \ddots & 0 \\ a_{1n} & \cdots & & a_{n-1,n} & a_{nn} \end{bmatrix}.$$

So when we add the two together, we get this:

$$\Delta + \Delta^{\top} = \begin{bmatrix} 2a_{11} & a_{12} & \cdots & & a_{1n} \\ a_{12} & \ddots & & \ddots & \vdots \\ \vdots & \ddots & & \ddots & a_{n-1,n} \\ a_{1n} & \cdots & & a_{n-1,n} & 2a_{nn} \end{bmatrix}.$$

We just need to subtract back the diagonal of A, which we will do using the matrix $diag(A)$ which has values $diag(A)_{ii} = a_{ii}$, and $diag(A)_{ij} = 0$ for any $i \neq j$:

$$A' = \Delta + \Delta^\top - diag(A) = \begin{bmatrix} a_{11} & a_{12} & \cdots & & a_{1n} \\ a_{12} & \ddots & & \ddots & \vdots \\ \vdots & & \ddots & & a_{n-1,n} \\ a_{1n} & \cdots & & a_{n-1,n} & a_{nn} \end{bmatrix},$$

which leaves A' to be a matrix consisting only of entries which were in the upper right triangle of A. A' is obviously symmetric, because $a'_{ij} = a'_{ji}$ for all i and j. Since the adjacency matrix is symmetric, the network A' represents is undirected.

Box 3.7.3 When is "ignoring" a triangle appropriate?

When we have an undirected network, it is often the case that the network will be stored only as a single "triangle" with the diagonal, since half of the matrix is redundant. Therefore, we can potentially save space by only storing a little over half of it (because we need to retain only one triangle plus the diagonal, and can ignore the other triangle of the matrix). So if we want the actual adjacency matrix, we need to "ignore" the uninformative triangle, and "retain" the informative one, like the procedure above.

So what does this mean in terms of the network itself? This means that the network originally had edge weights a_{ij}, where a_{ij} might not be equal to a_{ji}. Let's consider this in terms of the activity/hobby network. The activity/hobby network, which is undirected, perhaps has been stored in a representation where the entire lower left triangle is just zeros, for space purposes. When we then upper right symmetrize it, the network looks like this, using the `graspologic` function `symmetrize` with `method="triu"` (upper triangular symmetrization):

```
from graspologic.utils import symmetrize

# upper-triangle symmetrize the upper triangle
A_activity = symmetrize(A_activity_uppertri, method="triu")
```

We plot the two heatmaps in Figure 3.7.2.

Likewise, if the network only had the lower triangle stored, we could do the same thing but with `method="tril"` to retain the lower triangle of the matrix.

3.7.2.2 Taking a Function of the Two Values

There are many other ways we use a function of a_{ij} and a_{ji} to get a symmetric matrix (and an undirected network). One is to just average. That is, we can let the matrix A' be the matrix with entries $a'_{ij} = \frac{a_{ij}+a_{ji}}{2}$ for all i and j. In matrix form, this operation looks like this:

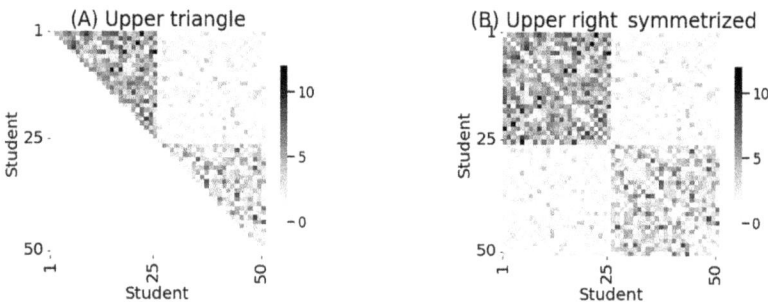

Figure 3.7.2 The matrices A_activity_uppertri and A_activity_triu_symmetrized showing (**A**) the upper triangle, and (**B**) the upper right symmetrized adjacency matrices.

$$A' = \frac{1}{2}\left(A + A^\top\right)$$

$$= \frac{1}{2}\left(\begin{bmatrix} a_{11} & \cdots & a_{1n} \\ \vdots & \ddots & \vdots \\ a_{n1} & \cdots & a_{nn} \end{bmatrix} + \begin{bmatrix} a_{11} & \cdots & a_{n1} \\ \vdots & \ddots & \vdots \\ a_{1n} & \cdots & a_{nn} \end{bmatrix}\right)$$

$$= \begin{bmatrix} \frac{1}{2}(a_{11} + a_{11}) & \cdots & \frac{1}{2}(a_{1n} + a_{n1}) \\ \vdots & \ddots & \vdots \\ \frac{1}{2}(a_{n1} + a_{1n}) & \cdots & \frac{1}{2}(a_{nn} + a_{nn}) \end{bmatrix}$$

$$= \begin{bmatrix} a_{11} & \cdots & \frac{1}{2}(a_{1n} + a_{n1}) \\ \vdots & \ddots & \vdots \\ \frac{1}{2}(a_{n1} + a_{1n}) & \cdots & a_{nn} \end{bmatrix}.$$

As we can see, for all of the entries, $a'_{ij} = \frac{1}{2}(a_{ij} + a_{ji})$, and also $a'_{ji} = \frac{1}{2}(a_{ji} + a_{ij})$. These quantities are the same, so $a'_{ij} = a'_{ji}$, and A' is symmetric. As the adjacency matrix is symmetric, the network that A' represents is undirected.

The asymmetry in the friendship network means student i might perceive their friendship with student j as being stronger or weaker than student j perceived about student i. Instead of just arbitrarily throwing one of those values away, we can average if it would better represent their friendship. This produces a single friendship strength a'_{ij} where $a'_{ij} = a'_{ji}$.

We can implement this with graspologic as follows:

```
# symmetrize with averaging
A_friend_avg_sym = symmetrize(A_friend, method="avg")
```

We encourage readers to plot the outcome and convince themselves that it is, in fact, symmetric using the is_symmetric() function.

We will will use the friendship network symmetrized by averaging (A_friend_avg_sym) in several of the following examples, which we will call the "undirected friendship network."

3.7.3 Diagonal Augmentation

Numerous techniques which operate on adjacency matrices require them to be *positive semidefinite*. We will explore this concept in Section 4.11.2. When we have a loopless network, a common practice is to set the diagonal to zero. This leads to adjacency matrices being *indefinite* (which means not positive semidefinite). This means that many network machine learning techniques cannot operate on these adjacency matrices. However, as we mentioned before, these entries are not actually zero, but simply do not exist, and so we need a way to represent them.

Diagonal augmentation is a procedure for imputing the diagonals of adjacency matrices for loopless networks. This gives us "placeholder" values that do not cause this issue of indefiniteness, and allow our techniques to work. For a simple network, the adjacency matrix will look like this:

$$A = \begin{bmatrix} 0 & a_{12} & \cdots & a_{1n} \\ a_{21} & \ddots & & \vdots \\ \vdots & & \ddots & a_{n-1,n} \\ a_{n1} & \cdots & a_{n,n-1} & 0 \end{bmatrix}.$$

What we do is impute the diagonal entries using the fraction of possible edges which exist for each node. This quantity is simply the node degree d_i (the number of edges which exist for node i) divided by the number of possible edges node i could have (which would be node i adjacent to each of the other $n-1$ nodes). Remembering that the degree matrix D is the matrix whose diagonal entries are the degrees of each node, the diagonal-augmented adjacency matrix is given by:

$$A' = A + \frac{1}{n-1}D = \begin{bmatrix} \frac{d_1}{n-1} & a_{12} & \cdots & a_{1n} \\ a_{21} & \ddots & & \vdots \\ \vdots & & \ddots & a_{n-1,n} \\ a_{n1} & \cdots & a_{n,n-1} & \frac{d_n}{n-1} \end{bmatrix}.$$

When the matrices are directed or weighted, the computation is a little different, but fortunately graspologic will handle this for us. Let's see how we would apply this to the directed friendship network:

```
from graspologic.utils import augment_diagonal

A_friend_aug = augment_diagonal(A_friend)
```

We will rotate back to the problem of positive semidefiniteness in Section 4.5 as it relates to statistical models for networks, and will pivot back again in Section 5.3 for the implications of this concept on adjacency matrices.

3.7.4   Regularizing the Edges of Weighted Networks

We are often concerned with the bias/variance trade-off. The *bias/variance trade-off* is an unfortunate side-effect that concerns how well a learning technique will generalize to new datasets [8].

1. *Bias* is an error from erroneous assumptions we make about the system that we are learning about. For instance, if we have a friendship network, we might make simplifying assumptions, such as an assumption that two athletes from different sports have an equally likely chance of being friends with a member of the band. This might be flat out false, as band members might be selectively better friends with athletes depending on which sports they play.
2. *Variance* is the degree to which an estimate will change when given new data. An assumption that a football player has a higher chance of being friends with a band member might make sense if the band performs at football games.

The "trade-off" is that these two factors tend to be somewhat at odds, in that raising the bias tends to lower the variance, and vice versa:

1. *High bias, but low variance*: Whereas a lower variance model might be better suited to the situation where the data we expect to see are noisy, it might not as faithfully represent the underlying dynamics we think the network possesses. A low variance model might ignore that athletes might have a different chance of being friends with a band member based on their sport all together. This means that while we won't get the student relationships correct, we might still be able to get a reasonable estimate that we think is not due to overfitting. In this case, we have smoothed away signal from the data at the expense of avoiding noise.
2. *Low bias, but high variance*: Whereas a low bias model might more faithfully model true relationships in our training data, it might fit training data a little too well. Fitting the training data too well is a problem known as *overfitting*. If we only had three football team members and tried to assume that football players were better friends with band members, we might not be able to well approximate this relationship because of how few individuals we have who reflect this situation.

Here, we show several strategies to reduce the variance (but, add bias) due to edge-weight noise in network machine learning.

3.7.5   Sparsification of the Network

The procedure of *sparsification* is one in which we take a network and remove edges from it, which is described by [9] and [10]. Removing edges, in terms of the adjacency matrix, is analogous to setting the corresponding adjacencies to zero. A matrix with many zero entries is called a *sparse* matrix. So, the reason we call the removal of the edges from a network sparsification is that we are producing a network with a sparse adjacency matrix.

Sparsification is a general class of edge regularization techniques, and includes many flavors. Here, we discuss a few of them. In network sparsification, we will often pick some property of the network (such as a particular edge weight) and remove edges in an attempt to preserve something about this particular property.

A useful tool to study how we might want to go about sparsifying the network is called the *edge-weight distribution* of our network sample, which is the distribution of values that the edge weights of the network take. The most common way to visualize the edge-weight distribution is an edge-weight histogram. This is similar to the node degree histogram we worked with in Section 3.6, but instead of node degrees, we look at the edge weights. Let's take a look at the friendship network, and then take a look at its edge-weight distribution. Because the friendship network is undirected, we need to remove its diagonal elements before we visualize the edge-weight distribution. We also remove edges with zero weights for visualization purposes:

```
def discard_diagonal(A):
    """
    A function that discards the diagonal of a matrix,
    and returns its non-diagonal edge-weights.
    """
    # create a mask that is True for the non-diagonal edges
    non_diag_idx = np.where(~np.eye(A.shape[0], dtype=bool))
    return A[non_diag_idx].flatten()

# obtain the non-diagonal edge-weights
friend_nondiag_ew = discard_diagonal(A_friend)
# get the non-zero, non-diagonal edge weights
friend_nondiag_nz_ew = friend_nondiag_ew[friend_nondiag_ew > 0]

# plot the histogram, as above
histplot(friend_nondiag_nz_ew, bins=20, binrange=(0, 1))
```

We show this plot in Figure 3.7.3(C).

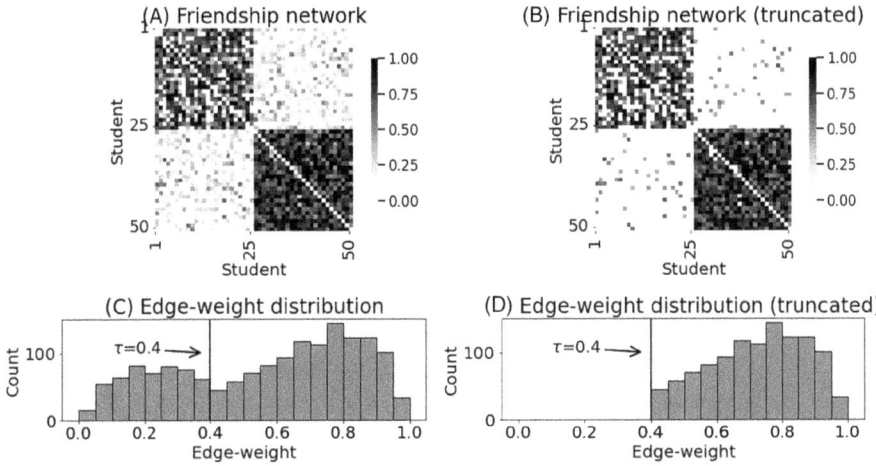

Figure 3.7.3 (**A**) The adjacency matrix before truncation. (**B**) The adjacency matrix after truncation. (**C**) The nonzero, nondiagonal edge weights before truncation. (**D**) The nonzero, nondiagonal edge weights after truncation at $\tau = 0.4$.

3.7.5.1   Truncation Removes the Smallest Edges

The simplest way to reduce the variance due to edge-weight noise is called edge truncation. *Edge truncation* is a process by which we choose some threshold value τ, and remove all of the weights which are smaller than τ but retain the weights that are bigger than τ. For edges that are equal to τ, what we will want to do depends on the strategy we are employing. We'll arbitrarily set nodes $\leq \tau$ to zero in our case.

The value of τ is typically chosen with one of the following two strategies:

1. Choose τ arbitrarily: After looking at our network and doing some preliminary visualizations, we might determine that our edge weights tend to be "multimodal". This means that when we look at the edge-weight distribution, we see multiple "clusters" of edge-weight bins which are larger, or smaller. For a lot of networks, these small edges might be very noise induced; that is, the small edges might just spuriously be close to, but not quite, zero, due to errors in the measuring process. We might just want to remove these edges entirely for subsequent analysis.
2. Choose τ using the quantile function: In this strategy, we start with a desired fraction q. Then, we pick τ such that a q fraction of the edges have a weight less than τ, and $1 - q$ fraction of the edges have a weight exceeding τ. Such a value of τ is picked through the quantile function, which we will learn more about shortly. We then identify the edges whose edge weights are below τ and then set these edge weights to 0, while the remaining edge weights are left unchanged. For instance, if we use a fraction of 0.5, this means that we take the smallest 50 percent of edges and set the weights to zero, while the largest 50 percent of edges retain their initial weights. There are two potential major pitfalls to this process, which we elaborate on below.

This is called truncation because we are taking the edge-weight distribution, and truncating (cutting it off) below the value τ.

With respect to what to do with edges that are equal to τ, when we choose a threshold arbitrarily, we can do whatever we want with them, as long as we are consistent if we have multiple networks we are truncating. What we mean by this is that we can select to remove edges less than or equal to this threshold, or retain edge weights greater than or equal to the threshold. When we truncate on the basis of a percentile, however, this is not quite the case. We will want to remove all the edges below τ, and truncate away the remaining edges equal to τ at random until we have truncated the desired fraction of edges in total.

Let's see how this works in practice. In the edge-weight histogram in Figure 3.7.3, we notice two "peaks" to the nonzero edge weights.

If we think that the smaller peak edge weights are spurious/noise, we might want a threshold somewhere in between the smaller and the larger peaks, like near 0.4, which is highlighted in 3.7.3(C).

```
def truncate_network(A, threshold):
    A_cp = np.copy(A)
    A_cp[A_cp <= threshold] = 0
    return A_cp

tau = 0.4
A_friend_trunc = truncate_network(A_friend, threshold=tau)
```

The next thing to look at is the adjacency matrix, before and after truncation. We show these plots in Figure 3.7.3(A) and 3.7.3(B). Notice that the smallest weight edges in the network (in this case, the ones with edge weights ≤ 0.4) have been replaced with zeros. As we can see, a lot of the edges in the upper right and upper left, which were previously small, are now zero. This is reflected in the edge-weight distribution:

```
friend_trunc_nondiag_ew = discard_diagonal(A_friend_trunc)
# get the non-zero, non-diagonal edge weights
friend_trunc_nondiag_nz_ew =
    friend_trunc_nondiag_ew[friend_trunc_nondiag_ew > 0]
histplot(friend_trunc_nondiag_nz_ew, bins=20, binrange=(0, 1))
```

which is shown in Figure 3.7.3(D). All of the edges with weights less than $\tau = 0.4$ have been truncated away.

A slight caveat to this procedure is that, if we use the percentile approach and the network is undirected, we need to exclude one triangle of the network to obtain the appropriate percentile. This is because when $a_{ij} = a_{ji}$, we would otherwise count an edge twice if we just used the adjacency matrix to obtain percentiles. We will see this more in the example on thresholding below.

3.7.5.2   Thresholding Converts Weighted Networks to Unweighted Networks

Closely related to truncation is the process of *thresholding*. Like truncation, we begin with a threshold τ, which is usually chosen arbitrarily or based on a quantile, as for truncation. However, there is one key difference: When we threshold a network, we set the edges below τ to zero, and the edges greater than τ to one. This has the effect of taking a weighted network, and effectively transforming it into an unweighted network.

We will show how to use the quantile approach to thresholding with the activity/hobby network. A *quantile* is a value where q fraction of the data is less than a value, and $1 - q$ fraction of the data exceeds a value. For instance, the 0.5 quantile of a set of data would correspond to the median, where 50 percent of the numbers are smaller than the median and 50 percent are larger than the median.

We will threshold by choosing τ such that τ is the median (0.5 quantile, or 50th percentile) of the edge-weight distribution. Remember, as we learned in Section 3.1, that if the network itself is loopless, the diagonal entries simply do not exist; 0 is simply a commonly used placeholder. For this reason, when we compute quantiles of edge weights, we need to exclude the diagonal if the network is loopless.

Since this network is undirected, we also need to restrict our attention to one triangle of the corresponding adjacency matrix. We choose the upper right triangle arbitrarily, as the adjacency matrix's symmetry means the upper right triangle and lower right triangle have identical edge-weight distributions. We can do this using numpy. This network is loopless and undirected, so we will want to exclude both the diagonal and only perform our analysis on a single triangle of the matrix:

```
# find the indices which are in the upper triangle and not in the
    diagonal
upper_tri_non_diag_idx = np.where(np.triu(np.ones(A_activity.shape),
    k=1).astype(bool))
q = 0.5 # desired percentile is 50, or a fraction of 0.5
```

> **Box 3.7.4** Why is thresholding with the quantile function desirable?
>
> Remember that in Section 3.3.1, we defined the network density for a simple network as:
>
> $$density(A) = \frac{\sum_{j>i} a_{ij}}{\binom{n}{2}}.$$
>
> If we threshold this network at a percentile of p, this corresponds to using the quantiling approach with a fraction of $q = \frac{p}{100}$. Ideally, we will set $1 - q$ fraction of the edges to 1, and a q fraction of the edges to zero. We will use a placeholder $q = \frac{p}{100}$ to denote the fraction of edges that we are setting to zero through a percentile.
>
> If we are able to do this perfectly, then $\sum_{j>i} a_{ij} = (1 - q)\binom{n}{2}$. Stated another way, $1 - q$ fraction of all possible edges in the resulting unweighted network will (ideally) exist.
>
> Therefore:
>
> $$density(A) = \frac{(1 - q)\binom{n}{2}}{\binom{n}{2}} = 1 - q.$$
>
> So when we threshold the network at a percentile p, and we are actually able to set a $q = \frac{p}{100}$ fraction of the edges to zero and a $1 - q$ fraction of the edges to one, we end with a network of density equal to $1 - q$. We will see conditions as to when this will, and will not, be possible to do later on.

```
histplot(A_activity[upper_tri_non_diag_idx].flatten())
# use the quantile function with the desired fraction q
tau = np.quantile(A_activity[upper_tri_non_diag_idx], q=q)
```

So, let's see what happens when we just compute τ using the q fraction of the non-diagonal, upper triangular entries of A, and then threshold A using τ. To do this, we will just check the number of edges greater than τ, and the number less than or equal to τ. Since we used $q = 0.5$ as our desired quantile, we should anticipate that these numbers should be very close to equal:

```
n_lteq_tau = np.sum(A_activity[upper_tri_non_diag_idx] <= tau)
n_gt_tau = np.sum(A_activity[upper_tri_non_diag_idx] > tau)
print("Number of edges less than or equal to tau:
    {}".format(n_lteq_tau))
print("Number of edges greater than to tau: {}".format(n_gt_tau))
```

The number of edges $\leq \tau$ are likely not close to equal the number of edges $> \tau$: They should be about 50 percent larger than the number of edges $> \tau$. So what happened?

3.7.5.3 The Duplicate Value Pitfall

Let's imagine an array that was $[1, 2, 3, 4]$ and $[1, 2, 2, 4]$, and we chose to threshold at the 50th percentile (the 0.5 quantile). The first array would give a 0.5

quantile of 2.5. If we thresholded with this value, we would get [0,0,1,1], and the number of elements retained after thresholding would be 50 percent ones and 50 percent zeros, like we expected. On the other hand, the 0.5 quantile of the second array is 2, and if we used the thresholding approach above we would get [0,0,0,1], which has 75 percent of the values taking 0 and 25 percent of the values taking one.

This means that if we pass in a quantile q and we expect that q fraction of the points will have a value of 0 after truncation/thresholding, we are going to need to be very careful with our data to handle points that are equal to the corresponding value of τ. To do this, one way is to assign edges less than τ to zero, and the edges greater than τ to one. Then, for edges equal to τ, we can to randomly assign them to a zero or one, until we obtain the desired threshold. This can be done with the pseudocode in Algorithm 3.1. We could write a similar utility for truncating with the quantile function.

Algorithm 3.1 Thresholding an adjacency matrix with random tiebreaking

---

Data: A: an adjacency matrix
        q: a fraction between 0 and 1
Result: an adjacency matrix thresholded at the q fraction.
1 Let d be the minimum nonzero difference between any two elements of A.
2 **for** i *in* $1:n$ **do**
3   **for** j *in* $1:n$ **do**
4   **if** $i = j$ *and A is hollow* **then**
5             $\epsilon_{ii} = 0$ for all i.
6   **else**
7   Let ϵ_{ij} be a random number between 0 and $\frac{d}{10}$.
8   **end**
9   **end**
10 **end**
11 **if** A *is symmetric* **then**
12     $\epsilon = \frac{\epsilon + \epsilon^{\top}}{2}$, which makes ϵ a symmetric matrix.
13 **end**
14 Compute the augmented adjacency matrix, $A' = A + \frac{\epsilon}{10}$.
15 Compute the appropriate threshold τ using A'.
16 Threshold A' by setting elements where $a'_{ij} > \tau$ to one, and $a'_{ij} < \tau$ to zero.

This algorithm adds a very small amount of noise to the matrix A that we are thresholding. Note that we take care to ensure that if A is hollow and the network is loopless, we do not add random noise to the diagonal. Otherwise, we might end up setting some diagonal elements to 1 when we threshold. Further, if A is symmetric and the network is undirected, we must add the same amount of noise to both entries a_{ij} and a_{ji} by symmetrizing the "noise matrix" ϵ. This noise is small enough that it is an order of magnitude (a factor of 10) smaller than the smallest appreciable difference in any two nonzero elements of A.

After we add this matrix to A, there is a probability of zero that any two elements of A will have the same value. Further, since we added noise that was an order of magnitude smaller than any nonzero differences of elements of A, it is impossible for an item that was originally greater than τ to now be less than the desired τ, and vice versa. This strategy is called a random tiebreaking, since we broke ties that occur at exactly τ randomly.

This can be implemented in Python as follows:

```python
from numpy import copy

def min_difference(arr):
    b = np.diff(np.sort(arr))
    return b[b>0].min()

def quantile_threshold_network(A, directed=False, loops=False, q=0.5):
    # a function to threshold a network on the basis of the
    # fraction q
    A_cp = np.copy(A)
    n = A.shape[0]
    E = np.random.uniform(low=0, high=min_difference(A)/10, size=(n, n))
    if not directed:
        # make E symmetric
        E = (E + E.transpose())/2
    mask = np.ones((n, n))
    if not loops:
        # remove diagonal from E
        E = E - np.diag(np.diag(E))
        # exclude diagonal from the mask
        mask = mask - np.diag(np.diag(mask))
    Ap = A_cp + E
    tau = np.quantile(Ap[np.where(mask)].flatten(), q=q)
    A_cp[Ap <= tau] = 0; A_cp[Ap > tau] = 1
    return A_cp

A_activity_thresholded03 = quantile_threshold_network(A_activity,
    q=0.3)
A_activity_thresholded07 = quantile_threshold_network(A_activity,
    q=0.7)
```

We visualize these two thresholded adjacency matrices along with the unweighted adjacency matrix in Figure 3.7.4.

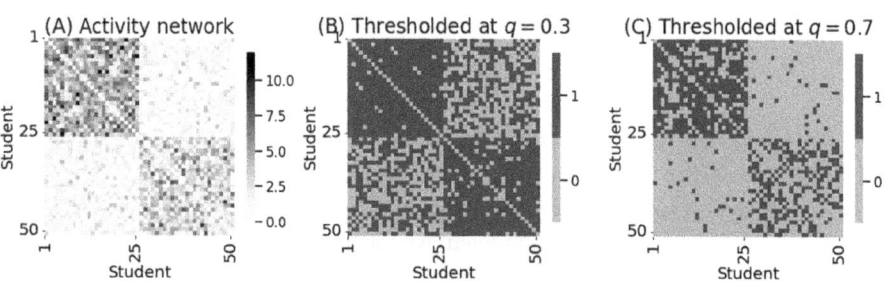

Figure 3.7.4 (**A**) The weighted adjacency matrix of the activity/hobby network. (**B**) The weighted adjacency matrix of the activity/hobby network after thresholding at a fraction of 0.3. (**C**) The weighted adjacency matrix of the activity/hobby network after thresholding at a fraction of 0.7.

Now, we confirm that we didn't run into the duplicate value pitfall. We will do this by writing a utility which computes the network density from an adjacency matrix for a simple network, and then illustrate that the fraction q that we indicated ends up being $1-$ the network's density, based on Box 3.7.4. Since $q = 0.3$ for the network we are checking below, we should obtain a network density of $1 - q = 0.7$:

```
from graspologic.utils import is_unweighted, is_loopless, is_symmetric

def simple_network_dens(X):
    # make sure the network is simple
    if (not is_unweighted(X)) or (not is_loopless(X)) or (not
        is_symmetric(X)):
      raise TypeError("Network is not simple!")
    # count the non-zero entries in the upper-right triangle
    # for a simple network X
    nnz = np.triu(X, k=1).sum()
    # number of nodes
    n = X.shape[0]
    # number of possible edges is 1/2*n*(n-1)
    poss_edges = 0.5*n*(n-1)
    return nnz/poss_edges

print("Network Density:
    {:.3f}".format(simple_network_dens(A_activity_thresholded03)))
# Network Density: 0.700
```

So our solution achieved the desired network density.

We call this the *duplicate value pitfall* because we can only run into it if our adjacency matrix has the same value duplicated multiple times.

3.7.5.4 The "Underly Ambitious" Pitfall

The next pitfall of using a fraction q is actually a special case of the duplicate value pitfall listed above: We might choose an underly ambitious fraction to truncate/threshold with. By *underly ambitious*, we mean that the adjacency matrix does not even have a $1 - q$ fraction of nonzero edges. When we threshold A with a fraction of q, we can spot this pitfall fairly easily by simply checking the fraction of 0-weight edges ahead of time.

For an example, let's consider a network where 50 percent of the possible edges are 0, and the other 50 percent are 1 (the network density is 0.5). If we were to choose a quantile of 0.3, quantiling will still only give us a network density of 0.5, and not 0.7 like we might have expected from Box 3.7.4.

Unfortunately, there is no quick fix like there was for the duplicate value pitfall; if we run into the underly ambitious pitfall and try to use the randomization procedure, the "solution" would end up setting edges with a value of zero in the adjacency matrix to one, which does not make much sense. To avoid this pitfall, we need to analyze our densities ahead of time if we want to use quantiling, and ensure that the fraction we choose is not underly ambitious.

If we had a collection of weighted networks that we wanted to threshold or truncate en masse using a fraction q, we could do this by plotting a histogram of the unweighted network densities (e.g., the ratio of edges to potential edges, ignoring weightedness), and ensuring that $1 - q$ is less than all of the unweighted network densities in our collection.

> **Box 3.7.5** With all these pitfalls, why would we quantile?
>
> When we analyze networks using summary statistics, it is often the case that we want to argue that our network summary statistic captures some sort of property of the networks that will subsequently be informative. Let's imagine that we have a collection of networks that are in one of two groups (such as brain networks from male worms and female worms), and we want to argue that the brains of female worms tend to be more clustered than the brains of male worms.
>
> Many network summary statistics that we might be interested in tend to be correlated with the network density. This means that when the network density is high, other summary statistics that we could use (such as the correlation coefficient) might be artificially higher or lower simply as a product of the network having more (or fewer) edges, rather. For this reason, if we want to analyze a collection of networks using summary statistics, it might make sense to analyze a collection of networks with the same network density. This is because in some sense, analyzing the networks with a similar network density will "decouple" this correlation with the network density, since the network density will no longer be changing across the networks.

3.7.5.5   When Can We Ignore these Pitfalls Entirely?

If our network fulfills two properties, we are guaranteed that we will not run into the quantiling pitfalls. First, if the network is *dense* (a network where all possible entries a_{ij} are nonzero, with arbitrarily small or large edge weights), we cannot possibly run into the underly ambitious pitfall, since that will only arise when there are zero-weight edges in the adjacency matrix. Second, if the adjacency matrix does not have any duplicate values, we cannot run into the duplicate value pitfall either, because we cannot have ties at the desired fraction if there are no duplicated values in the edge weights.

When considering when a network might run into these pitfalls using the adjacency matrix, be sure to only consider appropriate entries of the adjacency matrix. This means restricting analysis to the upper triangle or the lower triangle if the network is undirected, and removing the diagonal if the network is loopless.

3.8   Edge-Weight Global Rescaling

Sections 3.6 and 3.7 explored techniques for regularization. Building on this foundation, we now turn our attention to methods for rescaling edge weights in weighted networks. This section covers:

1. z-Score standardization of edge weights,
2. Ranking-based approaches for edge-weight normalization, and
3. Logarithmic transformation of edge weights.

Edge-weight rescaling helps compare networks with different edge-weight distributions or scales. These techniques serve to normalize network data, making them more suitable for comparative analyses and certain machine learning algorithms.

With weighted networks, it is often the case that we might want to reshape the distributions of edge weights to highlight particular properties. Notice that the edge weights for the friendship network takes values between 0 and 1, but the activity network takes values between 0 and almost 15. How can we possibly compare between these two networks where the edge weights take such different ranges of values? We might turn to standardization, which allows us to place values from different networks on the same scale.

3.8.1 *z*-Scoring Standardizes Edge Weights using the Normal Distribution

The first approach to edge-weight standardization is known commonly as z-scoring. Suppose that A is the adjacency matrix, with entries a_{ij}. With a z-score, we will rescale the weights of the adjacency matrix, such that the new edge weights (called z-scores) are approximately normally distributed. The reason this can be useful is that the normal distribution is pretty ubiquitous across many branches of science, and therefore a z-score is relatively easy to communicate with other scientists. Further, many things that exist in nature can be well approximated by a normal distribution, so it seems like a reasonable place to start to use a z-score for edge weights. To use the z-score, we will construct the z-scored adjacency matrix Z, whose entries z_{ij} are the corresponding z-scores of the adjacency matrix's entries a_{ij}. For a weighted, loopless network, we use an estimate of the mean, $\hat{\mu}$, and the unbiased estimate of the variance, $\hat{\sigma}^2$, which can be computed as follows:

$$\hat{\mu} = \frac{1}{n(n-1)} \sum_{i \neq j} a_{ij},$$

$$\hat{\sigma}^2 = \frac{1}{n(n-1)-1} \sum_{i \neq j} (a_{ij} - \hat{\mu})^2.$$

The z-score for the (i, j) entry is simply the quantity:

$$z_{ij} = \frac{a_{ij} - \hat{\mu}}{\hat{\sigma}}.$$

Since our network is loopless, notice that these sums are for all nondiagonal entries where $i \neq j$. If the network were not loopless, we would include diagonal entries in the calculation, and instead would sum over all possible combinations of i and j. The interpretation of the z-score z_{ij} is the number of stadard deviations that the entry a_{ij} is from the mean, $\hat{\mu}$.

We will demonstrate on the directed friendship network. We can implement z-scoring for a loopless directed network as follows:

```
from graspologic.utils import is_loopless, is_symmetric
from scipy.stats import zscore

def z_score_directed_loopless(X, undirected=False):
    if not is_loopless(X):
        raise TypeError("The network has loops!")
```

```
if is_symmetric(X):
    raise TypeError("The network is undirected!")
# the entries of the adjacency matrix that are not on the diagonal
non_diag_idx = np.where(~np.eye(X.shape[0], dtype=bool))
Z = np.zeros(X.shape)
Z[non_diag_idx] = zscore(X[non_diag_idx])
return Z

ZA_friend = z_score_directed_loopless(A_friend)
```

Note that in the above code snippet, we throw an error if the network is undirected (and the adjacency matrix is symmetric): Remember that we want to be careful to restrict our analysis to the upper triangle if the network is undirected and loopless. This won't really change the estimate of the mean, but the variance will be slightly different. The sums would be over $j > i$, and the normalizing factors would be $\binom{n}{2}$ instead of $n(n-1)$.

The theory for when, and why, to use z-scoring for network machine learning tends to go something like this: Many things tend to be normally distributed, so perhaps that is a reasonable expectation for our network, too. Unfortunately, we find this often to not be the case for network data. In fact, we often find that the specific distribution of edge weights itself often might be almost infeasible to identify in a population of networks, and therefore often irrelevant for subsequent analyses. In this case, we turn to ranking the edges.

3.8.2   Ranking Edges Preserves Ordinal Relationships

The idea behind ranking is as follows. We often don't know how the distribution of edge weights varies between a given set of networks. For this reason, we may want to virtually eliminate the impact of that distribution almost entirely. However, we know that if one edge weight is larger than another edge weight, we do in fact trust that relationship. What this means is that we want something which preserves ordinal relationships in our edge weights, but ignores other properties of the edge weights. An *ordinal relationship* just means that we have a natural ordering to the edge weights. This means that we can identify a largest edge weight, a smallest edge weight, and every position in between. When we want to preserve ordinal relationships in our network, we *pass the nonzero edge weights to ranks*. We will often use the abbreviation ptr to define this function because it is so useful for weighted networks. We pass nonzero edge weights to ranks as in Algorithm 3.2.

Next, we pass to ranks the directed friendship network using `graspologic`:

```
from graspologic.utils import pass_to_ranks

RA_friend = pass_to_ranks(A_friend)
```

A plot of the adjacency matrices before and after passing to ranks, as well as the edge-weight histograms before and after passing to ranks, is shown in Figure 3.8.1.

The edge weights for the adjacency matrix R after ptr have the interpretation that each entry r_{ij} which is nonzero is the fraction of nonzero edge weights that a_{ij}

Algorithm 3.2 Passing an adjacency matrix to ranks

Data: A is an adjacency matrix.

Result: The adjacency matrix, after passing to ranks.

1 Identify all of the nonzero entries of the adjacency matrix A.

2 Let n_{nz} be the number of nonzero entries of the adjacency matrix A.

3 Rank all of the nonzero edges in the adjacency matrix A, where for a nonzero entry a_{ij}, $rank(a_{ij}) = 1$ if a_{ij} is the smallest nonzero edge weight, and $rank(a_{ij}) = n_{nz}$ if a_{ij} is the largest edge weight. Ties are settled by using the average rank of the tied entries.

4 Report the weight of each nonzero entry (i, j) as $r_{ij} = \frac{rank(a_{ij})}{n_{nz}+1}$, and for each zero entry as $r_{ij} = 0$.

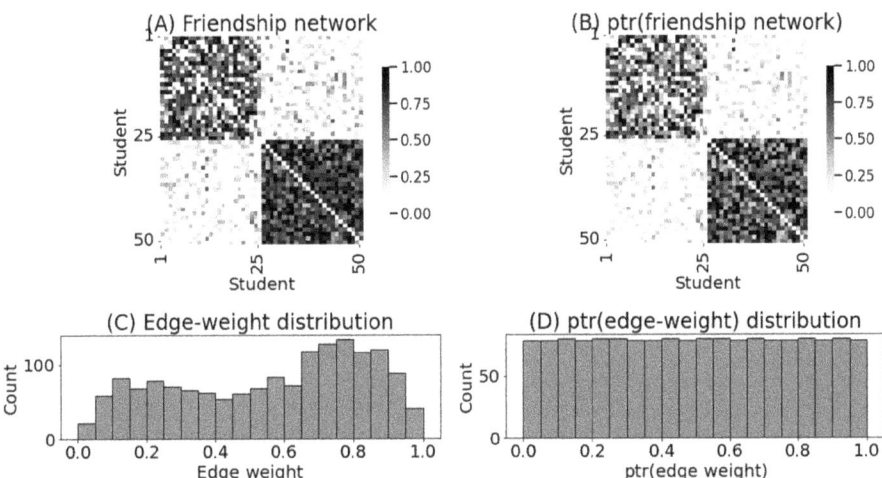

Figure 3.8.1 (**A**) The adjacency matrix before passing to ranks for the friendship network. (**B**) The adjacency matrix after passing to ranks. (**C**) The edge-weight histogram (including zero-weight edges) before passing to ranks. (**D**) The edge-weight histogram (including zero-weight edges) after passing to ranks.

exceeds. This is unique in that it is completely *distribution free*, which means that we do not need to assume anything about the distribution of the edge weights to have an interpretable quantity. On the other hand, the z-score has the interpretation of the number of standard deviations from the mean, which is only a sensible quantity to compare if the population of edge weights are normally distributed.

Another useful quantity related to pass to ranks is known as the zero-boosted pass to ranks. Zero-boosted pass to ranks is conducted as in Algorithm 3.3.

The edge weights for the adjacency matrix R' after zero-boosted `ptr` have the interpretation that each entry r'_{ij} is the quantile of that entry amongst all of the entries. Let's instead use zero-boosted `ptr` on our network:

```
RA_friend_zb = pass_to_ranks(A_friend, method="zero-boost")
```

Algorithm 3.3 Zero-boosted pass to ranks

Data: A is an adjacency matrix.

Result: The adjacency matrix, after passing to ranks.

1 Identify all of the nonzero entries of the adjacency matrix A and the zero-weighted entries of the adjacency matrix A.

2 Let n_{nz} be the number of nonzero entries of the adjacency matrix A, and n_z be the number of zero-weighted entries of the adjacency matrix A. Note that $n_{nz} + n_z = n^2$, since A has n^2 entries.

3 Rank all of the nonzero edges in the adjacency matrix A, where for a nonzero entry a_{ij}, $rank(a_{ij}) = 1$ if a_{ij} is the smallest nonzero edge weight, and $rank(a_{ij}) = n_{nz}$ if a_{ij} is the largest edge weight. Ties are settled by using the average rank of the two entries.

4 Report the weight of each nonzero entry (i, j) as $r'_{ij} = \frac{n_z + rank(a_{ij})}{n^2 + 1}$, and for each zero entry as $r'_{ij} = 0$.

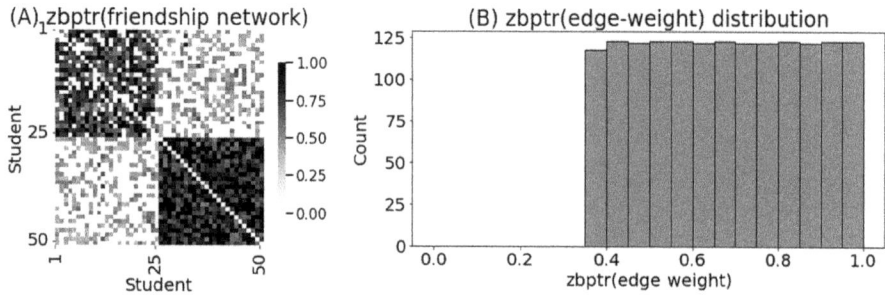

Figure 3.8.2 **(A)** The adjacency matrix, after zero-boosted `ptr`. **(B)** The edge-weight histogram, after zero-boosted `ptr`. Compare this to Figure 3.8.1(B) and 3.8.1(D), respectively.

We show the adjacency matrix after zero-boosted `ptr`, along with the edge-weight histogram (including zero-weight edges), in Figure 3.8.2.

3.8.3   Thresholding as a Decimation of Ranking

The thresholding approach we learned in Section 3.7.5.2 can be thought of as a *decimation* of ranking, assuming that the ranking implementation handles ties randomly (the implementation in `graspologic` does not, as ties are settled by the average rank, but we would encourage you to implement one that does as an exercise). This means that we are reducing the number of potential values that the resulting network weights can take (here, from normalized ranks to binary values). For instance, if we picked a threshold of 0.5, there is some corresponding rank (or value in between two ranks), where all of the elements of the adjacency matrix with a rank lower than a given threshold τ_r have corresponding weights lower than τ and all of the elements of the adjacency matrix with a rank higher than a given threshold τ_r have corresponding weights higher than τ. Then, we can simply threshold the ranked adjacency matrix using τ_r.

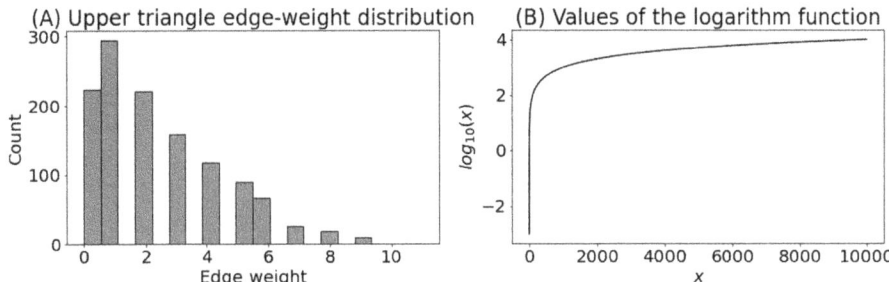

Figure 3.8.3 (**A**) The upper triangle edge-weight histogram for the activity/hobby network. Notice that the histogram "tails off" towards the right. (**B**) The value for the base-10 logarithm function for given values of x.

3.8.4 Logging Reduces Magnitudinal Differences between Edges

When we look at the distribution of upper triangle edge weights for the activity/hobby network or the friendship network, we notice a strange pattern, known as a right-skew. This is shown in Figure 3.8.3(A). Informally, a distribution is *right-skewed* if a large fraction of the points take relatively small values, and then a small portion of the points take relatively large values. Notice in this figure, for instance, that most points have an edge weight between 0 and 2, but and a small portion of points have an edge weight between 2 and 10. This is called a "right-skew" because the histogram "tails off" as the values go to the right (increase).

What if we want to make these large values more similar in relation to the smaller values, but we simultaneously want to preserve properties of the underlying distribution of the edge weights? Well, we can't use ptr`, because `ptr will throw away all of the information about the edge-weight distribution other than the ordinal relationship between pairs of edges. To interpret what this means, we might think that there is a big difference between sharing no interests compared to three interests in common, but there is not as much of a difference in sharing ten interests compared to thirteen interests in common.

To do this, we instead turn to the logarithm function. The logarithm function $log_{10}(x)$ is defined for positive values x as the value c_x where $x = 10^{c_x}$. In this sense, it is the "number of powers of ten" to obtain the value x. The logarithm function is shown in Figure 3.8.3(B).

As x increases, the log of x increases by a decreasing amount. Let's imagine we have three values, $x = 0.001$, $y = 0.1$, and $z = 10$. A calculator will give us that $log_{10}(x) = -3$, $log_{10}(y) = -1$, and $log_{10}(z) = 1$. Even though y is only 0.099 units bigger than x, its logarithm $log_{10}(y)$ exceeds $log_{10}(x)$ by two units. On the other hand, z is 9.9 units bigger than y, but yet its logarithm $log_{10}(z)$ is still the same two units bigger than $log_{10}(y)$. This is because the logarithm is instead looking at the fact that z is one power of ten, y is -1 powers of ten, and z is -3 powers of ten. The logarithm has collapsed the huge size difference between z and the other two values x and y by using exponentiation with base ten.

We can use the logarithm function to reduce the huge size difference between the values in our activity/hobby network. However, because $\log_{10}(0)$ is not defined, we need to augment the entries of the adjacency matrix if it contains zeros. To do this, we will "inflate" these values by a negligibly small magnitude. We show how to implement this in Algorithm 3.4.

Algorithm 3.4 Log transforming a network with zero-weight edges

---

Data: A is an adjacency matrix.

      b the base to log transform with.

Result: The adjacency matrix, after log transformation.

1 Identify the entries of A which take a value of zero.

2 Identify the smallest entry of A which is not zero, and call it a_m.

3 Compute a value ϵ which is an order of magnitude smaller than a_m. Since we are taking powers of b, a single order of magnitude would give us that $\epsilon = \frac{a_m}{b}$.

4 Take the augmented adjacency matrix A' to be defined with entries $a'_{ij} = a_{ij} + \epsilon$.

5 Log transform A' with a base of b.

The first process of this procedure is called a *zero augmentation*. We can code up the log transformation as follows:

```
def augment_zeros(X, base=10):
    if np.any(X < 0):
        raise TypeError("The logarithm is not defined for negative
            values!")
    am = np.min(X[np.where(X > 0)]) # the smallest non-zero entry of X
    eps = am/base # epsilon is one order of magnitude smaller than the
        smallest non-zero entry
    return X + eps # augment all entries of X by epsilon

def log_transform(X, base=10):
    """
    A function to log transform an adjacency matrix X, which may
    have zero-weight edges.
    """
    X_aug = augment_zeros(X, base=base)
    return np.log(X_aug)/np.log(base)

A_activity_log = log_transform(A_activity)
```

We plot the untransformed and log-transformed activity/hobby network in Figure 3.8.4.

When we plot the augmented and log-transformed data, we see that many of the edge weights we originally might have thought were zero if we only looked at a plot were, in fact, not zero (they were just small). In this sense, for nonnegative weighted networks, log transforming after zero-augmentation is often very useful for visualization to get a sense of the magnitudinal differences that might be present between edges, since we can get a better feel for how different the big weights are from the smaller weights.

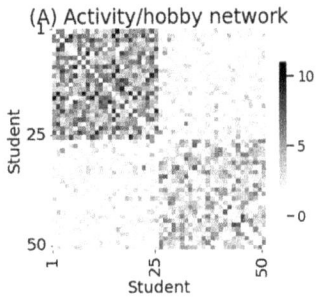 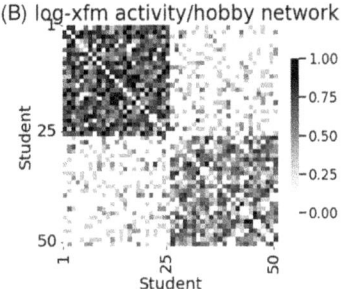

Figure 3.8.4 (**A**) The weighted adjacency matrix for the activity/hobby network. There are many small entries, and it is hard to discern which entries are zero from the entries that are just small. (**B**) The activity/hobby network, after log transformation. The edges which are zero are readily apparent in the plot, and we have a better sense of the range of nonzero elements visually (they tend to fall between 0 and 1, so are different by approximately a power of 10).

Bibliography

[1] Godsil C, Royle G. Algebraic Graph Theory. New York, NY, USA: Springer; 2001.

[2] Chung F. Spectral Graph Theory, vol. 92. American Mathematical Society; 1996.

[3] Li J, Guo JM, Shiu WC. Bounds on normalized Laplacian eigenvalues of graphs. J. Inequal. Appl. 2014 Dec.;2014(1):1–8.

[4] Chaudhuri K, Chung F, Tsiatas A. Spectral Clustering of Graphs with General Degrees in the Extended Planted Partition Model. In: Conference on Learning Theory. JMLR Workshop and Conference Proceedings; 2012, pp. 35.1–35.23.

[5] Amini AA, Chen A, Bickel PJ, Levina E. Pseudo-likelihood methods for community detection in large sparse networks. arXiv. 2012 Jul.

[6] Qin T, Rohe K. Regularized Spectral clustering under the degree-corrected stochastic blockmodel. arXiv. 2013 Sep.

[7] Barabsi AL. Network science. Phil. Trans. R. Soc. Lond. A. 2013 Mar.;371(1987): 20120375.

[8] Hastie T, Tibshirani R, Friedman JH. The Elements of Statistical Learning: Data Mining, Inference, and Prediction. New York, NY, USA: Springer; 2009.

[9] Spielman DA, Teng SH. Spectral sparsification of graphs. arXiv. 2008 Aug.

[10] Batson J, Spielman DA, Srivastava N, Teng SH. Spectral sparsification of graphs: theory and algorithms. Commun. ACM. 2013 Aug.;56(8):87–94.

4 Statistical Models of Random Networks

In Chapter 3, we explored ways to describe observed networks through both their representations (Section 3.4) and properties like density and degree distributions (Section 3.1). Unraveling this system's dynamics involves three steps: First, we make assumptions about the system (Chapter 4); second, we learn useful representations of the observed network(s) (Chapter 5); finally, we interpret how that representation informs our assumptions about the system (Part III).

We make assumptions about the system by assuming statistical models for our networks. A statistical model in network machine learning provides a mathematical framework describing how the underlying system generates the network we see.

We call the statistical model of a network, rather than its observation, a *random network*. The random network does not have edges, but edge probabilities. The rest of the book will either explicitly or implicitly assume a particular random network when we create representations in Chapter 5 and explore applications in Part III. These representations provide a framework from which we can interpret the results we obtain when using later techniques.

This chapter covers:

1. Section 4.1 covers the inhomogeneous Erdös–Rényi (IER) random network, the most general independent-edge network model.
2. Section 4.2 covers the Erdös–Rényi (ER) random network, the simplest network model.
3. Section 4.3 covers the stochastic block model (SBM), a model describing node community structure.
4. Section 4.4 covers the random dot product graph (RDPG), which we use in Part III to learn network representations.
5. Section 4.5 further explores the block matrix for SBMs, and when SBMs can be represented by RDPGs.
6. Section 4.6 discusses statistical properties of random networks.
7. Section 4.7 covers the degree-corrected SBM (DCSBM), an augmented SBM allowing for varying node connectivity.
8. Section 4.5 covers different types of block matrices for SBMs, and when these can be conceptualized using an RDPG.
9. Section 4.8 covers the structured independent-edge model (SIEM), which will later be used for investigating differences between groups of edges in a network.
10. Section 4.9 covers models for more than one network.
11. Section 4.10 covers the signal subnetwork (SSN) model for network-specific covariates.

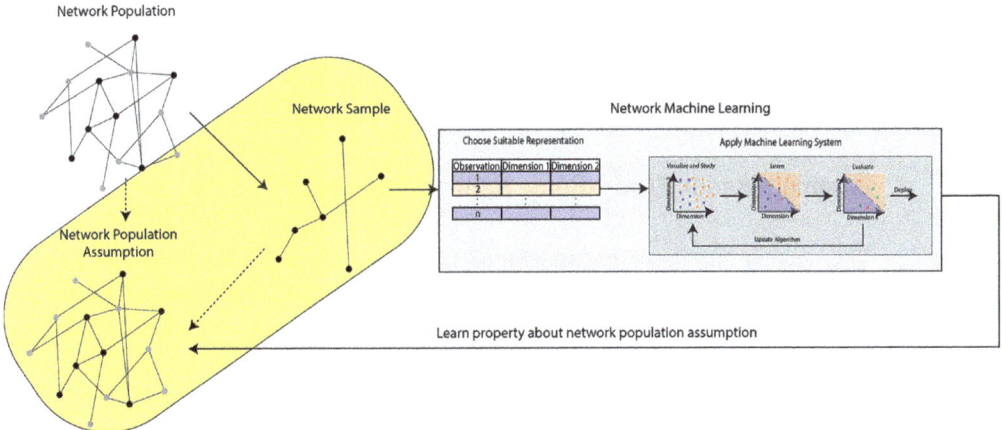

Figure 4.0.1 This chapter constructs assumptions about the random network governing a network sample.

We provide further technical discussion for statistical models in Appendix A. Figure 4.0.1 illustrates the role of statistical models in the network learning process. After data preprocessing, network machine learning methods compute properties of the networks. Making assumptions about the network sample using network models allows us to answer more specific questions about the network.

4.0.0.1 Defining Statistical Models

We will often explain statistical models through analogies with coin flipping. A biased coin lands on heads with a probability different from 0.5, meaning that over many flips, it might show heads more often than tails, or vice versa. When we flip a coin once, we don't know beforehand whether it will land on heads or tails, only the probability of each outcome.

By conceptualizing the coin as having a probability of heads, we assume a statistical model. We then use properties of this model to learn things about our underlying system. For instance, if we flip a coin 100 times and see 70 heads, we might have high confidence that the coin does not land on heads with probability 0.5. However, what if it landed on heads 7 times out of 10? Without having a statistical model, it is difficult to ascribe meaning to things that we learn about our data and confidence to conclusions we draw.

Network modeling follows a similar principle, especially for simple networks. Throughout this chapter, we will think of each edge of the network as a weighted coin. In a simple, unweighted network, edges either exist or don't exist, analogous to a coin landing on heads or tails. The probability of an edge existing might differ from 0.5; there could be a 0.7 chance that one edge exists, and a 0.4 chance for another.

When we construct models for networks, we prescribe sets of assumptions about how the "coin" for each edge behaves. We might ask: Do all edges in the network have equal probabilities of existing? Are there groups of nodes whose connecting edges share the same probabilities? What other ways can we describe the existence probabilities of edges?

We begin with conceptually simple models by allowing each edge to have its own probability. We then move into more complex models which can be used to build the representations we see in Chapter 5.

4.1   Inhomogeneous Erdös–Rényi Random Networks

This section introduces statistical models for random networks, beginning with the inhomogeneous Erdös–Rényi (IER) model. The IER model generalizes simpler network models by allowing each potential edge to have its own probability of existing, defined by a probability matrix.

We cover:

1. The Bernoulli model and its application to edge existence,
2. Probability matrices for describing edge probabilities,
3. Formal definition and properties of the IER model,
4. Simulating samples from IER random networks, and
5. Limitations of IER for practical modeling.

The IER model provides a foundation for understanding more structured network models introduced in subsequent sections. Its flexibility in specifying edge probabilities makes it a useful theoretical tool, though often impractical for real-world network modeling.

4.1.1   The Bernoulli Model

The "coin flip" model will be a foundational tool that will prove useful for conceptualizing networks. When we flip a coin, it will land on heads with some probability p, and on tails with a probability $1 - p$. Basic rules of probability tell us that the sum of the probabilities of all possible outcomes of a flip must be 1; therefore, if the coin lands on heads with probability p (so $P(\text{heads}) = p$):

$$1 = P(\text{heads}) + P(\text{tails})$$
$$= p + P(\text{tails}),$$

which implies that $P(\text{tails}) = 1 - p$. The idea is that the flipped coins are either heads or tails (they are *outcomes*, or *realizations*, which means that they have a fixed value), but the coin itself can land on either of these outcomes with a given probability. Unless $p = 1$ or $p = 0$, there is a nonzero chance of seeing either of the possible outcomes (heads or tails) in a given coin flip.

This simple example is known as the *Bernoulli model*, which describes two possible outcomes (1 or 0, which could be placeholders for heads and tails in our coin flip experiment), either of which occur randomly with a fixed probability. In this case, we would call the probability term the *parameter*, which is a value or set of values that defines specific behaviors of the model. Therefore, we say that a coin which lands on heads or tails with a fixed probability p is a *Bernoulli random variable* with parameter p. This is typically denoted in shorthand in statistics books by saying that the coin is *Bernoulli(p)*, or *Bern(p)*. This shorthand will typically include the model name (in this case, Bernoulli) and the parameters that govern the model (in this case, a probability, p).

4.1.1.1 A Note about Statistical Independence

Imagine that we have two random quantities; say, whether (or not) it is raining outside, and whether (or not) the grass is wet. If we have not looked outside (or checked the weather forecast), we might think that these things are random. We could imagine a statistical model, like coin flips, describing what is going on. However, these two random quantities are related. There are many reasons why the grass could be wet; perhaps there is a sprinkler in the yard, or there could be a pipe leak. Another reason is that it rained. If it did rain, the probability that we see wet grass rises dramatically.

Because rain raises the probability of wet grass, these two random quantities are related. In statistical terms, we would say that they are *statistically dependent*, which informally means that the probability of one event (here, whether or not the grass is wet) is related to the outcome of another event (here, whether or not it rained).

On the other hand, let's imagine that we have two coins (as previously), which each land on heads/tails with fixed probabilities. The two coins are different, so whether one coin lands on heads or tails has no probabilistic implications for whether the other coin lands on heads or tails. This gives us some intuition for the concept of *statistical independence*.

4.1.1.2 Details and Conventions for Random Quantities

When working with random quantities, it is important to clarify some conventions so that we have a good working idea of what is going on. In our coin flip example, we would use $\mathbf{x}$ to denote a random coin which has a scalar (univariate) value.

First, $\mathbf{x}$ is bold-faced and has nonitalic typesetting. Bold-face and nonitalic will be the convention that we use in this book to denote random quantities. This departs from the convention of many introductory statistics books such as [1], which often use capital letters (such as X) to denote random variables. We have adopted this alternative convention since we will often work with matrices or even random matrices, which are typically denoted with capital letters, so the bold-face gives us the flexibility to express random variables and matrices alike without overloading notation. In the coin flip example, we would say that $\mathbf{x}$ (the random process generating the result of the flip) is a $Bernoulli(p)$ random variable. This random variable has realizations x (note the lack of bold-face) which take values of 0 (tails) or 1 (heads). By *realizations*, we mean specific, deterministic outcomes of the random variable: what we observe after the randomness is gone. Realizations may also be referred to as *samples* or *observations* of random variables.

Second, note that $\mathbf{x}$ is lower case. Throughout this book, we will come across univariate quantities (such as integers or decimals) and multivariate quantities (such as matrices or vectors). That $\mathbf{x}$ is lower case denotes that its realizations x are univariate quantities (they are integers or decimals; in this case, 0s and 1s). If we write that $x = 0$ (we flipped the coin, and it landed on tails), this means that the realization x of $\mathbf{x}$ has the value of 0 (tails); there is nothing random about x since we already flipped the coin.

Vectors, Matrices, and Random Matrices

Throughout many sections of this book, we will see matrices whose elements can be random. While this might seem like it should be considerably more complicated, the idea is simple. If X is an $m \times n$ matrix, it can be written down like this:

$$X = \begin{bmatrix} x_{11} & \cdots & x_{1m} \\ \vdots & \ddots & \vdots \\ x_{n1} & \cdots & x_{nm} \end{bmatrix},$$

where each entry x_{ij} is univariate (note the lower case). All the same, we can have random matrices $\mathbf{X}$, which have $m \times n$ realizations. Therefore, the easiest thing to do would be to "denote" this random matrix the same way:

$$\mathbf{X} = \begin{bmatrix} \mathbf{x}_{11} & \cdots & \mathbf{x}_{1m} \\ \vdots & \ddots & \vdots \\ \mathbf{x}_{n1} & \cdots & \mathbf{x}_{nm} \end{bmatrix},$$

where each entry $\mathbf{x}_{ij}$ is a univariate random variable.

Analogously, we will often come across vectors. To denote vectors, we will adopt the convention of an arrow over top of a lower-case letter; for instance, an n-element vector might look like this:

$$\vec{x} = \begin{bmatrix} x_1 \\ \vdots \\ x_n \end{bmatrix},$$

with random vectors defined analogously to random matrices. For simplicity, we will always assume that vectors behave like single-column matrices. For instance, in the above example, we would say that $\vec{x}$ is a n-element vector, and has the properties of an $n \times 1$ matrix.

4.1.2   Probability Matrices

In Section 3.1.1, we developed our intuition for the adjacency matrix of a network with n nodes, which was an $n \times n$ matrix A. In the case of simple networks, each entry a_{ij} had a value of 1 (the edge exists) or 0 (the edge does not exist). In Section 1.3, we saw a number of reasons to think of A as imperfect. Like the coin, one approach would be to model some level of randomness to our network. Under this framework, we view an observed network A as a particular realization of a random network $\mathbf{A}$, just like the outcome of a coin (heads or tails) x is the realization of some underlying random process $\mathbf{x}$ (which is heads or tails with a probability).

This feels like our basic coin flip setup, in that we have two outcomes for each possible edge: It either exists, or it does not exist. We will commonly describe this using the probability matrix P, where the probability of an edge between two nodes i and j is described by p_{ij}.

If a network has n nodes, there are $n \times n$ possible potential edges. Therefore, we will want to keep track of $n \times n$ possible probabilities. A *probability matrix* is any

---

> **Remark 4.1.1** Naming conventions for IER random networks
>
> Sometimes, inhomogeneous Erdös–Rényi Random Networks are referred to as "independent-edge random networks." This alternative name calls attention to the fact that the only restriction placed by the model is the independent-edge assumption. Conveniently, these two possible names for the same concept both have the same first three letters for an abbreviation.

matrix which has values between 0 and 1. Stated another way, a probability matrix is just a matrix whose entries are probabilities.

Throughout this book, we will most often be concerned with probability matrices for random networks. As there are $n \times n$ possible potential edges, the probability matrix P for a random network with n nodes is therefore the $n \times n$ matrix:

$$P = \begin{bmatrix} p_{11} & \cdots & p_{1n} \\ \vdots & \ddots & \vdots \\ p_{n1} & \cdots & p_{nn} \end{bmatrix},$$

where each entry p_{ij} is a probability. An example probability matrix for a network with n nodes is illustrated in Figure 4.1.1(A).

Now that we know about Bernoulli random variables and probability matrices, we are ready to describe our first random network model.

4.1.3 The Inhomogeneous Erdös–Rényi (IER) Random Network Model

The IER random network is parametrized by a matrix of edge probabilities. In an IER random network, a probability matrix P with n rows and n columns defines each of the edge-existence probabilities for pairs of nodes in the network. For each pair of nodes i and j, we conceptualize the edge existence (or not) as a Bernoulli random variable, or coin flip, where the coin has a p_{ij} chance of landing on heads and a $1 - p_{ij}$ chance of landing on tails. For each pair of nodes in the network, we think of flipping the coin, and if it lands on heads (with probability p_{ij}), an edge exists. Each coin flip is performed independently of the coin flips for all of the other edges. If $\mathbf{A}$ has independent Bernoulli edges with a probability matrix P, we say that $\mathbf{A}$ is an $IER_n(P)$ random network.

Conventions for Directedness and Looplessness
In a loopless network, $\mathbf{a}_{ii} = 0$ for all nodes. Recall from Section 3.1.1 that this value of 0 is a symbolic placeholder, and is different from the use of 0 to denote the lack of existence of an edge. The edges on the diagonal do not "not exist"; they are impossible. For this reason, if a network is loopless, we typically define the network as such and ignore the diagonal of the probability matrix entirely.

In an undirected network, $a_{ij} = a_{ji}$. Likewise, random network models can also be undirected. If our network model specifies explicitly that the network is undirected, then $\mathbf{a}_{ij} = \mathbf{a}_{ji}$. If we assume that $\mathbf{a}_{ij}$ has a probability of p_{ij}, this means that $\mathbf{a}_{ji}$ will also have a probability of p_{ij}. Therefore, if we want the random network to produce undirected realizations, the probability matrix must be symmetric.

It is important to clarify that a symmetric probability matrix does not necessarily imply undirected network samples. To understand why this is the case, imagine if we have two coins which land on heads with the same probability. When we flip them, just because the probability is the same does not necessarily imply that they will both land on heads or both land on tails. Therefore, we need to explicitly specify in the model if the network is undirected that the probability matrix is symmetric and that $\mathbf{a}_{ij} = \mathbf{a}_{ji}$ for all nodes i and j.

In Remark 4.1.2, we discuss the statistical model for a simple IER network. A *statistical model* is a set of assumptions about how our data arose from a random process. For a random network $\mathbf{A}$ following the $IER_n(P)$ model, the model specifies the general assumptions (independent edges and the existence of edge probabilities), whereas the probability matrix P itself defines a specific random network. If we have another network $\mathbf{A}'$ following $IER_n(P')$ with a different probability matrix, it adheres to the same IER model assumptions but results in a distinct network due to the different P'.

Statistical network models provide a framework (assumptions), while parameters (the probability matrix) determine specific instances of the model within that framework.

Remark 4.1.2 What does a fully specified statistical model for a simple IER random network look like?

For all pairs of nodes i and j where $i > j$, $\mathbf{a}_{ij}$ is a $Bernoulli(p_{ij})$ random variable, which is independent of (does not depend on) the other potential edges of the random network.
For all pairs of nodes i and j where $i > j$, $\mathbf{a}_{ji} = \mathbf{a}_{ij}$. This ensures that the upper and lower triangles of the random adjacency matrix $\mathbf{A}$ are symmetric, so the random network is undirected.
For all nodes i, $\mathbf{a}_{ii} = 0$. This ensures that the diagonal of the random adjacency matrix $\mathbf{A}$ is 0, so the random network is loopless.

Notice that the only thing that has really changed is that we explicitly specify that the upper and lower triangles of the random adjacency matrix are symmetric, and that the diagonal is by default 0.

4.1.3.1 Generating a Realization from a Simple $IER_n(P)$ Random Network

The approach we use to describe random networks is called a *generative model*, which means that we have described a random object (the random network $\mathbf{A}$) in terms of the parameters of $\mathbf{A}$. In the case of IER random networks, we have described $\mathbf{A}$ in terms of a probability matrix, P.

Generative models for random objects are convenient in that we can easily adapt them to tell us how to simulate realizations. For instance, take a coin that lands on heads with some unknown probability p (the Bernoulli model). All that we know about the coin is that it has a probability of landing on heads, but not what that probability is. If we wanted to learn about this coin, how could we do it?

The easiest answer is to flip it a bunch of times, and analyze the outcomes that we observe. By flipping the coin, we are generating realizations: We generate some set of outcomes (heads or tails) of the random object, and then we can use the outcomes to estimate information about the generating process, the probability of landing on heads.

Likewise, we can use the generating model that underlies a random network $\mathbf{A}$ to generate a realization of $\mathbf{A}$, which is an actual network A. The procedure in Algorithm 4.1 will sample a network A from an $IER_n(P)$ random network.

Algorithm 4.1 Simulating a sample from an $IER_n(P)$ random network

---

Data: n a number of nodes

P a probability matrix with n rows and n columns

Result: The adjacency matrix of a sample from the random network.

1 **for** i *in* 1:n **do**
2   **for** $j > i$ **do**
3   Obtain a weighted coin (i, j) which has a probability p_{ij} of landing on heads, and a $1 - p_{ij}$ probability of landing on tails.
4   Flip the (i, j) coin, and if it lands on heads, the corresponding entry a_{ij} in the adjacency matrix is 1. If the coin lands on tails, the corresponding entry a_{ij} is 0.
5   Set $a_{ji} = a_{ij}$.
6   **end**
7 **end**
8 **return** A

Let's create an example. We will generate an unnecessarily complicated probability matrix to illustrate the flexibility of the IER model:

```python
import numpy as np
from graphbook_code import heatmap

def generate_unit_circle(radius):
    diameter = 2*radius + 1
    rx = ry = diameter/2
    x, y = np.indices((diameter, diameter))

    circle_dist = np.hypot(rx - x, ry - y)
    diff_from_radius = np.abs(circle_dist - radius)
    less_than_half = diff_from_radius < 0.5

    return less_than_half.astype(int)

def add_smile():
    canvas = np.zeros((51, 51))
    canvas[2:45, 2:45] = generate_unit_circle(21)
    mask = np.zeros((51, 51), dtype=bool)
    mask[np.triu_indices_from(mask)] = True
    upper_left = np.rot90(mask)
```

```
    canvas[upper_left] = 0
    return canvas

def smile_probability(upper_p, lower_p):
    smiley = add_smile()
    P = generate_unit_circle(25)
    P[5:16, 25:36] = generate_unit_circle(5)
    P[smiley != 0] = smiley[smiley != 0]

    mask = np.zeros((51, 51), dtype=bool)
    mask[np.triu_indices_from(mask)] = True
    P[~mask] = 0
    # symmetrize the probability matrix
    P = (P + P.T - np.diag(np.diag(P))).astype(float)
    P[P == 1] = lower_p
    P[P == 0] = upper_p
    return P

P = smile_probability(.95, 0.05)
heatmap(P, vmin=0, vmax=1, title="Probability matrix $P$")
```

The probability matrix is plotted in Figure 4.1.1(A). Next, we can generate a random sample of the $IER_n(P)$ random network, using the `sample_edges` function from `graspologic`:

```
from graspologic.simulations import sample_edges

A = sample_edges(P, directed=False, loops=False)
heatmap(A.astype(int), title="$IER_n(P)$ sample")
```

The heatmap is shown in Figure 4.1.1(B). We used this example to show that the key idea behind the IER network's probability matrix is simple: The entries can really be anything as long as they are probabilities (between 0 and 1) and the resulting matrix is symmetric in the case of undirected networks. There are no additional requirements nor parameters to add structure to the network.

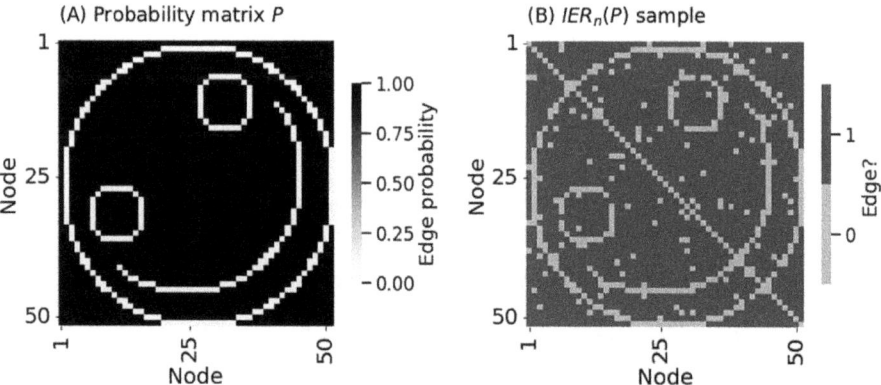

Figure 4.1.1 **(A)** The probability matrix for the $IER_n(P)$ random network. **(B)** An adjacency matrix sampled from the $IER_n(P)$ random network.

4.1.4   The Independent-Edge Random Network Models

4.1.4.1   How Many Unique Realizations are Possible for a Random Network with n Nodes?

For one coin, there are two possible outcomes: heads or tails. If we have two coins, the first coin could be heads or tails, and the second coin could be heads or tails. If the first coin were heads, there are two possible outcomes for the second coin. If the first coin were tails, there are two possible outcomes for the second coin. The total number of possible outcomes is the sum of the number of possible outcomes if the first coin is heads with the number of possible outcomes if the first coin were tails. With two coins, this gives us four possible outcomes. When we add a third coin, we repeat this calculation. If the first coin were heads, the second two coins could take any of four possible outcomes. If the first coin were tails, the second two coins could also take any of four possible outcomes. Therefore, with three coins, there are eight possible outcomes. Inductively, we see that with x coins, we have 2^x possible outcomes.

In Section 3.3.1, we determined that there are $\frac{1}{2}n(n-1)$ possible edges in a simple network, which we could represent using the notation $\binom{n}{2}$. In a realized network, each of these edges could exist or not exist, so, as in coin flips, there are two possibilities. The number of possible networks with n nodes is 2 to the power of the number of coin flips that are performed in the network.

Here, this is $2^{\binom{n}{2}}$. This quantity grows extremely quickly. In the code below, we calculate the number of possible networks for a given number of nodes in a network, but in a log scale, as powers of 10.

```python
import numpy as np
from math import comb

node_count = np.arange(2, 51)
log_unique_network_count = np.array([comb(n, 2) for n in
    node_count])*np.log10(2)
```

Figure 4.1.2 illustrates how quickly the number of unique networks grows. When n, the node count, is just 6, the number of possible networks is $2^{\binom{6}{2}} = 2^6$ which is over 32,000. When n is 15, the number of possible networks balloons up to $2^{\binom{15}{2}} = 2^{105}$ which is over 10^{30}. A naive approach to network learning might be to describe each

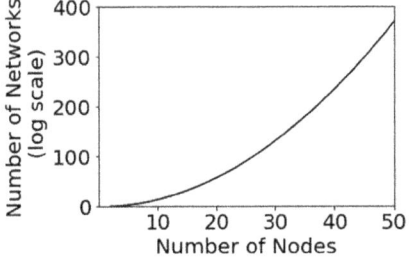

Figure 4.1.2 A log-scale plot of the number of possible networks for a given number of nodes.

possible network that could be observed. However, this is heavily impractical, as explained on Concept 4.1.3.

Concept 4.1.3 Why not just ascribe probabilities to each possible network?

The reason that we need a statistical model in the first place is that if we want to describe properties of the network, we need a framework in which we can analyze it. For $Bernoulli(p)$ coins, we affixed a probability to each possible outcome: Heads occurred with some probability (p) and tails occurred with some probability $(1 - p)$.

All the same, we could repeat this for networks with n nodes: We could affix a probability to each of the $2^{\binom{n}{2}}$ possible networks we could observe.

Describing each possible observable network for a given number of nodes is impossible, for the two reasons that we have given:

1. We could not possibly use a network with n nodes that we obtain to learn things about every possible network with n nodes, because our network is just one of many. If we flipped a coin once and obtained a result of heads, would we say we are extremely confident that the coin will never land on tails? This is the same problem we have with have with network data when we do not have a sufficiently straightforward model.
2. Even if we had more network samples, we could not possibly analyze nor even store this many possibilities, because for even modest choices of n, it is simply too many elements to keep track of: $2^{\binom{n}{2}}$ is a really big number when n is just 15; many of the real networks you will want to analyze might have hundreds, or thousands, of nodes.

These aspects are detailed at length in Appendix A.2.

4.1.4.2   Why Aren't $IER_n(P)$ Random Networks Used in Practice?

Instead of having $2^{\binom{n}{2}}$ parameters to estimate, the $IER_n(P)$ random networks reduce this to an $n \times n$ probability matrix with $\binom{n}{2}$ informative entries. This is because if the network is simple, the diagonal of the probability matrix contains no information (meaning n entries are not relevant), and the probability matrix is symmetric (so, of the remaining $n^2 - n$ entries, half of them are redundant). However, even this formulation is not particularly useful in practice, as discussed in Concept 4.1.4.

Throughout the remaining sections of this chapter, we will cover a family of networks known as the independent-edge random network models [2]. These are the random network models that can be specified with a probability matrix and the independent-edge assumption; that is, that the existence or not existence of edges does not impact the existence or not existence of other edges in the networks. Each network model, however, will place restrictions on the probability matrix P to simplify the learning task ahead of us. The goal is that these restrictions will simplify the network such that there are fewer parameters than $\binom{n}{2}$ to estimate, so that we can actually use observed networks to gain meaningful insights about the probability matrix.

> **Concept 4.1.4** Why not use $IER_n(P)$ random networks for everything?
>
> Ultimately, we want a network model wherein, for observed simple networks A, we can use estimates of the parameters and properties of the network model to learn something about the observed simple network. As previously, remember that the probability matrix for an n-node simple random network has $\binom{n}{2}$ informative entries. However, the observed simple network with n nodes also has $\binom{n}{2}$ informative entries.
>
> Therefore, if we wanted to learn about a probability p_{ij}, we would only have a single observed edge a_{ij} to learn from. This presents a similar issue to that of Concept 4.1.3: With one network observation, we would be attempting to learn about the probability a coin lands on heads or tails from the outcome of a single coin flip. We would need to use many network observations to estimate p_{ij} reasonably.

More technical details on inhomogeneous Erdös–Rényi random networks are in Appendix A.2.

4.2 Erdös–Rényi Random Networks

Building on the inhomogeneous Erdös–Rényi (IER) model introduced in Section 4.1, we now examine the simpler Erdös–Rényi (ER) random network model. The ER model simplifies the IER by using a single probability parameter for all edges. We cover:

1. Definition and properties of the ER model,
2. Relationship between ER and IER models,
3. Simulating samples from ER random networks,
4. Limitations and use cases for ER models, and
5. Concept of model generalization in network theory.

The ER model serves as a foundational concept in random graph theory, providing a baseline for understanding more complex network structures. Its simplicity makes it useful for developing intuition about random networks, though it often fails to capture the complexity of real-world networks.

To motivate new network models, we begin with a simple example, related to the friendship network which we learned about in Example 3.7.2. Consider a social network, with 50 students. The network has 50 nodes, where each node represents a single student in the network. Edges in the social network represent whether or not a pair of students are friends. What is the simplest way we can describe whether two people are friends?

Using the tools from Section 3.1, we represent this simple network as an adjacency matrix A whose entries a_{ij} are 1 if the students i and j are friends on the social networking site, and 0 if the students i and j are not friends on the social networking site. With 50 students the adjacency matrix A is going to be 50×50.

4.2.1   The Erdös–Rényi Random Network

The simplest random network model is called the Erdös–Rényi (ER) model, which was first described by [3] and [4]. In an ER random network, the edges depend only on a single shared probability, p, and each edge is independent of all other edges. For every edge $\mathbf{a}_{ij}$, a coin has a probability p of landing on heads, and $1 - p$ of landing on tails. Stated another way, every $\mathbf{a}_{ij}$ is a $Bernoulli(p)$ random variable; i.e., the same probability for all edges. If $\mathbf{A}$ has n nodes and independent edges with a single common probability p, we will say that $\mathbf{A}$ is an $ER_n(p)$ random network.

4.2.2   How Do We Simulate Samples of $ER_n(p)$ Random Networks?

The procedure in Algorithm 4.2 will generate a simple network A, where the underlying random network $\mathbf{A}$ is a simple $ER_n(p)$ random network.

Algorithm 4.2 Simulating a sample from a simple $ER_n(p)$ random network

Data: n a number of nodes
  p a probability of an edge existing
Result: The adjacency matrix of a sample from the random network.
1 Obtain a weighted coin which has a probability p of landing on heads, and a probability $1 - p$ of landing on tails. Note this probability p might differ from the "traditional" coin with a probability of landing on heads of approximately 0.5.
2 **for** i **in** 1:n **do**
3 | **for** $j > i$ **do**
4 | | Flip the coin once. If the coin lands on heads, let $a_{ij} = 1$. If the coin lands on tails, let $a_{ij} = 0$.
5 | | Let $a_{ji} = a_{ij}$.
6 | **end**
7 **end**
8 **return** A

4.2.3   When Do We Use an $ER_n(p)$ Network?

In practice, the $ER_n(p)$ model seems a little too simple to be useful. Why would it ever be useful to think that the best we can do to describe our network is to say that all connections exist with some shared probability? Does this not miss a lot of useful questions we might want to answer? Fortunately, there are a number of ways in which the simplicity of the $ER_n(p)$ model is useful. Given a probability and a number of nodes, we can easily describe the properties we would expect to see in a network if that network were ER. For instance, we can use statistical reasoning to describe the

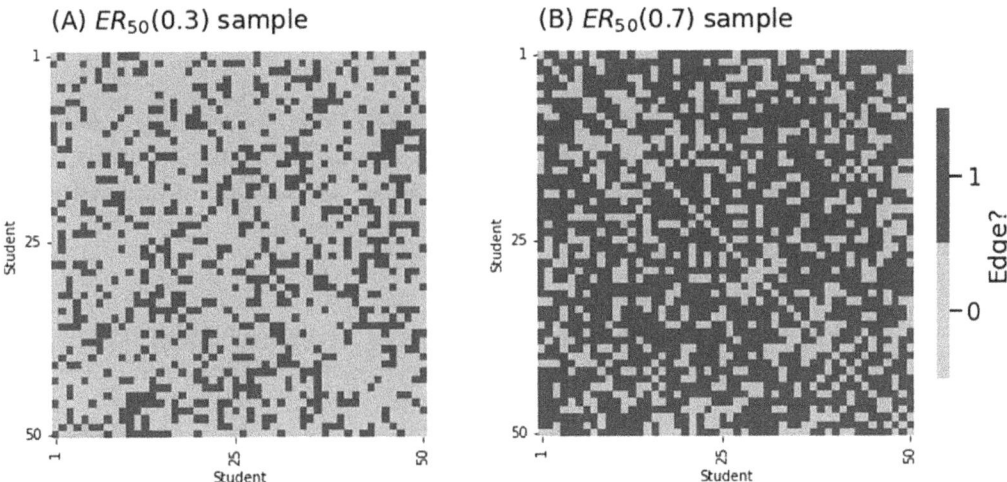

(A) $ER_{50}(0.3)$ sample   (B) $ER_{50}(0.7)$ sample

Figure 4.2.1 **(A)** A sample with $p = 0.3$. **(B)** A sample with $p = 0.7$. Notice that with higher probabilities, the samples from the random network have more edges.

approximate degree for each node of an $ER_n(p)$ random network, and we can easily characterize mathematical properties of its adjacency matrix.

We can reverse this idea, too: Given a network we think might not be ER, we could check whether it's different in some way from an $ER_n(p)$ random network. It is often useful to start with the simplest random network models when analyzing network data, and only turning to more complicated network models when the need arises, because the types of network models we choose will directly determine the types of questions we can answer later on. For instance, if half the nodes have a high degree (lots of edges), and half don't, the network is likely poorly described by an $ER_n(p)$ random network. In this case, we might look for more complex models that could describe our network.

In the next code block, we are going to sample a single $ER_n(p)$ network with 50 nodes and an edge probability p of 0.3:

```
from graphbook_code import draw_multiplot
from graspologic.simulations import er_np

n = 50 # network with 50 nodes
p = 0.3 # probability of an edge existing is .3

# sample a single simple adjacency matrix from ER(50, .3)
A = er_np(n=n, p=p, directed=False, loops=False)

# and plot it
draw_multiplot(A.astype(int), title="$ER_{50}(0.3)$ Simulation")
```

Our visualization is a heatmap and layout plot as in Section 3.4. The heatmap is shown in Figure 4.2.1(A).

> **Concept 4.2.1** Determining stochastic equivalence in independent-edge random networks
>
> When dealing with independent-edge random networks, we can make determinations about stochastic equivalence most by estimating the probability matrix. Two independent-edge random networks $A^{(1)}$ and $A^{(2)}$ are stochastically equivalent if their underlying probability matrices $P^{(1)}$ and $P^{(2)}$ are equal.

Next, let's see what happens when we use a higher edge probability, like $p = 0.7$:

```
p = 0.7 # network has an edge probability of 0.7

# sample a single adjacency matrix from ER(50, 0.7)
A = er_np(n=n, p=p, directed=False, loops=False)
```

We show the same plot for $p = 0.7$ in Figure 4.2.1(B). As the edge probability increases, the sampled adjacency matrix indicates that there are more connections in the network. This is because there is a higher chance of an edge existing when p is larger. Correspondingly, the network density (Section 3.3.1) increases.

4.2.4　Generalizing Network Models

We have discussed two random network models: the $ER_n(p)$ random networks, which have a probability parameter p, and the $IER_n(P)$ random networks, which have a probability matrix P. Take an $ER_n(p)$ random network $A^{(1)}$, for some fixed probability p. Remember that this means that for every pair of nodes i and j, $a_{ij}^{(1)}$ is $Bernoulli(p)$: each edge is a coin flip with probability p.

Next, take a second $IER_n(P^{(2)})$ random network $A^{(2)}$. What happens if every entry of $P^{(2)}$ is just p (that is, for all i and j, $p_{ij}^{(2)} = p$)? For every pair of nodes i and j, $a_{ij}^{(2)}$ is $Bernoulli(p)$, which is exactly what we saw above for the $ER_n(p)$ random network.

The word *stochastic* just means random, so $a_{ij}^{(1)}$ and $a_{ij}^{(2)}$ can be said to be *stochastically equivalent*: They have exactly the same governing rules (specified by a $Bernoulli(p)$ random variable) for all nodes i and j. Because both models make the same independence assumption (that the edges existing/not existing do not effect the existence/not existence of other edges), the random networks $A^{(1)}$ and $A^{(2)}$ themselves are also stochastically equivalent. We discuss more about how to identify stochastic equivalence in independent-edge random networks in Concept 4.2.1.

We could repeat this argument for any possible choice of p for the random network $A^{(1)}$: It does not matter if the probability is 0, 1, or any number in between, we could always find a stochastically equivalent $IER_n(P^{(2)})$ random network $A^{(2)}$. This motivates additional terminology: We say that a random network model is *contained* in another random network model if for every network in the first model, we can find a stochastically equivalent random network in the second model. In the above example, for instance, we would say that the $ER_n(p)$ random networks are contained in the $IER_n(P)$ random networks.

Conversely, we say that a random network model *generalizes* another random network model if for every network in the second model, we can find a stochastically equivalent random network in the first model. In the above example, we would say that the $IER_n(P)$ random networks from Section 4.1 generalize the $ER_n(p)$ random networks. More broadly, the $IER_n(P)$ random networks will generalize every random network model that we will learn in the upcoming sections.

4.3 Stochastic Block Models

Building on the Erdös–Rényi (ER) model from Section 4.2, we introduce the stochastic block model (SBM), which incorporates community structure into random networks. We cover:

1. Definition and components of the SBM,
2. Community assignment vectors and block matrices,
3. Simulating samples from SBM random networks,
4. Probability matrices for SBMs, and
5. Relationship between SBMs and ER models.

The SBM provides a more flexible framework for modeling networks with distinct node groups, or communities, addressing a number of limitations of simpler models like ER.

Let's imagine that we have 100 students, each of whom can go to one of two possible schools: school one or school two. We define a 100-node network, and each node represents a single student. The edges represent whether a pair of students are friends. It seems likely that if two students go to the same school, they have a higher chance of being friends than if they do not go to the same school. If we were to try to characterize this using an ER random network, we would run into a problem: We have no way to capture the impact that school has on friendships. To do this, we modify our $ER_n(p)$ model to include this complication.

The stochastic block model, or SBM, was first introduced by [5]. It captures the idea that edges are more likely to form within certain groups of nodes by assigning each of the n nodes in the network to one of K communities. A *community* is a group of nodes within a network which have similar properties. In our example, the communities would represent the two schools that students are able to attend. K here is a natural number which is typically greater than 1 (in the school example, K is 2). In general, communities are often nominal categories, which is detailed in Concept 4.3.1.

In an SBM, instead of describing all pairs of nodes with a fixed probability like with the ER model, we describe properties that hold for edges between pairs of communities.

4.3.1 The Community Assignment Vector

To describe an SBM random network, we proceed similarly to an ER random network, but with some extra information. An SBM random network has a parameter $\vec{z}$, a vector

---

> **Concept 4.3.1** Categorical values
>
> In machine learning, we will often come across *categorical values*: variables which can take on any one of K possible values. One example might be the primary colors (red, yellow, and blue). It is practically useful to denote each category with a number; e.g., red = 1, yellow = 2, and blue = 3.
>
> These numbers are often placeholders: Their numerical value holds no meaning. For instance, blue is not "two units" bigger than red; it is simply a different group. In this case, the set of possible categories is called *nominal*, which means that the only important feature of the categorical labels is that they are different.
>
> In other settings, the numbers might be meaningful. For instance, we could imagine asking people to rank preferred electoral candidates on a scale of unfavorable, neutral, and favorable. We can denote unfavorable = 1, neutral = 2, and favorable = 3. In this case, the numerical value holds meaning: these categories preserve favorability. Neutral (2) is greater than unfavorable (1), and neutral indicates that someone likes the candidate more than if they were unfavorable. These types of categories are referred to as *ordinal*, which means "order matters."
>
> In network machine learning, we often come across categorical values when dealing with communities of nodes. These are usually nominal categories, in that the main thing we convey via the community label is that the groups of nodes are different.

with a single element for each of the nodes. We call $\vec{z}$ the *community assignment vector*. For each node of our random network, z_i tells us which community the node is in. Specifically, $\vec{z}$ is a nominal categorical vector where each element z_i can take one of K possible values, where K is the total number of communities in the network.

For example, if we had an SBM random network with four nodes in total and two total communities, each element z_i can be either 1 or 2. If the first two nodes were in community 1, and the second two in community 2, we would say that $z_1 = 1$, $z_2 = 1$, $z_3 = 2$, and $z_4 = 2$, which means that $\vec{z}$ looks like:

$$\vec{z} = \begin{bmatrix} 1 \\ 1 \\ 2 \\ 2 \end{bmatrix}.$$

4.3.2 The Block Matrix

The other parameter for an SBM random network is called the block matrix, for which we will use the capital letter B. This matrix defines edge-existence probabilities between communities in the random network, and is therefore also a probability matrix. However, we will use the term *block matrix* to specifically mean a probability matrix which defines edge-existence probabilities between communities.

If there are K communities in the SBM random network, then B is a $K \times K$ matrix, with one entry for each pair of communities. For instance, if K were 2, B would be a 2×2 matrix, and would look like this:

> **Box 4.3.2** Simple SBMs have symmetric block matrices
>
> In the case of the simple networks, remember from Section 4.1 that since the adjacency matrix of a simple random network $\mathbf{A}$ is symmetric, that the probability matrix must also be symmetric; that is, $p_{ij} = p_{ji}$ for all i and j. For SBMs, notice that $p_{ij} = b_{z_i z_j}$, and $p_{ji} = b_{z_j z_i}$. Therefore, if the network is simple, $b_{z_i z_j} = b_{z_j z_i}$ for all i and j, and the block matrix B is symmetric.

$$B = \begin{bmatrix} b_{11} & b_{12} \\ b_{21} & b_{22} \end{bmatrix},$$

Each of the entries of B, which we denote as b_{kl}, is the probability of an edge existing between a node in community k and a node in community l.

4.3.3 Conceptualizing the SBM

We can also think about the SBM using coin flips. In our 2×2 example, if node 1 is in community 1 (since $z_1 = 1$) and node 2 is in community 1 (since $z_2 = 1$), we have a weighted coin which has a probability b_{11} (the first row, first column of the block matrix) of landing on heads, and a $1 - b_{11}$ chance of landing on tails. An edge between nodes one and two exists if the weighted coin lands on heads, and does not exist if that weighted coin lands on tails. If we wanted to describe an edge between nodes one and three instead, note that $z_3 = 2$. Therefore, the entry b_{12} is the probability of obtaining a heads for the weighted coin we flip this time.

The probability that an edge exists between nodes i and j is given by the block matrix entry $b_{z_i z_j}$. We will say that the random network has $Bernoulli(b_{z_i z_j})$ adjacency matrix entries $\mathbf{a}_{ij}$, where z_i is the community assignment for the ith node and z_j is the community assignment for the jth node. Therefore, the entries $\mathbf{a}_{ij}$ in the random network depend on both the block matrix B, as well as the communities of each node, given by z_i and z_j. As before, these entries are independent of all of the other entries in the random adjacency matrix. If $\mathbf{A}$ has n nodes with independent edges, a community vector $\vec{z}$, and a block matrix B, we say that $\mathbf{A}$ is an $SBM_n(\vec{z}, B)$ random network.

4.3.4 Simulating Samples of $SBM_n(\vec{z}, B)$ Random Networks

The procedure in Algorithm 4.3 will generate a simple network A, where the underlying random network $\mathbf{A}$ is a simple $SBM_n(\vec{z}, B)$ random network.

Let's work through the school example from the beginning of this section. We have 100 students, and each student goes to one of two possible schools. We already know the community assignment vector $\vec{z}$. We can assign node indices to students arbitrarily, so we assume that the first 50 students all go to the first school, and the second 50 students all go to the second school.

Algorithm 4.3 Simulating a sample from a simple $SBM_n(\vec{z}, B)$ random network

---

Data: n a number of nodes

$\vec{z}$ a community assignment vector for each of the n nodes to one of K communities

B a $K \times K$ probability matrix for each pair of the K communities

Result: The adjacency matrix of a sample from the random network.

1 For each pair of communities k and l, obtain a weighted coin (which we will call the (k, l) coin). This coin should have a b_{kl} chance of landing on heads, and a $1 - b_{kl}$ chance of landing on tails.

2 **for** i *in* 1: n **do**

3   **for** $j > i$ **do**

4   Flip the (z_i, z_j) coin, and if it lands on heads, the corresponding entry a_{ij} in the adjacency matrix is 1. If it lands on tails, the corresponding entry a_{ij} in the adjacency matrix is 0.

5   Let $a_{ji} = a_{ij}$.

6   **end**

7 **end**

8 **return** A

Let's plot what the community assignment vector looks like for the network:

```
from graphbook_code import plot_vector
import numpy as np

n = 100 # number of students

# z is a column vector of 50 1s followed by 50 2s
# this vector gives the school each of the 100 students are from
z = np.repeat([1, 2], repeats=n//2)
plot_vector(z, title="$\\vec z$, Node Assignment Vector",
            legend_title="School", color="qualitative",
            ticks=[0.5, 49.5, 99.5], ticklabels=[1, 50, 100],
            ticktitle="Student")
```

The community assignment vector is shown in Figure 4.3.1(A).

Let's assume that the students from the first school are more friendly than the students from the second school, so we'll say that the probability of two students who both go to the first school being friends is 0.6, and the probability of two students who both go to school two being friends is 0.4. Finally, let's assume that if one student goes to the first school and the other student goes to school two, the probability that they are friends is 0.1. This gives us the ingredients that we need to define the block matrix B.

We can make a block matrix and plot it using our `heatmap()` utility. When working with probabilities or probability matrices, we usually want to visualize these on a [0, 1] scale, which we can accomplish with the `vmin`, `vmax` arguments:

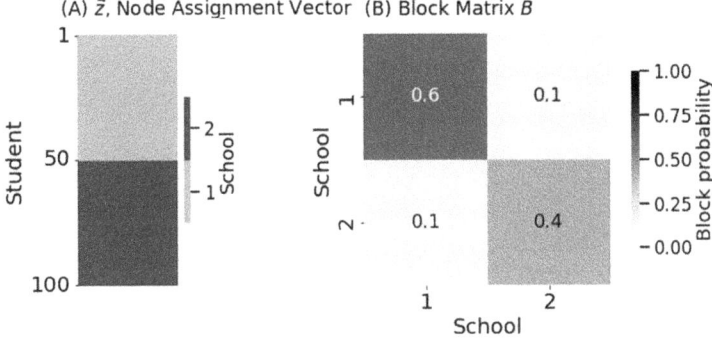

Figure 4.3.1 (**A**) The community assignment vector for each node (students). (**B**) The block matrix, which defines the probabilities of a pair nodes (students) from a given community having an edge.

```
from graphbook_code import heatmap

K = 2 # community count
# construct the block matrix B as described above
B = np.array([[0.6, 0.1],
              [0.1, 0.4]])

heatmap(B, xticklabels=[1, 2], yticklabels=[1,2], vmin=0,
        vmax=1, annot=True, xtitle="School",
        ytitle="School", title="Block Matrix $B$")
```

Figure 4.3.1(B) shows that the matrix B is a symmetric block matrix, since our network is undirected.

Finally, let's sample and plot a single network from the $SBM_n(\vec{z}, B)$ with parameters $\vec{z}$ and B:

```
from graspologic.simulations import sbm
from graphbook_code import draw_multiplot

# sample a graph from SBM_{100}(tau, B)
A, labels = sbm(n=[n//2, n//2], p=B, directed=False, loops=False,
    return_labels=True)
draw_multiplot(A, labels=labels, title="$SBM_n(z, B)$ Simulation");
```

The adjacency matrix is shown in Figure 4.3.2(A).

The students in the network are ordered by the school they are in (the first school and the second school, respectively). People from the first school are more connected than people from the second. This heatmap is *modular*: It has clear and apparent community structure. Connections between people from different schools appear to be less frequent than connections between people from the same school.

When the nodes are ordered by community, we will often observe a "patchy" structure. These visually salient subnetworks (see Section 3.5) are known as *modularity community subnetworks*. The (k, l) community subnetwork of the adjacency

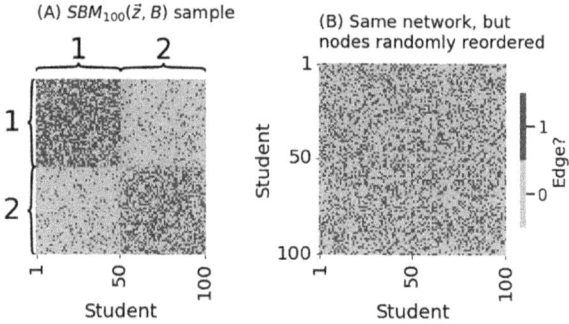

Figure 4.3.2 (**A**) The adjacency matrix for an $SBM_n(\vec{z}, B)$ simulation. The parameters are shown in Figure 4.3.1. (**B**) The same adjacency matrix, but with the nodes randomly reordered.

matrix corresponds to the connections between nodes in community k with nodes in community l. For instance, the $(1, 1)$ community subnetwork corresponds to the upper-left subnetwork of the adjacency matrix, induced by the nodes from community 1. The $(1, 2)$ community subnetwork of the adjacency matrix corresponds to the upper right subnetwork, which consists of nodes in communities 1 and 2, but only the edges from nodes in community 1 to nodes in community 2. The blocks (k, k) will be referred to as the *on-diagonal* community subnetworks, in that they are blocks occuring along the diagonal of the adjacency matrix. The community subnetworks (k, l) where $k \neq l$ will be referred to as the *off-diagonal* community subnetworks, in that they do not fall right along the diagonal of the adjacency matrix. Here, the on-diagonal community subnetworks have far more connections than the off-diagonal community subnetworks.

4.3.5   Modularity Is Not a Prerequisite for $SBM_n(\vec{z}, B)$ Random Networks

Something easy to mistake about a sample of an SBM is that it will not always have the obvious modular structure we can see in Figure 4.3.2(A) when we look at a heatmap. Rather, this modular structure is only obvious because the students are ordered according to the school they are in. What will happen if we look at the students in a random order? Will the structure in this network be obvious?

The answer is: No! Let's see what happens when we reorder the nodes randomly, and pretend we don't know the true community labels ahead of time:

```
import numpy as np

# generate a reordering of the n nodes
permutation = np.random.choice(n, size=n, replace=False)

Aperm = A[permutation][:,permutation]
yperm = labels[permutation]
heatmap(Aperm, title="Nodes randomly reordered")
```

In Figure 4.3.2(B), the students are not organized according to school, because they have been randomly reordered. It becomes difficult to figure out whether there are communities just by looking at the adjacency matrix, unless we are looking at a network in which the nodes are already arranged in an order which respects the community structure. By an order that respects the community structure, we mean that all of the nodes in the first community come first, followed by all of the nodes in the second community, followed by all of the nodes in the third community, so on and so forth up to the nodes of the community K.

In practice, this means that if we know ahead of time natural groupings of the nodes (such as knowing which school each student goes to) by way of node attributes, we can visualize our data according to that grouping. This property is covered in more depth by [6]. If we don't know anything about natural groupings of nodes, however, we are left with the problem of estimating community structure. A method called the spectral embedding which we will discuss in Section 5.3 can be paired with clustering techniques to allow us to estimate node assignment vectors. If we want, we can then use these estimates to reorganize the adjacency matrix into a more visually discernible modular structure.

4.3.6 Probability Matrix for SBM Random Networks

We can use the probability matrix to determine whether networks are stochastically equivalent (Concept 4.2.1). We want a procedure which takes a community assignment vector $\vec{z}$ and a block matrix B, and produces a probability matrix P where each entry $p_{ij} = b_{z_i z_j}$. We could do this by brute force, checking over each pair of nodes in an extremely lengthy for-loop. However, remember that in a simple network there are $\binom{n}{2}$ possible pairs of nodes, which is a large number for even modest choices of n. When $n = 1000$, for instance, this would be a for-loop with 499,500 iterations.

In practice, this can be accomplished more rapidly by exploiting the fact that the communities are nominal categories. We will begin by introducing the idea of the one-hot encoding, in Concept 4.3.3. Then, we will use this idea to express the probability matrix as a matrix product, which allows us to take advantage of accelerated libraries for matrix multiplication featured in modern programming languages.

We can leverage one-hot encodings to produce an interesting result. Using the rules of matrix multiplication, if $\vec{c}_i$ is a length-K vector and B is a $K \times K$ block matrix, then the product $\vec{c}_i^{\top} B$ is a $1 \times K$-dimensional matrix, consisting of the element-wise sum of the products of the rows of $\vec{c}_i$ with the columns of B:

$$\vec{c}_i^{\top} B = \begin{bmatrix} c_{i1} & \cdots & c_{iK} \end{bmatrix} \begin{bmatrix} b_{11} & \cdots & b_{1K} \\ \vdots & \ddots & \vdots \\ b_{K1} & \cdots & b_{KK} \end{bmatrix}$$

$$= \begin{bmatrix} \sum_{k=1}^{K} c_{ik} b_{k1} & \cdots & \sum_{k=1}^{K} c_{ik} b_{kK} \end{bmatrix}.$$

Let's take a look at this first value. The first entry is $\sum_{k=1}^{K} c_{ik} b_{k1}$. However, remember that the community assignment vector $\vec{c}_i$ takes a value of zero everywhere except at c_{iz_i}, where it has a value of 1. Therefore:

> **Concept 4.3.3** One-hot encodings
>
> When dealing with nominal categorical vectors such as a community assignment vector $\vec{z}$, remember that the vector has values z_i which take one-of-K possible values. While this defines the categories (which, here, are communities of nodes), we often cannot directly use the vector $\vec{z}$ mathematically since it is nominal (and therefore, the actual numbers themselves are not relevant).
>
> For this reason, we will typically resort to what is known as the one-hot encoding. A *one-hot encoding* of a nominal value z_i which takes one-of-K possible values is a length-K vector (one element for each category) $\vec{c}_i$, and has a value of 1 in the position corresponding to the category of z_i.
>
> For instance, let's imagine an SBM with two communities, where the first node is in community 1, so $z_1 = 1$. The one-hot encoding of z_1 will be a length-two vector, and will have the value:
>
> $$\vec{c}_1 = \begin{bmatrix} 1 \\ 0 \end{bmatrix}.$$
>
> Likewise, if $z_2 = 2$, the one-hot encoding of z_2 would be:
>
> $$\vec{c}_2 = \begin{bmatrix} 0 \\ 1 \end{bmatrix}.$$
>
> In general, the vector $\vec{c}_i$ will be such that $c_{iz_i} = 1$, and $c_{ij} = 0$ for all other entries.

$$\sum_{k=1}^{K} c_{ik} b_{k1} = c_{iz_i} b_{z_i 1} + \sum_{k \neq z_i} c_{ik} b_{k1}$$

$$= 1 b_{z_i 1} + \sum_{k \neq z_i} 0 b_{k1}$$

$$= b_{z_i 1}.$$

If you duplicate this argument over every entry of $\vec{c}_i^{\top} B$, it will become apparent that the result is:

$$\vec{c}_i^{\top} B = \begin{bmatrix} b_{z_i 1} & \cdots & b_{z_i K} \end{bmatrix}. \tag{4.1}$$

In effect, the product $\vec{c}_i^{\top} B$ has simply "pulled out" the appropriate row of B corresponding to the community of the node i. The product $\vec{c}_i^{\top} B$ can therefore be thought of as the "the block probabilities between the community of node i and any of the K possible communities."

What happens if we repeat the same procedure, but in reverse? This time, we will postmultiply $\vec{c}_i^{\top} B$ by the one-hot encoded community assignment vector $\vec{c}_j$ for some other node j. Remember that this one-hot encoding vector has K elements, so the product will just be a 1×1 matrix (it is just a scalar). When we do this multiplication, we obtain:

$$\vec{c}_i^\top B \vec{c}_j = \begin{bmatrix} b_{z_i 1} & \cdots & b_{z_i K} \end{bmatrix} \begin{bmatrix} c_{j1} \\ \cdots \\ c_{jK} \end{bmatrix}$$

$$= \sum_{k=1}^{K} b_{z_i k} c_{jk}.$$

Again, remember that the community assignment vector $\vec{c}_j$ takes a value of zero everywhere except at c_{jz_j}, where it has a value of 1. Therefore, we get that:

$$\sum_{k=1}^{K} b_{z_i k} c_{jk} = c_{jz_j} b_{z_i z_j} + \sum_{k \neq z_j} c_{jk} b_{z_i k}$$

$$= 1 b_{z_i z_j} + \sum_{k \neq z_j} 0 b_{z_i k}$$

$$= b_{z_i z_j},$$

so:

$$\vec{c}_i^\top B \vec{c}_j = b_{z_i z_j}. \tag{4.2}$$

This gives us a mathematical procedure that we can use to take an arbitrary pair of nodes in our network, and extract the appropriate block matrix entry from B corresponding to the communities i and j of these nodes.

The elegance of this result becomes apparent when we instead "stack" the one-hot encoded community assignment vectors for each node into a *one-hot encoded community assignment matrix* C, which is the $n \times K$ matrix:

$$C = \begin{bmatrix} \vdash & \vec{c}_1^\top & \dashv \\ & \vdots & \\ \vdash & \vec{c}_n^\top & \dashv \end{bmatrix}.$$

When we premultiply the block matrix B by C, the resulting product is a $n \times K$ matrix, where:

$$CB = \begin{bmatrix} \vdash & \vec{c}_1^\top & \dashv \\ & \vdots & \\ \vdash & \vec{c}_n^\top & \dashv \end{bmatrix} B.$$

Remember that matrix multiplication is performed by multiplying across the rows of the first matrix and down the columns of the second. Therefore, this product will be:

$$CB = \begin{bmatrix} c_1^\top B \\ \vdots \\ c_n^\top B \end{bmatrix},$$

which means that the K-element rows of this matrix are given by Equation (4.1).

Postmultiplication by $C^\top$ gives us:

$$CBC^\top = \begin{bmatrix} c_1^\top B \\ \vdots \\ c_n^\top B \end{bmatrix} \begin{bmatrix} \top & & \top \\ \vec{c}_1 & \cdots & \vec{c}_n \\ \bot & & \bot \end{bmatrix}.$$

Again, going across the rows of the first matrix and down the columns of the second gives us:

$$CBC^\top = \begin{bmatrix} \vec{c}_1^\top B \vec{c}_1 & \cdots & \vec{c}_1^\top B \vec{c}_n \\ \vdots & \ddots & \vdots \\ \vec{c}_n^\top B \vec{c}_1 & \cdots & \vec{c}_n^\top B \vec{c}_n \end{bmatrix}.$$

Note that the (i, j)th entry of this matrix has the form $\vec{c}_i^\top B \vec{c}_j$, which we learned in Equation (4.2) was just $b_{z_i z_j}$. This corresponds exactly to the probability of an edge between nodes i and j, from Section 4.3.3.

This gives us a procedure to construct a probability matrix for an SBM, using the result:

$$P = CBC^\top,$$

where C is the one-hot encoding matrix of the community assignment vector $\vec{z}$, and B is the corresponding block matrix.

Pseudocode is outlined in Algorithm 4.4 to perform this algorithmically.

Algorithm 4.4 Generating a probability matrix for a $SBM_n(\vec{z}, B)$ random network

Data: $\vec{z}$ a community assignment vector for each of the n nodes to one of K communities

  B a block matrix with K rows and K columns

Result: The probability matrix associated with the $SBM_n(\vec{z}, B)$.

1 Construct a matrix C with n rows and K columns; one row for each node, and one column for each community.

2 **for** i in $1{:}n$ **do**

3   **for** k in $1{:}K$ **do**

4   If $z_i = k$, let $c_{ik} = 1$. If $z_i \neq k$, let $c_{ik} = 0$.

5   **end**

6 **end**

7 Let $P = CBC^\top$. **return** A

Let's work through this using our school example, because it comes up a few times over the course of the book. We have 50 students attending school one (the first community), and 50 students attending school two (the second community). First, we need the code to produce the one-hot encoded community assignment matrix:

```
def ohe_comm_vec(z):
    """
    A function to generate the one-hot-encoded community
    assignment matrix from a community assignment vector.
    """
    K = len(np.unique(z))
    n = len(z)
    C = np.zeros((n, K))
    for i, zi in enumerate(z):
        C[i, zi - 1] = 1
    return C
```

And then we can use this to generate the probability matrix:

```
def generate_sbm_pmtx(z, B):
    """
    A function to generate the probability matrix for an
        SBM.
    """
    C = ohe_comm_vec(z)
    return C @ B @ C.T

# the community assignment vector
z = np.repeat([1, 2], 50)
# block matrix
B = np.array([[0.6, 0.1],
              [0.1, 0.4]])
# probability matrix
P = generate_sbm_pmtx(z, B)
```

The relationship between the community assignment vector, the one-hot encoded community assignment matrix, the block matrix, and the probability matrix is illustrated in Figure 4.3.3.

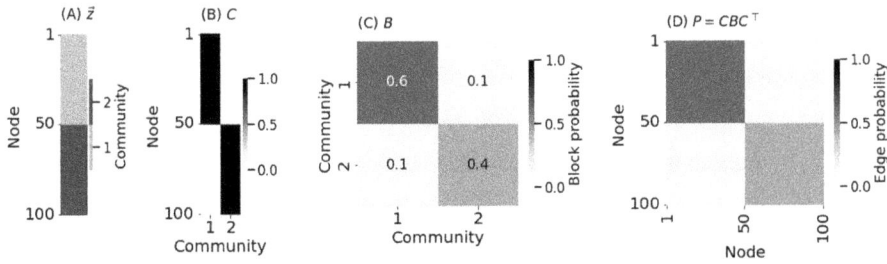

Figure 4.3.3 (**A**) The community assignment vector $\vec{z}$ and (**B**) the community assignment matrix C. Notice that each node has a value of 1 in the corresponding column in which the node is a community. The first 25 nodes have a value of 1 in column 1, and the second 25 nodes have a value of 1 in column 2. (**C**) The block matrix. (**D**) The probability matrix for each node pair.

4.3.7   SBMs Generalize ER Networks

To show that the SBMs generalize the ER networks from Section 4.2, we can use the logic that we developed in Section 4.2.4. If the SBM random networks generalize the ER random networks, this means that for any ER random network, we could find a stochastically equivalent SBM.

Take an $ER_n(p)$ random network $\mathbf{A}^{(1)}$. The probability matrix $P^{(1)}$ for $\mathbf{A}^{(1)}$ has entries $p_{ij}^{(1)} = p$. Our goal is to find another network (an SBM) that is stochastically equivalent to $\mathbf{A}^{(1)}$, for any choice of p. From Concept 4.2.1, we learned that this means that we need to find another $SBM_n(\vec{z}, B)$ random network $\mathbf{A}^{(2)}$, where $P^{(2)} = P^{(1)}$.

The simplest possible SBM would have a single community: $z_i = 1$ for every node i. Therefore, the one-hot encoded community assignment matrix C is just an $n \times 1$ matrix (it is a column-vector with n elements):

$$C = 1_n = \begin{bmatrix} 1 \\ \vdots \\ 1 \end{bmatrix}.$$

The symbol "1_n" is used to denote a vector of n-ones repeated.

With a single community, the block matrix B is just 1×1, also called a number. If we let $B = b_{11} = [p]$, applying the procedure from Section 4.3.6 gives us:

$$P^{(2)} = CBC^\top$$
$$= 1_n[p]1_n^\top,$$

where $C = 1_n$, and $B = [p]$ is just a 1×1 matrix (it is a scalar number). Remember that with matrix multiplication, scalar numbers can be brought to the front, so:

$$P^{(2)} = p1_n1_n^\top.$$

Notice that the product $1_n1_n^\top$ is an $n \times n$ matrix, where:

$$1_n1_n^\top = \begin{bmatrix} 1 \\ \vdots \\ 1 \end{bmatrix} \begin{bmatrix} 1 & \cdots & 1 \end{bmatrix}$$
$$= \begin{bmatrix} 1 & \cdots & 1 \\ \vdots & \ddots & \vdots \\ 1 & \cdots & 1 \end{bmatrix}. \tag{4.3}$$

Putting this together means that:

$$P^{(2)} = \begin{bmatrix} p & \cdots & p \\ \vdots & \ddots & \vdots \\ p & \cdots & p \end{bmatrix},$$

so $p_{ij}^{(2)} = p = p_{ij}^{(1)}$ for all i and j, and $P^{(1)} = P^{(2)}$. This result can be applied for any choice of p. Therefore, the $ER_n(p)$ random networks are contained in the $SBM_n(\vec{z}, B)$

random networks, and conversely, the $SBM_n(\vec{z}, B)$ random networks generalize the $ER_n(p)$ random networks.

4.3.8   SBMs Can (Uselessly) Generalize IER Random Networks

By the above formulation, we can also characterize the $IER_n(P)$ random networks using an $SBM_n(\vec{z}, B)$ random network: Choosing the number of communities to be equal to n (each node is in its own community) would yield the block matrix B being an $n \times n$ matrix of block probabilities. In this case, the "block probabilities" are probabilities for "blocks" of single nodes; the matrix behaves identically to an edge probability matrix P. Therefore, if $B = P$, then the $SBM_n(\vec{z}, B)$ random network with n communities is equivalent to an $IER_n(P)$ random network.

Such a random network is not particularly useful. The characterization of a simple network as an SBM still leaves us with $\binom{n}{2}$ probability terms to estimate, from a network with $\binom{n}{2}$ unique entries, which is the same problem from Concept 4.1.4. For this reason, later sections of this book will typically focus on SBMs where $K < n$, and we do not run into the problem of having a block matrix B equally as complicated as the probability matrix P.

4.4   Random Dot Product Graphs

Extending the concept of community structure from the SBM in Section 4.3, we introduce the random dot product graph (RDPG) model. In an RDPG, the manner in which a given node "behaves" in the greater network can be succinctly summarized with a single vector (of which there will be one per node in the network). Edge probabilities are defined using dot products between node-vectors.

We cover:

1. Definition and properties of the RDPG model,
2. Latent position matrices and their interpretation,
3. Simulating samples from RDPG random networks,
4. Probability matrices for RDPGs, and
5. Relationship between RDPGs and other network models.

The RDPG model defines a framework for representing complex network structures and relationships between nodes in a continuous vector space. Whereas we cannot use traditional machine learning techniques on sets of nodes and edges, we can use traditional machine learning techniques with data represented in continuous vector spaces. Because an RDPG expresses nodes as elements of this space, this framework will dominate much of the discussion in later parts of this book.

Take 100 people who live along a 100 mile long road, and each person is 1 mile apart. We create a network with nodes representing the people who live along this road, and the edges representing whether a given pair of people along the street are friends. However, there's a slight twist: The people at the ends of the road are party hosts. If someone lives closer to one party host, they are going to tend to go more frequently to that host's parties than the other party host. Consequently, when someone lives near a party host, they are going to tend to be better friends with other people who go to that host's parties more frequently. How could we model such a situation?

For each person i, we could have a vector $\vec{x}_i$, that looks like this:

$$\vec{x}_i = \begin{bmatrix} \frac{100-i}{100} & \frac{i}{100} \end{bmatrix}.$$

We could model the probability of two people i and j being friends with the inner product of the two vectors $\vec{x}_i^\top \vec{x}_j$. This quantity is the element-wise sum of the elements of each vector; that is:

$$\vec{x}_i^\top \vec{x}_j = \sum_{u=1}^{d} x_{id} x_{jd}.$$

For instance, $\vec{x}_1 = \begin{bmatrix} 1 \\ 0 \end{bmatrix}$, and $\vec{x}_{100} = \begin{bmatrix} 0 \\ 1 \end{bmatrix}$. Note that:

$$p_{1,100} = \vec{x}_1^\top \vec{x}_{100} = 1 \cdot 0 + 0 \cdot 1 = 0.$$

What happens in between?

Let's consider another person, person 30, who lives closer to person 1 than to person 100. Here, $\vec{x}_{30} = \begin{bmatrix} \frac{7}{10} \\ \frac{3}{10} \end{bmatrix}$. This gives:

$$p_{1,30} = \vec{x}_1^\top \vec{x}_{30} = \frac{7}{10} \cdot 1 + 0 \cdot \frac{3}{10} = \frac{7}{10}$$

$$p_{30,100} = \vec{x}_{30}^\top x_{100} = \frac{7}{10} \cdot 0 + \frac{3}{10} \cdot 1 = \frac{3}{10}.$$

So this means that person 1 and person 30 have a 70 percent probability of being friends, but person 30 and 100 have only a 30 percent probability of being friends.

The random dot product graph (RDPG), the formalization of this intuition, was first introduced by [7]. With the RDPG, we can generalize $ER_n(p)$ and certain $SBM_n(\vec{z}, B)$ random networks while retaining a discernable structure.

4.4.1   The Latent Position Matrix

We parameterize the RDPG using a matrix X called the *latent position matrix*. Each row $\vec{x}_i$ will be called the *latent position of the node i*. In matrix form, X looks like this:

$$X = \begin{bmatrix} \vdash & \vec{x}_1^\top & \dashv \\ \vdash & \vec{x}_2^\top & \dashv \\ & \vdots & \\ \vdash & \vec{x}_n^\top & \dashv \end{bmatrix}.$$

We will call the columns of X the *latent dimensions*, and the total number of columns the *latent dimensionality*. We will often use the letter d to denote the latent dimensionality of X. X has n rows (one for each node) and d columns (one for each latent dimension). The latent position of the node i, $\vec{x}_i$, is therefore a d-dimensional vector.

4.4.2　Conceptualizing the RDPG

We call this model the RDPG because the probabilities of edges existing are based on
dot products between pairs of latent positions for the different nodes in the network.
We will say that the random network has adjacency matrix entries $\mathbf{a}_{ij}$ which are
$Bernoulli(\vec{x}_i^\top \vec{x}_j)$, where $\vec{x}_i$ is the latent position for node i and $\vec{x}_j$ is the latent position
for node j. Therefore, the entries $\mathbf{a}_{ij}$ depend only on the latent positions of the nodes
i and j. As before, these entries are independent of all of the other entries in the
adjacency matrix. If $\mathbf{A}$ has n nodes with independent edges and a latent position matrix
X, we say that $\mathbf{A}$ is an $RDPG_n(X)$ random network.

4.4.3　How Do We Simulate Samples of $RDPG_n(X)$ Random Networks?

The procedure in Algorithm 4.5 will produce a simple network A, where the underlying random network $\mathbf{A}$ is a simple $RDPG_n(X)$ random network.

Algorithm 4.5 Simulating a sample from a simple $RDPG_n(X)$ random network

---

Data: n a number of nodes

$\vec{X}$ a latent position matrix whose rows indicate the d-dimensional latent
position vectors for each node

Result: The adjacency matrix of a sample from the random network.

1　**for** i *in* 1:n **do**
2　　**for** $j > i$ **do**
3　　　Obtain a weighted coin (i, j) which has a probability of $\vec{x}_i^\top \vec{x}_j$ of landing
　　　　on heads, and a $1 - \vec{x}_i^\top \vec{x}_j$ probability of landing on tails.
4　　　Flip the (i, j) coin, and if it lands on heads, the corresponding entry a_{ij} in
　　　　the adjacency matrix is 1. If the coin lands on tails, the corresponding
　　　　entry $a_{ij} = 0$.
5　　　Let $a_{ji} = a_{ij}$.
6　　**end**
7　**end**
8　**return** A

Let's return to the party example. We first must determine what our latent position
matrix looks like:

```
import numpy as np
from graphbook_code import lpm_heatmap

n = 100 # the number of nodes in our network
# design the latent position matrix X according to
# the rules we laid out previously
X = np.zeros((n,2))
for i in range(0, n):
    X[i,:] = [(n - i)/n, i/n]

lpm_heatmap(X, ytitle="Person", xticks=[0.5, 1.5], xticklabels=[1, 2],
            yticks=[0.5, 49.5, 99.5], yticklabels=[1, 50, 100],
            xtitle="Latent Dimension", title="Latent Position Matrix, X")
```

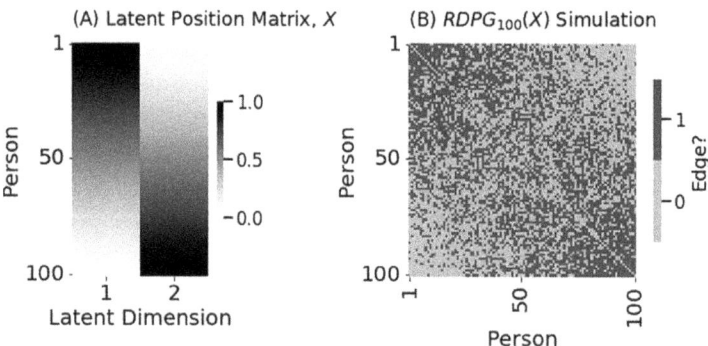

Figure 4.4.1 (**A**) The latent position matrix. (**B**) A sample of an $RDPG_n(X)$ random network.

This latent position matrix is shown in Figure 4.4.1(A). Next, we can use `graspologic` with this latent position matrix to sample an $RDPG_n(X)$ random network:

```
from graspologic.simulations import rdpg
from graphbook_code import heatmap

# sample an RDPG with the latent position matrix
# created above
A = rdpg(X, loops=False, directed=False)

# and plot it
heatmap(A.astype(int), xtitle="Person", ytitle="Person",
        title="$RDPG_{100}(X)$ Simulation")
```

A sample from the $RDPG_n(X)$ random network is shown in Figure 4.4.1(B).

4.4.4   Probability Matrix for RDPG Random Networks

In Concept 4.2.1, we learned that we can use the probability matrix to determine whether networks are stochastically equivalent. We want a procedure which takes a latent position matrix X whose rows are the latent positions $\vec{x}_i$ of each node i, and will produce a probability matrix P where each entry $p_{ij} = \vec{x}_i^\top \vec{x}_j$. As before, the brute force approach would work here, but we would strongly prefer to leverage matrix multiplication accelerations where possible due to the fact that most modern programming languages have accelerated matrix multiplication routines.

Fortunately, this is much more obvious than it was for the SBMs in Section 4.3.6. Notice that our goal is a procedure where we obtain P where $p_{ij} = \vec{x}_i^\top \vec{x}_j$. Remember that the latent position matrix looks like this:

$$X = \begin{bmatrix} \vdash & \vec{x}_1^\top & \dashv \\ & \vdots & \\ \vdash & \vec{x}_n^\top & \dashv \end{bmatrix}.$$

When we multiply X with its transpose, $X^\top$, the product ends up being this:

$$XX^\top = \begin{bmatrix} \vdash & \vec{x}_1^\top & \dashv \\ & \vdots & \\ \vdash & \vec{x}_n^\top & \dashv \end{bmatrix} \begin{bmatrix} \top & & \top \\ \vec{x}_1 & \cdots & \vec{x}_n \\ \bot & & \bot \end{bmatrix}.$$

The elements after matrix multiplication produce the (i, j)th value as the dot product of the ith row of the first matrix with the jth column of the second matrix. This product is:

$$XX^\top = \begin{bmatrix} \vec{x}_1^\top \vec{x}_1 & \cdots & \vec{x}_1^\top \vec{x}_n \\ \vdots & \ddots & \vdots \\ \vec{x}_n^\top \vec{x}_1 & \cdots & \vec{x}_n^\top \vec{x}_n \end{bmatrix}.$$

The (i, j)th entry $(XX^\top)_{ij} = \vec{x}_i^\top \vec{x}_j$, which was exactly our goal. Therefore:

$$P = XX^\top,$$

which gives us our expression for the probability matrix of an RDPG.

4.4.5 $RDPG_n(X)$ Random Networks Generalize a Broad Class of Problems

To show when the RDPGs generalize the ER and SBM random networks, we can turn to the logic that we developed in Section 4.2.4.

RDPG Random Networks Generalize the ER Random Networks
If the RDPG random networks generalize the ER random networks, then for any ER random network, we could find a stochastically equivalent RDPG.

Take an $ER_n(p)$ random network $\mathbf{A}^{(1)}$. The probability matrix $P^{(1)}$ for this network has entries $p_{ij}^{(1)} = p$. Our goal is to find another network $\mathbf{A}^{(2)}$ (an RDPG, with some latent position matrix X) that is stochastically equivalent to this network, for any choice of p. That is, we want a choice of $\vec{x}_i$ and $\vec{x}_j$, such that $\vec{x}_i^\top \vec{x}_j = p$, for all i and j.

This is quite easy to do. If the latent dimensionality $d = 1$, we can take $\vec{x}_i = [\sqrt{p}]$ for all nodes. That is, each latent position is just a scalar (the square root of p), and the "latent position matrix" is the $n \times 1$ matrix (a column-vector):

$$X = \sqrt{p}1_n,$$

where 1_n is the n-dimensional column-vector of 1s. Using the same logic that we used in Section 4.3.7:

$$P^{(2)} = XX^\top$$
$$= \sqrt{p}1_n\sqrt{p}1_n^\top$$
$$= p1_n1_n^\top,$$

which works because $\sqrt{p}$ is a scalar and therefore can be directly multiplied with the other $\sqrt{p}$. From Equation (4.3), we remember that:

$$P^{(2)} = \begin{bmatrix} p & \cdots & p \\ \vdots & \ddots & \vdots \\ p & \cdots & p \end{bmatrix},$$

so $p_{ij}^{(2)} = p = p_{ij}^{(1)}$ for all i and j, and $P^{(1)} = P^{(2)}$. This result can be applied for any choice of p. Therefore, the $ER_n(p)$ random networks are contained in the $RDPG_n(X)$ random networks, and conversely, the $RDPG_n(X)$ random networks generalize the $ER_n(p)$ random networks.

RDPG Random Networks Generalize Some SBM Random Networks
In certain situations, the $RDPG_n(X)$ model can generalize the $SBM_n(\vec{z}, B)$ model in Section 4.3. Imagine an $SBM_n(\vec{z}, B)$ random network $\mathbf{A}^{(1)}$, where C is the $n \times K$ one-hot encoded community assignment matrix with rows corresponding to nodes. Remember from Section 4.3.6 that the probability matrix is:

$$P^{(1)} = CBC^{\top}.$$

Likewise, if $\mathbf{A}^{(2)}$ is an $RDPG_n(X)$ random network, the probability matrix would be:

$$P^{(2)} = XX^{\top},$$

If the matrix B was "somehow" a product of another matrix (called a *square-root matrix*, written $\sqrt{B}$) with its transpose; that is:

$$B = \sqrt{B}\sqrt{B}^{\top}, \tag{4.4}$$

Then finding an $RDPG_n(X)$ random network that is stochastically equivalent to $\mathbf{A}^{(1)}$ would be possible. Notice that in this case:

$$P^{(1)} = C\sqrt{B}\sqrt{B}^{\top}C^{\top}.$$

If U and V are two matrices, then $(UV)^{\top} = V^{\top}U^{\top}$. Therefore, if we set $X = C\sqrt{B}$:

$$P^{(2)} = XX^{\top}$$
$$= C\sqrt{B}\left(C\sqrt{B}\right)^{\top}$$
$$= C\sqrt{B}\sqrt{B}^{\top}C^{\top}$$
$$= CBC^{\top} = P^{(1)}, \tag{4.5}$$

and our job would be done. Stated another way, if the relationship in Equation (4.4) is true, and the block matrix B has a square root, then the RDPG random networks would generalize the SBM random networks, and the SBM random networks would be contained by the RDPG random networks. However, the requirement that B has a square root is a bit more nuanced, and provides motivation for discussion in Section 4.5.

   Concept 4.4.1 roadmaps our discussions about network generalizations, and describes how the RDPG fits in to that picture.

Concept 4.4.1 The bigger picture of network generalization

The reason that we are discussing generalizations can be given most clearly through example. Imagine that you are learning how to knit, and that you want to knit a sweater. As you learn, you pick up many skills and abilities that also apply to simpler things. After finishing the sweater, you might want to knit a scarf, which is simpler than a sweater. The skills that you picked up to knit the sweater will probably generalize to your attempt to knit the scarf.

Similarly, for many sections of this book the RDPG will be a foundational model that we will build upon. In Chapter 5, we will focus most of our attention on developing machinery for estimating latent position matrices from network observations. The idea is that, just like knitting a sweater will give skills that generalize to knitting a scarf, developing machinery for one class of networks will generalize to other classes. If we develop machinery for the RDPGs and the RDPGs generalize a second random network model, the machinery we developed for the RDPGs generalizes to random networks described by the second random network model. We are working towards developing intuition that will give us a tool set that can deal with many problems, rather than a tool set which only applies to one problem. Chapters 7 through 9 will explore how to apply many of these techniques to real network learning problems and refine them for more specific network models.

4.5 Positive Semidefinite Matrices

We now take a break from defining new statistical models to explore the properties of positive semidefinite (PSD) matrices, which are symmetric, have nonnegative eigenvalues, and importantly, have square roots.

We cover:

1. Definition and properties of PSD matrices,
2. PSD block matrices in SBMs and their implications,
3. Relationship between PSD matrices and RDPGs,
4. Types of block matrices: homophilic, planted partition, kidney-egg, core–periphery, and disassortative, and
5. Generating latent position matrices for SBMs with PSD block matrices.

Positive semidefiniteness is a key property because any model with a PSD probability matrix can be thought of as an RDPG, motivating many of the representations we will discuss in Chapter 5.

In Section 4.4, we said that the probability matrix $P = XX^\top$ for $RDPG_n(X)$ random networks, where X was the latent position matrix. This means that P must be positive semidefinite for an RDPG.

There are multiple equivalent ways to define *positive semidefiniteness* (typically abbreviated PSD). In this book, we will borrow two definitions:

> **Concept 4.5.1** Matrix factorizations/decompositions
>
> If we have a matrix M, we say that M is *factorized* or *decomposed* if it can be expressed as a product of other matrices. For instance, if M is positive semidefinite, we can factorize or decompose it using the square-root matrix $\sqrt{M}$:
>
> $$M = \sqrt{M}\sqrt{M}^\top.$$
>
> There are many approaches with which we can obtain factorizations or decompositions of matrices, several of which will be useful for network learning problems.

1. If M is a real square symmetric matrix (that is, M has n rows and n columns, and $M = M^\top$), we say that M is *positive semidefinite* if and only if there exists another matrix $\sqrt{M}$ where $M = \sqrt{M}\sqrt{M}^\top$. In this case, understanding $\sqrt{M}$ to be the "square-root matrix" provides a reasonable level of intuition.
2. If M is a real square symmetric matrix, we say that M is positive semidefinite if and only if all of the eigenvalues are nonnegative.

The words "if and only if" can be taken to mean that the two statements are "equivalent characterizations" of one another. We could characterize a matrix as positive semidefinite either if it has a square-root matrix, or if all of its eigenvalues are nonnegative. Conversely, if we start by knowing that a real matrix is positive semidefinite, we also know that it has a square-root matrix and that its eigenvalues are nonnegative. Starting with $\sqrt{M}$ is often a more useful approach to construct positive semidefinite matrices, and checking for nonnegative eigenvalues is useful for verifying whether M is positive semidefinite. Concept 4.5.1 introduces the concept of a matrix factorization (or decomposition), which will be crucial for later sections.

To begin, we will work through a quick example. For $RDPG_n(X)$ random networks, if $P = XX^\top$, X is a square-root matrix for P. Therefore, we could say that the probability matrix P is positive semidefinite, and is factorized by the latent position matrix X and its transpose. Equivalently, we could check this with the following utility, which we will use in several sections of the book going forward:

```python
import numpy as np

def block_mtx_psd(B):
    """
    A function which indicates whether a matrix
    B is positive semidefinite.
    """
    return np.all(np.linalg.eigvals(B) >= 0)
```

4.5.1 Positive Semidefiniteness and Block Matrices

$SBM_n(\vec{z}, B)$ random networks can often share the positive semidefinite property, particularly with respect to the block matrix B.

We will restrict ourselves to the 2×2 case, in which we have two communities, so that we can build intuition for what a positive semidefinite block matrix looks like. In this case, the block matrix is:

$$B = \begin{bmatrix} b_{11} & b_{12} \\ b_{21} & b_{22} \end{bmatrix},$$

The existence of the square-root matrix $\sqrt{B}$ (in other words, that B is positive semidefinite) in the 2×2 case can be summarized succinctly with two conditions:

1. $b_{11} \geq 0$, and
2. The determinant of the block matrix is nonnegative; that is, $det(B) \geq 0$.

Since the block matrix B is also a probability matrix, condition 1 applies automatically: A probability cannot be negative. The determinant of a 2×2 matrix B is $b_{11}b_{22} - b_{21}b_{12}$. For this section, we will consider only simple $SBM_n(\vec{z}, B)$ random networks; from Remark 4.3.2, remember that this means that the block matrix will be symmetric, so $b_{12} = b_{21}$. Therefore, the determinant of a 2×2 symmetric matrix B is $b_{11}b_{22} - b_{21}^2$. So, condition two gives us that the block matrix will be positive semidefinite any time $b_{11}b_{22} \geq b_{21}^2$. When a matrix has all positive entries but is not positive semidefinite, we refer to the matrix as *indefinite*.

The Power of RDPGs
When this block matrix is positive semidefinite, as we explained in Equation (4.5), we could find a latent position matrix for the SBM:

$$P = XX^{\top},$$

which illustrates that the probability matrix for an SBM with a positive semidefinite block matrix is also positive semidefinite. This is because it can be factorized with a square-root matrix (here, the latent position matrix). So, to answer the question we left "hanging" at the end of Section 4.4.5, the RDPGs generalize SBMs with positive semidefinite block matrices (and conversely, the SBMs with positive semidefinite block matrices are contained by the RDPGs).

More broadly, to determine stochastic equivalence, we always will use a probability matrix. Imagine we have $\mathbf{A}^{(1)}$, a random network with a probability matrix $P^{(1)}$. If $P^{(1)}$ is positive semidefinite, we can find $\sqrt{P^{(1)}}$ where:

$$P^{(1)} = \sqrt{P^{(1)}}\sqrt{P^{(1)}}^{\top}.$$

Now, imagine that we have some RDPG $\mathbf{A}^{(2)}$, where the latent position matrix $X = \sqrt{P^{(1)}}$. Then the probability matrix for $\mathbf{A}^{(2)}$ is:

$$P^{(2)} = XX^{\top} = \sqrt{P^{(1)}}\sqrt{P^{(1)}}^{\top} = P^{(1)}.$$

Since $P^{(1)} = P^{(2)}$, $\mathbf{A}^{(1)}$ and $\mathbf{A}^{(2)}$ are stochastically equivalent by Concept 4.2.1. What this shows is that the RDPG random networks will generalize the entire class of random networks with positive semidefinite probability matrices, which is an extremely

---

Concept 4.5.2 The importance of RDPGs

By now, you should be starting to see the picture of why positive semidefiniteness, which we originally introduced in Concept 4.4.1, matters: Random networks with positive semidefinite probability matrices are generalized by RDPGs, which means that all machinery we will later develop for RDPGs applies (for free) to any random network with a positive semidefinite probability matrix.

---

useful property and will be very handy later on. This further solidifies the intuition that we developed in Concept 4.4.1, and is solidified by Concept 4.5.2.

A more nuanced question: What is a random network with a positive semidefinite probability matrix? To conceptualize what this means intuitively, we'll introduce various types of SBMs with two communities. These are covered in more technical depth in [8]. With the insight that we developed in Section 4.5.1, we will build intuition by classifying these block matrices as positive semidefinite (or not).

4.5.2   Erdös–Rényi Block Matrix

An SBM's block matrix is called *Erdös–Rényi* if all entries are equal. In the 2×2 symmetric case, this means that $b_{11} = b_{22} = b_{12} = p$:

$$B = \begin{bmatrix} p & p \\ p & p \end{bmatrix}.$$

If B has only one unique entry, and $\vec{z}$ is any community assignment vector, the resulting probability matrix will also have one unique entry. This is equivalent to the probability matrix for an $ER_n(p)$ network: We technically still have two communities, but they are completely indistinguishable.

Since we already showed that $ER_n(p)$ random networks are contained in the $RDPG_n(X)$ random networks, and $RDPG_n(X)$ can only have positive semidefinite probability matrices, this B matrix must be positive semidefinite.

To see this formally, notice that $b_{11} = b_{22} = b_{12}$ implies that $b_{11}b_{22} = b_{12}^2$, so the determinant of B is nonnegative.

4.5.3   Homophilic Block Matrices

An SBM's block matrix is called *homophilic* when the diagonal entries, b_{kk} for all communities k are greater than the off-diagonal entries b_{kl} where $k \neq l$:

$$B = \begin{bmatrix} b_{11} & b_{12} \\ b_{21} & b_{22} \end{bmatrix}$$

with $b_{11}, b_{22} > b_{12}, b_{21}$.

"Homophilic" roughly means "tending to form relationships with objects similar to oneself." In the context of a network, the nodes of an SBM with a homophilic block matrix are more probable to have connections with nodes from the same community than with different communities.

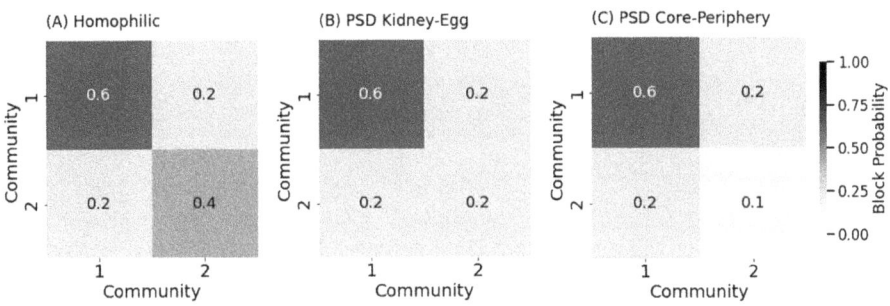

Figure 4.5.1 (**A**) A homophilic block matrix. (**B**) A positive semidefinite kidney-egg block matrix. (**C**) A positive semidefinite core–periphery block matrix.

Homophilic block matrices are positive semidefinite in general. We can see this easily for the 2×2 case using the determinant condition for B. Notice that since b_{11} and b_{22} are each greater than b_{21} and are nonnegative, their product will be greater than b_{21}^2.

Next, let's generate and plot a homophilic block matrix:

```
import numpy as np
from graphbook_code import heatmap

B = np.array([[0.6, 0.2],
              [0.2, 0.4]])
heatmap(B, title="A homophilic block matrix", annot=True, vmin=0,
    vmax=1)
block_mtx_psd(B)
# True
```

This block matrix is shown in Figure 4.5.1(A).

4.5.4   Planted Partition Block Matrix

A *planted partition* block matrix has equal on-diagonal entries; that is, $b_{11} = b_{22} = \cdots = b_{KK}$ for all K communities. Similarly, planted partition block matrices have equal off-diagonal entries; that is, $b_{12} = \cdots b_{1K} = b_{21} = \cdots b_{2K} = \cdots b_{K1} = \cdots = b_{KK-1}$:

$$B = \begin{bmatrix} b_{11} & b_{12} \\ b_{21} & b_{22} \end{bmatrix}$$

with $b_{11} = b_{22}, b_{12} = b_{21}$.

In our case, since we already know B is symmetric, this just means that $b_{11} = b_{22}$.

Using the determinant condition and the fact that $b_{11} = b_{22}$, this implies that a planted partition is positive semidefinite when $b_{11}^2 \geq b_{12}^2$. Since the entries of B are probabilities and therefore nonnegative, we can take square roots of both sides, and a sufficient condition is that $b_{11} \geq b_{12}$. When this condition is satisfied, we further clarify that the planted partition is homophilic, since it fulfills the homophily criterion given in Section 4.5.3.

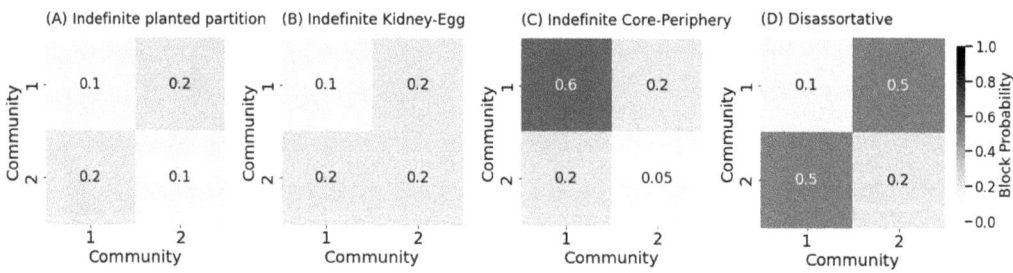

Figure 4.5.2 (**A**) An indefinite planted partition block matrix. (**B**) An indefinite kidney-egg block matrix. (**C**) An indefinite core–periphery block matrix. (**D**) A disassortative block matrix.

We can generate an indefinite planted partition block matrix with an example where the block matrix has off-diagonal entries that exceed the on-diagonal entries:

```
B_indef = np.array([[.1, .2],
                     [.2, .1]])
block_mtx_psd(B_indef)
# False
```

This is shown in Figure 4.5.2(A).

4.5.5   Kidney-Egg Block Matrices

A *kidney-egg* block matrix is a 2×2 block matrix where $b_{12} = b_{21} = b_{22}$:

$$B = \begin{bmatrix} b_{11} & b_{12} \\ b_{21} & b_{22} \end{bmatrix}$$

with $b_{12} = b_{21} = b_{22}$.

For this matrix to be positive semidefinite, the determinant condition along with $b_{12} = b_{21} = b_{22}$ gives us that $b_{11}b_{12} \geq b_{12}^2$. Dividing through by b_{12}, we can see that the kidney-egg block matrices are positive semidefinite with the same conditions as planted partition block matrices; that is, $b_{11} \geq b_{12}$. Next, we generate two kidney-egg block matrices, one of which is indefinite and one of which is positive semidefinite.

```
# a positive semidefinite kidney-egg block matrix
B_psd = np.array([[.6, .2],
                  [.2, .2]])
block_mtx_psd(B_psd)
# True

# an indefinite kidney-egg block matrix
B_indef = np.array([[.1, .2],
                    [.2, .2]])
block_mtx_psd(B_indef)
#False
```

We plot the positive semidefinite block matrix in Figure 4.5.1(B), and the indefinite block matrix in Figure 4.5.2(B).

4.5.6   Core–Periphery Block Matrices

Core–periphery block matrices have either b_{11} or b_{22} which are greater than all of the other entries of the block matrix:

$$B = \begin{bmatrix} b_{11} & b_{12} \\ b_{21} & b_{22} \end{bmatrix}$$

with $b_{11} > b_{22}, b_{12}, b_{21}$

or $b_{22} > b_{11}, b_{12}, b_{21}$.

This is called the core–periphery model because there are a group of nodes from a particular community (the *core*) that tend to be more strongly connected than nodes that are not in that community (the *periphery*). For instance, if community 1 were the core community, $b_{11} > b_{22}$ and $b_{11} > b_{12}$, then the nodes of community 1 would tend to heavily associate with other core nodes. However, the nodes of community 2 (the peripheral community) would have far fewer connections both with other peripheral nodes and with core nodes.

Core–periphery block matrices are a little bit harder to tie directly to positive semidefiniteness; the most precise that we can be is simply to say that $b_{11}b_{22} \geq b_{12}b_{21}$, which isn't particularly informative since that's just the criterion for positive semidefiniteness.

Let's show how this condition works with some more examples:

```
# a positive semidefinite core-periphery block matrix
B_psd = np.array([[.6, .2],
                  [.2, .1]])
block_mtx_psd(B_psd)
# True

# an indefinite core-periphery block matrix
B_indef = np.array([[.6, .2],
                    [.2, .05]])
block_mtx_psd(B_indef)
# False
```

The positive semidefinite core–periphery block matrix is shown in Figure 4.5.1(C), and the indefinite core–periphery block matrix is shown in Figure 4.5.2(C).

4.5.7   Disassortative Block Matrices

A block matrix is *disassortative* if b_{12} and b_{21} are greater than b_{11} and b_{22}:

$$B = \begin{bmatrix} b_{11} & b_{12} \\ b_{21} & b_{22} \end{bmatrix}$$

with $b_{11}, b_{22} < b_{12}, b_{21}$.

By definition, disassortative block matrices are not positive semidefinite. This is because $b_{11}b_{22} < b_{12}b_{21}$, since all of the entries of B are positive. There is no possible way that we could use a disassortative block matrix to construct an equivalent $RDPG_n(X)$.

Imagine that we have a simple network where the nodes are businesses, and each node is either a producer or a retailer (the two communities). An edge exists in the network if a relationship exists between two businesses. In general, producers will have business relationships with retailers, so the cross-community block probability b_{12} is high. However, producers will not tend to have business relationships with their competitor producers, and retailers will not tend to have business relationships with their competitor retailers, so the within-community block probabilities b_{11} and b_{22} are comparatively low.

We can generate a disassortative block probability matrix like this:

```
# an indefinite disassortative block matrix
B = np.array([[.1, .5],
              [.5, .2]])
block_mtx_psd(B)
# False
```

A plot of an indefinite block matrix is shown in Figure 4.5.2(D), and another example of a disassortative block matrix would be the indefinite planted partition block matrix shown in Figure 4.5.2(B).

4.5.8   How Do We Generate Latent Position Matrices for $SBM_n(\vec{z}, B)$ Random Networks with Positive Semidefinite Block Matrices?

When a real matrix M is positive semidefinite, we can obtain a square-root matrix $\sqrt{M}$ where $M = \sqrt{M}\sqrt{M}^\top$. This matrix can be generated through a process known as the Cholesky Decomposition [9]. This matrix $\sqrt{M}$ is also a square matrix; that is, it has K rows and K columns. This process will come in handy over the next few sections when we are dealing with positive semidefinite SBM block matrices and probability matrices, and we want to obtain a latent position matrix. We can do this with numpy, like so:

```
# homophilic, and hence positive semidefinite, block matrix
B = np.array([[0.6, 0.2],
              [0.2, 0.4]])

# generate square root matrix
sqrtB = np.linalg.cholesky(B)

# verify that the process worked through by equality element-wise
# use allclose instead of array_equal because of tiny
# numerical precision errors
np.allclose(sqrtB @ sqrtB.T, B)
# True
```

Next, we'll generate a community assignment vector, and then use the code that we first produced in Section 4.3.6 to obtain a one-hot encoding of the community assignment vector. We can then use that to produce a latent position matrix, using the instructions from Equation (4.5), by taking $X = C\sqrt{B}$:

```
from graphbook_code import ohe_comm_vec

def lpm_from_sbm(z, B):
    """
    A function to produce a latent position matrix from a
    community assignment vector and a block matrix.
    """
    if not block_mtx_psd(B):
        raise ValueError("Latent position matrices require PSD block
            matrices!")
    # one-hot encode the community assignment vector
    C = ohe_comm_vec(z)
    # compute square root matrix
    sqrtB = np.linalg.cholesky(B)
    # X = C*sqrt(B)
    return C @ sqrtB

# make a community assignment vector for 25 nodes / community
nk = 25
z = np.repeat([1, 2], nk)

# latent position matrix for an equivalent RDPG
X = lpm_from_sbm(z, B)
```

The resulting latent position matrix is shown along with the community assignment vector and the block matrix in Figure 4.5.3. Note that nodes with the same community have the same latent positions (rows of the latent position matrix X in Figure 4.5.3(C)).

Finally, we can verify that the latent position matrix and the process described in Section 4.3.6 to generate the probability matrix for an SBM produce the same probability matrix:

```
from graphbook_code import generate_sbm_pmtx

# generate the probability matrices for an RDPG using X and SBM
P_rdpg = X @ X.T
P_sbm = generate_sbm_pmtx(z, B)

# verify equality element-wise
np.allclose(P_rdpg, P_sbm)
# True
```

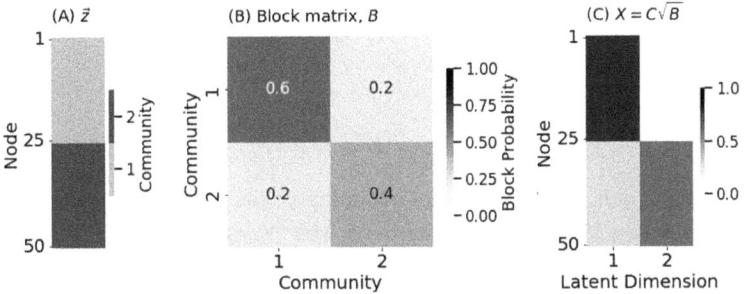

Figure 4.5.3 (**A**) The community assignment vector. (**B**) A homophilic block matrix, which is positive semidefinite. (**C**) The latent positions for an equivalent RDPG.

By Concept 4.2.1, this implies that the $RDPG_n(X)$ random network and the $SBM_n(\vec{z}, B)$ random network are the same.

4.5.9 The Latent Positions of Nodes in SBMs with Positive Semidefinite Block Matrices

In Figure 4.5.3(C), we made a particular note: The nodes in the same community of the network that we designed above appear to have the same latent positions. This is no fluke, and is more broadly a characteristic of nodes in the same community of any SBM random network with a positive semidefinite block matrix.

Suppose that we have an $SBM_n(\vec{z}, B)$ random network $\mathbf{A}$, where the block matrix B is positive semidefinite, and the SBM has K communities. Since B is positive semidefinite, $\mathbf{A}$ has a positive semidefinite probability matrix, which means that there is a stochastically equivalent $RDPG_n(X)$ random network. This is the conclusion that we reached in Section 4.5.1.

If C is the one-hot encoded community assignment matrix of $\mathbf{A}$, and $\sqrt{B}$ is the square-root matrix of B (which exists because B is positive semidefinite), a latent position matrix for such an RDPG would be:

$$X = C\sqrt{B}.$$

When we write out the rows of X and C, it looks like this:

$$\begin{bmatrix} \vdash & \vec{x}_1^\top & \dashv \\ & \vdots & \\ \vdash & \vec{x}_n^\top & \dashv \end{bmatrix} = \begin{bmatrix} \vdash & \vec{c}_1^\top & \dashv \\ & \vdots & \\ \vdash & \vec{c}_n^\top & \dashv \end{bmatrix} \sqrt{B},$$

where $\vec{x}_i^\top$ is the d-dimensional latent position for the node i, and $\vec{c}_1$ is the one-hot encoding of the community assignment for node i.

Matrix multiplication is performed by multiplying across the rows of the first matrix and down the columns of the second. Therefore, this product will be:

$$\begin{bmatrix} \vdash & \vec{x}_1^\top & \dashv \\ & \vdots & \\ \vdash & \vec{x}_n^\top & \dashv \end{bmatrix} = \begin{bmatrix} \vdash & \vec{c}_1^\top \sqrt{B} & \dashv \\ & \vdots & \\ \vdash & \vec{c}_n^\top \sqrt{B} & \dashv \end{bmatrix}. \tag{4.6}$$

Looking at each row of the left and right, this gives us that:

$$\vec{x}_i^\top = \vec{c}_i^\top \sqrt{B},$$

which we can transpose to obtain:

$$\vec{x}_i = \sqrt{B}^\top \vec{c}_i.$$

Remember that $\vec{c}_i$ is the one-hot encoding of the community assignment z_i; stated another way, $c_{iz_i} = 1$, and 0 otherwise. This means that for any other node j where $z_j = z_i$ (the nodes i and j are in the same community), $\vec{c}_i = \vec{c}_j$, because the community assignments are the same. Therefore:

$$\vec{x}_i = \sqrt{B}^\top \vec{c}_i$$
$$= \sqrt{B}^\top \vec{c}_j$$
$$= \vec{x}_j,$$

which is because $\vec{c}_i = \vec{c}_j$. Therefore, $\vec{x}_i = \vec{x}_j$ when $z_i = z_j$. Stated another way, nodes in the same community also share the same latent positions. This property will be useful for us in many future sections. In particular, this intuition will allow us to learn community labels for nodes (when we do not know community labels ahead of time) through community detection in Section 6.1, and will allow us to "untangle" the community structure from networks like those in Figure 4.3.2.

We show an example of a homophilic block matrix in Figure 4.5.3(A); the fact that it is homophilic also means that it is positive semidefinite. When we apply the conversion utility `lpm_from_sbm()`, we produce a latent position matrix in Figure 4.5.3(C). Notice that the rows for all of the nodes each of the two communities are equal.

Not All RDPGs Can Be Represented as SBMs, and Vice Versa
Section 4.5.9 provides us with insights into which situations SBMs can generalize RDPGs. The street example from the introduction of Section 4.4 provides a counter example indicating that not all $RDPG_n(X)$ random networks can be represented as $SBM_n(\vec{z}, B)$ random networks with fewer communities than nodes (that is, $K < n$ communities): In this example, all of the latent positions are different for each node. If it were possible to represent the street example as an $SBM_n(\vec{z}, B)$ random network with $K < n$ communities, a group of nodes with the same latent position vector would need to exist.

Likewise, as discussed earlier, RDPGs only generalize positive semidefinite RDPGs. This means that if we were to have an SBM with any of the indefinite block matrices from Figure 4.5.2, we would not be able to identify a latent position matrix for a corresponding RDPG such that the SBM with an indefinite block matrix and the RDPG have the same probability matrix. For the remainder of this book, when dealing with positive semidefinite matrices, we will abbreviate them as "PSD."

4.6 Properties of Random Networks

We now continue our break from defining new random network models to explore useful properties of random networks, extending the concepts introduced in Chapter 3 in the context of observed networks to random networks.

As we have discussed, unlike observed networks, random networks have nodes and random adjacency matrix entries $\mathbf{a}_{ij}$, which we describe using probability models (such as the $Bernoulli(p_{ij})$ random variable). In Sections 4.1, 4.2, 4.3, and 4.4, we introduced fundamental network models. This section clarifies the statistical properties of networks embodied by these assumptions. We cover:

1. Expected values for random quantities in networks,
2. Random node degree and expected degree,
3. Random network density and expected density, and
4. The population network Laplacian.

Understanding these properties helps with model selection and interpretation for real-world networks. Furthermore, understanding how the properties of networks behave under typical or atypical settings is crucial for developing downstream statistical inference techniques.

4.6.1   Expected Values

The principal result that we will use for this section is the expected value of binary quantities. If $\mathbf{x}$ is a random quantity that has the value 1 with probability p and 0 with probability $1 - p$, remember from Section 4.1.1 that $\mathbf{x}$ is a $Bernoulli(p)$ random variable. This is the equivalent of a coin flip experiment, where a value of heads is recorded as a 1, and a value of tails is recorded as a 0. The coin may or may not be fair, in that the probability that it lands on heads might differ from 0.5.

In this section, the outcome is not yet realized for the random quantity. Instead, we describe properties about the random quantity, which tell us information about how we expect it to behave. The expected value, denoted as $\mathbb{E}[\cdot]$, of a binary (0 or 1)-valued quantity $\mathbf{x}$ is:

$$\mathbb{E}[\mathbf{x}] = 0 Pr(\mathbf{x} = 0) + 1 Pr(\mathbf{x} = 1)$$
$$= Pr(\mathbf{x} = 1). \tag{4.7}$$

This can be informally thought of as the average value that the random quantity takes over infinitely many trials.

So, if a coin lands on heads (a value of 1) with probability 0.75, its expected value is 0.75.

Expected values behave linearly under finite sums. This means that if $\mathbf{x}$ and $\mathbf{y}$ are two random quantities, that:

$$\mathbb{E}[\mathbf{x} + \mathbf{y}] = \mathbb{E}[\mathbf{x}] + \mathbb{E}[\mathbf{y}]. \tag{4.8}$$

So, if $\mathbf{x}$ is a coin flip that lands on heads with probability 0.75 and $\mathbf{y}$ is a flip of a different coin that lands on heads with probability 0.25, the expected value of their sum is 1.0.

Next up is the rescaling property of expected values. If α is a constant (a nonrandom quantity), then:

$$\mathbb{E}[\alpha \mathbf{x}] = \alpha \mathbb{E}[\mathbf{x}]. \tag{4.9}$$

To make this more concrete, let's imagine that $\mathbf{x}$ is a coin flip that lands on heads with probability 0.75, and let's say that we decide to play a game where, if the coin lands on heads, we get \$5, but if it lands on tails we get \$0. Using this rule, we could just multiply the value of the coin flip outcome by 5 (if the coin lands on a 1, or heads, the outcome is 5, and if it lands on a 0, or tails, the outcome is $5 \cdot 0 = 0$). Stated another way, our profit from the game is $5\mathbf{x}$. Then the expected profit is:

$$\mathbb{E}[5\mathbf{x}] = 5\mathbb{E}[\mathbf{x}]$$

$$= 5 \cdot 0.75 = \frac{15}{4},$$

and we are expected to make \$3.75 from this game.

4.6.2   Edge Probabilities as Expected Values

In a random network, the edge $\mathbf{a}_{ij}$ is just a binary random variable, like $\mathbf{x}$.

Furthermore, if $\mathbf{A}$ is a $IER_n(P)$ random network, the probability matrix P has entries p_{ij} for each pair of nodes i and j that describe the probability that $\mathbf{a}_{ij}$ has a value of 1. Remember from Section 4.1.3 that this meant that $\mathbf{a}_{ij}$ was a $Bernoulli(p_{ij})$ random variable.

This means that we can compute the expected value of each adjacency in the network using the formula, as:

$$\mathbb{E}[\mathbf{a}_{ij}] = p_{ij}. \tag{4.10}$$

Crucially, this gives us the insight that the probability matrix can also be thought of as the expected value of the adjacency matrix for a random network:

$$\mathbb{E}[\mathbf{A}] = \begin{bmatrix} \mathbb{E}[\mathbf{a}_{11}] & \cdots & \mathbb{E}[\mathbf{a}_{1n}] \\ \vdots & \ddots & \vdots \\ \mathbb{E}[\mathbf{a}_{n1}] & \cdots & \mathbb{E}[\mathbf{a}_{nn}] \end{bmatrix} = P.$$

4.6.3   Random Node Degree

In Section 3.2.2 we defined the degree of a node i as:

$$d_i = degree(i) = \sum_{j \neq i} a_{ij}.$$

Similarly, we define the *random node degree* for a random network $\mathbf{A}$ as:

$$\mathbf{d}_i = \sum_{j \neq i} \mathbf{a}_{ij}.$$

This quantity is random, in that it is not necessarily any particular value: it takes a number of possible values with a probability. We can use Equation (4.8) to compute the expected degree:

$$\mathbb{E}[\mathbf{d}_i] = \mathbb{E}\left[\sum_{j \neq i} \mathbf{a}_{ij}\right]$$

$$= \sum_{j \neq i} \mathbb{E}[\mathbf{a}_{ij}], \tag{4.11}$$

Let's imagine that there are $n > 3$ nodes in the network, and $i = 1$. This means that:

$$\mathbb{E}[\mathbf{d}_1] = \mathbb{E}\left[\sum_{j \neq 1} \mathbf{a}_{1j}\right] = \mathbb{E}\left[\sum_{j \geq 2} \mathbf{a}_{1j}\right]$$

$$= \mathbb{E}[\mathbf{a}_{12}] + \mathbb{E}\left[\sum_{j \geq 3} \mathbf{a}_{1j}\right],$$

which is a direct application of the result of Equation (4.8). Next, we can write down $\mathbb{E}\left[\sum_{j \geq 3} \mathbf{a}_{1j}\right]$ as a sum of $\mathbb{E}[\mathbf{a}_{13}]$ and $\mathbb{E}\left[\sum_{j \geq 4} \mathbf{a}_{1j}\right]$, and we can continue this pattern all the way up to n to get the result in Equation (4.11).

Finally, remember that $\mathbb{E}[\mathbf{a}_{ij}] = p_{ij}$ by Equation (4.10). So, the *expected node degree* is:

$$\mathbb{E}[\mathbf{d}_i] = \sum_{j \neq i} p_{ij}. \tag{4.12}$$

Exercise 4.6.1 Degree homogeneity in an $SBM_n(\vec{z}, B)$ random network

Take an $SBM_n(\vec{z}, B)$ random network $\mathbf{A}$. Suppose that for n nodes, $n/2$ of the nodes are in community 1, and $n/2$ of the nodes are in community 2. Consider the block matrix:

$$B = \begin{bmatrix} 0.5 & 0.2 \\ 0.2 & 0.3 \end{bmatrix}.$$

1. With $n = 100$, compute the degree of each node in the network.
2. Repeat the above simulation $R = 100$ times, keeping track of your results in a data frame with the columns as the node index i, the community that the node i is in, the simulation replicate r, and the node degree $d_i^{(r)}$.
3. Compute the average degree for each node across all simulations. This should reduce your data frame to node index i, community that the node i is in, and the average node degree over all simulations.
4. Explain what you observe about the average degrees for each node in a particular community (the nodes of the same community have... average node degrees, and nodes in different communities have... average node degrees).
5. Establish an equation for the expected node degree for a node i, for each of the two communities. This should be a function of the entries of the block matrix B, given above. Explain how this supports your answer that you obtained in 4.

4.6.3.1 Random Network Density

The *density of a random network* $\mathbf{A}$ is defined as:

$$density(\mathbf{A}) = \frac{\sum_{j > i} \mathbf{a}_{ij}}{\binom{n}{2}}.$$

As before, this quantity is random, so it does not have any particular value. However, its expected value can be computed using the rules that we described above exactly.

First, notice that if the network has n nodes, $\binom{n}{2}$ is simply a constant. From Equation (4.9), this means that:

$$\mathbb{E}[density(\mathbf{A})] = \mathbb{E}\left[\frac{\sum_{j>i} \mathbf{a}_{ij}}{\binom{n}{2}}\right]$$

$$= \frac{1}{\binom{n}{2}}\mathbb{E}\left[\sum_{j>i} \mathbf{a}_{ij}\right].$$

Next, we can use the linearity argument from Equation (4.8) to obtain:

$$\mathbb{E}[density(\mathbf{A})] = \frac{1}{\binom{n}{2}}\sum_{j>i} \mathbb{E}[\mathbf{a}_{ij}]$$

$$= \frac{1}{\binom{n}{2}}\sum_{j>i} p_{ij}. \tag{4.13}$$

Using Equations (4.12) and (4.13), we can draw the same conclusions that we did in Section 3.2.2:

$$\mathbb{E}[density(\mathbf{A})] = \frac{\sum_{i=1}^{n} \mathbb{E}[\mathbf{d}_i]}{n(n-1)}. \tag{4.14}$$

Finally, from Section 3.2.2, remember that $d = \frac{1}{n}\sum_{i=1}^{n} d_i$ is the average degree of the nodes in a network A.

Likewise, $\mathbf{d} = \frac{1}{n}\sum_{i=1}^{n} \mathbf{d}_i$ is the average degree of nodes in a random network $\mathbf{A}$. Again, since this quantity is random, it can be summarized using expected values. Since n is a fixed number of nodes, then using the rescaling property of Equation (4.9):

$$\mathbb{E}[\mathbf{d}] = \mathbb{E}\left[\frac{1}{n}\sum_{i=1}^{n} \mathbf{d}_i\right]$$

$$= \frac{1}{n}\mathbb{E}\left[\sum_{i=1}^{n} \mathbf{d}_i\right].$$

Finally, using the linearity of sums in Equation (4.8):

$$\mathbb{E}[\mathbf{d}] = \frac{1}{n}\sum_{i=1}^{n} \mathbb{E}[\mathbf{d}_i].$$

Combining this with Equation (4.14):

$$\mathbb{E}[density(\mathbf{A})] = \frac{\mathbb{E}[\mathbf{d}]}{n-1}.$$

In the same way that the density of a network A could be conceptualized as the average degree of each node in the network, the expected density of a random network $\mathbf{A}$ can be conceptualized as the average expected degree of each node in the random network.

4.6.4　Population Network Laplacian

In Section 3.4.4, we defined the DAD Laplacian as a function of the adjacency matrix:

$$L = D^{-\frac{1}{2}} A D^{-\frac{1}{2}}. \tag{4.15}$$

The population network Laplacian $\mathcal{L}$ is to the random network $\mathbf{A}$ what the DAD Laplacian L was to the adjacency matrix A.

The *population network Laplacian* is:

$$\mathcal{L} = \mathcal{D}^{-\frac{1}{2}} P \mathcal{D}^{-\frac{1}{2}}. \tag{4.16}$$

The matrices $\mathcal{D}$ here are what is known as the *expected degree matrix*.

In the case of simple $IER_n(P)$ random networks, this is the diagonal matrix whose diagonal entries are:

$$\mathbb{E}[\mathbf{d}_i] = \sum_{j \neq i} p_{ij}. \tag{4.17}$$

The expected degree matrix looks like this:

$$\mathcal{D} = \begin{bmatrix} \mathbb{E}[d_1] & & \\ & \ddots & \\ & & \mathbb{E}[d_n] \end{bmatrix} = \begin{bmatrix} \sum_{j \neq 1} p_{1j} & & \\ & \ddots & \\ & & \sum_{j \neq n} p_{nj} \end{bmatrix}.$$

$\mathcal{D}$ is a diagonal matrix and is a function of the probability matrix P, like the degree matrix D was a function of the adjacency matrix A.

The diagonal entries of $\mathcal{D}$, $\mathbb{E}[d_i]$, give the expected number of edges for node i.

A natural choice for the inverted square-root matrix of $\mathcal{D}$ would be:

$$\mathcal{D}^{-\frac{1}{2}} = \begin{bmatrix} \frac{1}{\sqrt{\mathbb{E}[d_1]}} & & \\ & \ddots & \\ & & \frac{1}{\sqrt{\mathbb{E}[d_1]}} \end{bmatrix}.$$

Notice that as long as no node has a probability of zero of being connected to any other nodes in the network, each quantity on the diagonal exists and is finite. If any node i had a probability of zero of being connected to all of the other nodes of the network, then $\sum_{j \neq i} p_{ij} = \sum_{j \neq i} 0 = 0$, and hence, $\frac{1}{0} = \infty$. Therefore, for $\mathcal{D}^{-\frac{1}{2}}$ to be defined, then for every node i, at least one other node j must exist where $p_{ij} > 0$. This fact serves as motivation for the degree trimming preprocessing techniques we explored in Section 3.6.1.

With the restriction in mind, all of the entries along the diagonal of $\mathcal{D}$ will be positive. This means that their reciprocals $\frac{1}{\mathbb{E}[d_i]}$ and the square roots of their reciprocals $\frac{1}{\sqrt{\mathbb{E}[d_i]}}$ will also be positive.

We can think of $\mathcal{L}$ as the expected DAD Laplacian for a random network $\mathbf{A}$. It is defined equivalently to L in Equation (4.15), except instead of an observed adjacency matrix A, we are thinking about the expected adjacency matrix (the probability matrix, P) and the expected degree matrix $\mathcal{D}$ for the random network $\mathbf{A}$.

Performing the same multiplication as in Equation (4.15), we see that $\mathcal{L}$ has entries $\ell_{ij} = \frac{p_{ij}}{\sqrt{\mathbb{E}[d_i]}\sqrt{\mathbb{E}[d_j]}}$. Therefore, the interpretation of the (i, j)th entry of the population network Laplacian are that it is the probability p_{ij}, but normalized by the square root of the corresponding expected degrees of the incident nodes i and j.

4.7 Degree-Corrected Stochastic Block Models

We now return to building new statistical machinery. In Section 4.3, we introduced the SBM in order to model networks with simple community structure. However, the SBM is limited: Subnetworks of an SBM corresponding to communities are simply Erdös–Rényi random networks, with no way to distinguish between nodes. The Degree-Corrected Stochastic Block Model (DCSBM) addresses these limitations by augmenting the SBM with the flexibility to model networks with varying node degrees within communities, called node degree heterogeneity.

We cover:

1. Motivation and definition of the DCSBM,
2. Degree-correction vectors and their interpretation,
3. Simulating samples from DCSBM random networks,
4. Probability matrices for DCSBMs, and
5. The relationship between DCSBMs, SBMs, and RDPGs.

We should use the DCSBM as it provides us with more flexibility for modeling networks with varying node degrees within communities, in exchange for a slightly more complicated model.

Let's return to the school example that we covered in Section 4.3. There are 100 students, who each attend one of two schools. The edges of the network represent whether a pair of students are friends. If two students attend the same school, they have a higher chance of being friends than if they attend different schools.

In many real-world networks, using an SBM to model this network would work effectively. It captures "community structure" in a very succinct way. However, the SBM has a weakness. Within a given community, we have no way to represent fundamental differences between nodes. If node i and node j are both in the same community, they will have have the same expected node degree on average.

This means that, on average, students in the same school will all have the same number of friends. This is referred to as *degree homogeneity*: The expected degrees are the same for all nodes in the same community. This model often fails to capture complexity in the real world, where nodes often have different degrees and some are more "important" than others. Let's define this more formally.

4.7.1 Degree Homogeneity of the SBM

Let's imagine that $\mathbf{A}$ is an $SBM_n(\vec{z}, B)$ random network with two communities, and the node i is in community 1, so $z_i = 1$. The expected node degree from Section 4.6.3 for a node i in community 1 can be written:

$$\mathbb{E}[\mathbf{d}_i; z_i = 1] = \sum_{j \neq i} \mathbb{E}[\mathbf{a}_{ij}; z_i = 1] = \sum_{j \neq i} p_{ij}.$$

The semicolon means that we are calculating the expected degree for a node where $z_i = 1$. For the stochastic block model, this relationship is simple. If node i is in community 1, this sum can be split into:

$$\mathbb{E}[\mathbf{d}_i; z_i = 1] = \sum_{j:z_j=2} p_{ij} + \sum_{j:z_j=1 \text{ and } j \neq i} p_{ij}.$$

So we have split this into a sum over the nodes in community 2 (where $z_j = 2$) and the nodes that are not node i but are also in community 1. For nodes in community 2, $p_{ij} = b_{12}$. For nodes in community 1, $p_{ij} = b_{11}$. Finally, we will let n_k be a simple "counter" of the number of nodes in community k. Putting these facts together, we obtain:

$$\mathbb{E}[\mathbf{d}_i; z_i = 1] = n_2 b_{12} + (n_1 - 1) b_{11}.$$

Nothing in the result here depends on the node i, other than its community assignment z_i. When the random network $\mathbf{A}$ is an $SBM_n(\vec{z}, B)$ with K communities, we obtain a more general result, found in Concept 4.7.2.

Together, this means that for an $SBM_n(\vec{z}, B)$ random network with K communities, the nodes all have the same expected degree if they are in the same community. This is known as the *degree-homogeneity within-community* of the stochastic block model: All nodes in the same community have the same expected node degree. This was also the conclusion of Exercise 4.6.1.

The degree-corrected stochastic block model (DCSBM) corrects this limitation by incorporating a degree-correction vector, allowing us to convey the idea of "node importance": Some students may have more friends than others, beyond differences in school placement.

4.7.2   The Degree-Correction Vector

The first two parameters of the DCSBM are the same as the SBM, in that we have a community assignment vector and a block matrix.

The degree heterogeneity is conveyed via the *degree-correction vector* $\vec{\theta}$, which has n elements (one for each node). For each node i, the degree-correction factor θ_i "degree-corrects" the node i, by either "amplifying" its expected node degree when $\theta_i > 1$ (meaning, on average, node i will have more edges than it would if it were a node in an $SBM_n(\vec{z}, B)$), or "reducing" its expected node degree when $\theta_i < 1$ (meaning, on average, node i will have fewer edges than it would if it were a node in an $SBM_n(\vec{z}, B)$). Degree correction factors are always ≥ 0, so cannot have a negative degree-correction factor.

4.7.3   Conceptualizing the DCSBM

The DCSBM random network has adjacency matrix entries $\mathbf{a}_{ij}$, each of which is $Bernoulli(\theta_i \theta_j b_{z_i z_j})$, where z_i and z_j are the community assignments for the ith and jth node, and θ_i and θ_j the degree-correction factors for the ith and jth nodes. The probability that an edge exists between nodes i and j is given by the block matrix entry $\theta_i\theta_j b_{z_i z_j}$. Therefore, the entries $\mathbf{a}_{ij}$ in the random network depends on both the block matrix B and the communities z_i and z_j, and are altered by the degree-correction factors θ_i and θ_j. As before, every value in $\mathbf{A}$ is independent. With n nodes, the community vector $\vec{z}$, the degree-correction vector $\vec{\theta}$, and the block matrix B, we say that $\mathbf{A}$ is a $DCSBM_n(\vec{z}, \vec{\theta}, B)$ random network.

4.7.4   Probability Matrix for DCSBM Random Networks

In Section 4.7.2 that the DCSBM can be easily tied to the IER random networks from Section 4.1. Notice that above, we can take the probability $p_{ij} = \theta_i\theta_j b_{z_i z_j}$. This relationship demonstrates that there is a *slight* condition on the vector $\vec{\theta}$ in order to ensure that we create a valid random network model. For all pairs of nodes i and j, applying the degree-correction vector must result in values between 0 and 1, ensuring that it is a probability. We discuss methods to ensure this in Concept 4.7.1. We will assume that each θ_i is a value between 0 and 1, and therefore, the product of $\theta_i\theta_j$ and a probability $b_{z_i z_j}$ will also be between 0 and 1.

Concept 4.7.1 When is a degree-correction vector $\vec{\theta}$ valid?

Not every choice of a degree-correction vector is valid: The probability matrix $P = \Theta C B C^\top \Theta^\top$ must have entries between 0 and 1.

If we are using $DCSBM_n(\vec{z}, \vec{\theta}, B)$ for simulation, we can choose $\vec{\theta}$ such that the maximum value is 1, and then adjust B accordingly. The product of a degree-correction factor between 0 and 1 and a block probability also between 0 and 1 will always be a probability (between 0 and 1), so we are guaranteed to produce degree-correction factors generating valid probability matrices.

We can also select $\vec{\theta}$ such that for every community, all of the degree-correction factors within that community sum to 1 [10; 11]. This means that the entries θ_i will be strictly less than 1 if there are at least two nodes in a single community. The block matrix can then be adjusted such that it is no longer a probability matrix (taking values exceeding 0 or 1), so long as we can still end up with a valid probability matrix using $P = \Theta C B C^\top \Theta^\top$.

We prefer the first method for the purposes of this book, simply because it is easier to work with. When doing proofs with $DCSBM_n(\vec{z}, \vec{\theta}, B)$ random networks, the second method is often useful.

To determine stochastic equivalences, we need an efficient procedure to produce probability matrices. We can develop a method for generating P similar to the one for SBMs in Section 4.3.6, then verify that all entries of P are between 0 and 1. Matrix multiplications can accomplish this task.

We first define the $n \times n$ degree-correction matrix Θ, a diagonal matrix containing the degree-correction factors. We use the uppercase θ, since Θ is a matrix:

$$\Theta = \begin{bmatrix} \theta_1 & 0 & \cdots & 0 \\ 0 & \theta_2 & \ddots & \vdots \\ \vdots & \ddots & \ddots & 0 \\ 0 & \cdots & 0 & \theta_n \end{bmatrix}. \tag{4.18}$$

We recall from 4.3.6 that for an $SBM_n(\vec{z}, B)$ random network $\mathbf{A}'$, we can write the probability matrix as $P' = CBC^\top$, where C is the one-hot encoded community assignment matrix, and P' has entries $p'_{ij} = b_{z_i z_j}$:

$$P' = \begin{bmatrix} b_{z_1 z_1} & \cdots & b_{z_1 z_n} \\ \vdots & \ddots & \vdots \\ b_{z_n z_1} & \cdots & b_{z_n z_n} \end{bmatrix}.$$

Our goal is to "augment" P' by multiplying each row i of P' by the corresponding degree-correction factor θ_i, and each column j of P' by the corresponding degree-correction factor θ_j. This yields $\theta_i \theta_j b_{z_i z_j}$, which is our desired result.

Premultiplying by Θ yields:

$$\Theta P' = \begin{bmatrix} \theta_1 b_{z_1 z_1} & \cdots & \theta_1 b_{z_1 z_n} \\ \vdots & \ddots & \vdots \\ \theta_n b_{z_n z_1} & \cdots & \theta_n b_{z_n z_n} \end{bmatrix}.$$

Premultiplication by the diagonal matrix Θ has resulted in each row i of P' being multiplied by the degree-correction factor of the corresponding entry θ_i.

Similarly, postmultiplying by $\Theta^\top$ yields:

$$\Theta P' \Theta^\top = \begin{bmatrix} \theta_1^2 b_{z_1 z_1} & \cdots & \theta_1 \theta_n b_{z_1 z_n} \\ \vdots & \ddots & \vdots \\ \theta_n \theta_1 b_{z_n z_1} & \cdots & \theta_n^2 b_{z_n z_n} \end{bmatrix}.$$

Postmultiplication by the diagonal matrix Θ has resulted in each column j of P' being multiplied by the degree-correction factor of the corresponding entry θ_j.

This means that:

$$p_{ij} = \left(\Theta P' \Theta^\top \right)_{ij} = \theta_i \theta_j b_{z_i z_j}.$$

The entries of this matrix are exactly the probability of an edge existing in a $DCSBM_n(\vec{z}, \vec{\theta}, B)$ random network. The degree-correction factor $\vec{\theta}$ thus "inflates" or "deflates" the block probabilities of an $SBM_n(\vec{z}, B)$ based on each node's popularity θ_i or θ_j, relative other nodes in the same community.

Algorithm 4.6 can be used to generate a probability matrix for a $DCSBM_n(\vec{z}, \vec{\theta}, B)$ network. First, we generate a probability matrix for an $SBM_n(\vec{z}, B)$ random network as the "uncorrected probability matrix." We then apply the degree-correction by premultiplying and postmultiplying by Θ and $\Theta^\top$.

Algorithm 4.6 Generating a probability matrix for a $DCSBM_n(\vec{z}, \vec{\theta}, B)$

Data: n a number of nodes

$\vec{z}$ a community assignment vector of each node to one of K communities

$\vec{\theta}$ a degree-correction factor

B a block matrix with K rows and K columns

Result: A probability matrix for a $DCSBM_n(\vec{z}, \vec{\theta}, B)$.

1 Let $P' = CBC^\top$, as per Algorithm 4.4, where C is the one-hot encoding of $\vec{z}$.

2 Let Θ be the degree-correction matrix, defined as per Equation (4.18).

3 Let $P = \Theta P' \vec{\Theta}^\top$.

4 **return** P

4.7.5 Simulating Samples of $DCSBM_n(\vec{z}, \vec{\theta}, B)$ Random Networks

While `graspologic` and `networkx` do not have utilities built-in to simulate samples of a DCSBM directly, we can build our own tools. Algorithm 4.7 produces a network A, where the underlying random network $\mathbf{A}$ is a DCSBM random network.

Algorithm 4.7 Simulating a sample from a $DCSBM_n(\vec{z}, \vec{\theta}, B)$ random network

---

Data: n a number of nodes

$\vec{z}$ a community assignment vector of each of the n nodes to K communities

$\vec{\theta}$ a valid degree-correction vector for each of the n nodes

B a block matrix with K rows and K columns

Result: The adjacency matrix of a sample from the random network.

1 Define $P = \Theta CBC^\top \Theta^\top$ as per Algorithm 4.6.

2 Generate a sample A from an $IER_n(P)$ network, using Algorithm 4.1.

3 **return** A

Taking the students example from Section 4.3, we order students by their popularity using a degree-correction vector that declines from 1 to 0.5 in both the first and second community. Using the `generate_sbm_pmtx()` utility from Section 4.3.6, we use the logic developed in Algorithm 4.6 to augment the probability matrix with the degree-correction factor. We then write a function that generates samples from DCSBM random networks using the `sample_edges()` utility from `graspologic`:

```
import numpy as np
from graspologic.simulations import sample_edges
from graphbook_code import heatmap, plot_vector, \
    generate_sbm_pmtx

def dcsbm(z, theta, B, directed=False, loops=False, return_prob=False):
    """
    A function to sample a DCSBM.
    """
    # uncorrected probability matrix
```

```
Pp = generate_sbm_pmtx(z, B)
theta = theta.reshape(-1)
# apply the degree correction
Theta = np.diag(theta)
P = Theta @ Pp @ Theta.transpose()
network = sample_edges(P, directed=directed, loops=loops)
if return_prob:
    network = (network, P)
return network
```

Next, we can use this function to generate and plot samples of our DCSBM random network:

```
# Observe a network from a DCSBM
nk = 50 # students per school
z = np.repeat([1, 2], 50)
B = np.array([[0.6, 0.2], [0.2, 0.4]]) # same probabilities as from
    SBM section
theta = np.tile(np.linspace(1, 0.5, nk), 2)
A, P = dcsbm(z, theta, B, return_prob=True)

# Visualize
plot_vector(z, title="$\\vec z$", legend_title="School",
    color="qualitative",
        ticks=[0.5, 49.5, 99.5], ticklabels=[1, 50, 100],
        ticktitle="Student")
plot_vector(theta, title="$\\vec \\theta$",
        legend_title="Degree-Correction Factor",
        ticks=[0.5, 49.5, 99.5], ticklabels=[1, 50, 100],
        ticktitle="Student")
heatmap(P, title="$P = \\Theta C B C^\\top \\Theta^\\top$", vmin=0,
    vmax=1)
heatmap(A.astype(int), title="Sample of $DCSBM_n(\\vec z, \\vec
    \\theta, B)$")
```

Figure 4.7.1 visualizes the parameters for our sampled $DCSBM_n(\vec{z}, \vec{\theta}, B)$ random network. Note that the degree-correction factors in Figure 4.7.1(B) are higher for the first nodes in each community. This is reflected in the probability matrix in Figure 4.7.1(D), where the probabilities are highest in the upper left corners of each diagonal block, as these edges are between nodes with high degree-correction factors. In this sense, edges between pairs of nodes with high degree-correction factors will tend to exist more often than edges between pairs of nodes with lower degree-correction factors.

4.7.6   Why Is it Called a Degree-Corrected Stochastic Block Model?

To illustrate why this model is known as a "degree-corrected" SBM, we can use the two-community SBM example from Section 4.7.1.

Working through the first step to compute the expected degree of a node i for a $DCSBM_n(\vec{z}, \vec{\theta}, B)$ random network, we get:

$$\mathbb{E}[\mathbf{d}_i; z_i = 1] = \sum_{j \neq i} \mathbb{E}[\mathbf{a}_{ij}] = \sum_{j \neq i} \theta_i \theta_j b_{z_i z_j}.$$

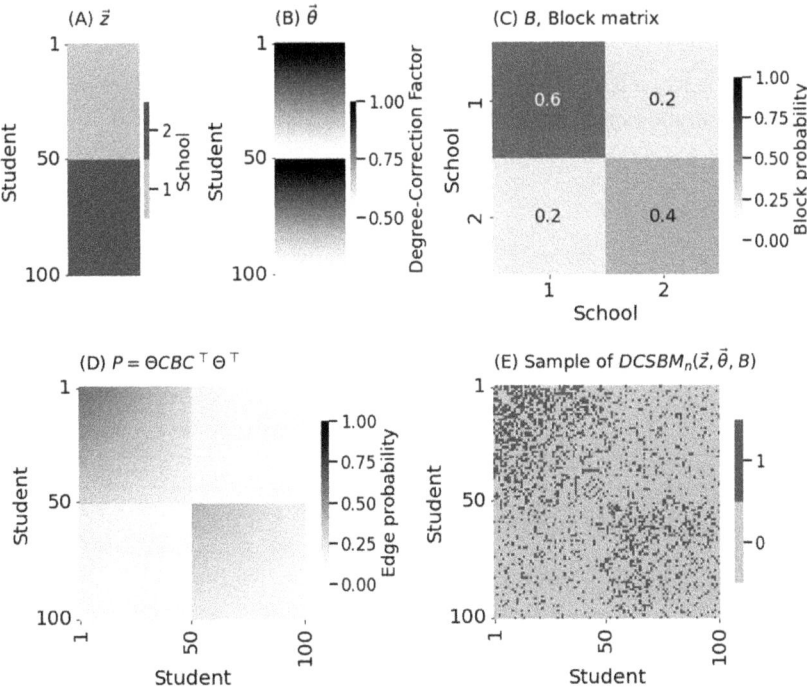

Figure 4.7.1 **(A)** The community assignment vector, **(B)** the degree-correction vector, and **(C)** the block probability matrix. **(D)** The probability matrix, calculated from the community assignment vector, the degree-correction vector, and the degree-correction factor. **(E)** A sample from a $DCSBM_n(\vec{z}, \vec{\theta}, B)$ random network, using the probability matrix from **(D)** coupled with an $IER_n(P)$ network sampler from `graspologic`.

Using a similar derivation as in Section 4.7.1, we obtain:

$$\mathbb{E}[\mathbf{d}_i; z_i = 1] = \theta_i \left(b_{12} \sum_{j:z_j=2} \theta_j + b_{11} \sum_{j:z_j=1 \text{ and } j \neq i} \theta_j \right).$$

The expected degree of the node i is thus "degree-corrected" by its degree-correction factor θ_i. For an arbitrary $DCSBM_n(\vec{z}, \vec{\theta}, B)$ random network with K communities, the expected node degree for a node in an arbitrary community k is shown in Concept 4.7.2.

The degree-correction factor θ_i therefore "corrects" the expected degree of the node i. That is, when θ_i is smaller (relative to the degree-correction factors of other nodes in the same community z_i as node i), the expected node degree is smaller. Similarly, when θ_i is larger, the expected node degree is larger.

The $DCSBM_n(\vec{z}, \vec{\theta}, B)$ random networks therefore allow us to incorporate our notion of node importance. Less important nodes can be equipped with smaller degree-correction factors, and will tend to have lower degrees. Conversely, more important nodes can be equipped with larger degree-correction factors, and will tend to have higher degrees.

Concept 4.7.2 The expected node degree for block models

If $\mathbf{A}$ is a $SBM_n(\vec{z}, B)$ random network with n nodes and K communities, then the expected degree of a node i in community k is:

$$\mathbb{E}[\mathbf{d}_i; z_i = k] = \sum_{l \neq k} n_l b_{lk} + (n_k - 1) b_{kk}.$$

If $\mathbf{A}$ is a $DCSBM_n(\vec{z}, \vec{\theta}, B)$ random network with n nodes and K communities, then the expected degree of a node i in community k is:

$$\mathbb{E}[\mathbf{d}_i; z_i = k] = \theta_i \left(\sum_{l \neq k} \left[b_{lk} \sum_{j:z_j=l} \theta_j \right] + b_{kk} \sum_{j:z_j=k \text{ and } j \neq i} \theta_j \right).$$

4.7.7   Generalization and DCSBMs

Take an $SBM_n(\vec{z}, B)$ random network $\mathbf{A}^{(1)}$. To illustrate that the DCSBMs generalize the SBMs, we need to find a DCSBM equivalent to this SBM for any choice of $\vec{z}$ and B. In other words, we seek a random network $\mathbf{A}^{(2)}$ with corresponding community-assignment vector $\vec{z}'$, degree-correction vector $\vec{\theta}'$, and a block matrix B' where $P^{(1)} = P^{(2)}$; that is, $\mathbf{A}^{(1)}$ and $\mathbf{A}^{(2)}$ are stochastically equivalent, by Concept 4.2.1.

Because $\mathbf{A}^{(1)}$ is an SBM, we can use the procedure of Section 4.3.6:

$$P^{(1)} = CBC^{\top},$$

where C is the one-hot encoding matrix of the community assignment vector $\vec{z}$. We can also write this as:

$$P^{(1)} = I_{n \times n} CBC^{\top} I_{n \times n}^{\top}, \qquad (4.19)$$

where $I_{n \times n}$ is the $n \times n$ identity matrix.

If we choose the community assignment vector and block matrix of $\mathbf{A}^{(2)}$ to be equal to those of $\mathbf{A}^{(1)}$, then:

$$P^{(2)} = \Theta' CBC^{\top} \Theta'^{\top}. \qquad (4.20)$$

This is because the one-hot encoding matrix and the block matrix of $\mathbf{A}^{(2)}$ are the same as for $\mathbf{A}^{(1)}$. Equation (4.19) and Equation (4.20) are almost the same, and would be identical if $\Theta' = I_{n \times n}$. This occurs when the degree-correction vector $\vec{\theta}' = 1_n$; that is, when the degree-correction factors are just 1 for all of the nodes in the network.

Therefore, choosing $\vec{\theta}' = 1_n$ gives us $P^{(1)} = P^{(2)}$, so $\mathbf{A}^{(1)}$ and $\mathbf{A}^{(2)}$ are stochastically equivalent. Our choices did not depend on the specific community assignment vector $\vec{z}$ nor the block matrix B of $\mathbf{A}^{(1)}$.

Therefore, for any SBM, we can always find a stochastically equivalent DCSBM by choosing the same community assignment vector and block matrix, and degree-correction factors of 1. Therefore, the DCSBMs generalize the SBMs, and conversely, the SBMs are contained in the DCSBMs.

Since SBMs generalize ER random networks, we can conclude by transitivity that the DCSBMs also generalize the ER random networks.

RDPGs Generalize PSD DCSBM Random Networks
From Algorithm 4.6, the probability matrix for a $DCSBM_n(\vec{z}, \vec{\theta}, B)$ random network $\mathbf{A}^{(1)}$ is $P^{(1)} = \Theta P' \Theta^\top$, where P' is the uncorrected probability matrix for an $SBM_n(\vec{z}, B)$ random network. With $P' = CBC^\top$:

$$P^{(1)} = \Theta CBC^\top \Theta^\top.$$

In Section 4.5.1, we concluded that we could produce a latent position matrix X for any positive semidefinite probability matrix. As it turns out, the condition for the probability matrix P of a $DCSBM_n(\vec{z}, \vec{\theta}, B)$ random network to be positive semidefinite is identical to that of an $SBM_n(\vec{z}, B)$ random network: The block matrix B must be positive semidefinite.

If the block matrix B is positive semidefinite, it has a matrix $\sqrt{B}$ where $B = \sqrt{B}\sqrt{B}^\top$, so the probability matrix for $\mathbf{A}^{(1)}$ can be written:

$$P^{(1)} = \Theta C \sqrt{B} \sqrt{B}^\top C^\top \Theta^\top$$
$$= \Theta C \sqrt{B} \left(\Theta C \sqrt{B}\right)^\top,$$

using rules for the transpose of a product of matrices.

If $X = \Theta C \sqrt{B}$ were a latent position matrix for some $RDPG_n(X)$ random network $\mathbf{A}^{(2)}$, then:

$$P^{(2)} = XX^\top = \Theta C \sqrt{B} \left(\Theta C \sqrt{B}\right)^\top$$
$$= \Theta C \sqrt{B} \sqrt{B}^\top C^\top \Theta^\top$$
$$= \Theta CBC^\top \Theta^\top = P^{(1)},$$

where we used the fact that $\sqrt{B}\sqrt{B}^\top = B$ when B is PSD. So $P^{(1)}$ and $P^{(2)}$ are equal, and therefore $\mathbf{A}^{(1)}$ and $\mathbf{A}^{(2)}$ are stochastically equivalent.

We can conclude that the RDPG random networks generalize the DCSBM random networks whenever the block matrix of the DCSBM is positive semidefinite.

We can design a utility for generating latent position matrices for DCSBM random networks with positive semidefinite block matrices:

```
from graphbook_code import lpm_from_sbm

def lpm_from_dcsbm(z, theta, B):
    """
    A function to produce a latent position matrix from a
    community assignment vector, a degree-correction
        vector,
    and a block matrix.
    """
```

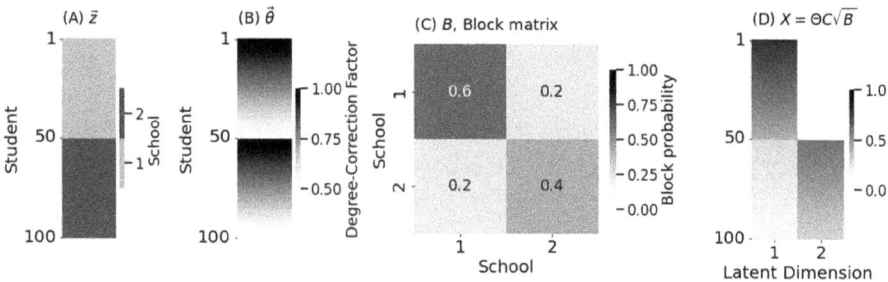

Figure 4.7.2 **(A)** The community assignment vector. **(B)** The degree-correction vector. **(C)** A homophilic block matrix, which is positive semidefinite. This block matrix is the same example shown in Figure 4.5.1(A). **(D)** The latent positions for an equivalent RDPG.

```
# X' = C*sqrt(B)
Xp = lpm_from_sbm(z, B)
# X = Theta*X' = Theta * C * sqrt(B)
return np.diag(theta) @ Xp

# make a degree-correction vector
theta = np.tile(np.linspace(1, 0.5, 50), 2)
X_dcsbm = lpm_from_dcsbm(z, theta, B)
```

Figure 4.7.2 shows the resulting latent position matrix, along with the community assignment vector, the degree-correction vector, and the block matrix. Nodes with the same community have similar latent positions, but have large magnitudes for the first few nodes in each community, and smaller magnitudes for the last few nodes in each community.

4.7.8   Nodes in the Same Community Have the Same Latent Position (Up to a Rescaling)

Section 4.5.9 showed that if $\mathbf{A}$ is an $SBM_n(\vec{z}, B)$ random network, we identify a stochastically equivalent $RDPG_n(X)$ random network by letting $X = C\sqrt{B}$. For a given node i, we found that the latent position was $\vec{x}_i = \sqrt{B}^\top \vec{c}_i$, where $\vec{c}_i$ was the one-hot encoding for the community of node i, z_i. This has the implication that latent positions for nodes in the same community are the same (since they have the same one-hot encoding, and $\sqrt{B}$ is fixed).

We learned in Section 4.7.7 that the latent position matrix for a $DCSBM_n(\vec{z}, \vec{\theta}, B)$, with a positive semidefinite block matrix (and hence probability matrix), was:

$$X = \Theta C \sqrt{B}.$$

This can be interpreted similarly to the result we obtained for the $SBM_n(\vec{z}, B)$ random networks.

The result from Equation (4.6) gives:

$$
\begin{bmatrix} \vdash & \vec{x}_1^\top & \dashv \\ & \vdots & \\ \vdash & \vec{x}_n^\top & \dashv \end{bmatrix}
=
\begin{bmatrix} \vdash & \vec{c}_1^\top \sqrt{B} & \dashv \\ & \vdots & \\ \vdash & \vec{c}_n^\top \sqrt{B} & \dashv \end{bmatrix},
$$

for an $SBM_n(\vec{z}, B)$ random network, where $\vec{c}_i$ is the one-hot encoding of the community for the ith node. In the $DCSBM_n(\vec{z}, \vec{\theta}, B)$ random network, using $X = \Theta C \sqrt{B}$, we instead obtain:

$$
\begin{bmatrix} \vdash & \vec{x}_1^\top & \dashv \\ & \vdots & \\ \vdash & \vec{x}_n^\top & \dashv \end{bmatrix}
=
\begin{bmatrix} \theta_1 & & \\ & \ddots & \\ & & \theta_n \end{bmatrix}
\begin{bmatrix} \vdash & \vec{c}_1^\top \sqrt{B} & \dashv \\ & \vdots & \\ \vdash & \vec{c}_n^\top \sqrt{B} & \dashv \end{bmatrix}.
$$

Multiplying by the diagonal matrix Θ:

$$
\begin{bmatrix} \vdash & \vec{x}_1^\top & \dashv \\ & \vdots & \\ \vdash & \vec{x}_n^\top & \dashv \end{bmatrix}
=
\begin{bmatrix} \vdash & \theta_1 \vec{c}_1^\top \sqrt{B} & \dashv \\ & \vdots & \\ \vdash & \theta_n \vec{c}_n^\top \sqrt{B} & \dashv \end{bmatrix}.
$$

Looking at each row, we obtain $\vec{x}_i^\top = \theta_i \vec{c}_i^\top \sqrt{B}$. Since θ_i is just a scalar, we can apply the transpose to find:

$$
\vec{x}_i = \theta_i \sqrt{B}^\top \vec{c}_i.
$$

Section 4.5.9 showed that if nodes i and j had the same community assignments and $z_i = z_j$, then $\vec{c}_i = \vec{c}_j$, since they will also have the same one-hot encodings. Therefore, if j is another node where $z_i = z_j$, it follows that:

$$
\vec{x}_j = \theta_j \sqrt{B}^\top \vec{c}_j
$$
$$
= \theta_j \sqrt{B}^\top \vec{c}_i,
$$

since $\vec{c}_i = \vec{c}_j$. Notice that since $\vec{x}_i = \theta_i \sqrt{B}^\top \vec{c}_i$, that $\sqrt{B}^\top \vec{c}_i = \frac{1}{\theta_i} \vec{x}_i$. Using this fact, we obtain that:

$$
\vec{x}_j = \frac{\theta_j}{\theta_i} \vec{x}_i.
$$

This illustrates that if a pair of nodes i and j are in the same communities, their latent positions will be almost equal. In particular, they will be constant multiples of one another. These constant multiples are given by the ratio of their respective degree-correction factors, $\frac{\theta_j}{\theta_i}$. Further, if nodes i and j from the same community have the same degree-correction factor, so that $\theta_i = \theta_j$, this argument shows that $\vec{x}_j = \vec{x}_i$.

Figure 4.7.2(D) illustrates the latent positions for a DCSBM with a PSD block matrix. The rows of the latent position matrix, the latent positions for each node, follow the same pattern of the degree-correction vector in Figure 4.7.2(B), though for nodes with higher degree-correction factors, the magnitudes are greater. This is because the degree-correction vector is rescaling the latent positions between nodes in the same community.

This shows us that some $RDPG_n(X)$ random networks cannot be represented as $DCSBM_n(\vec{z}, \theta, B)$ random networks with $K < n$. We can see this from the street example: There is no choice of degree-correction factors $\vec{\theta}$ which would allow us to rescale the latent position associated with a community and obtain the latent positions. The values of the latent dimensions from Figure 4.4.1 for the street example have a pattern of taking opposites: As the value in latent dimension one increases, the value in latent dimension two decreases, and vice versa (where all values of the latent position matrix were positive). Accounting for this with a degree-correction factor would require at least that the pattern is the same; both would have to be simultaneously increasing or decreasing owing to the fact that the latent position matrix has only positive entries. Likewise, owing to the same reasoning as with SBMs, RDPGs do not generalize DCSBMs with indefinite block probability matrices.

There are two takeaways:

1. When the underlying random network is an $SBM_n(\vec{z}, B)$ and the block matrix is PSD, all nodes within the same community have the same latent position vector.
2. When the underlying random network is a $DCSBM_n(\vec{z}, \vec{\theta}, B)$ and the block matrix is PSD, all nodes within the same community have the same latent position vector up to a rescaling by their degree-correction factor. If the nodes are in the same community and the degree-correction factor is the same, the nodes have the same latent position.

These findings can be summarized succinctly: As long as the block matrix of a block model is positive semidefinite, we can find a stochastically equivalent latent position matrix for an RDPG. Therefore, any procedure that can be used on RDPGs can also be applied to block models with positive semidefinite block matrices. We suggest revisiting Concept 4.4.1 in this light to appreciate its importance.

4.7.9   Exercises

Section 4.5 gives intuition on which block matrices are positive semidefinite in simple 2×2 cases. To solidify these concepts, we would recommend going through the exercises in Exercise 4.7.3 and Exercise 4.7.4.

4.8   Structured Independent-Edge Random Networks

In Sections 4.3, 4.4, and 4.7, the behaviors of the random network were directly tied to properties of the nodes (*node attributes*), such as communities, degree corrections, and latent positions. However, networks can also be defined using properties of the edges, known as *edge attributes*. To this end, we introduce the structured independent-edge model (SIEM), which creates edge probability structure. We cover:

1. Definition and components of the SIEM,
2. cluster assignment matrices and probability vectors,
3. Simulating samples from SIEM random networks,

Exercise 4.7.3 Core–periphery SBM and planted partition DCSBM equivalence

Imagine that we have a $DCSBM_n(\vec{z}, \vec{\theta}, B)$ with a planted partition block matrix B, with degree-correction vector $\vec{\theta}$ containing two unique values u and v. These unique values are chosen such that whenever $z_i = 1$, $\theta_i = u$, and whenever $z_i = 2$, $\theta_i = v$.

1. Generate a visualization of the probability matrix.
2. Use this visualization to show that there exists a core–periphery block matrix B' where $SBM_n(\vec{z}, B')$ and $DCSBM_n(\vec{z}, \vec{\theta}, B)$ have the same probability matrix.
3. Find a function of u,v, and B such that $B' = f(u, v, B)$.

Conclude that planted partition DCSBMs with the degree-correction vector having one unique value for each community are equivalent to core–periphery SBMs with a suitably chosen block matrix.

Exercise 4.7.4 Degree-correction factors "stretch" latent positions

Take a positive semidefinite block matrix B associated with a 2-community $SBM_n(\vec{z}, B)$ random network (for instance, a homophilic block matrix, with n taken to be any number of nodes). Compute the latent position matrix for the $SBM_n(\vec{z}, B)$ random network. This results in an $n \times 2$-dimensional latent position matrix.

Next, take a range of values for $\vec{\theta}$ (you can pick these however you like). Compute a latent position matrix for the corresponding $DCSBM_n(\vec{z}, \vec{\theta}, B)$ random network.

1. Take the latent position associated with community 1 from the SBM. Plot it as a point.
2. Overlay the latent positions associated with community 1 in the corresponding DCSBM in a different color.
3. Conclude that θ is "stretching" the latent positions of the corresponding SBM in a straight line.
4. Repeat for the latent position $\vec{y}$ associated with community 2.

Conclude that degree-correction factors for $DCSBM_n(\vec{z}, \vec{\theta}, B)$ random networks "stretch" the latent positions of $SBM_n(\vec{z}, B)$ random networks along a straight line, depending on the value of θ.

---

4. Relationship between SIEM and other network models, and
5. Applications and use cases for SIEM.

The SIEM can be used whenever we direct our focus on the relationships between objects, rather than the objects themselves. We later use this model in Section 6.3, where we build hypothesis tests to investigate differences in edges.

We now cover a statistical model for networks that generalizes the SBM from Section 4.3 a little differently than the IER network from Section 4.1. We will use the brain network from Section 4.2. Suppose $n = 100$ nodes are located in different areas of the brain, where each node is either on the left or right side (hemisphere). An edge exists if the two areas of the brain tend to be active together while a person interacts with the world. In general, nodes tend to be more active with other nodes from the same hemisphere. However, even though the left and right sides of the brain tend to have different functions, their nodes might still be active together, especially in the same region on both sides.

For instance, even though the motor cortex in the left hemisphere has a slightly different function than the motor cortex in the right hemisphere, the two hemispheres tend to activate concurrently. The right motor cortex provides movement for the left side of the body, and the left motor cortex provides movement for the right side of the body. When someone is moving around, many tasks will require them to use both sides of the body. This pattern, known as *bilateral homotopy*, also applies to many other areas in the brain. We ask: Do bilateral node pairs have higher connectivity than nonbilateral node pairs?

To answer this question, we need statistical models that capture what we understand about the system. Perhaps it is more likely that there will be edges between bilaterally symmetric node pairs. Based on what we know so far, we could achieve this property with an $IER_n(P)$ random network: Allow every pair of nodes in the network to have their own edge probability.

It is difficult to describe this system. On the one hand, we would like a simpler model than ascribing probabilities to every possible network configuration of an n-node simple network (of which there are $2^{\binom{n}{2}}$, as per Remark 4.1.3). On the other hand, this model still has $\binom{n}{2}$ parameters (the entries of the probability matrix P), one for each edge in the network, and this cannot be simplified further. This is dissimilar from the preceding models in this chapter, where we used objects like block matrices and latent position matrices to summarize P more succinctly. This is, in a sense, still equivalent to the coin flipping problem from Remark 4.1.3: To learn about a probability p_{ij}, we have only one edge a_{ij}. Learning about p_{ij} from a single edge a_{ij} is as impossible as trying to learn about the probability that a coin lands on heads from the outcome of a single coin toss.

In many cases, our data may only provide one network. Borrowing from previous techniques, we can "simplify" the network by using groupings of the edges, much like we did with the nodes of the network for SBMs.

4.8.1   The Structured Independent-Edge Model

The structured independent-edge model (SIEM) is parameterized by a cluster assignment matrix and a probability vector.

The Cluster Assignment Matrix
The $n \times n$ cluster assignment matrix Z assigns potential edges in the random network to clusters.

The $n \times n$ adjacency matrix $\mathbf{A}$ for a random network has entries $\mathbf{a}_{ij}$. The cluster assignment matrix takes each of these n^2 random variables, and uses a parameter z_{ij}

to indicate which of K possible clusters this edge is part of. In the brain example, for instance, we could take $z_{ij} = 1$ when the nodes i and j are bilateral pairs, and $z_{ij} = 2$ when the nodes i and j are not bilateral pairs. For simple networks, we'll also add the restriction that $z_{ij} = z_{ji}$ for all node pairs i and j. Since the networks are loopless, it doesn't matter what we do for the diagonal entries. We will typically arbitrarily set them to their own cluster 0 or **NA**.

The Probability Vector

The second parameter for the SIEM is a probability vector, $\vec{p}$. If there are K edge clusters in the SIEM, then $\vec{p}$ is a length-K vector. Each entry p_l indicates the probablity of an edge in the lth cluster existing in the network. For example, p_1 indicates the probability of an edge in the first edge cluster, p_2 indicates the probability of an edge in the second edge cluster, and so on. In the brain example, for instance, p_1 would represent the probability of an edge between a pair of nodes that represent the same brain area in opposite hemispheres (bilateral pairs), and p_2 would represent the probability of an edge between a pair of nodes that are not bilateral pairs.

4.8.2 Conceptualizing the SIEM

The random network has $Bernoulli(p_{z_{ij}})$ adjacency matrix entries $\mathbf{a}_{ij}$, where z_{ij} is the cluster assignment for edge (i, j), and $p_{z_{ij}}$ is the edge probability in cluster z_{ij}. Therefore, the entries $\mathbf{a}_{ij}$ in the random network depend on both the probability vector $\vec{p}$, and the clusters of each edge, given by z_{ij}. The entries in $\mathbf{A}$ are otherwise independent from each other. If $\mathbf{A}$ has n nodes, the cluster assignment matrix Z, and the probability vector $\vec{p}$, we say that $\mathbf{A}$ is an $SIEM_n(Z, \vec{p})$ random network.

4.8.2.1 How Do We Simulate Samples from an $SIEM_n(Z, \vec{p})$ Random Network?

The procedure in Algorithm 4.8 will generate an observation from an $SIEM_n(Z, \vec{p})$ random network $\mathbf{A}$.

In our brain example, let the first 50 nodes be the areas in the left hemisphere of the brain, and let the second 50 nodes be the areas of the right hemisphere of the brain. The nodes will be sequentially ordered, so that the first node of the left is a bilateral pair with the first node on the right, and so on for all 50 pairs of nodes. Further, it is much easier to encode NA as 0, so we fill the diagonal with 0s. These entries won't matter for the sample that we generate, since the networks will be loopless (and therefore, the diagonals ignored). We can generate a cluster assignment matrix like this:

```
import numpy as np

n = 100
Z = np.ones((n, n))
for i in range(0, int(n / 2)):
    Z[int(i + n / 2), i] = 3
    Z[i, int(i + n / 2)] = 3
Z[0:50, 0:50] = Z[50:100, 50:100] = 2
np.fill_diagonal(Z, 0)
```

Algorithm 4.8 Simulating a sample from an $SIEM_n(Z, \vec{p})$ random network

---

Data: n the number of nodes

         Z a matrix which assigns one of K edge clusters to each of the n^2 edges

         $\vec{p}$ a K-dimensional probability vector for each edge cluster

Result: The adjacency matrix of a sample from the random network.

1   For each of the K clusters, obtain K total weighted coins, where the kth coin lands on heads with probability p_k and tails with probability $1 - p_k$.

2   **for** i *in* 1:n **do**

3   **for** $j > i$ **do**

4   Flip the z_{ij} coin, and if it lands on heads, the corresponding entry in the adjacency matrix a_{ij} is 1. If it lands on tails, the coresponding entry in the adjacency matrix a_{ij} is 0.

5   Let $a_{ji} = a_{ij}$.

6   **end**

7 **end**

8 **return** A

We also visualize the cluster assignment matrix Z along with the hemisphere of each brain node:

```
from graphbook_code import heatmap

labels = np.repeat(["L", "R"], repeats=n/2)
heatmap(Z.astype(int), title="Cluster assignment matrix",
        inner_hier_labels=labels)
```

Figure 4.8.1(A) shows Z. Nodes in opposite hemispheres are in general assigned to cluster 1, and nodes that are in the same hemisphere to cluster 2. The white band across the diagonal corresponds to the self-loop edges, which are set to 0 arbitrarily.

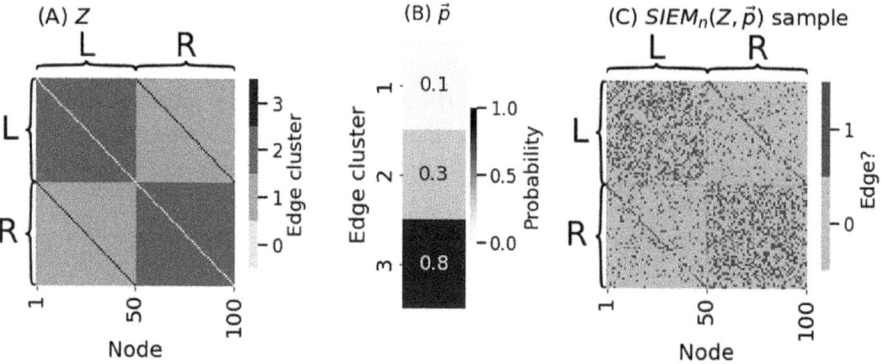

Figure 4.8.1 **(A)** The cluster assignment matrix Z, **(B)** the probability vector $\vec{p}$, and **(C)** a sample of an adjacency matrix from an $SIEM_n(Z, \vec{p})$ random network.

In the superdiagonal and subdiagonal entries, we see additional bands. These bands consist of the bilateral pairs of nodes; that is, pairs where the left hemisphere node and the right hemisphere node are in the same functional areas in each brain hemisphere. These edges are assigned to cluster 3. This pattern will manifest as an "offset" band, where the "offset" amount is simply the number of nodes between area u in the left hemisphere and area u in the right hemisphere (which, in this case, is 50).

The remaining off-diagonal entries are not bilateral pairs of nodes. These entries are assigned to cluster 1.

We will arbitrarily say that there is a 0.1 probability that an edge adjoining two nonbilateral pairs of nodes that are not in the same hemisphere (edge cluster 1) is connected, a 0.3 probability that an edge adjoining two nodes in the same hemisphere (edge cluster 2) is connected, and a 0.8 probability that an edge adjoining two bilateral pairs of nodes (cluster 3) is connected. The probability vector is shown in Figure 4.8.1(B). Then, we sample a network:

```
from graphbook_code import siem, plot_vector

p = np.array([0.1, 0.3, 0.8])
A = siem(n, p, Z)
plot_vector(p, title="probability vector", vmin=0, vmax=1, annot=True)
heatmap(A.astype(int), title="$SIEM_n(Z, \\vec p)$ sample",
        inner_hier_labels=labels)
```

Figure 4.8.1(C) shows the resulting adjacency matrix. Notice that the adjacency matrix reflects the same banding pattern as the cluster assignment matrix.

Exercise 4.8.1 Relationship between SIEMs and IERs

Explain why an $SIEM_n(Z, \vec{p})$ random network with $\binom{n}{2}$ edge clusters is stochastically equivalent to any $IER_n(P)$ random network. Use this and similar logic to Concept 4.3.8 to deduce why we focus on $SIEM_n(Z, \vec{p})$ random networks with fewer than $\binom{n}{2}$ edge clusters.

4.8.3 What Is the Relationship between SIEMs and SBMs?

In the preceding sections, we spent a lot of effort determining which networks generalize other networks. We can also do this for the $SIEM_n(Z, \vec{p})$ random networks.

Every simple $SBM_n(\vec{z}, B)$ random network with $K < n$ communities can be represented as a simple $SIEM_n(Z, \vec{p})$ random network with $L < \binom{n}{2}$ edge clusters. For each pair of communities k and k', we define a unique edge cluster l corresponding to the (k, k') community pairing. Next, for each pair of nodes i and j, we check which communities they are part of, and then define z_{ij} to be the edge cluster that corresponds to that pair of communities.

Finally, for the probability vector, we just take p_l for a given edge cluster l to be the entry of B corresponding to the communities mapped to edge cluster l. For instance, if communities k and k' mapped to edge cluster l, we take $p_l = b_{kk'}$. The resulting $SIEM_n(Z, \vec{p})$ random network has the same probability matrix as the $SBM_n(\vec{z}, B)$ random network, so all SBMs with $K < n$ have a stochastically equivalent SIEM with $L < \binom{n}{2}$.

The reverse is not true; consider, for instance, the smile face from Section 4.1 and Figure 4.1.1. We could have equivalently described this network by assigning the high-probability edges to cluster 1 (the dark portions), and the eyes, mouth, and head outline to cluster 2, with the corresponding probability vector suitably chosen. The face example cannot be represented using an $SBM_n(\vec{z}, B)$ random network with a number of communities $K < n$.

For this reason, the SIEM random networks with $L < \binom{n}{2}$ edge clusters generalize the SBM random networks with $K < n$ communities, but the reverse is not true. In later sections such as Section 6.3, we will develop statistical tools for SIEM random networks. Since the SBM random networks are contained in the SIEM random networks, these techniques will generalize to the SBM random networks. The SIEM will let us find differences between pairs of groups of edges, rather than just looking for differences between pairs of groups of nodes, since there can be complicated arrangements of edges which are not easily captured with the SBM.

4.9   Multiple Network Models

Up to this point, we have exclusively studied single network models. However, we are often in situations where we don't have just one network, but many. In this section, we explore two models for these situations: the joint random dot product graph (JRDPG), and the common subspace independent edge (COSIE) models. JRDPG is used in simple cases where we believe the collection of networks shares the same underlying structure, and we want to find a single latent space representation for all the networks. COSIE is used when the networks share a common structure, but there are network-specific variations.

We cover:

1. Joint random dot product graphs (JRDPG),
2. The common subspace independent edge (COSIE) model,
3. Correlated network models,
4. Simulating samples from multiple network models, and
5. Applications and use cases for multiple network models.

In Section 5.5 and Chapter 9, we will use these models to build network representations and explore their applications.

Imagine that we have a company with 100 total employees: 50 of these employees are network machine learning experts (ML), 25 are company administrative executives (AD), and 25 are marketing experts (MA). We study the social media habits of the employees on Facebook, Instagram, and LinkedIn. For a given social networking site, an edge is said to exist between a pair of employees if they are connected on the social media site (by being friends, following one another, or being connected, respectively). Individuals tend to most closely associate with the colleagues with whom they work most closely: Network machine learning experts are more connected with network machine learning experts, marketing experts are more connected with marketing experts, and so on and so forth. We will see below that all of the networks appear to have the same community organization, though on LinkedIn, we see that the administrative executives tend to be a little more connected than the other team members. This is reflected in the fact that there are more connections between admin members on LinkedIn and other team members.

We will use a homophilic stochastic block model from Section 4.5 for the Facebook and Instagram networks, and a homophilic degree-corrected stochastic block model (with slightly fewer connections for nonadmin team members, $\theta = 1$, and slightly more, $\theta = \sqrt{2}$, for admin team members) for the LinkedIn network. We will borrow the dcsbm function from Section 4.7, and the LabelEncoder from sklearn to encode our labels:

```python
from graspologic.simulations import sbm
import numpy as np
from graphbook_code import dcsbm
from sklearn.preprocessing import LabelEncoder

# Create block probability matrix B
K = 3
B = np.full(shape=(K, K), fill_value=0.15)
np.fill_diagonal(B, 0.4)

# degree-correct the different groups for linkedin
ml, admin, marketing = nks = [50, 25, 25]
theta = np.ones((np.sum(nks), 1))
theta[(ml):(ml + admin), :] = np.sqrt(2)

# our dcsbm function only works with communities encoded 1,2,...,K
# so we'll use a LabelEncoder to map labels to natural numbers
labels = np.repeat(["ML", "AD", "MA"], nks)
le = LabelEncoder().fit(labels)
z = le.transform(labels) + 1

# sample the random networks
A_facebook = sbm(n=nks, p=B)
A_insta = sbm(n=nks, p=B)
A_linkedin, P_linkedin = dcsbm(z, theta, B, return_prob=True)
```

Figure 4.9.1 illustrates heatmaps from each of the three networks. While the Facebook and Instagram networks do not look particularly different, the LinkedIn network appears to show that administrative members tend to have higher numbers of connections with other members.

As usual, the random network has an adjacency matrix denoted by $\mathbf{A}$, and has network samples A. When we have multiple networks, we will need to be able to index them individually. For this reason, this section will use the convention that a random network's adjacency matrix is denoted by $\mathbf{A}^{(m)}$, where m defines an index in our collection. The capital letter M defines the total number of random networks in the collection. In this case, M denotes a scalar number, rather than the usual matrix for capital letter notation.

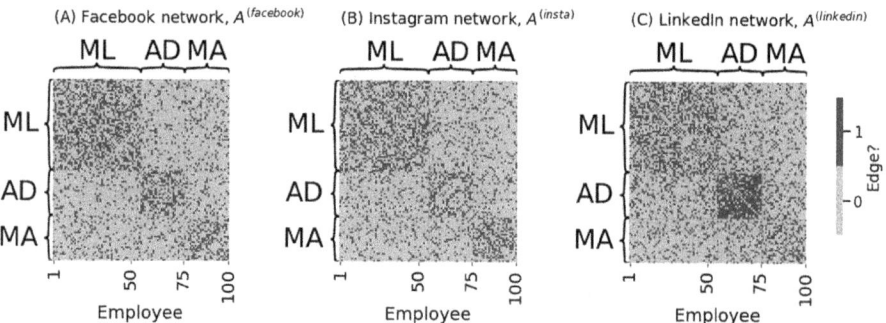

Figure 4.9.1 (**A**) Facebook social network. (**B**) Instagram social network. (**C**) LinkedIn social network. Notice that on LinkedIn, the administrators tend to have more edges.

Because we have connection networks for three sites, M is 3. When we use the letter m itself, we refer to an arbitrary random network among the collection of random networks, where m is between 1 and M. When we have M total networks, we will write down the entire collection of random networks using the notation $\{A^{(1)}, \ldots, A^{(M)}\}$. With what we already know, we could describe a random network $A^{(m)}$ with a single network model. For instance, if we thought that each social network could be represented by a different RDPG, we could have a different latent position matrix $X^{(m)}$ to define each of the three networks.

This setup, however, would neglect to describe the common structure shared by the three networks. In our example, for instance, each random network uses the same block matrix, despite the fact that the LinkedIn network used a degree-correction factor for the administrative team.

However, since we used a unique latent position matrix $X^{(m)}$ for each random network $A^{(m)}$, we have inherently ignored shared common structure. If we were to perform a task downstream, such as identifying which employees are in which community, we would have to analyze each latent position matrix individually.

In this section we will build on ideas from the random dot product graph (RDPG) and close variations. This is because the $RDPG_n(X)$ random networks can be used to describe all positive semidefinite $IER_n(P)$ networks. Using the RDPG gives us inherently flexible multiple random network models. One of our new models will use a "generalized" RDPG, which will allow us to generalize to arbitrary $IER_n(P)$ networks [12; 13].

4.9.1   The Joint Random Dot Product Graphs (JRDPG) Model

The Facebook and Instagram connections look qualitatively similar in our social network example. They seem to exhibit similar connectivity patterns between the different employee working groups, and we might even think that the two underlying random networks generating these two social networks are identical. In statistical science, we use the term *homogeneity* to describe a collection of M random networks with the same underlying random process. Let's put what this means into context using coin flips. If a pair of coins are *homogeneous*, then the probability that they land on heads is identical. The intuition we gain viewing edges as coin flips extends directly to collections of random networks.

4.9.1.1   Homogeneous and Heterogeneous Collections of Random Networks

A *homogeneous* collection of independent-edge random networks $\{\mathbf{A}^{(1)}, \ldots, \mathbf{A}^{(M)}\}$ has the same probability matrix P for each of the M random networks. Consequently, these random networks all have the same distribution. The probability matrix is the fundamental unit which can be used to describe independent-edge random networks, as we learned in Section 4.1. A *heterogeneous* collection of independent-edge random networks $\{\mathbf{A}^{(1)}, \ldots, \mathbf{A}^{(M)}\}$ has differing probability matrices for at least one of the M random networks; hence, they do not have the same distribution.

As we saw in Algorithm 4.4, the probability matrix P for an $SBM_n(\vec{z}, B)$ random network is a function of $\vec{z}$ and B. Therefore, the probability matrices $P^{(facebook)}$ and $P^{(insta)}$ for the Facebook and Instagram random networks $\mathbf{A}^{(facebook)}$ and $\mathbf{A}^{(insta)}$ are identical, because they share the same community assignment vector $\vec{z}$ and block matrix B.

4.9.1.2   Conceptualizing the $JRDPG_{n,M}(X)$ Model

The JRDPG is the simplest way to extend the RDPG random network model to multiple random networks. For each of our M total random networks, the edges depend on a single latent position matrix X. We say that a collection of random networks $\{\mathbf{A}^{(1)}, \ldots, \mathbf{A}^{(M)}\}$ with n nodes is $JRDPG_{n,M}(X)$ if each random network $\mathbf{A}^{(m)}$ is $RDPG_n(X)$ and if the M networks are independent. The joint random dot product graph model is formally described by [2], and is related to the omnibus embedding [14], which we will learn about in Section 5.5.

4.9.1.3   The JRDPG Model Does Not Allow Heterogeneity

Under the JRDPG model, each of the M random networks share the same latent position matrix. For an RDPG, the probability matrix $P = XX^\top$. So for all of the M networks, $P^{(m)} = XX^\top$ under the JRDPG model. hence, $P^{(1)} = P^{(2)} = \cdots = P^{(M)}$, and all of the probability matrices are identical. This means that the M random networks are a homogeneous collection of random networks. Consequently, the JRDPG can be thought of as M homogeneous and independent RDPGs.

From Section 4.3.6, we learned how to construct probability matrices from homophilic block matrices. Let's try this for the SBMs for Instagram and Facebook:

```
from graphbook_code import generate_sbm_pmtx, heatmap

# we already returned P_linkedin for the linkedin
# probability matrix from dcsbm() function
P_facebook_insta = generate_sbm_pmtx(z, B)

# when plotting for comparison purposes, make sure you are
# using the same scale from 0 to 1
heatmap(P_facebook_insta, vmin=0, vmax=1)
heatmap(P_linkedin, vmin=0, vmax=1)
heatmap(P_linkedin - P_facebook_insta, vmin=0, vmax=1)
```

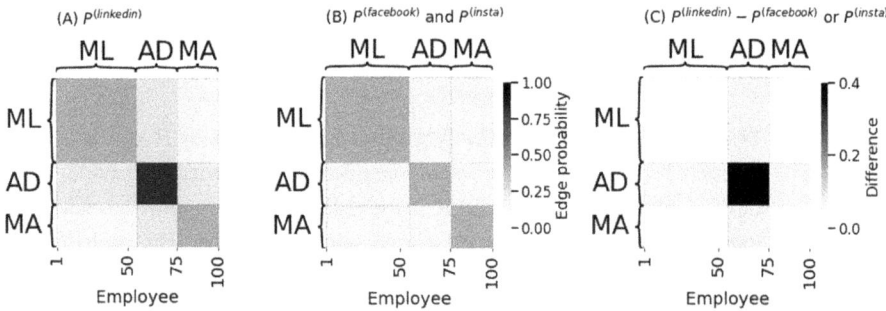

Figure 4.9.2 (**A**) The probability matrix for the random networks underlying LinkedIn, (**B**) the probability matrix for the random networks underlying Instagram and Facebook, $\mathbf{A}^{(1)}$ and $\mathbf{A}^{(2)}$, and (**C**) the difference between the probability matrices for LinkedIn and Instagram/Facebook.

Figure 4.9.2 illustrates heatmaps of the probability matrices. Because the probability matrices for Facebook and Instagram in Figure 4.9.2(B) are exactly identical (they are both functions of the same block matrix B), the collection of random networks $\left\{\mathbf{A}^{(facebook)}, \mathbf{A}^{(insta)}\right\}$ are homogeneous. We could model this pair of networks using the JRDPG due to their homogeneity and the fact that the underlying block matrices are homophilic (and hence, have a PSD matrix and probability matrix).

On the other hand, $\mathbf{A}^{(facebook)}$ an $\mathbf{A}^{(insta)}$ do not have the same probability matrix as $\mathbf{A}^{(linkedin)}$, as shown in Figure 4.9.2(C). This means that the collections of random networks $\left\{\mathbf{A}^{(facebook)}, \mathbf{A}^{(linkedin)}\right\}$, $\left\{\mathbf{A}^{(insta)}, \mathbf{A}^{(linkedin)}\right\}$, and $\left\{\mathbf{A}^{(facebook)}, \mathbf{A}^{(insta)}, \mathbf{A}^{(linkedin)}\right\}$ are heterogeneous, because their probability matrices are different.

So, unfortunately, the JRDPG cannot handle the heterogeneity between the random networks of Facebook and Instagram with the random network for LinkedIn. To avoid this restrictive homogeneity property of the JRDPG, we turn to a variation of the $IER_n(P)$ random network.

4.9.2 Common Subspace Independent Edge (COSIE) Model

We want a multiple network model which allows us to convey some shared structure, but which also lets us convey unique structure within different networks. In this section we describe the COSIE model, defined by a collection of score matrices and a shared low-rank subspace. In Section 5.5.3, we will learn about multiple adjacency spectral embedding (MASE), a technique which uses the COSIE model to conceptualize multiple network representations.

In our social network example, the employees on the administrative team had far more connections than usual among one another on LinkedIn. Figure 4.9.2 shows that the independent-edge random networks $\mathbf{A}^{(facebook)}$ and $\mathbf{A}^{(linkedin)}$ underlying the social networks $A^{(facebook)}$ and $A^{(linkedin)}$ are also different: The probability matrices $P^{(facebook)}$ and $P^{(linkedin)}$, and hence the generative model itself, are different.

Because of these extra connections in the LinkedIn network, we have heterogeneity (by way of the degree-correction factors for LinkedIn). This is despite the fact that there was shared structure (the block matrices underlying the $DCSBM_n(\vec{z}, \vec{\theta}, B)$ random network for LinkedIn and the $SBM_n(\vec{z}, B)$ random networks for Facebook/Instagram were the same).

Even though $P^{(facebook)}$ and $P^{(linkedin)}$ are not identical, we can see they still share some structure: The employee teams are the same between the two social networks, and much of the probability matrix is unchanged. COSIE allows us to model this using a shared latent position matrix to describe the similarities, and unique score matrices to describe the differences, for each of the random networks.

4.9.2.1   The Shared Latent Position Matrix

The *shared latent position matrix* S for the COSIE model is quite similar to the latent position matrix X for an RDPG. As in an RDPG, S is a matrix with n rows (one for each node) and d columns. The columns of S behave similarly to the columns of X, and d is referred to as the *latent dimensionality* of the COSIE random networks. Each row of the shared latent position matrix $\vec{s}_i$ denotes the shared latent position vector for node i.

We will add an additional restriction to S: It must have orthogonal columns. This means that for each column of S, the dot product of the column with itself is 1, and the dot product of the column with any other column is 0; the geometric interpretation is that the column-vectors are all at right angles to each other. This has the implication that $S^\top S = I$, the identity matrix. This gives a sense of uniform scale for all of the columns (scale 1) of the latent position matrix.

The shared latent position matrix conveys the common structure between the COSIE random networks, and will be a parameter for each of the neworks. With the JRDPG model, we were able to express the homogeneity of the social networks on Facebook and Instagram, but not the heterogeneity of the social network on LinkedIn. The shared latent position matrix S conveys the commonality among the three social networks.

Unfortunately, obtaining shared latent positions analytically is difficult. We will use the probability matrices $P^{(m)}$ combined with MASE, the technique we mentioned earlier in Section 5.5 to obtain them:

```
from graspologic.embed import MultipleASE as mase
from graphbook_code import lpm_heatmap

embedder = mase(n_components=3, svd_seed=0)
# obtain shared latent positions
S = embedder.fit_transform([P_facebook_insta, P_facebook_insta,
    P_linkedin])

lpm_heatmap(S)
```

Figure 4.9.3(A) shows the shared latent position matrix S. This matrix is arranged as in the figures in Section 4.4 on the $RDPG_n(X)$ random network, and can be interpreted similarly: The rows indicate nodes (employees), and the columns indicate latent dimensions. Each row $\vec{s}_i$ of S indicates the latent position of a given node i.

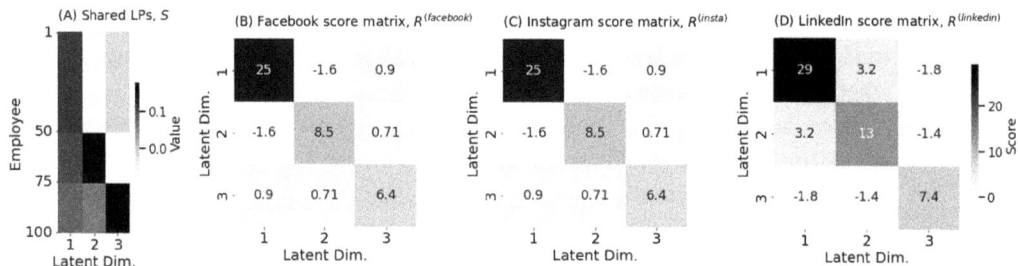

Figure 4.9.3 (**A**) The shared latent position matrix across all of the networks, (**B**) score matrix for the Facebook random network, (**C**) score matrix for the Instagram random network, and (**D**) score matrix for the LinkedIn random network.

One thing immediately jumps out: The latent positions are the same for all employees across a given community assignment (their role in the company). This makes sense given what we learned in Section 4.7.8 about nodes in the same community having the same latent position up to a rescaling.

The Facebook and Instagram networks are just $SBM_n(\vec{z}, B)$ random networks with a homophilic block matrix, so the latent positions should be identical across all nodes from a given community. For the LinkedIn network, the degree-correction factors are identical within each community, so it also makes sense that the latent positions should be identical across all nodes from a given community there, too.

In our example, the homophilic (and hence, positive semidefinite) block matrix B itself is identical across all of the networks. This means that for each network, using the results from Section 4.5.9, a node i in community 1 would have the latent position:

$$\vec{x}_i^{(facebook)\top} = \vec{x}_i^{(insta)\top} = \begin{bmatrix} 1 & 0 & 0 \end{bmatrix} \sqrt{B}$$

for both Facebook and Instagram. For LinkedIn, the latent position would be:

$$\vec{x}_i^{(linkedin)\top} = \theta_i \begin{bmatrix} 1 & 0 & 0 \end{bmatrix} \sqrt{B}.$$

In particular, $\vec{x}_i^{(linkedin)}$ is equivalent to $\vec{x}_i^{(facebook)}$ and $\vec{x}_i^{(insta)}$, up to the rescaling by θ_i (the degree-correction factor). If we repeat this for all of the communities, we would see that the shared latent positions for the LinkedIn network should just be a rescaling of the shared latent positions from the Facebook and Instagram networks.

We see from the shared latent position matrix that the COSIE model can capture what we already know: There is a strong degree of homogeneity across the different networks; the latent positions are identical (up to a rescaling), and we can represent them with the same shared latent position matrix.

4.9.2.2   Score Matrices

The shared latent position matrix for COSIE describes similarities; the score matrices describe differences.

The *score matrices* tell us how to assemble the shared latent position matrix to obtain a unique probability matrix for each network. The score matrix $R^{(m)}$ for a random network m has d columns and d rows. Therefore, it is a square matrix whose number of dimensions is equal to the latent dimensionality of the shared latent position matrix.

The probability matrix for each network under the COSIE model is:

$$P^{(m)} = SR^{(m)}S^\top$$

where, again, S is the shared latent position matrix. We can understand this equation by focusing on the first term $SR^{(m)}$. This uses the scores to express which latent position vectors in the shared latent position matrix are more or less important in the probability matrix $P^{(m)}$. In this sense, the score matrix tells us which combinations of latent positions determine the unique features of heterogeneous probability matrices.

In the social network example, we want the score matrices to indicate that Facebook and Instagram share a probability matrix, but Facebook and LinkedIn do not. Consequently, we would expect that the score matrices from Facebook and Instagram should be the same, but the score matrix for LinkedIn will be different. We can obtain these with the MASE object in graspologic:

```
import matplotlib.pyplot as plt

R_facebook = embedder.scores_[0]
R_insta = embedder.scores_[1]
R_linkedin = embedder.scores_[2]

# and plot them
smin = np.min(embedder.scores_)
smax = np.max(embedder.scores_)

fig, axs = plt.subplots(1, 3, figsize=(20, 7))
heatmap(R_facebook, vmin=smin, vmax=smax, ax=axs[0], annot=True,
    title="facebook score matrix")
heatmap(R_insta, vmin=smin, vmax=smax, ax=axs[1], annot=True,
    title="Instagram score matrix")
heatmap(R_linkedin, vmin=smin, vmax=smax, ax=axs[2], annot=True,
    title="LinkedIn score matrix")
```

Figure 4.9.3 shows the score matrices. The score matrices for Facebook and Instagram are identical, but the score matrix for LinkedIn is distinct.

4.9.2.3 Conceptualizing the COSIE Model

In the COSIE model, for each random network, the probability matrix $P^{((m)}$ depends on the shared latent position matrix S and the score matrix $R^{(m)}$. The probability matrix $P^{(m)}$ for the mth random network is defined so that $P^{(m)} = SR^{(m)}S^\top$. This means that each entry $p_{ij}^{(m)} = \vec{s}_i^\top R^{(m)}\vec{s}_j$. We say that a collection of random networks $\{A^{(1)}, \ldots, A^{(M)}\}$ with n nodes is $COSIE_{n,M}\left(S, R^{(1)}, \ldots, R^{(M)}\right)$ if each random network $\mathbf{A}^{(m)}$ is $IER_n(P^{(m)})$ and the networks are otherwise independent. Each of the M random networks share the same *orthogonal* latent position matrix S, but a unique score matrix $R^{(m)}$. This allows the random networks to share some underlying structure (which is conveyed by S) but with a unique combination of this shared structure (conveyed by $R^{(m)}$).

Since the probability matrix $P^{(m)} = SR^{(m)}S^\top$, two random networks with the same score matrix will be homogeneous (identically distributed), and two random networks with different score matrices will be heterogeneous (not identically distributed). In this way, we are able to capture the homogeneity between the random networks for Facebook and Instagram connections, while also capturing the heterogeneity between the random networks for Facebook and LinkedIn connections. The COSIE model is described by [13].

Exercise 4.9.1 Demonstrating properties of shared latent position matrices and score matrices

Demonstrate that you are able to recover the true probability matrices using the shared latent position matrices S and the score matrices R_facebook, R_insta, and R_linkedin.
Show that the true probability matrices P_facebook_insta and P_linkedin are identical to the probability matrices that you obtain using the shared latent positions and the score matrices by using np.allclose(), like we did in Section 4.5.8.

Connections with the GRDPG
The initial formulation of the COSIE model in [13] describes generalized random dot product graphs. These are equivalent to a broad class of models called IER networks, which we will introduce briefly in Section 5.7.3).

4.9.3   Correlated Network Models

In this section we explore correlated network models. Let's say that we have a group of people in a city, and we know that each person in our group has both a Facebook and a Instagram account. The nodes in the networks are the people who possess both social media accounts. The first network consists of Facebook connections, where an edge exists between two people if they are friends on Facebook. The second network consists of Instagram connections, where an edge exists between two people if they follow one another on Instagram. If two people are friends on Facebook, then there is a good chance that they follow one another on Instagram, and vice versa. How do we reflect this similarity through a multiple network model?

Network *correlation* between a pair of networks describes the property that the existence of edges in one network gives information about edges in the other network, as in this Facebook/Instagram example. We will focus on ρ-correlated network models. Given two random networks with the same number of nodes, each edge has a correlation of ρ between the two networks. A pair of random networks $\mathbf{A}^{(1)}$ and $\mathbf{A}^{(2)}$ are called ρ-*correlated* if for all pairs of indices i and j, corr$(\mathbf{a}_{ij}^{(1)}, \mathbf{a}_{ij}^{(2)}) = \rho$, where corr$(\mathbf{x}, \mathbf{y})$ is the Pearson correlation between two random variables $\mathbf{x}$ and $\mathbf{y}$. Otherwise, the edges are independent between the two networks. In our example, this is how we will model whether two people are friends on Facebook is correlated with whether they are following one another on Instagram.

Concept 4.9.2 The Pearson correlation

The Pearson correlation between two random variables $\mathbf{x}$ and $\mathbf{y}$ is defined as the covariance of the two variables divided by the product of their standard deviations, given by:

$$\mathrm{corr}(\mathbf{x}, \mathbf{y}) = \frac{\mathrm{cov}(\mathbf{x}, \mathbf{y})}{\sigma_x \sigma_y}$$

where $\mathrm{cov}(\mathbf{x}, \mathbf{y})$ is the covariance between $\mathbf{x}$ and $\mathbf{y}$, and σ_x and σ_y are their standard deviations. The symbol for correlation is typically "rho" (greek letter ρ). Since the correlation ρ is the same for all edges in the network in the formulations we are discussing, these models are typically referred to as the ρ-correlated network models. More complicated models may have more complicated correlation structures.

The Pearson correlation (defined in Concept 4.9.2) describes whether one variable being large or small gives information that the other variable is large or small. The correlation is positive and closer to 1 if one variable being large gives information that the other variable might also be large, it is close to -1 if one variable being large gives information that the might be small, and it is close to 0 if seeing the value of one variable does not provide much information about the the other. Applying this to networks, we see that if the two networks are positively correlated and we know that one of the edges $\mathbf{a}_{ij}^{(1)}$ has a value of one, then we have information that $\mathbf{a}_{ij}^{(2)}$ might also be one; and vice versa for taking values of zero. If the two networks are negatively correlated and we know that one of the edges $\mathbf{a}_{ij}^{(1)}$ has a value of one, then we have information that $\mathbf{a}_{ij}^{(2)}$ might be zero, and vice versa. If the two networks are not correlated ($\rho = 0$) we do not learn anything about edges of the second network by looking at edges from the first.

4.9.3.1 ρ-Correlated RDPG

The ρ-correlated RDPG is a relatively straightforward correlated network model, and is described by [15] and [16]. Since ER, SBM, and DCSBM random networks are special cases of the RDPG (as long as the block matrix is positive semidefinite), the ρ-correlated RDPG can be used to define a ρ-correlated ER, ρ-correlated SBMs, and ρ-correlated DCSBMs. For the normal RDPG, a latent position matrix X with n rows and a latent dimensionality of d is used to define the edge-existence probabilities for the networks $\mathbf{A}^{(1)}$ and $\mathbf{A}^{(2)}$. The difference with the ρ-correlated RDPG is that probabilities in $\mathbf{A}^{(2)}$ now depend on the outcome of observing an instance of $\mathbf{A}^{(1)}$.

Let's take a coin flip example. We begin by defining $\mathbf{A}^{(1)}$ as an $RDPG_n(X)$ random network. We define the second network $\mathbf{A}^{(2)}$ as follows. We use a coin for each edge (i, j), which has a probability that depends on the value that the corresponding edge in $\mathbf{A}^{(1)}$ takes. If the edge $\mathbf{a}_{ij}^{(1)}$ takes the value of one, then we use a coin which has a probability of $\vec{x}_i^\top \vec{x}_j + \rho(1 - \vec{x}_i^\top \vec{x}_j)$ of landing on heads. If the edge $\mathbf{a}_{ij}^{(1)}$ takes the value of zero, then we use a coin which has a probability of $(1 - \rho)\vec{x}_i^\top \vec{x}_j$ of landing on heads. We flip this coin, and if it lands on heads, then the edge $\mathbf{a}_{ij}^{(2)}$ takes the value of one. If it lands on tails, then the edge $\mathbf{a}_{ij}^{(2)}$ takes the value of zero. If $\mathbf{A}^{(1)}$ and $\mathbf{A}^{(2)}$ are ρ-correlated RDPGs with latent position matrix X and n nodes each, we say that the pair $\{\mathbf{A}^{(1)}, \mathbf{A}^{(2)}\}$ are $\rho RDPG_n(X)$.

How Do We Simulate Samples of $\rho RDPG_n(X)$ Random Networks?

The procedure in Algorithm 4.9 will produce a pair of networks $A^{(1)}$ and $A^{(2)}$ where the underlying random networks $\mathbf{A}^{(1)}$ and $\mathbf{A}^{(2)}$ are $\rho RDPG_n(X)$.

Algorithm 4.9 Simulating a paired sample of $\rho RDPG(X)$ random networks

---

Data: n a number of nodes

$\quad\quad$ X a latent position matrix with n rows and d columns

$\quad\quad$ ρ a correlation between the two networks that is between -1 and 1

Result: A pair of random networks which are ρ-correlated.

1   Simulate a sample $A^{(1)}$ which is a sample of an $RDPG_n(X)$ random network, using Algorithm 4.5.

2   **for** i *in* $1{:}n$ **do**

3   **for** $j > i$ **do**

4   **if** $a_{ij}^{(1)} = 1$ **then**

5   Obtain a coin which has a probability of landing on heads of $\vec{x}_i^\top \vec{x}_j + \rho(1 - \vec{x}_i^\top \vec{x}_j)$.

6   **end**

7   **else**

8   Obtain a coin which has a probability of landing on heads of $(1 - \rho)\vec{x}_i^\top \vec{x}_j$.

9   **end**

10   Flip the coin, and if it lands on heads, the corresponding entry $a_{ij}^{(2)}$ in the adjacency matrix is 1. If the coin lands on tails, the corresponding entry $a_{ij}^{(2)}$ is 0.

11   Set $a_{ji}^{(2)} = a_{ij}^{(2)}$.

12   **end**

13 **end**

14 **return** $A^{(1)}$ *and* $A^{(2)}$

Fortunately, `graspologic` makes sampling ρ-correlated RDPGs relatively simple. Let's use the Instagram/Facebook example from this section, and assert that the networks are not only identical in probability, but that they are also correlated.

Saying that the two networks are positively correlated is the same as saying that if we knew that a pair of people were friends on Facebook, then they would be more likely to be following one another on Instagram. We will start by generating latent position matrices for the Instagram/Facebook example using code from Section 4.5.8:

```
from graphbook_code import lpm_from_sbm
X_facebook_insta = lpm_from_sbm(z, B)
```

Let's see what happens when the underlying correlation is $\rho = 0.7$. To summarize the differences between the two networks, we'll count the total number of edges that differ between the two networks, the absolute difference matrix:

```
from graspologic.simulations import rdpg_corr

# generate the network samples
rho = 0.7
facebook_correlated_network, insta_correlated_network = rdpg_corr(
    X_facebook_insta, Y=None, r=rho
)

# the difference matrix
correlated_difference_matrix = np.abs(
    facebook_correlated_network - insta_correlated_network
)
# the total number of differences
correlated_differences = correlated_difference_matrix.sum()
```

Figure 4.9.4(A), (B), and (C) show heatmaps of the two networks, along with their difference matrix.

We also show the case where the underlying correlation is much lower, such as $\rho' = 0.0$ (the networks are *uncorrelated*).

```
rho_nil = 0.0
facebook_uncorrelated_network, insta_uncorrelated_network = rdpg_corr(
    X_facebook_insta, Y=None, r=rho_nil
)

# the difference matrix
uncorrelated_difference_matrix = np.abs(
    facebook_uncorrelated_network - insta_uncorrelated_network
)
# the total number of differences
uncorrelated_differences = uncorrelated_difference_matrix.sum()
```

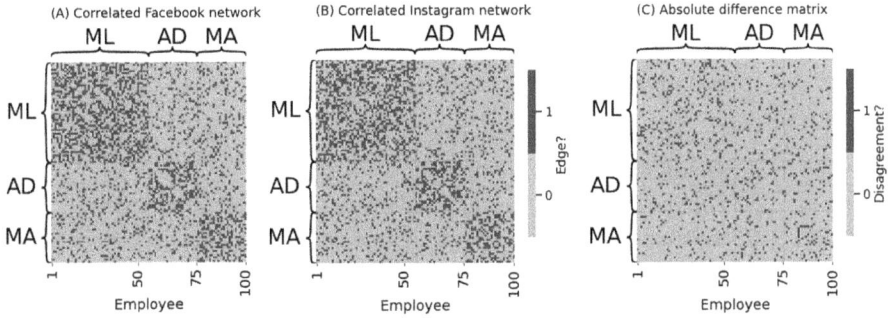

Figure 4.9.4 **(A)** The Facebook network. **(B)** The Instagram network. **(C)** The edges which differ between the two networks.

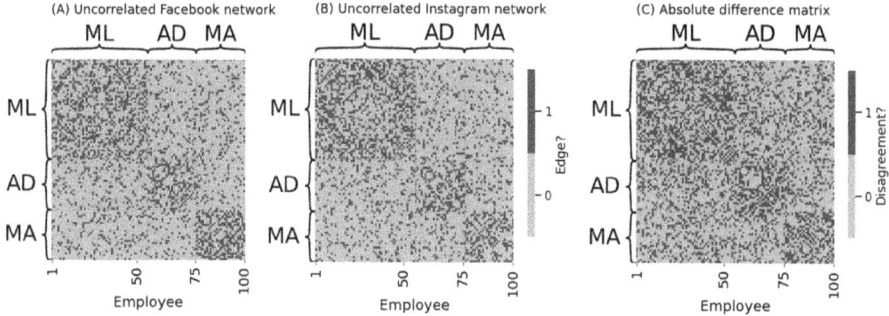

Figure 4.9.5 (**A**) The Facebook network. (**B**) The Instagram network. (**C**) The edges which differ between the two networks. Note that there are far more edges that differ than in Figure 4.9.4.

A heatmap of the two networks is shown in Figure 4.9.5(A) and (B), along with the difference matrix in Figure 4.9.5(C). In both Figure 4.9.4 and Figure 4.9.5, the Facebook and Instagram networks have identical latent position matrices, and the latent position matrices are the same for both scenarios. However, when the networks are correlated, the edges tend to be more similar between the two networks. When the networks are uncorrelated, the edges tend to differ more between the two networks.

Exercise 4.9.3 Negative ρ-correlated RDPGs

If we generated another simulation where the networks were anticorrelated, we could arbitrarily increase the magnitude of this difference. Try the simulation again with ρ having a negative value, and describe what you see. Repeat it a few times, setting ρ as low as -1, and describe your result.

Next, do the simulation again with $\rho = 1.0$. What do you notice?

4.10   Models with Covariates

We often have additional information for networks besides node or edge attributes. For example, a network might be labeled into a category. In this section, we explore network models that incorporate these *network attributes*.

We cover:

1. Definition and motivation for models with covariates,
2. The signal subnetwork model,
3. Simulating samples from models with covariates,
4. Relationship between covariate models and other network models, and
5. Applications and use-cases for models with covariates.

In Section 8.3 and Section 8.2, we will use these ideas to develop prediction models classifying networks into different classes.

Say we have a collection of networks representing the brains of $M = 200$ individuals 500,000 years into the future. These individuals are all either humans who have persisted with life-as-normal on Earth (earthlings), or astronauts who left for a planet with a different set of prominent colors and light content from Earth.

Let's define the network attributes, which in this case are network labels. For each individual m, a *covariate* y_i indicates whether the individual is an earthling (1) or an astronaut (2). Here, y_m is a categorical variable: We have two categories 1 and 2, and we chose people (earthlings) to be 1 and astronauts to be 2. The total number of categories, or *classes*, Y is 2. In the special case when categorical variables take one of two levels, we call them *binary* or *dichotomous* variables (two possible values).

Let's define the nodes in our astronaut example. Each brain network has five nodes, representing the sensory functions and modalities of the brain: the area responsible for sight (SI), the area responsible for language (L), the area responsible for hearing/emotional expression (H/E), the area responsible for thinking/movement (T/M), and the area responsible for basic survival functions such as heartbeat and breathing (BS). Edges represent whether pairs of brain areas can pass information to one another. There were evolutionary pressures on the astronauts towards people whose eyes could better adapt to the different set of colors and light on the new planet, so the vision node is expected to relate to the other nodes differently.

Let's say that we have observed pairs of data $\left(A^{(m)}, y_m\right)$, for m from 1 to $M = 200$. Each adjacency matrix $A^{(m)}$ is a 5×5 matrix, and the covariate y_m takes the value 1 if the mth individual is an earthling, and 2 if the mth individual is an astronaut. We want to predict the class for each individual (earthling or astronaut) using only their adjacency matrix $A^{(m)}$. We can see two example networks for the earthlings and the astronauts in the following:

```python
import numpy as np
from graspologic.simulations import sample_edges

nodenames = [
    "SI", "L", "H/E",
    "T/M", "BS"
]

# generate probability matrices
n = 5 # the number of nodes
P_earthling = 0.3*np.ones((n, n))
signal_subnetwork = np.zeros((n, n), dtype=bool)
signal_subnetwork[1:n, 0] = True
signal_subnetwork[0, 1:n] = True
P_astronaut = np.copy(P_earthling)
P_astronaut[signal_subnetwork] = np.tile(np.linspace(0.4, 0.9, num=4),
    2)

# sample two networks
A_earthling = sample_edges(P_earthling)
A_astronaut = sample_edges(P_astronaut)
```

Figure 4.10.1 compares the two adjacency matrices. By design, the edges in the first column and the first row, responsible for "sight," are different. However, there are

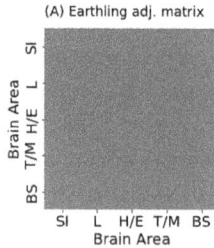 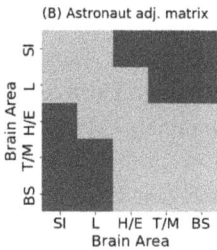

Figure 4.10.1 (**A**) A brain network of an earthling. (**B**) A brain network of an astronaut.

so few nodes that it would be impossible to make meaningful claims if we didn't know this in advance. Is there some way that we could "pool" across many networks, and gain insight by thinking about properties shared by all of the networks from a single class (astronaut vs. earthling)?

To devise a statistical model, we view each piece of data in our sample as an observation of a corresponding random variable. When we were dealing with multiple network models in Section 4.9, this meant that for each network $A^{(m)}$ there was a random network $\mathbf{A}^{(m)}$, and that this random network was the underlying process generating $A^{(m)}$. Now, for each data pair $\left(A^{(m)}, y_m\right)$, there exists a corresponding random network $\mathbf{A}^{(m)}$ and a corresponding random covariate $\mathbf{y}_m$, where $\left(\mathbf{A}^{(m)}, \mathbf{y}_m\right)$ is a sample of the random tuple $\left(\mathbf{A}^{(m)}, \mathbf{y}_m\right)$. So, for our multiple network model with covariates, we seek to describe both $\mathbf{A}^{(m)}$ and $\mathbf{y}_m$.

4.10.1   Signal Subnetwork Model

The astronauts are remarkably similar to the earthlings, except for the connections related to vision. In other words, the subnetwork comprised only of edges incident to the vision lobe carry the *signal disparity* between human and astronaut brains. We explored the concept of a subnetwork in Section 3.5.

If we were to just compare the adjacency matrices themselves, we would end up looking at a lot of extraneous information: Edges that do not show any difference between the humans and the astronauts. In a fixed sample of earthlings and astronauts, we might find disparities between these extraneous edges, but these disparities are just because of the particular sample of humans and astronauts that we chose and are not representative of actual differences. Instead, we want to identify the subset of edges and corresponding nodes, called the *signal subnetwork*, which actually carry the *signal*, the set of edges which show real differences between the earthlings and the astronauts. In the following, we plot the probability matrices for earthlings and astronauts:

```
# plot probability matrices and their differences on the same scale
heatmap(P_earthling, vmin=0, vmax=1)
heatmap(P_astronaut, vmin=0, vmax=1)
heatmap(np.abs(P_astronaut - P_earthling), vmin=0, vmax=1)
```

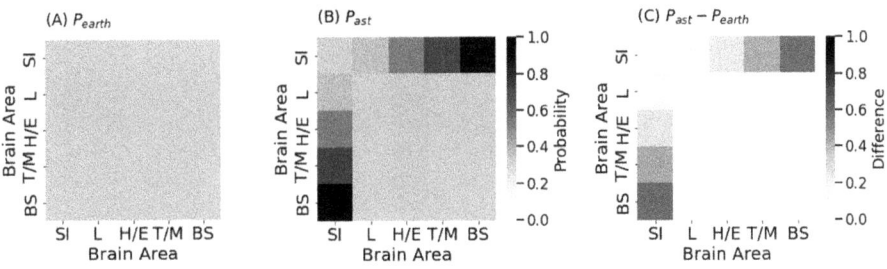

Figure 4.10.2 (**A**) The probability matrix for brain networks of earthlings. (**B**) The probability matrix for brain networks of astronauts. (**C**) The difference between the probability matrices for astronauts and humans. Notice that the the area responsible for sight, SI, has very different connection probabilities with all other brain areas.

Figure 4.10.2 explores these results in more detail. Notice that the entirety of the disparity between earthlings and astronauts (in terms of their probability matrices) shown in Figure 4.10.2(C) is captured by the edges which include a node involved in eyesight. We can observe this because only the first row and column of the matrix (corresponding to the node for sight, SI) is different between the two networks for all other pairs of nodes.

We explore this signal using the *signal subnetwork (SSN) model*, which models adjacency matrices where we have per-network attributes. To decide whether a network is from an earthling or an astronaut, we will look only at the signal subnetwork, and ignore the rest of the network entirely.

The core idea in the SSN model is that for each edge in the network, the probability of an edge existing (or not existing) depends on the class. There is a set of edges for which the class changes the probability, and another set of edges for which the class has no impact. For an edge (i, j) for classes y (in our case, either 0 or 1), we will use the notation $p_{ij}^{(y)}$ to denote the probability of an edge existing in class y.

The *signal subnetwork* [17] is a collection of edges $\mathcal{S}$, with elements (i, j) where i and j are nodes in the network between 1 and n, such that the following two conditions hold:

1. For each edge in the signal subnetwork, class membership changes edge probability. That is, if an edge (i, j) is in the signal subnetwork $\mathcal{S}$, then there exist two classes y and y' where $p_{ij}^{(y)} \neq p_{ij}^{(y')}$.
2. For each edge which is not in the signal subnetwork, class does not affect edge probability. That is, if an edge (i, j) is not in the signal subnetwork $\mathcal{S}$, then $p_{ij}^{(y)} = p_{ij}^{(y')}$. For this reason, if an edge is not in the signal subnetwork, we will use the notation $p_{ij} = p_{ij}^{(0)} = p_{ij}^{(1)} = \cdots = p_{ij}^{(Y-1)}$, where Y is the number of classes.

The signal subnetwork tracks the edges which have different probabilities for any pair of classes. For our earthlings versus astronauts example, this is the set of edges for which at least one node is in the visual region of the brain:

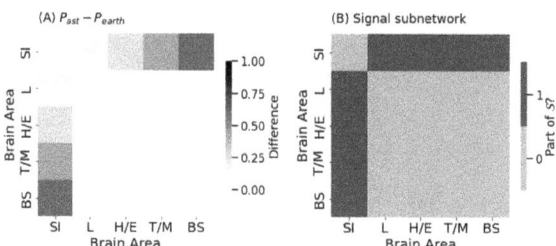

Figure 4.10.3 (**A**) The difference between the earthling and astronaut probability matrices. (**B**) The signal subnetwork.

```
# plot the signal subnetwork
ax = heatmap(signal_subnetwork)
```

Figure 4.10.3(B) shows a plot of the signal subnetwork. It is compared to the difference between the probability matrices for earthlings and astronauts in Figure 4.10.3(A). The signal subnetwork includes all edges in which the two probability matrices are different.

We can now formally define the signal subnetwork model. For each random tuple $(\mathbf{A}^{(m)}, \mathbf{y}_m)$, we first obtain a "class assignment" die with Y total sides. For a given face of the dice y, the probability that the dice lands on side Y is π_y. We flip the class assignment die, and if it lands on side y, then $\mathbf{y}_m$ takes the value y. Next, for each edge (i, j) which is not in the signal subnetwork $\mathcal{S}$, we obtain a "nonsignal" coin which has a probability of p_{ij} of landing on heads and $1 - p_{ij}$ of landing on tails. The edge $\mathbf{a}_{ij}$ exists if the coin lands on heads and does not exist if the coin lands on tails. Finally, for every edge (i, j) which is in $\mathcal{S}$, we check which class $\mathbf{y}_m$ indicates. If $\mathbf{y}_m$ is class y, we obtain a "signal" coin which has a probability of $p_{ij}^{(y)}$ of landing on heads, and a probability of $1 - p_{ij}^{(y)}$ of landing on tails. The edge $\mathbf{a}_{ij}$ exists if the coin lands on heads and does not exist if the coin lands on tails.

In summary, we will say that a collection of random network/covariate pairs $\{(\mathbf{A}^{(1)}, \mathbf{y}_1), \ldots, (\mathbf{A}^{(M)}, \mathbf{y}_M)\}$ with n nodes is $SSN_{n, M}(\vec{\pi}, P^{(1)}, \ldots, P^{(Y)}, \mathcal{S})$ if the following three conditions hold:

1. For every edge (i, j) which is in the signal subnetwork $\mathcal{S}$, there exists at least two classes y and y' where $p_{ij}^{(y)} \neq p_{ij}^{(y')}$.
2. For all edges (i, j) not in the signal subnetwork $\mathcal{S}$, edge probabilities are the same: $p_{ij} = p_{ij}^{(1)} = \cdots = p_{ij}^{(Y)}$.
3. Conditional on the class $\mathbf{y}_m$ being y, then $\mathbf{A}^{(m)}$ is $IER_n(P^{(y)})$, where $IER_n(P^{(y)})$ is from Section 4.1.

4.10.1.1 Simulating Samples of SSN Random Networks

Algorithm 4.10 generates a set of networks $\{A^{(1)}, \ldots, A^{(M)}\}$ and covariates $\vec{y}$ where the underlying random networks $\{\mathbf{A}^{(1)}, \ldots, \mathbf{A}^{(M)}\}$ and covariates $\vec{\mathbf{y}}$ are $SSN_{n, M}(\vec{\pi}, P^{(1)}, \ldots, P^{(Y)}, \mathcal{S})$ random networks.

Algorithm 4.10 Simulating samples from an $SSN_{n,M}(\vec{\pi}, P^{(0)}, \ldots, P^{(Y-1)}, \mathcal{S})$ random network

Data: n a number of nodes

M the total number of networks

$\pi_1, \ldots, \pi_Y$ the probability of a network being from a given class

$P^{(1)}, \ldots, P^{(Y)}$ the probability matrix associated with each class

$\mathcal{S}$ the signal subnetwork

Result: A collection of M networks with n nodes.

1 Obtain a dice with Y sides numbered from 1 to Y, that has a π_y chance of landing on the y side.

2 **for** m in $1{:}M$ **do**

3   Flip the Y-sided die, and if it lands on side y, assign the item m to class y. Call this class y_m.

4   Simulate an adjacency matrix $A^{(m)}$, using the procedure for an $IER_n(P^{(y)})$ network, in Algorithm 4.1.

5 **end**

6 **return** $\{(A^{(1)}, y_1), \ldots, (A^{(M)}, y_M)\}$

We can implement this programmatically as follows, where we sample $M = 200$ network/covariate pairs:

```
# sample the classes of each sample
M = 200 # the number of training and testing samples
pi_astronaut = 0.45
pi_earthling = 0.55
np.random.seed(0)
yvec = np.random.choice(2, p=[pi_earthling, pi_astronaut], size=M)

# sample network realizations given the class of each sample
Ps = [P_earthling, P_astronaut]

As = np.stack([sample_edges(Ps[y]) for y in yvec], axis=2)
```

4.11 The Big Picture of Random Network Models

At this point, we have studied many random network models. In this section, we take a bird's-eye view to summarize our major conclusions.

We cover the following:

1. Key parameters, edge probabilities, and node degree characteristics for each model,
2. Relationships between different models, including generalizations and special cases,
3. The role of positive semidefiniteness in connecting block models to random dot product graphs, and
4. A hierarchical framework for understanding the connections between different network models.

We will use these statistical models both explicitly and implicitly for the remainder of the book.

4.11.1   Parameters and Intuition

Here, we provide brief snippets about each random network model, and some basic intuition about how to think about them. To refresh us, the parameters of a random network are the descriptors that are necessary to fully specify the unique aspects of one random network under a given model. The edge probabilities delineate the probability of an edge existing or not existing between a given pair of nodes. The expected node degree is the expected number of edges for a given node, and may or may not depend on other features of that node (such as its community assignment, or its degree-correction factor). We will assume that each network has n nodes. If a network has community structure, we will use K to denote the number of communities. If the network has latent structure, we will use d to denote the latent dimensionality. If a network has edge clusters, K will instead be used to denote the number of edge clusters. If there are multiple networks, M will denote the number of networks. The collection of random networks that can be described with the indicated parameters is known as the *random network model*; for example, the Erdös–Renyi random network model is the collection of random networks that can be described with a single probability p.

Further, these random network models describe independent-edge random networks; that is, the existence or nonexistence of an edge does not provide information about the existence or nonexistence of another edge in the network (beyond what is conveyed by the parameters of each network). We will assume that all of the network models described below are for simple networks; that is, the networks are unweighted (edges either exist or do not exist), undirected (all edges are bidirectional; i.e., an edge from i to j implies an edge from j to i), and loopless (nodes cannot have edges to themselves).

Erdös–Renyi Random Networks (ERs)
- Parameters: p the edge probability.
- Edge probabilities: $\mathbb{E}[\mathbf{a}_{ij}] = p_{ij} = p$.
- Expected node degrees: All nodes have identical expected node degrees. $\mathbb{E}[\mathbf{d}_i] = (n-1)p$.
- Calculating the probability matrix: $P = p1_{n \times n}$, where $1_{n \times n}$ is an $n \times n$ matrix of ones.
- Specification: $\mathbf{A}$ is $ER_n(p)$.
- Intuition: The existence or nonexistence of edges in the network is random with the same probability.

Stochastic Block Model (SBMs)
- Parameters: $\vec{z}$ the length-n community assignment vector assigning each node to one of K communities, and B the $K \times K$ block probability matrix.
- Edge probabilities: $\mathbb{E}[\mathbf{a}_{ij}] = p_{ij} = b_{z_i z_j}$.

- Expected node degrees: All nodes in the same community have the same expected node degree

$$\mathbb{E}[\mathbf{d}_i ; z_i = k] = \sum_{l \neq k} n_l b_{lk} + (n_k - 1) b_{kk}.$$

- Calculating the probability matrix: $P = CBC^\top$, where C is the $n \times K$ one-hot encoding of the community assignment vector.
- Specification: $\mathbf{A}$ is $SBM_n(\vec{z}, B)$.
- Intuition: The existence or nonexistence of edges depends on the communities that nodes are assigned to.

Random Dot Product Graphs (RDPGs)
- Parameters: X the $n \times d$ latent position matrix.
- Edge probabilities: $\mathbb{E}[\mathbf{a}_{ij}] = p_{ij} = \vec{x}_i^\top \vec{x}_j$.
- Expected node degrees: $\mathbb{E}[\mathbf{d}_i] = \sum_{j \neq i}^n \vec{x}_i^\top \vec{x}_j$.
- Calculating the probability matrix: $P = XX^\top$.
- Specification: $\mathbf{A}$ is $RDPG_n(X)$.
- Intuition: The existence or nonexistence of edges depends on the latent positions of the incident nodes.

Degree-Corrected Stochastic Block Model (DCSBMs)
- Parameters: $\vec{z}$ the length-n community assignment vector assigning each node to one of K communities, $\vec{\theta}$ the length-n degree-correction vector, and B the $K \times K$ block probability matrix.
- Edge probabilities: $\mathbb{E}[\mathbf{a}_{ij}] = p_{ij} = \theta_i \theta_j b_{z_i z_j}$.
- Expected node degrees: The degree-correction factor "scales" the expected degree of a given node compared to other nodes in the same community

$$\mathbb{E}[\mathbf{d}_i ; z_i = k] = \theta_i \left(\sum_{l \neq k} \left[b_{lk} \sum_{j : z_j = l} \theta_j \right] + b_{kk} \sum_{j : z_j = k, j \neq i} \theta_j \right).$$

- Calculating the probability matrix: $P = \Theta C B (\Theta C)^\top$, where C is the $n \times K$ one-hot encoding of the community assignment vector, and Θ is the diagonal matrix whose entries are the degree-correction factors.
- Specification: $\mathbf{A}$ is $DCSBM_n(\vec{z}, \vec{\theta}, B)$.
- Intuition: The existence or nonexistence of edges depends on the community a node is assigned to, where the degree-correction factors θ_i or θ_j up- or down-weight the edge-existence probabilities.

Independent-Edge Erdös–Renyi (IER)
- Parameters: P, an $n \times n$ probability matrix.
- Edge probabilities: $\mathbb{E}[\mathbf{a}_{ij}] = p_{ij}$.
- Expected node degrees: $\mathbb{E}[\mathbf{d}_i] = \sum_{j \neq i} p_{ij}$.
- Calculating the probability matrix: The probability matrix is a parameter, and is just P.

- Specification: $\mathbf{A}$ is $IER_n(P)$.
- Intuition: The existence or nonexistence of edges is unstructured, other than the structure implied by the constraints of the network (independent-edge, unweighted, undirected, loopless).

Further technical details regarding single network models are provided in Appendix A.

Structured Independent-Edge Model (SIEM)

- Parameters: Z an $n \times n$ cluster assignment matrix for each edge to one of K edge clusters, and $\vec{p}$ a length-K probability vector for each of the K edge clusters.
- Edge probabilities: $\mathbb{E}[\mathbf{a}_{ij}] = p_{z_{ij}}$.
- Node degrees: $\mathbb{E}[\mathbf{d}_i] = \sum_{j \neq i} p_{z_{ij}}$.
- Specification: $\mathbf{A}$ is $SIEM_n(Z, \vec{p})$.
- Intuition: The existence or nonexistence of edges depends on the cluster a given edge is assigned to.

Joint Random Dot Product Graphs (JRDPG)

- Parameters: X the latent position matrix.
- Viewed as individual random networks (marginally), each of $\mathbf{A}^{(m)}$ are $RDPG_n(X)$.
- Viewed as a collection of random networks, $\mathbf{A}^{(m)}$ are independent.
- Specification: $\{\mathbf{A}^{(1)}, \ldots, \mathbf{A}^{(1)}\}$ are $JRDPG_{n,M}(X)$.
- Intuition: The collection of random networks $\{\mathbf{A}^{(1)}, \ldots, \mathbf{A}^{(1)}\}$ are independent $RDPG_n(X)$ random networks with homogeneous structure (the probability matrices are all the same).

Common Subspace Independent-Edge Model (COSIE)

- Parameters: V the $n \times d$ shared latent position matrix, and $R^{(m)}$ the $d \times d$ score matrix for each of the M networks.
- Viewed as individual random networks (marginally), each of $\mathbf{A}^{(m)}$ are $IER_n\left(P^{(m)}\right)$, where $P^{(m)} = VR^{(m)}V^{\top}$.
- Viewed as a collection of random networks, $\mathbf{A}^{(m)}$ are independent.
- Specification: $\{\mathbf{A}^{(1)}, \ldots, \mathbf{A}^{(1)}\}$ are $COSIE_{n,M}\left(V, \{R^{(1)}, \ldots, R^{(m)}\}\right)$.
- Intuition: The collection of random networks $\{\mathbf{A}^{(1)}, \ldots, \mathbf{A}^{(1)}\}$ are independent $IER_n\left(VR^{(m)}V^{\top}\right)$. The shared latent positions V convey shared structure across the networks, and the (potentially unique) score matrices $R^{(m)}$ delineate how to combine the shared latent positions for each network. This network model captures homogeneity across the networks through the shared latent positions and heterogeneity across the networks through the potentially unique score matrices.

Correlated Random Dot Product Graphs (ρRDPG)

- Parameters: ρ the correlation between the two networks, and X a latent position matrix.
- Viewed as individual random networks (marginally), each of $\mathbf{A}^{(m)}$ are $RDPG_n(X)$.

- Viewed as a pair of random networks (jointly), with $\mathbf{A}^{(1)}$ an $RDPG_n(X)$ random network, the edge probabilities for $\mathbf{A}^{(2)}$ are:

$$\mathbb{E}\left[\mathbf{a}_{ij}^{(2)}\right] = \begin{cases} \vec{x}_i^\top \vec{x}_j + \rho(1 - \vec{x}_i^\top \vec{x}_j), & \mathbf{a}_{ij}^{(1)} = 1 \\ (1 - \rho)\vec{x}_i^\top \vec{x}_j, & \mathbf{a}_{ij}^{(1)} = 0. \end{cases}$$

- Edge correlations: corr $\left(\mathbf{a}_{ij}^{(1)}, \mathbf{a}_{ij}^{(2)}\right) = \rho$.
- Specification: $\mathbf{A}$ is $SIEM_n(Z, \vec{p})$.
- Intuition: The two $RDPG_n(X)$ random networks $\mathbf{A}^{(1)}$ and $\mathbf{A}^{(2)}$ have edges which are correlated by ρ; that is, ρ conveys that edges existing in one network provide information about edges existing in the other network (ρ is positive), edges existing in one network are uninformative about the edges of the other network (ρ is near 0), or edges existing in one network provide information about edges not existing in the other network (ρ is negative).

Signal Subnetwork Model (SSN)
- Parameters: $\vec{\pi}$ the length-Y class assignment vector whose elements π_u delineate the probabilities of a network being in class y, a set of $n \times n$ probability matrices $P^{(y)}$ for all Y classes of networks, S the signal subnetwork which is a collection of edges.
- Edge probabilities: If an edge $(i, j) \in S$, then for at least two classes y and y', $p_{ij}^{(y)} \neq p_{ij}^{(y')}$. If an edge $(i, j) \notin S$, for all classes, $p_{ij}^{(1)} = \cdots = p_{ij}^{(Y)}$.
- Specification: $\left\{(\mathbf{A}^{(1)}, y_1), \ldots, (\mathbf{A}^{(1)}, y_1)\right\}$ are $SSN_{n,M}\left(\vec{\pi}, \left\{P^{(0)}, \ldots, P^{(Y)}\right\}, S\right)$.
- Intuition: The "signal subnetwork" delineates the edges which carry the "signal"; that is, the edges which differ across the two classes. Aside from the signal subnetwork edges, the remainder of the edges are identical across the networks.

4.11.2 Positive Semidefiniteness and Relating Block Models to RDPGs

As we learned in Section 4.5, positive semidefiniteness (PSD) is useful in that all positive semidefinite networks can be thought of as RDPGs. Particularly for block models (stochastic block models and degree-corrected stochastic block models), positive semidefiniteness of the block matrix means that the block matrix can be easily factorized by its square-root matrix:

$$B = \sqrt{B}\sqrt{B}^\top.$$

When the block matrix of a block model is PSD, we can find an equivalent RDPG. Stated another way, we could calculate a latent position matrix, where an RDPG with that latent position matrix has the same probability matrix as the original block model.

Latent Positions for SBMs
When $\mathbf{A}$ is $SBM_n(\vec{z}, B)$ where B is PSD, a latent position matrix can be calculated as $X = C\sqrt{B}$, which will have n rows and K latent dimensions (one for each community). The latent position for a given node is $\vec{x}_i = \sqrt{B}^\top \vec{c}_i$, where $\vec{c}_i$ is the

one-hot encoding of the community z_i for the node i. Consequently, for all nodes with the same community assignment, the latent positions are the same. For nodes with different community assignments, the latent positions may differ.

Latent Positions for DCSBMs
When $\mathbf{A}$ is $DCSBM_n(\vec{z}, \vec{\theta}, B)$ where B is PSD, a latent position matrix can be calculated as $X = \Theta C\sqrt{B}$, which will have n rows and K latent dimensions (one for each community). The latent position for a given node is $\vec{x}_i = \theta_i \sqrt{B}^\top \vec{c}_i$, where $\vec{c}_i$ is the one-hot encoding of the community z_i for the node i. Consequently, for all nodes with the same community assignment, the latent positions are the same, up to a rescaling by the degree-correction factor θ_i. In this sense, the degree-correction factor for a PSD DCSBM "stretches" the latent position associated with that community. For nodes with different community assignments, the latent positions may differ.

4.11.3   Stochastic Equivalence and a Hierarchy of Random Network Models

In Section 4.2.4, we introduced the idea of stochastic equivalence. Two random networks were stochastically equivalent if they had the same probability matrix. We used this idea to introduce the concept of "generalizations" of families of random network models; that is, one random network model (the "generalizing" model) generalizes the other (the "contained" model) if, for every random network in the contained model, we can identify a stochastically equivalent random network in the generalizing model.

Figure 4.11.1 summarizes these relationships. In this figure, there is a single shaded region for each random network model we have described. When one shaded region (the contained model) is contained in the other (the generalizing model), the indicated random network model is contained in the generalizing random network model.

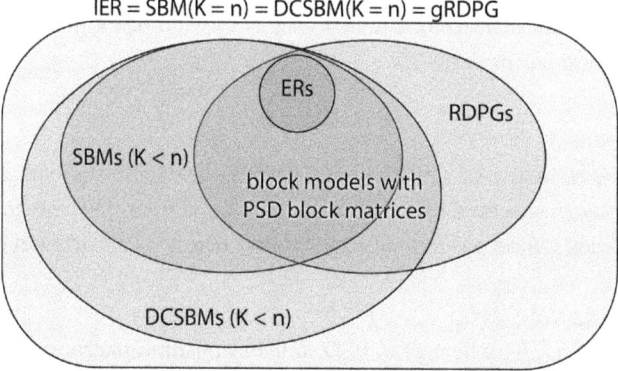

Figure 4.11.1 The hierarchy of random network models for single networks.

1. ERs are generalized by every other single network model.
2. SBMs with $K < n$ (each node is not assigned to its own unique community) are contained by DCSBMs, and SBMs with $K < n$ and PSD block matrices are contained by RDPGs.
3. DCSBMs with $K < n$ generalize SBMs, because they add an additional optional parameter (the degree-correction factors). SBMs and DCSBMs with indefinite block matrices are not RDPGs.
4. RDPGs generalize random networks with PSD probability matrices, such as ERs, and block models with PSD block matrices.
5. IER networks are the most general network models, and are equivalent to block models which allow noninformative communities (i.e., each node assigned to its own community). These are also equivalent to the generalized RDPG, or GRDPG, which we will briefly describe in Section 5.7.3 and in Appendix A.7.

It is useful to approach network modeling with this hierarchy of random networks in mind, due to the result of Concept 4.4.1: When we develop a technique for one random network model, the technique will apply "for free" to any random network model contained within it. In particular, when we develop tools for RDPGs, the techniques and intuition also apply to PSD SBMs and DCSBMs, since these are contained in the RDPGs.

Bibliography

[1] Casella G, Berger RL. Statistical Inference. Boston, MA, USA: Cengage Learning; 2001.
[2] Athreya A, Fishkind DE, Tang M, Priebe CE, Park Y, Vogelstein JT, et al. Statistical inference on random dot product graphs: A survey. J. Mach. Learn. Res. 2017 Jan.;18(1): 8393–8484.
[3] Erdös P, Rényi A. On random graphs I. Publicationes Mathematicae Debrecen. 1959;6:290.
[4] Gilbert EN. Random graphs. Ann. Math. Stat. 1959 Dec.;30(4):1141–1144.
[5] Holland PW, Laskey KB, Leinhardt S. Stochastic blockmodels: First steps. Social Networks. 1983 Jun.;5(2):109–137.
[6] Abbe E. Community detection and stochastic block models. arXiv. 2017 Mar.
[7] Young SJ, Scheinerman ER. Random dot product graphs for social networks. In: Algorithms and Models for the Web-Graph. Berlin, Germany: Springer; 2007, pp. 138–149.
[8] Chung J, Bridgeford E, Arroyo J, Pedigo BD, Saad-Eldin A, Gopalakrishnan V, et al. Statistical connectomics. Annu. Rev. Stat. Appl. 2021 Mar.;8(1):463–492.
[9] Horn RA, Johnson CR. Matrix Analysis. Cambridge, England, UK: Cambridge University Press; 2012.
[10] Karrer B, Newman MEJ. Stochastic blockmodels and community structure in networks. Phys. Rev. E. 2011 Jan.;83(1):016107.
[11] Qin T, Rohe K. Regularized spectral clustering under the degree-corrected stochastic blockmodel. arXiv. 2013 Sep.
[12] Rubin-Delanchy P, Cape J, Tang M, Priebe CE. A statistical interpretation of spectral embedding: The generalised random dot product graph. J. R. Stat. Soc. Ser. B Stat. Methodol. 2022 Sep.;84(4):1446–1473.

[13] Arroyo J, Athreya A, Cape J, Chen G, Priebe CE, Vogelstein JT. Inference for multiple heterogeneous networks with a common invariant subspace. J. Mach. Leran. Res. 2021;22(142):1–49.

[14] Levin K, Athreya A, Tang M, Lyzinski V, Priebe C. A Central Limit Theorem for an Omnibus Embedding of Multiple Random Dot Product Graphs. In: 2017 IEEE International Conference on Data Mining Workshops (ICDMW). 2017.

[15] Lyzinski V, Fishkind DE, Priebe CE. Seeded graph matching for correlated Erdös–Rényi graphs. J. Mach. Learn. Res. 2014 Jan.;15(1):3513–3540.

[16] Pantazis K, Athreya A, Arroyo J, Frost WN, Hill ES, Lyzinski V. The importance of being correlated: Implications of dependence in joint spectral inference across multiple networks. J. Mach. Learn. Res. 2022;23(141):1–77.

[17] Vogelstein JT, Roncal WG, Vogelstein RJ, Priebe CE. Graph classification using signal-subgraphs: applications in statistical connectomics. IEEE Trans. Pattern Anal. Mach. Intell. 2013 Jul.;35(7):1539–1551.

5   Learning Network Representations

In Chapter 3, we explored ways to describe and summarize observed networks. Chapter 4 introduced statistical models for random networks that could generate such observations. This chapter builds on these foundations to use our statistical models for learning useful representations, also called *embeddings*, of networks (the second to last step in Figure 5.0.1).

As we discussed in Section 1.3, networks are often not naturally suited to many traditional machine learning algorithms, which expect data in tabular form. Network embeddings address this challenge by transforming network data into vector representations that capture key structural properties. There are a variety of ways we can create these representations, one of which are called spectral embedding methods.

This chapter covers the following topics:

1. Section 5.1 introduces maximum likelihood estimation (MLE) for simple network models.
2. Section 5.2 motivates the need for network embeddings and contrasts networks with tabular data.
3. Section 5.3 presents adjacency spectral embedding (ASE) for learning latent position representations.
4. Section 5.4 covers Laplacian spectral embedding as an alternative to ASE.
5. Section 5.5 explores techniques for embedding multiple networks simultaneously.
6. Section 5.6 discusses joint representation learning incorporating node attributes.
7. Section 5.7 addresses estimating the appropriate latent dimension for embeddings.

Understanding the statistical models from Chapter 4 provides valuable context for this chapter. Moreover, they provide theoretical foundations for many of the applications we will examine in Chapter 7 and beyond. As readers progress through this chapter, we encourage them to regularly revisit the relevant statistical models in Chapter 4 when learning each new representation technique.

5.1   Maximum Likelihood Estimation

In Chapter 4, we introduced the concept of a random network, and began thinking of an observed network as a sample from its random network. Random network models are defined by their parameters. For example, an $SBM_n(\vec{z}, B)$ is defined by the parameters $\vec{z}$ and B. However, when we observe networks in the real world, we do not have

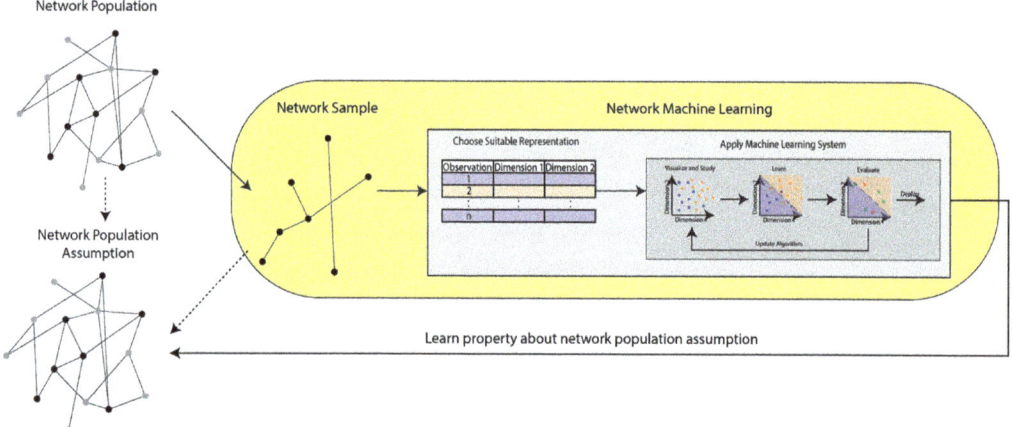

Network Population

Network Population
Assumption

Figure 5.0.1 The statistical learning pipeline. In this chapter, we will choose suitable representations for networks.

direct access to these parameters, and we must estimate them. This section explores methods for estimating parameters using a method common in statistical inference called *maximum likelihood estimation* (MLE).

We cover the following:

1. The basics of MLE,
2. MLE for the Erdös–Rényi , estimating the edge probability parameter, and
3. MLE for the stochastic block model, estimating the block probability matrix.

MLE is often used both explicitly and implicitly to build representations from observations of random variables, and works well when we have a firm understanding of the underlying behavior of our network. It is not particularly effective in more general cases, so the remainder of the chapter will focus on alternative strategies. Appendix B.1 provides more detailed mathematical derivations of MLE for network models.

Suppose we encounter a real-world network and wish to understand it better. We assume that this network is an observation of a random network characterized by certain parameters, but we do not know the parameters in advance. How do we estimate them?

We can often use MLE. The basics of MLE are discussed in Concept 5.1.1.

In this section, we will explore the MLE for our two most common graph models, the Erdös–Rényi (ER) random network and the stochastic block model. It is worth noting that both models, under the positive semidefinite assumption, can also be thought of as random dot product graphs. We will take advantage of this fact in Section 5.3.

5.1.1   Erdös–Rényi (ER)

Recall from Section 4.2 that the Erdös–Rényi (ER) random network has a single parameter: the probability of any edge existing, p.

Concept 5.1.1 The basics of MLE

In MLE, the objective is to find the parameter values that maximize the likelihood of the observed network under a given network model. This lets us use the data we have to estimate the parameters that generated them.

Mathematically, let $\mathcal{L}(\theta; A)$ denote the *likelihood function*, where θ represents the parameters of the model and A is the observed network. The MLE of θ is given by:

$$\hat{\theta}_{MLE} = \underset{\theta}{\operatorname{argmax}} \, \mathcal{L}(\theta; \mathbf{A}).$$

In practice, the negative natural logarithm of the likelihood function is often used to simplify calculations, because the logarithm has a property known as monotonicity, meaning that if $x > y$, then $\log(x) > \log(y)$. Therefore, if x is the maximizer of a function, then x is also the minimizer of the negative logarithm of that function. So, by minimizing the negative log likelihood, we maximize the likelihood.

Let's explore how we can use MLE to estimate p. Imagine we have a coin, but we don't know the probability of it landing on heads. However, we are allowed to flip it 100 times and then guess the probability of it landing on heads. After 100 flips, say it landed on heads 45 times. We flip again. What is our best guess for the probability that the coin will on heads?

If you thought it might be $\frac{45}{100}$, or the number of heads we got divided by the total number of coin flips, you would be right. This guess is the maximum likelihood estimate for a binary random variable.

The same principle applies to the ER random network. The best estimate of the probability of an edge existing in an ER random network is the ratio of the total number of edges in the simple network, $m = \sum_{j>i} a_{ij}$, divided by the total number of edges possible in the network, which is $\binom{n}{2}$.

Our result is:

$$\hat{p} = \frac{m}{\binom{n}{2}}.$$

The $\hat{}$ symbol means that $\hat{p}$ is an *estimate*: It is a function of the observed data that we use to describe the *estimand*, which is the parameter of the model that we want to learn about. In this case, since we are considering an $ER_n(p)$ model, our estimand is p.

Let's look at an example. We will use a sample of an ER random network, with 50 nodes and an edge probability of 0.3, similar to the example in Section 4.2. We begin by simulating and visualizing the appropriate network:

```
from graspologic.simulations import er_np
import numpy as np


p = 0.3
A = er_np(n=50, p=p)
```

Next, we fit the `ERAEstimator` from `graspologic`, and compare the true probability $p = 0.3$ to the estimated probability $\hat{p}$:

```python
from graspologic.models import ERAEstimator

model = ERAEstimator(directed=False, loops=False)
model.fit(A)
# obtain the estimate from the fit model
phat = model.p_
```

We can see how good the estimator performs by comparing it to the (true) population parameter, p:

```python
print("Difference between phat and p: {:.3f}".format(phat - p))
```

The estimate of the probability should end up close to the true value.

5.1.2 Stochastic Block Model

In Section 4.3, we said that the SBM, like the ER, is characterized by a probability parameter; in this case, a block probability matrix B. The entries in B, b_{kl}, denote the probabilities of edges existing between pairs of communities. When the other parameter for the SBM, the community assignment vector $\vec{z}$, is known, we can use similar strategies for learning about B.

As before, we will use the notation m_{kl} to denote the total number of edges between nodes in community k and nodes in community l, while n_{kl} represents the total possible number of edges between these communities. When we apply the MLE method to this model, we estimate b_{kl} by dividing m_{kl} by n_{kl}.

$$\hat{b}_{kl} = \frac{m_{kl}}{n_{kl}}.$$

To bring this back to our coin flip example, this is like saying that there is one coin (k, l) for each pair of communities in our network. We flip each coin once for every possible edge between those pairs of communities, n_{kl}. When that coin lands on heads, that edge exists, and when it lands on tails, that edge does not exist. Our best guess is just to count the number of heads we obtained, m_{kl}, and divide by the number of coin flips we made, n_{kl}.

In our Section 4.3 example, we had 100 students, each of whom were in one of two schools (school one and school two). If the students were both in school one, the probability that they were friends was 0.6, and if the students were both in school two, the probability that they were friends was 0.4. If the students attended different schools, the probability that they were friends was 0.1. This gave us a block matrix of:

$$B = \begin{bmatrix} 0.6 & 0.1 \\ 0.1 & 0.4 \end{bmatrix}.$$

Using this setup, we will simulate an appropriate SBM:

```
from graspologic.simulations import sbm

n = [50, 50]
B = np.array([[0.6, 0.1],
              [0.1, 0.4]])

A, z = sbm(n=n, p=B, return_labels=True)
```

A network sample is shown in Figure 4.3.1.

Next, we fit an appropriate SBM, and investigate the estimate of B:

```
from graspologic.models import SBMEstimator
from graphbook_code import heatmap

model = SBMEstimator(directed=False, loops=False)
model.fit(A, y=z)
Bhat = model.block_p_

# plot the block matrix vs estimate
heatmap(B, title="$B$ true block matrix", vmin=0, vmax=1, annot=True)
heatmap(Bhat, title=r"$\hat B$ estimate of block matrix", vmin=0,
    vmax=1, annot=True)
heatmap(np.abs(Bhat - B), title=r"$|\hat B - B|$", vmin=0, vmax=1,
    annot=True)
```

The difference between B and $\hat{B}$ is shown in Figure 5.1.1, and will tend to be quite small.

In this section, we have learned about estimating parameters for two types of simple networks. First, we have the $ER_n(p)$ random network. Here, edges are largely unstructured. Second, we have the $SBM_n(\vec{z}, B)$ network. For this, the network structure is predetermined by known community assignments and we only need to understand B.

For both types of random networks, we can accurately estimate the underlying probability parameters of these models using methods like MLE. These approaches allow us to make well-informed guesses about the likelihood of different types of

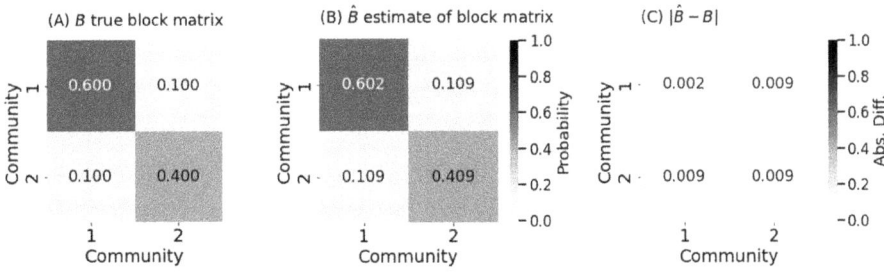

Figure 5.1.1 (**A**) The true block matrix underlying a random network. (**B**) The estimated block matrix from the network sample. (**C**) The difference between the estimated and true block matrices.

connections within these networks. Appendix B.1 provides technical details for MLE in ER and SBM random networks.

5.2   Why Do We Embed Networks?

We have been mentioning that a major topic of study in network machine learning is *representation learning*, which in our case often deals with embedding networks into modalities that we can understand as feature representations. We call these feature representations *tabular data* and the way we get to them an *embedding method*.

As we discussed in Section 1.1.1, tabular data are structured with rows representing observations and columns denoting features. This format simplifies the application of numerous ML algorithms such as neural networks, decision trees, or tasks such as classification, regression, and clustering. In this section, we explore the motivation behind representation learning. We cover the following topics:

1. The challenges of applying traditional machine learning algorithms to network data,
2. The concept of statistical dependence in network structures,
3. The need for transforming network data into tabular formats, and
4. How embeddings address the complex dependencies inherent in networks.

After giving proper motivation, we will dive into our first representation learning method, adjacency spectral embedding, in Section 5.3.

A common underlying assumption in machine learning is that each observation (row) is independent of others, reducing complex interdependences and correlations to simpler, feature-based relationships. However, in network data, this independence assumption crumbles. Each node is explicitly connected to others, resulting in a web of dependencies.

Network embeddings are a way of transforming network data into more digestible form for traditional ML algorithms. By projecting network data into a vector space (creating a "feature representation" for each node), we retain crucial information about node relationships while also structuring the data in a way that respects the expectations of these algorithms.

There is also a rich bidirectional relationship between networks and tabular data. Just as we can get from networks to tabular data, we can get from tabular data to networks. For instance, we can think of each row in our data matrix as a vector in Euclidean space. We can define its edge weight with other rows via some similarity or distance metric for that space, such as a Gaussian kernel, the Euclidean distance, or the cosine distance, and create a network accordingly. This method underlies numerous dimensionality reduction techniques, such as the diffusion map. Another strategy might be to find the nearest neighbors of the row vector, and construct a network using those neighbors. This idea underlies other techniques such as isomap.

The key with this example is less the specific techniques that are applied, and more the big picture of the implications of these problems on network data.

> **Case Study 5.2.1** Lobster dataset
>
> To better understand the concepts of this section, we will try to understand a lobster dataset [1]. Note that this dataset is not network valued. In this dataset, $n = 2560$ lobsters were collected by a team of university investigators in Norway. The data are encoded in a tabular format, where each row indicates the observation of a single lobster. For each lobster, the investigators measured the lobster's biological sex, the crusher claw width (CW), and the total length (TL) of the lobster. These attributes (or *features*) are encoded in the columns. Our question of interest is whether we can predict the crusher claw width using the lobster's biological sex and total length.

5.2.1   Statistical Dependence

To visualize whether we expect to find a relationship between the attributes measured in the lobster dataset, we use a scatter plot, shown in Figure 5.2.1. Each point represents the biological sex, claw width CW, and total length TL of a single lobster. There is clearly a positive association, where longer lobsters tend to have larger crusher claws. Further, it would appear that male lobsters tend to have a more dramatic increase in crusher claw width as total length increases.

In other words, this graph indicates a dependence between crusher claw width, lobster total length, and biological sex. Larger lobsters tend to have greater claw widths, and as males grow, their claw widths tend to grow faster than female claws.

It looks like we could fit a line between the total length and the crusher claw width for each lobster biological sex, and get a pretty good description of the relationship

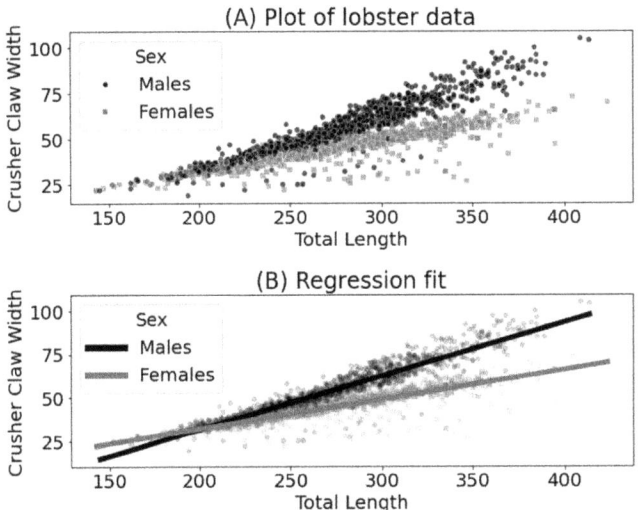

Figure 5.2.1 (**A**) A scatter plot of lobster total length against crusher claw width, separated by biological sex (shape + color). (**B**) A linear regression of the crusher claw width onto total length and biological sex, with an interaction term for biological sex and total length.

between the three features. A first-pass strategy would be to use a linear regression. In this case, based purely on the information we have gathered from visualizing the data, an appropriate model would regress the crusher claw width onto the lobster biological sex and total length, and allow for the biological sex to modify the relationship between total length and crusher claw width.

Figure 5.2.1(B) shows the results of this regression model. It appears that a relatively straightforward linear regression model does a good job of capturing what we intuitively derive from visualizing the data in Figure 5.2.1(A). We were able to explicitly describe a dependence that we expected, model it, and then capture it by fitting a regression model we believed to be appropriate.

It is almost never this easy to study a dependence, but it is often at least possible to do using an appropriate method. The key is that the traditional approach to dealing with dependencies when they arise in machine learning is to model them directly (like we did above) or indirectly (using latent models, for example, which we did not describe here, but which are discussed in [2]). When we have underlying dependencies in the data and want to account for them, our approach is to explicitly describe or isolate the dependence whenever possible. Further, if we are uncertain about dependencies in the model, we can often at least attempt to infer them implicitly.

5.2.2   How Can We Adapt Our Tabular Models to Networks?

This example, while trivial, gives us a good sense of some of the problems we will run into when we try to analyze network data.

The machine learning techniques and intuitions we build are usually designed for tabular data formats. Networks are not tabular at all; an observed network is a matrix and not a vector, and a node is defined within the adjacency matrix by its set of connections with other nodes. It is unclear at first glance how to adapt a network for the tabular setting.

The solution to this problem is a network embedding, which is first and foremost a tool. Embedding is the "bridge" which provides functionality to convert to tabular data. Embedding a network and then visualizing that embedding is also often the simplest way to quickly explore a network.

All networks have the same type of statistical dependence which arose in the lobster data, but on a much larger scale. When studying a dataset with two features there is one possible dependence that can arise: The first feature can be related to the second feature. When studying a dataset with three features like the lobster data, there are three possible pairwise dependencies that can arise: the first feature being related to the second, the second related to the third, or the first being related to the third. The number of possible pairwise dependencies with d features is $\frac{d(d-1)}{2}$. When d is small, this is manageable with explicit modeling (like we did previously for the lobsters). Even when d is fairly large, most dependencies are typically negligible.

Unfortunately, dependencies in networks are explicitly nonnegligible. The nodes and edges that make up the adjacency matrix have inherent dependencies: Each edge depends on a pair of nodes, so our network has at least $\binom{n}{2}$ dependencies to consider when determining how to learn from it. Stated another way, nodes could be related to one another explicitly (by a specific grouping, such as a community assignment) or implicitly (by the nodes having similarities depending on different aspects of them that are not immediately apparent at first glance), and these relationships convey dependencies between the edges or subnetworks of the network itself. When n is 50, a small sized network, $\binom{n}{2} = 1225$, which means that with just 50 nodes, we would have over a thousand possible dependencies.

Explicitly Delineating the Dependence Structure
Sometimes, we can take the easy way out with network data, like we might do with tabular data: We can simply ignore a lot of the dependencies that might exist. If we think that the nodes of our network are totally unrelated, we can learn from it by using strategies appropriate for ER random networks (Section 4.2). Remember that the ER random network made the assumption that all pairs of nodes have an equal connection probability that does not depend on any aspect of the individual nodes themselves (the edges are entirely independent).

If we are given some sort of a grouping between the nodes, such as a community assignment vector, we can learn from the network using strategies appropriate for SBM random network models (Section 4.3) and their cousins. Remember than the SBM random network models make the assumption that, once we know the community assignment $\vec{z}$ of a node, the edge probability is simply the appropriate entry of the block matrix. The SBM makes the crucial assumption that other than the community assignments and the block probabilities, edges are independent. These approaches make excellent first-passes, and can be combined with other techniques we will see arise in Part III.

If We Cannot Explicitly Delineate Dependencies, What Are We Left With?
We usually cannot immediately ignore dependence structures in networks. We might have a network where we do not know a good grouping of the nodes ahead of time, or we might want to learn appropriate groupings of nodes directly from the data. There might be dependencies that go beyond just a grouping of the nodes, or grouping nodes together might be entirely inappropriate. There are a variety of ways in which prescriptive applications of SBMs with known community assignment vectors and ERs are not entirely appropriate.

In the next few sections, we will start to learn embedding techniques to address these more complicated situations.

5.3   Adjacency Spectral Embedding

Section 4.4 introduced the random dot product graph (RDPG), a statistical model which parametrizes some positive semidefinite probability matrix P as the product of a latent position matrix X and its transpose: $P = XX^\top$. In this section, we learn how to estimate X from some adjacency matrix A using a technique called *adjacency spectral embedding* (ase).

We cover the following:

1. The mathematical foundations of ase, including eigendecomposition and singular value decomposition,
2. The process of embedding adjacency matrices into latent positions,
3. Limitations of ase for adjacency matrices and the transition to singular value decomposition,
4. Interpretation of ase results and their relationship to underlying network structure, and
5. The concept of nonidentifiability in network embeddings.

Intuition about positive semidefiniteness from Section 4.5 will be critical for the embedding approach that we learn in this chapter. We will heavily use both the eigen-decomposition and the singular value decomposition. For a refresher on eigendecom-position, see [3]. For singular value decomposition, read lectures 4 and 5 in [4]. One key result that we will use repeatedly throughout this section concerns matrix multiplications with diagonal matrices. Readers should work through Exercise 5.3.1 as a check for linear algebra background.

Exercise 5.3.1 Matrix multiplications with diagonal matrices

Suppose the A is a $n \times m$ matrix, D is a $m \times m$ square diagonal matrix, and B is a $n \times m$ matrix. Denote the columns of A and B by $\vec{a}_i$ and $\vec{b}_i$, respectively, and the diagonal elements of D by d_i; that is:

$$A = \begin{bmatrix} | & & | \\ \vec{a}_i & \cdots & \vec{a}_m \\ | & & | \end{bmatrix}, \quad D = \begin{bmatrix} d_1 & & \\ & \ddots & \\ & & d_m \end{bmatrix}, \quad B = \begin{bmatrix} | & & | \\ \vec{b}_i & \cdots & \vec{b}_m \\ | & & | \end{bmatrix}.$$

Show that:

$$ADB^\top = \sum_{i=1}^{m} d_i \vec{a}_i \vec{b}_i^\top,$$

using the rules of matrix multiplication, and expansion of the above sum. Note that $\vec{a}_i \vec{b}_i^\top$ is a matrix.

Imagine that we have a probability matrix P for a positive semidefinite, simple, independent-edge random network. Section 4.5 showed that any PSD real matrix has a real square-root matrix. Since the network is simple, it is undirected, and so P is symmetric.

If we let $X = \sqrt{P}$ be the square-root matrix for P, so that $P = XX^\top$, P is the probability matrix corresponding to an $RDPG_n(X)$ random network. For our purposes, we will assume that the network has n nodes, and X has a latent dimensionality of d which is less than the number of nodes. This implies that the rank of X is at most d (the rank of the matrix, the number of linearly independent columns, cannot exceed the number of columns).

5.3.1 Uses of the Eigendecomposition for Positive Semidefinite Probability Matrices

These facts provide us with useful information about the eigendecomposition of P. Specifically, we can factorize P into its eigenvalues and eigenvectors (called the *eigendecomposition* of P, another example of a matrix decomposition from Remark 4.5.1) and this provides us with latent position matrices for random networks. Note that these results only apply with symmetric, PSD probability matrices, where the matrix is guaranteed to decompose into a full set of eigenvalues and eigenvectors. Remember that the probability matrix for a network with n nodes is square ($n \times n$). If the network is simple, it is also symmetric (Section 4.1). Relevant conclusions for such a probability matrix are summarized in Concept 5.3.2.

Concept 5.3.2 The eigendecomposition of real symmetric matrices

Consider a real symmetric square matrix R. Diagonal symmetry in matrices guarantees a full eigendecomposition. The *eigendecomposition* of R is:

$$R = Q \Lambda Q^\top = \sum_{i=1}^{n} \lambda_i \vec{q}_i \vec{q}_i^\top,$$

where Λ is the diagonal matrix of the ordered (in decreasing order) eigenvalues λ_i of R, and Q is an orthogonal matrix whose columns $\vec{q}_i$ are eigenvectors of R. Throughout this book, we notate the eigendecomposition of a matrix R with $\text{evd}(R)$. A matrix W is *orthogonal* if it is square and $WW^\top = W^\top W = I$, the identity matrix.

If R is symmetric PSD and low rank, the eigenvalues have another interesting property, summarized in Concept 5.3.3.

Concept 5.3.3 The eigendecomposition of symmetric, PSD, low-rank matrices

Assume that R is an $n \times n$ real symmetric square matrix, the rank of R is $d' < n$, and R is positive semidefinite. If $R = Q \Lambda Q^\top$ is an evd of R, Λ will have d' positive eigenvalues, and the remaining $n - d'$ eigenvalues will be 0. So:

$$\lambda_1 \geq \lambda_2 \geq \cdots \geq \lambda_{d'} > 0 = \lambda_{d'+1} = \cdots = \lambda_n$$

For such a symmetric PSD and low-rank matrix R, notice that the evd is:

$$R = Q \Lambda Q^\top = \sum_{i=1}^{n} \lambda_i \vec{q}_i \vec{q}_i^\top$$

$$= \sum_{i=1}^{d'} \lambda_i \vec{q}_i \vec{q}_i^\top + \sum_{i=d'+1}^{n} \lambda_i \vec{q}_i \vec{q}_i^\top$$

$$= \sum_{i=1}^{d'} \lambda_i \vec{q}_i \vec{q}_i^\top,$$

where we used the fact that $\lambda_i = 0$ for the remaining $n - d'$ eigenvalues. For any $d > d'$:

$$\sum_{i=d'+1}^{d} \lambda_i \vec{q}_i \vec{q}_i^\top = \sum_{i=d'+1}^{n} \lambda_i \vec{q}_i \vec{q}_i^\top = 0,$$

because both the left and right of the equals sign have the value of 0 (since the eigenvalues are 0). If $d \geq d'$, then combining these facts gives:

$$R = \sum_{i=1}^{d} \lambda_i \vec{q}_i \vec{q}_i^\top$$

$$= \sum_{i=1}^{d'} \lambda_i \vec{q}_i \vec{q}_i^\top.$$

This fact leads to the observation noted in Concept 5.3.4.

Concept 5.3.4 reduced `evd` for symmetric, PSD, low-rank matrices

Assume that R is an $n \times n$ real symmetric square matrix, the rank of R is $d' < n$, and R is positive semidefinite. Then if $R = Q\Lambda Q^\top$ is a `evd` for R, for any $d \geq d'$:

$$R = Q_d \Lambda_d Q_d^\top,$$

where Q_d is a matrix whose columns are the first d columns of Q, and Λ_d is a $d \times d$ square matrix whose diagonal entries are the first d diagonal entries of Λ (the first d eigenvalues of R).

Remember that the RDPGs can characterize any random network with a PSD probability matrix, as we learned in Concept 4.5.2. If the latent position matrix X has d latent dimensions where $d < n$, then by definition, the rank of X is at most d. Further, the rank of a matrix is equal to the rank of its transpose, so the rank of $X^\top$ is at most d as well.

The rank of the product of two matrices is also upper-bounded by the ranks of the individual matrices. For instance, if $C = AB$, the rank of C is:

$$\text{rank}(C) \leq \min\left(\text{rank}(A), \text{rank}(B)\right). \tag{5.1}$$

In our case, since $P = XX^\top$ and X and $X^\top$ are rank at most d, P has a rank of at most d.

Applying this fact in conjunction with Concept 5.3.4, we see that if the probability matrix P is positive semidefinite, has rank at most d, and is symmetric, we obtain a characterization of latent positions of P where:

$$P = Q_d \Lambda_d Q_d^\top$$

$$= \left(Q_d \sqrt{\Lambda_d}\right)\left(Q_d \sqrt{\Lambda_d}\right)^\top = XX^\top, \quad X = Q_d \sqrt{\Lambda_d} \tag{5.2}$$

where $\sqrt{\Lambda_d}$ is the matrix whose entries are the square roots of the first d eigenvalues of P. Note that $\sqrt{\Lambda_d}$ is real, because the top d eigenvalues are positive by Concept 5.3.3, so their square root is defined.

We can put this entire procedure together using Algorithm 5.1, to obtain a latent position matrix for the random network.

Algorithm 5.1 Finding latent positions for a low-rank, symmetric, PSD probability matrix

---

Data: P an $n \times n$ symmetric PSD and square probability matrix of rank at most d.

Result: a latent position matrix for the random network.

1 Let $Q, \Lambda = \text{evd}(P)$ be the eigenvectors and eigenvalues of P.

2 Let $Q_d = \begin{bmatrix} \top & & \top \\ \vec{q}_1 & \cdots & \vec{q}_d \\ \bot & & \bot \end{bmatrix}$, and let $\Lambda_d = \begin{bmatrix} \lambda_1 & & \\ & \ddots & \\ & & \lambda_d \end{bmatrix}$ be the matrix whose

rows are the first d eigenvectors and the diagonal matrix whose entries are the first d eigenvalues of P.

3 Compute $\sqrt{\Lambda_d}$ to be the matrix whose entries are $\sqrt{\lambda_i}$, for all i from 1 to d.

4 Let $X = Q_d\sqrt{\Lambda_d}$.

5 **return** X

This gives us a method to compute a latent position matrix for the underlying random network, which has n rows (the same as the number of nodes) and d columns. We will call this process `eigembed(P)`.

5.3.1.1   Limitations of `eigembed` for Adjacency Matrices

These results are helpful when we know the probability matrix ahead of time. In fact, we even know how to determine whether the probability matrix is positive semidefinite, using the procedure that we developed in Section 4.5, where we simply checked whether all of the eigenvalues were nonnegative.

Unfortunately, in real data, we do not have the probability matrix; all we have is the network itself, usually in the form of an adjacency matrix. It would be helpful if we could simply plug the adjacency matrix into Algorithm 5.1, and obtain a reasonable estimate of latent positions. Unfortunately, while this matrix is real and symmetric, it is not necessarily positive semidefinite. This means that we cannot necessarily decompose it in the same way and obtain real estimates of latent position matrices.

Consider, for instance, the adjacency matrix for a 2×2 network:

$$A = \begin{bmatrix} 0 & 1 \\ 1 & 0 \end{bmatrix}.$$

From Section 4.5, for a 2×2 matrix to be positive semidefinite, its determinant has to be nonnegative: $det(A) \geq 0$. However, $det(A) = -1$, so this matrix is not positive semidefinite.

This means that none of the logic leading to Algorithm 5.1 applies to adjacency matrices. In this simple example, for instance, $\sqrt{\Lambda_d}$ would not even be a real matrix (it would be a complex matrix). In practice, the implications of this trivial example are

that we cannot always use the eigendecomposition to obtain real estimates of latent
position matrices from adjacency matrices.

5.3.2   The Singular Value Decomposition Allows Us to Estimate Latent Position Matrices

There is a closely related approach, the *singular value decomposition*, which we can
use to estimate latent position matrices regardless of the positive semidefiniteness of
P. Concept 5.3.5 summarizes useful results about the singular value decomposition.

Concept 5.3.5 The singular value decomposition of real matrices

If R is a real $n \times n$ square matrix of rank d, then the *singular value decomposition*
is the factorization:

$$R = U \Sigma V^\top = \sum_{i=1}^{n} \sigma_i \vec{u}_i \vec{v}_i^\top,$$

where Σ is the diagonal matrix of the nonnegative ordered *singular values* σ_i
of R, U is an orthogonal matrix whose n columns $\vec{u}_i$ are the n-dimensional *left
singular vectors* of R, and V is an orthogonal matrix whose n columns $\vec{v}_i$ are the
n-dimensional *right singular vectors* of R. Throughout this book, we notate the
singular value decomposition of a matrix R with $\mathrm{svd}(R)$.

When a matrix is positive semidefinite and low rank, such as the probability matrix
for an RDPG, we obtain a virtually equivalent result to Concept 5.3.4 (which was for
the evd) for the svd. This observation is noted in Concept 5.3.6.

Concept 5.3.6 svd of symmetric, PSD, low-rank matrices

If R is symmetric and PSD, then all left and right singular vectors $\vec{u}_i = \vec{v}_i$ for any
$\sigma_i > 0$.
If R is a real matrix that is rank $d' < n$ and has the svd $R = U \Sigma V^\top$, R will have
d' positive singular values, and the remaining $n - d'$ singular values will be 0. So:

$$\sigma_1 \geq \sigma_2 \geq \cdots \geq \sigma_{d'} > 0 = \sigma_{d'+1} = \cdots = \sigma_n.$$

For such a symmetric PSD and low-rank matrix R, the svd is:

$$R = U \Sigma V^\top = \sum_{i=1}^{n} \sigma_i \vec{u}_i \vec{v}_i^\top$$

$$= \sum_{i=1}^{d'} \sigma_i \vec{u}_i \vec{u}_i^\top + \sum_{i=d'+1}^{n} \sigma_i \vec{u}_i \vec{v}_i^\top,$$

where we used the fact that $\vec{u}_i = \vec{v}_i$ for the first d' singular values. Notice further that
$\sigma_i = 0$ for the the remaining $n - d'$ singular values, so:

$$R = \sum_{i=1}^{d'} \sigma_i \vec{u}_i \vec{u}_i^\top + \sum_{i=d'+1}^{n} 0\vec{u}_i \vec{v}_i^\top .$$

Because $0\vec{u}_i \vec{v}_i^\top = 0\vec{u}_i \vec{u}_i^\top = 0$, this implies that:

$$R = \sum_{i=1}^{d'} \sigma_i \vec{u}_i \vec{u}_i^\top + \sum_{i=d'+1}^{n} 0\vec{u}_i \vec{u}_i^\top .$$

Therefore:

$$R = U\Sigma U^\top ,$$

so the svd of a symmetric PSD and low-rank matrix R is also an evd of R. We can take this a final step further, in Concept 5.3.7.

Concept 5.3.7 svd gives an evd for positive semidefinite, low-rank matrices

If R is a symmetric PSD and low-rank matrix with rank $d' < n$, and the svd is given by $R = U\Sigma V^\top$, then $R = U\Sigma U^\top$ is also an evd for R.
Therefore, by Concept 5.3.4, for any $d \geq d'$:

$$R = U_d \Sigma_d U_d^\top$$

where U_d is the $n \times d$ matrix of the top d left singular vectors of R, and Σ_d is the $d \times d$ diagonal matrix of the top d singular values of R.

Together, when P is positive semidefinite, symmetric, has rank at most d, and the svd is given by $P = U\Sigma V^\top$, we obtain a characterization of latent positions of P using the left singular vectors and the singular values which is similar to the result we obtained in Equation (5.2):

$$P = XX^\top, \quad X = U_d\sqrt{\Sigma_d}. \tag{5.3}$$

Here, $\sqrt{\Sigma_d}$ is the matrix whose entries are the square roots of the first d singular values of P, and U_d are the first d left singular vectors of P. However, there is a subtle but impactful distinction to the result we obtained in Equation (5.2).

The left and right singular vector matrices U and V are by definition real matrices for any real matrix P (no requirement of positive semidefiniteness). Further, the singular values σ_i are always nonnegative, which means that they have a real square root. This means that any time we compute $U_d\sqrt{\Sigma_d}$ using the svd of a real matrix, we will end up with a real result.

The procedure in Algorithm 5.1 only produced a real matrix when the input matrix followed strict conditions that are not necessarily satisfied by adjacency matrices; particularly, positive semidefiniteness. However, the procedure we just developed can be applied to any real matrix and produce a real result, summarized in Algorithm 5.2.

> **Remark 5.3.8** `ase` tabularizes the adjacency matrix
>
> One of the challenges we noted in Section 1.3 and reiterated in Section 5.2 was that network learning differs fundamentally from traditional machine learning in that the data are not tabular. However, the embedding process has changed this: We have tabularized the network into a real estimated latent position matrix with n rows (one for each node) and d columns (one for each latent dimension). This provides us with a tabular data structure, which we can build upon later on to explore the nodes using more traditional machine learning approaches.

Algorithm 5.2 Estimating latent positions from adjacency matrices (`ase`)

Data: A an adjacency matrix for a simple network.

       d a target latent dimensionality.

Result: an estimate of a latent position matrix.

1 Let $U, \Sigma, V^\top = \mathrm{svd}(A)$ be the left singular vectors, the singular values, and the right singular vectors of A.

2 Let $U_d = \begin{bmatrix} \top & & \top \\ \vec{u}_1 & \cdots & \vec{u}_d \\ \bot & & \bot \end{bmatrix}$, and let $\Sigma_d = \begin{bmatrix} \sigma_1 & & \\ & \ddots & \\ & & \sigma_d \end{bmatrix}$ be the matrix whose

rows are the first d left singular vectors and the diagonal matrix whose entries are the first d singular values of A.

3 Compute $\sqrt{\Sigma_d}$ to be the matrix whose entries are $\sqrt{\sigma_i}$, for all i from 1 to d.

4 Let $\widehat{X} = U_d \sqrt{\Sigma_d}$.

5 **return** $\widehat{X}$

This process is known as the adjacency spectral embedding, or `ase`. It is called "adjacency" because unlike `eigembed`, it is able to operate on the adjacency matrix. "Spectral" means that its theoretical intuition relies on the eigenvalues/eigenvectors (the spectrum) of P. "Embedding" means that it finds a mathematical structure contained in another (in this case a tabular structure contained within the adjacency matrix, as explained in Remark 5.3.8). While we will not obtain the convenient equality in Equation (5.3) that the adjacency matrix is exactly equal to $\widehat{X}\widehat{X}^\top$ where $\widehat{X} = \mathrm{ase}(A)$, $\widehat{X}$ is a real matrix that we can study further.

Imagine we have an $SBM_n(\vec{z}, B)$ with 100 nodes, where the first 50 nodes are in community 1, and the second 50 nodes are in community 2. The block matrix will be homophilic, so by Section 4.5, the probability matrix is positive semidefinite.

```
from graspologic.simulations import sbm
from graphbook_code import generate_sbm_pmtx, lpm_from_sbm
import numpy as np

n = 100
# construct the block matrix B as described above
B = np.array([[0.6, 0.1],
              [0.1, 0.4]])
```

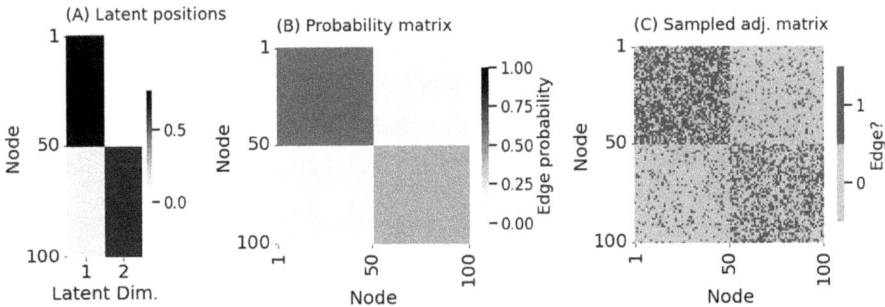

Figure 5.3.1 (**A**) Latent positions of the SBM random network, (**B**) the probability matrix of the SBM random network, and (**C**) a sampled adjacency matrix of the SBM random network.

```
# sample a graph from SBM_{100}(tau, B)
np.random.seed(0)
A, zs = sbm(n=[n//2, n//2], p=B, return_labels=True)

X = lpm_from_sbm(zs, B)
P = generate_sbm_pmtx(zs, B)
```

Figure 5.3.1 plots the latent positions, the probability matrix, and the network sample. The latent positions are all equal for nodes from the same community. In light of the results we explored in Section 4.7.8, we should expect this for an SBM random network with a positive semidefinite block matrix.

In the SBM we are studying above, the latent position matrix has two latent dimensions (one for each community). This is no coincidence, and the reason for this is important to understand. This insight is provided in Concept 5.3.9.

Next, we use `graspologic` to compute the `ase` of our network sample. We know that there are two communities, so we embed into two dimensions. This gives us an estimate of the latent position matrix:

```
from graspologic.embed import AdjacencySpectralEmbed as ase

d = 2 # the latent dimensionality
# estimate the latent position matrix with ase
Xhat = ase(n_components=d, svd_seed=0).fit_transform(A)
```

Using this estimate of the latent position matrix, we can visualize an estimate of the probability matrix, as:

$$\widehat{P} = \widehat{X}\widehat{X}^{\top}.$$

Let's do this with numpy:

```
Phat = Xhat @ Xhat.transpose()
```

Figure 5.3.2(A) and (C) plots the latent position matrix and probability matrix, and Figure 5.3.2(B) and (D) plots the estimated latent position matrix and estimated probability matrix.

> **Concept 5.3.9** Number of latent dimensions for positive semidefinite SBMs
>
> From Concept 4.3.3, the one-hot encoding matrix C has n rows and K columns (one for each community). For each community, all nodes have the same one-hot encoding. That is, for all nodes i and j where $z_i = z_j = k$ (nodes i and j are in the same community), $\vec{c}_i = \vec{c}_j$ (they have the same one-hot encoding). Further, the one-hot encodings for each community are distinct from one another. That is, any nodes i and j' where $z_i \neq z_{j'}$ (nodes i and j' are in different communities), $\vec{c}_i \neq \vec{c}_{j'}$ (they have different one-hot encodings). This means that C has K unique rows and is therefore rank K.
>
> Further, the positive semidefinite block matrix B will be full rank in general. With $P = CBC^\top$, we can identify an upper bound for the rank of the probability matrix using Equation (5.1):
>
> $$\text{rank}(P) \leq \min\left(\text{rank}(C), \text{rank}(B), \text{rank}(C^\top)\right).$$
>
> By the above, $\text{rank}(C) = K$, $\text{rank}(B) = K$, and $\text{rank}(C^\top) = K$, since matrices have the same rank as their transposes. Therefore, $\text{rank}(P) \leq K$.
> From Equation (5.3), $P = XX^\top$ where $X = U_d\sqrt{\Sigma_d}$, and d is $\geq$ the rank of P. Therefore, for a positive semidefinite SBM with K communities, we use K embedding dimensions, since the corresponding probability matrix P would have a rank of at most K.

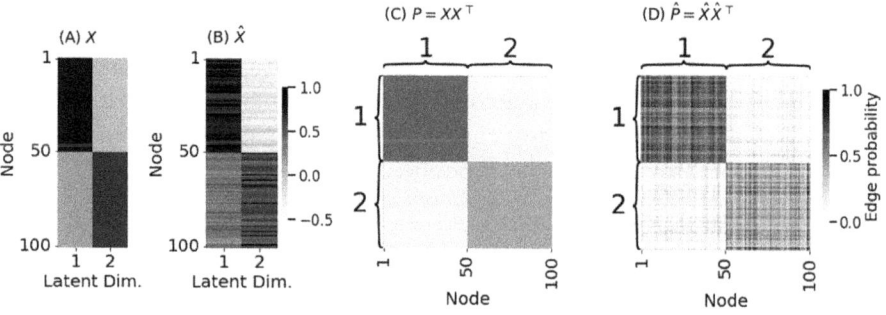

Figure 5.3.2 (**A**) The true latent positions, (**B**) the estimated latent positions, (**C**) the true probability matrix, and (**D**) the estimated probability matrix.

Comparing the latent positions in Figure 5.3.2(A) to the estimated latent positions in Figure 5.3.2(B), we see that the values are different; however, a major pattern remains the same. The estimated latent positions follow the general trend we would anticipate for the SBM; particularly, all of the nodes in the first community (the first 50 nodes) tend to have similar estimated latent positions, and all of the nodes in the second community (the second 50 nodes) tend to have similar estimated latent positions which are distinct from the first. In light of Section 4.7.8, the true latent positions are identical for nodes in the same community, so any estimated latent positions in this same community should be close to each other. Likewise, the probability matrix in Figure 5.3.2(C) is similar to the estimated probability matrix in Figure 5.3.2(D).

Now, let's consider what happens when we randomly reorder the nodes of the network, just like we did in Section 4.3.5:

```
vtx_perm = np.random.choice(n, size=n, replace=False)

# reorder the adjacency matrix
Aperm = A[tuple([vtx_perm])] [:,vtx_perm]
# reorder the community assignment vector
zperm = np.array(zs)[vtx_perm]

# compute the estimated latent positions using the
# permuted adjacency matrix
Xhat_perm = ase(n_components=2).fit_transform(Aperm)
```

Our adjacency matrix looks like Figure 5.3.3(A), and the estimated latent positions look like Figure 5.3.3(B). It is not quite as obvious now that the two communities of nodes in the network have similar latent positions looking only at the heatmap of $\hat{X}$ in (B), because these communities have been dispersed throughout the network.

5.3.2.1 The "Pairs Plot" for Estimated Latent Positions

Figure 5.3.3(C) visualizes tabular data structures to explore the latent structure with a *pairs plot*.

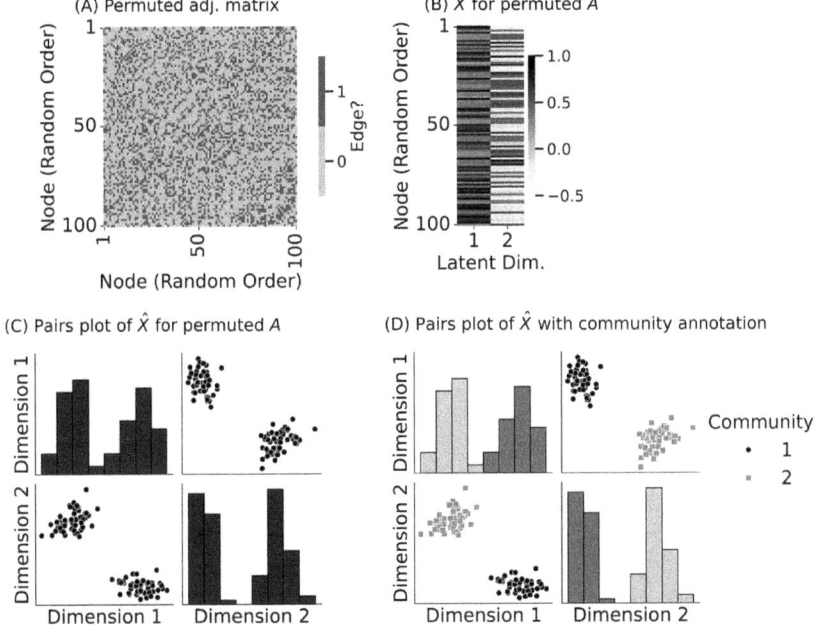

Figure 5.3.3 (**A**) The permuted adjacency matrix, (**B**) the estimated latent positions of the permuted adjacency matrix, (**C**) the pairs plot of the estimated latent positions of the permuted adjacency matrix, and (**D**) the pairs plot shown with the true community labels of the nodes.

To study the pairs plot, we can call the pair plotting utility directly from graspologic, which provides a wrapper for the pairplot function from seaborn designed for latent position matrices:

```
from graspologic.plot import pairplot

pairplot(Xhat, title=r"Pairs plot of $\hat X$")
```

Figure 5.3.3(C) shows the pairs plot for the estimated latent positions. The pairs plot is a $d \times d$ matrix of plots, where d is the total number of features of the matrix for which a pairs plot is being produced. It is called "pairs plot" because it plots pairs of dimensions.

For each off-diagonal plot, the kth row and lth column has the points (x_{ik}, x_{il}) for each node in the network. It is a scatter plot for each node of the kth dimension and the lth dimension of the matrix being plotted. There are two distinct looking "blobs" of point clouds in the pairs plot of $\hat X$ in Figure 5.3.3(C). These "blobs" are known as latent clusters. They are latent because they are unknown to us at the beginning of analysis, and clusters because they are groups of points. These clusters provide evidence for latent community structure in the network. The plot is symmetric, since the off-diagonal entries are mirror images of one another (one will be dimension k against dimension l, and the off-diagonal entry will be dimension l against dimension k).

The diagonal elements of the pairs plot represent histograms or density estimates (called *Kernel Density Estimates*, or KDEs) of the estimated latent positions for each dimension. If we do not include labels, we obtain histograms, which are scaled bins showing the number of points for a given dimension which fall into the indicated range. If we do pass in labels, we obtain density estimates, where higher densities indicate that more points have latent position estimates in that range. For instance, the top left density estimate is the density estimate of the first latent dimension for all nodes, the middle is a density estimate of the second latent dimension for all nodes, and so on.

When the number of embedding dimensions is two, showing a full pairs plot is redundant. In this case, we often simply show a scatter plot of dimension 1 against dimension 2.

Now, let's see what happens to the pairs plot for $\widehat X$, which we pass in the reordered community labels for the nodes:

```
fig = pairplot(Xhat_perm, labels=zperm, legend_name = "Community",
            title=r"Pairs plot of $\widehat X$ with community
                annotation",
            diag_kind="hist")
```

The resulting plot is shown in Figure 5.3.3(D). The two distinct clusters in Figure 5.3.3(C) each correspond to a single community in the underlying SBM random network. In fact, nodes of the same community tend to have estimated latent positions that are close together. We say vectors are "close together" with respect to the Euclidean distance, defined in Concept 5.3.10.

To evaluate this, we can compute the distance matrix of the estimated latent positions, D. We will use the the unpermuted points to make the conclusion more

---

Concept 5.3.10 Euclidean norms and the Euclidean distance

If $\vec{x} = (x_i)_{i=1}^d$ is a d-dimensional real vector, the *Euclidean norm* (or, 2-norm) is defined as:

$$\|\vec{x}\|_2 = \sqrt{\sum_{i=1}^n x_i^2}.$$

If $\vec{y} = (y_i)_{i=1}^d$ is a second d-dimensional real vector, the *Euclidean distance* is defined as:

$$d(\vec{x}, \vec{y}) = \|\vec{x} - \vec{y}\|_2 = \sqrt{(\vec{x} - \vec{y})^\top (\vec{x} - \vec{y})} = \sqrt{\sum_{i=1}^d (x_i - y_i)^2}.$$

---

immediate. Each entry D_{ij} corresponds to the distance $d(\hat{\vec{x}}_i, \hat{\vec{x}}_j)$ between all pairs of estimated latent positions. We can compute the pairwise distance matrix using `scipy`:

```
from scipy.spatial import distance_matrix

D = distance_matrix(Xhat, Xhat)
```

Figure 5.3.4 shows a plot of the pairwise distance matrix. Note that the pairwise distance matrices between the first 50 nodes (community 1, the upper left block of the pairwise distance matrix) and the second 50 nodes (community 2, the bottom right block of the pairwise distance matrix) are relatively small, but the pairwise distances between nodes from community 1 and nodes from community 2 (and vice versa, in the upper right and bottom left blocks of the pairwise distance matrix) are relatively

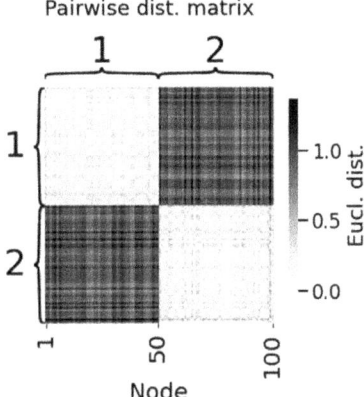

Figure 5.3.4 The pairwise distance matrix between the latent position vectors of all pairs of nodes.

large. This will be useful to us in Section 6.1 when we attempt to estimate underlying community structure from SBM random networks.

5.3.3   Why Do We Use `ase`?

The primary utility of `ase` is that it tabularizes an adjacency matrix into an $n \times d$ real matrix, where d is the number of embedding dimensions.

There are additional reasons to use `ase`.

`ase` Always Recovers Latent Positions for the Probability Matrix, given the Latent Dimensionality

Say we sample a network A from an $RDPG_n(X)$ random network with a latent position matrix X and latent dimensionality d. Using `ase(P,d)` gives us true latent positions for the probability matrix, which we found in Equation (5.3). We can embed our sample's adjacency matrix A using `ase` in the exact same way that we embed the underlying probability matrix P to get estimates of the latent positions. We can use `ase` even if A is not positive semidefinite, so we will always obtain a set of real latent positions for adjacency matrices.

`ase` Decouples Dependencies of the Random Network

Studying a latent position matrix X is statistically equivalent to studying P when P is a function of X, such as $P = XX^\top$. Since X is far simpler than P (it will usually have fewer columns, in practice), it will be easier to study.

Section 5.2 discussed the complexity of the dependency structure for a random network $\mathbf{A}$. This is because the inherent coupling of edges to nodes creates at least $\binom{n}{2}$ possible dependencies.

The probability matrix P defines the behavior of the random network $\mathbf{A}$. When P is positive semidefinite and $P = XX^\top$ for a set of latent positions, the dependency structure encoded by P is also encoded by X. This means that the latent positions, which often have a number of columns much less than the number of nodes, encode the complicated dependency structure of the underlying network.

Estimated Latent Positions from `ase` Are Directly Related to Latent Positions of Random Networks

Our discussion of `ase` has focused on the spectral embedding of P and its latent positions. In practice, we only have A, not P.

However, when A is a sample from a random network $\mathbf{A}$ with a positive semidefinite probability matrix P, the estimates of latent positions $\widehat{X}$ closely approximate the true latent positions X of $\mathbf{A}$ as the number of nodes in the network increases [5; 6; 7] (up to rotations and reflections, which is the focus of Section 5.5.1). Similarly, $\widehat{P}$ approximates P, with limit theorems showing convergence as the node count increases. Appendix B.2.1 details the theoretical advantages of `ase`.

These advantages do not apply to sparse networks, which we address in Section 6.2.

Results Hold for Nonpositive Semidefinite Probability Matrices
When we view a network as a sample of a random network with a symmetric PSD probability matrix, studying $\widehat{X}$ will be a good surrogate to use in place of studying X (since we cannot obtain X from a network adjacency matrix A). This is powerful because the set of $IER_n(P)$ random networks where the probability matrix is positive semidefinite include many complicated structures, such as those shown in Section 4.5, and extensions of these structures to more than two communities.

In fact, `ase` remains valid even outside of symmetric PSD probability matrices, as briefly discussed in Section 5.7.3. We explain `ase` using symmetric PSD probability matrices because this approach is intuitive and requires only college-level linear algebra. The general case requires complex analysis and advanced probability theory.

However, the applicability of these results outside of the symmetric PSD context indicates that they can be applied broadly and robustly.

5.4   Laplacian Spectral Embedding

Section 5.3 introduced the adjacency spectral embedding, `ase`, which finds embeddings through a spectral decomposition of the adjacency matrix. The Laplacian, introduced in Section 3.4.4, offers an alternative matrix representation of networks. This section explores *Laplacian spectral embedding* (`lse`), a method for creating embeddings from the Laplacian rather than the adjacency matrix.

We cover the following key concepts:

1. The motivation for using the Laplacian matrix instead of the adjacency matrix,
2. Different types of Laplacian matrices: standard, normalized, and regularized,
3. The process of Laplacian spectral embedding,
4. Advantages of `lse`, particularly for degree-corrected stochastic block models, and
5. Comparisons between `ase` and `lse` in various network scenarios.

`lse` provides a robust network embedding method less sensitive to degree heterogeneity than `ase`. This technique captures global structure and creates smooth, continuous embeddings, making it particularly useful for networks with varying node degrees.

Section 5.3 showed how adjacency spectral embedding, or `ase`, estimates latent positions (up to an orthogonal transformation) for positive semidefinite probability matrices. For homophilic $SBM_n(\vec{z}, B)$ random networks, estimated latent positions for nodes in the same community tend to be similar.

This similarity aligns with our observation in Section 4.7.8 that the true latent positions for nodes of the same community are identical. As noted in Section 5.3.3, the estimated latent position matrix produced by `ase` reasonably estimates the underlying network's latent positions, and will do better the more nodes there are. Therefore, the estimated latent positions for nodes in the same community will follow this pattern, and be very similar in large networks (see Appendix B.2).

However, $SBM_n(\vec{z}, B)$ random networks poorly represent many real-world networks. These models assume that the connection probability for a pair of nodes i and j

depends only on their community assignments z_i and z_j, as given by the block matrix entry $b_{z_i z_j}$ in Section 4.3. This assumption ignores the individual node characteristics, such as node popularity.

5.4.1 $DCSBM_n(\vec{z}, \vec{\theta}, B)$ Random Networks

Section 4.7 introduced the degree-corrected SBM random networks, or $DCSBM_n(\vec{z}, \vec{\theta}, B)$. As noted in Section 4.7.8, the latent positions for nodes of the same community in a $DCSBM_n(\vec{z}, \vec{\theta}, B)$ random network are identical up to a rescaling by the nodes' degree-correction factors θ_i and θ_j.

Using notation from Section 4.7.8, the latent position vectors for a $DCSBM_n(\vec{z}, \vec{\theta}, B)$ random network are:

$$\vec{x}_i^\top = \theta_i \vec{c}_i^\top \sqrt{B}$$

where $\vec{c}_i$ is a column-vector corresponding to the ith row of the one-hot encoding matrix of the community assignment vector $\vec{z}$. In this vector, $c_{ik} = 1$ when the node is in k, and 0 otherwise. Geometrically, θ_i "rescales" the vector $\vec{c}_i^\top \sqrt{B}$, where the vector $\vec{c}_i^\top \sqrt{B}$ is the same for the entire community.

We can make this more concrete with an example. We will use a $DCSBM_n(\vec{z}, \vec{\theta}, B)$ similar to the one in Section 4.7, but with more extreme degree-correction factors $\vec{\theta}$:

```
import numpy as np
from graphbook_code import dcsbm

nk = 150
z = np.repeat([1,2], nk)
B = np.array([[0.6, 0.2], [0.2, 0.4]])
theta = np.tile(6**np.linspace(0, -1, nk), 2)
np.random.seed(0)
A, P = dcsbm(z, theta, B, return_prob=True)
```

Next, we compute the ase of A, using the strategy from Section 5.3, and we compute a pairwise distance matrix:

```
from graspologic.embed import AdjacencySpectralEmbed as ase
from scipy.spatial import distance_matrix

d = 2 # the latent dimensionality
# estimate the latent position matrix with ase
Xhat = ase(n_components=d, svd_seed=0).fit_transform(A)
# compute the distance matrix
D = distance_matrix(Xhat, Xhat)
```

Figure 5.4.1(A) shows a scatter plot of the estimated latent positions, annotated with the community of each node. Scatter plots of estimated latent positions are illustrated on square axes, to highlight the structure and shape of the scattered points. The estimated latent positions appear to be "elongated" blobs for a given community. This means that the blobs are elliptical, where the red blob elongates towards the upper right, and the blue blob elongates towards the lower right in our figure.

We can understand this because the true latent positions for each node i are given by $\vec{x}_i = \theta_i \sqrt{B}^\top \vec{c}_i$, where $\vec{c}_i$ is a vector whose value $c_{ik} = 1$ if $z_i = k$, and 0 otherwise.

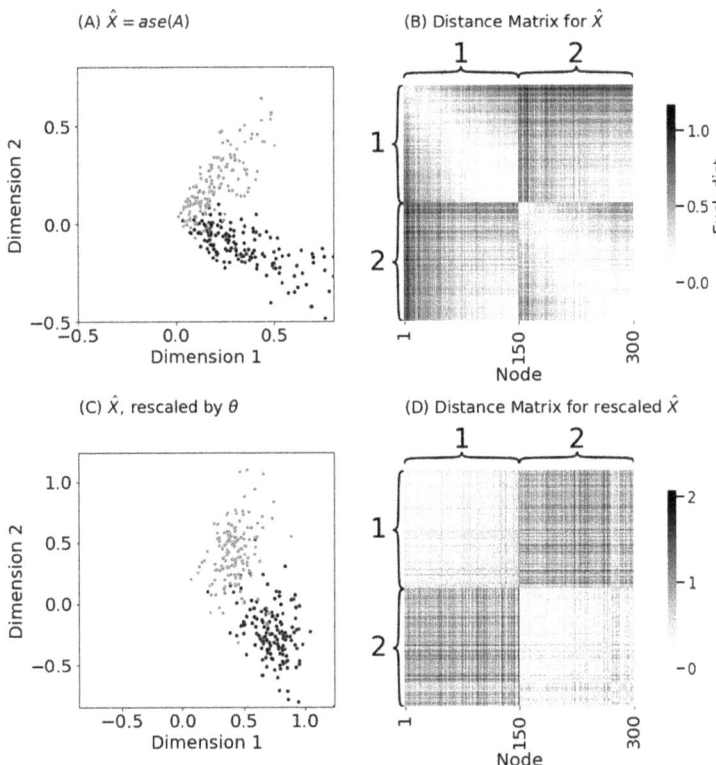

Figure 5.4.1 (**A**) The estimated latent positions for a network sample of a $DCSBM_n(\vec{z}, \vec{\theta}, B)$ random network, where color indicates community (gray $=$ community 1, black $=$ community 2), (**B**) the pairwise distance matrix, (**C**) the estimated latent positions, after normalizing by the degree-correction vector $\vec{\theta}$, and (**D**) the pairwise distance matrix, after normalizing the estimated latent positions by the degree-correction vector.

In this sense, the true latent positions are "stretched" by the degree-correction factors. Using an informal transitivity argument, the estimated latent positions are estimating the true latent positions which are stretched along an axis, so the estimated latent positions will also end up stretched along an axis.

The distance matrix in Figure 5.4.1(B) reveals a pattern. While nodes in the same community generally have similar distances, many nodes have smaller between-community distances than within-community distances. Dark gray bands in the distance matrix in the upper left and lower right blocks of the distance matrix show this, as well as light gray bands in the upper right and lower left blocks of the distance matrix.

Next, let's divide each latent position by the underlying degree-correction factor. The rows of `Xhat_rescaled` consist of the entries $\frac{\hat{x}_i^\top}{\theta_i}$, so we are "unstretching" each latent position by its degree-correction factor:

```
Xhat_rescaled = Xhat / theta[:,None]
D_rescaled = distance_matrix(Xhat_rescaled, Xhat_rescaled)
```

Figure 5.4.1(C) shows these rescaled latent positions, and Figure 5.4.1(D) shows the pairwise distance matrix. Notice that rescaling by the degree-correction factors

θ_i eliminated the "stretching" effect in the estimated latent positions. Further, the distances are now virtually devoid of the cross-community similarity: We are back to nodes of the same community having generally smaller distances that pairs of nodes in opposite communities.

This suggests that the degree-correction vector $\vec{\theta}$ can be used in conjunction with ase to recover rescaled latent positions where, after rescaling, the rescaled latent positions for nodes in the same community tend to be close together in Euclidean distance.

In practice, we do not have the degree-correction vector. It was a parameter of the random network, for which we only have a sample A.

5.4.2 The Laplacian Spectral Embedding

Recall from Section 4.5 that if P is symmetric PSD, ase(P) gives us two matrices U_d and Σ_d, where $Y = U_d\sqrt{\Sigma_d}$ is a latent position matrix for the random network:

$$P = YY^{\top}.$$

This procedure also works for functions of the probability matrix which preserve positive semidefiniteness. An interesting example would be multiplying by diagonal matrices that only take positive real values. If a matrix R is positive semidefinite, and a matrix D is diagonal with only positive values, then both DR and RD are also positive semidefinite.

5.4.2.1 The Population Network Laplacian

In Section 4.6.4, we introduced the population network Laplacian $\mathcal{L}$. We defined it as:

$$\mathcal{L} = \mathcal{D}^{-\frac{1}{2}} P \mathcal{D}^{-\frac{1}{2}}.$$

The diagonal matrix $\mathcal{D}$ is the expected degree matrix, and the diagonal entries $\mathbb{E}[\mathbf{d}_i]$ are the expected degrees of each of the nodes in the network. Assuming that every node i has at least one other node j where $p_{ij} > 0$, the diagonal entries are positive, and the inverse square-root matrix $\mathcal{D}^{-\frac{1}{2}}$ is just the diagonal matrix with entries $\frac{1}{\sqrt{\mathbb{E}[\mathbf{d}_i]}}$. Section 3.4.3 provided useful intuition transferable to these matrices.

When P is a positive semidefinite matrix, its positive semidefiniteness is preserved under multiplications (pre or post) with diagonal matrices whose diagonal only contains positive values. This means that if P is positive semidefinite, $\mathcal{D}^{-\frac{1}{2}} P$ is positive semidefinite. Since $\mathcal{D}^{-\frac{1}{2}} P$ is positive semidefinite, we can also postmultiply by another diagonal matrix $\mathcal{D}^{-\frac{1}{2}}$ and end up with a positive semidefinite matrix, so $\mathcal{L}$ is positive semidefinite too.

Likewise, when P is a rank d matrix, its rank is preserved under multiplications (premultiplications or postmultiplications) with diagonal matrices whose diagonal only contains positive values. By a similar argument, this means that if P is rank d, then $\mathcal{L}$ is rank d.

This population network Laplacian $\mathcal{L}$ has a special feature: It is normalized by the expected degrees of the nodes. We can see this by writing out the multiplication in Equation (4.16):

$$
\mathcal{L} =
\begin{bmatrix}
\frac{p_{11}}{\mathbb{E}[d_1]} & \cdots & \frac{p_{1n}}{\sqrt{\mathbb{E}[d_1]}\sqrt{\mathbb{E}[d_n]}} \\
\vdots & \ddots & \vdots \\
\frac{p_{n1}}{\sqrt{\mathbb{E}[d_1]}\sqrt{\mathbb{E}[d_n]}} & \cdots & \frac{p_{nn}}{\mathbb{E}[d_n]}
\end{bmatrix}.
$$

So, the population network Laplacian $\mathcal{L}$ has entries $\ell_{ij} = \frac{p_{ij}}{\sqrt{\mathbb{E}[d_i]}\sqrt{\mathbb{E}[d_j]}}$. This looks very similar to the DAD Laplacian from Section 3.4.4, except instead of adjacencies and node degrees, we have probabilities (expected values of the adjacency matrix entries, Section 4.6) and expected node degrees.

5.4.2.2   Estimating the Population Network Laplacian

The qualifications that we needed in Remarks 5.3.2 and Remarks 5.3.5 about the symmetric positive semidefiniteness of P and its rank $d \le n$ allowed us to conclude that:

$$
P = YY^\top,
$$

where P was the symmetric PSD probability matrix. We could compute such a Y for the probability matrix using either the eigendecomposition in Algorithm 5.1 or the singular value decomposition in Algorithm 5.2, and obtain latent positions that were equal to the true latent positions for an underlying $RDPG_n(X)$ random network (up to an orthogonal transformation, due to nonidentifiability, the focus of Section 5.5.2).

We also learned previously that the population network Laplacian $\mathcal{L}$ is both symmetric PSD and has a rank $d \le n$, so:

$$
\mathcal{L} = XX^\top,
$$

where X is an $n \times d$ real matrix, and is computed from the eigenvectors/values or the singular vectors/values using Algorithms 5.1 and 5.2 (with the same caveats). This X is similarly referred to as the latent positions. In this book, we will refer to this X as *latent positions of the population network Laplacian*, and it will always be clear from context whether it is the X computed from the adjacency matrix or the Laplacian.

Samples of networks A are not always positive semidefinite, discussed in Section 5.3. Similarly, even if $\mathcal{L}$ is positive semidefinite and rank d, the DAD laplacian L will not necessarily be positive semidefinite. Therefore, the procedure in Algorithm 5.1 is not guaranteed to produce a real result. However, the procedure in Algorithm 5.2 will still at least provide us with a real answer.

When we compute the DAD laplacian and then run the spectral decomposition approach, we term the strategy *Laplacian spectral embedding*, or `lse`, which is described in Algorithm 5.3.

We can now use `lse` to produce estimates of the latent positions for the population network laplacian $\mathcal{L}$, which is similar to the probability matrix (but regularized by the node degrees). Will this help us fix the degree-correction stretching problem that we noticed in Figure 5.4.1? Let's find out.

We can perform `lse` using `graspologic`:

```
from graspologic.embed import LaplacianSpectralEmbed as lse

d = 2 # embed into two dimensions
Xhat_lapl = lse(n_components=d, svd_seed=0).fit_transform(A)
D_lapl = distance_matrix(Xhat_lapl, Xhat_lapl)
```

Algorithm 5.3 Estimating latent positions from Laplacian matrices (`lse`)

Data: A an adjacency matrix for a simple network.

$\quad\quad$ d a target latent dimensionality.

$\quad\quad$ τ an optional regularizer.

Result: an estimate of a latent position matrix for the population network

$\quad\quad$ Laplacian.

1 Compute the degree matrix D of the network A.

2 Regularize the degree matrix with $D_\tau = D + \tau I_n$.

3 Compute the DAD Laplacian, $L = D_\tau^{-\frac{1}{2}} A D_\tau^{-\frac{1}{2}}$.

4 Let $U, \Sigma, V^\top = \text{svd}(L)$ be the left singular vectors, the singular values, and the right singular vectors of L.

5 Let $U_d = \begin{bmatrix} \uparrow & & \uparrow \\ \vec{u}_1 & \cdots & \vec{u}_d \\ \downarrow & & \downarrow \end{bmatrix}$, and let $\Sigma_d = \begin{bmatrix} \sigma_1 & & \\ & \ddots & \\ & & \sigma_d \end{bmatrix}$ be the matrix whose

rows are the first d left singular vectors and the diagonal matrix whose entries are the first d singular values of A.

6 Compute $\sqrt{\Sigma_d}$ to be the matrix whose entries are $\sqrt{\sigma_i}$, for all i from 1 to d.

7 Let $\widehat{X} = U_d \sqrt{\Sigma_d}$.

8 **return** $\widehat{X}$

We show the latent positions and the distance matrix estimated through `ase` and `lse` in Figure 5.4.2. Notice that when we tabularize A through `ase` in Figure 5.4.2(A), the estimated latent positions tend to be "elongated" along an axis as they were in Figure 5.4.1. This makes sense because the true latent positions are also "elongated" along an axis, and the amount of elongation is determined by the degree-correction factors (θ_i). `lse` eliminates some of this "elongating" effect. The "blobs" of nodes in the same community tend to be more similar in Figure 5.4.2(C). This is reflected in the distance matrix of Figure 5.4.2(D), where nodes in the same community tend to have smaller distances than nodes in different communities. This was not the case in Figure 5.4.2(B), where many nodes are more similar to nodes in the opposite community than in the same community.

5.4.3   When Do We Use `lse` over `ase`, and Vice Versa?

The primary difference between `lse` and `ase` is illustrated in Figure 5.4.2. `ase` will capture estimates of latent positions of the adjacency matrix, whereas `lse` will capture estimates of latent positions of the population network Laplacian. Loosely, this has the consequence that `lse` will produce "scaled" estimates of latent positions that have been adjusted for degree differences in the underlying network.

Often, we will want to learn about latent structures that are not related to the degrees of the nodes in the network. In such cases, the scaled estimates produced by `lse` will often make latent structure more obvious both visually (in heatmaps and pairs plots) and algorithmically (through the use of downstream models to identify latent structure from estimated latent positions).

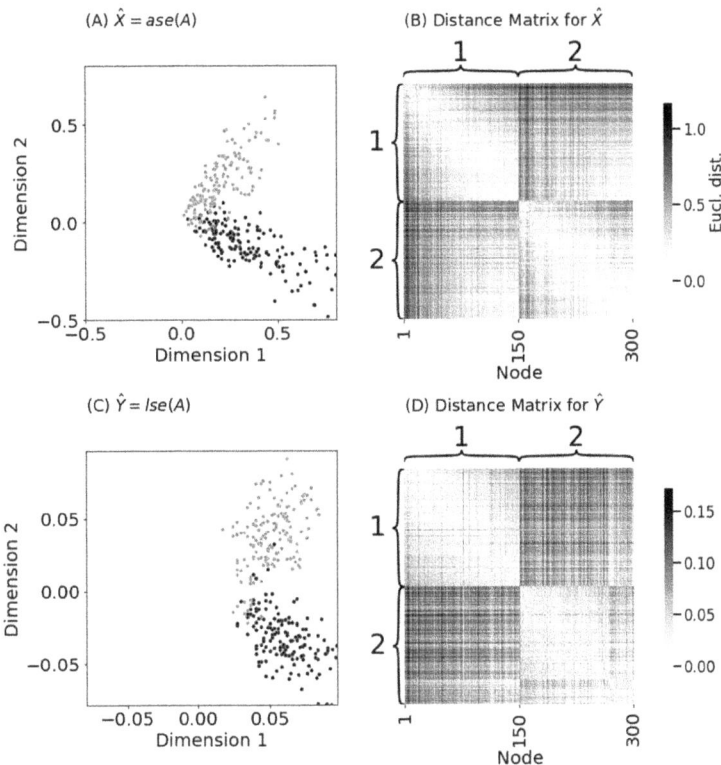

Figure 5.4.2 (**A**) The estimated latent positions, (**B**) the pairwise distances of estimated latent positions, (**C**) the estimated latent positions from lse, and (**D**) the pairwise distances of the estimated latent positions from lse.

An initial visualization to determine whether ase or lse is appropriate is the node degree histogram, which shows the degrees for each node in the network. Let's investigate this for the $DCSBM_n(\vec{z}, \vec{\theta}, B)$ sample we generated in Section 5.4.1:

```
import seaborn as sns
import pandas as pd

# compute the degrees for each node, using the
# row-sums of the network
degrees = A.sum(axis = 0)

# plot the degree histogram
df = pd.DataFrame({"Node degree" : degrees, "Community": z})
sns.histplot(data=df, x="Node degree", bins=20, color="black")
```

The key feature that we look for is whether the degree histogram is *right-skewed* or *heavy tailed*. Remember from Section 3.6 that a distribution is right-skewed if it "tails off" towards the relatively large values in the positive direction. In these situations, the node degrees are bounded below by zero (the networks are simple, so all the adjacencies a_{ij} are either 0 or 1, and the node degrees are sums of adjacencies).

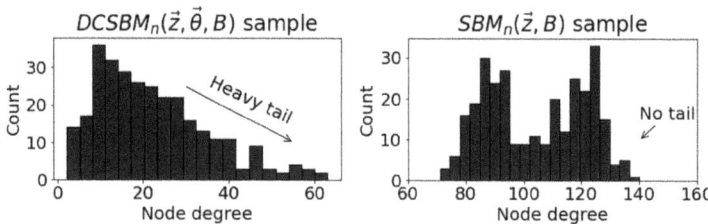

Figure 5.4.3 (A) The degree histogram for a $DCSBM_n(\vec{z}, \vec{\theta}, B)$ network, where the degree-correction factors are not equal for the nodes in the network. (B) The degree histogram for an $SBM_n(\vec{z}, B)$ network.

This is generally referred to as a "heavy-tailed degree distribution," since it can only "tail off" to the right. In Figure 5.4.3(A), the degree distribution for nodes across both communities tails off to the right. $DCSBM_n(\vec{z}, \vec{\theta}, B)$ random networks where the degree-correction factors θ_i tend to have mostly relatively small values but some relatively large values will tend to yield heavy tailed degree distributions.

This contrasts with $SBM_n(\vec{z}, B)$ random networks and $DCSBM_n(\vec{z}, \vec{\theta}, B)$ random networks where the degree-correction factor θ_i is constant for all nodes in the same community, which will tend to have symmetric degree distributions for each community.

```
Asbm = sbm([nk, nk], B)

# row-sums of the network
degrees_sbm = Asbm.sum(axis = 0)
```

The histogram for an $SBM_n(\vec{z}, B)$ random network is shown in Figure 5.4.3(B). Note that the degree histogram appears to have two "peaks," and neither peak is particularly heavy tailed (they both look fairly mirrored). This plot provides evidence that the degree-distribution is not heavy tailed.

Heavy-tailed degree distributions arise frequently in real data [8; 9; 10]. This pattern is particularly apparent in networks that share features of core–periphery networks from Section 4.5, where a selection of nodes (the *core*) have much higher node degrees than the nodes outside of the core (the *periphery*) [10]. This pattern can materialize concurrently with other patterns, such as the example that we saw above with a $DCSBM_n(\vec{z}, \vec{\theta}, B)$ network with heterogeneous degree correction factors and homophilic networks.

When we can identify a heavy-tailed degree distribution from visualizations such as the node degree histogram, lse may be advantageous to use over ase.

5.5   Multiple Network Representation Learning

When we explored statistical models of networks in Chapter 4, we found it desirable to have strategies for multiple network scenarios in Section 4.9. We now return to this situation in the new context of representation learning.

We cover the following:

1. Motivations for multiple network analysis,
2. The concept of joint matrices for multiple networks,
3. Parallel embedding techniques, including omnibus embedding (`omni`),
4. Fused embedding techniques, including multiple adjacency spectral embedding (`mase`),
5. Comparisons between `omni` and `mase`, discussing their strengths and use-cases, and
6. The challenge of alignment in multiple network settings.

We assume knowledge of COSIE (Section 4.9.2) and joint random dot product graphs (Section 4.9.1). We will return a third time to this scenario in the context of applications in Chapter 9.

When we have multiple networks, there are a variety of questions that we might want to ask. In this section, we'll focus on a few of these questions, and provide structured ways to learn representations of many networks that allow us to answer downstream questions. The $COSIE_{n,M}\left(S, R^{(1)}, \ldots, R^{(M)}\right)$ random networks in Section 4.9 will be critical for understanding many of the techniques that we cover in this section.

We will use a running example of brain networks, which we describe in Remark 5.5.1.

Box 5.5.1 Alien and human brain networks

We have been given the unique task of learning about a group of four recently discovered human-like alien life forms. When studying their brains (in a noninvasive way), we make the remarkable discovery that aliens and humans have brain areas that do similar things across species. These $n = 100$ brain areas will be the nodes of the network.

For both aliens and humans, there are two hemispheres (communities) in the brain. However, while human brains tend to have a homophilic structure (with more connections between nodes in the same hemisphere of the brain), alien brains tend to have a core–periphery structure, where the nodes in the left hemisphere (the core) are much more connected than nodes in the right hemisphere (the periphery). For this reason, we want to be able to obtain suitable representations of these networks to learn about the differences between human and alien brains.

Let's generate working examples.

```
from graspologic.simulations import sbm
import numpy as np
from sklearn.preprocessing import LabelEncoder

n = 100 # the number of nodes
M = 8 # the total number of networks
# human brains have homophilic block structure
Bhuman = np.array([[0.2, 0.02], [0.02, 0.2]])
```

```
# alien brains have a core-periphery block structure
Balien = np.array([[0.4, 0.2], [0.2, 0.1]])

# set seed for reproducibility
np.random.seed(0)

# generate 4 human and 4 alien brain networks
A_humans = [sbm([n // 2, n // 2], Bhuman) for i in range(M // 2)]
A_aliens = [sbm([n // 2, n // 2], Balien) for i in range(M // 2)]
# concatenate list of human and alien networks
networks = A_humans + A_aliens

# 1 = left hemisphere, 2 = right hemisphere for node communities
le = LabelEncoder()
labels = np.repeat(["L", "R"], n//2)
zs = le.fit_transform(labels) + 1
```

The collection networks is a list of adjacency matrices where the first four entries correspond to the human brains, and the second four entries correspond to the alien brains. labels corresponds to community labels for the nodes of the networks, where L is a placeholder for "left hemisphere," and R is a placeholder for "right hemisphere." We also fit a LabelEncoder to our labels, allowing us to map them to 0 and 1 in the form of the array zs. Having dummy placeholders for discrete community labels (such as zs) is often handy when we want to do things like run one-hot encodings, and more informative node labels (such as labels) are handy for when we want to visualize and plot. We can use our fit LabelEncoder, le, to easily convert between labels and their numerical mapping.

Figure 5.5.1 plots the human and alien brain networks, with nodes ordered by the node hemisphere (the "community"). Whereas the human brain networks tend to have more connections within the same hemisphere (the on-diagonal blocks), the alien brain networks tend to have high amounts of connections between nodes in the first community, and fewer connections between nodes in the second community. Our goal is to characterize the differences in network structure between humans and aliens.

In Sections 5.3 and 5.4, we learned two approaches for embedding networks with positive semidefinite probability matrices, ase and lse.

(A) Human Brain Networks   (B) Alien Brain Networks

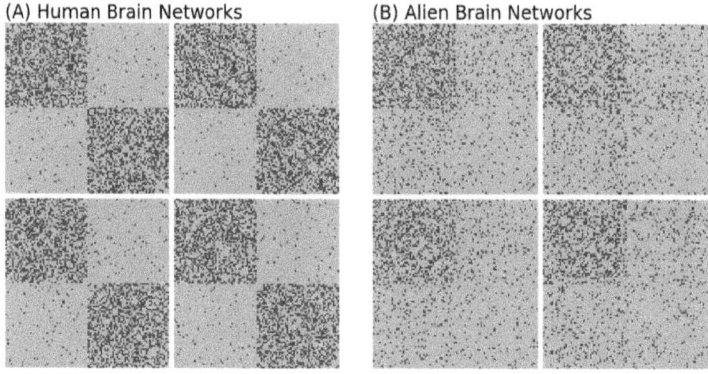

Figure 5.5.1 (**A**) The human brain networks, and (**B**) the alien brain networks.

When we have multiple networks, we could start by tabularizing them using embedding techniques and then comparing these tabular representations across the networks. However, this approach would end up being misleading due to nonidentifiability.

5.5.1   The Nonidentifiability Problem and Network Embeddings

Assume that we have a network $\mathbf{A}$ which is $RDPG_n(X)$, where X is the latent position matrix for $\mathbf{A}$, and $P = XX^\top$ is its probability matrix. In this case, X is the parameter for the RDPG random network.

In many univariate distributions, the parameters uniquely define a distribution. If $\mathbf{x}$ is a Gaussian random variable with two parameters, mean μ and variance σ, any random variable with a different mean or a different variance has a different distribution. If $\mathbf{x}$ is a coin that lands on heads with probability 0.5 (the parameter for the Bernoulli distribution), its behavior is distinct from a coin which lands on heads with probability 0.3.

In this sense, it might be surprising to know that there are infinitely many potential latent position matrices Y where the resulting probability matrix would be equal to P, even though $X \neq Y$. These latent position matrices consist of all possible rotations around and reflections across the origin of X. This is problematic, because P defines the distribution of $\mathbf{A}$.

In Concept 5.3.2, we learned that an *orthogonal matrix* W in d dimensions is any $d \times d$ matrix where $WW^\top = W^\top W = I_d$, the d-dimensional identity matrix. Imagine that Y is another latent position matrix, but is an *orthogonal transformation* of X. That means that there is an orthogonal matrix W where $Y = XW$. The probability matrix for the $RDPG_n(Y)$ network is:

$$P = YY^\top$$
$$= XW\,(XW)^\top,$$

because $Y = XW$. Applying the definition of a transpose, we get:

$$P = XWW^\top X^\top$$
$$= XI_d X^\top,$$

because W is an orthogonal matrix, so $W^\top W = WW^\top = I_d$ (where I_d is the rank-d identity matrix). Finally, since $XI_d = X$:

$$P = XX^\top.$$

This leads to the conclusion in Concept 5.5.2.

We can also think about this geometrically, with the understanding that orthogonal matrices in two dimensions are either rotations (of the points in two-dimensional space) or rotations combined with reflections (e.g., across axes).

First we will think of the orthogonal matrix as a rotation. Imagine that we have a simple latent position matrix X with two nodes and two latent dimensions ($d = 2$):

$$X = \begin{bmatrix} \vdash & \vec{x}_1^\top & \dashv \\ \vdash & \vec{x}_2^\top & \dashv \end{bmatrix}.$$

> **Concept 5.5.2** Nonidentifiability of RDPG random networks
>
> If Y and X are latent position matrices with d latent dimensions, W is a d-dimensional orthogonal matrix, and $Y = XW$ (Y is an orthogonal transformation of X), then $RDPG_n(X)$ random networks and $RDPG_n(Y)$ random networks have the same probability matrix. There is no reason that either of these latent position matrices would be better than the another, as they produce the same probability matrix.
>
> When dealing with single network questions, this is not much of a problem, as our main interest in single network questions is typically about latent positions of nodes relative to one another. However, when dealing with multiple network questions, this will be very impactful because we will need to take care to ensure that the latent positions are rotationally aligned between different networks.

When we compute the probability matrix with $P = XX^\top$, we get:

$$P = XX^\top = \begin{bmatrix} \vdash & \vec{x}_1^\top & \dashv \\ \vdash & \vec{x}_2^\top & \dashv \end{bmatrix} \begin{bmatrix} \top & \top \\ \vec{x}_1 & \vec{x}_2 \\ \bot & \bot \end{bmatrix}.$$

Thinking of each latent position $\vec{x}_i$ as a point in two dimensions, we see that $p_{ij} = \vec{x}_i^\top \vec{x}_j$. So, the matrix P is the set of dot products between the latent positions for all pairs of nodes. The dot product of two Euclidean vectors $\vec{x}_i$ and $\vec{x}_j$ is equivalent to:

$$\vec{x}_i \cdot \vec{x}_j = \|\vec{x}_i\| \|\vec{x}_j\| \cos \angle(\vec{x}_i, \vec{x}_j)$$

where $\angle(\vec{x}_i, \vec{x}_j)$ is the angle between $\vec{x}_i$ and $\vec{x}_j$. If we apply a rotation matrix W to X, we get:

$$\begin{aligned} Y = XW &= \begin{bmatrix} \vdash & \vec{x}_1^\top & \dashv \\ \vdash & \vec{x}_2^\top & \dashv \end{bmatrix} W \\ &= \begin{bmatrix} \vdash & \vec{x}_1^\top W & \dashv \\ \vdash & \vec{x}_2^\top W & \dashv \end{bmatrix}, \end{aligned}$$

so we could write $\vec{y}_i^\top = \vec{x}_i^\top W$: The rotated latent positions Y are all rotated by the same rotation matrix W.

When we rotate both vectors by the same angle, which is what happens when we apply the same rotation W to each of the latent positions, neither their lengths nor their angles with respect to each other change, so their dot product remains constant. Therefore, any rotation of a latent position matrix produces a network with the same probability matrix.

We can also think about the case where the matrix W' is a reflection of an axis across the origin. For instance, consider the matrix W' where:

$$W' = \begin{bmatrix} -1 & 0 \\ 0 & 1 \end{bmatrix}.$$

When premultiplied by a latent position matrix X with two latent dimensions, W' has the effect of "reflecting" the first latent dimension across the origin:

$$X = \begin{bmatrix} x_{11} & x_{12} \\ \vdots & \vdots \\ x_{n1} & n_{n2} \end{bmatrix}.$$

Applying the reflection W to X gives:

$$XW' = \begin{bmatrix} -x_{11} & x_{12} \\ \vdots & \vdots \\ -x_{n1} & x_{n2} \end{bmatrix}.$$

Therefore, the probability matrix is:

$$XW'(XW')^\top = \begin{bmatrix} -x_{11} & x_{12} \\ \vdots & \vdots \\ -x_{n1} & x_{n2} \end{bmatrix} \begin{bmatrix} -x_{11} & \cdots & -x_{n1} \\ x_{12} & \cdots & x_{n2} \end{bmatrix} = XX^\top,$$

because when computing the element-wise products of rows of XW' with columns of $(XW')^\top$, the negatives cancel.

In the general case (more than two latent dimensions), the concept of rotational and reflectional nonidentifiability is generalized as nonidentifiable up to an orthogonal transformation. Exercise 5.5.3 works through illustrating that orthogonal transformations are distance preserving.

Exercise 5.5.3 Orthogonal matrices are distance preserving

Assume X is a latent position matrix with n nodes in d dimensions, and W is a $d \times d$ orthogonal matrix. Further, assume that $Y = XW$ is an orthogonal transform of X. Let $\vec{x}_i$ be the latent position for each node. Using the definition of the Euclidean distance, the definition of an orthogonal matrix, and the fact that $\vec{y}_i = W^\top \vec{x}_i$, show that for any two nodes i and j:

$$\|\vec{x}_i - \vec{x}_j\|_2 = \|\vec{y}_i - \vec{y}_j\|_2$$

or that orthogonal transformations preserve distances between latent positions. Formally, a distance-preserving transformation is known as an *isometry*.

Why Are Rotations and Reflections Problematic?
As we mentioned in Section 5.5.2, the latent positions are nonidentifiable, in that for an $RDPG_n(X)$ with latent positions X, an $RDPG_n(XW)$ where W is a d-dimensional orthogonal matrix has the same probability matrix. The estimated latent positions $\widehat{X}$ share this issue. Let's estimate the latent positions for a single network from our example networks:

```
from graspologic.embed import AdjacencySpectralEmbed as ase

# embed the first network
Xhat = ase(n_components=2, svd_seed=0).fit_transform(A_humans[0])
```

We visualize the estimated latent positions as a scatter plot (a plot of $\widehat{X}$ similar to the pairs plot you learned in Section 5.3) in Figure 5.5.2(A). Next, we apply a rotation matrix W to $\widehat{X}$; in this case, the rotation matrix has the effect of a 90° clockwise rotation:

```
# a rotation by 90 degrees
W = np.array([[0, -1], [1, 0]])
Yhat = Xhat @ W
```

The points after rotation are illustrated in Figure 5.5.2(B), with the points before rotation shown in light gray. The rotation clockwise follows the arrows. Notice that the two "blobs" are rotated clockwise by 90° around the origin.

Despite the fact that the latent positions of $\widehat{X}$ and $\widehat{Y}$ are different (they are rotated), they produce the same probability matrix:

```
# check that probability matrix is the same
np.allclose(Yhat @ Yhat.transpose(), Xhat @ Xhat.transpose())
# returns True
```

We can similarly reflect across the first latent dimension:

```
# a reflection across first latent dimension
Wp = np.array([[-1, 0], [0, 1]])
Zhat = Xhat @ Wp
# check that the probability matrix is the same
# check that probability matrix is the same
np.allclose(Zhat @ Zhat.transpose(), Xhat @ Xhat.transpose())
# returns True
```

Figure 5.5.2(C) illustrates the points after reflection, with the points before reflection shown in light gray. The reflection across the origin of the first latent dimension (dotted arrow) follows the arrows. Notice that the two "blobs" are reflected across the dotted line.

This becomes problematic if we want to compare embeddings from different adjacency matrices. Consider, for instance, an embedding of the third human network. The human networks are samples of the same SBM random network, so they are stochastically equivalent (they have the same probability matrix). As a result, the network samples look virtually indistinguishable, as shown in Figure 5.5.3(A) and

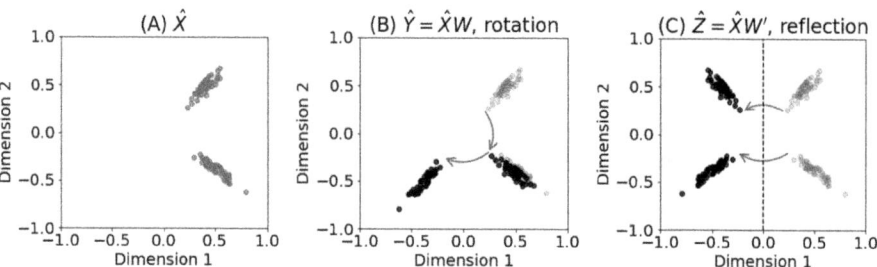

Figure 5.5.2 (**A**) The estimated latent positions, (**B**) the estimated latent positions, but rotated by 90°, and (**C**) the estimated latent positions, but reflected across the first latent dimension.

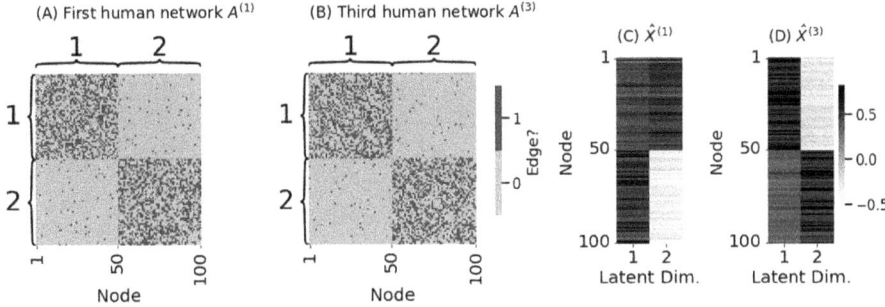

Figure 5.5.3 (**A**) A network sample for the first human, (**B**) a network sample for the third human, (**C**) estimated latent positions for the first human, and (**D**) estimated latent positions for the third human.

Figure 5.5.3(B). Our intuition would suggest that since their latent positions could be calculated to be the same, we should obtain estimated latent positions that at least look similar between the two:

```
# embed the third human network
Xhat3 = ase(n_components=2, svd_seed=0).fit_transform(A_humans[3])
```

Figure 5.5.3(C) and Figure 5.5.3(D) plot the estimated latent positions. Although nodes within the same community for both networks have similar latent positions, the actual values are dissimilar across the two networks.

To get a sense of how dissimilar, we will introduce a generalization of the Euclidean distance but for matrices, known as the Frobenius distance, in Concept 5.5.4. Small Frobenius distances indicate that a pair of matrices are similar in value, and larger Frobenius distances indicate that a pair of matrices are more dissimilar in value.

Concept 5.5.4 The Frobenius norm

The Frobenius norm can be thought of as a generalization of the Euclidean norm from Concept 5.3.10 to matrices. If A is a $n \times m$ real matrix with entries a_{ij}, the Frobenius norm is:

$$\|A\|_F = \sqrt{\sum_{i=1}^{n}\sum_{j=1}^{m} a_{ij}^2}.$$

The Frobenius norm is equivalent to "unrolling" a matrix into a vector, and then finding its Euclidean norm.

If B is a second $n \times m$ real matrix with entries b_{ij}, the Frobenius distance is:

$$\|A - B\|_F = \sqrt{\sum_{i=1}^{n}\sum_{j=1}^{m} (a_{ij} - b_{ij})^2}.$$

Next, we will embed an alien network. From Figure 5.5.1, the alien and the human networks look nothing alike, so we would anticipate that their estimated latent positions should be different. However, this is not the case:

```
# embed the first alien network
Xhat_alien = ase(n_components=2, svd_seed=0).fit_transform(A_aliens[0])

# compute frob norm between first human and third human net
# estimated latent positions
dist_firsthum_thirdhum = np.linalg.norm(Xhat - Xhat3, ord="fro")
print("Frob. norm(first human, third human) =
    {:3f}".format(dist_firsthum_thirdhum))
# Frob. norm(first human, third human) = 8.798482

# compute frob norm between first human and first alien net
# estimated latent positions
dist_firsthum_alien = np.linalg.norm(Xhat - Xhat_alien, ord="fro")
print("Frob. norm(first human, alien) =
    {:3f}".format(dist_firsthum_alien))
# Frob. norm(first human, alien) = 5.991560
```

The estimated latent positions for our first human network are, somewhat surprisingly, more similar to the estimated latent positions for the first alien network (the Frobenius norm is smaller) than they are to the estimated latent positions for the third human network. This, problematically, shows that estimated latent positions are not directly comparable when dealing with multiple networks. We summarize these crucial points, and how they relate to the previous Section 5.3 on the ase, in Remark 5.5.5.

5.5.2   Different Types of Multiple Network Representation Learning

In this section we explore general approaches for multiple network representation learning. We need to obtain representations of our networks which are comparable so that we can learn from them downstream, and there are at least two ways we could do this: in parallel, or by fusing representations. Each of these eventually results in one or many latent position representation for our networks.

Every multiple network representation learning strategy that we describe in this section entails constructing a *joint matrix*: A single matrix derived from multiple networks, which represents all of them. The specifics of this construction depend on which multiple network representation learning technique we use.

Below, we summarize each approach:

- Fused network embedding: Embed into separate representations first. Then, fuse those representations into a joint matrix, from which separate embeddings living in the same space can be pulled out.
- Parallel network embedding: Create a joint matrix first. Then, use it to create every network representation in parallel.

Fused Network Embedding
In fused network embedding, we first obtain representations from each network, either with adjacency spectral embedding or with some other single network representation

> **Remark 5.5.5** A quick rundown of nonidentifiability
>
> In this section, we reached three conclusions:
>
> 1. Positive semidefinite random networks have infinitely many possible latent position matrices. These latent position matrices are all orthogonal transformations of one another (and there are infinitely many possible orthogonal matrices). In two dimensions, these matrices rotate and reflect the latent positions.
> 2. Estimates of latent positions suffer from a similar limitation in that they will only be similar to the underlying latent position matrix up to an orthogonal transformation. However, the infinitely many equivalent estimates of latent positions (the infinitely many possible orthogonal matrices) all produce the same estimated probability matrix which closely approximates the true probability matrix (Figure 5.3.2), and they are isometries (Exercise 5.5.3). When dealing with single network questions, these facts imply that nonidentifiability can largely be ignored.
> 3. Estimates of latent positions from different networks naively obtained through naive applications of ase and lse cannot be directly compared across multiple networks. This is because the latent positions may not be aligned (Figure 5.5.3). The remainder of this section will develop embedding techniques to address this issue when dealing with multiple networks.

learning strategy. Next, we combine these embeddings into a joint matrix, and then we learn from this joint matrix using sequential approaches (such as additional embeddings of the joint matrix). This approach is summarized in Figure 5.5.4. Multiple adjacency spectral embedding (mase), which we will learn about in Section 5.5.3, is an example of this approach.

This approach is effective when our networks have shared structure, where the final embedding describes shared structure across the nodes of the networks, and when we obtain other descriptive features about the joint embedding that describe particularities about the individual networks as they relate to this shared structure. It can also be useful when we only have embeddings, but not the original matrix.

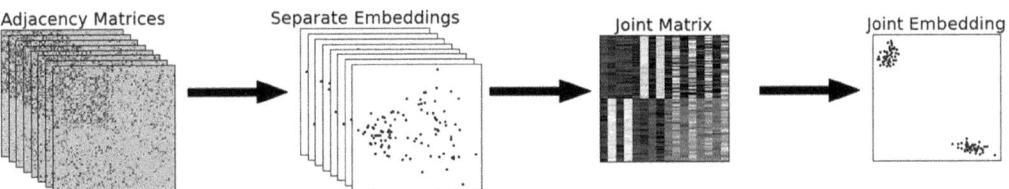

Figure 5.5.4 Fused embedding is the process of embedding networks to obtain separate representations, combining these representations to obtain a joint matrix, and then obtaining a representation of the joint matrix.

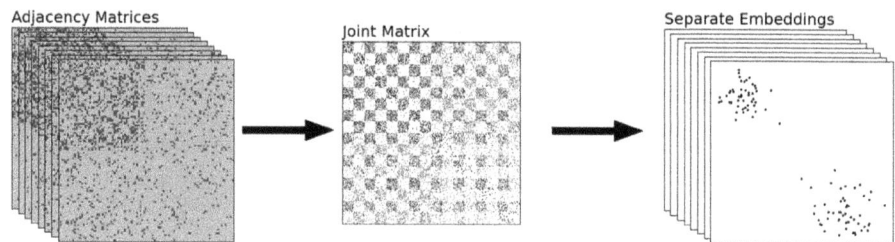

Figure 5.5.5 Parallel embedding is the process of combining networks to acquire a joint matrix, and then embedding the result to obtain separate network representations.

Parallel Network Embedding

There are situations in which we might want to keep our embeddings separate, but we still want them to coexist in a related latent space. For example, we noticed in Section 5.5.2 that embeddings are often orthogonal transformations of each other due to nonidentifiability. Parallel network embedding allows us to avoid this by generating separate embeddings using a single joint matrix. When we approach multiple network representation learning in this manner, we can directly compare the embeddings of the separate networks. An example of parallel embedding is the omnibus embedding (omni), and is illustrated in Figure 5.5.5. We will explore omni in depth in Section 5.5.4.

This approach is effective when we want to study each of our networks individually, but we still want to be able to compare them to each other.

In Sections 5.5.3 and 5.5.4, we explore the strengths and weaknesses of fused and parallel embedding techniques: mase and the omnibus embedding (omni).

5.5.3   Multiple Adjacency Spectral Embedding

Multiple adjacency spectral embedding, or mase, is a fused embedding technique which concatenates and then reembeds separate latent positions into a single space. There is also a sense in which it is parallel: We will learn that we can still "distill" out separate representations for each network. The advantage of mase is that it is flexible to different ways networks can present in real data; we only need the nodes of the different networks to be aligned and have similar "meaning" across the networks. This means that node 1 in network 1 has the same literal interpretation as node 1 in networks 2 through m, and this is true for all n nodes of the network. In our brain networks, for instance, node 1 is the first region, node 2 is the second region, and so forth. Regions have the same label across all networks in the collection.

The goal of mase is to embed the networks into a shared space with shared latent dimensions, while separately preserving any differences between them.

mase is based on the common subspace independent-edge (COSIE) model in Section 4.9.2. With the COSIE model, there might be some underlying homogeneity across networks: In the brain networks, for instance, the same communities might exist across all networks. In the real world, brain networks may be distinct for one reason or another in terms of their underlying probability matrix, but still share fundamental

> **Remark 5.5.6** Graph matching
>
> Ensuring that nodes align across networks is sometimes nontrivial. For situations in which we don't know in advance which nodes across networks correspond to each other, we can approximate their alignment with graph matching. We learn about this technique in Section 7.3.

properties. The COSIE model allowed us to capture both the homogeneity and heterogeneity across different networks simultaneously.

We have already been exposed to `mase` in Section 2.5, when we used it in our starting project. Let's use `mase` on the human and alien brains. Then, we will dig deeper into what is happening under the hood.

```
from graspologic.embed import MultipleASE as mase

# Use mase to embed everything
mase = mase(n_components=2, svd_seed=0)
# fit_transform on the human and alien networks simultaneously
latents_mase = mase.fit_transform(networks)
```

5.5.3.1 How Does `mase` Work?

Embedding Networks

The first step in `mase` is to embed each network. This step is discussed for `ase` in Section 5.3 and `lse` in Section 5.4.

If we do not know ahead of time how many dimensions we want to embed into, it is a good rule of thumb to over-embed rather than to under-embed. If we embed into too few dimensions, we risk discarding latent structure (and will therefore have no hope of finding it downstream). In general, for the first step of `mase`, a good rule-of-thumb for embedding dimensions is $\log_2(n)$. When n is 100 as in our example, this is about 7:

```
from graspologic.embed import AdjacencySpectralEmbed as ase

dhat = int(np.ceil(np.log2(n)))
# spectrally embed each network into ceil(log2(n)) dimensions with ASE
separate_embeddings = [ase(n_components=dhat,
    svd_seed=0).fit_transform(network) for network in networks]
```

We plot the spectral embeddings of the networks for an human and an alien (showing only the first two dimensions) in Figure 5.5.6. Notice that the separate embeddings individually preserve the community structure across both humans and aliens. Figure 5.5.7(A) shows the embeddings across all networks as heatmaps. For the rest of the section, we will use these eight human/alien networks.

These embeddings do not live in the same latent space just yet. They may be rotated from each other due to nonidentifiability, and the embeddings may not be directly comparable.

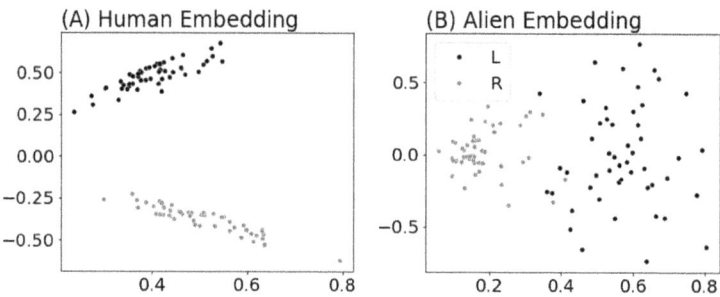

Figure 5.5.6 (**A**) The spectral embedding for a human network, and (**B**) the spectral embedding for an alien network.

Calculating a Shared Latent Space
Our goal is to find some reasonable way to fuse together these individual embeddings into a shared space.

We can concatenate each of our individual network embeddings horizontally. Because the rows of these matrices are all aligned, meaning, row 1 corresponds to node 1 for all matrices, we can think of each node as having (in this case) Md latent dimensions: There are d latent dimensions for each of the M networks. In this case, since $\hat{d} = 7$ and $M = 8$, each node has $7 \times 8 = 56$ latent dimensions associated with it (seven per network).

This process produces an $n \times Md$ matrix, where n is the number of nodes (the rows of the resulting matrix), and Md is the number of latent dimensions associated with each node (the columns of the resulting matrix). This is the joint matrix for mase, since it is a composition of information from the M total networks. We can use numpy to construct the joint matrix:

```
# Concatenate the embeddings horizontally into a single n x Md matrix
joint_matrix = np.hstack(separate_embeddings)
```

The joint matrix is plotted in Figure 5.5.7(B).

When we look at the joint matrix oriented in this manner, we see the redundant information that we will exploit in our next step. In particular, the first and second columns of every embedding look like they tend to separate the first 50 nodes (which were the left hemisphere) from the next 50 nodes (the right hemisphere). Successive dimensions look like noise.

We can exploit this redundancy of some of the qualitative features, despite the fact that the columns are not exactly identical in their behavior (for instance, for some of the networks, the second embedding dimension has high values for the first 50 nodes and low values for the second 50 nodes, or low values for the first 50 nodes and high values for the second 50 nodes). The important idea is that there is some notion of similar information being conveyed that we can use to simplify the problem.

Embedding the Joint Matrix to Create a Joint Embedding
We want to address the fact that there is redundant information common to many of these embeddings, and some information common to only a subset of these

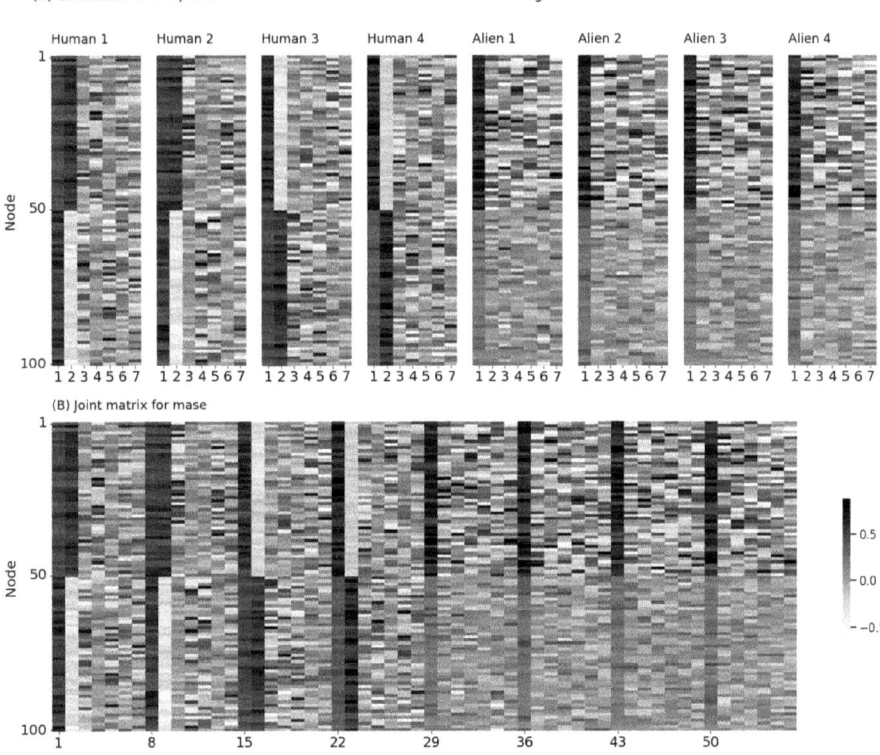

Figure 5.5.7 (**A**) The separate embeddings for each network. (**B**) The joint matrix, which concatenates the separate embeddings for each network (horizontally).

embeddings. This redundancy is not entirely consistent from embedding to embedding, nor even within network groupings (human versus alien). The patterns in some of the human and alien network embeddings are different, even though the underlying $SBM_n(\vec{z}, B)$ random networks are homogeneous for networks in the same group. This is an instance of the nonidentifiability problem from Section 5.5.2 and illustrated in Figure 5.5.2.

Fortunately, spectral embedding is an ideal candidate for picking out these sorts of "redundancies" that arise across columns of our matrix. Spectral embedding allows us to capture the redundancy of the qualitative aspects of these columns, and to obtain the general idea of what they each convey numerically. For this, we will use another spectral embedding. The process is nearly identical to what we did for ase in Algorithm 5.2, in that we perform svd, and retain the top d left singular vectors. This is called an *unscaled spectral embedding*, because (unlike for ase) we are not weighting the left singular vectors by the square roots of their singular values.

We use this process to embed the joint matrix, obtaining a joint embedding. We will embed into two dimensions, because there are two communities, as per Concept 5.3.9:

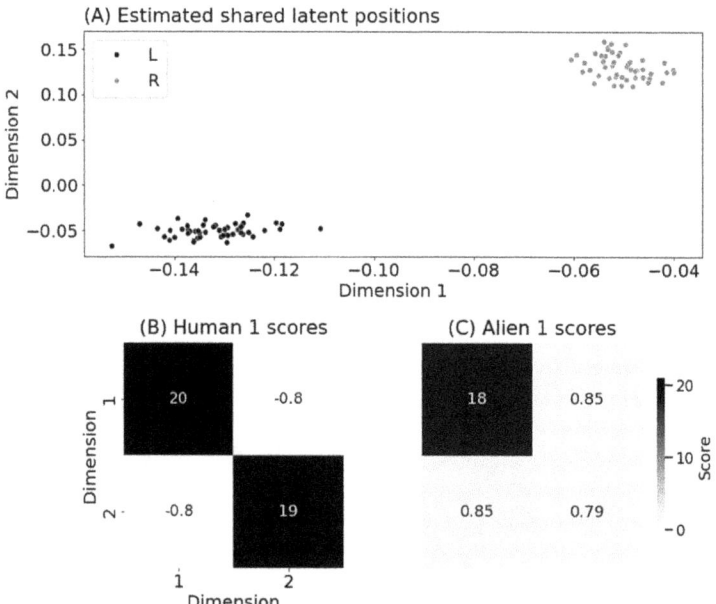

Figure 5.5.8 (**A**) The estimated shared latent positions of the human and alien brains. (**B**) The estimated scores for the first human network. (**C**) The estimated scores for the first alien network.

```
def unscaled_embed(X, d, seed=0):
    np.random.seed(seed)
    U, s, Vt = np.linalg.svd(X)
    return U[:,0:d]

Shat = unscaled_embed(joint_matrix, 2)
```

The result of this unscaled embedding is an *estimate of the shared latent positions*, and is denoted by the matrix $\widehat{S}$. $\widehat{S}$ has n rows and d columns, so each row $\widehat{s}_i$ is an estimate of the shared latent position of node i.

We plot the estimate of the shared latent positions $\widehat{S}$ in Figure 5.5.8(A). Note that the estimated shared latent positions convey the shared structure between human and alien brains: The left and right hemispheres are appreciably different. It is in this sense that mase is a fused embedding technique. Now, we distill out separate representations for each network and explore the sense in which it can also be parallel.

Building Representations for Each Network

How is our joint embedding related to the separate, original networks? Under the COSIE model in Section 4.9.2, the probability matrix for the ith network could be described as:

$$P^{(i)} = SR^{(i)}S^\top \tag{5.4}$$

where S conveyed the homogeneity across all M networks (the *shared latent positions*), and $R^{(i)}$ conveyed the unique aspects of the probability matrix for a network i (the unique *score matrices*).

Also, remember that in the COSIE model, we assumed that S was orthogonal. For an orthogonal matrix S with n rows and n columns, $S^\top S = SS^\top = I_n$. We can use this to understand $R^{(i)}$ by premultiplying by $S^\top$ and postmultiplying by S in Equation (5.4):

$$S^\top P^{(i)} S = S^\top S R^{(i)} S^\top S$$
$$\Rightarrow R^{(i)} = S^\top P^{(i)} S, \tag{5.5}$$

After the simplification, $R^{(i)}$ represents a transformed version of the $P^{(i)}$ matrix. This is analogous to looking at the structure of the ith network from the perspective of the basis from all of the networks provided by S: We can think of $R^{(i)} = S^\top P^{(i)} S$ as an orthogonal transform of the probability matrix of a specific network $P^{(i)}$ into the basis defined by the columns (the shared latent positions) of S.

In practice, we have two problems:

1. Estimates of the shared latent positions are not necessarily orthogonal, and
2. We do not directly observe the probability matrix.

We discuss these problems in more detail below.

Estimates of the Shared Latent Positions Are Not Orthogonal

We usually do not have the shared latent positions S. In practice, we only have access to an estimate of the shared latent positions $\widehat{S}$, the first d columns of the left singular vectors U of the joint matrix. While the full left singular vector matrix is orthogonal (by definition of the svd, in Remark 5.3.5), it is helpful to reduce the dimensionality when we embed below the number of nodes in the network so that we can learn from the shared latent position matrix later. Unfortunately, this disrupts the orthogonality, and $\widehat{S}$ is no longer orthogonal when we discard the last $n - d$ columns. This is because orthogonal matrices must be square, and a matrix with n rows and $n - d$ columns is not square.

We Do Not Observe the Probability Matrix

A hurdle that we experienced in the ase was that we could obtain a perfect estimate of the latent position matrix (up to an orthogonal transformation) if we knew the probability matrix. In practice, however, we never have a true probability matrix; we only see observations of adjacency matrices.

Instead, we simply embedded the adjacency matrix. We settled on this approach for ase because the eigendecomposition procedure in Algorithm 5.1 would not work unless the matrix was positive semidefinite, but we had no such restriction with the ase procedure in Algorithm 5.2 using svd. Likewise, no part of the procedure for mase is restricted to positive semidefiniteness to obtain a real answer.

These limitations may feel impactful. However, we can ignore them for the time being as we did with ase because our estimates are generally "close enough." Using Equation (5.5) for the score matrices, we can simply plug in the estimate of the shared latent positions for S, and the adjacency matrix $A^{(i)}$ for the probability matrix, to obtain an estimate of the score matrix:

$$\widehat{R}^{(i)} = \widehat{S}^\top A^{(i)} \widehat{S}.$$

Let's do this in practice with our networks:

```
# stack the networks into a numpy array
As_ar = np.asarray(networks)
# compute the scores
scores = Shat.T @ As_ar @ Shat
```

We plot the estimated score matrices in Figure 5.5.8(B) and (C) for a human and alien network, respectively. Notice in particular that the human networks and the alien networks leverage different combinations of the two latent dimensions to "reconstruct" the score matrix, much like in Section 4.9.2.2 when the Facebook/Instagram and LinkedIn networks used different score matrices to convey the disparate structure in the networks. In particular, the second estimated shared latent dimension, which conveys the disparity between the left and right communities, is much different for the human and alien networks. This highlights that the human and alien networks have disparate community structure (humans have a homophilic structure, aliens a dissassortative structure) through the latent dimension which distinguish the communities.

We use this with the COSIE model in Equation (5.4) to obtain:

$$\hat{P}^{(i)} = \widehat{S}\hat{R}^{(i)}\widehat{S}^{\top}.$$

Let's see how this works out in practice, by computing the true probability matrix for the humans and aliens, and comparing it to the estimated probability matrix for the humans and aliens. We compute the true probability matrix using the results from Section 4.3.6.

```
from graphbook_code import generate_sbm_pmtx

Phum = generate_sbm_pmtx(zs, Bhuman)
Palien = generate_sbm_pmtx(zs, Balien)
Pests = Shat @ scores @ Shat.T
```

The true probability matrices for humans and aliens are shown in Figure 5.5.9(A) and (C), and are compared to the estimated probability matrices for a human and an alien in Figure 5.5.9(B) and (D). Note that mase is able to recover both the homophilic structure of the human brain networks and the core–periphery structure of the alien brain networks through unique combinations of the estimated shared latent positions in Figure 5.5.8(A), which separated the left and right communities.

Using mase in Practice
The mase algorithm is shown in Algorithm 5.4.

You can run the mase algorithm using graspologic, which streamlines the procedure that we outlined above:

```
from graspologic.embed import MultipleASE as mase

d = 2
mase_embedder = mase(n_components=d)
# obtain an estimate of the shared latent positions
Shat = mase_embedder.fit_transform(networks)
```

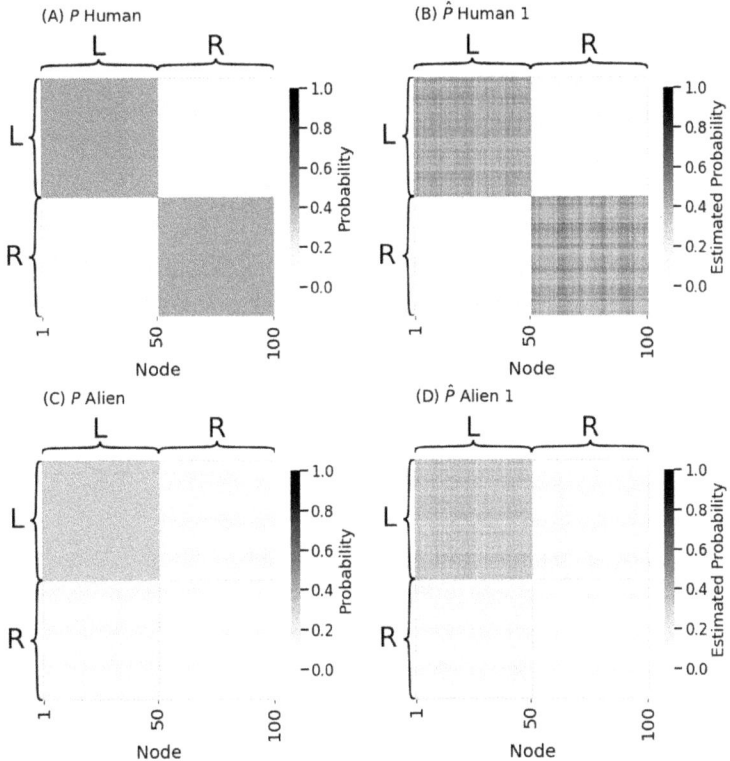

Figure 5.5.9 (**A**) The probability matrix for human networks, (**B**) the estimated probability matrix for the first human network, (**C**) the probability matrix for alien networks, and (**D**) the estimated probability matrix for the first alien network.

```
# obtain an estimate of the scores
Rhat_hum1 = mase_embedder.scores_[0]
# obtain an estimate of the probability matrix for the first human
Phat_hum1 = Shat @ mase_embedder.scores_[0] @ Shat.T
```

5.5.4 Omnibus Embedding

The *omnibus embedding* (omni) is a parallel embedding technique that embeds networks separately while keeping them all in the same latent space, so that they will be properly rotated to align with one another. This allows us to compare separate network representations directly. omni does not attempt to separately identify shared and unique structure across networks, unlike mase (which considered shared structure via the estimated shared latent positions S and unique structure through the separate estimated score matrices for each network $R^{(i)}$).

5.5.4.1 How Does omni Work?

The omnibus embedding works by:

1. Assembling individual adjacency matrices together into a single joint matrix, called the *omnibus matrix*,

---

Algorithm 5.4 Multiple adjacency spectral embedding (`mase`)

Data: $A^{(1)}, \ldots, A^{(M)}$ a collection of M networks with n nodes.
  d the desired latent dimensionality.

Result: the estimated shared latent position matrix and the estimated score matrices.

1 For each $A^{(i)}$, obtain $\widehat{X}^{(i)} = \text{ase}\left(A^{(i)}, \log_2(n)\right)$, for $i = 1, \ldots, M$, via Algorithm 5.2.

2 Let $J = \begin{bmatrix} \widehat{X}^{(1)} & \cdots & \widehat{X}^{(M)} \end{bmatrix}$ be the joint matrix, consisting of a column-wise concatenation of the individual estimated latent position matrices.

3 Let $U, \Sigma, V = \text{svd}(J)$.

4 Let $\widehat{S} = U_d$, the first d columns of the left singular vectors of J.

5 Let $\hat{R}^{(i)} = \widehat{S}^\top A^{(i)} \widehat{S}$, for $i = 1, \ldots, M$.

6 **return** $\widehat{S}, R^{(1)}, \ldots, R^{(M)}$

---

2. Embedding the omnibus matrix with `ase`, and
3. Extracting latent position estimates for each network from this embedding.

Computing the Omnibus Matrix

The first step in `omni` is to compute the omnibus matrix, which is the joint matrix used by `omni`. The *omnibus matrix* for a collection of M networks with n nodes is the $Mn \times Mn$ matrix O, where for each $n \times n$ block $O^{(i,j)}$:

$$O^{(i,j)} = \frac{1}{2}\left(A^{(i)} + A^{(j)}\right).$$

The resulting (i, j) block of the omnibus matrix is itself an $n \times n$ matrix, and the Omnibus matrix looks like this:

$$O = \begin{bmatrix} O^{(1,1)} & \cdots & O^{(1,M)} \\ \vdots & \ddots & \vdots \\ O^{(M,1)} & \cdots & O^{(M,M)} \end{bmatrix} = \begin{bmatrix} A^{(1)} & \cdots & \frac{1}{2}\left(A^{(1)} + A^{(M)}\right) \\ \vdots & \ddots & \vdots \\ \frac{1}{2}\left(A^{(1)} + A^{(M)}\right) & \cdots & A^{(M)} \end{bmatrix}.$$

By construction, the omnibus matrix is symmetric with respect to the blocks themselves: $O^{(i,j)} = O^{(j,i)}$. However, if these individual blocks are not themselves symmetric, the omnibus matrix might not be symmetric. Since the blocks of the omnibus matrix are combinations of adjacency matrices, and adjacency matrices are symmetric when the underlying networks are undirected, the omnibus matrix is symmetric when the collection of networks are undirected.

Let's consider only the first two networks (human networks), and construct a simple omnibus matrix from these. We can do this with `numpy`:

```
omni_ex = np.block(
    [[networks[0], (networks[0]+networks[1])/2],
     [(networks[1]+networks[0])/2, networks[1]]]
)
```

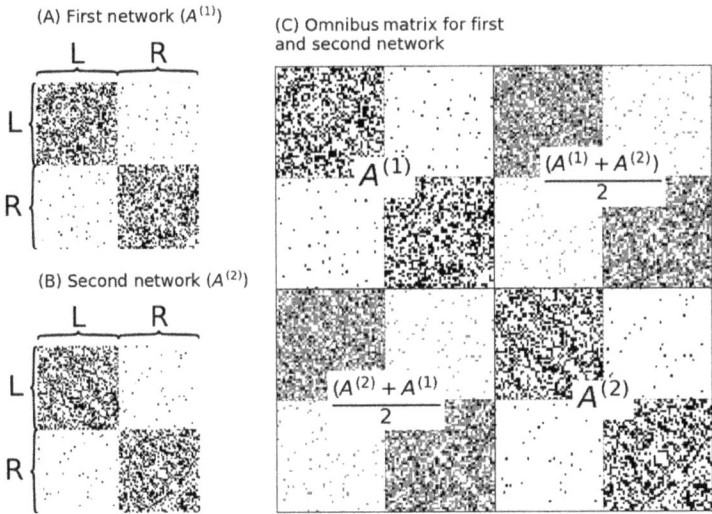

Figure 5.5.10 (**A**) The first human network, (**B**) The second human network, and (**C**) the omnibus matrix of the first two human networks.

We visualize this small omnibus matrix in Figure 5.5.10. We illustrate the first two networks in 5.5.10(A) and 5.5.10(B), and the resulting omnibus matrix of the first two networks in 5.5.10(C).

We can use `graspologic` to obtain the omnibus matrix for our collection of networks:

```
from graspologic.embed.omni import _get_omni_matrix
omni_mtx = _get_omni_matrix(networks)
```

The full omnibus matrix for all eight networks is shown in Figure 5.5.11(A). We can conceptualize the omnibus matrix as the adjacency matrix of a new (weighted) network from a collection of networks, where all the nodes from each network form a single node in the new network. A subnetwork induced on the omnibus matrix by the nodes from a single network is the original network itself (the on-diagonal blocks of the omnibus matrix $O^{(i,i)}$). The subnetwork formed by the nodes of a network i and the nodes of another network j provides information about how similar (or different) the networks i and j are (the off-diagonal blocks of the omnibus matrix $O^{(i,j)}$). This incorporation of information about each network in relation to the other networks is what will allow `omni` to properly orient the latent positions across the collection of networks.

Embedding the Omnibus Matrix
The next step is to embed the omnibus matrix using `ase`. This creates an estimate of the latent position matrix for the omnibus matrix itself. When the $Mn \times Mn$ omnibus matrix is embedded into d dimensions, we obtain an estimated latent position matrix with $Mn \times d$ dimensions. A good rule of thumb for the omnibus embedding is to use $\log_2(n)$ embedding dimensions.

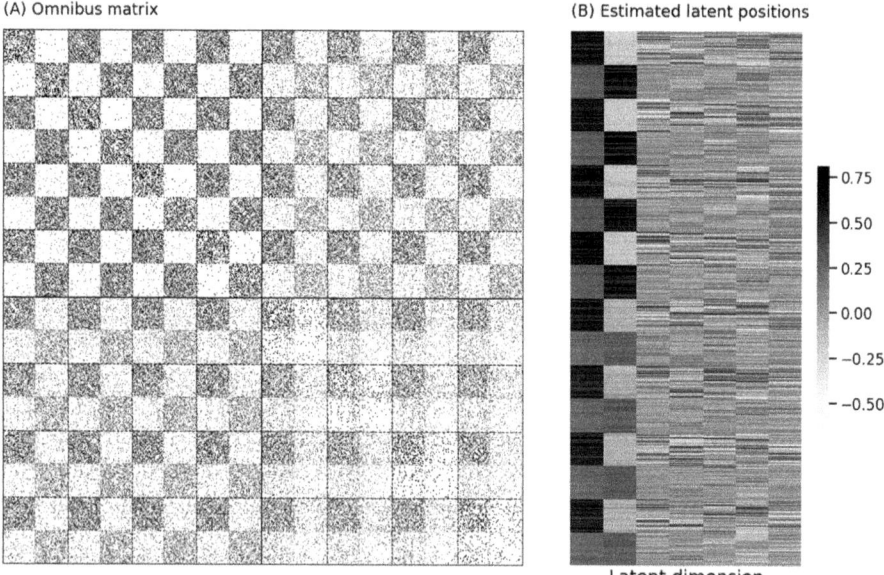

(A) Omnibus matrix

(B) Estimated latent positions

Latent dimension

Figure 5.5.11 (**A**) The omnibus matrix, and (**B**) the embedded omnibus matrix.

```
from graspologic.embed import AdjacencySpectralEmbed as ase

dhat = int(np.ceil(np.log2(n)))
Xhat_omni = ase(n_components=dhat, svd_seed=0).fit_transform(omni_mtx)
```

The estimated latent positions for the omnibus matrix are shown in Figure 5.5.11.

Extracting Oriented Estimated Latent Positions

The last step of omni is to obtain the properly oriented latent position estimates for each network. We conceptualize the omnibus matrix as the adjacency matrix for a new network, where the Mn nodes of this new network are the n nodes of each of the original M networks. The $Mn \times d$ estimated latent position matrix looks like this:

$$\widehat{X} = \begin{bmatrix} \widehat{X}^{(1)} \\ \widehat{X}^{(2)} \\ \vdots \\ \widehat{X}^{(M)} \end{bmatrix},$$

where each set of $n \times d$ estimated latent positions $\widehat{X}^{(i)}$ correspond to the estimated latent positions for the network $A^{(i)}$.

To obtain the latent positions for each network explicitly, we can reshape the $Mn \times d$ matrix into an $m \times n \times d$ tensor, and look at the individual slices of the tensor corresponding to the estimated latent position matrix for each network. We can do this with numpy:

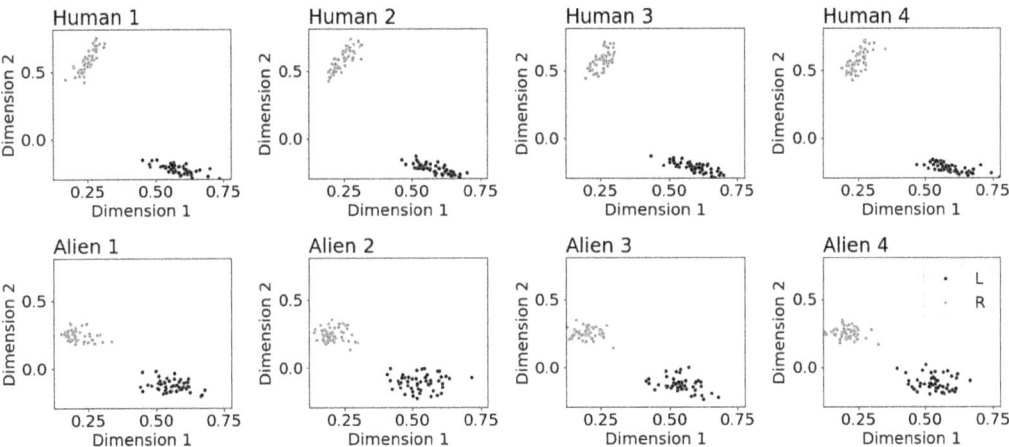

Figure 5.5.12 The estimated latent positions for each network.

```
M = len(networks)
n = len(networks[0])

# obtain an M x n x d tensor
Xhat_tensor = Xhat_omni.reshape(M, n, -1)
# the estimated latent positions for the first network
Xhat_human1 = Xhat_tensor[0,:,:]
```

The estimated latent positions for each network are illustrated in Figure 5.5.12 for all of the networks in our collection. The second and third dimensions capture most of the signal disparity between the human and alien networks, so we show scatter plots for these two dimensions. Note that the human networks appear to have the nodes in the same relative positions, and the alien networks appear to have the nodes in the same relative positions, which is a function of the alignment (e.g., lack of nonidentifiability) created by omni. Had we embedded the networks separately, this would not have been the case. On the other hand, the human brain network nodes and the alien brain network nodes appear to have different patterns in the embeddings, which is a function of the unique disparities between human and alien brain networks.

Using omni in Practice

The procedure for the omni embedding is outlined in Algorithm 5.5.

We can run omni using `graspologic`:

```
from graspologic.embed import OmnibusEmbed as omni

# obtain a tensor of the estimated latent positions
Xhat_tensor = omni(n_components=int(np.log2(n)),
    svd_seed=0).fit_transform(networks)
# obtain the estimated latent positions for the first human
# network
Xhat_human1 = Xhat_tensor[0,:,:]
```

Algorithm 5.5 Omnibus embedding (omni)

Data: $A^{(1)}, \ldots, A^{(M)}$ a collection of M networks with n nodes.

    d the desired latent dimensionality.

Result: estimated latent positions for each network.

1 Compute the $Mn \times Mn$ omnibus matrix O, where each $n \times n$ submatrix
$O^{(i,j)} = \frac{1}{2}\left(A^{(i)} + A^{(j)}\right)$.

2 Embed the omnibus matrix to produce estimated latent positions for the omnibus network, $\widehat{X} = \text{ase}(O, d)$, according to Algorithm 5.2.

3 Let $\widehat{X}^{(i)}$ be the $n \times d$ matrix consisting of the $(i - 1) \cdot n + 1$ through $i \cdot n$ rows of $\widehat{X}$.

4 **return** $\widehat{X}^{(1)}, \ldots, \widehat{X}^{(M)}$

Relating omni *to the JRDPG*

Recall from Section 4.9 that a homogeneous collection of random networks $\{\mathbf{A}^{(1)}, \ldots, \mathbf{A}^{(M)}\}$ has identical underlying probability matrices. We say that $\{\mathbf{A}^{(1)}, \ldots, \mathbf{A}^{(M)}\}$ are $JRDPG_{n,M}(X)$ where the probability matrix $P = XX^\top$. Each network $\mathbf{A}^{(m)}$ are individually independent $RDPG_n(X)$ random networks.

When we produced an embedding of each network using omni, we produce estimates $\widehat{X}^{(i)}$ for each of our M networks. With this framework in mind, the estimates $\widehat{X}^{(i)}$ are comparable, in that if two networks are homogeneous, their estimated latent positions are similar. Although the JRDPG model underlies the omni embedding (which assumes homogeneity), the embedding has the property that if networks are heterogeneous, their omni estimated latent positions will be dissimilar. Crucially, however, they will be aligned to one another; that is, without the nonidentifiability problem. This means that omni embedding allows our estimated latent positions $\widehat{X}^{(i)}$ to be directly compared, and significant differences between our them can provide evidence that they are dissimilar. Figure 5.5.12 showed this when we saw that the human embeddings and alien embeddings were homogeneous within species (human vs. human, or alien vs. alien), but heterogeneous across species (human vs. alien).

Using omni, we can obtain estimates of probability matrices like this:

```
Phat_hum1 = Xhat_human1 @ Xhat_human1.T
```

Repeating this for both human and alien networks, we see that this conceptual model does a reasonable job of estimating the underlying probability matrices for our networks, similar to mase.

5.5.5   omni **versus** mase

Both omni and mase will produce estimated latent representations of collections of networks which are comparable downstream during analysis. These techniques take a collection of networks and tabularize them so that we can compare them directly with downstream machine learning methods.

Mase embeds each network individually prior to the construction of the joint matrix, by first taking the ase of each individual network. The joint matrix is an

$n \times Md$ matrix, where d is the number of embedding dimensions used in the `ase` substep of `mase` (and is usually taken to be $\log_2(n)$). This matrix is manageable in size and scale for successive operations, as the number of elements scales on the order of $n\sqrt{n}$ and M.

`Omni` has a substantial limitation: the construction (and embedding) of the omnibus matrix. The omnibus matrix scales in size with $(Mn)^2$. When we have many networks and M is large, or when we have many nodes per network and n is large, this can be computationally prohibitive. The `svd` can become intractable to compute with sizable matrices, and in these situations `mase` might be simpler to incorporate.

Both `omni` and `mase` are simple to use, and have similar theoretical underpinnings (`mase` on the COSIE model, and `omni` on the JRDPG model, with established theoretical underpinnings for heterogeneous RDPG models). While the COSIE model makes explicit use of shared structure, there is nothing prohibiting the COSIE model from incorporating little to no shared structure across the collection of networks if none is present. We could imagine a situation in the worst case where there is no shared structure in which the estimated "shared" latent positions could be taken to be unique latent positions for each network. Then, the score matrices for each network could leverage only the unique latent positions for that specific network and simply have scores of 0 for the estimated shared latent positions that are associated with other networks. For this reason, when we want to exploit or highlight shared or unique structures across a collection of networks, `mase` is a sensible choice.

A nice feature of `omni` is that it produces latent position estimates for each network, rather than just unique score matrices for each network. This means that for each network, we end up with a d-dimensional representation for each node. To learn about disparities across networks downstream at the node-wise level, this might be a reasonable starting point for analysis, and could be easier to incorporate with tabular machine learning techniques.

For these reasons, if computational time or spatial considerations need to be made, or if we anticipate some amount of shared structure in our networks, `mase` will be a reasonable choice. If we do not anticipate shared structure in our networks, either `mase` or `omni` are principled approaches. Finally, if we want to maintain separate network representations but we want to avoid dealing with nonidentifiability, we will tend to use `omni`.

Appendix B.3.1 provides technical details on `omni` and `mase` embeddings.

5.6   Joint Representation Learning

Building on the covariate representation models introduced in Section 4.10, we now introduce representation learning methods for incorporating both network topology and node attributes into a single, unified representation.

We cover the following:

1. Motivation for combining network structure with node attributes,
2. The covariate-assisted spectral embedding (CASE) technique,

3. Construction of similarity matrices from node covariates,
4. Methods for balancing the influence of network structure and node attributes,
5. Considerations for positive semidefiniteness in joint embeddings, and
6. Extensions and variations of joint representation learning techniques.

Joint representation learning allows for the integration of multiple data modalities, leveraging both network structure and node-level information. This approach builds upon the network models with covariates introduced in Section 4.10 and extends the spectral embedding techniques covered in Sections 5.3 and 5.4. While conceptually similar to the multiple network representations explored in Section 5.5, joint embeddings focus on integrating different types of information within a single network, rather than combining information from multiple networks.

In many problems, a network might be more than just the *network topology*, or the information contained in its collection of nodes and edges. If we were investigating a social network, we might have access to extra information about each person; for example, their height or their age. If we were investigating an infectious disease network, we might incorporate vaccine coverage, population movement, or disease variant. When we embed a network, it seems like we should be able to use these extra bits of information – node, edge, or network attributes – to improve our analysis. We briefly discussed the theory around networks with covariates in Section 4.10. Here, we will expand on this theory with techniques and tools that jointly use both the covariates and the network topology to create and learn from new representations of the network. These techniques and tools are called joint representation learning.

There are two primary reasons that we might want to explore using node covariates in addition to topological structure. First, they might improve our standard embedding algorithms like ase and lse. For example, if the latent structure of the covariates of a network lines up with the latent structure of its topology, then we might be able to reduce noise when we embed, even if the communities in our network don't overlap perfectly with the communities in our covariates. Second, figuring out what the clusters of an embedding actually mean can sometimes be difficult. Covariates create a natural structure that we can explore. Covariate information in brain networks showing us where in the brain each node is, for instance, might let us better understand the types of characteristics that distinguish between different brain regions.

In this section, we will explore *covariate-assisted spectral embedding* (case), a variation on spectral embedding [11]. In case, instead of embedding just the adjacency matrix or the Laplacian, we will combine the Laplacian and the covariates into a new matrix and embed that.

We will invent toy data representing Wikipedia pages, described in Case Study 5.6.1. Let's first generate the data:

```
from graspologic.simulations import sbm
import numpy as np

n = 200 # total number of nodes
# first two communities are the ''core'' pages for statistics
# and computer science, and second two are the ''peripheral'' pages
# for statistics and computer science.
```

Case Study 5.6.1 Wikipedia pages

We can illustrate how using covariates might help us by using a model in which some of our community information is in the covariates and some is in our topology. Let's imagine we have a network of $N = 200$ nodes representing Wikipedia pages for two complementary fields: computer science and statistics. A pair of Wikipedia pages have an edge if both of the Wikipedia pages link to one another.

Unfortunately in our network, there is an extremely prominent core: The top 50 computer science Wikipedia pages and the top 50 statistics Wikipedia pages overwhelmingly cross-link to one another, and do not tend to link to the peripheral and more specialized pages nearly as much.

When we attempt to embed this network using a strategy like `ase`, the embedding will probably differentiate the strong core very easily from the periphery, but will not parse out the "subject-matter specific" signal of retaining the differences between computer science and statistics articles.

Fortunately, we have another piece of information: whether a given page cites each of the 20 most influential statisticians of all time. This is a simple indicator for each statistician: A value of 1 is recorded for page i and statistician k if statistician k is cited by page i.

```
B = np.array([[.4, .3, .05, .05],
              [.3, .4, .05, .05],
              [.05, .05, .05, .02],
              [.05, .05, .02, .05]])

# make the stochastic block model
np.random.seed(0)
A, labels = sbm([n // 4, n // 4, n // 4, n // 4], B,
    return_labels=True)
# generate labels for core/periphery
co_per_labels = np.repeat(["Core", "Periphery"], repeats=n//2)
# generate labels for statistics/CS.
st_cs_labels = np.repeat(["Stat", "CS", "Stat", "CS"], repeats=n//4)
```

The network is shown in Figure 5.6.1(A), and we show the results of an `lse` of the network into two dimensions in Figure 5.6.1(B). Note that in embedding this network, we can only distinguish the core nodes (from both computer science and statistics) from the periphery nodes (from both computer science and statistics), but we cannot differentiate between the two subject materials.

Next, we will focus on generating the covariates associated with each node. We have a simple binary indicator for each page, indicating whether any of our 20 influential statisticians are cited. For statistics pages, there is a 50 percent chance that each of the 20 statisticians are cited. However, for computer science pages, there is only a 5 percent chance that each of the 20 statisticians are cited. We can generate these covariates using numpy:

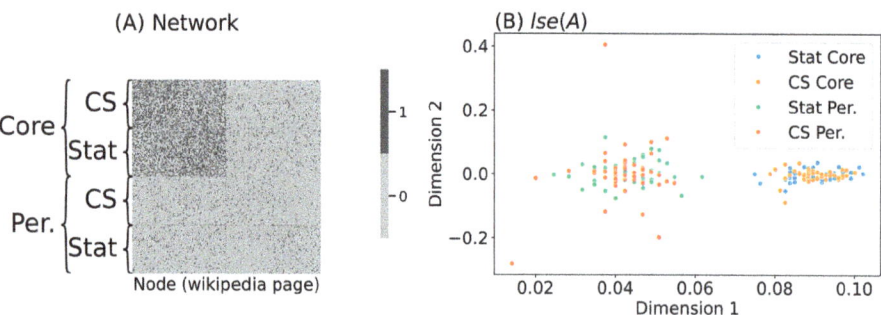

Figure 5.6.1 **(A)** The Wikipedia network, and **(B)** an `lse` of the Wikipedia network.

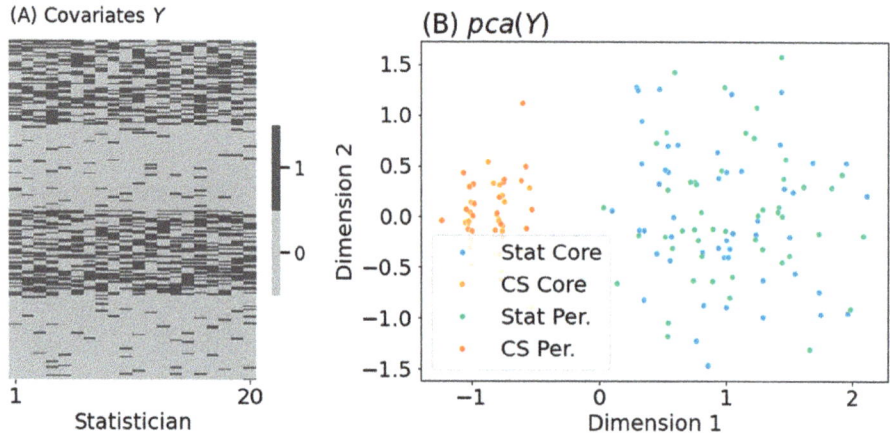

Figure 5.6.2 **(A)** The covariates associated with each wikipedia page, and **(B)** a `pca` of the covariate data.

```
trial = []
for label in st_cs_labels:
    if "Stat" in label:
        # if the page is a statistics page, there is a 50% chance
        # of citing each of the scholars
        trial.append(np.random.binomial(1, 0.5, size=20))
    else:
        # if the page is a CS page, there is a 5% chance of citing
        # each of the scholars
        trial.append(np.random.binomial(1, 0.05, size=20))
Y = np.vstack(trial)
```

The covariate matrix is plotted in Figure 5.6.2(A). Next, we perform a `pca` with the covariates, to determine whether we could learn the four communities (core and periphery of statistics and computer science) using only the covariate data. We will build PCA ourselves to show the similarity of the method with `ase` or `lse`. In practice one would usually use `sklearn`'s implementation, `sklearn.decomposition.PCA`.

```
def embed(X, d=2, seed=0):
    """
    A function to embed a matrix.
    """
    np.random.seed(seed)
    Lambda, V = np.linalg.eig(X)
    return V[:, 0:d] @ np.diag(np.sqrt(np.abs(Lambda[0:d])))

def pca(X, d=2, seed=0):
    """
    A function to perform a pca on a data matrix.
    """
    X_centered = X - np.mean(X, axis=0)
    return embed(X_centered @ X_centered.T, d=d, seed=seed)

Y_embedded = pca(Y, d=2)
```

We plot the resulting embedding in Figure 5.6.2(B). This time, we have excellent separation of the statistics and computer science pages, but we cannot differentiate the core from the periphery.

5.6.1   Covariate-Assisted Spectral Embedding

Covariate-assisted spectral embedding, or case, is a simple way of combining our network and our covariates into a single model. In the most straightforward version of case, we take a weighted combination of the network's Laplacian L and a similarity matrix for our covariates, $YY^\top$.

Let's take a look at the network Laplacian and the covariate similarity matrix $YY^\top$:

```
from graspologic.utils import to_laplacian

# compute the network Laplacian
L_wiki = to_laplacian(A, form="DAD")
# log transform, strictly for visualization purposes
L_wiki_logxfm = np.log(L_wiki + np.min(L_wiki[L_wiki > 0])/np.exp(1))

# compute the node similarity matrix
Y_sim = Y @ Y.T
```

The network Laplacian and the node similarity matrix are shown in Figure 5.6.3. Note that we used a log-transform strategy to visualize the log-transformed Laplacian after adding a suitably small offset ϵ. This is because many of the network weights are extremely small, so the color scale was not particularly informative of the Laplacian itself.

Each matrix appears to preserve disparate properties of the underlying network: Its topology, reflected in the network Laplacian, conveys the topological disparities between the core and peripheral pages in our network. On the other hand, the covariate metadata associated with each node in the network conveys the content disparities between the statistics and computer science nodes.

Remark 5.6.2 Connections to Principal Components Analysis (pca)

The rows of the matrix Y, denoted by $\vec{y}_i$, are each 20-dimensional vectors, where each entry has a value of 0 of 1. The matrix product $YY^\top$ has entries containing the dot product of each $\vec{y}_i$ with each $\vec{y}_j$:

$$\left(YY^\top\right)_{ij} = \vec{y}_i^\top \vec{y}_j = \sum_{k=1}^{20} y_{ik} y_{jk}.$$

In this case, since the values of our covariate matrix can take only 0s and 1s, these dot products simply count the number of times Wikipedia page i and Wikipedia page j both cite the same scholar. We can conceptualize the uncentered, unrescaled covariance matrix $YY^\top$ as giving a degree of "similarity" in the covariates for each of our nodes.

Much like ase exploits latent structure in the adjacency matrix to determine an appropriate embedding, a pca exploits latent structure in the covariances of our data matrix (here, our covariates, Y) to embed a given dataset. Typically, a pca of Y would spectrally embed the centered and rescaled sample covariance matrix S, with entries:

$$s_{ij} = \frac{1}{n-1}(\vec{y}_i - \bar{y})^\top(\vec{y}_j - \bar{y}),$$

where $\bar{y} = \frac{1}{n}\sum_{i=1}^{n}\vec{y}_i$ is the sample mean of the rows of Y (i.e., the samples are mean-centered), and $\frac{1}{n-1}$ is a rescaling factor.

This is similar yet distinct from the procedure that we are using here, because we will not typically take the centering (by the mean $\bar{y}$) nor the rescaling steps.

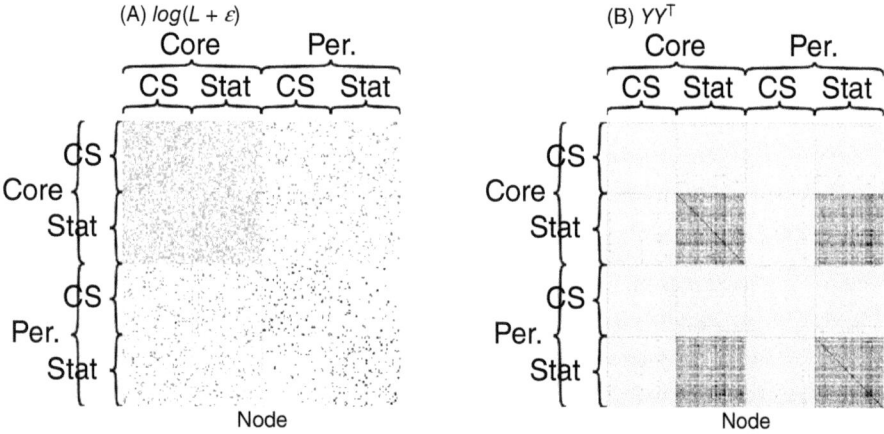

Figure 5.6.3 Visualizations of (**A**) the log-transformed network Laplacian, and (**B**) the covariate similarity matrix.

Combining Information from the Network Topology and the Covariates
The matrix we embed with `case` is a linear combination of the network Laplacian L and the covariate similarity matrix $YY^\top$. It is typically represented like this:

$$L + \alpha YY^\top.$$

The weight α is a hyperparameter to the `case` technique. We will often want to select it with respect to a downstream task of interest.

```python
from graspologic.embed import AdjacencySpectralEmbed as ase

def case(A, Y, weight=0, d=2, tau=0, seed=0):
    """
    A function for performing case.
    """
    # compute the laplacian
    L = to_laplacian(A, form="R-DAD", regularizer=tau)
    YYt = Y @ Y.T
    return ase(n_components=2, svd_seed=seed).fit_transform(L +
        weight*YYt)

embedded = case(A, Y, weight=.002)
```

For instance, if we had a high-level goal of producing an embedding which preserved both topological properties of the network (such as the core and peripheral components) as well as covariate-derived properties of the network (such as statistics and computer science components), a heuristic might be to try numerous weights α, and evaluate the resulting embeddings for each choice of α. A suitable choice of α would preserve the community groupings.

Figure 5.6.4 explores various network embeddings with different choices of α. Note that for low choices of α, the embedding resembles that of the topology-only `lse` in

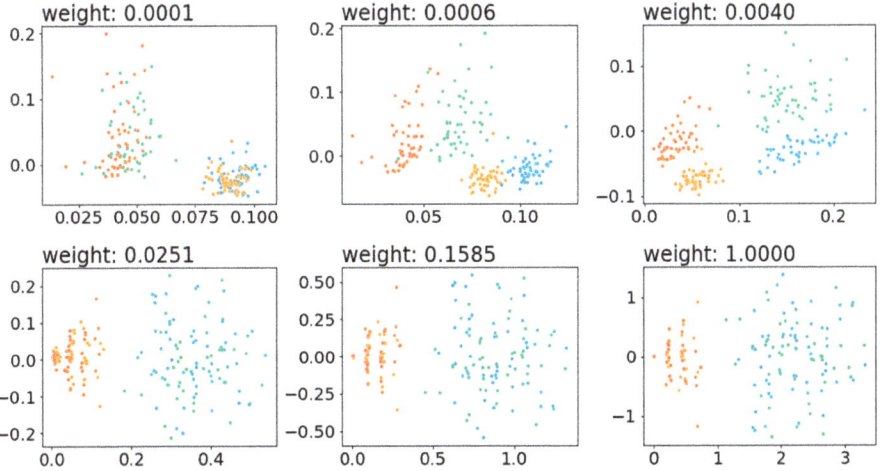

Figure 5.6.4 The network embedding using both the network topology and the node covariates for $L + \alpha YY^\top$, for different choices of weight α.

Figure 5.6.1(B). For large choices of α, the embedding closely resembles that of the covariate-only embedding in Figure 5.6.2(B). For the intermediate choices, such as $\alpha = 0.0006$ or $\alpha = 0.004$, the embedding appears to leverage information across both the covariates and the network topology, and both the core or periphery and subject matter (statistics or computer science) structures are preserved.

In practice, we can often use grid-like search approaches like those in Figure 5.6.4 to determine which weight values produce good community separation. If we know community separations ahead of time, we could compute centers for our communities and then use metrics like the silhouette score (discussed in Appendix C.1), which measures community separation, to automate this process. If we do not know community separations ahead of time, we can use automated approaches such as community detection (discussed in Section 6.1).

5.6.1.1   Automatic Weight Selection

In general, it is ideal to perform joint representation learning with an approach like case with a downstream machine learning task in mind. This is because the weight selection procedure of case is a search over hyperparameters, and it is difficult to determine what an appropriate hyperparameter choice is without any way to evaluate it. For instance, in Figure 5.6.3, we determined "ideal" weight selections to be on the basis of how well different weights established community structure for known communities. We could make such a search more quantitative by incorporating a procedure which quantifies "community separation" between groups of nodes.

While we cannot automatically determine an "ideal" weight in terms of an arbitrary downstream task, we can take principled steps to ensure that the two components of case (the normalized Laplacian and the covariate similarity matrix) are contributing equally to the embedding process.

When embedding symmetric matrices, we need to keep in mind that the points we are plotting are the components of the eigenvectors with the biggest eigenvalues. When embedding into two-dimensional space, for instance, the x-axis values are the components of the eigenvector with the biggest eigenvalue, and the y-axis values are the components of the eigenvector with the second-biggest eigenvalue. This means that we should be thinking about how much information is being contributed to the biggest eigenvalue/eigenvector pairs.

Let's think about this more deeply. If we have a relatively small weight α, $YY^\top$ will contribute only a small amount to the largest eigenvalue/eigenvector pair. If we have a relatively large weight, $YY^\top$ will contribute a large amount to the largest eigenvalue/eigenvector pair. A prudent starting point, therefore, might be the ratio of the largest eigenvalue of L to the largest eigenvalue of $YY^\top$:

$$\alpha_0 = \frac{\lambda_1(L)}{\lambda_1(YY^\top)}.$$

The `case` procedure can be automated in `graspologic`, with:

```
from graspologic.embed import CovariateAssistedEmbed as case

embedding = case(alpha=None, n_components=2).fit_transform(A,
    covariates=Y)
```

The `alpha` parameter will specify a specific weight.

5.6.2 Considerations for Positive Semidefiniteness

As we will see in Section 5.7.3, most of the techniques discussed so far operate well under the homogeneous setting captured by the GRDPG. This setting extends the intuition of what we have discussed in the positive semidefinite case to the nonpositive semidefinite case.

case does not quite fall into the same theoretical framework as the other algorithms described in this section, despite sharing conceptual and intuitive similarities. If we have reason to believe that the random network underlying our data is not positive semidefinite, such as identifying a disassortative block structure (from Section 4.5), we can alter the Laplacian to be positive semidefinite by instead embedding $LL + \alpha YY^\top$. This can be done in `graspologic` with:

```
embedding = case(assortative=False, n_components=2).fit_transform(A,
    covariates=Y)
```

When we are not sure whether the structure of the network contains positive semidefinite or nonpositive semidefinite structure in the underlying random network, the nonassortative case tends to perform nearly as well under assortative structures, and far better under nonassortative structures [11].

5.6.3 Extensions of `case`

We might want to consider other possible similarity functions than simply the inner product $\vec{y}_i^\top \vec{y}_j$ for covariate assisted embedding techniques. For instance, `graspologic` also allows centering and scaling steps to be taken, in much the same vein as the typical preprocessing steps for pca described in Remark 5.6.2. We could further generalize this strategy to other similarity functions entirely, or try different ways of combining the two matrices.

5.7 Estimating Latent Dimensionality and Nonpositive Semidefiniteness

Chapter 5 has covered a variety of approaches that enable us to use embedding techniques such as ase, lse, mase, omni, or case to obtain estimates of latent position matrices. However, we ignore a crucial question: How many dimensions should we embed into?

This section introduces techniques to predict the embedding dimension $\hat{d}$. We also explore the implications of nonpositive semidefinite probability matrices.

We cover:

- The scree plot as a visualization tool for embedding dimensionality,
- Automatic elbow selection techniques for estimating latent dimensions, and
- The consequences of embedding matrices that lack positive semidefiniteness and the generalized random dot product graph (GRDPG).

Estimating the correct latent dimensionality is critical for the effectiveness of the embedding techniques introduced in Sections 5.3 and 5.4. The methods presented here form the foundation for more advanced applications in community detection (Section 6.1) and network comparison (Section 7.1).

In this section, we will use the following SBM as our example network:

```python
from graspologic.simulations import sbm
import numpy as np

# block matrix
n = 100
B = np.array([[0.6, 0.2], [0.2, 0.4]])
# network sample
np.random.seed(0)
A, z = sbm([n // 2, n // 2], B, return_labels=True)
```

5.7.1   The Scree Plot

Throughout any investigation into spectral embeddings, one of the critical summary statistics to look at with respect to the matrix being embedded is its scree plot.

The *scree plot* shows the singular values of the embedding matrix (the diagonal entries of the singular value matrix Σ) in sequential (descending) order by their indices; the first (biggest) singular value is in the beginning, and the last (smallest) singular value is at the end. We can find the singular values like this:

```python
from scipy.linalg import svdvals

# use scipy to obtain the singular values
s = svdvals(A)
```

And we can visualize the scree plot like this:

```python
from pandas import DataFrame
import seaborn as sns
import matplotlib.pyplot as plt


def plot_scree(svs, title="", ax=None):
    """
    A utility to plot the scree plot for a list of singular values
    svs.
    """
```

Concept 5.7.1 Orthogonal matrices

When A is a square adjacency matrix for n nodes with svd given by $A = U\Sigma V^\top$, U and V are square orthogonal matrices; that is, $U^\top U = V^\top V = I_n$. Applying standard definitions of matrix multiplication, we see that:

$$U^\top U = \begin{bmatrix} \vdash & \vec{u}_1^\top & \dashv \\ & \vdots & \\ \vdash & \vec{u}_n^\top & \dashv \end{bmatrix} \begin{bmatrix} \top & & \top \\ \vec{u}_1 & \cdots & \vec{u}_n \\ \bot & & \bot \end{bmatrix}$$

$$= \begin{bmatrix} \vec{u}_1^\top \vec{u}_1 & \cdots & \vec{u}_1^\top \vec{u}_n \\ \vdots & \ddots & \vdots \\ \vec{u}_n^\top \vec{u}_1 & \cdots & \vec{u}_n^\top \vec{u}_n \end{bmatrix} = \begin{bmatrix} 1 & & \\ & \ddots & \\ & & 1 \end{bmatrix} = I_n.$$

Therefore, for any i, we obtain that $\vec{u}_i^\top \vec{u}_i = \|\vec{u}_i\|_2 = 1$ (the left singular vectors are normalized to have a Euclidean norm of 1; i.e., their "length" is 1), by using the definition of the Euclidean norm from Concept 5.3.10. As an aside, note also that for any pair $i \neq j$, that $\vec{u}_i^\top \vec{u}_j = 0$. Identical results apply to the right singular vectors.

```
if ax is None:
    fig, ax = plt.subplots(1,1, figsize=(10, 4))
sv_dat = DataFrame({"Singular Value": svs, "Dimension": range(1,
    len(svs) + 1)})
sns.scatterplot(data=sv_dat, x="Dimension", y="Singular Value",
    ax=ax)
sns.lineplot(data=sv_dat, x="Dimension", y="Singular Value", ax=ax)
ax.set_xlim([0.5, len(s)])
ax.set_title(title)

plot_scree(s, title="Scree plot of $L$")
```

Figure 5.7.1(A) shows the scree plot. A singular value can be thought of as quantifying to the relative amount of "information" that a corresponding left or right singular vector contains about its underlying matrix.

To formalize this intuition, recall Exercise 5.3.1. If $A = U\Sigma V^\top$ is an svd of A, that:

$$A = U\Sigma V^\top = \sum_{i=1}^{n} \sigma_i \vec{u}_i \vec{v}_i^\top. \tag{5.6}$$

By Concept 5.7.1, note that the left and right singular vectors $\vec{u}_i$ and $\vec{v}_i$ are normalized to have unit length; that is, $\vec{u}_i$ and $\vec{v}_i$ have a Euclidean norm of 1. With this intuition in mind, we can think of the singular value σ_i as "weighting" the matrix $\vec{u}_i \vec{v}_i^\top$ such that it is responsible for a greater proportion of the sum that produces A. Since the singular values are nonnegative and decreasing ($\sigma_1 \geq \sigma_2 \geq \cdots \geq \sigma_n \geq 0$), each sequential singular value and left or right singular vector is less important, in that its weight in the overall sum is smaller.

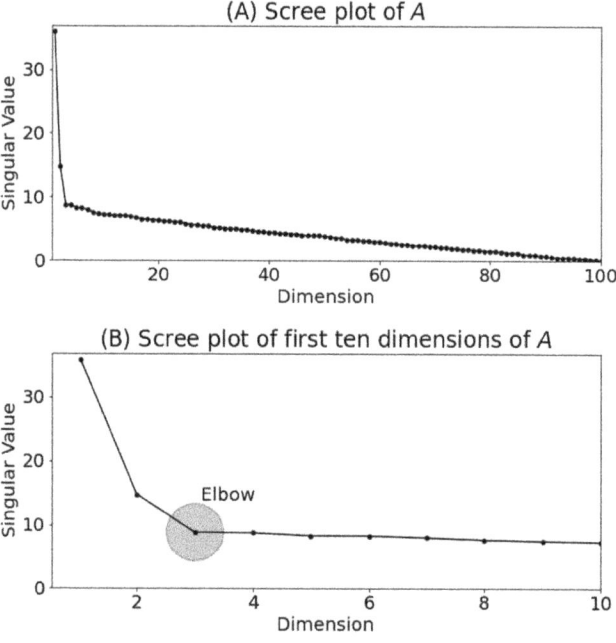

Figure 5.7.1 (**A**) The scree plot of singular values of A, and (**B**) the scree plot of the first ten singular values of A, with the elbow annotated.

In Figure 5.7.1(B), we isolate the first ten dimensions from the scree plot. Notice that there's a marked area called the "elbow." In this area, singular values stop changing in magnitude as much when they get smaller: Before the elbow, the singular values decline rapidly, and after the elbow, the singular values "level off." This is called an elbow because the plot looks somewhat like an arm when viewed from the side.

In an SBM with two communities such as our example here, we found in Concept 5.3.9 that the rank of the probability matrix (and the true latent dimensionality of the random network) would be at most 2; therefore, applying Concept 5.3.6, we would anticipate at most two nonzero singular values, and the remaining singular values would have a value of 0. In practice, when we look at adjacency matrices (instead of probability matrices), the singular values can be thought of as a "noisy" version of the observations we made about the singular values of a probability matrix. The location of the elbow in the scree plot gives a rough indication for how many "true" dimensions the latent representation has; singular values after the elbow are quite small. Taken in light of Equation (5.6), this indicates that these successive dimensions do not weight very heavily in the svd for the adjacency matrix, and in this sense, tend to be largely "noise."

The Balancing Act of Elbow Selection
When a network has fewer nodes, or when its adjacency matrix is sparse because it has very few nonzero entries, its scree plot tends to be messy. There may be multiple elbows, and it may be unclear where we should "draw the line" and cut off extraneous

singular values. By removing too many dimensions, we may end up cutting off dimensions that contain latent structure in the estimated latent positions. By removing too few dimensions, we may be left with too many noisy latent dimensions, and learning about the network later might be overly complicated. Manually choosing an estimated latent dimensionality is a balancing act, and often more of an art than a science.

5.7.2   Automatic Elbow Selection

The visual method of estimating latent dimensionality using elbow location is inherently subjective. Real data will rarely have a prominent elbow like our simulated network in Figure 5.7.1. In general, embedding into more dimensions than necessary tends to be less problematic than embedding into too few dimensions; if one chooses a latent dimensionality overly aggressively, one may discard a useful signal entirely, which cannot be recovered during a downstream analysis.

graspologic automates the process of finding an elbow using a popular method developed in 2000 by Dr. Thomas Minka at MIT called minka, from [12]. We won't get into the specifics of how it works here, but it generally does a fairly good job at automatic elbow selection. In graspologic, when we do not specify a number of embedding dimensions via the n_components argument, the elbow selection is done automatically with minka:

```
from graspologic.embed import AdjacencySpectralEmbed as ase

# use automatic elbow selection
Xhat_auto = ase(svd_seed=0).fit_transform(A)
```

The number of columns of Xhat_auto.shape[1] gives the dimensionality estimated by graspologic.

5.7.3   What Happens for non-PSD Probability Matrices?

Throughout this book, we have made a strong assumption: We conceptualize our underlying random networks to have positive semidefinite probability matrices. This has convenient implications for us.

First, we are able to find latent position matrices with $DCSBM_n(\vec{z}, \vec{\theta}, B)$ and $SBM_n(\vec{z}, B)$ random networks with PSD block matrices exactly and succinctly, taking the probability matrices to be:

$$P_{sbm} = CBC^\top$$
$$P_{dcsbm} = \Theta CBC\Theta^\top.$$

Since B is positive semidefinite, it has an exact real square-root matrix. This allows us to obtain exact (real) representations of latent positions:

$$X_{sbm} = C\sqrt{B}$$
$$X_{dcsbm} = \Theta C\sqrt{B},$$

where we would always be able to compute $\sqrt{B}$ in an exact form using the Cholesky decomposition, as we did in Section 4.5.

PSD structure also arises readily in real data. Many block matrix structures from Section 4.5 appear in a positive semidefinite manner. Grasping core intuition about random networks where the underlying block matrices are positive semidefinite will play an important role in conceptualizing real problems.

However, it is useful to explore what happens when we depart from this assumption. This section will explore the consequences (or lackthereof) of nonpositive semidefiniteness.

The Generalized Random Dot Product Graph

Even if P is not positive semidefinite, it can still be decomposed in the form [6; 7]:

$$P = X I_{p,q} X^\top, \tag{5.7}$$

where X is the real latent position matrix. Since X is a $n \times d$ matrix, $I_{p,q}$ will be a $d \times d$ square matrix. In particular, $I_{p,q}$ will be a special "variation" of the identity matrix. It will be a diagonal matrix whose diagonal entries are p consecutive 1s, followed by q consecutive -1s. Since a $d \times d$ diagonal matrix has d diagonal elements, we have the restriction that $p + q = d$.

Notice that if $p = d$, then $q = 0$ and therefore $P = XX^\top$, so P is positive semidefinite because it can be decomposed into the product of a real matrix and itself. However, if $p < d$ and consequently $q > 0$, this matrix is not necessarily positive semidefinite.

Even when P is not positive semidefinite, `ase` can still recover estimates $\hat{X}$ of X (up to an orthogonal transformation) that are reasonable [7], in the same sense that `ase` was reasonable for networks with underlying positive semidefinite probability matrices (Section 5.3.3). Further, these latent positions X share several of the convenient features that latent position matrices for positive semidefinite $SBM_n(\vec{z}, B)$ and $DCSBM_n(\vec{z}, \vec{\theta}, B)$ random networks share in Section 4.7.8.

If the random network is an $SBM_n(\vec{z}, B)$, PSD block matrix or not, the latent position vectors $\vec{x}_i$ from the decomposition in Equation (5.7) will still be the same for all nodes in the same community. If the random network is a $DCSBM_n(\vec{z}, \vec{\theta}, B)$, PSD block matrix or not, the latent position vectors $\vec{x}_i$ from the decomposition in Equation (5.7) will also be the same (up to a rescaling by the degree-correction factor) for all nodes in the same community.

The fact that `ase` (and likewise, `lse`, `omni`, and `mase`) can recover reasonable estimates $\hat{X}$ of X suggests that we can still use $\hat{X}$ to recover latent structure in the estimates of the latent positions produced with these strategies, even if positive semidefiniteness is not a reasonable assumption about the networks.

This way of representing P given in Equation (5.7) is known as the generalized random dot product graph, or $GRDPG_n(X)$ model with "signature" (p, q). This model is equivalent hierarchically in Figure 4.11.1 to the $IER_n(P)$ simple random networks. For a simple random network, for every probability matrix P, there exists some latent position matrix X that has $d \leq n$ latent dimensions and I_{p+q} where

$P = XI_{p,q}X^\top$. This makes the GRDPG an extremely powerful theoretical tool for network embeddings, because it can be used to conceptualize any probability matrix. The GRDPG is analyzed in more depth in Appendix A.7.

To motivate the utility of the `ase` outside of positive semidefinite contexts, let's perform `ase` on a sample of an $SBM_n(\vec{z}, B)$ random network with a disassortative block matrix from Section 4.5. Remember that disassortative block matrices have off-diagonal entries greater than the on-diagonal entries, so the determinant is negative by design and the block matrix is not PSD:

```python
from graspologic.embed import AdjacencySpectralEmbed as ase
from scipy.spatial import distance_matrix

nk = 50 # the number of nodes in each community
B_indef = np.array([[.1, .5], [.5, .2]])
np.random.seed(0)
A_dis, z = sbm([nk, nk], B_indef, return_labels=True)
Xhat = ase(n_components=2, svd_seed=0).fit_transform(A_dis)
D = distance_matrix(Xhat, Xhat)
```

Figure 5.7.2(A) visualizes a sample of the random network with a non-PSD probability matrix, where it is evident that between-community connections (the off-diagonal blocks of the adjacency matrix in the upper right and lower left corners) are more frequent than within-community connections (the on-diagonal blocks of the adjacency matrix). This reflects the idea that the underlying random network has a non-PSD probability matrix. The estimated latent positions are shown in Figure 5.7.2(B). Notice that even though the block matrix (and consequently the probability matrix) of the underlying random network is not PSD, `ase` still produced a meaningful embedding, in that nodes from the same community are still more similar than nodes from different communities. This insight can be confirmed by looking at the pairwise distance matrix (Figure 5.7.2(C)). While some of the strategies we discussed were developed prior to these results, such as the `omni` embedding [13], it is likely that they produce principled estimates of latent positions even under certain types of non-PSD structure.

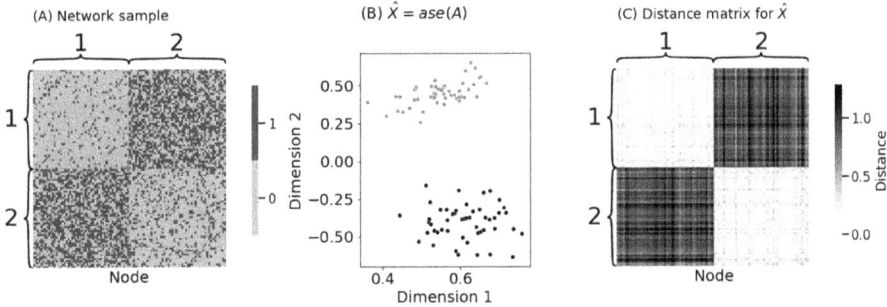

Figure 5.7.2 (**A**) A sample of a random network with an indefinite block matrix, and hence indefinite probability matrix, (**B**) a scatter plot of the estimated latent positions via `ase`, and (**C**) the distance matrix between pairs of estimated latent positions.

Hopefully, this provides a level of credence to the idea that spectral embeddings are flexible, and can be used to derive latent structure from network samples across many (not just PSD) contexts.

Bibliography

[1] Sørdalen TK, Halvorsen KT, Vøllestad LA, Moland E, Olsen EM. Marine protected areas rescue a sexually selected trait in European lobster. Evol. Appl. 2020 Oct.;13(9):2222–2233.

[2] Hastie T, Tibshirani R, Friedman JH. The Elements of Statistical Learning: Data Mining, Inference, and Prediction. New York, NY, USA: Springer; 2009.

[3] Axler S. Linear Algebra Done Right. Cham, Switzerland: Springer International Publishing; 2015.

[4] Trefethen LN, Bau D. Numerical Linear Algebra. Society for Industrial and Applied Mathematics; 1997.

[5] Sussman DL, Tang M, Fishkind DE, Priebe CE. A consistent adjacency spectral embedding for stochastic blockmodel graphs. J. Am. Stat. Assoc. 2012 Sep.;107(499):1119–1128.

[6] Athreya A, Fishkind DE, Tang M, Priebe CE, Park Y, Vogelstein JT, et al. Statistical inference on random dot product graphs: a survey. J. Mach. Learn. Res. 2017 Jan.;18(1):8393–8484.

[7] Rubin-Delanchy P, Cape J, Tang M, Priebe CE. A statistical interpretation of spectral embedding: The generalized random dot product graph. J. R. Stat. Soc. Ser. B Stat, Methodol. 2022 Sep.;84(4):1446–1473.

[8] Qin T, Rohe K. Regularized spectral clustering under the degree corrected stochastic blockmodel. arXiv. 2013 Sep.

[9] Muldoon SF, Bridgeford EW, Bassett DS. Small-world propensity and weighted brain networks. Sci. Rep. 2016 Feb.;6(22057):1–13.

[10] Prakash BA, Sridharan A, Seshadri M, Machiraju S, Faloutsos C. EigenSpokes: Surprising patterns and scalable community chipping in large graphs. In: Advances in Knowledge Discovery and Data Mining. Berlin, Germany: Springer; 2010. p. 435–448.

[11] Binkiewicz N, Vogelstein JT, Rohe K. Covariate-assisted spectral clustering. Biometrika. 2017 Jun.;104(2):361–377.

[12] Minka T. Automatic choice of dimensionality for PCA. Adv. Neural Info. Proc. Syst. 2000;13.

[13] Levin K, Athreya A, Tang M, Lyzinski V, Priebe C. A Central Limit Theorem for an Omnibus Embedding of Multiple Random Dot Product Graphs. In: 2017 IEEE International Conference on Data Mining Workshops (ICDMW). 2017.

Part III

Applications

6   Applications for a Single Network

In Part II, we came quite a long way. We first defined a number of random network models in Chapter 4. Then, given data – network observations – Chapter 5 used these models to transform our observations into useful representations.

Now, we show what can be done with our representations. Chapter 6 begins by exploring applications for single networks. We then compare two networks in Chapter 7, and many networks in Chapter 8. We conclude with a discussion on deep learning methods in Chapter 9. The process is described on the right of Figure 6.0.1.

We begin by deriving insights from a single network:

1. Section 6.1 introduces the community detection problem, and how we can use network embeddings to impute community labels for our network.
2. Section 6.2 investigates different notions of sparsity and how they relate to random networks and network adjacency matrices.
3. Section 6.3 tests whether groups of edges differ in the network.
4. Section 6.4 determines appropriate levels of model complexity for our network.
5. Section 6.5 introduces the vertex nomination problem, which allows us to find nodes that are "similar" to reference nodes.
6. Section 6.6 embeds new nodes into an existing network embedding.

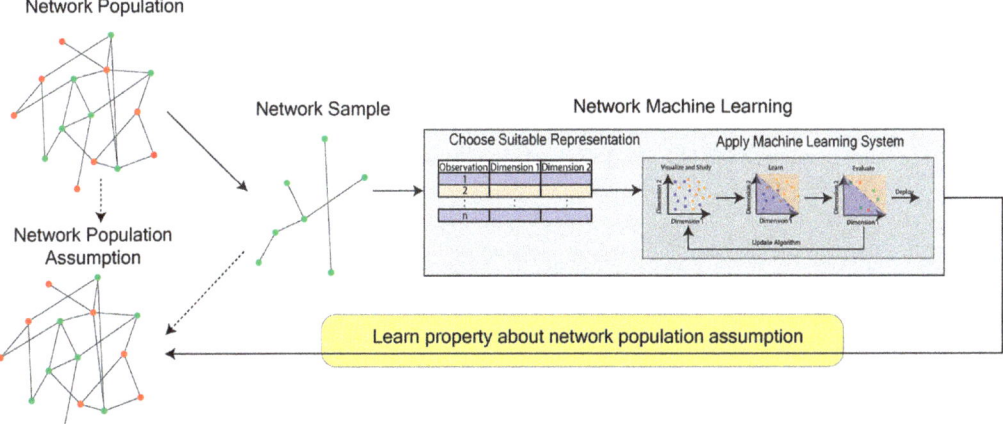

Figure 6.0.1 The statistical learning pipeline. In this chapter, we will learn to apply network machine learning systems to make inferences about the underlying network population.

6.1   The Community Detection Problem

Until now, when dealing with stochastic block models, we assumed that we knew the community assignments ahead of time. In Section 4.7.8, we saw that nodes within the same community share identical latent positions, up to degree correction. We also learned how spectral embedding techniques like `ase` and `lse` can estimate these latent positions up to an orthogonal transformation from observed networks (Sections 5.3 and 5.4).

This section tackles the practical challenge of estimating community structure when true community labels are unknown. We will:

1. Estimate latent community assignments from spectral embeddings,
2. Evaluate the homogeneity of estimated communities,
3. Assess the distinctness of detected communities, and
4. Explore techniques for determining the number of communities.

To do this, we assume familiarity with several concepts from unsupervised learning, including the K-means algorithm, the adjusted Rand index (ARI), confusion matrices, and the silhouette score. Appendix C.1 details the silhouette score, and Online Appendix D.2 covers the other concepts.

Let's revisit the Section 5.4 example of communities in schools. We sampled from a homophilic $DCSBM_n(\vec{z}, \vec{\theta}, B)$ random network which originally had two communities. Here we will sample from a similar random network with three communities instead of two. We will also permute the nodes of the matrix randomly, since in practice, nodes will not initially be ordered to reflect community structure:

```
import numpy as np
from graphbook_code import dcsbm

nk = 100 # 100 nodes per community
K = 3 # the number of communities
n = nk * K # total number of nodes

zs = np.repeat(np.arange(K)+1, repeats=nk)
# block matrix and degree-correction factor
B = np.array([[0.7, 0.2, 0.1], [0.2, 0.5, 0.1], [0.1, 0.1, 0.4]])
theta = np.tile(np.linspace(start=0, stop=1, num=nk), reps=K)
# generate network sample
np.random.seed(0)
A = dcsbm(zs, theta, B)

# permute the nodes randomly
vtx_perm = np.random.choice(n, size=n, replace=False)
Aperm = A[vtx_perm, :][:,vtx_perm]
zperm = zs[vtx_perm]
```

The network probability matrix is shown in Figure 6.1.1(A), and the adjacency matrix is shown in Figure 6.1.1(B). Looking at the adjacency matrix, there is no obvious structure to the network.

If we were to make a histogram of the node degrees, we would see that the network appears to be slightly heavy-tailed, and so the reasoning in Section 5.4.3 would

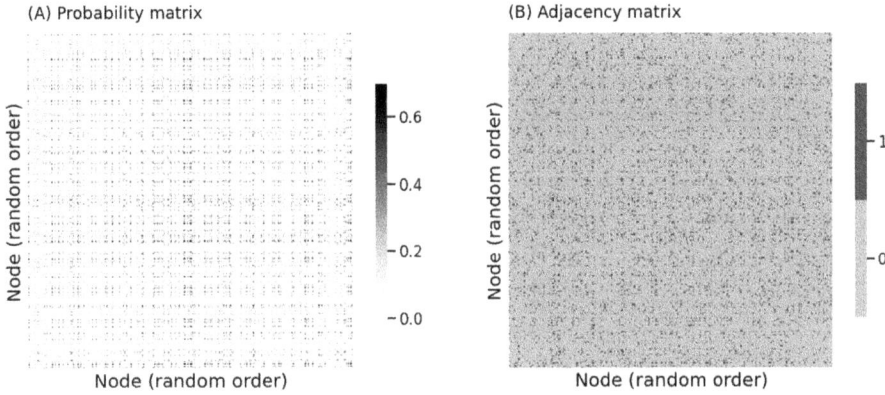

Figure 6.1.1 (**A**) The probability matrix for the $DCSBM_n(\vec{z}, \vec{\theta}, B)$ random networks, and (**B**) a sample of the random network.

encourage the use of `lse`. However, for the purposes of this section, we will proceed with `ase`.

6.1.1 Spectral Clustering with a Predefined Number of Communities

When we embed a network with a predefined number of communities K, the true number of embedding dimensions is usually taken to be the number of communities. Concept 5.3.9 discussed the reasoning for this.

In our example, since $K = 3$, we embed with three embedding dimensions:

```
import scipy as sp
from graspologic.embed import AdjacencySpectralEmbed as ase

Xhat = ase(n_components=3, svd_seed=0).fit_transform(Aperm)
D = sp.spatial.distance_matrix(Xhat, Xhat)
```

Figure 6.1.2(A) plots the second and third embedding dimensions as a scatter plot. Even though the nodes in `Aperm` were completely randomized, the estimated latent positions still retain a "blob" structure, where groups of nodes in the same community look spatially close to one another. This is reflected in the distance matrix in Figure 6.1.2(B), where we can see that the within-community pairwise distances are usually smaller than the between-community pairwise distances.

6.1.1.1 Estimating Community Assignments via `KMeans`

We will use `sklearn`'s implementation of `KMeans`, an unsupervised clustering algorithm, to estimate the latent community assignment vector. We denote this estimate by $\hat{\vec{z}}$:

```
from sklearn.cluster import KMeans

labels_kmeans = KMeans(n_clusters = 3,
    random_state=0).fit_predict(Xhat)
```

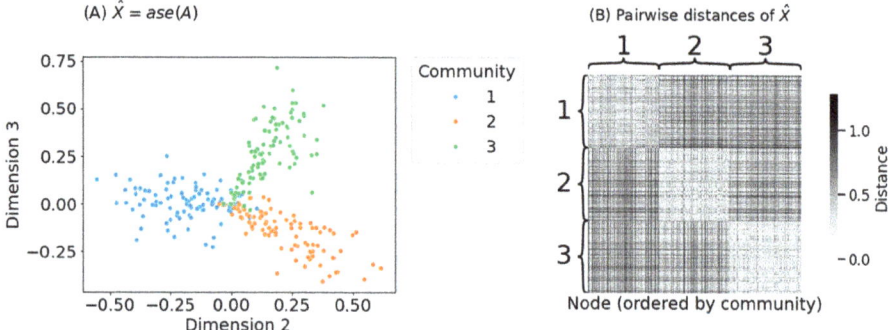

Figure 6.1.2 (**A**) A spectral embedding of the randomly ordered adjacency matrix. (**B**) The pairwise distances between the estimated latent positions for each pair of nodes. Note that nodes are ordered by community, rather than randomly as in Figure 6.1.1.

As this procedure is fully unsupervised, there is no reason for the labels to "align" with true descriptors (such as communities) with the nodes. In this case, we have no reason to believe that community 1 produced by KMeans will correspond to community 1 in our network. For this reason, we need to be careful when evaluating unsupervised clustering techniques.

Evaluating the Clustering

Because we are using simulated data, the true community labels are already known. When we know true node labels ahead of time, we can leverage special tools to evaluate clustering performance. The first of these is the confusion matrix, produced with sklearn's confusion_matrix(). The confusion matrix is a table that illustrates how an unsupervised classification model stratifies points into predicted labels on the basis of a known set of true labels.

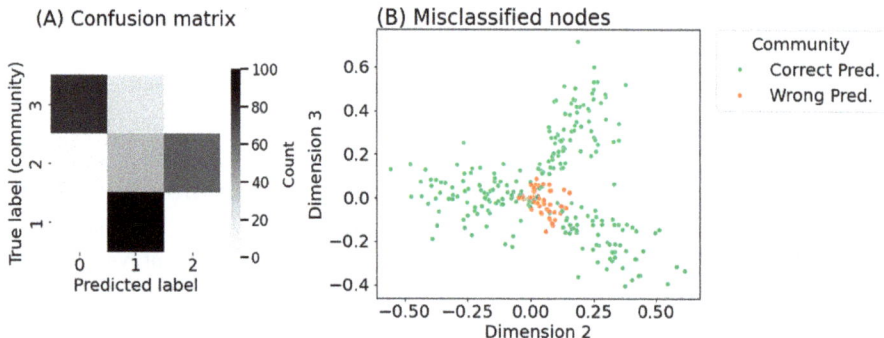

Figure 6.1.3 (**A**) The confusion matrix. (**B**) The estimated latent positions, along with whether the node was classified correctly (or not) after realigning the predicted communities with the true communities.

```
from sklearn.metrics import confusion_matrix

# compute the confusion matrix between the true labels z
# and the predicted labels labels_kmeans
cf_matrix = confusion_matrix(zperm, labels_kmeans)
```

Figure 6.1.3(A) shows the confusion matrix. When we have a clustering that aligns well with the true labels, the predictions tend to be homogeneous: A particular true label will correspond to a particular predicted label, and vice versa. We can evaluate this homogeneity using the adjusted Rand index (ARI), where a score of closer to 1 indicates that the true and predicted labels are perfectly homogeneous:

```
from sklearn.metrics import adjusted_rand_score

ari_kmeans = adjusted_rand_score(zperm, labels_kmeans)
print(ari_kmeans)
# 0.490
```

A score of 0 indicates that the predicted community labels do not align with the true labels, and a score of 1 indicates that the predicted communities perfectly align with the true labels.

Evaluating the Error Rate

By remapping the labels, we can evaluate the error rate. From the confusion matrix in Figure 6.1.3, we have a reasonable pattern:

1. Nodes assigned a predicted label of 0 tend to correspond to community 3,
2. Nodes assigned a predicted label of 1 tend to correspond to community 1, and
3. Nodes assigned a predicted label of 2 tend to correspond to community 2.

It seems clear that this would make for a reasonable correspondence between the predicted and true labels. A *correspondence* between two sets (in this case, the predicted and true labels for node communities) is a mapping that pairs the elements of one set to elements in another set.

Results that are not as homogeneous as they are here can be complicated, and we will not discuss them here. We can remap the labels with graspologic's remap_labels() utility:

```
from graspologic.utils import remap_labels

labels_kmeans_remap = remap_labels(zperm, labels_kmeans)
```

With the labels from KMeans properly aligned to the true community labels, we can evaluate the error rate of our function with numpy like this:

```
# compute which assigned labels from labels_kmeans_remap differ from
    the true labels z
error = zperm - labels_kmeans_remap
# if the difference between the community labels is non-zero, an error
    has occurred
error = error != 0
error_rate = np.mean(error) # error rate is the frequency of making an
    error
```

In Figure 6.1.3(B), we visualize the misclassified points as a function of the data matrix that is being leveraged to estimate community assignments, the estimated latent position matrix. We do a good job of classifying points in the "arms" of the individual blobs of nodes (the *clusters*), but tend to do worse for the points that are located between the clusters of nodes. This happens because of the manner in which predicted community labels are applied by KMeans. See Box 6.1.1 and Online Appendix D.2 for more detailed commentary about why this happens.

Box 6.1.1 Why does KMeans perform well for clustering samples of block models?

When we cluster points using KMeans, we will tend to identify clusters which correspond to blobs of points in our data which have similar pairwise (often Euclidean) distances. Points are assigned to the cluster that they are closest to, and as the KMeans algorithm iterates, it attempts to identify cluster centers which minimize the cumulative pairwise distance from each set of points to the nearest cluster.

Recall from Section 4.7.8 that with stochastic block models, the true underlying latent positions are identical for all nodes in the same community, and from Section 5.3 that the estimated latent positions tend to "approximate" the true latent positions. The estimates will retain this feature and the estimated latent positions will be similar (in terms of their Euclidean distance) if they are in the same community for the stochastic block model.

In the case of the degree-corrected stochastic block model, the underlying latent positions are identical up to a rescaling along the direction of the community-specific latent position vector. This will tend to materialize as elliptically shaped "blobs" in the estimated latent positions along the direction of the rescaling in the underlying community-specific latent position vector. This is undesirable when we try to cluster, because KMeans is effectively "penalizing" a difference between a point and the community center symmetrically in Euclidean space. In reality, we would want the "penalty" to be applied asymmetrically. Because degree heterogeneity is a common problem with real networks, we are often motivated to use other clustering techniques such as GMM which are more adaptive to rescalings along the community-specific latent position vectors. See Exercise 6.1.2.

6.1.2   Spectral Clustering with an Undefined Number of Communities

In real data, we almost never have a beautiful canonical modular structure that makes choosing a number of communities obvious. Further, by applying unsupervised clustering algorithms in the first place and attempting to learn community labels from the data, it's likely that we will not know reasonable community labels in advance. This means that we will very rarely know the "true" number of communities, K, nor the number of embedding dimensions ahead of time.

To estimate the community assignment vector in this case, we use a procedure similar to the one we used in Section 6.1. We embed, but because we do not know

---

Exercise 6.1.2 Using GMM for clustering samples of block models

Here we walk through the steps for using GMM for clustering. First, simulate from a $DCSBM_n(\vec{z}, \vec{\theta}, B)$ random network, like we did above, but skew the degree-correction vector more dramatically, with $K = 2$ communities.

1. Spectrally embed the adjacency matrix into two dimensions, and illustrate that the estimated latent positions appear to be elliptical.
2. Apply GMM to cluster the estimated latent positions, using GaussianMixture from sklearn. Use the techniques that we described in this section to evaluate the clustering procedure.
3. Following the tutorial [1], plot the community centers (the means_ attribute of the instantiated class) estimated by GMM, and plot ellipses reflecting the estimated covariance (the covariances_ attribute) about the community centers.
4. For each point in the network, compute the probability that the point is from its assigned cluster, using the predict_proba() function from the GaussianMixture object. Plot the estimated latent positions, with the color going from low probability (red) to high probability (green).

Use the objective function for GMM to argue that GMM tends to penalize points less if they are farther away from the community center but along the principal axis of the community-specific ellipse, and more if they are farther away from the community center but not along the principal axis of the community-specific ellipse. Argue why this makes sense in the context of the $DCSBM_n(\vec{z}, \vec{\theta}, B)$ random network underlying the network sample by discussing the degree-correction factor heterogeneity.

Box 6.1.3 Nomenclature about clusters and communities

With unsupervised classification, groups of points that are assigned to the same group by the trained classifier are typically called a *cluster*. However, in our case, they are more than just clusters: They are predicted node community labels. For this reason, when we are referring specifically to the assignments themselves, we will often refer to this concept as "predicted communities" or something of the like. When we are referring to "blobs of points," we will often default to calling them clusters of points.

---

the number of communities we are looking for, we use automatic elbow selection from Section 5.7. When we do not specify a number of dimensions explicitly, graspologic does this by default:

```
Xhat = ase(svd_seed=0).fit_transform(Aperm)
print("Estimated number of dimensions: {:d}".format(Xhat.shape[1]))
# Estimated number of dimensions: 3
```

Examining the pairs plot, we again find that dimensions 2 and 3 show stratified blobs in the estimated latent positions, in Figure 6.1.2(A).

Since we do not know the optimal number of communities K nor the true community assignments, we must choose an unsupervised clustering technique which allows us to compare clusterings with different choices of community counts.

The Silhouette Score

We can use the silhouette score (Appendix C.1) to deduce a reasonably appropriate number of communities. We first choose a range of communities that we think might be appropriate for our network. For instance, we think there might be as many as 10 communities in our dataset. We perform a clustering using unsupervised learning for all possible numbers of communities, from 2 to the maximum number of communities we think could be reasonable. Then, we compute the silhouette score for predictions with each number of communities. Finally, we choose the predictions corresponding to the number of communities that has the highest silhouette score.

Let's see how to do this, using `graspologic`'s `KMeansCluster()` function:

```
from graspologic.cluster import KMeansCluster

km_clust = KMeansCluster(max_clusters = 10, random_state=0)
labels_kmclust = km_clust.fit_predict(Xhat)
```

To determine an optimal number of clusters, we visualize the silhouette score as a function of the number of clusters:

```
import seaborn as sns
from pandas import DataFrame as df

nclusters = range(2, 11) # graspologic nclusters goes from 2 to
    max_clusters
silhouette = km_clust.silhouette_ # obtain the respective silhouettes

# place into pandas dataframe
ss_df = df({"Number of Communities": nclusters, "Silhouette Score":
    silhouette})
sns.lineplot(data=ss_df, x="Number of Communities", y="Silhouette
    Score")
```

In Figure 6.1.4(A), we look at the number of communities as a function of the silhouette score. Notice that `KMeans` with silhouette score analysis determines that the optimal number of communities is $\hat{K} = 4$.

Figure 6.1.4(B) shows the predicted communities for each node coloring the estimated latent dimensions. It appears that `KMeans` has been "fooled" by the elliptical, nonspherical embeddings, and determined that optimal unsupervised classification performance could be achieved by adding a fourth community to the center of the estimated latent positions. This is because `KMeans` and the silhouette score penalize all dimensions equally, which might not always be desirable.

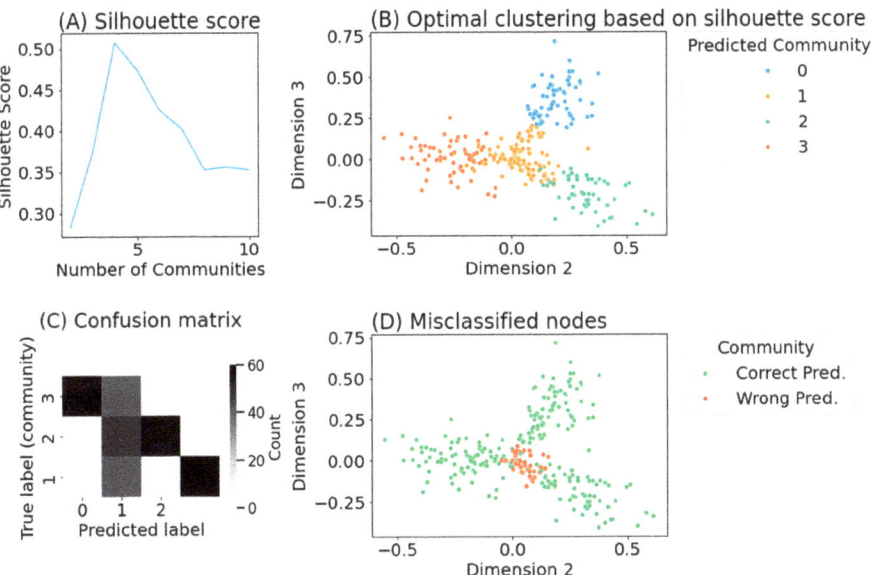

Figure 6.1.4 (**A**) An analysis of the silhouette scores as a function of the number of communities, (**B**) the predicted communities for each node, (**C**) the confusion matrix with $\hat{K} = 4$, and (**D**) the misclassified points.

Interpreting Community Predictions

To determine what the predicted communities correspond to, we plot the confusion matrix as a function of the true node community in Figure 6.1.4(C). The "arms" of the ellipses in Figure 6.1.4(B) correspond to predicted labels of 0, 2, and 3 respectively, and nearly perfectly correspond with the true underlying node communities 1 through 3 respectively in Figure 6.1.4(C). On the other hand, the 1 community at the center of the arms does not correspond to any specific true label particularly well, and is an agglomeration of points at the bases of the arms across all three true communities. We visualize the points that are misclassified in Figure 6.1.4(D), which correspond to the points assigned to the 1 community.

Determining What Predicted Communities Mean

By now, we know how to apply spectral clustering to network data and evaluate it when we have a single node covariate. However, real data typically have many covariates associated with each node, some of which might not even have discrete (one of K) labels. For instance, in Figure 2.6.1, each node had a spatial position. This would not be an easy framework for interpreting our communities.

For this reason, there is an art in determining what predicted communities mean, much like many other applications of unsupervised learning. For instance, we may have to determine which lobe of the brain each spatial position listed above falls into to obtain a sensible interpretation of the communities.

In many contexts, we might not even know what these predicted communities correspond to at all, and we might have to rethink how the network was collected and work from the ground up to try to find meaning in the predicted communities. In this sense, once we perform community detection and identify stable communities, our role as a network learning scientist has really just started.

6.1.3   Extending Community Detection to Other Formulations

Algorithm 6.1 provides a generic formulation of the community detection process for network data with adjacency representations using KMeans and ase. These procedures generalize readily to alternative approaches in which the network data can be represented as a matrix.

Algorithm 6.1 Unsupervised spectral community detection from network data with KMeans

Data: A the adjacency matrix of your network.
  d Optionally, a number of embedding dimensions.
  K Optionally, a number of communities.
Result: predicted community assignments.
1 Let $\widehat{X} = \text{ase}(A, d)$. If the dimensionality d is unspecified, estimate it through elbow selection in Section 5.7.
2 Train a KMeans classifier, using the representation $\widehat{X}$, to identify K communities. If the number of communities is unspecified, evaluate the classifier over a range of reasonable numbers of communities, and evaluate the clusterings using a predefined evaluation metric. Represent this trained classifier as the community centers $\hat{\mu}_k$ for each community k.
3 For all points, compute $d_{ik} = \|\hat{\vec{x}}_i - \hat{\mu}_k\|_2$, or the distance from each node i's estimated latent position to the community center k, for all communities.
4 Let $\hat{z}_i = \text{argmin}_k d_{ik}$ be the predicted community for node i, which is the community corresponding to the center that is closest to the estimated node latent position for node k.
5 **return** $\hat{z}$

For instance, we could substitute lse for ase, and potentially be more robust to degree variation in the network. If we had many networks with an underlying shared structure, we could run mase on our collection of networks, and use unsupervised learning techniques to learn about the underlying shared latent position matrix. If we had particular node covariates that we wanted to incorporate into our clustering, we could use case to embed a weighted combination of the network topology with node-specific covariates, and produce communities that might meaningfully inform our ability to learn from our network data. Further, we could look to nonspectral embedding techniques as well to learn latent representations. We discuss a few in Chapter 9.

Finally, as we covered in Exercise 6.1.2, there are many other unsupervised learning techniques such as GMM that we could leverage to estimate community labels from our network. If we do not specify the number of communities ahead of time and wish to evaluate a range of possible numbers of communities, it is important to choose evaluation criteria that will reflect our choice of clustering technique. GMM gives us flexibility in terms of degree-heterogeneities that may materialize in our embeddings. These heterogeneities make the naive Euclidean distance potentially unsuitable if the communities in our network are elliptical. The evaluation criteria that we used for KMeans (the silhouette score) also uses Euclidean distance, and therefore might run into similar issues if used as a metric for identifying a suitable number of communities. For this reason, it is useful to think about other evaluation metrics as well. In GMM, for instance, a popular choice is the number of communities which minimizes the Bayesian information criterion (BIC), another metric used to determine the optimal number of clusters that measures the trade-off between the likelihood and the complexity of the model.

6.2 Sparsity and Storage

In Section 3.3.1, we introduced the network density as a key descriptive property of networks. Building on this foundation, we now explore the related and more applied concept of network sparsity, which has important implications for both the theoretical analysis and practical handling of large-scale networks. Large networks, in particular, benefit from a rigorous treatment of sparsity, because in practice nodes in large networks often have few edges relative to the total possible edge count. Using sparse methods in these common cases can dramatically improve computational efficiency.

This section will cover the following:

1. Introduction to network sparsity and its relationship to density,
2. Formal definitions and mathematical properties of sparse networks,
3. Implications of sparsity for network learning algorithms,
4. Efficient data structures and storage methods for sparse networks, and
5. Computational advantages of leveraging sparsity in network analysis.

We will begin by revisiting the concept of network density and showing how it relates to sparsity. Then, we will define sparse networks, building on the properties of random networks discussed in Section 4.6. This section assumes familiarity with concepts such as sequences, algorithmic complexity, and asymptotic notation, summarized in Concept 6.2.2. For readers seeking additional background on algorithmic complexity, see the Wikipedia page on the topic [2].

To illustrate the ideas in this section, we will use a working example of academic scholars, introduced in Case Study 6.2.1.

We can produce our network with the following code, similarly to how we generated a $DCSBM_n(\vec{z}, \vec{\theta}, B)$ sample in Section 4.7. We separate out the construction of the probability matrix here so that we don't have to sample the entire network every time:

```
import numpy as np
from graspologic.simulations import sample_edges
from graphbook_code import generate_sbm_pmtx
```

> **Case Study 6.2.1** Network of academic scholars
>
> The nodes of a toy network represent academic scholars in computer science from K universities. For every university, we select 10 scientists at random from the community. An edge exists if a pair of researchers have coauthored a paper together. Researchers who work with more people will have more edges, and consequently, a higher node degree.
>
> Most researchers publish many papers with their working groups. Every researcher will publish at least one paper with someone else at the same university, so the within-university probability will be 1. The between-university probability will be 0.01, meaning the network is extremely homophilic.
>
> Let us say that 70 percent of the researchers are junior members of a research group: They are not yet running a lab, so most of their work occurs with close collaborators at their university. These researchers have a degree-correction factor that is $Beta(1,4)$ distributed; this means that their degree-correction factors will be between 0 and 1, but will tend to be low (on average, $\frac{1}{1+4} = \frac{1}{5}$).
>
> On the other hand, 30 percent of the researchers are lab leaders; they spend a lot of time working with researchers both within and outside of their university. These researchers will have degree-correction factors that are $Beta(2,1)$ distributed. In this case, the degree-correction factors will be between 0 and 1, but will tend to be higher (on average, $\frac{2}{1+2} = \frac{2}{3}$).

```python
def academic_pmtx(K, nk=10, return_zs=False):
    """
    Produce probability matrix for academic example.
    """
    n = K*nk
    # get the community assignments
    zs = np.repeat(np.arange(K)+1, repeats=nk)
    # randomly generate proteges and lab leaders
    unif_choices = np.random.uniform(size=n)
    thetas = np.zeros(n)
    # 90% are proteges
    thetas[unif_choices > .1] = np.random.beta(1, 5, size=(unif_choices
        > .1).sum())
    # 10% are lab leaders
    thetas[unif_choices <= .1] = np.random.beta(2, 1,
        size=(unif_choices <= .1).sum())
    # define block matrix
    B = np.full(shape=(K,K), fill_value=0.01)
    np.fill_diagonal(B, 1)
    # generate probability matrix for SBM
    Pp = generate_sbm_pmtx(zs, B)
    Theta = np.diag(thetas)
    # adjust probability matrix for SBM by degree-corrections
    P = Theta @ Pp @ Theta.transpose()
    if return_zs:
        return P, zs
    return P
```

```
def academic_example(K, nk=10, return_zs=False):
    P = academic_pmtx(K, nk=nk, return_zs=return_zs)
    if return_zs:
        return (sample_edges(P[0]), P[1])
    else:
        return sample_edges(P)
```

Concept 6.2.2 Asymptotic notation

Asymptotic notation is a description of what happens at the limits of the domains of functions. Suppose that $f(x)$ and $g(x)$ are two functions defined for real values x. Common asymptotic notations include:

1. $f(x) = \mathcal{O}(g(x))$: "$f(x)$ is big-O of $g(x)$" means that $g(x)$ is a rate that upper-bounds $f(x)$. Formally, there exists a constant multiplier c and a value x_c where for any value $x \geq x_c$:

$$|f(x)| \leq cg(x).$$

The intuition is to establish $g(x)$ as a ceiling function that bounds the growth of $f(x)$, allowing for a proportional scaling factor c.

2. $f(x) = o(g(x))$: "$f(x)$ is little-o of $g(x)$" means that for any positive constant ϵ, there exists an x_ϵ where for any value $x \geq x_\epsilon$:

$$|f(x)| \leq \epsilon g(x).$$

The intuition is that $g(x)$ is growing so much faster than $f(x)$ for large values of x, that if we chose any arbitrarily miniscule multiplier ϵ, we could find a value x_ϵ where $g(x)$ is still going to be much larger than $|f(x)|$, even after we rescale by ϵ, for any $x \geq x_\epsilon$.

The key distinction between big-$\mathcal{O}$ and little-o notation is that for big-$\mathcal{O}$ notation, we only need to be able to find a single choice of a constant c where the inequality holds. However, for little-o notation, the relationship can be found for any choice of a constant ϵ.

In this sense, for a function $f(x)$ to be big-$\mathcal{O}$ of $g(x)$, it can be growing at the same speed, or slower, than $g(x)$, just as long as it is eventually (for all $x \geq x_c$) multiplicatively close for some factor c. On the other hand, for $f(x)$ to be little-o of $g(x)$, it must be so much smaller than $g(x)$ that we could always go "farther out" in the domain (x) and have the inequality hold.

6.2.1   Formal Definitions of Sparse Networks

Let's imagine that we have a collection of random networks $\{A^{(1)}, A^{(2)}, \ldots\}$. This collection is called a *sequence of random networks*, because we assume that the collection contains a random network $A^{(n)}$ for every possible indexing value of n (extending all the way out to infinity). In this case, $A^{(n)}$ is a random network with n nodes. The collection is called a *sequence* because there is an order (the number of nodes in the network).

A Formal Definition of Sparsity
A sequence of networks is *sparse* if:

$$\mathbb{E}\left[\sum_{j>i} \mathbf{a}_{ij}^{(n)}\right] = \mathcal{O}\left(\binom{n}{2}\right). \tag{6.1}$$

For a network $\mathbf{A}^{(n)}$ with n nodes, $\mathbb{E}\left[\sum_{j>i} \mathbf{a}_{ij}^{(n)}\right]$ can be thought of as the expected number of edges in the network, and $\binom{n}{2}$ is the (constant) number of potential edges in the network. With the characterization of asymptotic notation in Concept 6.2.2 in mind, this means that, "the expected number of edges in the networks grows much slower than the number of potential edges."

By the definition of asymptotic notation $\mathcal{O}(\cdot)$, this means that for any value $\epsilon > 0$, we can find an n_ϵ where for all $n \geq n_\epsilon$:

$$\mathbb{E}\left[\sum_{j>i} \mathbf{a}_{ij}^{(n)}\right] \leq \epsilon \binom{n}{2}. \tag{6.2}$$

Let's see how this looks for the academic random networks in Case Study 6.2.1. The degree-correction factors give the probability matrix some element of randomness, so we won't get exactly the same results every time if we do not use random seeds. We will run the simulation and average over 50 repetitions per setting to account for this added source of randomness:

```
import pandas as pd
from tqdm import tqdm # optional

results = []
nrep = 50
for K in tqdm(np.linspace(start=2, stop=128, num=10, dtype=int)):
    for j in range(nrep):
        P = academic_pmtx(K)
        n = P.shape[0]
        results.append({"Count": np.triu(P, k=1).sum(), "Edges":
            "Expected",
                    "#Nodes": n, "Index": j})
        results.append({"Count": n*(n - 1)/2000, "Edges":
            "Potential/1000",
                    "#Nodes": n, "Index": j})

df = pd.DataFrame(results)
df_mean=df.groupby(["Edges", "#Nodes"])[["Count"]].mean()
```

We normalize the number of potential edges by a factor of 1000 so that these two values could exist on the same plot (the number of potential edges grows quickly). Figure 6.2.1(A) shows a plot of the number of potential edges $\binom{n}{2}$ against the number of expected edges:

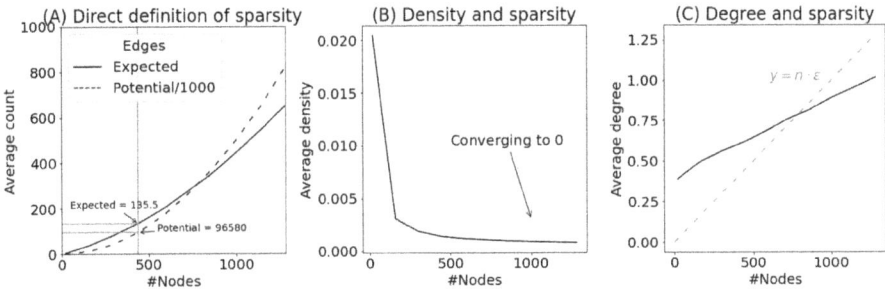

Figure 6.2.1 (**A**) The direct definition of sparsity, (**B**) the equivalent definition of sparsity using the expected network density, and (**C**) the equivalent definition of sparsity using the expected average node degree.

```
ax = sns.lineplot(data=df, x="#Nodes", y="Count", hue="Edges")
```

The number of potential edges is growing much faster with the number of nodes than the average number of expected edges. If $\epsilon = 0.00145$, for instance, with $n_\epsilon = 440$ (vertical gray bar), then the number of potential edges, (bottom horizontal line) is 96,580 (follow the horizontal line to the y-axis, and then multiply by 1000). The average number of edges, (top horizontal line) is about 140 (follow the horizontal line to the y-axis). Note that $140 \approx 96{,}580 \cdot \epsilon$. For any choice of $n > n_\epsilon$, the average number of edges is less than the number of potential edges multiplied by such a choice of ϵ. We could repeat this process for any choice of ϵ, however small (noting that we might have to make our simulation have a much higher number of nodes for extremely small values of ϵ).

Relating Sparsity to the Network Density
Assume that we are given a value $\epsilon > 0$, and n_ϵ is chosen such that Equation (6.2) holds for all $n \geq n_\epsilon$.

Dividing through by $\binom{n}{2}$ we see that for this ϵ and n_ϵ pair and see that it is also true that for all $n \geq n_\epsilon$:

$$\mathbb{E}\left[density\left(\mathbf{A}^{(n)}\right)\right] = \frac{\mathbb{E}\left[\sum_{j>i} a_{ij}^{(n)}\right]}{\binom{n}{2}} \leq \epsilon, \tag{6.3}$$

where we used the definition of the expected density from Section 4.6.3.1. This shows that another equivalent characterization of sparse networks is:

$$\mathbb{E}\left[density\left(\mathbf{A}^{(n)}\right)\right] = \mathcal{O}(1).$$

that is, the expected density is decreasing to 0 as the number of nodes grows.

We can repeat this with our experimental data by simply dividing the number of expected edges by the number of potential edges (adjusting for the normalization we made), like so:

```
df_wide = pd.pivot(df_mean.reset_index(), index="#Nodes",
    columns="Edges", values="Count")
# remember normalizing constant of 100 for potential edges
df_wide["Density"] =
    df_wide["Expected"]/(1000*df_wide["Potential/1000"])
df_wide = df_wide.reset_index()
# plot it
sns.lineplot(data=df_wide, x="#Nodes", y="Density", color="black")
```

Figure 6.2.1(B) shows that for any choice of ϵ, we could choose some value n_ϵ where the expected density is less than ϵ.

Relating Sparsity to the Expected Average Node Degree
In Section 4.6.3.1, we wrote the expected network density as:

$$\mathbb{E}\left[density\left(\mathbf{A}^{(n)}\right)\right] = \frac{\mathbb{E}[\mathbf{d}^{(n)}]}{n-1},$$

where $\mathbb{E}[\mathbf{d}^{(n)}] = \frac{1}{n}\sum_{i=1}^{n}\mathbb{E}[\mathbf{d}_i^{(n)}]$ was the expected average node degree.

Similarly, for the same choice of ϵ and n_ϵ as in Equation (6.3), if Equation (6.3) holds for any $\epsilon > 0$ and $n \geq n_\epsilon$, it is also the case that:

$$\mathbb{E}\left[density\left(\mathbf{A}^{(n)}\right)\right] = \frac{\mathbb{E}[\mathbf{d}^{(n)}]}{n-1} \leq \epsilon$$

$$\Rightarrow \mathbb{E}[\mathbf{d}^{(n)}] \leq (n-1)\epsilon \leq n\epsilon,$$

where the last inequality is because $\epsilon > 0$, so $(n-1)\epsilon \leq n\epsilon$. This shows that in a sparse collection of networks, the expected node degree $\mathbb{E}\left[\mathbf{d}^{(n)}\right] = \mathcal{O}(n)$.

This gives us our final equivalent characterization of sparse networks as networks where the expected average degree grows sublinearly with the number of nodes in the network.

We can perform such an experiment as before using pandas, as:

```
df_wide["Degree"] = df_wide["Density"]*(df_wide["#Nodes"] - 1)
sns.lineplot(data=df_wide, x="#Nodes", y="Degree", color="black")
```

Figure 6.2.1(C) shows a diagonal line growing with a rate proportional to n for $\epsilon = 0.001$. Notice that the average node degree is growing slightly slower than the diagonal line (sublinearly). Again, we could repeat this process for any choice of ϵ, however small (noting that we might have to make our simulation have a much higher number of nodes for extremely small values of ϵ).

Equivalent Characterizations of Sparsity
In total, we have three identical characterizations of *sparse networks*:

1. The expected number of edges grows slower than the total number of potential edges: $\mathbb{E}\left[\sum_{j>i}\mathbf{a}_{ij}^{(n)}\right] = \mathcal{O}\left(\binom{n}{2}\right)$,
2. The expected network density decreases as the number of nodes grows: $\mathbb{E}\left[density\left(\mathbf{A}^{(n)}\right)\right] = \mathcal{O}(1)$, and

3. The expected average degree grows slower than the number of nodes in the network: $\mathbb{E}[\mathbf{d}^{(n)}] = \mathcal{O}(n)$

Concept 6.2.3 Ultrasparse networks

A further class of sparse networks, the *ultrasparse* networks, is a collection of networks where $\mathbb{E}[\mathbf{d}^{(n)}] = \mathcal{O}(1)$. This means that the expected average degree is constant, so the nodes in the network will have an average degree that does not grow as more nodes are added to the network.

Our example academic scholars networks do not appear to be ultrasparse, because the expected average node degree is growing (albeit, slower than the number of nodes is increasing). To determine whether the sparsity is leveling off to some finite number or growing to infinity as $n \to \infty$ would require background in real analysis.

6.2.2 Data Wrangling and Matrix Sparsity

In addition to network sparsity being a substantial nuisance when running many standard network learning techniques, it also plays a big role in the data wrangling step for network data. *Data wrangling* refers to the process of manipulating data into a format that makes them more appropriate and valuable for analytical purposes. An $n \times d$ matrix with nonnegative entries is said to be *sparse* if most of its entries are zero. On the other hand, an $n \times d$ matrix with nonnegative entries is said to be *dense* if none of its entries are zero.

We say that a matrix is *sufficiently sparse* with respect to some sparse algorithm if the matrix has enough of a fraction of the entries being zero that the sparse algorithm has a faster runtime than its dense counterpart.

Let's explore some applications of matrix sparsity. Our working example will be a sample of our academic networks from Case Study 6.2.1, with $K = 10$ communities and $n = 1000$ nodes:

```
np.random.seed(0)
K = 10; nk = 100
P, zs = academic_example(K, nk=nk, return_zs=True)
A = sample_edges(P)

print(f"# Non-zero entries: {A.sum().astype(int)}")
# Non-zero entries: 5308

print(f"# Number of entries: {A.size}")
# Number of entries: 1000000
```

Figure 6.2.2(B) plots the adjacency matrix for our example.

Storage Implications of Sparse Adjacency Matrices with Network Data
Throughout this book, we typically encounter networks as dense adjacency matrices. This means that we store the entire adjacency matrix (all $n \times n$ entries). When the

adjacency matrix is sufficiently sparse, this is an extremely inefficient approach to storing network data.

The academic network has $n = 1000$ nodes. The simplest way to store its adjacency matrix, as an $n \times n$ matrix, means that we have 1,000,000 entries. Each of these entries defaults to a `float64` in numpy, which is a 64-bit number. This means that our network, occupies $1000^2 \cdot 64 = 64$ million bits (Mb), or $64/8 = 8$ million bytes (MB).

We have many redundancies. First, the network is simple, so edges are unweighted. When the edges are unweighted, we only need a single bit to represent each edge. Unfortunately, RAM is divided by bytes, so the best we can do is 1 byte per entry using standard `python` approaches. We will cast each entry of A to a `uint8`, which is an 8-bit unsigned integer. That it is unsigned simply means that the entry cannot be negative. Let's see how much space we save:

```
print(f"Size in KB: {A.nbytes/1000:.3f} KB")
# Size in KB: 8000.000 KB

B = A.astype(np.uint8)
print(f"Size in KB: {B.nbytes/1000:.3f} KB")
# Size in KB: 1000.000 KB
```

Byte separation aside, this is still considerably more space than necessary. First, the total number of entries being stored is $1000^2 = 1$ million, but there are only $\binom{1000}{2} = 499,500$ unique entries (remember that a simple network is loopless and undirected, which means that we only need to keep track of the upper triangle of the adjacency matrix, and we can ignore the diagonal entries entirely) so we are overcounting by about a factor of two.

This means that we could simply ignore everything but the upper triangle, and still recover the entire adjacency matrix. Let's see how to do this with `scipy` sparse matrices:

```
import scipy.sparse as sparse

Btriu = sparse.triu(B)
print(f"Size in KB: {Btriu.data.size/1000:.3f}")
# Size in KB: 2.654 KB
```

This has reduced the size of the network from 8000 KB to just 2.390 KB, which is smaller by a factor of about 400.

How did `scipy` do this?

Let's just print out `Btriu` and see what `scipy` did:

```
Btriu
# <1000x1000 sparse matrix of type '<class 'numpy.uint8'>'
#    with 2654 stored elements in COOrdinate format>
```

`COOrdinate` format is an efficient way to represent the entries of a sparse adjacency matrix. To illustrate the `COOrdinate` format, imagine that we have the simple 5×5 adjacency matrix for a network with five nodes shown as follows:

Table 6.1. The adjacency matrix in Equation (6.4), in COOrdinate format. For larger networks, this pattern would continue for every nonzero entry in the adjacency matrix in the upper right triangle.

Row	Column	Value
0	1	1
1	3	1
2	2	1

$$A = \begin{bmatrix} 0 & 1 & 0 & 1 \\ 1 & 0 & 0 & 0 \\ 0 & 0 & 0 & 1 \\ 1 & 0 & 1 & 0 \end{bmatrix}. \tag{6.4}$$

scipy stores the matrix as shown in Table 6.1. It looks at each nonzero edge in the upper triangle of the adjacency matrix for the network (for instance, $a_{12} = 1$, so we will arbitrarily call this the first edge), and then records the row and column of those edges. The second edge is $a_{14} = 1$, and the third edge is $a_{34} = 1$. The adjacencies in the lower triangle (a_{21}, a_{41}, and a_{43}) are redundant, so they are omitted from the representation entirely.

In effect, scipy ignored storing the matrix entry-wise: It simply stored the rows and columns of the upper triangular nonzero entries of B, each as a single byte. Next, it stored the total size of the matrix in another spot (which was 1000×1000) so that we could "recover" the entire matrix B from the COOrdinate format in Btriu. When the underlying network is simple, we can just use utilities from Section 3.7.2 to symmetrize Btriu if we want to recover the original matrix A.

```
from graspologic.utils import symmetrize

# cast the sparse matrix back to a dense matrix,
# and then triu symmetrize with graspologic
A_new = symmetrize(Btriu.todense(), method="triu")
np.array_equal(A_new, A) # True
```

With sufficiently sparse adjacency matrices, we can exploit this structure to get vastly improved storage compression. Since sizable networks tend to be sufficiently sparse, the most common storage format we will find with simple networks is something similar to this COOrdinate format, called an edge list, which is a csv (comma-separated values), ssv (space-separated values), or tsv (tab-separated values) file, as shown in Table 6.2 for the simple example in Equation (6.4). With csv or ssv formats, instead of having tabs separate the node indexing columns of the edge list, we could also have spaces or commas (or any suitable delimiter).

The appropriate format for storing networks differ depending on their properties. When networks are simple, an edgelist, where each line indicates the node indices of nonzero entries in the upper triangle of the adjacency matrix, works well. When the network is weighted, there is often a third column corresponding to the edge weight,

Table 6.2. The upper triangle of the adjacency matrix, stored as a `tsv` (tab-separated values) file, for the adjacency matrix in Equation (6.4).

Node 1	Node 2
1	2
1	4
2	3

which is redundant in unweighted networks. When the network is directed, the lower triangle entries are also typically stored. When the network is undirected but may include loops, the edgelist will typically include the all nodes in the upper triangle in addition to the diagonal.

With so many possible representations of networks in edgelist or sparse formats, it is imperative to first ascertain the underlying properties of the networks we work with. Understanding these properties will indicate how to properly "unpack" an edgelist or sparse representation to recover an adjacency matrix.

Algorithmic Implications of Matrix Sparsity

When we represent the adjacency matrix using sparse formats, we benefit by leveraging algorithms designed for sparse data. Let's see, for instance, how long it takes for `scipy` to run a sparse `svd` when we pass the data in a dense format (a standard `numpy` array) and use a standard `svd`, compared to when we use a sparse format and use a partial `svd`, to embed into 20 dimensions. A full `svd` for an $n \times n$ square matrix will compute all n left and right singular vectors (along with their singular values). A partial `svd` will only compute the top (or bottom) subset of these:

```
import time
import scipy as sp

# a naive full svd on the dense matrix
timestart = time.time()
U, S, Vh = sp.linalg.svd(A)
Xhat = U[:, 0:10] @ np.diag(np.sqrt(S[0:10]))
timeend = time.time()
print(f"Naive approach: {timeend - timestart:3f} seconds")
# we get about 0.55 seconds

# a sparse svd on the sparse matrix
Acoo = sparse.coo_array(A)
timestart = time.time()
U, S, Vh = sp.sparse.linalg.svds(Acoo, k=10)
Xhat = U @ np.diag(np.sqrt(S))
timeend = time.time()
print(f"Sparse approach: {timeend-timestart:3f} seconds")
# we get about .01 seconds
```

We see roughly a factor of ten speed improvement (depending on the hardware). As matrices grow in size, and have an increasingly small fraction of their entries being nonzero, sparse approaches tend to dramatically outperform naive implementations.

When data get large enough, we may not even be able to execute standard functions on standard arrays, and might be required to use sparse approaches.

6.2.3 Practical Applications of Network and Matrix Sparsity

Matrix and network sparsity have a unique interplay when dealing with network data represented as an adjacency matrix. This case we will consider deals directly with a familiar strategy: spectral embeddings of network data. For this example, we will see a unique problem that the adjacency spectral embedding can run into with sparse networks with sparse adjacency matrices.

Let's consider our example from Section 6.2 with $K = 10$ communities and $n = 1000$ nodes. The underlying probability matrix and the adjacency matrix for the network are shown in Figure 6.2.2(A) and (B) respectively. We can see fairly prominent modular structure, so we could try a spectral embedding and a clustering (Chapter 5 and Section 6.1) to identify community assignments. To determine whether `lse` or `ase` is appropriate for our data, we compute the node degrees like we did in Section 5.4:

```
degrees = A.sum(axis=0)
```

The degree distribution for the network is shown in 6.2.2(C). It looks right-skewed or heavy-tailed, so it would be appropriate to do a spectral embedding with `lse` (Section 5.4).

We will look at the top five left singular vectors of the DAD Laplacian. `lse` is a function of these vectors (rescaled by the singular values) in Algorithm 5.3. We will do this with `scipy`'s faster sparse `svd` (note: this will still take some time).

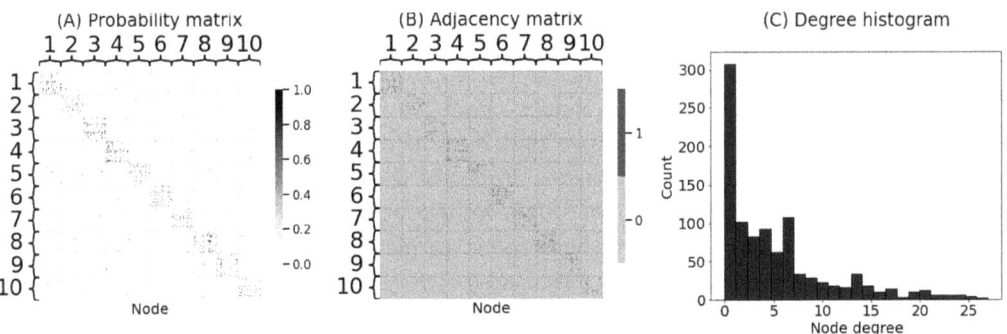

Figure 6.2.2 (**A**) The probability matrix, (**B**) the adjacency matrix, and (**C**) the heavy-tailed degree histogram for a network from a sparse sequence of networks.

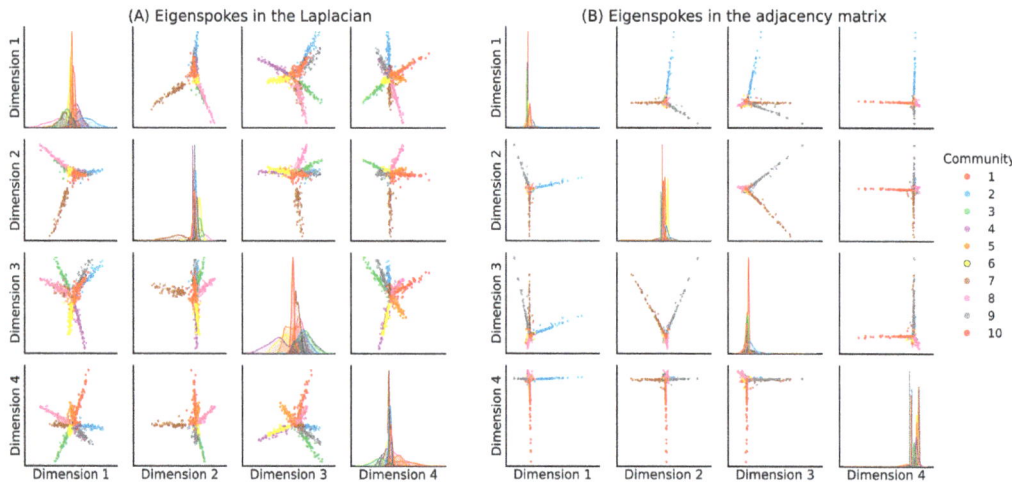

Figure 6.2.3 **(A)** Eigenspokes in the singular vectors of the Laplacian, and **(B)** moderate spokes in the singular vectors of the adjacency matrix.

```
from graspologic.utils import to_laplacian
from graspologic.plot import pairplot

# use sparse svd, so that we don't need to compute
# 1000 singular vectors and can just calculate the top 10
U, S, Vh = sp.sparse.linalg.svds(to_laplacian(A), k=10, random_state=0)
# plot the first 4
pairplot(U[:,0:4], labels=zs, title="Eigenspokes in the Laplacian")
```

We visualize the top four singular vectors as a pairplot in Figure 6.2.3(A). Each node is a point in this plot. What we notice is rather unusual. In many dimensions, such as dimensions 2 and 3, nodes appear to have an "all or nothing" pattern: Entire communities of nodes have a 0 along almost all of the singular vectors, except for the long spoke that they stretch along. For instance, in dimension 2, notice that the brown community has a long spoke pattern, and the other communities are bunched up. In dimension 3, we can see that the purple and yellow communities stretch downwards along the spoke, and the other communities are bunched in the top. Along many of the other dimensions, such as 3 and 4, almost all of the nodes simply have a value of 0.

This "all-or-nothing" pattern is what is known as an *EigenSpoke* [3]: Some communities are clearly separated along a subset of axes, but have no separation along other axes. This all-or-nothing EigenSpoke behavior presents a challenge for techniques like KMeans and GMM, which tend to favor spherical and elliptical "blobs" respectively.

It seems pretty clear from Section 6.1 that we don't have the setup that KMeans or GMM do well in (structured blobs in the pairplots), so let's try looking at the singular vectors associated with the ase instead of the lse:

```
U, S, Vh = sp.sparse.linalg.svds(A, k=10, random_state=0)
# plot the first 4
fig = pairplot(U[:,0:4], labels=zs, title="Eigenspokes in the
    adjacency matrix")
```

These aren't quite "EigenSpokes," in that the spokes aren't as apparent as they were with the Laplacian, but they are still quite spokey in shape. Here, too, naive community detection approaches like KMeans will not work well, even though some of the communities look less poorly separated. This would be clear if we were to visualize the distance matrix between pairs of nodes, as in Section 5.4, armed with the intuition from Section 6.1 about KMeans for community detection in mind.

As it turns out, spectral approaches do not work well with sparse networks. For this reason, we can identify when we might run into these patterns by looking at the sparsity of its adjacency matrix. We will typically run into sparse network troubles when the number of edges is "close to" the number of nodes in the network, and when it is far less than the number of potential edges. We can calculate these with:

```
print("# Expected edges: {:.2f}".format(np.triu(P).sum()))
# Expected edges: 2654.00
print("# True edges: {:d}".format(np.triu(A).sum().astype(int)))
# True edges: 2654
print("# Potential edges: {:d}".format(int(K*nk*(K*nk - 1)/2)))
# Potential edges: 499500
```

When the number of observed edges is orders of magnitude less than the number of potential edges, many naive spectral techniques (such as ase, lse, and derived approaches like mase and omni) will probably not produce embeddings which will easily facilitate downstream analysis like community detection [4]. We may need to turn to alternative techniques such as [5; 6] to achieve high performance in these settings, where we incorporate different functions of the adjacency matrix that are better behaved for sparse regimes all together or apply penalties to nodes with low degrees to, in some sense, force the embeddings to avoid spoke-like patterns, or turn to other analysis techniques entirely. While these situations are not common in most network learning problems, knowing when they might occur and how to discern them (through visualization via pairs plots or other heuristics, such as looking at network density) are valuable tools for your arsenal.

Remark 6.2.4 Simulating EigenSpokes is not an exact science

We know that EigenSpokes can arise in sparse networks, but we don't know how to reliably obtain them from random network samples.

Changing seeds may result in needing to run simulations a few more times to produce "EigenSpoke"-like patterns that run perfectly parallel along eigenvectors. This shouldn't be too difficult; running the examples in this section yields spokes about 20 percent of the time and nonsensical embeddings in the other cases.

Network Sparsity and Sparse Matrices

In Section 6.2, we defined sparsity as a property that occurs over a sequence of random networks. Next, we showed that when a network had relatively few entries so that its adjacency matrix was sparse, we could identify odd behaviors in particular algorithms like the `lse` and `ase`. These two ideas feel at odds because the definition of sparsity does not apply to network samples; however, in practice, we only have network samples.

In Section 5.3.3, we justified the use of `ase` by arguing that, when we have a network sample from a random network, as the network gets larger and larger, the estimated latent position matrix gets increasingly close to the true latent position matrix of the underlying random network. However, the underlying random network must have a probability matrix that obeys certain conditions [5; 7] that ensure that the sequence of networks are not sparse.

When networks fail to satisfy these conditions, the naive `ase` loses its meaning. As the number of nodes increases, instead of the estimated latent position matrices getting increasingly close to the true latent position matrix of the underlying random network, the estimates become increasingly nonsensical. At some level, we lose the ability to say that the estimated latent position matrix $\hat{X}$ is a reasonable estimate of the true underlying latent position matrix X. This is why we observed "puzzling" behaviors in the spectral embeddings of realizations of sparse networks.

Concept 6.2.5 Complementary definitions of sparsity

Network sparsity is a property of an underlying sequence of random networks (with nodes and potential edges), but *matrix sparsity* is a property of the adjacency matrix (or a function thereof, such as a network Laplacian) for an actual network (with nodes and edges).

A network with a sufficiently sparse adjacency matrix will often run into problems associated with sparse sequences of random networks, and samples from sparse sequences of networks with enough nodes will often have sufficiently sparse adjacency matrices which cause odd results in network learning algorithms, so these two definitions prove complementary in network science.

6.3   Testing for Differences between Groups of Edges

In Chapter 4, we explored stochastic block models (Section 4.3) and their degree-corrected variants (4.7). We also introduced the structured independent edge model, or SIEM (Section 4.8), which generalizes the SBM by allowing for more flexible edge clustering. All $SBM_n(\vec{z}, B)$ random networks can be reformulated as $SIEM_n(Z, \vec{p})$ random networks. This section uses the SIEM to develop statistical tests for determining whether different groups of edges differ from one another. As the SIEM generalizes stochastic block models, these techniques readily apply to SBMs.

We cover the following topics:

1. Review of the SIEM framework and its relationship with SBMs,
2. Introduction to hypothesis testing in the context of edge groups,
3. Development of test statistics for comparing edge probabilities across clusters,

4. Application of these tests to SBMs for comparing community-level connectivity, and

5. Discussion of practical considerations and limitations of edge group testing.

We begin by revisiting the SIEM framework, where the parameter Z defines individual edge clusters and the vector $\vec{p}$ specifies edge probabilities for each cluster.

Whenever a network has a set of node or edge groupings, we can conceptualize it as a sample of an $SIEM_n(Z, \vec{p})$ random network. We learned in Section 5.1 how to estimate probabilities from collections of edges, and these strategies apply readily to the $SIEM_n(Z, \vec{p})$ random networks.

By the argument we made regarding maximum likelihood estimation, if we have a network sample with edge clusters given by the matrix Z, we can compute the estimated probability for edges in cluster k with:

$$\hat{p}_k = \frac{\sum_{i,j:z_{ij}=k} a_{ij}}{n_k},$$

where n_k is the total number of edges that are assigned to cluster k, and is given by $\sum_{i,j:z_{ij}=k} 1$. The denominator sums over all possible edges in cluster k, and the numerator sums only edges in k which exist.

Let's return to the $SIEM_n(Z, \vec{p})$ brain hemisphere example from Section 4.8, and use a probability vector $\vec{p}^\top = [0.4, 0.6]$. We can build the edge cluster assignment matrix and a probability vector like this:

```
import numpy as np
from graphbook_code import siem

n = 100
Z = np.ones((n, n))

# Fill the upper and lower 50th diagonals with 2
# and the main diagonal with 0
np.fill_diagonal(Z[:, 50:], 2)
np.fill_diagonal(Z[50:, :], 2)
np.fill_diagonal(Z, 0)

p = [0.4, 0.6]
np.random.seed(0)
A = siem(n, p, Z)
```

Figure 6.3.1(A) shows the edge cluster assignment matrix Z. A sample of the network is shown in Figure 6.3.1(B). The edges corresponding to edge cluster 2 in Figure 6.3.1(A) stand out from the other edges in the adjacency matrix (B), but it looks far from definitive. We can compute the estimated edge probabilities (per edge cluster) using the below code:

```
est_pvec = {k: A[Z == k].mean() for k in [1, 2]}
print(est_pvec)
# {1: 0.3955102040816327, 2: 0.6}
```

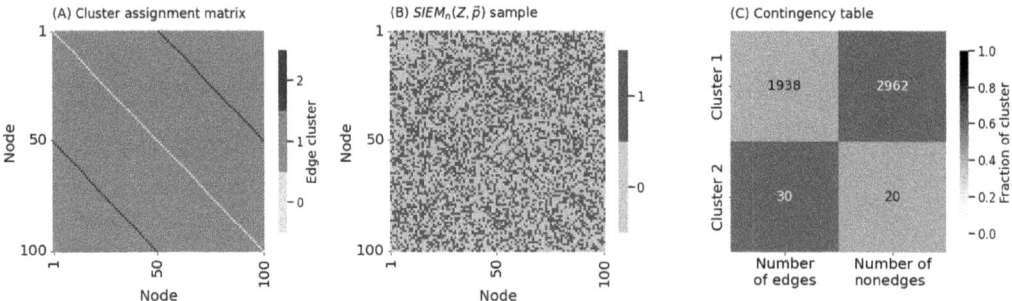

Figure 6.3.1 (**A**) The edge-cluster assignment matrix, (**B**) the adjacency matrix, and (**C**) a contingency table for the two edge clusters in the network sample.

The estimated edge probabilities appear to be quite different from just looking at the sample. When we observe the sample, we don't initially know whether the underlying random network truly has a different probability for each edge cluster. This means that if we want to determine whether the estimated edge probabilities are appreciably different, we have some work to do.

6.3.1   Two-Sample Hypothesis Testing

With two samples of data, a key question is determining whether their differences are due to random chance, or whether the samples were drawn from fundamentally different distributions. This is known as a *two-sample test*.

A sample of an $SIEM_n(Z, \vec{p})$ random network A has binary edges a_{ij}. For a pair of communities k and l (which are two of the K total clusters in our network), we want to choose between two possible scenarios that describe their respective probability distributions. These scenarios are known as *hypotheses* for a hypothesis test. In this case our hypotheses are:

$$H_0: p_k = p_l \text{ against } H_A: p_k \neq p_l.$$

In general, we assume that the *null hypothesis*, H_0, represents an "uninteresting" or "default" effect for our system. In our example, our null hypothesis is that $p_k = p_l$, or that the underlying probabilities are identical between the two clusters (the two clusters are not different in probability). The capital H denotes that this is a hypothesis, and the lower-case 0 just indicates "null".

The *alternative hypothesis* H_A is the scenario in which H_0 is false. This will typically denote the "interesting" effect that we wish to illustrate that is supported by our real data. In our example, the alternative hypothesis is that $p_k \neq p_l$, or that the underlying probabilities differ between the two edge clusters.

We read the hypothesis as: We are testing H_0 the null that $p_k = p_l$ and the underlying probabilities are identical against H_A the alternative that $p_k \neq p_l$ and the underlying probabilities differ.

Hypothesis tests come from a branch of statistics known as *statistical inference*, which attempts to make informed decisions about a population based on data sampled from it. We perform statistical inference with hypothesis tests by looking at how well aligned our data are with an assumption by proceeding with the assumption that the null hypothesis is true. This means that either the data look like what we would expect under the null hypothesis, or the data do not look like what we would expect under the null hypothesis. We convey the degree to which the data look different from what we would expect under the null hypothesis with the p-value, which is explained in Concept 6.3.1.

Concept 6.3.1 The p-value is the unit used for decision making in hypothesis tests

When performing hypothesis tests, we fundamentally use the *p-value* for decision making. The p-value is:

$$p = Pr\left(\text{we falsely reject } H_0 \text{ in favor of } H_A \big| H_0 \text{ is true}\right).$$

The vertical bar in statistics means "conditioned on," which means that the probability is being computed under the assumption that the null hypothesis is true. The implications of this statement are critical to a quality statistical analysis. For a hypothesis test, we first begin by deciding the assumptions that we have about how the system behaves. For network science, these assumptions are conveyed by the statistical models in Chapter 4.

After we assume the statistical model, our hypotheses typically reflect possible ways in which the data might behave with respect to the parameters of our model. For instance, in the $SIEM_n(Z, \vec{p})$ model, we assume that the edges $\mathbf{a}_{ij}$ are independent coin flips with probability given by $p_{z_{ij}}$.

Finally, we usually structure the null hypothesis as a distribution with well-known properties. If we were to flip two coins with potentially different probabilities of landing on heads, we can explicitly determine the amount of variation that we would expect in the number of heads that two identical coins would receive in a particular number of coin flips.

Intuitively, if we flip two coins ten times each and one gets three heads and the other seven, we can quantify whether the number of heads that we obtain is "close enough" to the level of variability that we would expect if the coins had the same probability of landing on heads.

6.3.2   Two-Sample Hypothesis Testing with Binary-Valued Data

In the coin flip example of Concept 6.3.1, we might construct a two-sample hypothesis that:

$$H_0: p_1 = p_2 \text{ against } H_A: p_1 \neq p_2, \tag{6.5}$$

where p_1 is the probability that the first coin lands on heads, and p_2 is the probability that the second coin lands on heads. When each of the two samples (the ten coin flips

Table 6.3. A contingency table for the coin flip example in Concept 6.3.1.

	Number of heads	Number of tails
Coin 1	3	7
Coin 2	7	3

from each of the two coins) are independent and have binary-valued outcomes (heads or tails), a common summary measure is a contingency table. The contingency table is shown in Table 6.3.

The contingency table conveys everything of statistical value between our two samples of data (the columns) and is known as a test statistic. A *test statistic* is a quantity computed from data (here, the contingency table) that is used for statistical inference. Since each of the two samples were composed of independent coin flips of coins where each flip of a given coin has the same probability of landing on heads, we have no reason to believe that anything other than the number of heads and tails in ten flips is important for ascertaining whether there is a difference between the coins.

One method of testing the hypothesis in Equation (6.5) is *Fisher's exact test*. This test computes the probability of observing the contingency table in Table 6.3 if both columns have independent, binary entries where the underlying random events (the coin flips) have the same probability.

We can assemble our contingency table using numpy arrays, and we can perform Fisher's exact test using scipy:

```python
from scipy.stats import fisher_exact
import numpy as np

# assemble the contingency table indicated
table = np.array([[3, 7], [7, 3]])
_, pvalue = fisher_exact(table)
print(f"p-value: {pvalue:.3f}")
# p-value: 0.179
```

Given that one coin obtained three heads and seven tails and the other obtained seven heads and three tails, we conclude that there is a 17.9 percent chance that the contingency table that we observed in Table 6.3 (or one with a more extreme disparity in the number of heads and tails, such as two and eight) could have been observed if both of the coins had the same true probabilities of landing on heads.

At this point, we may suspect that the coins are not identical. However, perhaps we made erroneous assumptions somewhere along the way, or perhaps we want to be extra safe before we make a determination.

For this reason, statisticians usually choose a decision threshold ahead of time, known as the α (alpha) of the test. The α indicates a threshold for the p-values noteworthy enough to declare that the data do not support the null hypothesis. A commonly chosen threshold which we will use throughout this book is $\alpha = 0.05$, which means that we will decide that our data do not support the null hypothesis when p-values are below 0.05.

Here, we would determine that the data are insufficient to reject the null hypothesis that the coins have the same underyling probability, since the p-value of $0.179 > 0.05$.

Faithfully Representing Underlying Network Structure
In Section 3.7.5.2, we learned that when networks are undirected and loopless (both of which are true for simple networks), it is imperative to be careful when computing summary statistics from data.

A common strategy is to compute summary statistics entirely from one "triangle" from the adjacency matrix; we use the upper triangle throughout this section. When performing hypothesis testing, the amount of variation to be expected is directly tied to the sample size. The adjacency matrix is simply a representation of our simple network: It can be misused in that a_{ji} is not relevant if we have already included a_{ij} in our analysis. These two entries are *deterministically identical* (they are always the same) as a property of the network (simple networks are undirected), and deterministic features are not relevant to statistics since there is no randomness. Likewise, if the network is loopless, we must exclude the diagonal.

When two coins are flipped 10 times and one yields 3 heads but the other 7 heads, the p-value is only 0.179. However, if the coins are flipped 20 times and one yields 6 heads but the other 14 heads, the p-value plummets to 0.026, despite the fact that the "rate of heads" in each sample was the same.

In much the same way, had we analyzed all of the adjacency matrix instead of just the upper triangle, the number of edges would be artificially inflated (by way of the deterministic identicality of the upper and lower triangles) and we would artificially add the diagonal placeholders (the network is loopless, so the diagonal values of 0 are simply placeholders).

With larger experiments, we can be more confident that smaller amounts of variability are not random, so it is important not to artificially "double" the number of edges that we count or include placeholders such as the diagonal.

6.3.3 Applying Hypothesis Testing to Samples of $SIEM_n(Z, \vec{p})$ Random Networks

We can apply hypothesis testing for detecting differences in estimated probabilities for samples of $SIEM_n(Z, \vec{p})$ random networks. We begin by constructing contingency tables, as we did with coin flips in the previous section. We can do this with numpy, by simply counting the number of edges that had a value of 1 and 0 for each cluster. Since the network is simple, we take care not to double-count edges in the lower triangle nor include the diagonal:

```
# compute an upper-triangular mask to only look at the
# upper triangle since the network is simple (undirected and loopless)
upper_tri_mask = np.triu(np.ones(A.shape), k=1).astype(bool)
column_clust1 = [
    A[(Z == 1) & upper_tri_mask].sum(),
    (A[(Z == 1) & upper_tri_mask] == 0).sum(),
]
column_clust2 = [
    A[(Z == 2) & upper_tri_mask].sum(),
```

```
    (A[(Z == 2) & upper_tri_mask] == 0).sum(),
]
cont_tabl = np.vstack((column_clust1, column_clust2))
```

The resulting contingency table is plotted as a heatmap in Figure 6.3.1(C).
    We can apply Fisher's exact test to this contingency table:

```
_, pvalue = fisher_exact(cont_tabl)
print(f"p-value: {pvalue:.5f}")
# p-value: 0.00523
```

We end up with a p-value that is close to zero. With our decision threshold still at $\alpha = 0.05$, the p-value of our test is $< \alpha$. Therefore, we have evidence to suggest that we should reject the null hypothesis.

6.3.4   Caveats of Hypothesis Testing

Now that we have covered some basics about how to perform hypothesis tests with random networks, we hope to emphasize a few misconceptions about hypothesis testing that permeate science. Even without a substantial background in statistics, these tips can hopefully give some insight into interpreting statistical analyses in the remainder of this book and in applying hypothesis tests. These caveats are not limited in applicability to network data alone.

Statistical Models Are Almost Always Wrong
True or false, in the context of a hypothesis test performed on real data, do not mean true or false in the traditional sense. A hypothesis test is tied directly to the statistical model used to describe the data: A hypothesis can be true or false with respect to a statistical model which is assumed to be true, but hypotheses on the basis of real data can either be supported by the data or unsupported by the data.

    This is because statistical models used to describe real data are not true. This statement applies to network data or nonnetwork data. This does not invalidate the approaches in Chapters 4 and 5, nor does it invalidate every statistical method developed over the past hundred years, which rest on similar sets of assumptions.

    While these assumptions are imperfect, they still allow us to describe behaviors that arise in our network data (or any data for that matter). This allows us to be specific about a context in which our results can be interpreted. In the absence of this context, we would have no way to determine whether irregularities in our data are anomalous or whether they are the result of the normal variation that we can expect from imperfect data.

Parameters of the Underlying Model
Hypothesis tests make statements about the true parameters of a statistical model based on data and dependent on assumptions made about the statistical model. For example, in coin flipping, we consider the actual probabilities p_1 and p_2 (true probabilities of heads) rather than $\hat{p}_1$ or $\hat{p}_2$ (estimated probabilities of heads).

Even if the statistical model used is correct (e.g., in simulations), analysis rarely provides the true underlying parameters. Flipping a fair coin 101 times (with a true probability of 0.5 for heads) will not yield exactly 50.5 heads. We can only conclude that a hypothesis (about the true parameters of the assumed statistical model) is supported or unsupported by the data.

The Null Hypothesis

Statistical hypothesis testing makes statements about whether we have evidence or not that the null hypothesis is unsupported by the data. These are the only two outcomes for a typical hypothesis test with real data. In the first outcome, where the null hypothesis is unsupported by the data, we "reject the null hypothesis in favor of the alternative hypothesis." The possible second outcome is that we "cannot reject the null hypothesis." Note that this second outcome makes no statement about the null hypothesis being supported by the data: We do not accept a null hypothesis, we simply do not have enough evidence to reject it.

Consider, for instance, the example from Section 6.3.2 where we flipped two coins 10 times, and saw three heads for one coin and seven heads for the other coin. Just because the p-value (0.179) exceeded $\alpha = 0.05$ does not mean that the data provide evidence that the null hypothesis is true (the coins have the same probability). There just is not enough evidence (yet) to support that they are different. If we performed our experiment again with more coin flips, we might be able to obtain that evidence. This point is frequently misunderstood and misapplied by many excellent scientists.

6.4 Model Selection with Stochastic Block Models

We have now thought about block models in some applied scenarios, including community assignment estimation (Section 6.1) and testing for differences between edge clusters (Section 6.3).

This section focuses on differentiating between possible block matrix structures and selecting the appropriate model, leveraging the various structures introduced in Section 4.5 to develop a systematic approach for model selection. We will:

1. Introduce the concept of model selection for stochastic block models,
2. Explore methods for choosing between models of different complexity,
3. Apply the principle of parsimony in model selection,
4. Demonstrate a step-by-step procedure for model comparison using the likelihood ratio statistic, and
5. Walk through a practical example using a simulated network.

Section 4.5 covered many separate models to describe 2×2 random networks with block structures. Some of the models could fully describe others, but not necessarily the other way around. For instance, a homophilic block matrix could be further categorized as a planted partition block matrix, but not vice versa. Understanding model selection builds on the community detection ideas introduced in Section 6.1 to give us a systematic way to balance model complexity with explanatory power.

Let's imagine that we have a network sample with a set of community assignments for each node. In the following code, we will take a look at one such sample from an $SBM_n(\vec{z}, B)$ random network with a homophilic block matrix:

```
import numpy as np
from graspologic.simulations import sbm

nk = 50 # 50 nodes per community
K = 2 # the number of communities
n = nk * K # total number of nodes

zs = np.repeat(np.arange(1, K+1), repeats=nk)
# block matrix
B = np.array([[0.6, 0.3],[0.3, 0.5]])
# generate network sample
np.random.seed(0)
A = sbm([nk, nk], B)
```

A plot of the true underlying block matrix is shown in Figure 6.4.1(A), and the adjacency matrix is shown in Figure 6.4.1(B).

From what we learned in Section 5.1, given a network and a set of community assignments, a logical step to learn more about the network is to estimate the block probability matrix. We can do this using the following code:

```
from graspologic.models import SBMEstimator

# instantiate the class object and fit
model = SBMEstimator(directed=False, loops=False)
model.fit(A, y=zs)
# obtain the estimate of the block matrix
Bhat = model.block_p_
```

The estimated block matrix is shown in Figure 6.4.1(C). The estimated probabilities support a homophilic structure: The two on-diagonal entries exceed the estimated off-diagonal entries.

However, in Section 6.3, a key focus was determining when differences between estimated probabilities indicated that the true underlying probabilities differed. Even though two probability estimates might be different, we leverage statistical strategies

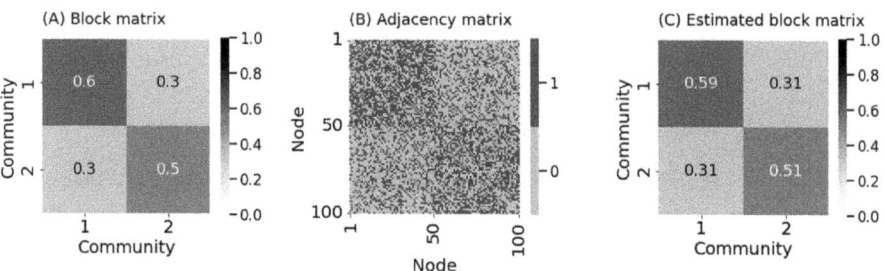

Figure 6.4.1 **(A)** The true block matrix underlying the $SBM_n(\vec{z}, B)$ random network, **(B)** a sample of the random network, and **(C)** the estimated block matrix.

to determine whether these differences are more or less than we would expect given natural variation that can arise in the data. When the observed differences are less than we would expect with natural variability, we determined that we did not have evidence to reject the null hypothesis. When the observed differences exceed what we would expect with natural variability, we determined the data supported rejecting the null hypothesis.

6.4.1   Model Selection and Random Networks

Model selection is the task of selecting among several possible statistical models which we think may describe our sample. We do this using quantitative strategies to determine which statistical models are best supported by the data.

Remark 6.4.1 Model selection with coin flips

In Section 6.3.2, we introduced a simple two-sample test for coin flip data to determine whether the two coins had the same probability. The null hypothesis was $H_0: p_1 = p_2$, against $H_A: p_1 \neq p_2$.

This question can be approached as a two-sample test, which we described in Section 6.3.2. Our question can also be thought of as determining whether or not there were really two samples of data in the first place.

Under our null hypothesis, we are asking whether a coin with the same probability was used for both of the samples. Under the alternative hypothesis, we are asking whether two fundamentally different coins were used for each of the samples.

So, the null can be reformulated as: Can the two samples be described using the same probability term, or can the two samples be best described using different probability terms? Stated another way, does the most reasonable model for the data have one parameter (the same probability term, for both samples), or should we describe it with two parameters (a unique probability term for each sample)?

In Remark 6.4.1, we introduce the idea of model selection in terms of whether a collection of twenty coin flips (from two samples of data) should be described using a single probability term for all twenty coin flips, or whether each of the ten coin flips should be described using two probability terms.

We can formulate our block matrices under the same light. The block matrix for a simple $SBM_n(\vec{z}, B)$ random network is organized as:

$$B = \begin{bmatrix} b_{11} & b_{12} \\ b_{12} & b_{22} \end{bmatrix}.$$

The symmetry of B is because the underlying simple random network is undirected (so $b_{21} = b_{12}$). We want to ask formally: Do the data provide us with enough evidence to support the homophilic network not being a planted partition (does $b_{11} \neq b_{22}$)? Further, is there any reason to believe that there is block structure?

From the estimated block matrix in Figure 6.4.1(C), it seems at first glance that the network is homophilic – but "seems at first glance" is not quantitative enough.

As we move to inceasingly complicated models, there is concurrently a trade-off known as model parsimony. *Model parsimony* is the idea that simpler models with fewer parameters are preferable to complicated models with more parameters, provided both models describe the data equally well. This idea ties directly into the bias/variance trade-off, which we discussed in Section 3.6.

This can be interpreted rigorously by considering the extremes. In the simplest case, we could have a random network model with a single parameter (an $ER_n(p)$ random network). In the most complicated case, we could have an $IER_n(P)$ random network with a unique probability term p_{ij} for each edge.

With most datasets, we can find a "happy medium" of parsimony, where the model is complicated enough that it describes our system faithfully, but not so complicated that we end up overfitting when we use our network sample to analyze it. Through model selection, we attempt to develop principled strategies that allow us to favor parsimonious models that are complicated enough to describe the data efficiently, but not so complicated that our data cannot support the downstream conclusions that we develop.

6.4.1.1   Sequentially Nested Hypotheses

In model selection, we will exploit the fact that we have nested hypotheses with 2×2 block matrices. A hypothesis H_1 is *nested* in another hypothesis H_2 if, whenever H_1 is true, H_2 is true too.

In the coin flip example, we can reformulate our two hypotheses H_0 and H_A as a sequence of nested hypotheses. If H_0 is true, the model could be described with a single probability term $p_1 = p_2 = a$. On the other hand, if H_A is true, the model can be described by $p_1 = b$ and $p_2 = c$. If H_A is nested in H_0, then even if we use two numbers b and c as the probabilities of p_1 and p_2, we could always just set $b = c$, and end up with the model in H_0. If in the underlying system it is the case that $p_1 \neq p_2$ (and H_A is true), then we need the additional delineation of terms b and c. On the other hand, if in the underlying system it is the case that $p_1 = p_2$, we can get away with just the one term.

Sequentially Nested Hypotheses for Network Data
To consider the idea of sequentially nested hypotheses for network data, let's think about the setting that we have with our 2×2 block matrix. In this case, we have three groups of edges:

1. The group of edges where both nodes are from community one,
2. The group of edges where one node is from community one and the other from community two, and
3. The group of edges where both nodes are from community two.

For each edge, we can build an edge group assignment matrix, which reconceptualizes our $SBM_n(\vec{z}, B)$ random network as an $SIEM_n(Z, \vec{p})$ random network. This is simply to ease our ability to index the adjacency matrix by groups of nodes:

```
# upper left has a value of 1, lower right has a value of 2,
# and upper right, bottom left have a value of 3
Z = np.array(zs).reshape(n, 1) @ np.array(zs).reshape(1, n)
# make lower right have a value of 3
Z[Z == 4] = 3
```

This gives us three "samples" (to borrow the analogy from our coin flip model) of data. Visually, the model looks homophilic, so this motivates the following sequentially nested hypotheses:

1. H_0: The block matrix is Erdös–Rényi, where $b_{11} = b_{12} = b_{22} = a$.
2. H_1: The block matrix is a planted partition, where $b_{11} = b_{22} = a$, but $b_{12} = b$, and $a > b$. Note that H_0 is nested in H_1, as if H_0 were true, H_1 would also be true if we were to choose b where $a = b$.
3. H_2: The block matrix is homophilic with potentially heterogeneous on-diagonal blocks, where $b_{11} = a$, $b_{12} = b$, and $b_{22} = c$, and $b_{11}, b_{22} > b_{12}$. Note that H_1 is nested in H_2, as if H_1 were true, H_2 would be true with a choice of c where $c = a$.

Testing Sequentially Nested Hypotheses
We first ask how to determine which of these sequentially nested hypotheses to pick. In the two hypothesis case, we tested the null hypothesis against the alternative hypothesis. In this case, we have three hypotheses, so we need a different strategy.

Statisticians have come up with a simple but elegant solution to this problem. We start with the simplest model that we could have (H_0). We add a single layer of complexity in the scope of the models that we think could be reasonable (H_1), and simply test H_0 as the null hypothesis against H_1 as the alternative hypothesis.

For a sequence of nested hypotheses with N levels, for a hypothesis at level n to be reasonable, then the hypothesis at level $n - 1$ has to be more reasonable than the one at level $n - 2$ first. This amounts to determining that if the model has a homophilic block matrix with a heterogeneous on-diagonal block structure, we should first know whether a homophilic block matrix makes sense in the first place. We follow this pattern backwards, which leads to the insight that we should begin at H_0 against H_1.

Once we test H_0 against H_1, we have two routes: Either the data do not support H_0 and we reject H_0 in favor of H_1, or we do not have evidence to reject H_0. If we do not have evidence to reject H_0, we stop, since we only want to use complicated models when strictly necessary (e.g., when we do not have evidence to reject the simpler model). We repeat this process over and over again, in the process known as *forwards model selection*, in Algorithm 6.2.

6.4.2 Applying Sequentially Nested Hypotheses to Network Data

With network data, the network samples have binary adjacency matrix entries a_{ij} (which take values of 0 or 1). When we have two samples of data, a suitable representation was the contingency table in Table 6.3. When we have three samples of binary data, what else can we use?

Algorithm 6.2 Forwards model selection

Data: $H_0, H_1, \ldots, H_N$ a sequence of sequentially nested hypotheses delineating different models to describe the data.

Result: The deepest hypothesis that is not rejected against the next sequential alternative.

1 Set $n = 1$, and `stop=False`.
2 **while** `stop = False` **do**
3   Test H_{n-1} as the null hypothesis against H_n as the alternative hypothesis.
4   **if** *no evidence to reject H_{n-1}* **then**
5   Let `stop=True`.
6   **else**
7   **if** $n = N$ **then**
8   Let `stop=True`
9   **end**
10   Let $n = n + 1$.
11   **end**
12 **end**
13 **return** H_{n-1}

Table 6.4. A contingency table with three samples.

	Number of edge	Number of nonedges
Edge group 1		
Edge group 2		
Edge group 3		

The best way to summarize these data is another contingency table. The contingency table for a three-sample example is laid out in Table 6.4.

In the two-sample case with two columns, Fisher's exact test is the preferred statistical test. However, most formulations of Fisher's exact test (such as those implemented by `scipy`) only work with two samples and not three. For this reason, we turn to the likelihood ratio test, discussed briefly in Concept 6.4.2.

Applying this to our sequentially nested hypotheses, we can test whether the block model is Erdős–Rényi against whether it is homophilic planted partition directly, using the 2×2 contingency table in Table 6.5. This produces a test statistic $\ell^{(1,0)}$ (the log likelihood ratio statistic), which has higher values when it is more likely that the data do not support the null hypothesis. In this case, the log likelihood ratio statistic between hypotheses n and n' is:

$$\ell^{(n,n')} = \log\left(\frac{\mathcal{L}(\mathcal{D}; H_n)}{\mathcal{L}(\mathcal{D}; H_{n'})}\right),$$

where $\mathcal{L}(\mathcal{D}; H_n)$ is the likelihood of observing the data $\mathcal{D}$ under the hypothesis H_n (the statistic $\ell^{(n,n')}$ is the log of a "ratio" of likelihoods). By properties of the logarithm, this is equivalent to:

Concept 6.4.2 The likelihood ratio test for $K \times 2$ contingency tables

The *likelihood ratio test* can be used to determine whether a categorical grouping of binary data (summarized by a contingency table) into one of K categories shows differences across the categories. As an asymptotic test, it works best with large samples, unlike Fisher's exact test which is preferable for smaller samples. Though exact tests are generally preferable, the likelihood ratio test suffices for our purposes. In this context, we construct a contingency table by counting the number of edges and nonedges across the different (community, community) pairings of edges.

The test produces a statistic X that increases as the K groups differ more. If the edges in the network are independent, and if the (community, community) pairings have no bearing on the probability of an edge existing, the test statistic X will have approximately a χ-squared distribution for large enough networks. By comparing the observed X to this distribution, we obtain a p-value that quantifies how anomalous our observed data are under the null hypothesis.

$$\ell^{(n,n')} = \log \mathcal{L}(\mathcal{D}; H_n) - \log \mathcal{L}(\mathcal{D}; H_{n'}). \qquad (6.6)$$

Intuitively, this test statistic is comparing the log likelihood ratio of observing data $\mathcal{D}$ under the alternative hypothesis H_n with the log likelihood ratios of observing the data $\mathcal{D}$ under some null hypothesis $H_{n'}$ that is nested in H_n. When this statistic has larger values, the log likelihood (and consequently the likelihood) of observing the data under the alternative hypothesis H_n is higher than it is under the null hypothesis.

We can use this to test H_0 that the model is Erdös–Rényi against H_1 that the model is a homophilic planted partition. We perform this test by comparing $\ell^{(1,0)}$ to the χ-squared distribution. To do so, we must also know the degrees of freedom for the likelihood ratio test statistic under the null hypothesis. The degrees of freedom is the number of parameters that are removed from the model in the simpler hypothesis compared to the more complicated hypothesis. Here, since an Erdös–Rényi block matrix has a single parameter (a) but the homophilic planted partition block matrix has two parameters (a and b), the number of degrees of freedom is 1.

In our data, the first step is to establish a model with the desired contingency table. We do this by using a `pandas` dataframe where the rows are edges, the first column indicates the value of the adjacency matrix for that particular edge, and the second column indicate the edge group. Here, the edge group delineates whether or

Table 6.5. Contingency table for testing whether a block model is Erdös–Rényi against whether it is homophilic planted partition.

	Number of edges	Number of nonedges
$(1,1)$ or $(2,2)$ blocks		
$(1,2)$ block		

not the edge is in an off-diagonal block or an on-diagonal block, which includes the parameters relevant to the hypothesis delineated by H_1 (that the network is a planted partition):

```
import statsmodels.api as sm
import pandas as pd
import statsmodels.formula.api as smf
from scipy import stats as spstat

# upper triangle since the network is simple (undirected and loopless)
upper_tri_non_diag = np.triu(np.ones(A.shape), k=1).astype(bool)

df_H1 = pd.DataFrame({"Value" : A[upper_tri_non_diag],
        "Group": (Z[upper_tri_non_diag] != 2).astype(int)})
```

Then, we run a logistic regression model using the `statsmodels` package. We use it to compute the log likelihood ratio statistic. The log likelihood ratio statistic built-in to statistical modeling software will almost always correspond to the $\ell^{(n,0)}$; that is, it will compare the log likelihood ratio of the data under our present hypothesis H_n with the null hypothesis (there is no difference across the samples). We can therefore compute $\ell^{(1,0)}$ directly from the model, and compare to a χ-squared distribution with one degree of freedom:

```
# fit the logistic regression model, regressing the outcome (edge or
    no edge)
# onto the edge group (on-diagonal or off-diagonal), the grouping
# corresponding to H1
model_H1 = smf.logit("Value ~ C(Group)", df_H1).fit()

# compare the likelihood ratio statistic to the chi2 distribution
# with 1 dof to see the fraction that is less than l1
dof = 1
print(f"p-value: {spstat.chi2.sf(model_H1.llr, dof):.3f}")
# p-value: 0.00000
```

Once we know that the data support rejecting the null hypothesis, we run a second test, using the contingency table in Table 6.6. However, as we just learned in the preceding paragraph, the log likelihood ratio statistic directly output by the fit model is:

$$\ell^{(2,0)} = \mathcal{L}(\mathcal{D}; H_2) - \log \mathcal{L}(\mathcal{D}; H_0)$$

which we can use directly to test H_0 that the network is Erdös–Rényi against H_2 that the network is homophilic with potentially heterogeneous on-diagonal blocks.

Table 6.6. Contingency table for testing whether a block model is Erdös–Rényi against whether it is homophilic planted partition.

	Number of edges	Number of nonedges
(1, 1) block		
(1, 2) block		
(2, 2) block		

Importantly, note that this is not the comparison we want to make: Rather, we want to compare whether H_1 the network is a homophilic planted partition against H_2 that the network is homophilic with potentially heterogeneous on-diagonal blocks. A more suitable log likelihood ratio statistic would intuitively be:

$$\ell^{(2,1)} = \mathcal{L}(\mathcal{D}; H_2) - \log \mathcal{L}(\mathcal{D}; H_1),$$

but this is not what statistical modeling software will give us out-of-the-box. Fortunately, this statistic $\ell^{(2,1)}$ is trivial to derive from what we have already learned. Note that:

$$\ell^{(2,0)} - \ell^{(1,0)} = \log \mathcal{L}(\mathcal{D}; H_2) - \log \mathcal{L}(\mathcal{D}; H_0) -$$
$$(\log \mathcal{L}(\mathcal{D}; H_1) - \log \mathcal{L}(\mathcal{D}; H_0))$$
$$= \log \mathcal{L}(\mathcal{D}; H_2) - \mathcal{L}(\mathcal{D}; H_1)$$
$$= \log \left(\frac{\mathcal{L}(\mathcal{D}; H_2)}{\mathcal{L}(\mathcal{D}; H_1)} \right) = \ell^{(2,1)}.$$

So, to compare $\mathcal{L}(\mathcal{D}; H_2)$ with $\mathcal{L}(\mathcal{D}; H_1)$, a suitable approach would be to look at the statistic $\ell^{(2,0)} - \ell^{(1,0)}$. More generally, we have that the log likelihood ratio statistic for hypotheses H_n and H_n' when $H_{n'}$ is nested in H_n is:

$$\ell^{(n,n')} = \ell^{(n,0)} - \ell^{(n',0)}.$$

This means we can directly compare sequential nested hypotheses to one another using sequential log likelihood ratio statistics. Additionally, this result is a basis for why likelihood ratio tests are a powerful tool in the broader field of statistical analysis.

As before, the number of degrees of freedom is the difference between the number of possible parameters in the larger model that allows for a homogeneous block model with potential on-diagonal heterogeneity in the block matrix (here, three; a unique parameter for a, b, and c) and the number of possible parameters in the smaller planted partition model (which was two, a unique parameter for a and b, with $c = a$). This gives us that there is one degree of freedom for our likelihood ratio test:

```
df_H2 = pd.DataFrame({"Value": A[upper_tri_non_diag],
                "Group": Z[upper_tri_non_diag].astype(int)})
model_H2 = smf.logit("Value ~ C(Group)", df_H2).fit()
lr_stat_H2vsH1 = model_H2.llr - model_H1.llr
print(f"p-value: {spstat.chi2.sf(lr_stat_H2vsH1, 1):.7f}")
# 0.00008
```

The p-value is below $\alpha = 0.05$ for this test, too. So, we reject the null hypothesis that the underlying block matrix is a homophilic planted partition, and we conclude that the underlying block matrix is homophilic with heterogeneous on-diagonal blocks.

6.5 The Vertex Nomination Problem

In Section 4.3, we introduced the $SBM_n(\vec{z}, B)$ random network as a conceptual model for many real-world networks. Chapter 5 built spectral embedding techniques that assume an $RDPG_n(X)$, and which can be applied to SBMs. Section 6.1 explored community detection methods for estimating network structure when we do not know the node community in advance. However, in some applications, we do have partial community information. This section addresses the vertex nomination problem, which aims to identify nodes without community assignments that are most similar to a set of nodes with known assignments [8].

We cover the following:

1. Define the vertex nomination problem and its importance in network analysis,
2. Introduce the concept of seed nodes and their role in vertex nomination,
3. Develop spectral vertex nomination techniques using estimated latent positions,
4. Explore extensions of vertex nomination to related problems, and
5. Discuss alternative approaches to vertex nomination beyond spectral methods.

The vertex nomination problem bridges the gap between fully labeled and unlabeled network data, providing a framework for prioritizing nodes for further investigation.

This approach is particularly useful in applications such as social network analysis, where partial information about network covariate structure is often available.

In Case Study 6.5.1, we explore an example in which the vertex nomination problem can be used in practice: human trafficking. This case study will serve as our motivating example for the remainder of the section.

Case Study 6.5.1 Human trafficking and the vertex nomination problem

One of the most important jobs for law enforcement officers is to maintain an understanding of the business dealings of criminals. In recent years, the internet has become a popular medium for sharing and organizing illicit activity. The US Department of Defense released the Memex tool, which facilitates precise searches over isolated web domains.

This has allowed investigators to develop a network with tens of thousands of nodes [8; 9], which represent individual web pages for job postings on the internet. An edge exists between a pair of nodes if the contact information (phone number) or the region (city) on the contact information is the same. A small number of nodes in the network were identified directly as being tied to human trafficking through the content on the webpage or the URL itself. The goal is to produce the set of remaining nodes for which the human trafficking status is unknown which are most likely to be tied to human trafficking, so that the postings can be further monitored and investigated by law enforcement.

We will use an $SBM_n(\vec{z}, B)$ random network with $n = 1000$ nodes representing web pages. The community of each node represents whether the web page is associated with human trafficking: 100 will be associated with human trafficking and 900 will not be associated with human trafficking. Of the 100 web pages associated with human trafficking, we will only know the community label for 20 of them.

```
from graspologic.simulations import sbm

# first 100 nodes are traffickers, second 900 are non-traffickers
ns = [100, 900]
B = np.array([[0.3, 0.1], [0.1, 0.2]])
np.random.seed(0)
A = sbm(ns, B)
```

Figure 6.5.1(A) shows a plot of the adjacency matrix, with the nodes organized by community.

The nomination task here is not just about classification, it is about prioritization. Of the remaining 980 web pages, we want to produce a list of the remaining nodes, which are organized in the order we should prioritize them for further investigation. If we are successful, our nomination list should contain the remaining 80 nodes in the human trafficking community as the highest priority, and the 900 nodes unassociated with human trafficking as lower priority.

6.5.1   The Seed Nodes

The key idea for addressing the vertex nomination problem is the use of *seed nodes*, which are nodes in a network for which we know the true label.

In this case, we know the node labels for 20 of the human traffickers. We will assume that the seed nodes are a random subset of human traffickers.

```
# the number of seed nodes
nseeds = 20
# The first ns[0] nodes are the human traffickers, so choose 20 seeds
# at random
seed_ids = np.random.choice(ns[0], size=20)
```

6.5.2   Spectral Vertex Nomination (svn)

The first step to spectral vertex nomination is to use a spectral embedding to obtain estimated latent positions. We can do this with ase:

```
from graspologic.embed import AdjacencySpectralEmbed as ase

Xhat = ase(n_components=2, svd_seed=0).fit_transform(A)
```

In Figure 6.5.1(B), the estimated latent positions for the seed (the web pages confirmed to be associated with human trafficking, in black) and nonseed (for which the human trafficking status is unknown, in gray) nodes are shown. Based on Sections 5.3 and 6.1, nodes in the same community tend to have similar estimated latent positions. This was a consequence of the fact that the underlying latent positions are identical for nodes in the same community, which we learned from Section 4.7.8.

In Section 5.3, we used the Euclidean distance from Concept 5.3.10 to quantify what we meant by nodes from the same community having "similar" estimated latent

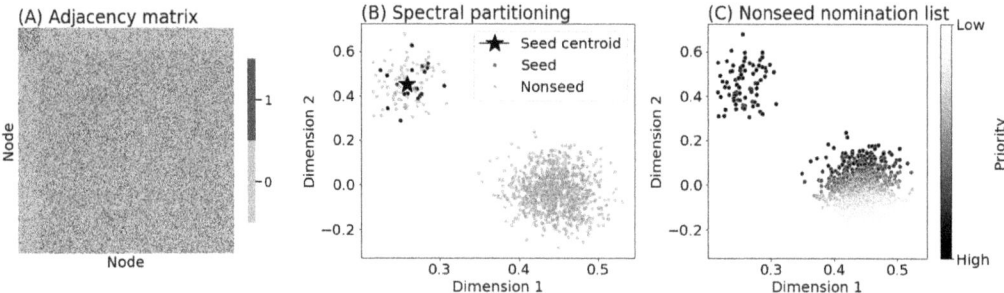

Figure 6.5.1 (**A**) The adjacency matrix for the web page network. (**B**) The estimated latent positions for the nodes in the web page network (faint points). The centroid of the seed nodes is annotated directly. (**C**) The nomination priorities for each of the unlabeled nodes. Nodes which are closer to the seed centroid have higher priority.

positions. When we used KMeans to estimate the unknown community assignments in Section 6.1, the key idea was that we could exploit the fact that nodes in the same community had similar latent positions to identify clusters of nodes which had similar latent positions. This resulted in community-specific mean vectors $\vec{\mu}_k$, and we assigned points to communities depending on their proximity to the community-specific mean vectors.

Here, we use a similar insight. We already know the community assignments for the seed vectors in our community of interest, and all nodes i from the same community have the same underlying latent position $\vec{x}_i$. This property does not hold in the estimated latent positions $\hat{\vec{x}}_i$ for the nodes in the same community, since the latent positions are imperfectly estimated, which we know from Section 5.3.

Since the underlying latent positions of the random network are the same, a reasonable estimated latent position for the community can be obtained by performing a spectral clustering via KMeans:

```
from sklearn.cluster import KMeans

# community detection with kmeans
km_clust = KMeans(n_clusters=2, random_state=0)
km_clust.fit(Xhat)
labels_kmeans = km_clust.fit_predict(Xhat)
```

For each seed node, we can obtain the surrogate for the estimated latent position associated with the community of the seeds by simply finding which of the communities the seeds tended to be assigned to, and then using the centroid associated with this community to find nodes most similar to the seed nodes:

```
from graphbook_code import ohe_comm_vec

# estimated community assignment matrix
Chat = ohe_comm_vec(labels_kmeans)

# get the community (class) with the most seeds
comm_of_seeds = np.argmax(Chat[seed_ids,:].sum(axis=0))
```

```
# get centroid of the community that seeds tend to be
# assigned to
centroid_seeds = km_clust.cluster_centers_[comm_of_seeds]
```

Figure 6.5.1(B) indicates the centroid of the community that the most seed nodes were assigned to with the large star.

Finally, using the Euclidean distance, we can estimate the spatial proximity for each unlabeled node to the centroid that the most the seed nodes were assigned to. We will use this spatial proximity to the centroid as a surrogate for unlabeled nodes being "similar" to the seed nodes in producing our nomination list:

```
from scipy.spatial.distance import cdist
from scipy.stats import rankdata

# compute the distance to the centroid for all estimated latent
    positions
dists_to_centroid = cdist(Xhat, centroid_seeds.reshape(1,
    -1)).reshape(-1)
# compute the node numbers for all the nonseed nodes
nonseed_bool = np.ones((np.sum(ns)))
nonseed_bool[seed_ids] = 0
nonseed_ids = np.array(np.where(nonseed_bool)).reshape(-1)

# isolate the distances to the centroid for the nonseed nodes
nonseed_dists = dists_to_centroid[nonseed_ids]
```

To produce the nomination list, we can sort the distances of the nonseed nodes to the centroid, return the index-sorted ordering, and then output our nomination list by reordering the nonseed indices in order of their distances. The following code will do this:

```
# produce the nomination list
nom_list_nonseeds = np.argsort(nonseed_dists).reshape(-1)
# obtain a nomination list in terms of the original node ids
nom_list = nonseed_ids[nom_list_nonseeds]
```

In Figure 6.5.1(C), we show the nomination priorities for each of the unlabeled nodes by their spatial proximity to the seed centroid. The unlabeled nodes that are closest to the seed centroid tend to have smaller distances, and are hence higher priority in the nomination list (with a smaller numerical label in nom_list).

This procedure is known as the "Spectral Partitioning Nomination Scheme," or sp, and has been studied in several areas of application [8; 9].

6.5.3   Extensions to Other Problems

There are many alternative ways to approach the vertex nomination problem. Let's take a look at a few of them. None of these approaches are "better" or "worse" than others, and each can be leveraged to answer a different network learning question [8; 9; 10; 11; 12]. For any vertex nomination problem, we will need to tailor the strategy based on the network data.

Different Strategies for Spectral Partitioning
We assumed that our network had two communities, and two embedding dimensions, which was largely a function of visual simplicity when viewing the node nominations in Figure 6.5.1(C). However, there is no reason to assume the number of communities or the number of embedding dimensions ahead of time, and we could have used dimensionality selection as in Section 5.7, automated the community selection procedure like we did in Section 6.1, or substituted different clustering algorithms and different notions of similarity.

For instance, GMM is a popular choice for community detection in [9], where the notion of similarity is the probability density of a particular unlabeled point given the mean and variance of the cluster the most seeds are assigned to. This enables robustness to networks where the underlying random network is $DCSBM_n(\vec{z}, \vec{\theta}, B)$, as we learned in Section 6.1.

We also could have used the lse instead of ase as our embedding method if we wanted to use a method more invariant to node degree.

Extending Spectral Partitioning to Related Problems
The spectral partitioning nomination scheme can be extended directly to many other related problems. A key limitation here is that we are assuming that our nodes are in one of two groups, and all of the labeled nodes that we pass in are associated with the same group. Our goal is to prioritize nodes that are also likely from that group.

On the other hand, we could have identified nomination lists on a per-seed-node basis; for example, for each seed node, we could have found a set of unlabeled nodes that have spatially proximal estimated latent positions. This extension provides the intuitive foundation for the *graph matching problem* [8; 12], in Section 7.3.

Ignoring Partitioning Techniques
We could have ignored partitioning and latent community detection approaches entirely, and simply estimated the "centroid" directly by taking the average estimated latent position of all of the seed nodes.

6.6   Out-of-Sample Embedding

So far, the networks we have been using have been relatively small. However, as networks grow larger, the computational cost of embedding methods can become a significant concern. We explored sparse methods for the large network setting in Section 6.2. Now, we address the challenge of embedding large-scale networks and introduce efficient strategies for handling network growth.

We will cover the following topics:

1. Introduction to algorithmic complexity in the context of network embedding,
2. Time and space complexity of spectral embedding methods,
3. Challenges of frequent reembedding in growing networks,

4. Out-of-sample embedding techniques for efficient updating of network representations, and
5. Methods for reusing existing embeddings to incorporate new nodes.

We will begin by discussing the concept of algorithmic complexity, focusing on time complexity (the computational time required) and space complexity (the memory usage in RAM). We will examine how these factors impact the scalability of spectral embedding methods like the singular value decomposition (SVD), which poorly scales as $\mathcal{O}(n^3)$ in time and $\mathcal{O}(n^2)$ in space.

We will then build on our understanding of spectral embedding from Section 5.3 to explore how out-of-sample embedding techniques can alleviate the computational burden of repeatedly embedding large, growing networks. These methods allow us to efficiently update network representations by embedding new nodes without recomputing the entire embedding. Out-of-sample techniques can be particularly valuable in dynamic network settings, such as social networks, where the network structure evolves over time.

Imagine a network where nodes are web pages and edges are whether a pair of web pages cross-link to one another. The network is huge, with $n = 10^9$ nodes, and we suspect that there are homophilic communities (they have high within-community block probabilities). For any given day, we want to have a record of the estimated communities that exist in the network. We learned how to address this task in Section 6.1: We begin by embedding the network, and then we train an unsupervised classifier to identify estimated community structure from the estimated latent positions.

The next day, another $n' = 3$ web pages are added to the network. We could simply reexecute the procedure from the previous day; however, because of time and space complexities, this can quickly become cumbersome and costly.

We would like to find a procedure to estimate the embeddings for our new nodes without recomputing the svd. This is the problem that out-of-sample embedding addresses.

6.6.1   Out-of-Sample Embeddings, a Disclaimer

When we assume that a network A is a sample of an underlying random network $\mathbf{A}$ as in Section 5.3.3, the estimates of latent positions produced by ase tend to be close to the true underlying latent positions in the network (up to an orthogonal transformation). As the network grows, these estimates get increasingly better (on average). This means that if we embedded a network with $n + n'$ nodes, the embedding will be fractionally better than if we had just used n nodes.

This difference, however, will not be particularly substantial if $n \gg n'$. Outside of network learning domains, it is often the case that we might train a machine learning model, and then apply the learned model to new data, without recomputing. In much the same way, we might be willing to trade a slight loss in the precision of our embedding for greater computational and algorithmic efficiency. In these cases, we can use an *out-of-sample embedding*, or oose [13; 14], to embed new nodes (the "out-of-sample" nodes) into an existing latent space computed using only the original nodes (the "in-sample" nodes).

When we do this, we obtain estimated latent positions for our new nodes in a shared space between the new and old nodes. While we might still want to occasionally recompute the full embedding, in the short term we can save a lot of computational resources and still obtain good enough estimated latent positions for downstream analyses.

6.6.2   Adjacency Matrix and Adjacency Vectors for each New Node

For the out-of-sample embedding, we first need an n-node network (the "in-sample" nodes). The crucial ingredient that we will need for the out-of-sample nodes are instructions that tell us how the out-of-sample nodes are connected to the "in-sample" nodes. This is accomplished via adjacency vectors, which can be thought of as behaving like the rows of an adjacency matrix. An *adjacency vector* for a node j in relation to an n-node network is a length-n vector $\vec{a}_j$, where a_{ij} indicates whether node i and node j are connected.

For demonstration purposes, we will generate a sample from an $SBM_n(\vec{z}, B)$ random network with $n + n'$ nodes. The in-sample nodes will be 50 nodes from community 1, and 50 nodes from community 2. The out-of-sample nodes will be 1 node from community 1, and 2 nodes from community 2:

```
import numpy as np
from graspologic.simulations import sbm

# the in-sample nodes
n = 100
nk = 50
# the out-of-sample nodes
np1 = 1; np2 = 2
B = np.array([[0.6, 0.2], [0.2, 0.4]])
# sample network
np.random.seed(0)
A, zs = sbm([nk + np1, nk + np2], B, return_labels=True)
```

Next, we will remove the n' "out-of-sample" nodes with `graspologic`. This will give us an $n \times n$ adjacency matrix corresponding to the subnetwork induced by the in-sample nodes, and an $n \times n'$ matrix A' of adjacency vectors, which indicate the connectivity of out-of-sample nodes to in-sample nodes:

```
from graspologic.utils import remove_vertices

# the indices of the out-of-sample nodes
oos_idx = [nk, nk + np1 + nk, nk + np1 + nk + 1]
# get adjacency matrix and the adjacency vectors A prime
Ain, Aoos = remove_vertices(A, indices=oos_idx, return_removed=True)
```

In Figure 6.6.1(A), we plot the adjacency matrix of the in-sample nodes. Note the modular community structure. In Figure 6.6.1(B), we show the adjacency vectors for each of the three out-of-sample nodes, in relation to the in-sample nodes

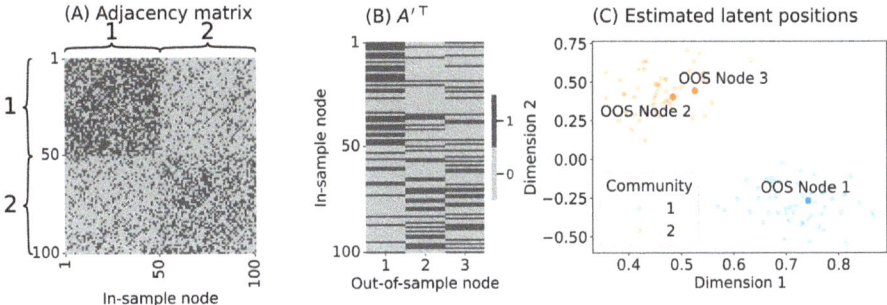

Figure 6.6.1 (**A**) The adjacency matrix for the in-sample nodes. (**B**) The adjacency vectors (columns) for each of the three out-of-sample nodes. (**C**) The estimated latent positions for each of the in-sample nodes (faint blue and red) with the estimated latent positions for the out-of-sample nodes (bold red and blue dots).

from Figure 6.6.1(A). Further, notice that the out-of-sample nodes tend to follow the patterns from their respective communities; out-of-sample node 1 is in community 1, and tends to have more connections with nodes of community 1. Out-of-sample nodes 2 and 3 are in community 2, and tend to have more connections with nodes of community 2.

6.6.3   The Probability Vector for an Out-of-Sample Node

If we add an out-of-sample node j to our simple network, the adjacency matrix for the new network is:

$$A = \begin{bmatrix} A & \vec{a}_j \\ \vec{a}_j^\top & 0 \end{bmatrix},$$

where the j simply denotes that we added the node j to the network, and $\vec{a}_j$ is the adjacency vector for node j. If we assume that this new network is a sample from an $RDPG_{n+1}(X')$ random network, the latent position matrix is:

$$X' = \begin{bmatrix} \vdash & \vec{x}_1^\top & \dashv \\ & \vdots & \\ \vdash & \vec{x}_n^\top & \dashv \\ \vdash & \vec{x}_j^\top & \dashv \end{bmatrix} = \begin{bmatrix} \vdash & X & \dashv \\ \vdash & \vec{x}_j & \dashv \end{bmatrix}, \tag{6.7}$$

where $\vec{x}_j$ is the latent position (the quantity that we want to obtain) associated with our out-of-sample node j, and X is a matrix comprised of latent positions for the other n nodes.

For an $RDPG_{n+1}(X')$ random network, for all pairs of nodes i and i', $p_{ii'} = \vec{x}_i^\top \vec{x}_{i'}$. Therefore, the matrix product $X\vec{x}_j$ is:

$$X\vec{x}_j = \begin{bmatrix} \vdash & \vec{x}_1^\top & \dashv \\ & \vdots & \\ \vdash & \vec{x}_n^\top & \dashv \end{bmatrix} \vec{x}_j = \begin{bmatrix} \vec{x}_1^\top \vec{x}_j \\ \vdots \\ \vec{x}_n^\top \vec{x}_j \end{bmatrix} = \begin{bmatrix} p_{1j} \\ \vdots \\ p_{nj} \end{bmatrix} = \vec{p}_j,$$

where we used the standard rules of matrix multiplication for the second equality, and then used the definition of p_{ij} for the in-sample nodes. We will call this vector $\vec{p}_j$ the probability vector of node j, which has entries p_{ij} for all n in-sample nodes. In particular, this implies that:

$$X\vec{x}_j - \vec{p}_j = \vec{0} = \begin{bmatrix} 0 \\ \vdots \\ 0 \end{bmatrix}, \tag{6.8}$$

where $\vec{0}$ is the n-dimensional 0 vector.

6.6.4   Estimating the Out-of-Sample Node's Latent Position

Our goal is to obtain an estimate of $\vec{x}_j$. In Equation (6.8), we have two unobserved quantities, X and $\vec{p}_j$ (the probability vector for the node j).

6.6.4.1   Estimating the Unobserved Quantities
The Latent Positions of the In-Sample Nodes
Using the notation of Equation (6.7), the probability matrix for our $RDPG_{n+1}(X')$ random network is:

$$P' = X'X'^\top = \begin{bmatrix} & X & \\ \vdash & \vec{x}_j^\top & \dashv \end{bmatrix} \begin{bmatrix} X^\top & \vec{x}_j \\ & \end{bmatrix}$$

$$= \begin{bmatrix} XX^\top & X\vec{x}_j \\ \vec{x}_j^\top X & \vec{x}_j^\top \vec{x}_j \end{bmatrix},$$

where $XX^\top$ is a $n \times n$ probability matrix, $\vec{x}_j^\top X$ is a $1 \times n$ probability vector, $X\vec{x}_j$ is a $n \times 1$ probability vector, and $\vec{x}_j^\top \vec{x}_j$ is a probability. In particular, $P = XX^\top$ is a probability matrix for the subnetwork induced by the first n nodes, and the first n nodes (the in-sample nodes) are an $RDPG_n(X)$ random network.

By the logic that we developed in Section 5.3, we can use ase to estimate latent positions for the in-sample nodes. We do this using graspologic:

```
from graspologic.embed import AdjacencySpectralEmbed as ase

oos_embedder = ase()
# estimate latent positions for the in-sample nodes
# using the subnetwork induced by the in-sample nodes
Xhat_in = oos_embedder.fit_transform(Ain)
```

The in-sample estimated latent positions are shown in Figure 6.6.1(C), with the faint colored nodes. The estimated latent positions are as-described for the estimated latent positions of a two-community $SBM_n(\vec{z}, B)$ random network: two relatively homogeneous (in terms of the latent positions) clusters of nodes. Remember that this is a function of the fact that the latent positions for an $SBM_n(\vec{z}, B)$ random network are identical within-community as-per Section 4.7.8, and the estimated latent positions are estimating the latent positions.

The Probability Vector

Next, we'll estimate $\vec{p}_j$ by solving a least-squares optimization problem.

In Section 5.1, we covered a basic result from probability theory for finding maximum likelihood estimates for coin flips. Recall that we concluded that, if a coin that lands on heads with probability p is flipped m times, giving samples of coin flips y_i, a reasonable estimate of the probability that the coin lands on heads is given by the maximum likelihood estimate (MLE):

$$\hat{p} = \frac{1}{m} \sum_{i=1}^{m} y_i,$$

which is simply the fraction of the m coin flips that landed on heads.

A direct extension of this is that, if we flip the coin only once, the MLE would just be the outcome of that coin flip. With an identical rationale, we estimate $\vec{p}_j$ using:

$$\hat{p}_{ij} = a_{ij}.$$

We estimate the probability $\hat{p}_{ij}$ between an in-sample node i and an out-of-sample node j using the adjacency value a_{ij} between them. Accumulating these $\hat{p}_{ij}$ into a vector over all i in-sample nodes, we will estimate $\hat{\vec{p}}_j$ with $\vec{a}_j$.

$\hat{X}$ is only an estimate of X, and is also inexact (see Section 5.3.3). Likewise, it is unlikely that $\hat{p}_{ij} = p_{ij}$; that is, estimating the probability that the in-sample node i and the out-of-sample node j are connected with a single observation from the adjacency vector is probably not going to give us a particularly exact solution.

We will instead define a least-squares problem using what we established in Equation (6.8) (see Concept 6.6.1 for a refresher). For a more detailed overview, check out [15].

Since our estimates of X via $\hat{X}$ and $\vec{p}_j$ via $\vec{a}_j$ are imperfect, when we plug these into Equation (6.8), our equation becomes:

$$\hat{X}\vec{x}_j - \vec{a}_j = \vec{e}_j,$$

where $\vec{e}_j$ is an n-dimensional error term. In an ideal world, $\vec{e}_j$ would be exactly the zero vector, but since we imperfectly estimated X and $\vec{p}_j$ with $\hat{X}$ and $\vec{a}_j$, this will not be the case. For this reason, we turn to least-squares regression.

Using the normal equations in Remark 6.6.1, the estimate of $\vec{x}_j$ that minimizes the mean-squared error is given by:

$$\hat{\vec{x}}_j = \left(\hat{X}^\top \hat{X} \right)^{-1} \hat{X}^\top \vec{a}_j. \tag{6.9}$$

This estimate $\hat{\vec{x}}_j$ is known as the *least-squares out-of-sample embedding* of the out-of-sample node j.

Concept 6.6.1 Ordinary least-squares (OLS) regression

We observe n samples y_i, along with a set of features $\vec{x}_i$, which is a d-dimensional feature vector for each sample i. The goal of least-squares regression is to identify a set of d coefficients $\vec{\beta}$, where for all n samples:

$$\vec{y} = \begin{bmatrix} y_1 \\ \vdots \\ y_n \end{bmatrix} = X\vec{\beta} = \begin{bmatrix} \vdash & \vec{x}_1^\top & \dashv \\ & \vdots & \\ \vdash & \vec{x}_n^\top & \dashv \end{bmatrix} \begin{bmatrix} \beta_1 \\ \vdots \\ \beta_d \end{bmatrix}.$$

By subtracting $X\beta$ from both sides, we obtain:

$$\vec{y} - X\vec{\beta} = \vec{0}.$$

Unfortunately, samples are noisy in practice, So we are limited to getting a close approximation of each sample:

$$y_i - \vec{x}_i^\top \beta = r_i, \text{ and consequently, } \vec{y} - X\beta = \vec{r},$$

where r_i is known as the residual or error associated with sample i in the regression. We want this residual to be as small as possible. To accomplish this, we minimize the *mean-squared error*, defined as:

$$MSE(\vec{\beta}) = \frac{1}{n} \sum_{i=1}^{n} (r_i)^2 = \frac{1}{n} \|X\vec{\beta} - \vec{y}\|_2^2.$$

Our goal is to find the choice of $\vec{\beta}$ that minimizes the mean-squared error. With a bit of calculus, the solution to this is given in closed form by:

$$\hat{\vec{\beta}} = (X^\top X)^{-1} X^\top \vec{y},$$

which is the *least-squares estimate*.

In the general case when we have n' out-of-sample nodes with adjacency vectors to the in-sample nodes, the least-squares out-of-sample embedding (least-squares oose) for the out-of-sample nodes can be found using the procedure in Algorithm 6.3.

Algorithm 6.3 Least-squares out-of-sample embedding (least-squares oose)

Data: An estimated latent position matrix $\hat{X}$ for the in-sample nodes.
A', an $n \times n'$ matrix whose columns $\vec{a}_j$ indicate the adjacency vectors $\vec{a}_j$ for each of the n' out-of-sample nodes with the in-sample nodes.
Result: $d \times n'$ matrix, whose columns indicate the estimated latent positions for each of the n' out-of-sample nodes.

1 Let $\hat{X}' = \left(\hat{X}^\top \hat{X} \right)^{-1} \hat{X}^\top A'$.

2 **return** $\hat{X}'$

We can perform embed the least-squares `oose` using `graspologic`:

```
Xhat_oos = oos_embedder.transform(Aoos)
```

Figure 6.6.1(C) shows the embedding for the out-of-sample nodes. Note that out-of-sample node 1 was in community 1, and has an estimated latent position near those of the in-sample nodes from community 1. Likewise, the out-of-sample nodes 2 and 3 were in community 2, and have estimated latent positions near the in-sample nodes from community 2. In this sense, least-squares oos has preserved the relative homogeneity in the latent positions within-community for the out-of-sample nodes with respect to the in-sample nodes, without requiring the in-sample network to be reembedded.

6.6.5   Computational Considerations

Recomputing spectral embeddings for a network with n nodes when n' nodes are added would require the computation of an `svd`. The time complexity of the `svd` is $\mathcal{O}\left((n + n')^3\right)$, and the space complexity is $\mathcal{O}\left((n + n')^2\right)$.

On the other hand, the least-squares solution in Algorithm 6.3 has a time complexity of $\mathcal{O}\left(d^2(n + n')\right)$. If the embedding is meaningful, the number of estimated latent dimensions is usually far less than the number of nodes. So this approach has far improved time scalability over reembedding the entire network, because for networks with large numbers of nodes $(n + n')^3$ will be much larger than $d^2(n + n')$.

Space-wise, when the number of in-sample nodes exceeds the number of estimated latent dimensions and the number of out-of-sample nodes, the space complexity to solve a least-squares problem is $\mathcal{O}\left(d(n + n')\right)$. Note that $d(n + n')$ is much less than $(n + n')^2$, so the least-squares problem can be solved with far less space than recomputing the embedding.

Bibliography

[1] Gaussian Mixture Model Ellipsoids; 2023. [Online; accessed Apr. 12, 2023.]

[2] Contributors to Wikimedia projects. Big O notation – Wikipedia; 2023. [Online; accessed Apr. 10, 2023.]

[3] Prakash BA, Sridharan A, Seshadri M, Machiraju S, Faloutsos C. EigenSpokes: Surprising patterns and scalable community chipping in large graphs. In: Advances in Knowledge Discovery and Data Mining. Berlin, Germany: Springer; 2010, pp. 435–448.

[4] Lei J, Rinaldo A. Consistency of spectral clustering in stochastic block models. arXiv. 2013 Dec.

[5] Krzakala F, Moore C, Mossel E, Neeman J, Sly A, Zdeborová L, et al. Spectral redemption in clustering sparse networks. Proc. Natl Acad. Sci. USA. 2013 Dec.;110(52):20935–20940.

[6] Chen Y, Sanghavi S, Xu H. Clustering sparse graphs. Adv. Neur. Info. Proc. Syst. 2012;25.

[7] Athreya A, Fishkind DE, Tang M, Priebe CE, Park Y, Vogelstein JT, et al. Statistical inference on random dot product graphs: A survey. J. Mach. Learn. Res. 2017 Jan.;18(1):8393–8484.

[8] Fishkind DE, Lyzinski V, Pao H, Chen L, Priebe CE. Vertex nomination schemes for membership prediction. Ann. Appl. Stat. 2015 Sep.;9(3):1510–1532. [Online; accessed Apr. 16, 2023.]

[9] Yoder J, Chen L, Pao H, Bridgeford E, Levin K, Fishkind D, et al. Vertex nomination: The canonical sampling and the extended spectral nomination schemes. arXiv. 2018 Feb.

[10] Coppersmith GA, Priebe CE. Vertex nomination via content and context. arXiv. 2012 Jan.

[11] Coppersmith G. Vertex nomination. WIREs Comput. Stat. 2014 Mar.;6(2):144–153.

[12] Fishkind DE, Adali S, Patsolic HG, Meng L, Singh D, Lyzinski V, et al. Seeded graph matching. Pattern Recognit. 2019 Mar.;87:203–215.

[13] Levin K, Roosta F, Mahoney M, Priebe C. Out-of-Sample Extension of Graph Adjacency Spectral Embedding. In: International Conference on Machine Learning. PMLR; 2018, pp. 2975–2984.

[14] Bengio Y, Paiement Jf, Vincent P, Delalleau O, Roux N, Ouimet M. Out-of-sample extensions for LLE, isomap, MDS, eigenmaps, and spectral clustering. Adv. Neur. Info. Proc. Syst. 2003;16.

[15] Géron A. Hands-On Machine Learning with Scikit-Learn and TensorFlow. Sebastopol, CA, USA: O'Reilly Media, Inc.; 2017.

7 Applications for Two Networks

This chapter focuses on the case of two networks. With two networks, we encounter additional algorithmic complexities, but we can also address new questions.

When we have two sufficiently similar networks, we can make explicit comparisons across them. We assume the networks have the same nodes, with only the edges differing. In this case, we can learn properties of network models and make comparisons between the networks by studying how these properties change between them. We end the chapter by discussing strategies to align (or, *match*) the nodes when they are permuted (or, nonoverlapping, in the case where networks only share a subset of nodes) between the networks.

Here are the main topics we cover:

1. Section 7.1 introduces two-sample testing for networks, and how we can use bootstrapping coupled with our statistical models to compare networks.
2. Section 7.2 covers two-sample testing for stochastic block models (SBMs). We develop machinery specific to SBMs that explicitly leverages their block structure.
3. Section 7.3 discusses the graph matching problem. We address the challenge of identifying a correspondence, or a way to match, the nodes from one network to the nodes of another, and techniques for overcoming problems where some of the nodes may not be the same from one network to the next.

These tools are essential for analyzing evolving networks, comparing networks from different sources, and integrating network data across multiple domains.

7.1 Two-Sample Testing for Networks

Coauthored with Sambit Panda

In Chapter 5, we introduced several spectral embeddings for networks, including `ase` and `lse`. Chapter 6 demonstrated how these tools enable various network analyses, such as for community detection (Section 6.1), vertex nomination (6.5), and out of sample embedding (6.6). Remark 5.5.5 highlighted a limitation: Nonidentifiability prevents direct comparison of spectral embeddings across networks.

We now turn to techniques comparing two networks. We begin by extending the two-sample testing framework from Section 6.3, which compared edge clusters within a single network. Our goal is to determine whether two network observations are sampled from the same random network, or from different random networks.

We will:

1. Develop statistical tests for comparing latent position matrices across networks,
2. Introduce nonparametric techniques for testing differences in network distributions,
3. Explore methods to evaluate structural changes in networks over time, and
4. Examine applications of two-sample testing in network comparison problems.

We apply these techniques to SBMs in Section 7.2. Section 8.1 extends these ideas to timeseries sequences of networks.

We return to the alien and human brain networks example from Box 5.5.1. There are $n = 100$ brain areas, which represent the nodes of the network. This time, we find a third group of aliens, and their brain structure is much more similar to humans than our original group of aliens (they are still homophilic). However, this group of aliens tends to have heterogeneities in the node degrees: Nodes with lower indices have a higher degree than nodes with higher indices. The human brains tend to have more homogeneous structurings.

Imagine that we have one human brain and one alien brain:

```
from graspologic.simulations import sbm
import numpy as np
from graphbook_code import dcsbm, generate_dcsbm_pmtx, \
                  generate_sbm_pmtx


n = 100 # the number of nodes
# human brains have homophilic block structure
Bhum = np.array([[0.2, 0.02], [0.02, 0.2]])
# alien brains add degree-correction
theta_alien = np.tile(np.linspace(1.5, 0.5, n // 2), 2)

# generate human and alien brain network
np.random.seed(0)
A_human, z = sbm([n // 2, n // 2], Bhum, return_labels=True)
A_alien = dcsbm(z, theta_alien, Bhum)

Phum = generate_sbm_pmtx(z, Bhum)
Palien = generate_dcsbm_pmtx(z, theta_alien, Bhum)
```

Plots of the networks are shown in Figure 7.1.1, where their underlying probability matrices are shown in parts (A) and (C). Note that the degree-correction factor for the alien brain network has led to the nodes with lower indices in each community having higher probabilities of being connected to other nodes. Samples of the human and alien brain networks are in (B) and the alien brain network in (D). It is less obvious that the networks are different when we look at the network samples.

Just like when we were flipping coins we could not immediately conclude that two coins were different because they produced a different number of heads in a given number of flips, it would be unwise to conclude that the networks differ fundamentally (that is, they have different probability matrices) because the samples look different.

For this reason, it is important for us to build out our two-sample testing procedures, so that we can determine whether the networks differ.

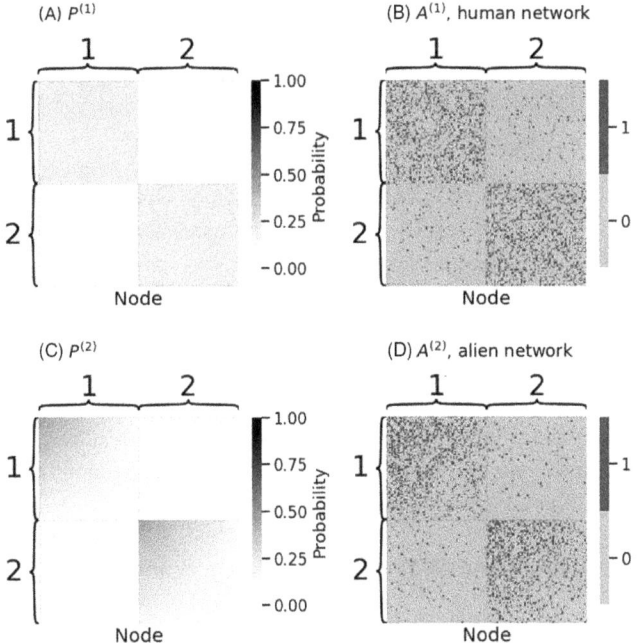

(A) $P^{(1)}$

(B) $A^{(1)}$, human network

(C) $P^{(2)}$

(D) $A^{(2)}$, alien network

Figure 7.1.1 (**A**) Probability matrix underlying human brain network, (**B**) brain network from human, (**C**) probability matrix underlying alien brain network, and (**D**) brain network from alien.

7.1.1   Two-Sample Tests and Random Networks

When we observe two random networks $\mathbf{A}^{(1)}$ and $\mathbf{A}^{(2)}$, we first need to determine appropriate models. If we make the assumption that these random networks are $IER_n\left(P^{(m)}\right)$ from Section 4.1, the broadest class of independent-edge random network models, then the probability matrix encodes the differences between the two random networks. Therefore, our question is:

$$H_0: P^{(1)} = P^{(2)} \text{ against } H_A: P^{(1)} \neq P^{(2)}, \tag{7.1}$$

or whether the edge probability matrices are the same (under the null hypothesis) against that the edge probability matrices differ (under the alternative hypothesis). This is exactly the same question asked about determining whether two coins are different, but generalized to $n \times n$ probability matrices.

The $IER_n\left(P^{(m)}\right)$ random networks are difficult to deal with directly using only a single network sample. This means that testing the hypotheses in Equation (7.1) is impractical with only two networks, because there is only one sample $a_{ij}^{(m)}$ to base the estimate of $p_{ij}^{(m)}$ on.

7.1.2   Latent Position Testing

For this reason, it is typical to make further assumptions about the network structure. From Section 5.3, it is often reasonable to assume that the random networks are

$RDPG_n\left(X^{(m)}\right)$, with latent position matrices $X^{(m)}$. The latent position matrix $X^{(m)}$ fully describes the probability matrix $P^{(m)}$, so it would be equivalent to compare the latent positions directly:

$$H_0: X^{(1)} = X^{(2)} \text{ against } H_A: X^{(1)} \neq X^{(2)}, \tag{7.2}$$

Unfortunately, owing to the nonidentifiability problem in Section 5.5.2, this hypothesis would not be entirely accurate as-written. For a network with a latent position matrix $X^{(m)}$, for any $d \times d$ orthogonal matrix W:

$$P^{(m)} = X^{(m)} X^{(m)\top} = X^{(m)} W W^\top X^{(m)\top}.$$

This means that even if $P^{(1)}$ and $P^{(2)}$ were identical, they could still have different latent position matrices; particularly, if W is a $d \times d$ orthogonal matrix, we could have $X^{(2)} = X^{(1)}W$ be an orthogonal transform of the first latent position matrix. For this reason, we will make our hypothesis "robust" to this challenge, and test:

$$H_0: X^{(1)} = W X^{(2)} \text{ for some orthogonal matrix } W$$
$$H_A: X^{(1)} \neq W X^{(2)} \text{ for any orthogonal matrix } W. \tag{7.3}$$

The null hypothesis is that the latent positions are identical up to an orthogonal transform (for some possible orthogonal matrix), and our alternative hypothesis is that the latent positions are not orthogonal transforms of one another (for any possible orthogonal matrix).

7.1.2.1 Learning Orthogonal Transforms from the Data

From Section 5.3, we know that we can obtain estimates of $X^{(m)}$ by using the ase, where $\widehat{X}^{(m)} = \text{ase}\left(A^{(m)}\right)$. How do we account for the possibility that $X^{(1)}$ and $X^{(2)}$ are orthogonal transforms of one another?

The Orthogonal Procrustes Problem

To estimate a possible orthogonal transform, we will need to set up an optimization problem. Our goal is to find the best possible orthogonal transform of $X^{(2)}$ onto $X^{(1)}$. This method involves a matrix norm, the Frobenius norm, which we introduced in Concept 5.5.4.

By the "best" possible orthogonal transform, we mean the orthogonal transform where the Frobenius distance between $X^{(1)}$ and $X^{(2)}$ is minimized. We can describe our goal as:

$$\text{find } W \text{ where } \left\| X^{(1)} - X^{(2)} W \right\|_F \text{ is minimized.}$$

We can equivalently write this goal as:

$$\widehat{W} = \text{argmin}_W \left\| X^{(1)} - X^{(2)} W \right\|_F. \tag{7.4}$$

The idea is that if $X^{(1)}$ and $X^{(2)}$ are orthogonal transforms of one another, the solution to this optimization problem is the $d \times d$ orthogonal matrix $\widehat{W}$ that properly aligns them. If such a matrix exists, the function $\left\| X^{(1)} - X^{(2)} \widehat{W} \right\|_F$ that we are minimizing will have a value of 0 when we find the correct orthogonal matrices because the transformed latent position matrices will be identical. The problem of solving for optimal orthogonal transforms in Equation (7.4) is known as the *orthogonal Procrustes problem*.

In practice, we only have estimates $\widehat{X}^{(1)}$ and $\widehat{X}^{(2)}$, so we will not find the perfect orthogonal transform of $\widehat{X}^{(1)}$ onto $\widehat{X}^{(2)}$ (even if such an orthogonal transform exists for $X^{(1)}$ and $X^{(2)}$, because estimates using samples from random networks are imperfect). Therefore, when we minimize $\left\| \widehat{X}^{(1)} - \widehat{X}^{(2)} W \right\|_F$, we will just want the $\widehat{W}$ that makes them the most similar in terms of the Frobenius distance. If $X^{(1)}$ and $X^{(2)}$ are the same, we would expect that $\left\| \widehat{X}^{(1)} - \widehat{X}^{(2)} \widehat{W} \right\|_F$ would take a small value.

We can code this up as:

```
from scipy.linalg import orthogonal_procrustes
from graspologic.embed import AdjacencySpectralEmbed as ase

d = 2
# estimate latent positions for alien and human networks
Xhat_human = ase(n_components=d).fit_transform(A_human)
Xhat_alien = ase(n_components=d).fit_transform(A_alien)
# estimate best possible orthogonal transform of Xhat_alien to
    Xhat_human by
# solving orthogonal procrustes problem
W = orthogonal_procrustes(Xhat_alien, Xhat_human)[0]
observed_norm = np.linalg.norm(Xhat_human - Xhat_alien @ W, ord="fro")
```

This gives us the value shown in Figure 7.1.2(A), in red.

Estimating a p-Value
In Section 6.3.1, we looked at how well the data reflect the null hypothesis. Here, this is whether the latent positions for our networks are identical up to an orthogonal transform.

With estimates computed from the data, we can determine directly by the nature of the data and our assumptions exactly how "anomalous" the observed difference is relative to what we would expect under the null hypothesis. In the case of the contingency tables from Section 6.3.1, Fisher's exact test used the assumptions that the two

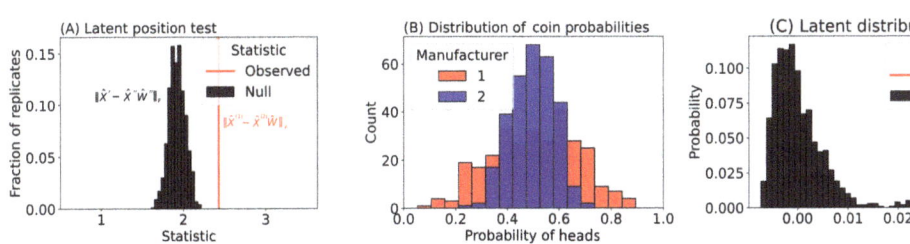

Figure 7.1.2 **(A)** The observed statistic from the data (red) compared to a histogram from the $r = 100$ parametric replicates (black). **(B)** A comparison of the probabilities for two buckets of coins of landing on heads, where each coin has a different probability. **(C)** The observed statistic from the data (red) compared to a histogram from the $r = 100$ replicates (black). Figures were produced with `nrep=1000` to smooth out the null distributions, rather than `nrep=100` as indicated in the text.

samples were independent binary events to compute how anomalous the contingency table that we observed was.

In this case, however, without more assumptions we can't quite compute this value exactly. In the interest of keeping assumptions to a minimum, a popular strategy is to use a *bootstrap*, a technique which attempts to quantify the sampling distribution of some numerical quantity that is computed from the data (a *statistic*). The *sampling distribution* refers to the distribution of the statistic, in this case $\left\| \widehat{X}^{(1)} - \widehat{X}^{(2)} \widehat{W} \right\|_F$.

To do this, we will use the parameter $\widehat{X}^{(1)}$ as the latent position matrix to generate two new random networks, $\mathbf{A}'$ and $\mathbf{A}''$. Then, we will generate two new samples of these random networks:

```python
from graspologic.simulations import rdpg

def generate_synthetic_networks(X):
    """
    A function which generates two synthetic networks with
    same latent position matrix X.
    """
    A1 = rdpg(X, directed=False, loops=False)
    A2 = rdpg(X, directed=False, loops=False)
    return A1, A2

Ap, App = generate_synthetic_networks(Xhat_human)
```

We then use these two new networks, and again estimate latent position matrices for these:

```python
def compute_latent(A, d):
    """
    A function which returns the latent position estimate
    for an adjacency matrix A.
    """
    return ase(n_components=d).fit_transform(A)

Xhat_p = compute_latent(Ap, d)
Xhat_pp = compute_latent(App, d)
```

Finally, just like we aligned $\widehat{X}^{(1)}$ and $\widehat{X}^{(2)}$ via the "optimal orthogonal transform" $\widehat{W}$, we will align $\widehat{X}'$ and $\widehat{X}''$ via the "optimal orthogonal transform" $\widehat{W}'$. Then, we recompute our statistic of interest $\left\| \widehat{X}' - \widehat{X}'' \widehat{W}' \right\|_F$ using these new samples, where the underlying latent positions were truly identical:

```python
def compute_norm_orth_proc(A, B):
    """
    A function which finds the best orthogonal transform
    of B onto A, and then computes and returns the norm.
    """
    R = orthogonal_procrustes(B, A)[0]
    return np.linalg.norm(A - B @ R)

norm_null = compute_norm_orth_proc(Xhat_p, Xhat_pp)
```

We keep repeating this process. Over time, we get some idea of what $\left\| \widehat{X}^{(1)} - \widehat{X}^{(2)} \widehat{W} \right\|_F$ would look like if the true latent positions $X^{(1)}$ and $X^{(2)}$ were identical up to an orthogonal transform by W. This is known as a *parametric bootstrap*. It is called *parametric* because we are using the assumption that the networks are RDPGs to generate what $\widehat{X}^{(1)}$ and $\widehat{X}^{(2)}$ would look like under the null hypothesis.

The statistics we generate in this matter are collectively called the *parametric null replicates*. Figure 7.1.2(A) indicates these in black. These statistics are less extreme than the one that we observed from the data, shown in red.

The following code will repeat this procedure $r = 100$ times (the number of parametric null replicates), and keep track of the computed statistics under the null hypothesis:

```
def parametric_resample(A1, A2, d, nreps=100):
    """
    A function to generate samples of the null distribution under H0
    using parametric resampling.
    """
    null_norms = np.zeros(nreps)
    Xhat1 = compute_latent(A1, d)
    for i in range(0, nreps):
        Ap, App = generate_synthetic_networks(Xhat1)
        Xhat_p = compute_latent(Ap, d)
        Xhat_pp = compute_latent(App, d)
        null_norms[i] = compute_norm_orth_proc(Xhat_p, Xhat_pp)
    return null_norms

nreps = 100
null_norms = parametric_resample(A_alien, A_human, 2, nreps=nreps)
```

What we see is that $||\widehat{X}^{(p)} - \widehat{X}^{(r)}\widehat{W}||_F$ is much larger than the almost all of the values of $||\widehat{X}' - \widehat{X}''\widehat{W}'||_F$ that we calculated. We will use this to estimate a p-value, and we will say that the p-value of H_0 against H_A is the fraction of times that when the underlying latent positions were equal (for each replicate of our parametric bootstrap), the value of the statistic that we calculated from the observed data exceeded the statistic that we calculated from the replicate. We add one to the numerator and denominator, since we observed one instance of a value at least as big as that in the observed data: the observed data themselves.

This means our p-value is:

```
pval = ((null_norms >= observed_norm).sum() + 1)/(nreps + 1)
print(f"estimate of p-value: {pval:.5f}")
# estimate of p-value: 0.00990
```

We then repeat this process, but we use $A^{(2)}$ as our reference network instead of $A^{(1)}$. The overall p-value is the maximum of the two p-values produced with this procedure.

This is called the *latent position test*, and it is implemented directly by graspologic. Note that the p-value that we obtain from this process will likely differ every time we run the test, since there is randomness in the generation process of the A's and the A''s for every time we repeated the comparison. Making the number of repetitions larger by setting n_bootstraps to a higher value will tend to yield more stable p-value estimates for when we estimate p-values using resampling techniques:

```
from graspologic.inference import latent_position_test

nreps = 100 # the number of null replicates
lpt = latent_position_test(A_human, A_alien, n_bootstraps = nreps,
    n_components=d, workers=-1)
print("estimate of p-value: {:.5f}".format(lpt[1]))
# estimate of p-value: 0.00990
```

The p-value is low, and below a typical decision threshold of $\alpha = 0.05$. This means we have evidence to reject the null hypothesis in favor of the alternative: The latent position matrix for a human brain network differs from the latent position matrix for an alien brain network (by more than just an orthogonal transform).

Next, let's see what happens if we have two networks with the same underlying latent position matrices. We'll make a second network from a human, and use the latent position test to determine whether the networks have identical latent position matrices (up to an orthogonal transform):

```
# generate a new human brain network with same block matrix
A_human2 = sbm([n // 2, n // 2], Bhum)

lpt_hum2hum = latent_position_test(A_human, A_human2,
    n_bootstraps=nreps, n_components=d, workers=-1)
print("estimate of p-value: {:.5f}".format(lpt_hum2hum[1]))
# estimate of p-value: 0.41584
```

The p-value is relatively large, so with $\alpha = 0.05$, we fail to reject the null hypothesis. We conclude that our data do not support that our two human networks have different underlying latent position matrices. The latent position test is described in [1].

7.1.3 Latent Distribution Testing

The latent position test allows us to determine whether the latent position matrices for two random networks differ, using the realizations of our network with the estimated latent position matrices. With latent distribution testing, we instead ask: Are the latent positions themselves fundamentally different, across all nodes, for the two random networks?

To motivate a latent distribution test, we start with another coin example. Imagine that two people have containers of 300 coins that were created by different coin manufacturers. Each container has coins that are not necessarily fair (their probabilities of landing on heads may differ slightly from 0.5, due to, say, manufacturing tolerances in coin construction). Each of these 300 coins can be identified as the coin $\mathbf{x}_i^{(1)}$ or $\mathbf{x}_i^{(2)}$, the ith coin in each of the two containers from the different coin manufacturers.

The outcomes $\mathbf{x}_i^{(1)}$ and $\mathbf{x}_i^{(2)}$ are random. These coins all have different probabilities of landing on heads, $\mathbf{p}_i^{(1)}$ and $\mathbf{p}_i^{(2)}$, again for each of the manufacturers respectively, and the probabilities that the coins land on heads is random too. Let's say, for sake of example, that on average, both coin manufacturers produce fair coins (the average probability of landing on heads is 0.5). However, for one manufacturer of coins,

---

Concept 7.1.1 The basics of the Beta distribution

The *Beta distribution* is a continuous probability distribution for probabilities. In particular, if $\mathbf{p}$ is a $Beta(\alpha, \beta)$ random variable, samples p are probabilities (they are values which will fall between 0 and 1). The expected value of $Beta(\alpha, \beta)$ random variables is given by:

$$\mathbb{E}[\mathbf{p}] = \frac{\alpha}{\alpha + \beta},$$

and the variance of $Beta(\alpha, \beta)$ random variables is given by:

$$\text{var}(\mathbf{p}) = \frac{\alpha\beta}{(\alpha + \beta)^2(\alpha + \beta + 1)}.$$

---

the variability of this probability exceeds the other. We can do this with the Beta distribution, described in Concept 7.1.1:

```
ncoins = 300 # the number of coins in each container

# the probabilities from container 1 landing on heads
# with a much larger variance
pi1 = np.random.beta(a=4, b=4, size=ncoins)

# the probabilities of container 2 landing on heads,
# with a much smaller variance
pi2 = np.random.beta(a=15, b=15, size=ncoins)
```

Using the logic that we have developed thus far, we could directly compare the coins themselves to test whether each individual coin is different from one manufacturer to the next. However, there are more interesting questions that we could ask about the coins from the different manufacturers. In particular, we might ask, even though the two containers may contain coins with the same probability (on average) of landing on heads, does one manufacturer have tighter tolerances for their coins' variability? Formally, we might ask:

$$H_0: \text{var}\left(\mathbf{p}_i^{(1)}\right) = \text{var}\left(\mathbf{p}_i^{(2)}\right) \text{ against } H_A: \text{var}\left(\mathbf{p}_i^{(1)}\right) \neq \text{var}\left(\mathbf{p}_i^{(2)}\right).$$

Histograms of the probabilities $p_i^{(m)}$ underlying the 300 coins for each bucket are illustrated in Figure 7.1.2(B). Note that even though the two containers appear to contain coins with approximately the same average probability of landing on heads (about 0.5), the second manufacturer has much tighter tolerances than the first manufacturer. The histogram for the second manufacturer is much narrower than the first, indicating that the second manufacturer has lower variance to the probabilities of the coins landing on heads.

Much the same, we could assume that not only are the latent positions for humans and aliens different, but random too, like the probabilities of the coins. When we say that the latent position matrices are random, we mean that the latent position vectors

Concept 7.1.2 Independence testing and two-sample testing

A common scenario in machine learning involves two random quantities, $\mathbf{x}_i$ and $\mathbf{y}_i$. We suspect that for each i, $\mathbf{x}_i$ and $\mathbf{y}_i$ are drawn in a related manner. This idea is captured by a "joint distribution," meaning that $(\mathbf{x}_i, \mathbf{y}_i)$ for each i are sampled from some distribution $F_{\mathbf{x}, \mathbf{y}}$. For example, a joint distribution could be the *multivariate normal distribution*, where each dimension of a random vector follows a normal distribution. If we assume that the pair $(\mathbf{x}_i, \mathbf{y}_i)$ are multivariate normally distributed, then $\mathbf{x}_i$ is a $\mathcal{N}(\mu_x, \sigma_x)$ random variable, $\mathbf{y}_i$ is a $\mathcal{N}(\mu_y, \sigma_y)$ random variable, and $\text{corr}(\mathbf{x}_i, \mathbf{y}_i) = \rho$ is their correlation.

A formulation of our question is known as the *independence testing problem* and can be written:

$$H_0 : F_{x,y} = F_x F_y \text{ against } H_A : F_{x,y} \neq F_x F_y$$

which tests whether $\mathbf{x}_i$ and $\mathbf{y}_i$ are independent against the alternative they are not. The independence testing problem assumes nothing about the distribution or nature of $\mathbf{x}_i$ or $\mathbf{y}_i$ (they could be either random variables or vectors, for instance). If $\mathbf{y}_i$ takes one of two possible values, the two-sample test can be reformulated as an independence test. Thus, independence tests can serve as an alternative for two-sample tests.

$\vec{x}_i^{(1)}$ and $\vec{x}_i^{(2)}$ for each of the n total nodes may not be fixed quantities, but observations of random variables $\vec{\mathbf{x}}_i^{(1)}$ and $\vec{\mathbf{x}}_i^{(2)}$ associated with probability distributions.

The idea is that the latent position vectors for each node $\vec{\mathbf{x}}_i^{(1)}$ and $\vec{\mathbf{x}}_i^{(2)}$ may have underlying parameters as well, just like the random probabilities of heads for the coins in our earlier example. The characteristics that determine how the human or alien latent position vectors can be realized are governed by the distributions of these vectors. We use the symbol $F^{(1)}$ and $F^{(2)}$, respectively, to denote the distribution of the humans' latent position vectors and the aliens' latent position vectors, respectively. When we ask questions about whether $\mathbf{P}^{(1)}$ and $\mathbf{P}^{(2)}$ differ, we are no longer checking whether the latent positions themselves are different, but whether the distributions of these latent positions are different. Note that the latent position vectors $\vec{\mathbf{x}}_i^{(m)}$ are random, and consequently, the latent position matrices $\mathbf{X}^{(m)}$ are also random. Since $\mathbf{P}^{(m)} = \mathbf{X}^{(m)} \mathbf{X}^{(m)\top}$, the probability matrices are random as well. Hence, the probability matrices are bold-faced here.

As before, we will design null and alternative hypotheses. The null hypothesis will be that $H_0: F^{(1)} = F^{(2)} W$, which means that the distributions of the latent positions are the same. Like before, we allow for a possible orthogonal matrix W. The alternative hypothesis will be that the latent positions for the humans and the aliens have a different distribution for any possible orthogonal transformation, $H_A: F^{(1)} \neq F^{(2)} W$.

We will assume as little as possible about the distributions for the latent positions. Two good ways to do this are by using distance correlation [2] or the multiscale generalized correlation (MGC) [3], which are two approaches for independence testing. The connection between independence testing and two-sample testing is described briefly in Concept 7.1.2. For this we can use `graspologic`, through the `latent_distribution_test` function:

```
from graspologic.inference import latent_distribution_test

nreps = 100
approach = 'mgc' # the strategy for the latent distribution test
ldt_dcorr = latent_distribution_test(A_human, A_alien, test=approach,
    metric="euclidean", n_bootstraps=nreps, workers=-1)
print("estimate of p-value: {:.5f}".format(ldt_dcorr.pvalue))
# estimate of p-value: 0.00990
```

For the latent distribution test, we again look at the *p*-value:

```
print("estimate of p-value: {:.4f}".format(ldt_dcorr[1]))
```

The null replicates against the observed test statistic are shown in Figure 7.1.2(C). For more details on this approach, check out [4].

7.1.4   The Latent Distribution Test versus the Latent Position Test

The latent distribution test is nonparametric because it does not make the assumption that the networks are RDPGs with fixed latent position matrices. In this sense, the latent distribution test tends to be a little bit more general than the latent position test, and will tend to be more conservative. In statistics, a *conservative* test is a testing procedure which tends to err on the side of caution: The *p*-values, and consequently the conclusions, will tend to err towards shying away from rejecting the null hypothesis. When we obtain results in favor of rejecting H_0 in favor of H_A with conservative tests (such as a small *p*-value), we have a little bit more confidence that our results hold up to scrutiny. This comes with the caveat that, since the test is conservative (and therefore will tend to prioritize rejecting H_0 in favor of H_A only when the data support a high degree of evidence to do so), that we will end up with fewer discoveries of potentially truthful differences between our networks.

Moreover, the latent position test assumes that the two networks are node-matched: Node 1 in the first network has the same interpretation as node 1 in the second network, and so on for all n nodes in the network. The latent distribution test does not make this rather limiting assumption: We can perform a latent distribution test when the nodes differ both in interpretation (nodes don't need to be matched) and in number. This makes the latent distribution test more flexible than the latent position test.

Generalizing to Other Network Models

The results in this section generalize directly to all random network models which can be described as $RDPG_n(X)$ random networks. This includes any network model where the probability matrix has a positive semidefinite structure. As we learned in Section 4.5, many network models have this structure, such as DCSBMs and SBMs with positive semidefinite block matrices.

The utility of these techniques, however, generalizes beyond just the $RDPG_n(X)$ random networks, and probably (but not provably) includes some types of GRDPG random networks. This is because the primary piece of information that is needed to motivate the techniques described here is that $\widehat{X}^{(1)}$ and $\widehat{X}^{(2)}$ are reasonable (unbiased and consistent) estimates of the latent position matrices $X^{(1)}$ and $X^{(2)}$ (up to an orthogonal transformation). In Section 5.7.3, we saw that spectral embedding techniques can produce similarly reasonable estimates of latent position matrices for GRDPG random networks. While there is no direct theory that asserts that the latent position and latent distribution tests are appropriate for GRDPG, it is reasonable to expect them to apply for GRDPG (with potentially nonpositive semidefinite probability matrices), and this is empirically true in practice. For the latent position test, a key modification would be that the parametric bootstrap would need to consider samples from GRDPG random networks, and not $RDPG_n(X)$ random networks.

Appendix A.6 discusses the foundational assumptions for the latent distribution test, the a posteriori random dot product graph. Appendix B.2 discusses the implications of latent distribution testing with respect to spectral embeddings.

7.2   Two-Sample Testing for SBMs

In Section 7.1, we introduced a framework for comparing two networks using latent position testing. We found that for networks characterized by RDPGs, we could test whether the latent positions for the underlying RDPGs are the same by taking advantage of the orthogonal Procrustes method to find orthogonal transformations that allow us to avoid the nonidentifiability problem. This approach extends to positive semidefinite block models, including SBMs (Section 4.3) and DCSBMs (Section 4.7), as discussed in Section 4.11.3.

While the latent position test is generalizable, it may disregard specific features of block models that could yield more sensitive and specific tests. This section develops machinery tailored to SBMs, leveraging their explicit community structure. We will:

1. Explore how incorporating model-specific features can improve test sensitivity,
2. Develop test statistics that explicitly account for SBM community structure,
3. Compare the performance of SBM-specific tests to more general approaches, and
4. Discuss practical considerations for choosing between general and specific tests.

SBMs are a widely used model in network analysis, and model-specific tests can often detect differences with smaller sample sizes than more general approaches. Building model-specific intuition for this model can therefore be helpful for building model-specific intuition more generally. This exploration builds on concepts from maximum likelihood estimation (Section 5.1), hypothesis testing (Section 6.3), and model selection (Section 6.4).

In Section 4.5.8, we learned that the latent position matrix for positive semidefinite block matrices is a function of the community assignment vector and the block matrix. Therefore, if two networks have the same community assignment vectors but their positive semidefinite block matrices are unequal, their latent position matrices are unequal. In this case, we can use the machinery that we developed in Section 7.1 directly to test whether the block matrices are unequal.

However, we can approach this question more directly for SBMs by testing whether the block matrices are unequal directly. In Case Study 7.2.1, we develop an interstate traffic pattern example we will work with for this section.

Case Study 7.2.1 Traffic patterns

Transit planners are determining how to allocate resources for a new high-speed rail project. To do so, the planners seek to understand vehicular traffic patterns, to prioritize which routes could benefit from additional public transit options, and how those options could be best offered to offset traffic congestion. We have two networks which summarize the traffic patterns amongst $n = 100$ interstate exits (represented by the nodes in our network) across $K = 3$ states (represented by the communities in our network). The first 45 exits are in New York (NY, the first community), the second 30 exits are in New Jersey (NJ, the second community), and the third 25 exits are in Pennsylvania (PA, the third community).

We measure the number of drivers who commute from one exit to another over the course of a month through highway toll records. If more than 1000 drivers make the commute more than five times over a single interval, we add an edge between the pair of exits. We know that people commute more frequently within their state, so the probability that an edge exists between pairs of exits in the same state exceeds the probability that an edge exists between pairs of exits which are not in the same state. Further, people tend to commute more frequently to states they are next to; e.g., drivers are more likely to commute to New York from New Jersey than from Pennsylvania, because Pennsylvania is generally farther away from New York than New Jersey.

The first goal for transit planners is to determine whether there is a time effect to the highway networks; that is, whether (and how) the networks differ during the day versus night. We measure over two time windows: 7 a.m. and 7 p.m. (covering the bulk of the work day), and between 7 p.m. and 7 a.m. (covering the bulk of night time). We know that a lot of people in New Jersey tend to commute to New York for the work day, so the probability of an edge existing between a New Jersey exit and a New York exit are higher during the day than the night.

Let's generate the community assignment vector and the block matrices for the day and night time for Case Study 7.2.1. The day time network will be network (1), and the night time network will be network (2):

```
import numpy as np
from graspologic.simulations import sbm

ns = [45, 30, 25] # number of exits

states = ["NY", "NJ", "PA"]
# z is a column vector indicating which state each exit is in
z = np.repeat(states, ns)

Bnight = np.array([[.3, .2, .05], [.2, .3, .05], [.05, .05, .3]])
```

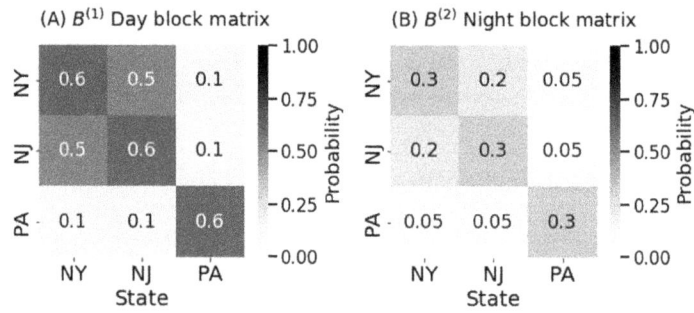

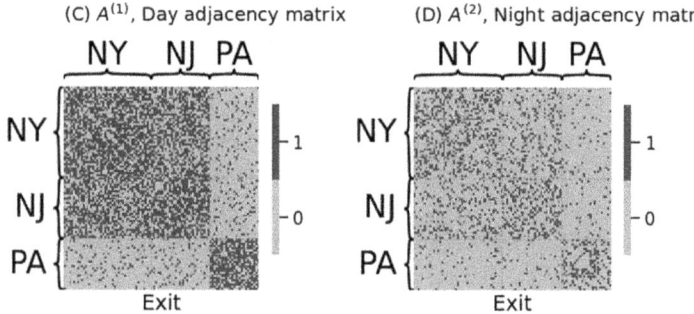

Figure 7.2.1 (**A**) The block matrix for night time, (**B**) the block matrix for day time, (**C**) the adjacency matrix for night time, and (**D**) the adjacency matrix for day time.

```
Bday = Bnight*2 # day time block matrix is generally 50% more than
    night

# people tend to commute from New Jersey to New York during the day
# at anomalously high rates
Bday[0, 1] = .5; Bday[1,0] = .5

np.random.seed(0)
Anight = sbm(ns, Bnight)
Aday = sbm(ns, Bday)
```

The block matrices, and the two network samples, are shown in Figure 7.2.1.

7.2.1   Block Matrices in an SBM

For Case Study 7.2.1, we know ahead of time that the block matrices for the SBMs are different. We would like a method of testing this formally. We will start by defining what we mean by "different." We introduce some new variables for the block matrices during the day time $(B^{(1)})$ and at night time $(B^{(2)})$ clearly. The block matrices are:

$$B^{(1)} = \begin{bmatrix} b_{11}^{(1)} & b_{12}^{(1)} & b_{13}^{(1)} \\ b_{21}^{(1)} & b_{22}^{(1)} & b_{23}^{(1)} \\ b_{31}^{(1)} & b_{32}^{(1)} & b_{33}^{(1)} \end{bmatrix} ; \quad B^{(2)} = \begin{bmatrix} b_{11}^{(2)} & b_{12}^{(2)} & b_{13}^{(2)} \\ b_{21}^{(2)} & b_{22}^{(2)} & b_{23}^{(2)} \\ b_{31}^{(2)} & b_{32}^{(2)} & b_{33}^{(2)} \end{bmatrix} .$$

We want to test the null hypothesis that the block matrices are the same, H_0: $B^{(1)} = B^{(2)}$, against the alternative hypothesis that the block matrices are different, H_A: $B^{(1)} \neq B^{(2)}$. Two matrices are equal if all of the entries are identical, and unequal if at least one of the entries is unequal. We can reformulate the null and alternative hypotheses with this logic.

For the null hypothesis, H_0: $B^{(1)} = B^{(2)}$, the statement is equivalent to saying that for all pairs of communities k and l, $b_{kl}^{(1)} = b_{kl}^{(2)}$. We will write each of these statements down as individual hypotheses for all pairs of communities, using the convention $H_{0,kl}$: $b_{kl}^{(1)} = b_{kl}^{(2)}$.

Therefore, the null hypothesis H_0 is equivalent to saying that for every pair of communities k and l, $H_{0,kl}$ is true.

For the alternative hypothesis, H_A: $B^{(1)} \neq B^{(2)}$, the statement is equivalent to saying that for at least one pair of communities k and l, $b_{kl}^{(1)} \neq b_{kl}^{(2)}$. We will write down each of these statements as well as individual hypotheses for all pairs of communities using the convention $H_{A,kl}$: $b_{kl}^{(1)} \neq b_{kl}^{(2)}$. Therefore, the alternative hypothesis H_A is equivalent to saying that for at least one pair of communities k and l, $H_{A,kl}$ is true.

Testing whether a pair of block probabilities between communities k and l are the same, $H_{0,kl}$, against whether the pair of block probabilities between communities k and l are different, $H_{A,kl}$, is again the two-sample testing problem from Section 6.3.1. We addressed this problem using Fisher's exact test, and that is what we will do here, too.

Remember that with Fisher's exact test, when we want to compare two probabilities, we construct a contingency table. In this case, we will have $\binom{K}{2} + K$ contingency tables (one for each unique pair of communities, plus the on-diagonal blocks where both nodes have the same community). An example is shown in Table 7.1.

In Table 7.1, entry a is the total number of edges between nodes of community k with nodes of community l in the day time network, and b the number of nonedges. The entry c the total number of edges between nodes of community k with nodes of community l in the night time network, and d the number of nonedges.

We implement this using `numpy` and `scipy` for each pair of communities. To identify which adjacency matrix entries correspond to a given pair of communities, we use `np.outer`. Since the network is simple, we also exclude the on-diagonal entries, and avoid double counting by only looking at the upper right triangle of the adjacency matrix:

Table 7.1. An example of a contingency table for testing for a difference in the block matrices between two SBMs. Note that $\binom{K}{2} + K$ of these contingency tables are constructed, corresponding to the contingency tables between nodes in community k and l for all possible pairs of communities (including the K community-to-community pairs).

	Number of edges	Number of nonedges
Day time	a	b
Night time	c	d

```
from scipy.stats import fisher_exact

K = 3
Pvals = np.empty((K, K))
# fill matrix with NaNs
Pvals[:] = np.nan

# get the indices of the upper triangle of Aday
upper_tri_idx = np.triu_indices(Aday.shape[0], k=1)
# create a boolean array that is nxn
upper_tri_mask = np.zeros(Aday.shape, dtype=bool)
# set indices which correspond to the upper triangle to True
upper_tri_mask[upper_tri_idx] = True

for k in range(0, K):
    for l in range(k, K):
        comm_mask = np.outer(z == states[k], z == states[l])
        table = [[Aday[comm_mask & upper_tri_mask].sum(),
                 (Aday[comm_mask & upper_tri_mask] == 0).sum()],
                 [Anight[comm_mask & upper_tri_mask].sum(),
                 (Anight[comm_mask & upper_tri_mask] == 0).sum()]]
        Pvals[k,l] = fisher_exact(table)[1]
```

This gives us a matrix of p-values, corresponding to tests of $H_{0,kl}$ against $H_{A,kl}$ for all pairs of communities k and l. However, directly attempting to interpret these p-values may be misleading.

7.2.1.1   Adjusting for Multiple Comparisons

When performing multiple statistical tests, we run into the multiple hypothesis correction problem. Imagine that we have 5000 coins, and each of these coins has a true probability of landing on heads of 0.5. We flip each coin 500 times, and for each coin i, we estimate the probability that the coin lands on heads by just counting the number of heads and dividing by 500. For each coin, we want to test whether the probability that the coin lands on heads is different from 0.5: We test $H_0^{(i)}: p^{(i)} = 0.5$ against $H_A^{(i)}: p^{(i)} \neq 0.5$. For this problem, an appropriate statistical test is known as the *binomial test*, a way of testing whether the data support (or do not support) a probability being equal to a fixed constant. Let's run our experiments:

```
import numpy as np
from graspologic.simulations import er_np
import seaborn as sns
from scipy.stats import binomtest

ncoins = 5000 # the number of coins
p = 0.5 # the true probability
n = 500 # the number of flips

# the number of heads from each experiment
experiments = np.random.binomial(n, p, size=ncoins)

# perform binomial test to see if the number of heads we obtain
#    supports that the
```

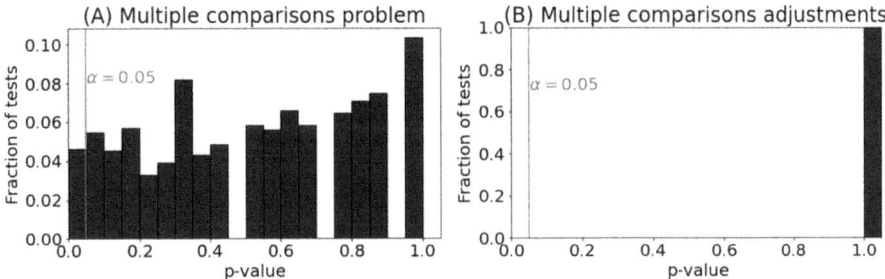

Figure 7.2.2 (**A**) a histogram of the p-values before multiple comparisons adjustment, and (**B**) a histogram of the p-values after adjusting for multiple comparisons, by preserving the FWER via Holm–Bonferroni correction.

```
# true probabiily is 0.5
pvals = [binomtest(nheads_i, n, p=p).pvalue for nheads_i in
    experiments]
```

A histogram of the p-values from all 5000 tests (one for each coin) is shown in Figure 7.2.2(A). In general, we will fail to reject the null hypothesis. This is great, since p_i is, in fact, 0.5 as specified by the null hypothesis $H_0^{(i)}$. However, for a portion of the tests, we are wrong. We obtain many p-values which are under our decision threshold of $\alpha = 0.05$, and would incorrectly reject the null hypothesis in favor of the alternative, that p_i is not 0.5. This is both wrong and extremely problematic. The p-value was defined in Concept 6.3.1 as the probability that the null hypothesis (here, that $p_i = 0.5$) would be incorrectly rejected in favor of the alternative hypothesis (here, that $p_i \neq 0.5$). If the null hypothesis were true, we would expect to see p-values of at most α being reported about α of the time (this assumes all of the coins are independent, but even when they are not all independent, we still obtain a similarly shocking conclusion). This means that with $n = 5000$ tests and $\alpha = 0.05$, we would expect to be wrong about $n \cdot \alpha = 250$ times.

The essential problem is that while each test individually only has an $\alpha = 0.05$ chance of incorrectly rejecting the null hypothesis (when it is true), by running multiple tests, we have increased the familywise error rate to be well north of $\alpha = 0.05$. The *familywise error rate* (FWER) is the probability that we make an error and incorrectly reject the null hypothesis for any one of the hypothesis tests we ran. Collectively, this issue is known as the *multiple comparisons problem*. See [5] for more detail.

One focus of statistics in recent decades has been the development of methods which, in effect, inflate the p-values based on the number of tests that we perform, so that we run into this issue at much lower rate than $n \cdot \alpha$ of the time. These strategies are collectively known as *multiple comparisons adjustments*. There are many methods for multiple comparison adjustments implemented in common statistical libraries. In Python, given a list of p-values `pvals`, we can simply adjust the p-values using the `multipletests()` method from `statsmodels`. This will give protection for this "multiple comparisons" issue in analyses in exchange for more conservative tests: The tests will tend away from rejecting the null hypothesis, as-per the definition in Section 6.3.1.

Let's see what happens when we adjust our *p*-values here using a popular method called *Holm–Bonferroni adjustment* [6]:

```
from statsmodels.stats.multitest import multipletests

alpha = 0.05 # the desired alpha of the test
_, adj_pvals, _, _ = multipletests(pvals, alpha=alpha, method="holm")
```

Figure 7.2.2(B) shows a histogram of the *p*-values after adjustment. After adjusting for multiple comparisons, we end up with all of the *p*-values being 1. Therefore, we no longer incorrectly reject the null hypothesis after adjustment.

In general, for multiple hypothesis correction, we recommend using Holm–Bonferroni correction, encoded with the parameter `method="holm"`. We recommend the use of the Holm–Bonferroni procedure because it ensures that our *p*-values produced by using multiple statistical tests controls the FWER with no additional restrictions on the hypotheses being tested. While other adjustment techniques may situationally give more precise *p*-values, they typically make assumptions about relationships between the hypotheses that entail a more nuanced discussion.

Let's adjust our *p*-values for the pairwise community comparisons for our networks, upper right symmetrize the resulting matrix of *p*-values (because we only ran tests on the upper right triangle of the adjacency matrix), and then plot the result:

```
from graspologic.utils import symmetrize

Pvals_adj = multipletests(Pvals.flatten(),
    method="holm")[1].reshape(K, K)
Pvals_adj = symmetrize(Pvals_adj, method="triu")
```

The matrix of *p*-values (after adjustment for multiple comparisons) is shown in Figure 7.2.3(A). The *p*-values are all extremely small, so we can conclude that the block matrices $B^{(1)}$ and $B^{(2)}$ differ for all entries. The *p*-value for the test of H_0 that the block matrices are identical against H_A that the block matrices are different can be taken to be the minimum of all of the adjusted *p*-values, due to the fact that the block matrices are different if any individual entries are different:

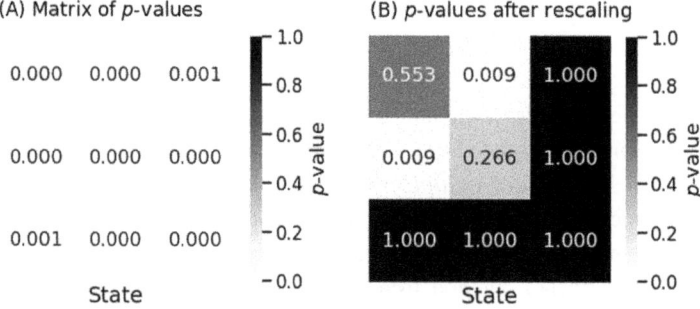

Figure 7.2.3 **(A)** The *p*-values for test of a difference between the Case Study 7.2.1 block matrices, and **(B)** *p*-values for test of a difference between the block matrices, after rescaling.

```
pval_dif = Pvals_adj.min()
print(f"p-value of block matrix difference: {pval_dif:.4f}")
# p-value of block matrix difference: 0.0000
```

This is so small that it rounds to 0. With $\alpha = 0.05$ as usual, we reject the null hypothesis that the block matrices are identical in favor of the alternative that the block matrices are different.

7.2.2   Testing for whether the Block Matrices in an SBM Are Rescalings

In Section 4.6.3 we learned a useful summary statistic for random networks, the expected density:

$$\mathbb{E}[density(\mathbf{A})] = \frac{\sum_{i=1}^{n} \mathbb{E}[\mathbf{d}_i]}{n(n-1)},$$

which is the expected average degree of each node in the network, divided by the maximum possible degree each node could have.

The network density plays a large role in virtually every property of networks which we estimate in machine learning, including the block matrices. From Concept 4.7.2, for a $SBM_n(\vec{z}, B)$ random network, the average degree for a node in community k is:

$$\mathbb{E}\left[\mathbf{d}_i^{(m)}; z_i = k\right] = \sum_{l \neq k} n_l b_{lk}^{(m)} + (n_k - 1)b_{kk}^{(m)}$$

so it is clear that the expected node degree is a function of the block matrix. Recalling from Equation (4.14) that the expected density is a function of the expected degrees:

$$p^{(m)} = \mathbb{E}\left[density\left(\mathbf{A}^{(m)}\right)\right] = \frac{\sum_{i=1}^{n} \mathbb{E}\left[\mathbf{d}_i^{(m)}; z_i = k\right]}{n(n-1)},$$

by transitivity, the expected density is a function of the block matrix. Note in a network with known communities, $\vec{z}$ is fixed, so $\mathbb{E}[\mathbf{d}_i; z_i = k]$ is equivalent to $\mathbb{E}[\mathbf{d}_i]$ (which is the original notation used in Equation (4.14)) for a node i in community k, since expected values are over random quantities (and z_i is not random). We could also reverse this argument, and establish a relationship between the block matrices and the expected density in the network.

This means that if the expected densities are different, the block matrices will, by default, also be different.

For instance, in our example, we know that the block matrix indicated that in general there are twice as many edges during the daytime than during the night. As effective transit planners, we want to identify the fine points to anomalies in the traffic patterns. We want to find the topological differences between the two networks that go above and beyond a simple rescaling. That is, that the day time driving patterns between New Jersey and New York exits exceed the two times increase in traffic we otherwise saw. For this reason, we revamp our hypothesis.

We tested the null hypothesis $H_0: B^{(1)} = B^{(2)}$ that the two block matrices are the same against the alternative $H_A: B^{(1)} \neq B^{(2)}$ that the block matrices differ. Now, our null hypothesis becomes $H_0: B^{(1)} = \beta \cdot B^{(2)}$ that the two block matrices are the same up to a rescaling against $H_A: B^{(2)} \neq \beta \cdot B^{(2)}$, that they differ even after possible rescalings.

In this case, we choose the value β to be the difference in expected network densities between the day time and night time networks, that is, the quantity $\beta = \frac{p^{(1)}}{p^{(2)}}$. In practice, we use an estimate of this quantity, $\hat{\beta} = \frac{\hat{p}^{(1)}}{\hat{p}^{(2)}}$, where $\hat{p}^{(1)}$ is the network density of the day time network and $\hat{p}^{(2)}$ is the network density of the night time network. Accepting the alternative hypothesis here means that the block matrices of the day and night time network are not simply multiples of each other.

Case Study 7.2.2 Bilateral symmetry in fruit fly brains

In the 1860s, a scientist named Paul Broca definitively established that the brain of human beings is asymmetric: Different sides of the brain are responsible for related but distinct functions [7]. Broca discovered that patients with brain lesions to the same area of the left frontal portion of the brain experienced similar symptoms of speech loss. The fact that two patients with similar lesions experienced the same symptoms provided evidence that brain function was *localized*. Later observations made by psychologists led to conclusions that took this a step further, showing that different hemispheres of the brain were responsible for different functions.

In a recent paper [8], investigators were able to demonstrate a similar "localization of connectivity" in the wiring of the brain itself. The investigators used connectomes of a fruit fly, where the nodes were individual neurons and the edges were individual synapses. Using statistical methods based on the techniques outlined in this section, they were able to show that some types of cells in the brain had totally different densities of edges between the two hemispheres. After accounting for these hemisphere density disparities, specific neural cell types still showed disparate connectivity patterns, indicating asymmetry and localization of function in insect brains.

We address this problem similarly to Section 7.2.1, but instead use the χ-squared test for nonunity probability ratios from [9]. We covered the χ-squared test in Section 6.4 when we were covering model selection. Whereas before, the χ-squared test allowed us to test whether our grouping of the edges in the network had differing probabilities based on the edge group, the nonunity probability ratio test allows us to incorporate the rescaling parameter β. We implement this using `graspologic`. This approach is described in [8]:

```
from graspologic.inference import group_connection_test

stat, pval_diff_rescale, misc = group_connection_test(Aday, Anight,
    labels1=z, labels2=z, density_adjustment=True)
Pval_adj_rescaled = np.array(misc["corrected_pvalues"])
print(f"p-value of block matrix difference, after rescaling:
    {pval_diff_rescale:.4f}")
# p-value of block matrix difference, after rescaling: 0.0087
```

This new matrix of *p*-values is shown in Figure 7.2.3(B). After we adjust the block matrix for changes in network density, the difference in the block probability for traveling between New York and New Jersey is still significant.

Therefore, after adjusting for density, we can still reject the null hypothesis in favor of the alternative that the block matrices for day and night time are different. This difference can be accounted for by different traffic patterns between New York and New Jersey in day time versus night time, that exceed simple traffic density differences. For an example of the use of these strategies in practice, see Case Study 7.2.2.

7.3   The Graph Matching Problem

Coauthored with Ali Saad-Eldin

So far in Part III, we have explored methods for comparing networks under the assumption that they have the same nodes, and that those networks are node-aligned. However, real-world networks rarely have index-aligned nodes, and the networks that we wish to compare often have varying numbers of nodes. Figure 4.3.2 showed us that simply reordering node indices dramatically alters an adjacency matrix.

These challenges motivate the *graph matching problem*, which addresses the challenge of identifying node correspondences between networks.

We will:

1. Define the graph matching problem and its importance in network comparison,
2. Explore intuitive approaches for aligning nodes across networks,
3. Introduce optimization-based methods for graph matching, and
4. Discuss applications and limitations of graph matching techniques.

Graph matching will allow us to make principled comparisons from one network to the next if the networks are not node-aligned. While a rigorous treatment requires a background in nonlinear optimization, our focus will be on building intuition. Graph matching gives us a basic and regularly useful tool for multinetwork analysis.

7.3.1   A Failure of Brute Force

To begin to understand the graph matching problem, we will revisit the stochastic block model in Section 4.3.5. We saw that, when the nodes were ordered by community, we obtained a prominent modularity pattern characteristic of many of the block models that we have seen so far in the book (Figure 4.3.2(A)). However, when we reordered the nodes in the adjacency matrix randomly (and changed nothing else about the network), the adjacency matrices looked radically different, despite the fact that the underlying networks remained otherwise the same. Without knowing in advance, how could we have discovered that the networks were identical up to a permutation of node indices?

If we did not already know the sorting, we might simply take a brute-force approach: Iterate over every possible way that one could sort the nodes of one network, and continue until we reach a sorting that perfectly matches the other network.

Unfortunately, this solution has a number of limitations. First, for network pairs with n nodes, there are $n!$ possible mappings. This means that when $n = 100$, there are more than 10^{157} possible matchings, a computationally infeasible number of possibilities. Our task is to figure out which mapping is best without the computationally intractable task of checking each one. For a thorough review of the history of different ways of approaching this problem, see [10].

The social network example in Case Study 7.3.1 will motivate the remainder of the section.

Case Study 7.3.1 Graph matching across social networks

Suppose all Instagram users' names and handles have been somehow been deleted, and our task is to recover the lost information. We have a resource to help with this task: the Facebook social network. We know all Facebook users and who they are friends with. Since only the Instagram usernames are lost, we can still see which unnamed Instagram users follow each other. Our goal is to use the Facebook network connectivity data to relabel the Instagram network. In other words, we are "aligning" or "matching" Instagram to Facebook.

In the two social networks, each user is a node. An edge in Facebook exists if two users are friends, and an edge in Instagram exists if two users follow each other. We will define the Facebook and Instagram networks as F and I respectively, with associated adjacency matrices $A^{(F)}$ and $A^{(I)}$. Our goal is for one of the Instagram users to be assigned the user name of the Facebook user with the most connections in common. This is done for the whole network, with the end result being that overall the structure is preserved.

7.3.2   Defining a Similarity Network

To begin to address the graph matching problem, we first must define a notion of similarity for two networks via a metric $f\left(A^{(1)}, A^{(2)}\right)$. We want this metric to be small when the two networks are similar, and large when they are not. For graph matching, we use the squared Frobenius distance from Concept 5.5.4:

$$f\left(A^{(1)}, A^{(2)}\right) = \left\|A^{(1)} - A^{(2)}\right\|_F^2.$$

To understand this metric, consider the best possible case where the two networks are identical; that is, $A^{(1)} = A^{(2)}$:

$$
A^{(1)} = \begin{array}{c} \\ 0 \\ 1 \\ 2 \end{array}
\begin{array}{ccc} 0 & 1 & 2 \\ \left[\begin{array}{ccc} 0 & 1 & 1 \\ 1 & 0 & 1 \\ 1 & 1 & 0 \end{array}\right] \end{array},
\qquad
A^{(2)} = \begin{array}{c} \\ 0 \\ 1 \\ 2 \end{array}
\begin{array}{ccc} 0 & 1 & 2 \\ \left[\begin{array}{ccc} 0 & 1 & 1 \\ 1 & 0 & 1 \\ 1 & 1 & 0 \end{array}\right] \end{array}
$$

$$A^{(1)} - A^{(2)} = \begin{array}{c} \\ 0 \\ 1 \\ 2 \end{array} \begin{array}{ccc} 0 & 1 & 2 \\ \left[\begin{array}{ccc} 0 & 0 & 0 \\ 0 & 0 & 0 \\ 0 & 0 & 0 \end{array}\right] \end{array}$$

$$\left\| A^{(1)} - A^{(2)} \right\|_F^2 = 0.$$

The difference will be a matrix of all zeros, and taking the squared Frobenius norm will yield $f\left(A^{(1)}, A^{(2)}\right) = 0$. This is because all of the element-wise differences $a_{ij}^{(1)} - a_{ij}^{(2)}$ are zero, and hence both their square (and sum) will also be zero. Next, we remove one edge from $A^{(2)}$:

$$A^{(1)} = \begin{array}{c} \\ 0 \\ 1 \\ 2 \end{array} \begin{array}{ccc} 0 & 1 & 2 \\ \left[\begin{array}{ccc} 0 & 1 & 1 \\ 1 & 0 & 1 \\ 1 & 1 & 0 \end{array}\right] \end{array}, \qquad A^{(2)} = \begin{array}{c} \\ 0 \\ 1 \\ 2 \end{array} \begin{array}{ccc} 0 & 1 & 2 \\ \left[\begin{array}{ccc} 0 & 1 & 1 \\ 1 & 0 & 0 \\ 1 & 0 & 0 \end{array}\right] \end{array}$$

$$A^{(1)} - A^{(2)} = \begin{array}{c} \\ 0 \\ 1 \\ 2 \end{array} \begin{array}{ccc} 0 & 1 & 2 \\ \left[\begin{array}{ccc} 0 & 0 & 0 \\ 0 & 0 & 1 \\ 0 & 1 & 0 \end{array}\right] \end{array}$$

$$\left\| A^{(1)} - A^{(2)} \right\|_F^2 = 2.$$

Because these networks are unweighted and undirected, we are effectively counting the total number of disagreements in the adjacency matrices between $A^{(1)}$ and $A^{(2)}$.

7.3.2.1 Graph Matching Small Networks

We will use I and F for the Instagram and Facebook networks respectively. We first use a four-person subgraph for simplicity. Our two networks, with adjacency matrices $A^{(I)}$ and $A^{(F)}$, then have four nodes each: $\{0, 1, 2, 3\}$ for $A^{(I)}$, and $\{a, b, c, d\}$ for $A^{(F)}$. We will assume we have a node correspondence:

- Person 0 on Instagram is person a on Facebook,

- Person 1 on Instagram is person b on Facebook,

- Person 2 on Instagram is person c on Facebook,

- Person 3 on Instagram is person d on Facebook.

A *correspondence* is a mapping from one set of items to those of another. Here, we have a correspondence between each user's profile on Instagram and Facebook. We say that a node in one network is *matched* to a node in the other if the two nodes are linked by the correspondence. For instance, in the above correspondence, person 1 on Instagram is matched to person b on Facebook. When all of the nodes from two networks are matched, we will refer to the networks themselves as matched (or, alternatively, *aligned*).

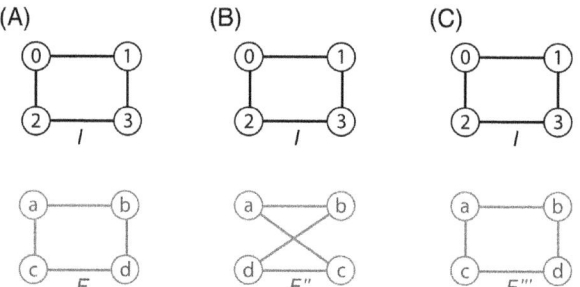

Figure 7.3.1 (**A**) The social networks, with the nodes aligned. (**B**) The social networks, with the nodes misaligned. (**C**) The social networks, with the nodes misaligned, but with the topology of the network identical.

The Importance of Node Ordering

The adjacency matrices of the two networks are equal to each other when the nodes are laid out for $A^{(I)}$ as $\{0, 1, 2, 3\}$, and when the nodes are laid out for $A^{(F)}$ as $\{a, b, c, d\}$. Figure 7.3.1(A) illustrates the two networks with their nodes laid out with respect to the node correspondence. Below, we compare the two adjacency matrices, and find that the absolute difference matrix $\left|A^{(F)} - A^{(I)}\right|$ is a matrix of zeros (the two adjacency matrices are identical).

$$
A^{(F)} = \begin{array}{c} \\ 0 \\ 1 \\ 2 \\ 3 \end{array} \begin{array}{cccc} 0 & 1 & 2 & 3 \\ \left(\begin{array}{cccc} 0 & 1 & 1 & 0 \\ 1 & 0 & 0 & 1 \\ 1 & 0 & 0 & 1 \\ 0 & 1 & 1 & 0 \end{array} \right) \end{array}, \qquad
A^{(I)} = \begin{array}{c} \\ a \\ b \\ c \\ d \end{array} \begin{array}{cccc} a & b & c & d \\ \left(\begin{array}{cccc} 0 & 1 & 1 & 0 \\ 1 & 0 & 0 & 1 \\ 1 & 0 & 0 & 1 \\ 0 & 1 & 1 & 0 \end{array} \right) \end{array}
$$

$$
\left|A^{(F)} - A^{(I)}\right| = \begin{bmatrix} 0 & 0 & 0 & 0 \\ 0 & 0 & 0 & 0 \\ 0 & 0 & 0 & 0 \\ 0 & 0 & 0 & 0 \end{bmatrix}.
$$

If we permute the node indices of both networks and the permuted nodes still respect the node correspondence, the Frobenius difference between their adjacency matrices will be the same as if the networks were not permuted at all (here, 0).

We reorder the nodes for Instagram and Facebook as $\{2, 0, 1, 3\}$ and $\{c, a, b, d\}$ respectively. We will call these new adjacency matrices $A^{(I)'}$ and $A^{(F)'}$ respectively:

$$
A^{(I)'} = \begin{array}{c} \\ 2 \\ 0 \\ 1 \\ 3 \end{array} \begin{array}{cccc} 2 & 0 & 1 & 3 \\ \left[\begin{array}{cccc} 0 & 1 & 0 & 1 \\ 1 & 0 & 1 & 0 \\ 0 & 1 & 0 & 1 \\ 1 & 0 & 1 & 0 \end{array} \right] \end{array}, \qquad
A^{(F)'} = \begin{array}{c} \\ c \\ a \\ b \\ d \end{array} \begin{array}{cccc} c & a & b & d \\ \left[\begin{array}{cccc} 0 & 1 & 0 & 1 \\ 1 & 0 & 1 & 0 \\ 0 & 1 & 0 & 1 \\ 1 & 0 & 1 & 0 \end{array} \right] \end{array}
$$

$$
\left|A^{(I)'} - A^{(F)'}\right| = \begin{bmatrix} 0 & 0 & 0 & 0 \\ 0 & 0 & 0 & 0 \\ 0 & 0 & 0 & 0 \\ 0 & 0 & 0 & 0 \end{bmatrix}.
$$

Even though the ordering of the nodes is different, the first node for Instagram is node 2 and the first node for Facebook is node c (which was a matching noted by our correspondence), the second node for Instagram is 0 and the second node for Facebook is node a (a matching noted by our correspondence), and so on. The node orderings preserve the correspondence between the nodes of Instagram with the nodes of Facebook.

Networks Rarely Come Preordered

The ordering of the nodes in a network's adjacency matrix may often be arbitrary, which can make it hard to tell whether two networks are the same.

Let's say we had an arbitrary ordering of the nodes for Facebook. The nodes are ordered $\{a,b,d,c\}$ instead of $\{a,b,c,d\}$. Instagram's nodes are still ordered as $\{0,1,2,3\}$. Figure 7.3.1(B) illustrates this. We use $A^{(F)''}$ to denote the new ordering. The adjacency matrices are no longer equal:

$$
A^{(I)} = \begin{array}{c} \\ 0 \\ 1 \\ 2 \\ 3 \end{array} \begin{array}{cccc} 0 & 1 & 2 & 3 \\ \left[\begin{array}{cccc} 0 & 1 & 1 & 0 \\ 1 & 0 & 0 & 1 \\ 1 & 0 & 0 & 1 \\ 0 & 1 & 1 & 0 \end{array} \right] \end{array}, \quad A^{(F)''} = \begin{array}{c} \\ a \\ b \\ d \\ c \end{array} \begin{array}{cccc} a & b & d & c \\ \left(\begin{array}{cccc} 0 & 1 & 0 & 1 \\ 1 & 0 & 1 & 0 \\ 0 & 1 & 0 & 1 \\ 1 & 0 & 1 & 0 \end{array} \right) \end{array} \quad (7.5)
$$

$$
\left| A^{(I)} - A^{(F)''} \right| = \begin{bmatrix} 0 & 0 & 1 & 1 \\ 0 & 0 & 1 & 1 \\ 1 & 1 & 0 & 0 \\ 1 & 1 & 0 & 0 \end{bmatrix}.
$$

Our similarity metric changes as well: $f\left(A^{(I)}, A^{(F)''}\right) = 8$, since there are eight entries which are different in the adjacency matrices between $A^{(I)}$ and $A^{(F)''}$. The network is undirected, so adjacency disagreements are effectively counted twice: A single edge disagreement for an edge (i, j) also yields a disagreement for edge (j, i). By comparing the networks with the nodes misaligned, we have broken the node correspondence between the nodes of Instagram and Facebook. Note, however, that two matrices having a difference matrix of 0s does not necessarily imply that the nodes are ordered acccording to the node correspondence. In Remark 7.3.2, we explore how an incorrect node correspondence may still yield identical adjacency matrices.

Let's explore how to manipulate our adjacency matrices such that we can find alignments that match well.

7.3.3 Permutation Matrices

Permutation matrices are commonly used as a method to move the rows and columns of a square matrix. A *permutation matrix* is a matrix where, for every row and column, exactly one entry has a value of one and the rest are zero.

7.3.3.1 $P^{\top}A$ Permutes Rows

Consider the matrix A shown in Figure 7.3.2(A.I), where all entries of the first row have a value of one, all entries of the second row have a value of two, all entries of the

> **Remark 7.3.2** Low numbers of edge disagreements do not imply node correspondence
>
> We mix the ordering of the nodes for Facebook a third time, instead using $\{b,a,d,c\}$, to yield another adjacency matrix $A^{(F)'''}$, illustrated in Figure 7.3.1(C). Note that the adjacency matrices are identical for $A^{(F)'''}$ and $A^{(I)}$, despite the face that the nodes for Facebook are not ordered with respect to the node correspondence of the Instagram network:
>
> $$A^{(I)} = \begin{matrix} & \begin{matrix} 0 & 1 & 2 & 3 \end{matrix} \\ \begin{matrix} 0 \\ 1 \\ 2 \\ 3 \end{matrix} & \begin{bmatrix} 0 & 1 & 1 & 0 \\ 1 & 0 & 0 & 1 \\ 1 & 0 & 0 & 1 \\ 0 & 1 & 1 & 0 \end{bmatrix} \end{matrix}, \qquad A^{(F)'''} = \begin{matrix} & \begin{matrix} b & a & d & c \end{matrix} \\ \begin{matrix} b \\ a \\ d \\ c \end{matrix} & \begin{bmatrix} 0 & 1 & 1 & 0 \\ 1 & 0 & 0 & 1 \\ 1 & 0 & 0 & 1 \\ 0 & 1 & 1 & 0 \end{bmatrix} \end{matrix}$$
>
> $$\left| A^{(I)} - A^{(F)'''} \right| = \begin{bmatrix} 0 & 0 & 0 & 0 \\ 0 & 0 & 0 & 0 \\ 0 & 0 & 0 & 0 \\ 0 & 0 & 0 & 0 \end{bmatrix}.$$
>
> The fact that the adjacency matrices can be identical even when we do not have a correspondence of the nodes between the two networks presents a challenge and limitation for the graph matching problem. If two networks are identical (up to an ordering of the nodes), there may be multiple ways to orient the nodes of the networks to give no edge disagreements. We could have multiple different networks where the topology is the same.

third row have a value of three, and all entries of the fourth row have a value of four. We can apply a permutation matrix P to swap the rows around with the following heuristic: If the matrix P has the value one in entry p_{ij}, then in the resulting matrix $P^\top A$, the row j will be the row i from the matrix A we permuted.

In Figure 7.3.2(A.II), the values in p_{12}, p_{21}, p_{33}, and p_{44} are all one. We reorder the rows of A so that in $P^\top A$ the top row is the second row from the original matrix (and has a value of two), the second row will be the first row from the original matrix, the third row will be the third row from the original matrix, and the fourth row will be the fourth row from the original matrix.

We apply this "row" permutation with the matrix multiplication $P^\top A$:

```
import numpy as np

A = np.array([
    [1,1,1,1],
    [2,2,2,2],
    [3,3,3,3],
    [4,4,4,4]
])

P = np.array([
```

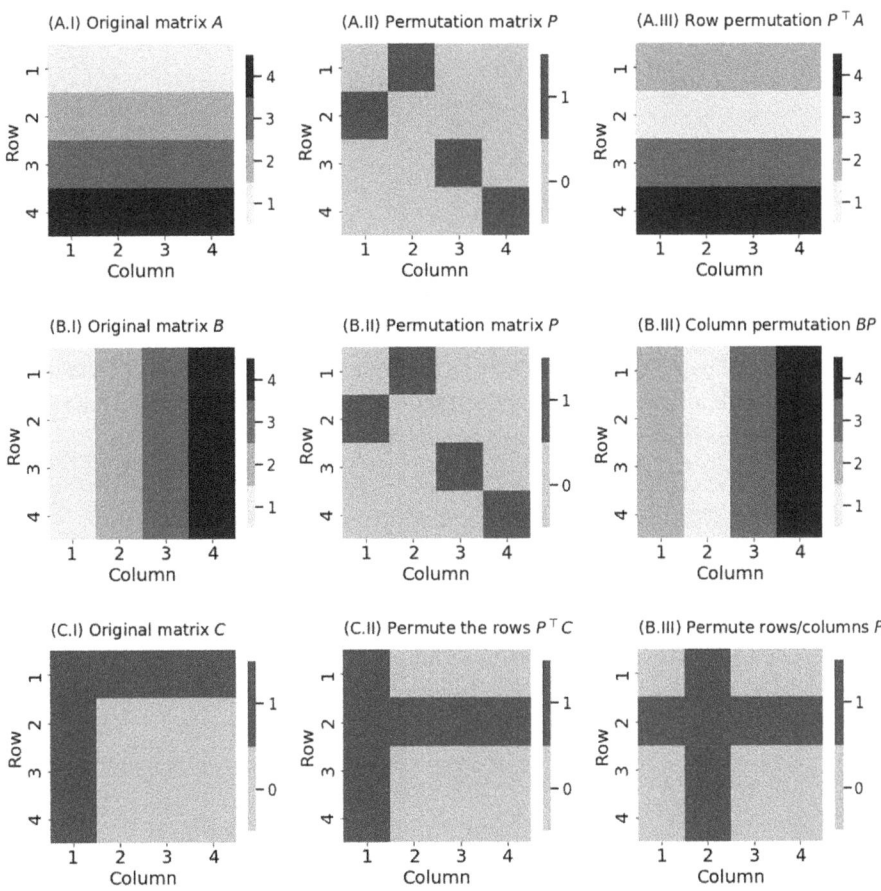

Figure 7.3.2 Row (**A**) shows a row permutation via premultiplication by $P^\top$, row (**B**) shows a column permutation via postmultiplication by P, and row (**C**) shows a row and column permutation via premultiplication by $P^\top$ and postmultiplication by P.

```
    [0,1,0,0],
    [1,0,0,0],
    [0,0,1,0],
    [0,0,0,1]
])

row_reordering = P.T @ A
```

Figure 7.3.2(A.III) shows a plot of the resulting row permutation.

7.3.3.2 BP **Permutes Columns**

Column permutations behave similarly. Consider a matrix B, where the first column has a value of one, the second column has a value of two, the third column has a value of three, and the fourth column has a value of four, shown in Figure 7.3.2(B.I). We use the same permutation matrix, where here, p_{ij} indicates that column j of the new matrix BP will be column i from the matrix B before the permutation was applied. This permutation is shown again in Figure 7.3.2(B.II). We apply the column permutation matrix as BP:

```
B = np.array([
    [1,2,3,4],
    [1,2,3,4],
    [1,2,3,4],
    [1,2,3,4]
])

column_reordering = B @ P
```

Figure 7.3.2(B.III) shows a plot of the resulting column permutation. The column with a value of one has been "shifted" to column four, and the values of columns one through three are now two through four respectively.

7.3.3.3 $P^{\top}CP$ Permutes Rows and Columns ConCurrently

We can apply these operations sequentially to concurrently reorder both rows and columns. Consider a permutation matrix where row/column one of the original matrix becomes row/column two of the new matrix, and likewise, row/column two of the original matrix becomes row/column one of the new matrix. We consider the matrix C shown in Figure 7.3.2(C.I) where the first row and first column both have entries of all ones, and the rest of the matrix has the value zero.

```
C = np.array([
    [1,1,1,1],
    [1,0,0,0],
    [1,0,0,0],
    [1,0,0,0]
])

row_reordering_C = P.T @ C
row_column_reordering = row_reordering_C @ P
```

When we premultiply by $P^{\top}$, we end up swapping row one with row two, as we would expect from Figure 7.3.2(A). When we postmultiply $P^{\top}C$ by P, we end up swapping columns one and two, as we would expect from Figure 7.3.2(B). This results in concurrently swapping the rows and columns one and two, shown in Figure 7.3.2(C.III). If C were an adjacency matrix with nodes indexed $\{1,2,3,4\}$, this would have the effect of permuting the node ordering of the adjacency matrix to $\{2,1,3,4\}$.

7.3.3.4   Permutations on Adjacency Matrices

For our networks, the indexing for the adjacency matrix, (i, j), is over a single set: the nodes. Therefore, if we want to change node indices, we need to permute both the rows and the columns of the adjacency matrix concurrently. If we had a permutation of the nodes given by P, we would reorder the adjacency matrix by permuting the rows and columns of A by using $P^{\top}AP$.

Suppose we want to "undo" a permutation with matrix P. We recall that every row and every column in a permutation matrix has a single entry which takes a value of one. Assume that $p_{ij} = 1$, which means that if we were to use P as a row permutation we would flip rows i and j, and as a column permutation we would flip columns i and j. If we were to use it for both a row and column permutation, we would flip rows/columns i and j.

If for any pair of indices $p_{ij} = 1$, then $(P^{\top})_{ji} = 1$: The (i, j) entry of the transpose is also one. This is just the definition of the matrix transpose operation. Let's look at what happens when we multiply $P^{\top}$ and P together:

$$P^{\top}P = \begin{bmatrix} (P^{\top})_{11} & \cdots & (P^{\top})_{1n} \\ \vdots & \ddots & \vdots \\ (P^{\top})_{n1} & \cdots & (P^{\top})_{nn} \end{bmatrix} \begin{bmatrix} p_{11} & \cdots & p_{1n} \\ \vdots & \ddots & \vdots \\ p_{n1} & \cdots & p_{nn} \end{bmatrix}.$$

When we use the definition of the transpose, this becomes:

$$P^{\top}P = \begin{bmatrix} p_{11} & \cdots & p_{n1} \\ \vdots & \ddots & \vdots \\ p_{1n} & \cdots & p_{nn} \end{bmatrix} \begin{bmatrix} p_{11} & \cdots & p_{1n} \\ \vdots & \ddots & \vdots \\ p_{n1} & \cdots & p_{nn} \end{bmatrix}.$$

The resulting matrix $P^{\top}P$ has entries i, j where:

$$(P^{\top}P)_{ij} = \sum_{k=1}^{n} p_{ik}p_{jk}. \tag{7.6}$$

But, as we know, for a particular row i and column k, exactly a single entry has a value of one (this is the definition of a permutation matrix). This means that for any $i \neq j$, $p_{ik}p_{jk}$ will be equal to zero, because two different rows of the same column k cannot both take the value of one.

If $i = j$, then there must be some k where $p_{ik} = 1$, because at least one entry of each row of P must be one by definition. Since $i = j$, $p_{jk} = 1$.

Therefore, $(P^{\top}P)_{ij} = 1$ if $i = j$, and $(P^{\top}P)_{ij} = 0$ everywhere else. This is the definition of the identity matrix, so $P^{\top}P = I_{n \times n}$. Since the transpose of the identity matrix is also the identity matrix, $PP^{\top} = I_{n \times n}$, too.

Using these facts, we arrive at Concept 7.3.3.

Concept 7.3.3 Unshuffling a shuffled adjacency matrix

Suppose that B is a shuffling of the adjacency matrix A by P; that is, $B = P^{\top}AP$. Letting $P_u = P^{\top}$, permuting the rows and columns of B by P_u gives:

$$P_u^{\top}BP_u = PBP^{\top},$$

where we used that $P_u = P^{\top}$. Writing B as $P^{\top}AP$:

$$P_u^{\top}BP_u = PP^{\top}APP^{\top}$$
$$= A,$$

because $PP^{\top} = I_{n \times n}$. Thus B can be unshuffled to recover A by permuting B with the matrix $P_u = P^{\top}$, and P is an orthogonal matrix.

7.3.3.5   Permutation Matrices for Network Matching

Let's return to Case Study 7.3.1 for Instagram and Facebook. We have a node correspondence where person 0 from Instagram is the same as person a from Facebook, person 1 from Instagram is the same as person b from Facebook, and so on.

We assume that the nodes from Instagram are given to us in order, $\{0, 1, 2, 3\}$, shown in Figure 7.3.3(A). In the ideal case, the nodes from Facebook would respect the node correspondence and be ordered as $\{a, b, c, d\}$. The problem we illustrated in Equation (7.5) was that, if the nodes for Facebook were ordered $\{a, b, d, c\}$, then $f\left(A^{(I)}, A^{(F'')}\right) = 8$, shown in Figure 7.3.3(B).

We want to construct a permutation matrix P which will preserve the indices of a and b, but swap nodes c and d. We can do this using the following:

```
insta = np.array([
    [0,1,1,0],
    [1,0,0,1],
    [1,0,0,1],
    [0,1,1,0]
])

facebook_permuted = np.array([
    [0,1,0,1],
    [1,0,1,0],
    [0,1,0,1],
    [1,0,1,0]
])

# the permutation to unshuffle the facebook
# permuted adjacency matrix
Pu = np.array([
    [1,0,0,0],
    [0,1,0,0],
```

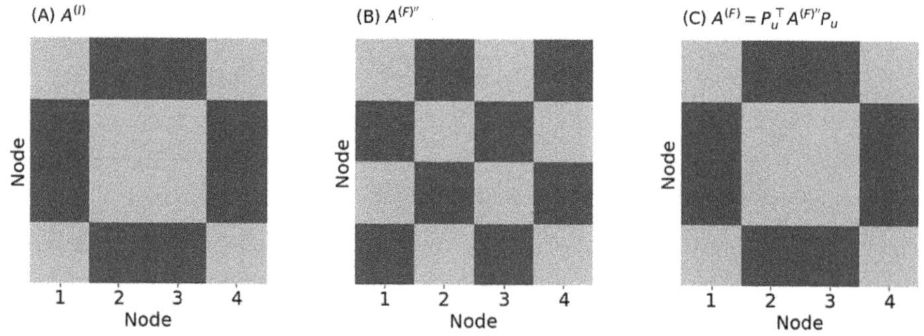

(A) $A^{(I)}$ (B) $A^{(F)''}$ (C) $A^{(F)} = P_u^\top A^{(F)''} P_u$

Figure 7.3.3 **(A)** The adjacency matrix for Instagram $A^{(I)}$. **(B)** The permuted adjacency matrix for Facebook, $A^{(F'')}$. **(C)** The unpermuted adjacency matrix for Facebook, after swapping nodes c and d via an unshuffling permutation matrix. Since node correspondences are not typically known at the time of analysis in graph matching problems and the numbering of nodes is arbitrary, the numbering of nodes in the axes do not necessarily correspond to a node correspondence. Here, for instance, if we were to provide the true identities of the nodes, (A) would be labeled 0, 1, 2, and 3, (B) would be labeled a, b, d, and c, and (C) would be labeled a, b, c, d.

```
    [0,0,0,1],
    [0,0,1,0]
])
```

```
fb_unpermuted = Pu.T @ facebook_permuted @ Pu
```

The permuted Facebook adjacency matrix (after unshuffling) is shown in Figure 7.3.3(C). The permutation matrix swaps nodes c and d, to recover the original node correspondence between Instagram and Facebook, and the networks are identical after premultiplying and postmultiplying by the permutation matrix.

We now define a function which creates random permutation matrices.

```
def make_random_permutation(n, random_seed=0):
    """
    A function that generates a random permutation matric $P$ for n
        elements.

    1. Generate indices from 0 to n-1
    2. shuffle those indices
    3. Place 1s in the matrix P at the positions defined by the
        shuffled indices.
    """
    rng = np.random.default_rng(seed=random_seed)
    starting_indices = np.arange(n)
    destination_indices = rng.permutation(n)
    P = np.zeros(shape=(n,n))
    P[destination_indices, starting_indices] = 1
    return P
```

We are ready to formalize graph matching as an optimization problem in Concept 7.3.4. We then explore methods for solving it.

Concept 7.3.4 Formalizing the graph matching problem

We can now formalize the graph matching problem. For two adjacency matrices A, B, we seek to minimize:

$$g_P(A, B) = \left\| A - P^\top B P \right\|_F^2$$

over all possible P, with the restriction that P is a permutation matrix. Minimizing this cost function finds the matrix P that permutes the rows and columns of B such that it is as close as possible to A in squared Frobenius norm. Intuitively, the solution to the graph matching problem identifies the "optimal" (in terms of the squared Frobenius distance) unshuffling matrix for B with respect to A.

Gradient Descent, a Brief Refresher

To solve the optimization problem defined in Concept 7.3.4, we will employ an algorithm closely related to *gradient descent*. Gradient descent works to minimize a cost

(A)   (B)

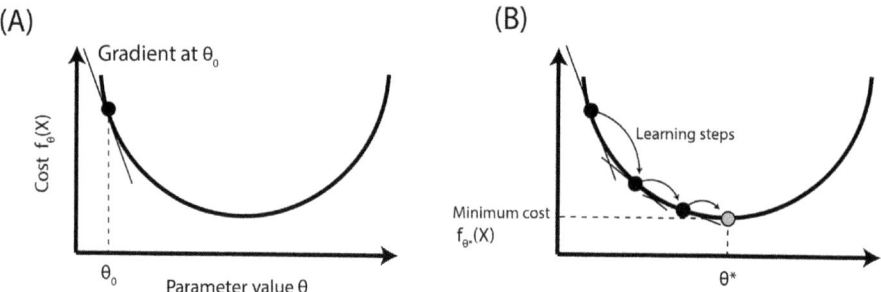

Figure 7.3.4 (**A**) The cost function with an initial starting position, and (**B**) the cost function, optimized via gradient descent.

function, by taking steps in the direction of a local gradient (closely related to a higher dimensional version of the derivative) with respect to some parameter. Once the gradient is zero, a local minimum has been found and the algorithm is stopped.

This process is illustrated in Figure 7.3.4 for a one-dimensional parameter θ. The y-axis represents the cost $f_\theta(X)$ of a particular parameter choice θ, given the data X (solid line).

In Figure 7.3.4(A), an initial parameter value θ_0 is chosen to begin the optimization routine. The gradient is computed at the point θ_0. With one parameter, this gradient is the slope of the tangent line to $f_\theta(X)$ at θ_0 (solid line). Since the slope is negative, this indicates that increasing the value of the parameter an arbitrarily small amount past θ_0 will decrease the cost. If the slope were positive, decreasing the value of the parameter an arbitrarily small amount past θ_0 would decrease the cost. Figure 7.3.4(B) illustrates the effects of repeating this process. Successive "learning steps" repeat this process until the tangent line has a slope of zero, at which point a local minimum for the cost function $f_\theta(X)$ at θ^* has been found.

To perform gradient descent, we first choose a suitable initial position. We then gradually improve the cost function one step at a time until the gradient is within ϵ of zero. It is not guaranteed that gradient descent will find a global minimum, only that it will find a local minimum to the initial position as long as the function is sufficiently smooth.

7.3.4   Solving the Graph Matching Problem

To solve the optimization problem defined in Concept 7.3.4, we will employ an optimization strategy known as the fast approximate quadratic (FAQ) algorithm [11]. FAQ uses a slight variation on gradient descent to find a local solution to the graph matching problem, which is otherwise computationally intractable.

We will match two networks with a known node mapping that preserves a common network structure. To do this, we simulate a single sample from an $ER_{12}(0.5)$ random network. Then, we generate B by randomly permuting the node labels of A.

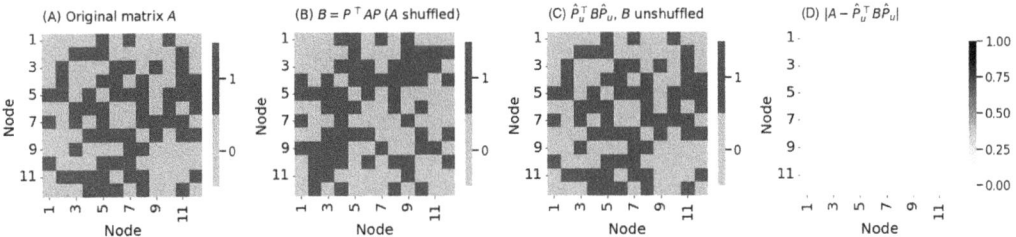

Figure 7.3.5 (**A**) The original adjacency matrix, (**B**) the shuffled adjacency matrix B, using the random permutation P, (**C**) the unshuffling of B, after graph matching to A, and (**D**) the edge disagreement matrix.

```
from graspologic.simulations import er_np

n = 12
p = 0.5

np.random.seed(0)
A = er_np(n=n, p=p)
# make a random permutation matrix
P = make_random_permutation(n)
B = P.T @ A @ P
disagreements = np.linalg.norm(A - B)**2
```

The network sample is shown in Figure 7.3.5(A), and the network after a random shuffling of the nodes is shown in Figure 7.3.5(B).

Now, we create a model to solve the graph matching problem using the `graph_match` function. We pass in two networks, A and B, that we wish to "match." We pass the random seed `rng=0` to ensure reproducibility.

Remark 7.3.5 Seeds vs. random seeds

There will be two uses of the word "seed" being used in this chapter. The first is a random seed, passed into random functions for reproducibility to ensure that they always return the same output. The second is a network seed, which is a set of nodes for whom the correspondence between two networks is already known. We will always use "random seed" to refer to the former, and "seed" to refer to the latter.

```
from graspologic.match import graph_match

gmp = graph_match(A,B, n_init=10, rng=0)
```

The `graph_match()` function initializes and returns a `MatchResult` object after solving the graph matching problem for two input adjacency matrices A and B. After fitting, the `MatchResult` features two attributes of note, `indices_A` and `indices_B` (the "permuted indices"); `indices_A` and `indices_B` are such that `indices_A[i]` is the node from the first input matrix that is matched to `indices_B[i]` the node from the second input matrix. When A and B are the same size, the behavior defaults to matching nodes of B to nodes of A; for example, `indices_A = np.arange(0, n)` for a network with n nodes (A is not resorted).

We can use these indices to construct an "unshuffling" permutation matrix for network B. Our goal is to construct an unshuffling matrix for B, where `Pu[i,j] = 1` if node j in B should be moved to position i in the "unshuffling" of B with respect to A. This logic follows directly from the intuition learned in Section 7.3.3.

```
def make_unshuffler(destination_indices):
    """
    A function which creates a permutation matrix P from a given
        permutation of the nodes.
    """
    n = len(destination_indices)
    Pu = np.zeros((n, n))
    starting_indices = np.arange(n)
    Pu[destination_indices, starting_indices] = 1
    return Pu

Pu = make_unshuffler(gmp.indices_B)
B_unshuffled = Pu.T @ B @ Pu
disagreements = np.linalg.norm(A - B_unshuffled)**2
print(f"Disagreements: {int(disagreements):d}")
# Disagreements: 0
```

In this case, we are estimating the unshuffling matrix, so we produce an estimate $\hat{P}_u$. When we unshuffle B with $\hat{P}_u$, we obtain the matrix $\hat{P}_u^\top B \hat{P}_u$, which is shown in Figure 7.3.5(C). Note that there are no edge disagreements between $\hat{P}_u^\top B \hat{P}_u$ and A, shown in Figure 7.3.5(D).

Because the algorithm is randomly initialized, unlucky readers using different random seeds may not get a perfect unshuffling.

7.3.4.1   The Match Ratio of Nodes

We can evaluate the quality of an unshuffling using the proportion of nodes which are correctly matched to their partners in the other network, called the *match ratio*.

Recall that given a permutation matrix P, the "unshuffling permutation matrix" P_u was $P_u = P^\top$. By definition of a permutation matrix, we found in Section 7.3.3 that $PP^\top = P^\top P = I_{n \times n}$, the identity matrix. This followed directly from Equation (7.6), by noting that the kth column of P could have only a single entry with a value of 1 (by definition of a permutation matrix), so p_{ik} and p_{jk} would only be nonzero when $i = j$. Since $P_u = P^\top$, $PP_u = P_u P = I_{n \times n}$.

Consequently, if we have an estimate of an unshuffling matrix $\hat{P}_u$ and the true permutation matrix P, we can count "correct matches" by looking at the diagonal entries of $\hat{P}_u P$. This is because $(\hat{P}_u P)_{ii} = 1$ whenever a node i is properly unshuffled, and is zero otherwise.

With this in mind, we can just take the match ratio to be the fraction of times the diagonal of $\hat{P}_u P$ or $P \hat{P}_u$ is 1:

$$\text{match ratio}(P, \hat{P}_u) = \frac{1}{n} \sum_{i=1}^{n} \mathbb{1} \left\{ (\hat{P}_u P)_{ii} = 1 \right\}$$

$$= \frac{\text{trace}(\hat{P}_u P)}{n}.$$

Remember that P is a permutation matrix and P_u is an estimated unshuffling matrix.

The function $\mathbb{1}\{x\}$ is an indicator that has a value of 1 if the statement inside the braces is true, and 0 if it is false. Here, it has a value of 1 if $(\hat{P}_u P)_{ii} = 1$, and a value of 0 if $(\hat{P}_u P)_{ii} \neq 1$. We write a simple utility to do this, and then call it on our permutation and unshuffling matrix to see that the match ratio is 1 here (we perfectly unshuffled B):

```
def match_ratio(P, Pu):
    n = P.shape[0] # the number of nodes
    return (np.diag(Pu @ P) == 1).sum()/n

print(f"match ratio: {match_ratio(P, Pu):.3f}")
# match ratio: 1.000
```

As before, you may not necessarily receive identical results to us, as the `GraphMatch` object relies on random initializations.

7.3.5 Seeded Graph Matching (SGM)

As networks become larger, they quickly become difficult to match. One method to mitigate this difficulty is to use seeds. *Seeds* are a subset of a node correspondence between two networks that we already know before we perform the graph matching. For example, if we are given the Instagram and Facebook networks I and F with 225 nodes each, we might already know 10 node matches between I and F. Having this prior information dramatically improves our ability to match the networks.

To demonstrate the effectiveness of seeded graph matching (SGM) [12; 13], we will apply the algorithm on a pair of simpler correlated SBM networks, which is an adaptation of the ρ-correlated $RDPG$ from Section 4.9.3. Like the ρ-correlated $RDPG$, we have two normal SBMs, but edges $\mathbf{a}_{ij}^{(1)}$ and $\mathbf{a}_{ij}^{(2)}$ in the SBMs will have correlation ρ.

Note that unlike preceding examples, the underlying networks for this example are not completely identical (even when unshuffled), but in general closely related (the networks are correlated). This scenario is far more realistic when attempting to align two networks in practice; the two networks will often be similar but with a few underlying differences (for instance, the networks may represent a different social network, where individuals may follow/be followed by similar but not identical people). This is because of the fact that networks that we encounter often reflect some degree of randomness in their behavior, as-per Section 1.3.

The block matrix is:

$$B = \begin{bmatrix} 0.7 & 0.1 & 0.4 \\ 0.1 & 0.7 & 0.1 \\ 0.4 & 0.1 & 0.7 \end{bmatrix}.$$

The first 75 nodes in the network will be from community one, the second 75 nodes in the network will be from community two, and the third 75 nodes in the network will be from community three:

```
from graspologic.simulations import sbm_corr

n_per_block = 75
n_blocks = 3
block_members = np.repeat(n_per_block, repeats=n_blocks)
n_nodes = block_members.sum()
rho = 0.5
block_probs = np.array(
    [[0.7, 0.1, 0.4],
     [0.1, 0.3, 0.1],
     [0.4, 0.1, 0.7]]
)

np.random.seed(0)
A1, A2 = sbm_corr(block_members, block_probs, rho)
disagreements = np.linalg.norm(A1 - A2)**2
print(f"Disagreements (Unshuffled): {int(disagreements):d}")
# Disagreements (Unshuffled): 8041
```

Figure 7.3.6(A) and (B) shows the networks $A^{(1)}$ and $A^{(2)}$. The networks have a similar topological structure. However, even when perfectly unshuffled, there are still edge disagreements, because the networks have differing (albeit, correlated) topologies.

To emphasize the effectiveness of SGM, as well as why having seeds is important, we will randomly shuffle the vertices of network B.

```
P = make_random_permutation(n_nodes)
A2_shuffle = P.T @ A2 @ P
disagreements_shuffled = np.linalg.norm(A1 - A2_shuffle)**2
print(f"Disagreements (Shuffled): {int(disagreements_shuffled):d}")
# Disagreements (Shuffled): 22201
```

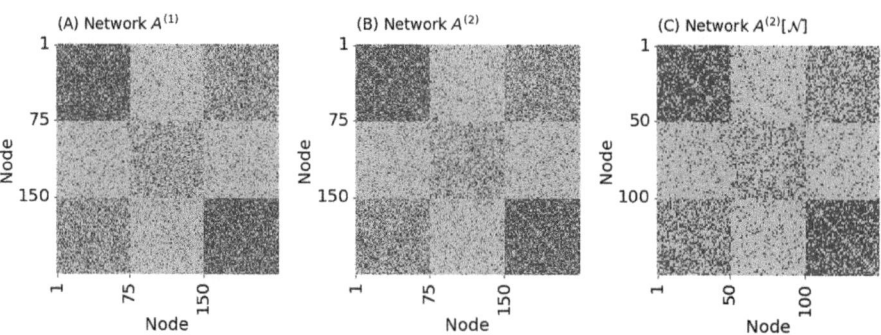

Figure 7.3.6 **(A)** The network $A^{(1)}$, **(B)** the network $A^{(2)}$ which is ρ-correlated to $A^{(1)}$, and **(C)** the network $A^{(2),r}$, $A^{(2)}$ with 25 nodes removed per community.

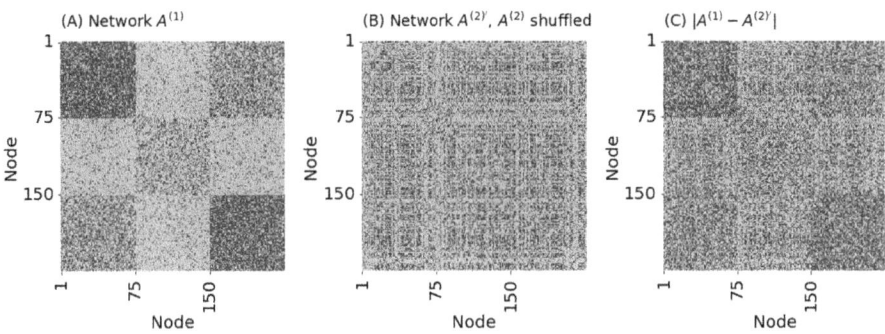

Figure 7.3.7 (**A**) The original network $A^{(1)}$, (**B**) the shuffled network $A^{(2)'}$ which is a shuffling of a network ρ-correlated to $A^{(1)}$, and (**C**) the edge disagreements between $A^{(1)}$ and $A^{(2)'}$.

We will call the version of $A^{(2)}$ after shuffling $A^{(2)'}$. The network $A^{(1)}$ and the shuffled network $A^{(2)'}$ are shown in Figure 7.3.7, along with the edge disagreements. Note that the number of disagreements has increased considerably after shuffling.

Matching the Networks without Seeds
First, we will run SGM on network $A^{(1)}$ and the shuffled network $A^{(2)'}$ with no seeds. We use the code for computing the unshuffling matrix, the match ratio, and the number of edge disagreements that we developed previously.

```
# fit with A and shuffled B
gm = graph_match(A1, A2_shuffle, rng=0)

# obtain unshuffled version of the shuffled B
P_unshuffle_noseed = make_unshuffler(gm.indices_B)
A2_unshuffle_noseed = P_unshuffle_noseed.T @ A2_shuffle @
    P_unshuffle_noseed

# compute the match ratio
match_ratio_noseed = match_ratio(P, P_unshuffle_noseed)
print(f"Match Ratio, no seeds: {match_ratio_noseed:.3f}")
# Match Ratio, no seeds: 0.004

disagreements_noseed = np.linalg.norm(A1 - A2_unshuffle_noseed)**2
print(f"Disagreements, no seeds: {int(disagreements_noseed):d}")
# Disagreements, no seeds: 12810
```

The original network $A^{(1)}$, the unshuffled network $\hat{P}_u^\top A^{(2)'} \hat{P}_u$, and the edge disagreements between the original network and the shuffled correlated network (after unshuffling is estimated without seeds) are shown in Figure 7.3.8. While the predicted unshuffling for $A^{(2)'}$ was relatively successful in recovering the basic structure of the network $A^{(1)}$, we see that the number of edge disagreements between them is still quite high, and the match ratio of successfully unshuffled nodes is quite low (it is about 0). Note that edge disagreements are fairly frequent.

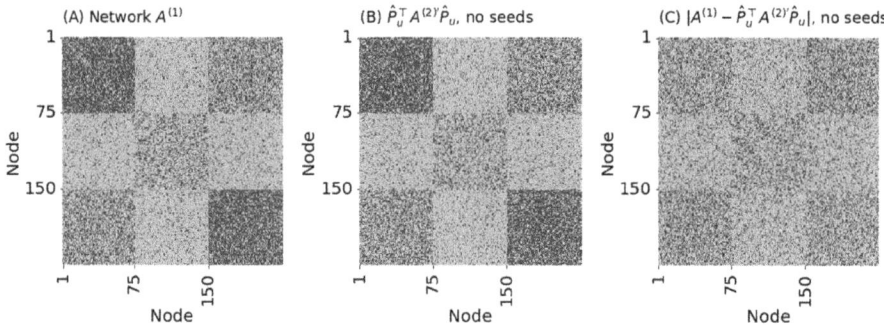

Figure 7.3.8 (**A**) The original network $A^{(1)}$, (**B**) the unshuffling of the correlated network $\hat{P}_u^\top A^{(2)'} \hat{P}_u$, and (**C**) the edge disagreements between the original network and the unshuffled network.

Matching the Networks with Seeds

Next, we run SGM with 10 seeds randomly selected from the optimal permutation vector found earlier. Although 10 seeds is only about 4 percent of the 225 node network, we will observe next how much more accurate the matching will be compared to having no seeds. First we add a helper function, which takes a permutation matrix and a desired number of seeds, and indicates where the identified seed nodes (from the unshuffled network) would be permuted to (after shuffling):

```
def gen_seeds(P, n_seeds, random_seed=0):
    """
    A function to generate n_seeds seeds for a pair of matrices A1 and
        P^TA2P
    which are initially matched, but P has been applied to permute the
        nodes
    of A2.
    """
    rng = np.random.default_rng(seed=random_seed)
    n = P.shape[0]
    # obtain n_seeds random seeds from 1:n
    seeds = rng.choice(n, size=n_seeds, replace=False)
    # use the permutation matrix to find where each seed was permuted to
    seeds_permuted = [np.where(P[i, :] == 1)[0] for i in seeds]
    return (seeds, seeds_permuted)
```

Next, we run seeded graph matching, using the `graph_match` function from `graspologic`, by passing seeds as parameters:

```
nseeds = 10 # the number of seeds to use
# select ten nodes at random from A which will serve as seeds

# obtain seeds for nodes of A1 with nodes of A2 after shuffling
seedsA1, seedsA2_shuffled = gen_seeds(P, nseeds)

# run SGM with A1 and shuffled A2, but provide the seed nodes from A
    as ref_seeds
```

```
# and the corresponding position of these seed nodes after shuffling
    as permuted_seeds
sgm = graph_match(A1, A2_shuffle, partial_match=(seedsA1,
    seedsA2_shuffled), rng=0)
P_unshuffle_seeds = make_unshuffler(sgm.indices_B)
A2_unshuffle_seeds = P_unshuffle_seeds.T @ A2_shuffle @
    P_unshuffle_seeds

match_ratio_seeds = match_ratio(P, P_unshuffle_seeds)
print(f"Match Ratio, seeds: {match_ratio_seeds:.3f}")
# Match Ratio with seeds: 1.000

disagreements_seeds = np.linalg.norm(A1 - A2_unshuffle_seeds)**2
print(f"Disagreements, seeds: {int(disagreements_seeds):d}")
# Disagreements, seeds: 8041
```

The resulting unshuffling steps for $A^{(2)'}$ are shown in Figure 7.3.9. Compared to Figure 7.3.8, we can see that the unshuffling produces far fewer edge disagreements than when we used unseeded graph matching. Further, using just 10 seeds (about 4 percent of the nodes in the network), the match ratio increased to at or near perfect.

Our conclusions can be summarized as follows:

1. When two networks have misaligned nodes, in that the nodes are not ordered the same but the networks are otherwise identical, graph matching strategies can often efficiently recover an unshuffling matrix to align the nodes between the two networks.
2. When two networks have misaligned nodes and the underlying networks are closely related (but not identical; e.g., they are conceptually correlated), graph matching strategies will generally reasonably match the overall topological structure of the two networks, but will often produce poor matches. Narrowing down the scope of the problem (via known seed nodes, where we know the matching ahead of time) can often still yield precise solutions.

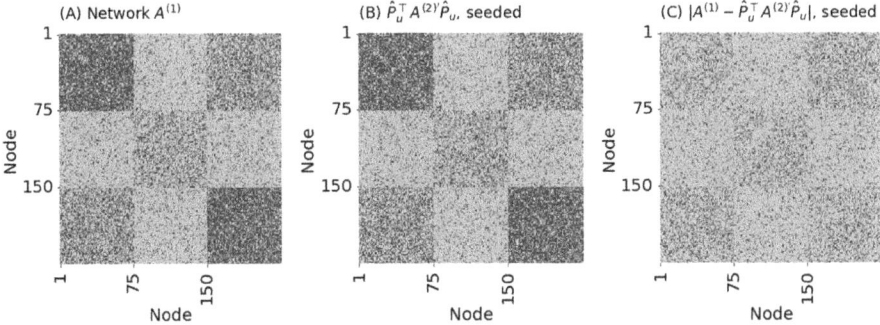

Figure 7.3.9 (**A**) The original matrix $A^{(1)}$, (**B**) the unshuffling of the shuffled and correlated matrix $\hat{P}_u^\top A^{(2)'} \hat{P}_u$, and (**C**) the edge disagreements when we graph match using seeds.

7.3.6   Padded Graph Matching

So far, we have assumed that the two networks being matched must have the same number of nodes. In practice, this is a restrictive limitation. Suppose we want to match the nodes in a smaller network to a larger network, or vice versa.

We will do this through a technique called *padded graph matching*, in which we add new nodes to the smaller network until it has the same number of nodes as the larger network, and then we run graph matching on the resulting networks with an equal number of nodes. We have two techniques for adding these isolated nodes: naive and adopted padding.

For these examples, we'll adjust our correlated network slightly from Section 7.3.5. Our first network $A^{(1)}$ will be the same one we sampled previously from the ρ-SBM. For $A^{(2)}$, we'll arbitrarily take out the last 25 nodes of each block. This new network will be called $\mathcal{A}^{(2)}[\mathcal{N}]$. Here, the notation $A^{(2)}[\mathcal{N}]$ denotes that it is the subnetwork of $A^{(2)}$ induced by the set of nodes $\mathcal{N}$, where $\mathcal{N}$ are the nodes that we want to retain:

```
from graspologic.utils import remove_vertices

nremove = 25

# nodes to remove from A2
n_nodes_A2_N = n_nodes - nremove*n_blocks
base_range = np.arange(n_per_block - nremove, n_per_block)
block_offsets = np.array([0, 75, 150])

# repeat a base range for each block and add block offsets
nodes_to_remove = np.repeat(base_range, len(block_offsets))
nodes_to_remove += np.tile(block_offsets, nremove)
N = np.setdiff1d(np.arange(n_nodes), nodes_to_remove)

# use the remove_vertices function to compute
# the subnetwork induced by the nodes nodes_to_retain
A2_N = remove_vertices(A2, nodes_to_remove)
```

In the foregoing code, we took care to obtain node indices of the nodes from $A^{(2)}$ that are retained in $A^{(2)}[\mathcal{N}]$ so that we will be able to evaluate our graph matching after we apply graph matching techniques. The network $A^{(2)}$ with the last 25 nodes removed from it is shown in Figure 7.3.6(C). This network $A^{(2)}[\mathcal{N}]$ and its corresponding underlying random network $\mathbf{A}^{(2)}[\mathcal{N}]$ have only 150 instead of 225 nodes.

Our task is to match the 150 nodes in $A^{(2)}[\mathcal{N}]$ to their corresponding matched pair in $A^{(1)}$.

We want to match $A^{(2)}[\mathcal{N}]$ to a subnetwork of $A^{(1)}$ induced by the nodes for which there is a corresponding matched pair. That is, we add the additional hurdle that we must figure out which nodes in the larger network $A^{(1)}$ actually have a matched pair in $A^{(2)}[\mathcal{N}]$, and ignore the other nodes entirely. The induced subnetwork of $A^{(1)}$ by the retained nodes, $A^{(1)}[\mathcal{N}]$ can be obtained like this:

```
A1_N = remove_vertices(A1, nodes_to_remove)
```

Crucially, while in simulations we know which nodes are missing from $A^{(2)}$ (given by the set `nodes_to_remove` in the code above), in real data we do not know which nodes are missing.

7.3.6.1 Naive Padded Graph Matching

Through *naive padding*, we simply add isolate nodes to the smaller network until the number of nodes in $A^{(2)}[\mathcal{N}]$ are equal to the number of nodes in $A^{(1)}$. From Section 3.6, we know that isolate nodes do not have any edges in the network. The naive padded version of $A^{(2)}[\mathcal{N}]$ can be obtained like this:

```
A2_N_padded = np.pad(
    A2_N,
    pad_width=[(0,nremove*n_blocks), (0, nremove*n_blocks)]
)
```

The padded network is shown in Figure 7.3.10(B), and we will refer to it notationally as $A^{(2)}[\mathcal{N}]^+$, where the superscript "+" denotes that it is padded. Naive graph matching proceeds rather simply by matching $A^{(1)}$ with $A^{(2)}[\mathcal{N}]^+$.

This padding procedure occurs under-the-hood when we call `graph_match` from `graspologic` with two adjacency matrices that have an unequal number of input nodes with the argument `padding="naive"`. As before, we can leverage seeds to improve our matches, being careful to choose seeds from nodes that are "retained"; that is, we want to make sure our seeds are actual nodes in the network (and not isolates). We do this by choosing seed nodes from $A^{(2)}[\mathcal{N}]$, and then using the inducing set $\mathcal{N}$ to determine the nodes of $A^{(1)}$ that these seeds correspond to:

```
nseeds_padded = 10

rng = np.random.default_rng(seed=0)
# obtain which nodes of A2 will be the seeds to use, from the retained
    nodes in the network
```

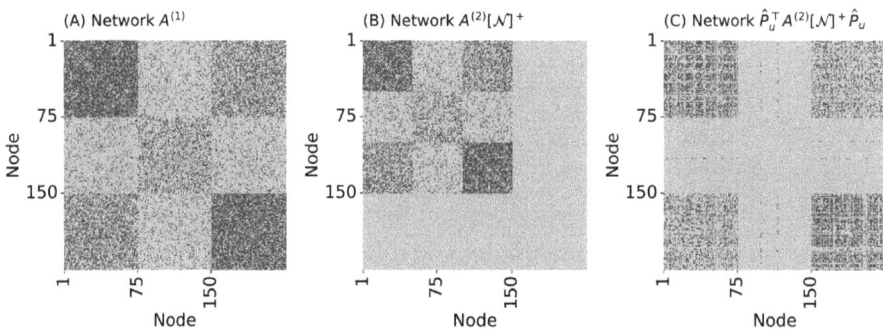

Figure 7.3.10 **(A)** The original network $A^{(1)}$ that we wish to align to, **(B)** the network $A^{(2)}$ is ρ-correlated with A, has 25 nodes per community removed to form $A^{(2)}[\mathcal{N}]$, and then has 75 isolates added (naively) to create the padded network $A^{(2)}[\mathcal{N}]^+$, and **(C)** the padded network $A^{(2)}[\mathcal{N}]^+$ after graph matching with naive padding.

```
seeds_A2_N = rng.choice(n_nodes_A2_N, size=nseeds_padded,
    replace=False)

# obtain the nodes in A1
seeds_A1 = N[seeds_A2_N]

# run SGM with A1 and the induced subnetwork of A2
# since we didn't shuffle A(2), we do not need
# to worry about permuting the seeds
sgm_naive = graph_match(A1, A2_N, partial_match=(seeds_A1, seeds_A2_N),
                padding="naive", rng=0, n_init=5)

# unshuffle A2_N using indices_B
P_unshuffle = make_unshuffler(sgm_naive.indices_B)
A2_N_unshuffle_seeds_naive = P_unshuffle.T @ A2_N @ P_unshuffle
```

As discussed, under the hood, naive padded graph matching adds nodes to construct $A^{(2)}[\mathcal{N}]^+$, and then aligns $A^{(2)}[\mathcal{N}]^+$ to the nodes of $A^{(1)}$ using the isolated padding nodes. To illustrate the limitations of this process, we can apply the unshuffling (from above) to the network $A^{(2)}[\mathcal{N}]^+$ with isolated padding nodes. Note that indices_A[i] indicates the node from $A^{(1)}$ that is matched to indices_B[i] in $A^{(2)}[\mathcal{N}]$. Therefore, the nodes matched to the nodes $\mathcal{N}$ are given by indices_A. We can use this to construct the original network, adding back the isolated padding nodes, using a numpy indexing grid:

```
A2_naive_full = np.zeros(A1.shape)
A2_naive_full[np.ix_(sgm_naive.indices_A, sgm_naive.indices_A)] =
    A2_N_unshuffle_seeds_naive
```

The network $A^{(2)}[\mathcal{N}]^+$ after unshuffling is shown in Figure 7.3.10(C). Unfortunately, The naive matching of $A^{(2)}[\mathcal{N}]^+$ after padding looks nothing like $A^{(1)}$. Particularly, notice that all of the "padding nodes" (with no edges) were simply "matched" with the second community of nodes. There is a large "hole" in the matched network in the middle, with very few edges. Consequently, the number of edge disagreements is high. To compute the edge disagreements, we look at the subnetwork $A^{(1)}[\mathcal{N}]$ induced by the nodes retained in $A^{(1)}$, and compare these to the unshuffled $A^{(2)}[\mathcal{N}]$ (without padding nodes):

```
A1_induced = remove_vertices(A1, nodes_to_remove)
disagreements_naive = np.linalg.norm(A1_induced -
    A2_N_unshuffle_seeds_naive)**2
print(f"Disagreements, naive padding: {int(disagreements_naive):d}")
# Disagreements, naive padding: 9058
```

which produces a high number of edge disagreements.

This happened because we effectively treated the new isolated nodes of $A^{(2)}[\mathcal{N}]^+$ after padding as "equal" to the original nodes of $A^{(2)}[\mathcal{N}]$ (which are actual nodes in the underlying network $A^{(2)}$). This allowed nodes that didn't really exist to play a substantial role in the matching. Note that in $A^{(1)}$, the second community of nodes (nodes 75 through 150) appear to have lower degrees than the other nodes of the network (there are fewer edges from nodes in community two to other nodes). The padded isolate nodes of $A^{(2)}[\mathcal{N}]^+$ ended up being aligned to these low-degree nodes of $A^{(1)}$.

Looking in 7.3.10(C), the average degree for nodes aligned with community two nodes (of $A^{(1)}$) are lower than the average degree for nodes aligned with those in communities one and three. This can be discerned by noting that there are far fewer edges with nodes in the second community. Formally, the subnetwork induced by the isolates of $A^{(2)}[\mathcal{N}]^+$ (the extra nodes that we added) were aligned with the subnetwork induced by the nodes with lowest degree in $A^{(1)}$. These nodes with the lowest degree in $A^{(1)}$ are typically called the *lowest density subnetwork* of $A^{(1)}$, in that their edge density is lowest. It is often the case that when using naive padded matching, isolated padding nodes of the network with smaller size will be aligned to low density subnetworks of the larger network.

7.3.6.2 Adopted Padded Graph Matching

Instead of having our match driven by the padding nodes in $A^{(2)}[\mathcal{N}]^+$ to the lowest density subnetwork of $A^{(1)}$ as is done by naive padding, we want to match $A^{(2)}[\mathcal{N}]$ (the unpadded network) to the best fitting induced subnetwork of $A^{(1)}$. The key difference is that, in the ideal case, the subnetwork induced on $A^{(1)}$ is the set of nodes which are actually present in $A^{(2)}[\mathcal{N}]$. Stated another way, we want to align $A^{(2)}[\mathcal{N}]^+$ to $A^{(1)}$, but with the padding nodes minimally impactful on the resulting matching quality.

To do this, we use a strategy called *adopted padding*, which is performed using `padding="adopted"` for the `GraphMatch` module. Adopted padding renormalizes both adjacency matrices so that the matching places greater weight on the subnetwork induced by nonpadding nodes, and very little weight on the padding nodes. Through adopted padding, we first normalize $A^{(1)}$ and $A^{(2)}[\mathcal{N}]$, to form $\tilde{A}^{(1)}$ and $\tilde{A}^{(2)}[\mathcal{N}]$, by multiplying the networks by 2, and then subtracting a matrix of 1s. We pad $\tilde{A}^{(2)}[\mathcal{N}]$ like we did before, adding isolated padding nodes until the two networks have the same number of nodes.

```
A1tilde = 2 * A1 - np.ones(A1.shape[0])
A2tilde_N = 2*A2_N - np.ones(A2_N.shape[0])
A2tilde_N_padded = np.pad(A2tilde_N, [(0,nremove*n_blocks), (0,
    nremove*n_blocks)])
```

These normalized networks are illustrated in Figure 7.3.11(A, B). The intuition of how the adopted padding procedure downweights padding isolated nodes is discussed in Remark 7.3.6.

```
# run SGM with A1 and A2[N] with nodes removed
sgm_adopted = graph_match(A1, A2_N, partial_match=(seeds_A1,
    seeds_A2_N), padding="adopted", rng=0, n_init=5)

# unshuffle A2[N] using the permutation identified
P_unshuffle_ad = make_unshuffler(sgm_adopted.indices_B)
A2_N_unshuffle_seeds_adopted = P_unshuffle_ad.T @ A2_N @ P_unshuffle_ad

A2_adopted_full = np.zeros(A1.shape)
A2_adopted_full[np.ix_(sgm_adopted.indices_A, sgm_adopted.indices_A)]
    = A2_N_unshuffle_seeds_adopted
```

Remark 7.3.6 Adopted padding and the value of normalization

Adopted padding downweights padded isolate nodes in the cost function through a specific normalization scheme, such that they will matter less in the cost function. Through this normalization, edges $\tilde{a}_{ij}^{(m)}$ will have a weight of 1, nonedges $\tilde{a}_{ij}^{(m)}$ will have a weight of -1, and padding nodes $\tilde{a}_{ij}^{(m)}$ will have edges with a weight of 0. To understand the impact of this normalization, consider the objective function, the squared Frobenius distance, before any permutation has been applied to either of the networks:

$$\|\tilde{A}^{(1)} - \tilde{A}^{(2)}[\mathcal{N}]^+\|_F^2 = \sum_{i=1}^{n} \sum_{j=1}^{n} \left(\tilde{a}_{ij}^{(1)} - \tilde{a}^{(2)}[\mathcal{N}]_{ij}^+ \right)^2.$$

When node i or node j are padding nodes for the second network, $\tilde{a}^{(2)}[\mathcal{N}]_{ij}^+ = 0$, and the squared difference is at most 1 (since $\tilde{a}_{ij}^{(1)}$ is 1 if there is an edge or -1 if there is no edge). However, when node i and j are both not padding nodes for the second network, the difference has a value of 2 and a squared difference of 4 (if the edges disagree) or 0 (if the edges do not disagree). Therefore, in the objective function, disagreements arising from padding nodes are "downweighted" relative to differences arising from nonpadding nodes, as disagreements have a higher cost when they occur due to nonpadded nodes. Consider how, in contrast, naive padded graph matching weights disagreements equally, regardless of whether they are due to padding isolated nodes or nonpadding nodes.

The unshuffled network (with padded isolate nodes) is illustrated in Figure 7.3.11(C). Note that the isolated nodes tend to be dispersed to the last few nodes of each community, which is consistent with the nodes that were originally removed from the network. They are not restricted to the nodes in the lowest density induced subnetwork, as in Figure 7.3.10(C). The networks appear to be much better aligned.

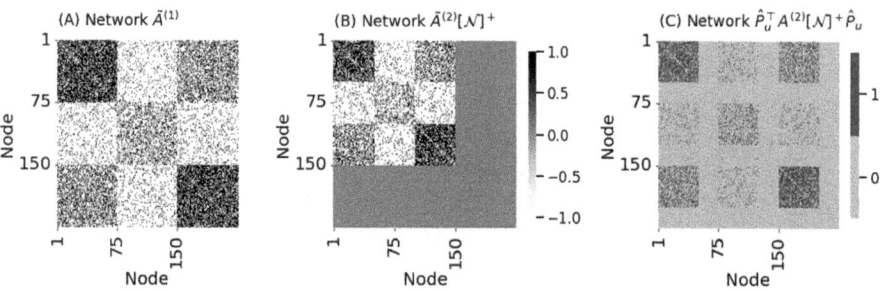

Figure 7.3.11 (**A**) The normalized network $\tilde{A}^{(1)}$, (**B**) the normalized network $\tilde{A}^{(2)}[\mathcal{N}]^+$, and (**C**) the network $A^{(2)}[\mathcal{N}]^+$ after alignment to $A^{(1)}$, which is aligned using $\tilde{A}^{(1)}$ and $\tilde{A}^{(2)}[\mathcal{N}]^+$ via adopted padding.

To evaluate this padding scheme, we evaluate the matching ratio on the subnetwork induced by the nonpadding nodes. In the ideal case, since we did not apply any permutations to $A^{(2)}[\mathcal{N}]$ (and only removed nodes), the permutation matrix should be the identity matrix, in that no nodes were sorted. Further, to compute the number of disagreements, we compare $A^{(2)}[\mathcal{N}]$ after unshuffling to $A^{(1)}[\mathcal{N}]$, using the `remove_vertices` utility from `graspologic`:

```
match_ratio_adopted = match_ratio(np.eye(A1_induced.shape[0]),
    P_unshuffle_ad)
print(f"Match Ratio, adopted padding: {match_ratio_adopted:.3f}")
# Match Ratio, adopted padding: 0.887

disagreements_adopted = np.linalg.norm(A1_induced -
    A2_N_unshuffle_seeds_adopted)**2
print(f"Disagreements, adopted padding:
    {int(disagreements_adopted):d}")
# Disagreements, adopted padding: 4186
```

Using adopted matching has yielded a nearly perfect match ratio, and the number of disagreements has been dramatically reduced. Compare this to naive padded matching from Figure 7.3.10, where the naive approach resulted in only isolates being matched to nodes in community two. See also Remark 7.3.7.

Remark 7.3.7 Vertex nomination via seeded graph matching

It is often the case that we have two networks $A^{(1)}$ and $A^{(2)}$, and we might want to ask which node or set of nodes in a second network are "maximally similar" to a given node (or set of nodes) of interest in the first network. Let's call this node $i^{(1)}$. This can be thought of as a form of the vertex nomination problem from Section 6.5, where we have a node of interest (or set of nodes of interest) and want to produce a nomination list of possible nodes in the network $A^{(2)}$ that our node(s) of interest in the network $A^{(1)}$ are most similar to.

Because we use stochastic gradient descent, the solution to the graph matching problem is nondeterministic, in that running it twice might produce a slightly different matching. We estimate a nomination list by computing the number of times each node $j^{(2)}$ in network 2 are matched to node $i^{(1)}$. Then, we can order the nomination list by the nodes that are most frequently matched to node $i^{(1)}$. This procedure is known as `VNviaSGM` [14].

Bibliography

[1] Tang M, Athreya A, Sussman DL, Lyzinski V, Park Y, Priebe CE. A semiparametric two-sample hypothesis testing problem for random graphs. J. Comput. Graph. Stat. 2017 Apr.;26(2):344–354.

[2] Székely GJ, Rizzo ML, Bakirov NK. Measuring and testing dependence by correlation of distances. Ann. Stat. 2007 Dec.;35(6):2769–2794.

[3] Vogelstein JT, Bridgeford EW, Wang Q, Priebe CE, Maggioni M, Shen C. Discovering and deciphering relationships across disparate data modalities. eLife. 2019 Jan.

[4] Alyakin A, Agterberg J, Helm HS, Priebe C. Correcting a nonparametric two-sample graph hypothesis test for graphs with different numbers of vertices. arXiv: Methodology. 2020.

[5] Ryan TA. Multiple comparisons in psychological research. Psychol. Bull. 1959 Jan.;56(1):26–47.

[6] Holm S. A simple sequentially rejective multiple test procedure. Scand. J. Stat. 1979;6(2):65–70.

[7] Springer SP, Deutsch G. Left Brain, Right Brain: Perspectives From Cognitive Neuroscience (Series of Books in Psychology). W. H. Freeman and Company/Worth Publishers; 2001.

[8] Pedigo BD, Powell M, Bridgeford EW, Winding M, Priebe CE, Vogelstein JT. Generative network modeling reveals quantitative definitions of bilateral symmetry exhibited by a whole insect brain connectome. eLife. 2023 Mar.

[9] Dunnett CW, Gent M. Significance testing to establish equivalence between treatments, with special reference to data in the form of 2X2 tables. Biometrics. 1977 Dec.;33(4): 593–602.

[10] Livi L, Rizzi A. The graph matching problem. Pattern Anal. Appl. 2013 Aug.;16(3): 253–283.

[11] Vogelstein JT, Conroy JM, Lyzinski V, Podrazik LJ, Kratzer SG, Harley ET, et al. Fast approximate quadratic programming for graph matching. PLoS One. 2015 Apr.;10(4):e0121002.

[12] Fishkind DE, Adali S, Patsolic HG, Meng L, Singh D, Lyzinski V, et al. Seeded graph matching. Pattern Recognit. 2019 Mar.;87:203–215.

[13] Lyzinski V, Fishkind DE, Priebe CE. Seeded graph matching for correlated Erdös–Rényi graphs. J. Mach. Learn. Res. 2014 Jan.;15(1):3513–3540.

[14] Patsolic HG, Park Y, Lyzinski V, Priebe CE. Vertex nomination via seeded graph matching. Stat. Anal. Data Min.: The ASA Data Sci. Journal. 2020 Jun.;13(3):229–244.

8   Applications for Multiple Networks

This chapter covers applications of network machine learning when working with numerous networks, extending beyond the single and paired network scenarios covered in Chapters 6 and 7. This chapter presents several key techniques and use-cases.

Many of the approaches in previous chapters can be adapted for multiple network settings. For instance, the community detection methods in Section 6.1 can be extended by examining embeddings or properties of the shared latent position matrices obtained through the multiple adjacency spectral embedding (mase) technique introduced in Section 5.5.3, or of the Omnibus technique introduced in Section 5.5.4.

This chapter covers the following topics:

1. Section 8.1 introduces anomaly detection in time series of networks, exploring how to identify significant changes in network structure over time.
2. Section 8.2 discusses incoherent signal subnetwork estimation, a technique for identifying important edges that differentiate between classes of networks.
3. Section 8.3 builds on the previous section by introducing coherent signal subnetwork estimation, which leverages additional network structural information to improve edge selection.

These techniques are most useful when we can collect many networks representing individual observations. Taking a large network and breaking it apart into subnetworks can also lead to use cases for this line of research.

8.1   Anomaly Detection in Timeseries of Networks

In Part III, we have explored methods for analyzing static networks and comparing pairs of networks. However, many real-world systems generate *longitudinal* networks that evolve over time, which are expressed as a sequence. This section aims to detect anomalous networks in longitudinal network data.

Anomaly detection focuses on identifying significant changes in network structure over time, either globally or within specific node subgroups. We will:

1. Define anomaly detection in the context of time-varying networks,
2. Develop methods for quantifying network changes between timepoints,
3. Explore techniques for identifying anomalous subgroups of nodes, and
4. Discuss challenges in distinguishing meaningful changes from noise.

Across a longitudinal sequence of networks, the nodes remain the same, but the edges vary depending on the timepoint. We consider a network in a timeseries sequence "anomalous" if a subset of nodes exhibits concurrent behavior changes compared to recent time points, while the remaining network structure remains relatively stable. We build from the two-sample testing foundation introduced in Section 7.1.

An exploration of longitudinal network analysis provides a foundation for studying dynamic systems, detecting critical transition points, and identifying localized changes in complex networks.

We will explore longitudinal network data in the context of sea slug nervous systems, discussed in Case Study 8.1.1.

Case Study 8.1.1 Brain networks of sea slugs

There is a particular type of sea slug with sensitive gills on the outside of its body. When the gills sense any stimulus, they reflexively withdraw into the body. When the gill response is repeatedly triggered without a negative effect on the slug, the response diminishes [1; 2]. However, when an electrical shock is administered, such as by a predator, the response returns. Foundational experiments on these slugs, called *Aplysia*, formed the basis for our physiological understanding of memory in the brain and led to the Nobel Prize in Physiology or Medicine by Eric Kandel in 2000.

Suppose we study these slugs, and we generate multiple brain networks of the same slug over a time period. We define each node as a single neuron and edges as connections between neurons. Each timepoint is associated with a gill response stimulation: Some timepoints are before the slug learns not to withdraw its gills, some are after learning, and some are after an electrical shock is administered. We hypothesize that the networks will differ after learning and after the administration of an electrical shock. Given the time-varying networks, how do we figure out which timepoints these are?

Collecting brain networks is a noisy process (Section 1.3). Random noise might lead to spurious changes in edges at different timepoints. We want to figure out if there are timepoints where there are changes in the network that exceed that of normal measurement variation; changes in the underlying process (the random network) that is generating our network observations.

The sea slug brain is measured at $T = 12$ points in time where the gill response occurs. Each network has 90 nodes representing neurons, in one of three communities of nodes. Although the actual *Aplysia* nervous system circuit controlling gill withdrawal is more complex, we will pretend that these communities represent peripheral motor neurons (responsible for movement and reflexes), the abdominal ganglion (responsible for determining whether the slug should reflex), and ocular neurons (responsible for sight). A pair of nodes are connected if the neurons they represent are both firing at that timepoint.

For the first six timepoints, the slug contracts its gills to protect them from damage. The network has a strong affinity structure: Within-community connections exist with probability 0.4, and between-community connections exist with probability 0.05.

After the sixth timepoint, the slug begins to learn that the water squirts are harmless, its hippocampus begins to block the gill withdrawal reflex, and the slug retracts its gills less. During this time there is a degree augmentation (see the DCSBM in Section 4.7) in the nodes of the brain network, via a degree-correction vector $\vec{\theta}$. By the seventh timepoint, the sea slug stops reflexing its gills all together, once it has learned that the splashes are harmless.

After the ninth timepoint, an electrical shock is administered to the slug prior to the water squirt, and the slug "forgets" that the water squirt itself is harmless. At this time point, the sea slug returns to its original brain patterns. We can generate the networks like this:

```
import numpy as np
from graspologic.simulations import sbm
from graphbook_code import dcsbm

# the block matrix for the neurons before learning
B0 = 0.05*np.ones((3, 3))
np.fill_diagonal(B0, 0.4)

nk = 40
ns = np.repeat(nk, 3)

theta = np.tile(np.linspace(np.sqrt(2), np.sqrt(2) - 1, nk), 3)
zs = np.repeat([1,2,3], nk)

T = 12
np.random.seed(0)
networks = np.array([sbm(ns, B0) if (t < 6 or t >= 9) else dcsbm(zs,
    theta, B0) for t in range(T)])
```

The simulated networks are illustrated in Figure 8.1.1. After learning in Figure 8.1.1(B), the nodes in the lower half of each community appear to have more edges than the nodes in the upper half of each community. After an electric shock is administered in Figure 8.1.1(C), this pattern returns to the baseline response from Figure 8.1.1(A).

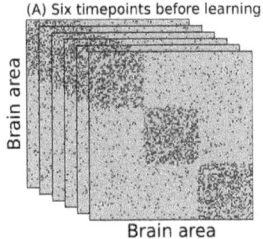
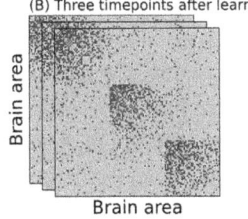
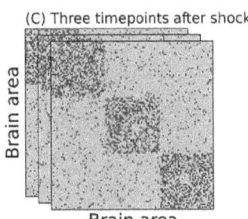

Figure 8.1.1 (**A**) The simulated networks, before learning, (**B**) the simulated networks, after learning, and (**C**) the simulated networks, after an electric shock is administered.

8.1.1   Detecting Anomalies using Network Models

Our goal is to detect the timepoints at which there are the largest changes in the network: We would like to determine at exactly which timepoint the shock occurred. If the network $A^{(t)}$ is a realization of a random network $\mathbf{A}^{(t)}$ with probability matrix $P^{(t)}$, we want to identify the timepoints t where the probability matrix changes for the current timepoint compared to the preceding timepoint $P^{(t)} \neq P^{(t-1)}$.

This gives us the hypotheses:

$$H_0^{(t)}: P^{(t)} = P^{(t-1)} \text{ against } H_A^{(t)}: P^{(t)} \neq P^{(t-1)}$$

for every timepoint t.

If there were only two timepoints in total and $T = 2$, this is equivalent to the hypotheses in Equation (7.1) from Section 7.1.

Because the networks appear to have a homophilic structure, the underlying random networks are likely positive semidefinite using the logic developed in Section 4.5. Therefore, the networks can be generalized by RDPGs, so it is sensible to use the latent position test from Section 7.1.2:

$$H_0^{(t)}: X^{(t)} = WX^{(t-1)} \text{ for some orthogonal matrix } W,$$
$$H_A^{(t)}: X^{(t)} \neq WX^{(t-1)} \text{ for any orthogonal matrix } W.$$

In practice, we found in Equation (7.4) that we could estimate the best possible orthogonal transform of the second estimated latent position matrix onto the first by solving the orthogonal Procrustes problem. We perform these latent position tests for all timepoints from 2 to T, by sequentially comparing a given timepoint t to the previous timepoint $t - 1$.

Each of these $T - 1$ tests gives us an estimated p-value, $\hat{p}^{(t)}$, using the parametric bootstrap procedure from Section 7.1.2 [3]. We consider a timepoint *anomalous* if $\hat{p}^{(t)} \leq \alpha$, where as usual, we use $\alpha = 0.05$.

The Multiple Comparisons Problem, Revisited

In the case where there is no longitudinal effect, that is, the underlying networks are identical across time, we run into the *multiple comparisons problem* from Section 7.2, where if the null hypothesis is true and there is no effect, we would expect about α fraction of tests run to have a p-value $\leq \alpha$.

If the error rate for an individual test at a given timepoint is α, the familywise error rate (FWER) for making an error for any of the $(T - 1)$ tests is $(T - 1)\alpha$. So if we have T timepoints and there is no longitudinal effect, we would expect a proportion of about $(T - 1)\alpha$ of the tests to falsely reject the null hypothesis in favor of the alternative hypothesis.

Section 7.2 addressed this issue with the Holm–Bonferroni adjustment [4], which we will also use here.

Corrected *p*-value for test of anomalies from one timepoint to next

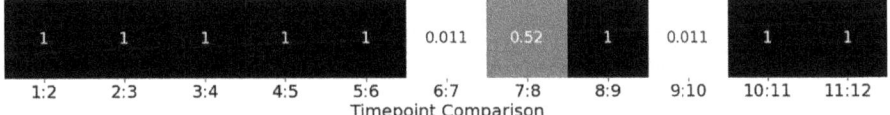

Timepoint Comparison

Figure 8.1.2 The *p*-values from the latent position test for each pair of adjacent timepoints in the longitudinal sequence of networks.

8.1.2 Applying Anomaly Detection to Simulated Networks

Let's see how we can implement the ideas from Section 8.1.1 for anomaly testing. We obtain estimated *p*-values by using the latent position test from Section 7.1.2. This code may take a minute or two to run, so we include tqdm in the loop:

```
from graspologic.inference import latent_position_test
import warnings
from tqdm import tqdm

warnings.filterwarnings('ignore')
pvalues = [latent_position_test(networks[t + 1], networks[t],
    n_components=3,
                    n_bootstraps=1000, workers=-1)[1] for t in
                    tqdm(range(T-1))]
```

Next, we adjust for multiple comparisons, using the multipletests() function from statsmodels:

```
from statsmodels.stats.multitest import multipletests

alpha = 0.05
_, adj_pvals, _, _ = multipletests(pvalues, alpha=alpha, method="holm")
```

The resulting adjusted *p*-values are shown in Figure 8.1.2. Recall that in timepoints 7 through 9, the slug "learned" that the water squirts are harmless. Therefore, for all pairs of timepoints from 1 to 6, 7 to 9, and 10 to 12, we should not be able to identify any difference. However, from 6 to 7 (when the slug learned) and from 9 to 10 (when the slug was shocked, and unlearned) we should be able to detect a difference. For these comparisons, the *p*-values (after adjustment) are below our detection threshold of $\alpha = 0.05$, indicating that we have evidence to reject the null hypothesis, and we find that the networks are different. We have found that the networks have detectable anomalies at these timepoints.

8.2 Testing for Significant Edges in Incoherent Signal Subnetworks

In Section 4.10, we introduced the concept of signal subnetworks (SSNs) using an example of earthling and astronaut brain networks. This section builds on that foundation to develop methods for identifying signal edges within these networks.

We will revisit the SSN model, building on Sections 3.5 and 4.10, where edge probabilities depend on both network class (earthling or astronaut) and membership in the signal network. We will:

1. Formalize the concept of incoherent signal subnetworks,
2. Develop statistical tests to identify significant edges across the network,
3. Explore methods to estimate incoherent signal subnetworks from data,
4. Develop strategies to use estimated signal subnetworks to classify network data, and
5. Discuss the challenges and limitations of incoherent SSN analysis.

These techniques analyze networks where only a subset of edges carries meaningful signal. This exploration extends our earlier work in Section 5.6 on network models with covariates, applying it to the practical problem of detecting evolved differences in brain connectivity.

An incoherent subnetwork estimator focuses exclusively on the importance of individual edges, often quantified by statistical measures such as Fisher's exact test p-values. In Section 8.3, we will explore coherent signal subnetworks, which incorporate network structure to improve classification accuracy and reduce sample-specific noise.

This section builds upon the Bayes plugin classifier (also called the Naive Bayes classifier). For a brief refresher, we recommend reviewing Online Appendix D.3.

We will consider how to statistically identify changes in a hypothetical sight-related node (SI) in the astronaut brain example from Section 4.10.

We begin by simulating data. We will have $M = 200$ people, and each person will be an earthling (class 1) with probability 0.55 or an astronaut (class 2) with probability 0.45:

```python
import numpy as np

pi_astronaut = 0.45
pi_earthling = 0.55
M = 200

# roll a 2-sided die 200 times, with probability 0.55 of landing on
    side 1 (earthling)p
probability
# and probability 0.45 of landing on side 2 (astronaut)
classnames = ["Earthling", "Earthling"]
np.random.seed(0)
ys = np.random.choice([1, 2], p=[pi_earthling, pi_astronaut], size=M)
print(f"Number of individuals who are earthlings: {(ys == 1).sum():d}")
print(f"Number of individuals who are astronauts: {(ys == 2).sum():d}")
```

Next, we construct probability matrices for each class. The probabilities for edges in which a node is in the sight area are higher for the astronauts than for the earthlings:

```python
n = 5
P_earthling = np.full(shape=(n, n), fill_value=0.3)

nodenames = [
    "SI", "L", "H/E",
```

```
    "T/M", "BS"
]

signal_subnetwork = np.full(shape=(n, n), fill_value=False)
signal_subnetwork[1:n, 0] = True
signal_subnetwork[0, 1:n] = True
P_astronaut = np.copy(P_earthling)

# probabilities for signal edges are higher in astronauts than
    earthlings
P_astronaut[signal_subnetwork] = np.tile(np.linspace(0.4, 0.9, num=4),
    reps=2)
```

In Figures 4.10.2 and 4.10.3, we saw that the probability matrices differed between the astronauts and the earthlings for all edges that included a node from the sight area (SI). These edges comprised the "signal subnetwork" (*SSN*).

Algorithm 4.10 gave us a procedure that we could use to generate samples of *SSN* networks:

```
from graspologic.simulations import sample_edges

# the probability matrices for each class
Ps = [P_earthling, P_astronaut]

# sample networks with the indicated probability matrix
np.random.seed(0)
As = np.stack([sample_edges(P=Ps[y-1]) for y in ys], axis=2)
```

Given a collection of networks from multiple classes, we will find the set of edges which differ most between the classes. We will then use this information to classify brain networks as earthling or astronaut.

We need to do the following:

1. We only look at *signal edges* which are in the *signal subnetwork*, and ignore edges which are not in the signal subnetwork. Edges which are not in the signal subnetwork are simply noise, since they have the same connection probability between the classes, and therefore are not useful for differentiating between the classes.
2. We incorporate these signal and nonsignal edges into a structured classifier, which predicts whether a network is from an earthling or astronaut.
3. We incorporate information about the network structure into our classifier.

8.2.1 Using *Edge Importances* to Estimate the Signal Subnetwork

We start by detecting which edges carry signal given a collection of networks with class labels.

To do this, we will return to Fisher's exact test from Section 6.3.1 and Table 7.1.

For a single edge, we test whether the probabilities for that edge differ between earthling and astronaut brain networks: $H_A: p_{ij}^{(0)} \neq p_{ij}^{(1)}$, against the null hypothesis

Table 8.1. A contingency table for edge existences or nonexistences between each of the two classes.

	Number of networks where edge (i, j) exists	Number of networks where edge (i, j) does not exist
Earthlings	a	b
Astronauts	c	d

that $H_0\colon p_{ij}^{(0)} = p_{ij}^{(1)}$. The desirable property of Fisher's exact test is that, when there is more evidence that the data do not support H_0, the p-value will tend to be smaller and we would tend to reject the null hypothesis. When there is more evidence to support H_0, the p-value will tend to be larger and we often would not have evidence to reject the null hypothesis. We will exploit this feature in our design of a classifier for earthlings versus astronauts. For each edge (i, j), we construct the table shown in Table 8.1 in Python as follows, for the edge from the sight area to the basic survival area:

```
def generate_table(As, ys, i, j):
    """
    A function to generate a contingency table for a given edge.
    """
    # count the number of earthlings with edge i,j
    a = As[i,j,ys == 1].sum()
    # count the number of astronauts with edge i,j
    b = As[i,j,ys == 2].sum()

    c = len(As[i,j,ys == 1]) - a
    d = len(As[i,j,ys == 2]) - b

    edge_tab = np.array([[a, b], [c, d]])
    return edge_tab

# edge (0, 4) corresponds to SI to BS
edge_tab = generate_table(As, ys, 0, 4)
print(edge_tab)
```

Next, we compute Fisher's exact test p-value, using `scipy`:

```
from scipy.stats import fisher_exact

_, pval = fisher_exact(edge_tab)
print(f"p-value: {pval:.4f}")
# p-value: 0.0000
```

The p-value for this edge is small, which tells us that we have evidence to reject the null hypothesis in favor of the alternative hypothesis that the edge from SI to BS shows a disparity between earthlings and astronauts.

Let's see what happens when we repeat this process for a nonsignal edge. We arbitrarily choose the edge between hearing/emotion (H/E) and language (L) areas, corresponding to $i = 2$ (H/E) and $j = 1$ (L):

```
_, pval = fisher_exact(generate_table(As, ys, 2, 1))
print(f"p-value: {pval:.4f}")
# p-value: 0.7600
```

Here we do not have evidence to reject the null hypothesis that the edge from L to H/E areas has the same probability in earthlings and astronauts.

By construction, the *p*-value for signal edges will usually be smaller than the *p*-value for nonsignal edges. We could still certainly get samples of data where this is not the case, analogous to flipping a fair coin 10 times and obtaining 10 heads, even if the coin has a probability of 0.5 of landing on heads.

We can use Fisher's exact test to quantify how "important" an edge is for differentiating the two classes, also known as an *edge importance* statistic. In this case, an edge importance statistic with a higher value indicates that the edge is more important for the class differentiation task. We will do this by ranking the *p*-values from largest (lower ranks) to smallest (higher ranks), where the edges with the higher ranks are more important for differentiating the classes.

Since the networks are loopless, we can ignore the diagonal, and since the networks are undirected, we can compute the *p*-values for a single triangle and then symmetrize the resulting Fisher *p*-value matrix. Then, we rank the edges, from largest to smallest, in terms of the *p*-values using `scipy`. The `scipy` function `rankdata()` natively ranks values from smallest to largest, so to rank positive data from largest to smallest, we first negate the matrix of Fisher test *p*-values:

```
from graspologic.utils import symmetrize
from scipy.stats import rankdata

fisher_mtx = np.empty((n, n))
fisher_mtx[:] = np.nan

for i in range(0, n):
    for j in range(i+1, n):
        fisher_mtx[i, j] = fisher_exact(generate_table(As, ys, i, j))[1]
fisher_mtx = symmetrize(fisher_mtx, method="triu")
# use rankdata on -fisher_mtx, to rank from largest p-value to
    smallest p-value
edge_imp = rankdata(-fisher_mtx, method="dense",
    nan_policy="omit").reshape(fisher_mtx.shape)
np.fill_diagonal(edge_imp, 0)
```

Figure 8.2.1(B) shows the resulting edge importance matrix, along with the signal subnetwork in Figure 8.2.1(A). Notice that edges which are in the signal subnetwork tend to have higher edge importances.

We can use this to estimate what is known as an *incoherent* signal subnetwork by finding the edges corresponding to the *K* highest edge importances.

We can implement this process using `graspologic` to estimate the signal subnetwork. Here we estimate a signal subnetwork with eight edges:

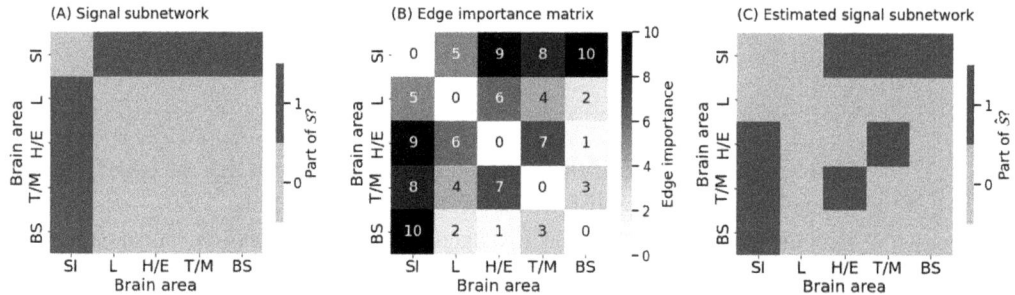

Figure 8.2.1 (**A**) The signal subnetwork for the earthling and astronauts, (**B**) the edge importances for differentiating earthlings from astronauts, and (**C**) the estimated signal subnetwork.

```
from graspologic.subgraph import SignalSubgraph

K = 8 # the number of edges in the subgraph
ssn_mod = SignalSubgraph()
# graspologic signal subgraph module assumes labels are 0, ..., K-1
# so use ys - 1 to rescale from (1, 2) to (0, 1)
ssn_mod.fit_transform(As, labels=ys - 1, constraints=K);

sn_est = np.zeros((n,n)) # initialize empty matrix
sn_est[ssn_mod.sigsub_] = 1
```

The estimated signal subnetwork $\widehat{S}$ with $K = 8$ edges is shown in Figure 8.2.1(C). Notice that when we ran the simulation, our results were imperfect: While six of eight of the estimated signal edges are in the true signal subnetwork, we got two edges incorrect. In the event that the difference in probabilities between the classes is large, as was the case for the six edges we got correct, this procedure will tend to reach reasonably stable conclusions, in that our estimates will faithfully reflect the underlying signal subnetwork. However, when the difference in probabilities between the classes is smaller (such as for the SI and L edge, which we got wrong) we might estimate the signal subnetwork incorrectly for a given number of networks M.

8.2.2   Building a Classifier using the Estimated Signal Subnetwork

We can use our estimated signal subnetwork $\widehat{S}$ to devise a network classifier, which will take new networks and assign them to their most probable class.

We will use a binary Naive Bayes classifier. For details on the Naive Bayes classifier, see Online Appendix D.3 and the original paper on signal subnetworks [5].

8.2.2.1   Network classification

The Bayes plugin classifier from `sklearn`, `BernoulliNB`, is designed for binary data features such as the adjacency matrix of an unweighted network. Online Appendix D.3 contains derivations and intuition behind the Bayes plugin classifier. We start by putting our data into a matrix `BernoulliNB` can work with. Our estimated signal subnetwork $\widehat{S}$ is returned in graspologic as a [2 x K] matrix, where K is the number of edges in the signal subnetwork. The first row is the row index of the entry of the signal subnetwork, and the second row is the column index of the entry in the signal subnetwork. We need to turn this into an [M x K] matrix which we will call the data matrix D, where M is the total number of networks and K is the number of edges in the signal subnetwork. Each entry of this matrix d_{mk} will represent the adjacency matrix value of the mth individual for the kth element of the signal subnetwork. We can do this as follows:

```
D = As[ssn_mod.sigsub_[0], ssn_mod.sigsub_[1],:].T
```

Next, we create a Bayes plugin classifier, and fit it using the classes $\vec{y}$ for all of our samples:

```
from sklearn.naive_bayes import BernoulliNB

classifier = BernoulliNB()
# fit the classifier using the vector of classes for each sample
classifier.fit(D, ys)
```

To evaluate our classifier's performance, we will create 200 new "hold-out" networks that were not used for training and find the classification accuracy. If $h_{\hat{\theta}}\left(A^{(m)}\right)$ is the predicted class (either earthling, 0, or astronaut, 1) for a new held-out sample $A^{(m)}$ for the Naive Bayes classifier after training with parameters $\hat{\theta} = (\widehat{S}, K)$, the classification accuracy for M' held-out samples is the average number of correct answers produced by the classifier:

$$\frac{1}{M'}\sum_{m=1}^{M'} \mathbb{1}\left\{h_\theta\left(A^{(m)}\right) = y_m\right\}.$$

We generate our held-out samples:

```
# number of holdout samples
Mp = 200
# new random seed so heldout samples differ
np.random.seed(123)
y_heldout = np.random.choice([1, 2], p=[pi_earthling, pi_astronaut],
    size=Mp)
# sample networks with the appropriate probability matrix
A_heldout = np.stack([sample_edges(Ps[y-1]) for y in y_heldout],
    axis=2)

# compute testing data on the estimated signal subnetwork
D_heldout = A_heldout[ssn_mod.sigsub_[0], ssn_mod.sigsub_[1],:].T

yhat_heldout = classifier.predict(D_heldout)

# classifier accuracy is the fraction of predictions that are correct
heldout_acc = np.mean(yhat_heldout == y_heldout)
print(f"Classifier Testing Accuracy: {heldout_acc:.3f}")
# Classifier Testing Accuracy: 0.810
```

This results in a classifier with accuracies between 70 percent and 85 percent.

Let's put this all together with a single function, which will use the training data to estimate a signal subnetwork and train a Bayes plugin classifier, and will produce accuracies using a separate set of "testing" networks:

```
def train_and_eval_ssn(Atrain, ytrain, Atest, ytest, K):
    """
    A function which trains and tests an incoherent signal subnetwork
    classifier with K signal edges.
    """
    ssn_mod = SignalSubgraph()
    ssn_mod.fit_transform(Atrain, labels=ytrain - 1,
        constraints=int(K));

    Dtrain = Atrain[ssn_mod.sigsub_[0], ssn_mod.sigsub_[1],:].T
    classifier = BernoulliNB()
    # fit the classifier using the vector of classes for each sample
    classifier.fit(Dtrain, ytrain)

    # compute testing data on the estimated signal subnetwork
    Dtest = Atest[ssn_mod.sigsub_[0], ssn_mod.sigsub_[1],:].T
    yhat_test = classifier.predict(Dtest)

    # classifier accuracy is the fraction of predictions that are
    #    correct
    return (np.mean(yhat_test == ytest), ssn_mod, classifier)
```

8.2.2.2   Parameter Selection for Signal Subnetworks

We need a way to determine an appropriate number of signal edges to include in our estimated signal subnetwork.

Similar to other machine learning techniques, we will use *cross validation*, a commonly used procedure in which we split the dataset into some number of approximately equally sized splits (called *folds*), and then we train a machine learning model using a subset of the folds (the *training folds*). We then test the trained model on the excluded subset of the folds (the *testing folds*). We use a trained machine learning model which maximizes accuracy on the testing folds, and break ties using other heuristics (for instance, selecting the simplest trained model that achieves maximal accuracy).

Algorithm 8.1 describes the procedure for estimating the optimal number of signal edges for network classification using signal subnetworks.

We implement this strategy using $L = 20$ folds, and consider signal subnetworks with sizes ranging from 2 to 20 signal edges. We proceed with increments of 2 because our networks are undirected, which means that edge (i, j) and edge (j, i) will contain identical information. We consider a maximum of 20 signal edges because the networks are loopless, so there are a maximum of 20 possible signal edges in the network.

We can implement 20-fold cross validation using `sklearn`. This procedure might take several minutes, even on the small networks that we have been working with so far:

Algorithm 8.1 Estimating the number of signal edges using cross validation

---

Data: A set of networks and class labels $(A^{(m)}, y_m)$, for $m = 1, \ldots, M$.

$\quad$ K' the maximum number of possible signal edges.

$\quad$ L the number of folds to use for cross validation.

Result: K^* the optimal number of signal edges.

1 Split the indexing set $\{1, \ldots, M\}$ into L folds of approximately equal size at random.

2 **for** $k = 1, \ldots, K'$ **do**

3 $\quad$ **for** $l = 1, \ldots, L$ **do**

4 $\quad\quad$ Let n_l denote the number of samples in fold l.

5 $\quad\quad$ Let $\hat{S}$ be the estimated signal subnetwork with k signal edges, which is estimated using the networks from the training folds $l' \neq l$.

6 $\quad\quad$ Train a Naive Bayes classifier using the training folds to produce a network classifier $h_{\hat{\theta}}$, which takes networks and produces class predictions.

7 $\quad\quad$ Let $a_{k,l}$ be the testing accuracy using the testing fold l.

8 $\quad$ **end**

9 $\quad$ Let $a_k = \frac{1}{n} \sum_{l=1}^{L} n_l a_{k,l}$ be the testing accuracy over all L folds for k signal edges.

10 **end**

11 Let $K^* = \mathrm{argmax}_k a_k$ be the number of signal edges which maximizes the testing accuracy. If there are multiple numbers of signal edges that maximize the testing accuracy, break ties by choosing the smallest such number of signal edges.

12 **return** K^*.

```
from sklearn.model_selection import KFold
import pandas as pd

kf = KFold(n_splits=20, shuffle=True, random_state=0)
xv_res = []
for l, (train_index, test_index) in enumerate(kf.split(range(0, M))):
    A_train, A_test = As[:,:,train_index], As[:,:,test_index]
    y_train, y_test = ys[train_index], ys[test_index]
    nl = len(test_index)

    for k in np.arange(2, 20, step=2):
        acc_kl, _, _ = train_and_eval_ssn(A_train, y_train, A_test,
            y_test, k)
        xv_res.append({"Fold": l, "k": k, "nl": nl, "Accuracy": acc_kl})
xv_data = pd.DataFrame(xv_res)

def weighted_avg(group):
    acc = group['Accuracy']
    nl = group['nl']
    return (acc * nl).sum() / nl.sum()

xv_acc = xv_data.groupby(["k"]).apply(weighted_avg)
print(xv_acc)
```

Table 8.2. The average testing accuracy as a function of the number of signal edges. With six or eight signal edges, the optimal average testing accuracy is achieved, indicated by the light gray rows.

Number of signal edges	Average testing accuracy
2	0.795
4	0.795
6	0.830
8	0.830
10	0.820
12	0.825
14	0.825
16	0.820
18	0.820

With our data, this produces Table 8.2. Because the simulation data used for this section were produced randomly, our results might be slightly different from run to run. In the simulation shown here, we reach optimal average testing accuracy with six or eight signal edges.

Once we have identified the optimal number of signal edges using cross validation, we would estimate a signal subnetwork and train a classifier using the full training data with the optimal number of signal edges, and evaluate our signal subnetwork and the resulting classifier using any remaining held-out data. Since in this case we have a tie in testing accuracy between six and eight signal edges, by convention, we would typically choose the optimal model based on whichever is simpler. In this case, since six signal edges is a simpler (but equally performant) model than eight signal edges, we would use six signal edges. We can train a signal subnetwork classifier with six signal edges and evaluate it on the held-out data as follows:

```
acc, ssn_est, classifier_est = train_and_eval_ssn(As,
    ys, A_heldout, y_heldout, 6)
```

To summarize, we estimated a signal subnetwork from a set of networks that are in one of K classes. We then covered how to use this estimated signal subnetwork to train a classifier which uses the signal edges to make predictions of the class for new networks. We learned how to use cross validation to tune the number of edges in the estimated signal subnetwork, so that we could identify the number of edges in the signal subnetwork which maximized the downstream classification accuracy for new networks.

8.3   Building Coherent Signal Subnetworks

In Section 8.2, we explored incoherent signal subnetwork estimators. However, the signal subnetwork estimator used in Section 8.2 was incoherent: It did not consider network structure when selecting edges, and focused only on edges with the highest importance. Incoherent subnetwork estimators often miss important edges, such as the connection between the sight (SI) and language (L) areas (Figure 8.2.1(C)). This signal edge carries subtle but crucial signals (Figure 4.10.2(C)).

This section introduces coherent signal subnetwork estimators to address these limitations, which leverage the structure of the network by using elements of its structure: nodes, edges, or other network attributes.

We will focus on:

1. Defining coherent signal subnetwork estimators and their advantages,
2. Developing methods that leverage multiple network elements (nodes, edges, attributes),
3. Comparing coherent and incoherent estimators in terms of Bayes accuracy, and
4. Discussing the implications for optimal classifier performance.

Classifiers that leverage all signal edges in their predictions achieve a higher *Bayes accuracy* [5; 6], which is the highest possible classification accuracy achievable by a classifier that knows the true data generating distribution. Optimal performance requires leveraging information from all signal edges.

We again use the earthling and astronaut setting from Section 4.10. This time, we obtain 200 training and testing samples explicitly:

```python
import numpy as np
from graspologic.simulations import sample_edges

nodenames = [
    "SI", "L", "H/E",
    "T/M", "BS"
]

# generate probability matrices
n = 5 # the number of nodes
P_earthling = 0.3*np.ones((n, n))
signal_subnetwork = np.zeros((n, n), dtype=bool)
signal_subnetwork[1:n, 0] = True
signal_subnetwork[0, 1:n] = True
P_astronaut = np.copy(P_earthling)
P_astronaut[signal_subnetwork] = np.tile(np.linspace(0.4, 0.9, num=4),
    2)

# sample the classes of each sample
M = 200 # the number of training and testing samples
pi_astronaut = 0.45
pi_earthling = 0.55
np.random.seed(0)
ytrain = np.random.choice([1,2], p=[pi_earthling, pi_astronaut],
    size=M)
ytest = np.random.choice([1,2], p=[pi_earthling, pi_astronaut], size=M)

# sample network realizations given the class of each sample
Ps = [P_earthling, P_astronaut]
np.random.seed(0)
Atrain = np.stack([sample_edges(Ps[y-1]) for y in ytrain], axis=2)
Atest = np.stack([sample_edges(Ps[y-1]) for y in ytest], axis=2)
```

Let's consider what is happening using coin flips. The edge (SI, L) could be represented by a coin that lands on heads with probability 0.4 for astronauts, but 0.3 for earthlings. Given a set of networks of earthlings and astronauts, we could think about the existence or not existence of this particular edge in our heads or tails framework. There is a chance that the rate we see heads for astronauts is the same, or even less, than the rate we see heads for earthlings.

Imagine another experiment for a nonsignal edge, such as $(BS, H/E)$, between the basic survival node and the hearing/emotion node. This nonsignal edge could be represented by a coin which lands on heads with probability 0.3 for both astronauts and earthlings. In a given set of networks of earthlings and astronauts, Figure 8.2.1(C) shows that it is still possible that we see more heads in one group or the other, leading to the nonsignal edge mistakenly being identified as a signal edge by our procedure for estimating signal subnetworks.

When we have many nonsignal edges, and only a small subset of signal edges, the chances of us running into this problem increases. This is closely related to the multiple comparisons problem from Section 6.3.1, where we might see spuriously small p-values (and consequently, high edge importances) in nonsignal edges due to random chance a fraction of the time.

8.3.1   Building a Coherent Signal Subnetwork Estimator

To reduce this type of sample-specific noise, we can build a coherent signal subnetwork estimator by using more information about our networks: the nodes that the edges are between. We start by computing the ranked significance matrix as we did before. However, when we pick the edges to include or exclude, we first choose the V nodes (the *signal nodes*) with the highest ranked significances. We then identify the K signal edges using only edges which are incident to a signal node.

The procedure to build a coherent signal subnetwork estimator is described in Algorithm 8.2.

This procedure sets an initial threshold c at the maximum ranked edge importance. It then counts how many edges connected to each node meet or exceed this threshold. The top V signal nodes are those with the most edges at or above the threshold. The algorithm lowers the threshold iteratively until it finds V nodes that each have at least K edges above the importance threshold. The final *coherent signal subnetwork* estimate consists of these V nodes and their top K edges.

We can do this using `graspologic` using multiple constraints, as follows, where we compute both incoherent and coherent signal subnetwork estimates:

```
from graspologic.subgraph import SignalSubgraph
K = 8 # the number of signal edges
V = 1 # the number of signal nodes

# the incoherent signal subnetwork estimator
ssn_est_inco = SignalSubgraph()
ssn_est_inco.fit_transform(Atrain, labels=ytrain-1, constraints=K)

# the coherent signal subnetwork estimator
```

Algorithm 8.2 Building a coherent signal subnetwork estimator

---

Data: A set of networks and class labels $(A^{(m)}, y_m)$, for $m = 1, \ldots, M$.

    V the number of signal nodes.

    K the number of signal edges.

Result: $(\mathcal{S}, \mathcal{V})$ a set of signal edges and signal nodes in the network.

1 Compute the ranked significance matrix R, which is an $n \times n$ matrix whose entries r_{ij} are the ranked significance for edge i and j.

2 Initialize $c = \max_{i,j} r_{ij}$, and let $w_c = 0$.

3 **while** $w_c < K$ **do**

4   For each node i, let $w_{i,c} = \sum_{j=1}^{n} \mathbb{1}\left\{r_{ij} \geq c\right\}$ be the number of edges for node i where the ranked significance is at least c.

5   Rank the nodes according to which node has the number of signal edges exceeding the threshold c. Denote the ith largest node by $w_{(i),c}$.

6   Let $w_c = \sum_{i=1}^{V} w_{(i),c}$ be the sum of the number of edges each of the top V-ranked nodes have at least at the threshold c.

7   Let $c = c - 1$.

8 **end**

9 Let $\mathcal{V}$ be the node set of the top V nodes identified in the final iteration of the preceding while loop.

10 Let $\mathcal{S}$ be the top K signal edges where at least one node for each edge is in the signal node set $\mathcal{V}$.

11 **return** $(\mathcal{S}, \mathcal{V})$.

```
ssn_est_coherent = SignalSubgraph()
ssn_est_coherent.fit_transform(Atrain, labels=ytrain-1,
    constraints=[K, V])
```

We can build the signal subnetwork estimates as follows:

```
ssn_coherent = np.zeros((n, n))
ssn_incoherent = np.zeros((n, n))

ssn_incoherent[ssn_est_inco.sigsub_] = 1
ssn_coherent[ssn_est_coherent.sigsub_] = 1
```

A visualization of the true signal subnetwork, the incoherent signal subnetwork, and the coherent signal subnetwork is shown in Figure 8.3.1. The incoherent signal subnetwork estimate will sometimes have spurious, nonsignal, edges included. The coherent signal subnetwork overcomes this potential hurdle by leveraging other topological properties of network data, such as the nodes themselves.

Now, we can put this together for training and evaluating coherent signal subnetworks:

```
from sklearn.naive_bayes import BernoulliNB

def train_and_eval_coherent_ssn(Atrain, ytrain, Atest, ytest, K, V):
```

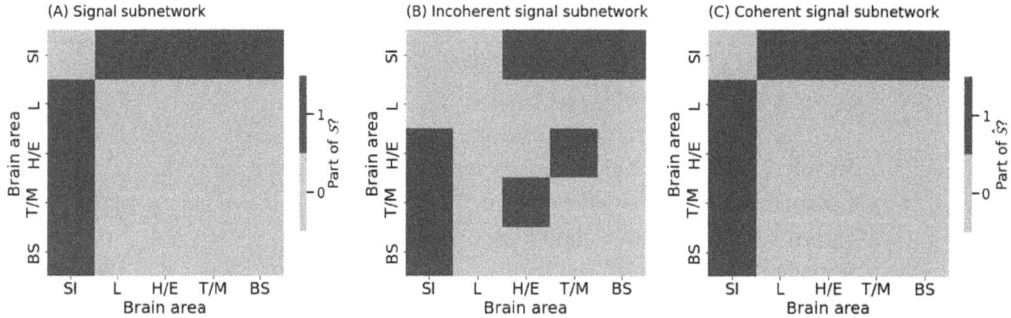

Figure 8.3.1 (**A**) The true signal subnetwork, (**B**) the incoherent signal subnetwork estimate, and (**C**) the coherent signal subnetwork estimate.

```
"""
A function which trains and tests an incoherent signal subnetwork
classifier with K signal edges and V signal nodes.
"""
ssn_mod = SignalSubgraph()
ssn_mod.fit_transform(Atrain, labels=ytrain-1, constraints=[int(K),
    int(V)]);

Dtrain = Atrain[ssn_mod.sigsub_[0], ssn_mod.sigsub_[1],:].T
classifier = BernoulliNB()
# fit the classifier using the vector of classes for each sample
classifier.fit(Dtrain, ytrain)

# compute testing data on the estimated signal subnetwork
Dtest = Atest[ssn_mod.sigsub_[0], ssn_mod.sigsub_[1],:].T
yhat_test = classifier.predict(Dtest)

# classifier accuracy is the fraction of predictions that are
    correct
return (np.mean(yhat_test == ytest), ssn_mod, classifier)
```

Parameter Selection for Coherent Signal Subnetworks

We again turn to cross-validation for parameter selection for coherent signal sub-networks. In Algorithm 8.1, we addressed parameter selection for incoherent signal subnetworks. We can use the same intuition to develop a method to parameter select for coherent signal subnetworks. In this case, we can simply add an additional loop to our computation, where we also tune over the number of signal nodes to include in the estimate.

```
from sklearn.model_selection import KFold
import pandas as pd
from tqdm import tqdm

kf = KFold(n_splits=20, shuffle=True, random_state=0)
xv_res = []
for l, (train_index, test_index) in tqdm(enumerate(kf.split(range(0,
    M)))):
```

```
    A_train, A_test = Atrain[:,:,train_index], Atrain[:,:,test_index]
    y_train, y_test = ytrain[train_index], ytrain[test_index]
    nl = len(test_index)

    for k in np.arange(2, n*(n-1), step=2):
        for v in range(1, n+1):
            try:
                acc_kl, _, _ = train_and_eval_coherent_ssn(A_train,
                    y_train, A_test, y_test, k, v)
                xv_res.append({"Fold": l, "k": k, "nl": nl, "v": v,
                    "Accuracy": acc_kl})
            except:
                xv_res.append({"Fold": l, "k": k, "nl": nl, "v": v,
                    "Accuracy": np.nan})
xv_data = pd.DataFrame(xv_res)

def weighted_avg(group):
    acc = group['Accuracy']
    nl = group['nl']
    return (acc * nl).sum() / nl.sum()

xv_acc = xv_data.groupby(["k",
    "v"]).apply(weighted_avg).reset_index(name='Accuracy')
# convert the pandas dataframe (long format) to a data matrix (wide
    format)
df_hm = xv_acc.pivot(index="k", columns="v", values="Accuracy")
```

We made a slight augmentation to the code, including a `try`/`except` block. The reason for this is that 20 signal edges is only possible with 5 signal nodes, so for any number of signal nodes less than 5, we will not be able to find a signal subnetwork with 20 signal edges. Figure 8.3.2(A) plots the accuracies as a heatmap.

While many combinations produce the highest cross-validated accuracy, we again opt for the simplest model in terms of the number of free parameters with this accuracy to avoid overfitting. In this case, the simplest model which attains the highest cross-validated accuracy has 1 signal node and 6 signal edges. When we refit this model on the full training data, we get:

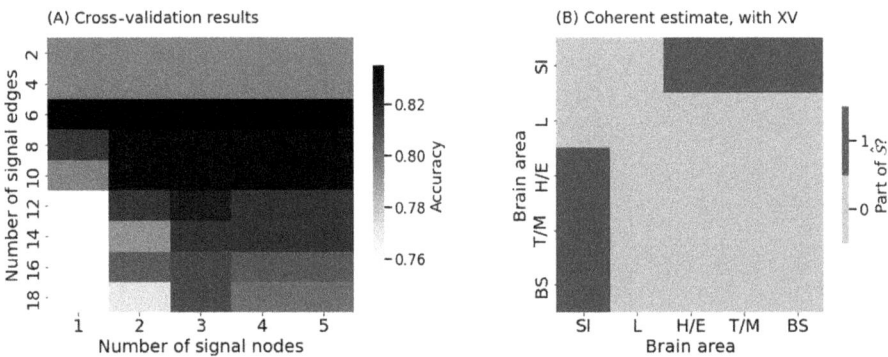

Figure 8.3.2 **(A)** The cross-validated accuracy as a heatmap for a coherent SSN, as a function of the number of signal nodes and edges, and **(B)** the estimated signal subnetwork from the training data with the "optimal" number of signal nodes and signal edges.

```
# the coherent signal subnetwork estimator, using the parameters from
    xv
ssn_est_coherent_xv = SignalSubgraph()
ssn_est_coherent_xv.fit_transform(Atrain, labels=ytrain-1,
    constraints=[6, 1])

ssn_coherent_xv = np.zeros((n, n))
ssn_coherent_xv[ssn_est_coherent_xv.sigsub_] = 1
```

which is the signal subnetwork shown in Figure 8.3.2(B). The testing accuracy on the held-out testing data can be computed as previously. Note that in this example the incoherent signal subnetwork and the coherent signal subnetwork perform similarly with cross-validation. We use a simpler example because estimating signal subnetworks can be extremely time consuming when the number of nodes is large. For networks that are larger in size with comparatively few signal nodes carrying most of the signal subnetwork, the difference in performance can be greater, with coherent estimates having far better performance and generally far fewer parameters. This yields more generalizable models less subject to overfitting to nonsignal edges.

Bibliography

[1] Carew TJ, Castellucci VF, Kandel ER. An analysis of dishabituation and sensitization of the gill-withdrawal reflex in Aplysia. Int. J. of Neuroscience. 1971 Aug.;2(2):79–98.
[2] Kandel ER. The molecular biology of memory storage: a dialogue between genes and synapses. Science (New York, NY). 2001 Nov.;294(5544):1030–1038.
[3] Tang M, Athreya A, Sussman DL, Lyzinski V, Park Y, Priebe CE. A semiparametric two-sample hypothesis testing problem for random graphs. J. Comput. Graph. Stat. 2017 Apr.;26(2):344–354.
[4] Holm S. A simple sequentially rejective multiple test procedure. Scan. J. Stat. 1979;6(2):65–70.
[5] Vogelstein JT, Roncal WG, Vogelstein RJ, Priebe CE. Graph classification using signal-subgraphs: Applications in statistical connectomics. IEEE Trans. Pattern Anal. Mach. Intell. 2013 Jul.;35(7):1539–1551.
[6] Fukunaga K. Introduction to Statistical Pattern Recognition (Computer Science & Scientific Computing). Cambridge, MA, USA: Academic Press; 1990.

9   Deep Learning Methods

Previous chapters of this book have focused on understanding and leveraging network representations with well-developed theory, often focusing on linear representations. In the case of the spectral embedding (Section 5.3), for instance, we constructed a tabular array from a network and used traditional techniques like K-means for community detection (Section 6.1). We learned how this representation was derived from $RDPG_n(X)$ random networks from Section 4.4, and how it could be used as a conceptual basis to make explicit assumptions about the network. Section 7.1, for instance, used the $RDPG_n(X)$ assumption to compare two networks.

We now investigate newer techniques for creating representations that use deep learning methods. These techniques become powerful in domains with vast amounts of training data. For instance, Deepmind's AlphaFold famously used a graph neural network as part of its architecture by modeling the protein structure prediction problem as a spatial graph, where the amino acids in the protein sequence are represented as nodes and their possible interactions as edges [1]. This was made possible by the Protein Data Bank, which contains hundreds of thousands of carefully curated protein structural data generated using biochemical methods over many years [2].

In this chapter:

1. Section 9.1 introduces graph neural networks, or GNNs, a broad class of techniques which use deep learning to investigate graph-valued data.
2. Section 9.2 explores diffusion-based methods, which use random walks on networks to develop representations.

In contrast to previous chapters, deep learning methods are often developed through experimentation rather than by explicit theoretical deduction. However, many of the conceptual steps we have taken for preceding models can be used to understand the internal representations generated by GNNs, and random walks are often explicitly used to create useful representations.

We begin our discussion by introducing the concept of a GNN through the case study of a drug discovery problem, in which we learn molecule representations. We then explore random walks using the familiar New York Bridge example from Section 3.1.

9.1   Graph Neural Networks

Coauthored with Jason Yim

We now move beyond spectral techniques to explore neural network approaches to creating and using network representations. This section explores graph neural networks (GNNs). GNNs extend traditional neural network architectures to operate directly on graph-structured data. GNNs exploit network topology to iteratively update node representations along neural network layers. The final representations can be used to predict node labels, network labels, edge existence, and more.

We cover:

1. Introducing the basic concepts and architecture of GNNs,
2. Examining how GNNs process and leverage network structure,
3. Exploring applications of GNNs in tasks such as node classification and link prediction,
4. Comparing GNN performance to traditional network analysis methods, and
5. Discussing the advantages and limitations of GNN approaches.

Neural networks are fundamentally representation learners. The middle layers of a network can be thought of as simply preparing the data for whatever the neural network is trying to do in its loss function. They are particularly powerful for large-scale networks and when node or edge features are available alongside topology.

We begin our discussion of graph neural networks through a drug discovery example. We can think of molecules as networks: An atom can be thought of as a node, and an atomic bond as an edge. Molecules in chemistry are also often described through alphabetic formulas: The letters represent atoms, and the subscripts represent the number of atoms in the molecule. For instance, the formula for water, H_2O, means that there are two hydrogen atoms and a single oxygen.

A fundamental problem for many pharmaceutical and chemistry investigations involves the analysis of molecules that might be useful for clinical purposes. A *clinically useful molecule* is a molecule which has properties which, for one reason or another, might make it beneficial for humans. For instance, people who have had headaches have probably become familiar with the the pain-relieving molecule $C_{13}H_{18}O_2$, or Ibuprofen (Advil).

Many of the drugs that we are familiar with on an everyday basis have been discovered totally by accident: for instance, the drug penicillin [3], which is a family of molecules having a core structure of $C_9H_{11}N_2O_4S$ that are crucial for their antibacterial properties.

Unfortunately, finding these "happy accident" molecules has become increasingly infrequent. When a condition needing treatment is identified, pharmacologists face enormous hurdles for finding candidate treatment molecules. The molecules must be:

1. nontoxic to humans,
2. an appropriate size,
3. be readily absorbed by humans, and
4. able to address the condition of interest.

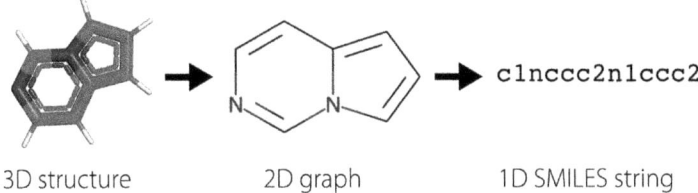

3D structure   2D graph   1D SMILES string

Figure 9.1.1 A SMILES string for the molecule $C_7H_6N_2$, or pyrrolo[1,2-c]pyrimidine. In the 2D graph, angle locations represent carbon atoms; two parallel lines represent double-bonded carbon atoms; and the two Ns represent nitrogens. Hydrogen atoms are implicit in the structure.

Achieving all of these aims is difficult in terms of time, labor, and risk to human participants in drug trials. Determining definitive, or at least suggestive, evidence that the molecule will achieve any or all of these conditions before running live human tests can save the company billions of dollars and can save participants in drug trials unnecessary exposure to harm.

Running laboratory tests to screen these molecules is an expensive, time-consuming, and skilled labor-intensive process: What are the companies left to do?

Many drug companies utilize virtual screening methods in which computational methods are used to quickly search large libraries of molecules to filter ones with the desirable properties. Success in virtual screening methods are determined by the accuracy and speed of the computational approach. For instance, molecular dynamics simulates the physical movement of each atom and particle, but requires an intractable number of numerical calculations that makes it infeasible to use in practice. Instead, methods have been built around succinct two-dimensional (2D) representations of molecules, by compressing them into one-dimensional (1D) simplified molecular input line-entry system (SMILES) [4; 5; 6] strings. These strings summarize the structural relationships between different atoms through the chemical bonds connecting them without any loss-of-information. SMILES strings are known as *fingerprints* for the molecules, and are illustrated in Figure 9.1.1.

Using SMILES, practioners have built statistical models to estimate correlations between SMILES and different molecular properties. Traditional methods have relied on building hand-crafted features derived from SMILES and optimizing simplistic statistical models to predict molecular properties from fingerprints of the molecules.

This too, however, is extremely labor intensive and requires direct human intervention to decipher the features used for statistical learning. With some clever manipulation, scientists have identified an ingenius approach to turn molecular screening into a network learning problem.

9.1.0.1   Obtaining a Network from a Molecule

We described molecule as a group of atoms which are bonded together. We also said that we could think of molecules as networks, where atoms are nodes and bonds are edges.

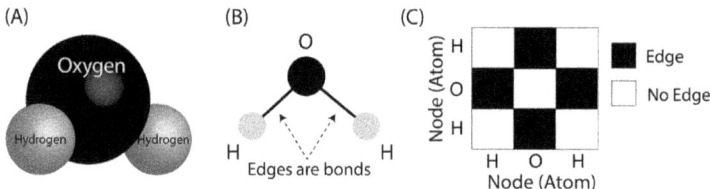

Figure 9.1.2 (A) A molecular structure for water (H_2O), **(B)** a network representation of a water molecule, and **(C)** the network as an adjacency matrix.

Let's see how this would work with the molecular formula of water, H_2O. In water, the oxygen atom sits in the middle, and there are hydrogens on each side. The process of turning a molecule into a network is illustrated in Figure 9.1.2. The structure of a molecule is identified through experimentation by chemists (Figure 9.1.2(A)). Figure 9.1.2(B) shows how the atoms (oxygen and two hydrogens) become the nodes of the network, and the bonds between the oxygen atom and the hydrogens become the edges. Figure 9.1.2(C) illustrates the network as an adjacency matrix.

The SMILES string for water is just O. Given this string, the molecular structure, and consequently the network and the adjacency matrix, are fully determined. The inverse is also true: Given a network and the other attributes of the atomic structure, the fingerprint can be determined. This means that implicitly, computational strategies which produce desirable representations of the fingerprints produce a desirable representation for the network itself.

We will focus our attention on the first hurdle faced by pharmacologists. Provided a SMILES fingerprint for a molecule, we will use network machine learning to determine whether the molecule is toxic or nontoxic.

9.1.1   Preprocessing SMILES Fingerprints

We will be using one of the datasets packaged in `MoleculeNet` [7]. PyTorch Geometric (PyG) [8; 9] provides a convenient module to access it. We first import the module `MoleculeNet` then extract the `ClinTox` dataset [10]. The dataset may take a minute to download. It has a total of 1478 molecules labeled with their presence or absence of toxicity – determined from clinical trials. Since this is a binary classification task, we observe there are two classes.

```
from torch_geometric.datasets import MoleculeNet

dataset = MoleculeNet(root='data/clintox', name='ClinTox')
print(f'Dataset: {dataset}\nNumber of molecules/graphs:
    {len(dataset)}\nNumber of classes: {dataset.num_classes}')
```

Let's look at a few molecules to understand their network structure. Each molecule has a known three-dimensional (3D) structure and an associated SMILES string. We pick out two arbitrary molecules from the dataset, and take a look first at their SMILES string:

```
mols = dataset[26], dataset[83]
for m in mols:
    print(m.smiles)
```

Next, we can draw the molecular structures for the two molecules:

```
from rdkit import Chem
from rdkit.Chem.Draw import rdMolDraw2D
from IPython.display import SVG

smiles = [Chem.MolFromSmiles(m.smiles) for m in mols]
d2d = rdMolDraw2D.MolDraw2DSVG(600,280,300,280)
d2d.drawOptions().addAtomIndices = True
d2d.DrawMolecules(smiles)
d2d.FinishDrawing()
SVG(d2d.GetDrawingText())
```

The molecules illustrated with the atom indices are plotted in Figure 9.1.3(A). The networks each have a different number of nodes (atoms). Further, each node has a number which uniquely identifies that node in the molecule. These molecules have been analyzed with cheminformatics software, RDKit [11], and also come with a set of node attributes for descriptive characteristics of that node in the particular molecule. While these node attributes are not relevant for our example, they have substantial real-world applications to optimize predictive accuracy. Let's take a look at the number of atoms and the number of atomic features now:

```
for i,m in enumerate(mols):
    print(f'Molecule {i+1}: Number of atoms={m.x.shape[0]}, Features
        per atom={m.x.shape[1]}')
```

The edges of the network are the bonds between different pairs of atoms. Using the SMILE fingerprint, we can also obtain information of the bonds of the network. Let's take a look at the indices of the bonds.

```
d2d = rdMolDraw2D.MolDraw2DSVG(600,280,300,280)
d2d.drawOptions().addBondIndices = True
d2d.DrawMolecules(smiles)
d2d.FinishDrawing()
SVG(d2d.GetDrawingText())
```

Especially for larger molecules, the adjacency matrices for molecular networks tend to be extremely sparse (see Section 6.2). For a simple network, the adjacency matrix has $\binom{n}{2} = \frac{1}{2}n(n-1)$ possible edges. So, if we store the entire adjacency matrix, we need to keep track of $\frac{1}{2}n(n-1)$ entries.

In a sparse adjacency matrix, the total number of edges might be considerably less than this. Since an edge is indexed by two nodes, if two times the number of edges is less than $\binom{n}{2}$, we can save a lot of space by storing and operating on the adjacency matrix using edgelists as in Section 6.2.2.

In Section 6.2.2, we discussed how to use scipy for sparse matrices without having to construct the adjacency matrix in its entirety. An equivalent construct for

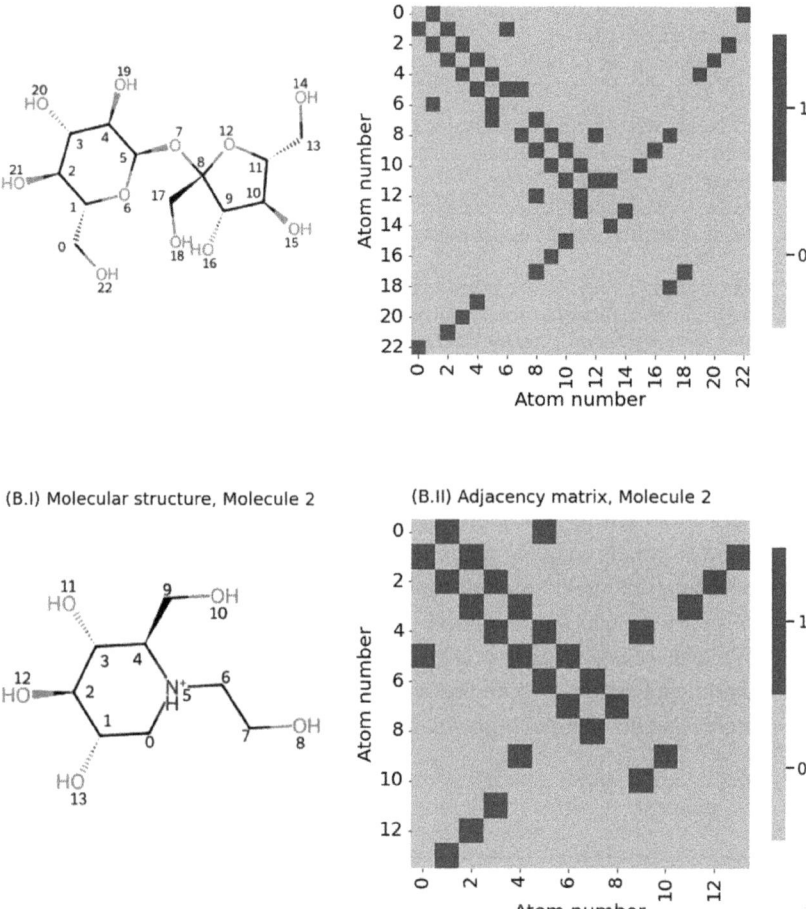

Figure 9.1.3 Example of two molecule adjacency matrices. Hydrogen atoms are not considered nodes. Carbon atoms are denoted by angles in the structure. (**A.I**) The first molecule. (**A.II**) The first molecule as an adjacency matrix. (**B.I**) The second molecule. (**B.II**) The second molecule as an adjacency matrix.

graph neural networks are `pytorch` sparse arrays such as those we leverage here. Sparse arrays in `pytorch` operate faster and more efficiently on sparse matrices than nonsparse approaches.

To build an adjacency matrix that we can visualize using the traditional heatmap, we need to first construct the adjacency matrix from the edgelist:

```
import numpy as np

_process = lambda x: [e[0] for e in np.split(x, 2)]
def adj_from_edgelist(molecule):
    """
    A function that takes a molecule edgelist and produces an adjacency
        matrix.
```

```
"""
# the number of nodes is the number of atoms (rows of .x attribute)
n = molecule.x.shape[0]
# the adjacency matrix is n x n
A = np.zeros((n, n))
edgelist = m.edge_index.numpy()
# loop over the edges e_k, and for each edge, unpack the
# nodes that are incident it. for this pair of nodes,
# change the adjacency matrix entry to 1
for e_k, (i, j) in enumerate(zip(*_process(edgelist))):
    A[i, j] = 1
return A
```

Now that we can produce adjacency matrices from sparse edgelists, we can convert the molecules to adjacency matrices, and then plot them using heatmaps:

```
from graphbook_code import heatmap

for m_i, m in enumerate(mols):
    A = adj_from_edgelist(m)
    heatmap(A)
```

The molecules are shown with their adjacency matrices in Figure 9.1.3. Notice that in the molecule shown in Figure 9.1.3(A.I), that an oxygen atom (index 7) is bonded to two carbon atoms (the "points" of the hexagon are carbon atoms), which have indices 5 and 8 respectively. When we look at the adjacency matrix in Figure 9.1.3(A.II), the row corresponding to atom index 7 shows that it is connected to atom indices 5 and 8, as desired.

Empirically, the first molecule is nontoxic, whereas the second is extremely toxic. We turn to graph neural networks to learn this property.

9.1.2   Graph Neural Networks (GNNs)

As it turns out, using only the adjacency matrix, we can do a pretty good job of determining whether a molecule is toxic or nontoxic. We will use a neural network approach for this task. See [12] or [13] for a comprehensive reference. Because the terminology can be confusing here, we will always use "network" to refer to our adjacency matrix and "neural network" or an abbreviation thereof (e.g., GNN) to refer to the algorithmic technique.

This task requires approaches different from those we have covered in earlier chapters. Previously, we assumed some knowledge of the structure of the data ahead of time. This assumption allowed us to assume a sensible statistical model from Chapter 4. We could then use this model for downstream statistical inference tasks.

When dealing with large molecular networks, problems arise with this approach. It is often unclear which statistical models are appropriate, and identifying the core features we want to capture for unseen molecules can be arduous, time consuming, and require substantial domain expertise. GNNs can often offer practical solutions in such a situation. A *graph neural network* is just a neural network, but modified for use with graph (or network)-valued data.

GNNs have desirable properties that can help us to overcome some of these hurdles: They are universal approximators and they are efficient to optimize. They also require comparatively few statistical assumptions. However, they can be slow, difficult to train, and data hungry compared to traditional approaches.

9.1.2.1 GNNs are Universal Approximators

In some cases, the features that determine a network's classification label can be straightforward and easily identifiable. For instance, a social network's sparsity might determine whether it represents a small, tight-knit community or a large city.

However, in many cases, the features are not nearly so simple. In the case of molecule classification, the features are not completely understood even by the most preeminent experts in organic chemistry. This is true in many more fields than pharmacology.

GNNs provide a framework for constructing universal approximators for network-valued data. The idea behind a *univeral approximator* is that, whatever the relationship between the data (the network) and the outcome of interest (in our example, toxic or nontoxic) happens to be, a properly chosen GNN is always capable of approximating the relationship [14], contingent on the amount and quality of training data. This is extremely appealing in fields for which domain expertise is less helpful and we have large quantities of training data.

In our example, there are hundreds of thousands of molecules that have been studied by pharmacologists for toxicity, so we have a substantial backlog of data where we know ahead of time whether the molecule is toxic or not.

9.1.2.2 GNNs Are Easy and Efficient to Optimize

A plethora of software libraries have been built for neural network training and optimization once we have a large volume of training data. Neural networks also require access to graphical processing units (GPUs), which are custom-built for accelerating large matrix multiplications. GNNs are widely used in practice because they can scale to very large and high-dimensional datasets due to the tight coupling of engineering progress/technical advances in GPU performance and mathematical theory.

9.1.2.3 Graph Convolutional Networks for Drug Discovery

For drug discovery, a preeminent technique for the construction of neural networks is to construct a graph convolutional network (GCN). This approach searches for a latent (unknown) embedding for each node in a given molecule network, and then we use the resulting node embeddings to identify a latent embedding for the entire molecule. In this investigation, we will assume that we have M total training networks and M' testing (validation) networks, where each network m (a single molecule) has n_m nodes in the network. Recall that in this case, network refers to the data (here, individual molecules, consisting of atoms and bonds), and GCN or GNN refers to the algorithm.

Unlike many of the multinetwork examples we have studied so far, the number of nodes, n_m, may not be constant across the networks: Each molecule is likely to be composed of differing numbers of atoms. The graph convolutional network procedure

[15] overcomes this hurdle. The idea is, for each node, to aggregate information from neighboring nodes. GCNs can therefore save memory cost and focus on local features by analyzing the properties of nodes within a neighborhood, rather than looking at all of the nodes in the network simultaneously. They then trickle this relational information from neighbors outwards in the network. As the information flows deeper through the neural network across sequential layers, each node is able to obtain and aggregate relational information from nodes which are not neighbors. This process is repeated for each node in the network in each pass. We begin with node features $\vec{x}_i^{(0)}$, which in our case, describe properties of the atoms that comprise our molecule.

We can write the aggregation step for layers $k \geq 1$ for a node i as:

$$\vec{a}_i^{(k)} = \bigoplus_{j \in \mathcal{N}(i)} \phi^{(k)} \left(\vec{x}_j^{(k-1)} \right),$$

where:

- $\vec{x}_j^{(k-1)}$ denotes node features for node j in layer $(k-1)$. The number of node features (for a given node in the actual network) in a given layer corresponds to the number of hidden channels in the GCN.
- $\bigoplus$ denotes an aggregation function such as sum, mean, or max.
- $\phi^{(k)}$ denotes a transformation of the features of the embedding from the preceding layer $k-1$ of neighbor j to i.
- $\vec{a}_i^{(k)}$ denotes the relational information for a node i that it receives from its neighbors $\mathcal{N}(i)$.

The aggregation step summarizes information from the node features at layer $k-1$ of neighbors of the node i. These are then combined via a propagation step to produce the hidden embedding $\vec{x}_i^{(k)}$ for a node i in layer k:

$$\vec{x}_i^{(k)} = \theta^{(k)} \left(\vec{x}_i^{(k-1)}, \vec{a}_i^{(k)} \right) = \sigma \left(\beta_0^{(k)} + \beta_1^{(k)} \vec{x}_i^{(k-1)} + \beta_2^{(k)} \vec{a}_i^{(k)} \right),$$

where:

- $\beta_0^{(k)}$ is an offset term.
- $\beta_1^{(k)}$ and $\beta_2^{(k)}$ are terms which indicate the extent to which the new embedding for layer k of node i should reflect the previous embedding $\vec{x}_i^{(k-1)}$ versus the relational information from neighbors of node i summarized in $\vec{a}_i^{(k)}$.
- σ is a nonlinear activation function.

In this case, the nonlinear activation function is applied to a weighted sum of the hidden embedding $\vec{x}_i^{(k-1)}$ for the node i at the previous layer $k-1$ with the aggregation of information from its neighbors at the previous layer $k-1$ via $\vec{a}_i^{(k)}$.

Figure 9.1.4 illustrates the aggregation and the propagation steps of a GCN. The network itself is illustrated with solid nodes and solid edges; the aggregation and propagation steps (of the GCN) are illustrated with dashed nodes and dashed edges. Directionality of information flow in the GCN is illustrated with arrows. Note that the transformations $\phi^{(k)}$ that denote aggregations from the neighbors j of a node i, and the manner in which the aggregations are combined with preceding embeddings

(A) Layer *k-1*   (B) Layer *k*

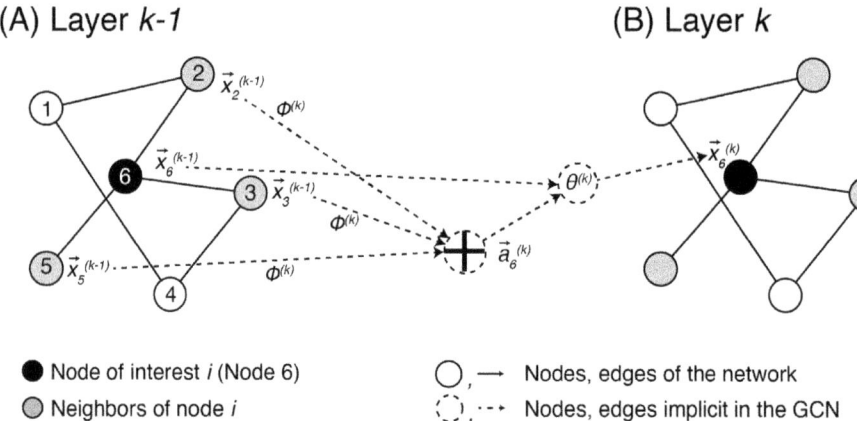

● Node of interest i (Node 6)   ○, → Nodes, edges of the network
◉ Neighbors of node i ⌒, --→ Nodes, edges implicit in the GCN

Figure 9.1.4 The aggregation and propogation steps of a GCN, for a network with six nodes.

$\theta^{(k)}$, are agnostic the specific node/neighbors i and j. The dashed arrows are implicit operations that occur in the GCN.

We denote the parameter set for the GCN with the short-hand (θ, ϕ), which is used to represent the set of possible weights and settings for the various functions and transformations used across layers of the GCN. θ and ϕ are parametrized functions for each layer; this short-hand should not suggest that these are specific scalar parameters θ and ϕ for the GCN. Rather, we leave the notation as θ and ϕ to denote that the parameters for these functions may vary depending on what the user chooses.

9.1.3   Training GNNs

Training deep learning and optimization-focused algorithms is somewhat different from other domains of machine learning. We first partition our dataset into training and testing data. For our use-case, each data point is one of our M networks. Training occurs over many iterations through the shuffled training data, called *epochs*. In each of the R epochs, the training data are partitioned into B batches. Each batch is run through the neural network in a *forward pass*, which produces a *prediction*. The prediction and the ground truth labels are then put into a loss function, which is to be minimized. To adjust the neural network for the next forward pass, the gradient of its parameters with respect to the loss is calculated. The parameters are then adjusted according to that gradient using an *optimizer* such that the loss is lower on the next forward pass.

The workflow for graph neural network training for molecule classification is illustrated in Figure 9.1.5.

We split a dataset into training and testing sets below. We use `pytorch`'s `dataset` and `DataLoader` objects, which make the process of loading, transforming, shuffling, and splitting a dataset into batches easy.

(A)   (B)   (C)

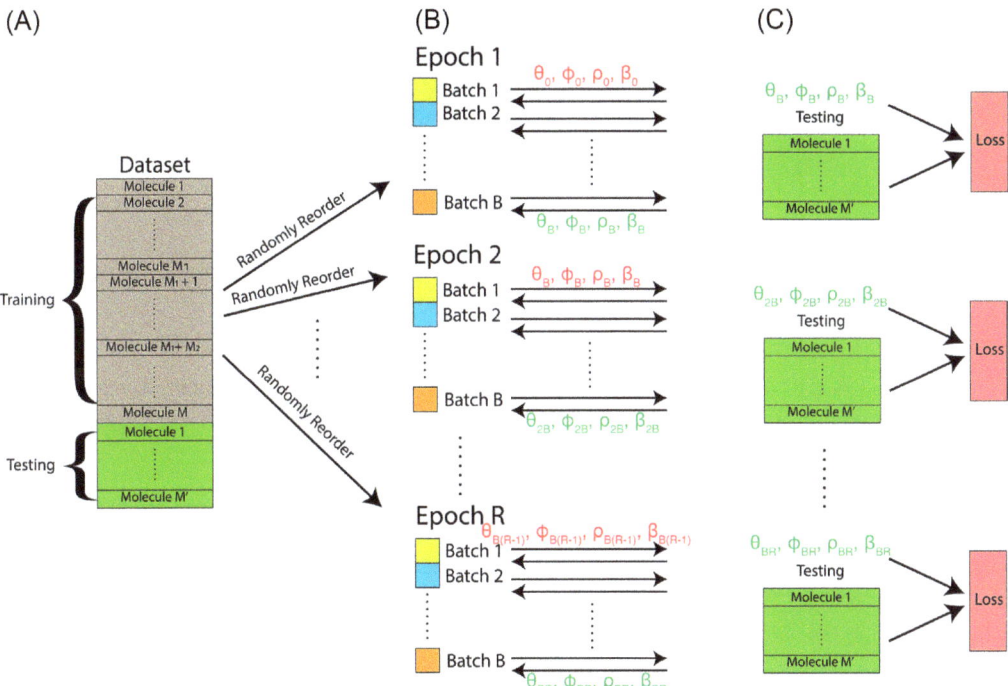

Figure 9.1.5 The training and evaluation procedure for a GNN. (**A**) The dataset is split into training and testing sets, and the training molecules are randomly reordered for each epoch. Each epoch consists of all M molecules randomly reordered. (**B**) Each epoch is split into B batches each of which have M_b molecules. Each batch is iteratively passed through the network (forward pass) and weights updated (backward pass), shown in more depth in Figure 9.1.6 and 9.1.7. (**C**) At the end of an epoch, we use the parameters and the GNN with the held-out testing data to assess performance.

```
import torch
# for notebook reproducibility
torch.manual_seed(12345)

dataset = dataset.shuffle()

train_dataset = dataset[:-150]
test_dataset = dataset[-150:]

print(f'Number of training networks: {len(train_dataset)}')
print(f'Number of test networks: {len(test_dataset)}')
```

Once we have the dataset parsed into training and testing sets, we define a `DataLoader` which subsets the data into 64 molecule-sized batches. The testing `DataLoader` remains unshuffled for reproducibility.

```
from torch_geometric.loader import DataLoader

train_loader = DataLoader(train_dataset, batch_size=64, shuffle=True)
test_loader = DataLoader(test_dataset, batch_size=64, shuffle=False)
```

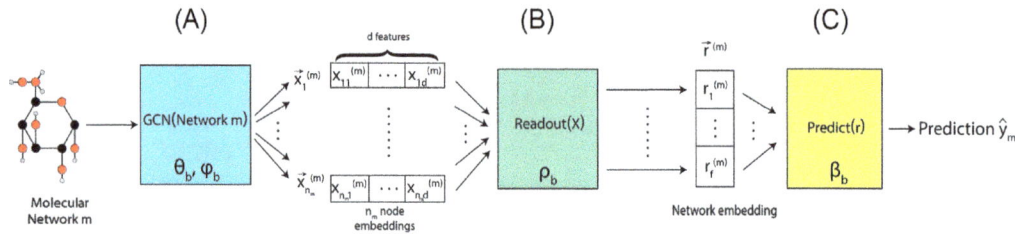

Figure 9.1.6 A molecule m has a predicted label computed, using **(A)** a graph convolutional layer, **(B)** a readout layer, and **(C)** a prediction layer.

A `pytorch` `DataLoader` can iterate through batches sequentially until it has gone through all the data, at which point a new epoch begins. When the next epoch begins, the `train_loader` data will be shuffled.

```
for step, data in enumerate(iter(train_loader)):
    print(f'Step {step + 1}:')
    print(f'Number of networks in the current batch: {data.num_graphs}')
    print(data)
```

The Forward Pass
The forward pass begins on a single batch b, of which there are B in total. We assume that there are M_b molecules in total in batch b.

For a given network m, we begin by passing the network through the graph convolutional layer, denoted by GCN (Network m), shown in Figure 9.1.6(A). The GCN has parameters θ_b and ϕ_b, the specific choice of weights and transformations for the GCN that will be used for batch b. The graph convolutional layer produces embedding vectors for each of the n_m nodes. In this way, we end up with an *embedding matrix* $X^{(m)}$, which has n_m nodes and d latent dimensions. This is conceptually similar to the omnibus embedding in Section 5.5.4, but allows greater flexibility in the characteristics of the embeddings. The caveat is that, when the number of training samples are smaller, the regularization inherent to the omnibus embedding can be advantageous to avoid overfitting.

Given the node embedding matrix $X^{(m)}$, we pass to a readout layer denoted by Readout(X), Figure 9.1.6(B). This layer has parameters ρ_b, which indicate how the n_m separate node embeddings should be aggregated by the readout algorithm. The readout layer produces a single embedding for the entire network, an f-dimensional vector denoted $\vec{r}^{(m)}$. In our case, the readout layer simply averages the node embeddings.

Given the network embedding $\vec{r}^{(m)}$, we are ready to make a prediction for our network Predict $\left(\vec{r}^{(m)}\right)$, Figure 9.1.6(C). The prediction function has parameters β_b, and in our simple binary example is a linear layer. This layer produces a weighted sum of all f dimensions (with weights denoted by the parameter set β_b). If the weighted sum exceeds a particular value (the *offset* β_0), the layer predicts that the network is in class 1. Otherwise, it predicts that the network is in class 0. It looks like this:

$$\text{Predict}\left(\vec{r}^{(m)}\right) = 1\left\{\sum_{j=1}^{f}\beta_j r_j^{(m)} > \beta_0\right\} = \begin{cases} 1, & \text{class 1} \\ 0, & \text{class 0.} \end{cases}$$

We can define this using `torch` as follows:

```
from torch import nn
from torch.nn import Linear
import torch.nn.functional as F
from torch_geometric.nn import GCNConv
from torch_geometric.nn import global_mean_pool

torch.manual_seed(12345)
class GCN(nn.Module):
    def __init__(self, hidden_channels):
        super(GCN, self).__init__()
        self.conv1 = GCNConv(dataset.num_node_features, hidden_channels)
        self.conv2 = GCNConv(hidden_channels, hidden_channels)
        self.conv3 = GCNConv(hidden_channels, hidden_channels)
        self.lin = Linear(hidden_channels, dataset.num_classes,
            bias=False)

    def forward(self, x, edge_index, batch):

        # 1. Obtain node embeddings via convolutional layers
        x = self.conv1(x, edge_index)
        x = x.relu()
        x = self.conv2(x, edge_index)
        x = x.relu()
        x = self.conv3(x, edge_index)

        # 2. Readout layer to produce network embedding
        x = global_mean_pool(x, batch) # [batch_size, hidden_channels]

        # 3. Apply a prediction classifier to the network embedding
        x = self.lin(x)

        return x

model = GCN(hidden_channels=64)
print(model)
```

The forward pass is applied to all of the molecules in a single batch, as shown in Figure 9.1.7(A). The pass is applied to all networks with the same parameters $(\theta_b, \phi_b, \rho_b, \beta_b)$ for a given batch, as indicated by Figure 9.1.7(B). Once predictions are made for all M_b molecules, the prediction loss is computed, which is a scalar quantity that we seek to minimize. The prediction loss is denoted by $\text{Loss}\left(\hat{y}_b\right)$, where $\hat{y}_b$ are the class predictions (toxic or nontoxic) for molecules in batch b. Inherently, since the predictions used to compute the loss are all produced by the particular parameters used for the forward pass $(\theta_b, \phi_b, \rho_b, \beta_b)$, the loss is also a function of the parameters.

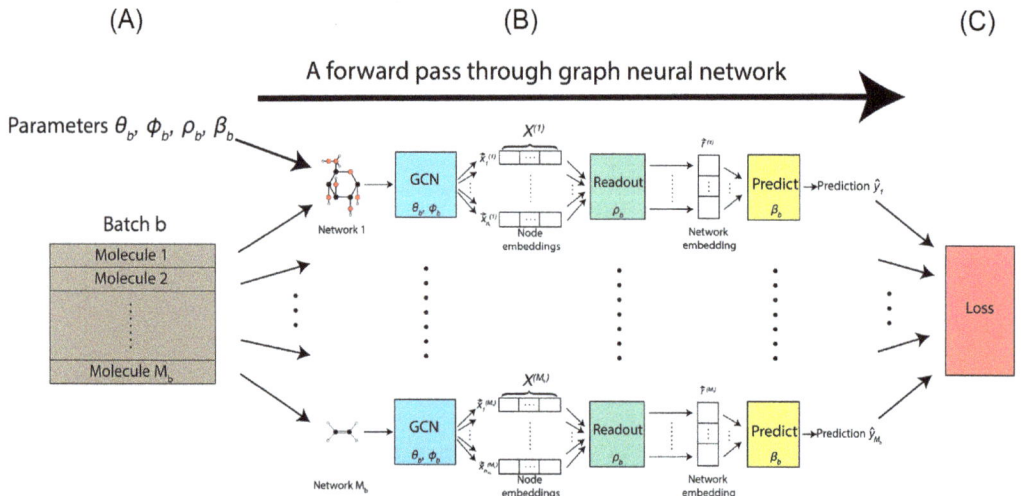

Figure 9.1.7 A single forward pass through the graph neural network for the M_b molecules in batch b.

The Backward Pass
The predictions (and consequently, the loss) produced for a given batch b are inherently a function of the parameters we used in the forward pass $\mathcal{W} = (\theta, \phi, \rho, \beta)$. In this context, we use the set $\mathcal{W}$ as a short-hand for all of the parameters to the neural network (the convolutional layer, the readout layer, and the prediction layer).

When the convolutional layer, the readout layer, and the prediction layers are chosen using differentiable functions (meaning, we can compute the derivative with respect to the parameters), we can use this differentiability in conjunction with the particular loss function we employed (in this case, the cross-entropy loss) to determine how the loss function behaves when we change the parameters slightly. This is done by taking the derivative of the loss with respect to each of the parameters. These are partial derivatives of the form $\frac{\partial \text{Loss}}{\partial w_i}$, where w_i denotes a particular parameter from the parameter set $\mathcal{W}$. The vector of all such partial derivatives is the loss gradient with respect to the parameters, $\nabla_{\mathcal{W}}\text{Loss}$. In practice, neural network layer parameters are often organized as matrices. In this case, the collection of partial derivatives is represented by the Jacobian matrix, which contains the partial derivatives of the loss with respect to each element of the parameter set $\mathcal{W}$.

We use the loss gradient to make small updates to the parameter values via gradient descent (similar to Figure 7.3.4), using an optimizer. When we combine the use of random batches with gradient descent, the trained parameters behave similarly to the parameters which would be obtained from looking at the entire epoch.

Our new set of updated parameters is given by $(\theta_{b+1}, \phi_{b+1}, \rho_{b+1}, \beta_{b+1})$.

Repeat for the Entire Epoch
After we complete a forward and backward pass, we repeat this process for each batch until we get to the end of an epoch. This is illustrated in Figure 9.1.8(A). When we get to the end of an epoch, we use the held-out testing data to estimate the testing accuracy

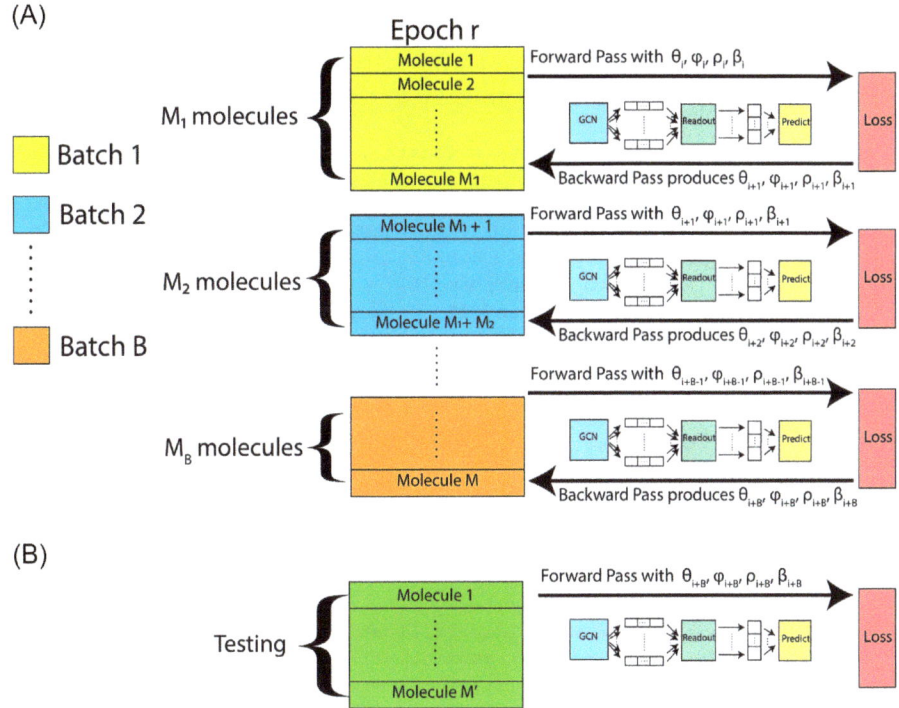

Figure 9.1.8 (**A**) We repeat forward and backwards passes over each batch within the epoch, starting with parameters $(\theta_i, \phi_i, \rho_i, \beta_i)$, and ultimately ending up with parameters $(\theta_{i+B}, \phi_{i+B}, \rho_{i+B}, \beta_{i+B})$. (**B**) The parameters from the final batch are assessed on the held-out testing set.

with the parameters we obtain from the final backwards pass. The testing data are fed through the neural network forwards, and then we compute the testing accuracy, as illustrated in Figure 9.1.8(B).

Putting it All Together
Now that we understand each piece individually, we are ready to look at what the whole process looks like. The training data are randomly reordered into R epochs, and then each epoch is split into B batches, illustrated in Figures 9.1.5(A) and (B). The parameters from the preceding epoch (or, if this is the first epoch, just initialization parameters) begin the first forward pass, and then forwards and backwards passes are alternated with the parameters updated accordingly after each batch is passed through, shown in Figure 9.1.5(B). At the end of the epoch, the resulting parameters Figure 9.1.5(C) are analyzed with the held-out testing data are used for validation. The parameters from the epoch with the best performance on the testing data are ultimately returned as the trained model parameters.

```
model = GCN(hidden_channels=64)
optimizer = torch.optim.Adam(model.parameters(), lr=0.0001)
criterion = torch.nn.CrossEntropyLoss()
```

```
def train():
  model.train()
  for data in train_loader: # Iterate in batches over the training
      dataset.
    out = model(data.x.float(), data.edge_index, data.batch) #
        Perform a single forward pass.
    # Handle a pyg bug where last element in batch may be all zeros
        and excluded in the model output.
    # https://github.com/pyg-team/pytorch_geometric/issues/1813
    num_batch = out.shape[0]
    loss = criterion(out, data.y[:num_batch, 0].long()) # Compute
        the loss.

    loss.backward() # Derive gradients.
    optimizer.step() # Update parameters based on gradients.
    optimizer.zero_grad() # Clear gradients.

def test(loader):
  model.eval()
  correct = 0
  for data in loader: # Iterate in batches over the training/test
      dataset.
    out = model(data.x.float(), data.edge_index, data.batch)
    pred = out.argmax(dim=1) # Use the class with highest
        probability.
    num_batch = pred.shape[0]
    correct += int((pred == data.y[:num_batch, 0]).sum()) # Check
        against ground-truth labels.
  return correct / len(loader.dataset) # Derive ratio of correct
      predictions.

R = 10 # number of epochs
for epoch in range(0, R):
  train()
  train_acc = test(train_loader)
  test_acc = test(test_loader)
  print(f'Epoch: {epoch:03d}, Train Acc: {train_acc:.4f}, Test Acc:
      {test_acc:.4f}')
```

To learn more about GNNs, we recommend a dedicated textbook on the topic, such as [16; 17].

9.2   Random Walks and Diffusion-Based Methods

This section introduces an alternative approach to directly learn network representations: analyzing random walks on networks. A random walk is a stochastic process, where we start at a node and take random steps to neighboring nodes. The behavior of these walks is determined by the network's topology, including nodes, edges, and potentially edge weights if the network is weighted. Random walk techniques build on the basic network properties and descriptive statistics introduced in Sections 3.1 and 3.2 to provide a dynamic view of network structure.

In this section, we will:

1. Introduce the concept of random walks on networks,
2. Explore how random walks can generate training data for graph neural networks models,
3. Demonstrate how neural networks can analyze random walks to uncover network properties, and
4. Discuss techniques for tuning random walks to capture specific network characteristics.

Random walk methods offer a complementary approach to spectral techniques. They are particularly useful for capturing local network structure and can be effective in tasks such as node classification and link prediction. Random walk methods also naturally allow the model to learn nonlinear relationships between nodes in the graph. However, random walk methods are inherently stochastic, require hyperparameter tuning, and are built on less solid theoretical foundations.

9.2.1 A Simplified First-Order Random Walk on a Network

Consider a simplified approach for a first-order random walk on the New York Bridge network example from Section 3.1. We will define the nodes and edges of the network so that the nodes are the five boroughs (Staten Island SI, Brooklyn BK, Queens Q, the Bronx BX, and Manhattan MH). The edges (i, j) exist if one can travel from borough i to borough j along a bridge.

Our example data are:

```
import numpy as np

# define the node names
node_names = np.array(["SI", "MH", "BK", "Q", "BX"])
# define the adjacency matrix
A = np.array([[0,0,1,0,0], # Staten Island neighbors Brooklyn
            [0,0,1,1,1], # Manhattan Neighbors all but Staten Island
            [1,1,0,1,0], # Brooklyn neighbors all but Bronx
            [0,1,1,0,1], # Queens neighbors all but Staten Island
            [0,1,0,1,0]]) # Bronx neighbors Manhattan and Queens
```

Figure 3.1.2 shows the network.

Suppose we are in a Manhattan conference, and we decide to randomly explore the city. When we are in some borough i, we will determine the next borough to explore with random chance. To define a first-order random walk, we first introduce the Markov chain and the Markov property.

9.2.1.1 Markov Chains and the Markov Property

A *finite-space Markov chain* is a model of a random system in which we have a finite sequence of possible states which can occur (for example, the boroughs we will visit on a day t) and the probability of the next state depends only on our current state. We only need to think about finite-space Markov chains, because networks have a finite collection of possible states (the nodes being visited). We represent our Markov chain by the sequence $s_0, s_1, s_2, \ldots$, where each s_t takes the value of one of the n total nodes in the network.

In our definition of the finite-space Markov chain, we require that the probability of each event depends only on the previous state. This is called the *Markov property*. For example, if we were in Manhattan at time $t - 1$ ($s_{t-1} = v_{MH}$) and in Brooklyn at time t ($s_t = v_{BK}$), the next step in the Markov chain s_{t+1} would not depend on the fact that we already saw Manhattan.

First-Order Random Walks on a Network as a Markov Chain

To explore Markov chains, we define a first-order random walk in our New York boroughs. The current borough, i, has d_i possible neighboring boroughs, where d_i is the degree of node i. We visit one of the other nodes in the network as follows. If an edge exists from borough i to borough j, we will visit borough j with probability $\frac{1}{d_i}$. We will visit the neighbors of each borough at random, depending only on whether we can get to the next borough along an edge of the network. This is called a *first-order random walk* because we ignore everything about the path we have taken to get to our current borough to date, except for the fact that we are at that borough now. If the node is not a neighbor of our current borough, we will visit it with probability 0.

Formally, if we are in node i at time t (that is, $s_t = i$), the probability of going to another node j is defined as:

$$p_{ij} = \begin{cases} \frac{1}{d_i}, & \text{edge } (i, j) \text{ exists} \\ 0, & \text{edge } (i, j) \text{ does not exist.} \end{cases} \tag{9.1}$$

These probabilities, called the *transition probability* from node i to node j, are always the same and have nothing to do with which nodes we have visited yet. To avoid confusion, we use the notation p_{ij} instead of $p_{ij}^{(t+1)}$.

Since the transition probabilities are unchanging in time, they are often organized into an $n \times n$ matrix called the *transition probability matrix P* with entries p_{ij} defined as above. In this case, the transition probability matrix can be arranged like this:

```
# compute the degree of each node
di = A.sum(axis=0)
# the probability matrix is the adjacency divided by
# degree of the starting node
P = (A / di).T
```

Figure 9.2.1(B) shows a heatmap of the transition probability matrix, with the corresponding layout plot for the network in Figure 9.2.1(A). Notice that if we are in Staten Island, there is only one borough we can go from here, so with probability 1, we will visit its only neighbor: Brooklyn. If we are in Manhattan, we could go to any of its three neighbors (Brooklyn, Queens, or Bronx), with equal probability $\frac{1}{3}$. This continues for each node in the network until we have successfully generated the transition probability matrix P. Since the transition probability entries p_{ij} are normalized only by the degree d_i of the node i, the transition probability matrix is not necessarily symmetric, even if the network is undirected (and has a symmetric adjacency matrix).

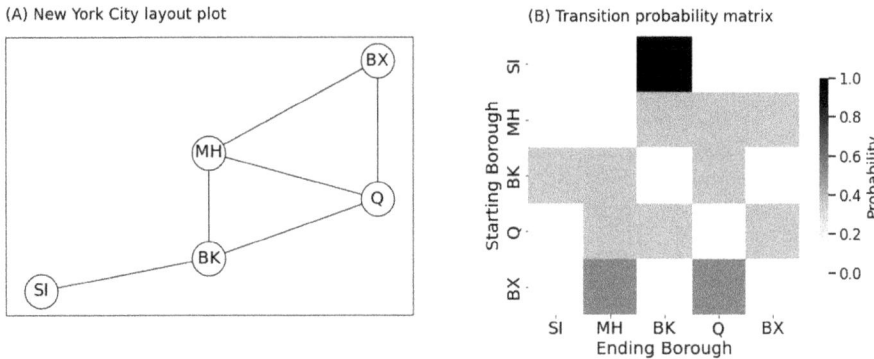

Figure 9.2.1 **(A)** The New York bridge network, and **(B)** the transition probability matrix for the network.

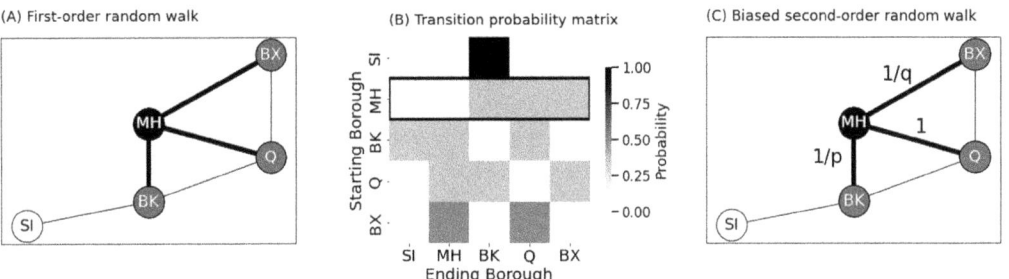

Figure 9.2.2 **(A)** The possible next nodes that can be accessed from MH, **(B)** their corresponding probabilities, and **(C)** the bias vectors for a biased second-order random walk.

See [18] for more information on the properties of transition probability matrices and Markov chains.

We use the transition probability matrix to generate a random walk on the New York City boroughs. We start our random walk through the city in Manhattan, such that $s_0 = v_{MH}$ (Figure 9.2.2(A)). Next, we visit either Brooklyn, the Bronx, or Queens with probability $\frac{1}{3}$, and Staten Island with probability 0. The nodes with nonzero transition probabilities are illustrated in dark gray, and are connected to MH via edges, shown in dark black. Staten Island is inaccessible directly from MH, and is in white. The corresponding transition probabilities for each of the nodes in the network are highlighted in Figure 9.2.2(B).

We then choose the next node using the probability vector of the next step in the random walk given the current step in the transition probability matrix P. We denote this probability vector with $\vec{p}_i$.

Notice that this is just the entries of the ith row of the transition probability matrix, which can be calculated using the relationship:

$$\vec{p}_i = P^\top \vec{x}^{(i)}$$

where $\vec{x}^{(i)}$ is the vector which has a value of 0 for all entries except for entry i, where it has a value of 1. This pulls out the ith row of P, because every multiplication except for those against the ith column of $P^\top$ will be 0.

We can pick the next node easily by just using numpy:

```
x0 = np.array([0,1,0,0,0]) # x vector indicating we start at MH
ps0 = P.T @ x0 # p vector for timestep 1 starting at node MH at time 0
# choose the next node using the probability vector we calculated
next_node = np.random.choice(range(0, len(node_names)), p=ps0)
print(f"Next node: {node_names[next_node]:s}")
```

This gives us a realization of the new node s_1, conditional on the starting node being $s_0 = v_{MH}$. We can generate a T-step first-order random walk along the network G by repeating this approach, as explained in Algorithm 9.1.

Algorithm 9.1 First-order random walk on a network

Data: A the adjacency matrix for an n-node network.
  s_0 the index of the node from which the random walk will begin.
  T the number of steps to take in the random walk.
Result: $\vec{s} = (s_0, s_1, \ldots, s_T)$ is a length $T + 1$ vector, defining the nodes of the random walk on the network.

1 Construct the degree matrix for the network, D, and let P be defined as described in Equation (9.1).
2 Initialize $\vec{x}^{(s_0)}$ to be the length n vector where $x_{s_0}^{(s_0)} = 1$, and 0 otherwise.
3 **for** t **in** 1: T **do**
4 $\quad$ Construct a vector $\vec{p}_{s_{t-1}} = P^\top \vec{x}^{(s_{t-1})}$.
5 $\quad$ Obtain an n-sided die, where the probability of landing on side j is $p_{s_{t-1}j}$.
6 $\quad$ Roll the die, and let s_t be the side that the die lands on.
7 $\quad$ Let $\vec{x}^{(s_t)}$ be the vector where $x_{s_t}^{(s_t)} = 1$, and 0 otherwise.
8 **end**
9 **return** $\vec{s}$.

9.2.2 Markov Chains, Random Walks, and Embedding Networks

In the opening of Section 9.2, we said we were going to cover how to use a random walk to embed our network. To this end, we introduce a slight variation of the random walk called the *second-order biased random walk*.

9.2.2.1 Second-Order Biased Random Walk

In our first-order random walk, it is possible to walk in circles. For example, we could explore from Manhattan to Brooklyn, and then to Staten Island, back to Brooklyn, back to Staten Island, and so forth. This is possible because of the Markov property: We ignored the previous places we had been when making the decision for where to go from our current borough.

The in–out parameter q modifies the transition probability from step s_t based on whether a potential next node j is connected to the previous node s_{t-1}. Specifically, if node j and node s_{t-1} are not connected, the probability of transitioning to j is scaled by a factor of q.

The In–Out and Return Parameters

The steps in our random walk, $\{s_0, s_1, \ldots, s_{t-1}, s_t, \ldots\}$, were sequences of random variables which took on values of nodes in the network. Assume that we have a random walk such that we know our previous state, $s_{t-1} = s_{t-1}$, and we are currently at node i, $s_t = i$.

The *in-out* parameter q modifies the transition probability from step s_t based on whether a potential next node j is connected to the previous node s_{t-1}. Specifically, if node j and node s_{t-1} are not connected, the probability of transitioning to j is scaled by a factor q.

If $q > 1$, then $\frac{1}{q}$ will be very small, and we will be biased against visiting nodes that are not connected to the previous node we visited (we "stay in" with nodes connected to those we just visited). If $q < 1$, then $\frac{1}{q}$ will be big, and we will be biased towards visiting nodes which are not connected to the previous node we visited (we "move out"). This can be understood in terms of breadth-first and depth-first searches, as explained in Concept 9.2.1.

The *return* parameter p indicates a bias of $\frac{1}{p}$ that we will go back to the previous node s_{t-1}. If p is large, $\frac{1}{p}$ will be small, and we will be biased against visiting the previous node. If p is small, then $\frac{1}{p}$ will be big, and we will be biased towards visiting the previous node. In Concept 9.2.2, we explain how the return parameter can yield different exploratory strategies about particular nodes in the network.

If a node satisfies neither of these conditions, the bias factor is just left at 1. Together, these relationships are summarized with the *second-order bias factors* $\alpha_{ij}(p, q, s_{t-1})$ starting at node $s_t = i$ and proceeding to node j with parameters p and q for the next step $t + 1$ given that we just left state s_{t-1} as:

$$\alpha_{ij}(p, q, s_{t-1}) = \begin{cases} \frac{1}{p}, & s_{t-1} = j \\ 1, & s_{t-1} \neq j \text{ and the edge } (j, s_{t-1}) \text{ exists} \\ \frac{1}{q}, & s_{t-1} \neq j \text{ and no edge } (j, s_{t-1}) \text{ exists.} \end{cases} \tag{9.2}$$

The corresponding second-order bias vector is $\vec{\alpha}_i(p, q, s_{t-1})$, which is a vector of each of the bias factors for all of the other n nodes in the network. These are called second order because they depend on the preceding node, s_{t-1}, as well as the current node i.

Figure 9.2.2(C) shows the bias factors overlaid on the adjacency matrix for our network. The current node is Manhattan ($s_t = v_{MH}$) and is shown in black, and the previous node was Brooklyn ($s_{t-1} = v_{BK}$). We just visited node BK, so the bias factor will be $\frac{1}{p}$. The node for Bronx does not have an edge back to Brooklyn, so taking it gets us "out," and the bias factor will be $\frac{1}{q}$. The nodes Queens, Manhattan, and Staten Island all have edges to Brooklyn, so the bias is 1.

We bias against returning with a large return parameter $p = 5$, and a small in–out parameter $q = \frac{1}{2}$, like this:

Concept 9.2.1 The in–out parameter and network searches

A random walk gives us an approach to "search" through the network, iterating over the nodes. We can understand this trade-off in terms of a homophilic network, with higher densities of within-community connections than between-community connections, shown in Figure 9.2.3, where we have a small network with three communities. For each of the two walks, we start at location s_0. The steps of the walk are annotated in sequential order.

A *breadth-first search* (BFS) tends to favor walks that explore local nodes with high interconnectedness, and prioritizes visiting all of the nodes in a community before moving on to new communities. When $q > 1$, the search is more BFS-like; we will tend to prioritize walking over nodes which are interconnected with nodes we have recently visited, and our random walks will tend to more fully explore a single community before moving to new communities. In Figure 9.2.3(A), we illustrate a walk over the nodes where $q > 1$. For instance, after s_3, we would be biased to take a step towards the top black node, which is also connected to the node from s_2 because $q > 1$.

A *depth-first search* (DFS) is a search strategy that tends to favor exploring novel regions of the network, and in so doing, prioritizing exploring all of the communities at a shallow depth over visiting all of the nodes within a community. In Figure 9.2.3(B), we illustrate a walk over the nodes where $q < 1$. After s_2, we are biased against taking a step to the unexplored top black node, and instead make a step towards the white node at s_3 because it is not connected to the node from s_1, as $q < 1$.

(A)   (B)

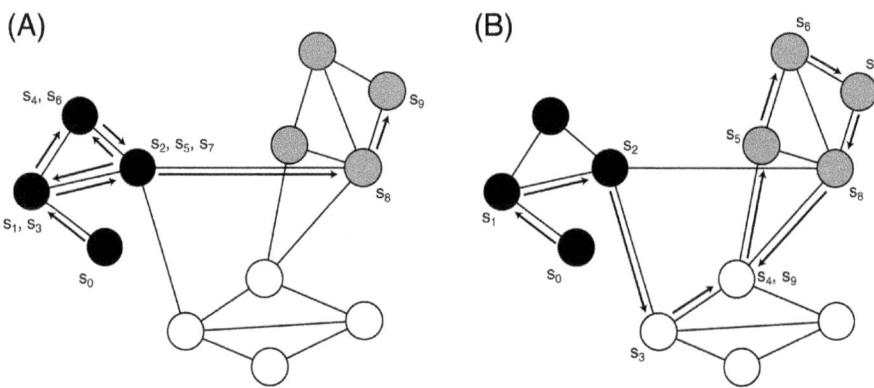

Figure 9.2.3 (A) A breadth-first, local neighborhood sampling walk, and (B) a depth-first, moderate exploration walk.

```
p = 5 # return parameter
q = 1/2 # in-out parameter
bias_vector = np.ones(len(node_names))
bias_vector[node_names == "BX"] = 1/q
bias_vector[node_names == "BK"] = 1/p
```

Concept 9.2.2 The return parameter and neighborhood exploration

The return parameter of a second-order biased random walk directly ties into our ability to explore the local neighborhood about particularly interconnected nodes. A *neighborhood* of width ϵ about a node i is the collection of nodes that i is connected to with a shortest path of length ϵ. The concept of the shortest path can be reviewed in Section 3.2.3.

When the return parameter is low ($p < 1$), we will tend to favor walks where we return back to nodes that we have just visited at the previous step. This gives us a greater chance to explore the local neighborhood of width 1 about particular nodes. For instance, Figure 9.2.3(A) shows an example of a walk with a high return parameter. Notice that from s_1 to s_4, we are able to visit all of the local neighborhood of the left-most node in the black community, due to the fact that we routinely return back to this node.

When the return parameter is high ($p > 1$), we will tend to favor walks that do not regularly return back to nodes, as in Figure 9.2.3(B). Instead, we tend to favor more exploratory steps towards nodes we have not recently visited.

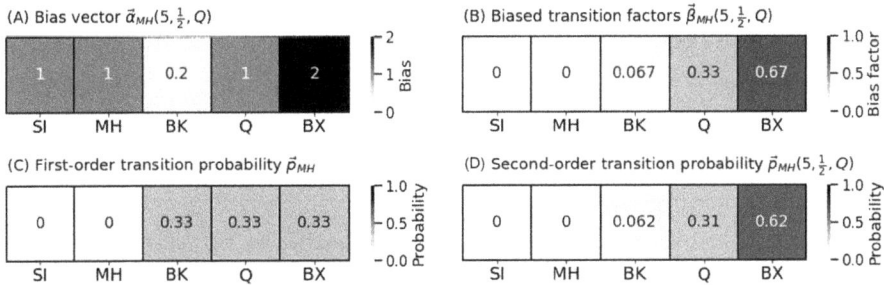

Figure 9.2.4 With with $p = 5$ and $q = \frac{1}{2}$ for $n = 5$ where $s_t = MH$ and $s_{t-1} = BK$, (**A**) the bias vector, (**B**) the second-order biased transition factors, (**C**) the first-order transition probabilities, and (**D**) the second-order biased transition probabilities.

The resulting bias vector is shown in Figure 9.2.4(A).

Adjusting the Transition Probabilities with the Bias Vector

In our second-order random walk, instead of the transition probabilities being a function only of the current state s_t, they are also a function of the preceding state s_{t-1}. This means that our transition probability matrix will look different based on which node we just came from. The transition probabilities will be defined using the notation $p_{ij}(p,q,s_{t-1})$, where s_{t-1} is the preceding node, i is the current node, j is any other node in the network, and p and q are the return and in–out parameters.

We first define the *second-order biased transition factors*:

$$\beta_{ij}(p,q,s_{t-1}) = \alpha_{ij}(p,q,s_{t-1})p_{ij} \tag{9.3}$$

where p_{ij} are the first-order Markov transition probabilities. The biased transition factors combine the bias factor with the transition probability from the first-order Markov chain.

We upweight or downweight (or don't change it at all, if the bias factor is 1) the transition probability p_{ij} based on the bias factor $\alpha_{ij}(p,q,s_{t-1})$. These are no longer probabilities, because starting at a node i, we might end up with the bias-adjusted transition factors no longer summing to one because we did not require anything about how $\alpha_{ij}(p,q,s_{t-1})$ behaved across all possible nodes j.

We now use the biased transition factors to compute the *second-order biased transition probabilities*. These are normalizations of the bias transition factors where we normalize to make sure that they all sum up to one (and hence, produce a valid transition probability from node i outwards):

$$p_{ij}(p,q,s_{t-1}) = \frac{\beta_{ij}(p,q,s_{t-1})}{\sum_{j'=1}^{n} \beta_{ij'}(p,q,s_{t-1})}. \tag{9.4}$$

In the denominator, we normalize the biased transition factor by the sum of all the other biased transition factors from node i to any other nodes j' in the network.

Next, we show how this computation works to update the transition probability vector from the Manhattan node to node j given a previous node of Brooklyn. We start with the first-order transition probability vector $\vec{p}_i$:

```
xt = [0, 1, 0, 0, 0] # starting vector at MH
pst = P.T @ xt # probability vector is Pt*x
```

This is illustrated in Figure 9.2.4(A). The next step is to compute the second-order biased transition factors:

```
bias_factors = pst*bias_vector
```

This is shown in Figure 9.2.4(B). And finally, we normalize the bias-adjusted transition factors to obtain the second-order biased transition probabilities:

```
biased_pst = bias_factors/bias_factors.sum()
```

We compare the first-order transition probabilities to the second-order biased transition probabilities in Figure 9.2.4(C) and 9.2.4(D), respectively. As we can see, our tendency to return to Brooklyn (since we were just there in the previous step, $s_{t-1} = v_{BK}$) has decreased from the first-order transition probability to the second-order biased transition probability, owing to the fact that the return parameter is big ($p = 5$). Further, our tendency to move out to Bronx (since Bronx has no edges to Brooklyn) has increased from the first-order transition probability to the second-order biased transition probability, owing to the fact that the in–out parameter is small ($q = 0.5$). The transition probability for the remaining node with a bias of 1, Queens, is less affected from the first-order to the second-order biased transition probability.

We use the second-order biased transition probabilities to decide where to go next, as we did before:

```
# choose the next node using the second-order biased transition
    probability
next_node = np.random.choice(range(0, len(node_names)), p=biased_pst)
print(f"Next node: {node_names[next_node]:s}")
```

The procedure for generating a second-order biased random walk is described in Algorithm 9.2. We assume $T > 1$ in the algorithm as if $T = 1$, the second-order biased random walk would be a first-order random walk as in Algorithm 9.1.

Algorithm 9.2 Second-order biased random walk

Data: A the adjacency matrix for an n-node network.

      s_0 the index of the node from which the random walk will begin.

      T the number of steps to take in the random walk, where $T > 1$.

      q the in–out parameter.

      p the return parameter.

Result: $\vec{s} = (s_0, s_1, \ldots, s_T)$ is a length $T + 1$ vector, defining the nodes of the random walk on the network.

1 Construct the degree matrix for the network, D, and let P be defined as described in Equation (9.1).

2 Perform a first-order random walk from s_0 to s_1, using the procedure in Algorithm 9.1 with $T = 1$, to obtain the first-order random walk (s_0, s_1).

3 Initialize $\vec{x}^{(s_1)}$ to be the length n vector where $x_{s_1}^{(s_1)} = 1$, and 0 otherwise.

4 **for** t in $2: T$ **do**

5   Compute the bias vector $\vec{a}_{s_{t-1}}(p, q, s_{t-2})$, using the equation described in Equation (9.2).

6   Compute the first-order transition probability vector, $\vec{p}_{s_{t-1}} = P^\top \vec{x}^{(s_{t-1})}$.

7   Compute the second-order bias factor vector $\vec{\beta}_{s_{t-1}}(p, q, s_{t-2})$, using Equation (9.3) with the transition probability vector $\vec{p}_{s_{t-1}}$.

8   Normalize the second-order bias factors $\beta_{s_{t-1}j}(p, q, s_{t-2})$ for each node j in the network, using Equation (9.4) to obtain the second-order biased transition probabilities $p_{s_{t-1}j}(p, q, s_{t-2})$.

9   Obtain a n-sided die, where the probability of landing on side j is $p_{s_{t-1}j}(p, q, s_{t-2})$.

10   Roll the die, and let s_t be the side that the die lands on.

11   Let $\vec{x}^{(s_t)}$ be the length n vector where $x_{s_t}^{(s_t)} = 1$, and 0 otherwise.

12 **end**

13 **return** $\vec{s}$.

9.2.3   Embedding with the `node2vec` Algorithm

Now that we know about second-order biased random walks, we can leverage random walks to produce structured embeddings.

    `word2vec` is a technique developed in 2013 by a team of researchers at Google led by Tomas Mikolov [19; 20]. It takes text along with a desired number of embedding dimensions d, and embeds every possible word in the text into d dimensions such that words which tend to be used in similar contexts or have similar meaning are closer together. Thus `word2vec` can be thought of as a preprocessing step to turn the collection of words into d-dimensional representations. This embedding can then be used for many problems using different downstream algorithms. `node2vec` [21] takes `word2vec` and applies it to nodes instead of words.

For each node in our network, we generate a second-order biased random walk with parameters (p, q) of length T starting at that node. This gives us a collection of random walks with disparate starting nodes. We repeat this procedure r times for each starting node to give us a set of rn random walks of length T.

Next, we "pretend" that node indices are words, and we feed the collections of random walks into the `word2vec` algorithm as our text along with the desired number of embedding dimensions d. We now explore how `word2vec` works.

9.2.3.1   One-Hot Encoding the Nodes

The first step is to convert each of the n nodes in the network into vectors. We can do this with one-hot encoding: For a given node i, we can one-hot encode the node with the vector $\vec{x}^{(i)}$, where $x_i^{(i)} = 1$, and 0 otherwise.

9.2.3.2   The Skip-Gram Algorithm

We next input our one-hot encodings to the skip-gram algorithm, which `word2vec` uses to implicitly obtain node embeddings. Skip-grams use neural networks, which adds a level of ambiguity for our nomenclature. To avoid confusion, when referring to the neural network itself, we will explicitly call it a "neural network" or "NN." When referring to the network that we want to embed, we will refer to it as just the "network."

The skip-gram algorithm seeks to achieve a solution for the following problem: Given a one-hot encoding of a node i in the network, identify the probability that at a "nearby" position in the corpus of random walks is another node j, for each of the n nodes in the network.

Sliding Windows to Generate Training/Testing Samples

To estimate the probability that at a "nearby" position in the set of random walks is another node j, for each of the n nodes in the network, we generate training and testing data using a *sliding window* with a fixed width ω.

In Figure 9.2.5(A), we look at the process of sliding a window over a random walk t of width $\omega = 2$. The sliding window is constructed about a *center* node, illustrated in white. The *context* nodes, illustrated in gray, are what we want the model to predict when given the center node.

Figure 9.2.5(B) shows the center and context nodes that will form the training set for our NN. In this case, the center node's one-hot encoding $\vec{x}^{(i)}$ will be the input to the NN, and the context node's one-hot encoding $\vec{x}^{(j)}$ will be the expected output for the NN. Together, these form a sample $(\vec{x}^{(i)}, \vec{x}^{(j)})$.

As in Section 9.1, we split all of these samples into a training set and a testing set, and we randomly reorder the training set into R epochs, each of which contain every training sample in a random order (see Figure 9.1.5).

Defining the Learning Problem

For our learning problem, we want to learn the context given the center node. For each training sample, we use the center of the sliding window $\vec{x}^{(i)}$ to produce estimated

(A)   (B)

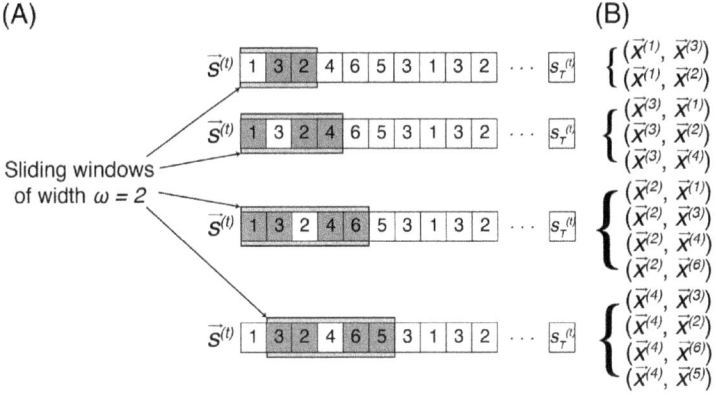

Figure 9.2.5 (A) Sliding windows moving over a generated random walk, and **(B)** training sample pairs which are generated from the window.

probability vectors $\hat{p}^{(i)}$ that are n-dimensional, with a single entry for each possible node in the network.

If our procedure is successful, the probabilities of context nodes from our training samples about a given center node will be higher than the probabilities of noncontext nodes about a given center node. For our cost function, we'll minimize the cross-entropy loss between the context nodes from the training samples and the predictions produced by the NN. We denote this by $L(\theta)$, for the parameters θ for our NN:

$$L(\theta) = -\sum_{i=1}^{N} \left\langle \vec{y}^{(i)}, \log\left(\hat{\vec{p}}^{(i)}\right)\right\rangle.$$

In the equation above, N is the number of training samples, $\vec{y}^{(i)}$ is the context for the ith sample (usually this is a one-hot vector representing the actual context node), and $\hat{\vec{p}}^{(i)}$ is the estimated probability vector output by the neural network for the center node of the ith sample. The log function applies element-wise to the vector $\hat{\vec{p}}^{(i)}$. The summand can be written:

$$-\left\langle \vec{y}^{(i)}, \log\left(\hat{\vec{p}}^{(i)}\right)\right\rangle = -\sum_{j'=1}^{N} y_{j'}^{(i)} \log\left(\hat{p}_{j'}^{(i)}\right).$$

For noncontext nodes j', $y_{j'}^{(i)} = 0$, so only the predicted probability of the context node contributes to this sum. For the context node j, $y_{j}^{(i)} = 1$. A higher probability $\hat{p}_{j}^{(i)}$ for the context node results in $\log\left(\hat{p}_{j}^{(i)}\right)$ closer to zero, yielding a smaller positive value for $-\left\langle \vec{y}^{(i)}, \log\left(\hat{\vec{p}}^{(i)}\right)\right\rangle$ (less loss). Conversely, a lower probability $\hat{p}_{j}^{(i)}$ for the context node results in a more negative $\log\left(\hat{p}_{j}^{(i)}\right)$, yielding a larger positive value for $-\left\langle \vec{y}^{(i)}, \log\left(\hat{\vec{p}}^{(i)}\right)\right\rangle$ (more loss).

The cost function $L(\theta)$ sums the cross-entropy loss over all training samples, and the goal of learning is to adjust the parameters θ to minimize this sum.

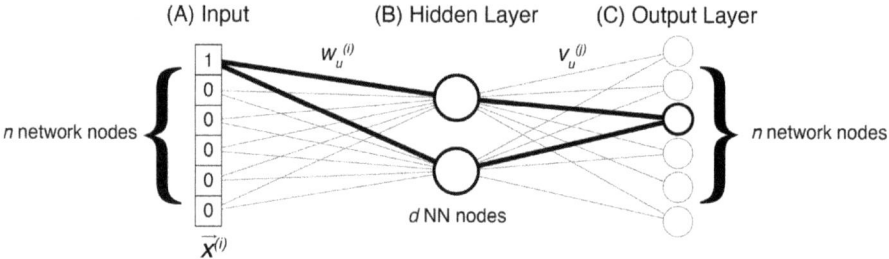

Figure 9.2.6 (**A**) The input to the network, (**B**) the hidden layer with d hidden NN nodes, and (**C**) the output layer.

Architecture of the Network

The network architecture for the skip-gram model is shown in Figure 9.2.6. Figure 9.2.6(A) is the input, which is the one-hot encoding for a center node of a given window in a random walk, which we will denote by i. In the figure, we illustrate the one-hot encoding for node 1 in the network. For each possible center node i in the network, a set of weights $w_u^{(i)}$ connects the node i to hidden layer u, for each of the d hidden layers in the network. The number of hidden nodes is the number of "embedding dimensions" for word2vec. This is illustrated in Figure 9.2.6(B). For each node, this gives us an associated d-dimensional vector of weights:

$$\vec{w}^{(i)} = \left[w_1^{(i)} \quad \cdots \quad w_d^{(i)} \right]^{\top}$$

where d is the number of nodes in the hidden layer.

These weights are captured in the weight matrix W, which has a single row for each possible node in the network:

$$W = \begin{bmatrix} \vdash & \vec{w}^{(1)\top} & \dashv \\ & \vdots & \\ \vdash & \vec{w}^{(n)\top} & \dashv \end{bmatrix}.$$

Premultiplying the one-hot encoding vector $\vec{x}^{(i)}$ by the transpose of this weight matrix W, notice that:

$$W^{\top} \vec{x}^{(i)} = \sum_{j=1}^{n} x_j^{(i)} \vec{w}^{(j)},$$

$$= \vec{w}^{(i)},$$

because $x_j^{(i)}$ is 0 for any $j \neq i$ and 1 exactly where $j = i$.

The idea here is that the weights connecting the input and hidden layers define a latent representation of the node i, which is the vector $\vec{w}^{(i)}$.

Finally, the output layer has n nodes, one for each node in the network, illustrated in Figure 9.2.6(C). The set of output weights $v_u^{(j)}$ connect the hidden node u to the output node j. With the hidden layers as the rows and the outputs as the columns, this produces a $d \times n$ matrix V for us, with columns $\vec{v}^{(j)}$ for each node in the network. The probability that a node i has a node j at least ω close (the window width) is:

$$p_j^{(i)} = \sigma\left(V^\top \vec{w}^{(i)}\right)_j = \frac{\exp\left(\vec{v}^{(j)\top}\vec{w}^{(i)}\right)}{\sum_{j'=1}^{n}\exp\left(\vec{v}^{(j')\top}\vec{w}^{(i)}\right)}. \tag{9.5}$$

Notice that the exponential function $\exp(\cdot)$ can only have positive values for finite inputs, regardless of the product between $\vec{v}^{(j)}$ and $\vec{w}^{(i)}$. Therefore, the numerator of the above equation indicates that the weights $\vec{w}^{(i)}$ and $\vec{v}^{(j)}$ convey a level of similarity between nodes i and j, in that when the value is high, they tend to be within an ω-width window of one another.

Finally, we normalize this quantity by looking at the other nodes which node i could have been close to in the random walk. This function $\sigma(\cdot)$ is known as the *softmax* activation function [22], commonly used in the output layer for neural networks which predict probabilities of sets of different outcomes. Here, we have n possible outcomes that we are predicting (whether a given node j is a context node for center node i, where nodes j range from 1 to n).

The quantity $\sigma\left(\vec{w}^{(i)\top} V\right)_j$ can be thought of as an estimate of the probability of the context being node j given that node i is the center node, and is denoted by $p_j^{(i)}$. The vector $\vec{p}^{(i)}$ is a length n vector, whose entries $p_j^{(i)}$ denote the probability of node j being contexts for center node i:

$$\vec{p}^{(i)} = \left[p_1^{(i)} \quad \cdots \quad p_n^{(i)}\right]^\top.$$

In total, the parameters θ for our NN are the two weight matrices, denoted by the set $\{W, V\}$.

Training the Network
As in Section 9.1, we split the samples produced by Figure 9.2.5(B) into training and testing sets, reorder the elements of the training set into epochs and then split the epochs into B batches.

For a given parameter set $\theta = \{W, V\}$, we feed a batch of training samples through the network one at a time, as indicated in Figure 9.2.7. The procedure is below:

1. Compute the one-hot encoding of center node i, as $\vec{x}^{(i)}$.
2. Obtain the ith row of the weight matrix W, by taking $\vec{w}^{(i)} = W^\top \vec{x}^{(i)}$.
3. Predict probabilities for each possible output node j being a context node for i, with $p_j^{(i)} = \sigma\left(V^\top \vec{w}^{(i)}\right)_j$, according to Equation (9.5).

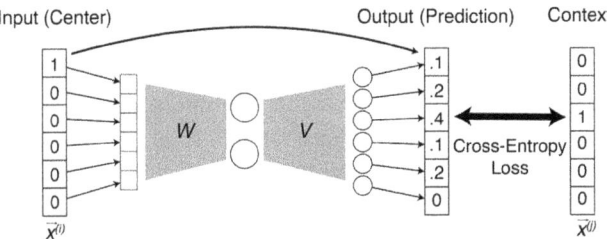

Figure 9.2.7 A forwards pass through a skip-gram network for a single training example, with a center node i and a context node j.

> **Concept 9.2.3** Using NNs and GNNs to obtain latent embeddings
>
> This section illustrates a use-case for neural networks. As we discussed in Section 9.1, neural networks and GNNs applied to network data that are structured typically perform an "embedding" step of some form, whether it is explicitly or implicitly incorporated into the architecture.
>
> To obtain a latent embedding, we can simply "remove" sets of layers of the NN, and learn about the network using the latent representation learned in the preceding layers. In this section, we illustrate that by just ignoring the output softmax layer, we can obtain the node2vec embedding of the network. In some sense, these successive layers existed solely so that the preceding layers (the weight matrix W) would be part of a sensible learning task.

This procedure gives us a probability vector $\vec{p}^{(i)}$. We repeat this process across an entire batch.

Now, we need the gradients of the loss function $L(\theta)$ with respect to the weight matrices W and V. This quantity can be written as $\nabla_{W,V} L(W, V)$, which has entries of the form $\frac{\partial L(W,V)}{\partial w_{ik}}$ or $\frac{\partial L(W,V)}{\partial v_{kj}}$ for each node i and j, and each embedding dimension k. As we saw in Figure 7.3.4, these gradients indicate how the loss $L(W, V)$ changes when we alter the matrix parameters W and V of our NN for each entry. We make a backwards pass using gradient descent to update our weight matrices to form W' and V', as in Figure 9.1.8. We repeat this procedure for all batches in our epoch.

When we finish off the epoch, we compute the cross-entropy loss on the held-out testing samples. We repeat this process over and over again for each epoch, until we reach our stopping criterion (which is typically convergence of the cross-entropy loss on the held-out testing samples).

Obtaining an Embedding from the Skip-Gram Model

After training, we take the weight matrix W, which has n rows and d columns, and use each row $\vec{w}^{(i)}$ as the embedding for node i. Nodes which tend to be along random walks together tend to end up closer in the embedding space, and nodes which do not tend to be along random walks together tend to end up further in the embedding space.

Conceptually, if two nodes tend to fall along similar positions in random walks, it would be desirable if they have similar predicted context nodes, which were computed from $\vec{p}^{(i)} = \sigma\left(V\vec{w}^{(i)}\right)$ for a given node i. This is because if, say, node 2 tends to fall in a similar context to node 1, and node 3 tends to occur in a similar context to node 2, it is quite likely that node 3 and node 1 also fall into similar contexts. This is because of the fact that context, in this case, was enforced using a window of fixed width ω, which means that nodes within a window of one another will necessarily have a subset of nodes falling between the two that are in each of their contexts. Since V is fixed for any given center node i, the only way that this can be the case is if the word embeddings $\vec{w}^{(i)}$ are similar, which satisfies our original aim.

9.2.3.3 Using node2vec with Network Data

To illustrate the utility of node2vec, we will construct an example that is a little bit different from what we are used to (see also Concept 9.2.3). We will use a 4-community SBM, where the block matrix has both affinity and core–periphery structure, as described in Section 4.5. The idea here is that there are two "communities" of nodes which have higher within-community probabilities than between-community probabilities, and within each community there are "subcommunities" which have higher average node degrees (the core) and lower average node degrees (the periphery):

```python
from graphbook_code import dcsbm

nk = 100 # 100 nodes per community
zs = np.repeat([1, 2], nk)
B = np.array([[0.6, 0.3], [0.3, 0.6]])
theta = b = np.repeat([1, .2, 1, .2], nk // 2)
deg_map = {1: "Core", 0.2: "Per."}

zs_deg = [f"{deg_map[theta[i]]:s}" for i in range(len(theta))]
zs_aug = [f"{z:d}, {deg:s}" for z, deg in zip(zs, zs_deg)]

A, P = dcsbm(zs, theta, B, return_prob=True)
```

We show the probability matrix and a realization in Figure 9.2.8(A) and Figure 9.2.8(B), respectively.

Let's try embedding this example using node2vec. We're going to set $p = 1$, $q = 10$ for now. We will generate 500 random walks starting at each node ($r = 500$), each walk will have a length of 200 steps ($T = 200$). We will begin by prioritizing walking in breadth-first way, with $q = 10 > 1$:

```python
from graspologic.embed import node2vec_embed
import networkx as nx
p=1; q=10; T=200; r=500
d = 4

np.random.seed(0)
Xhat1, _ = node2vec_embed(nx.from_numpy_array(A),
```

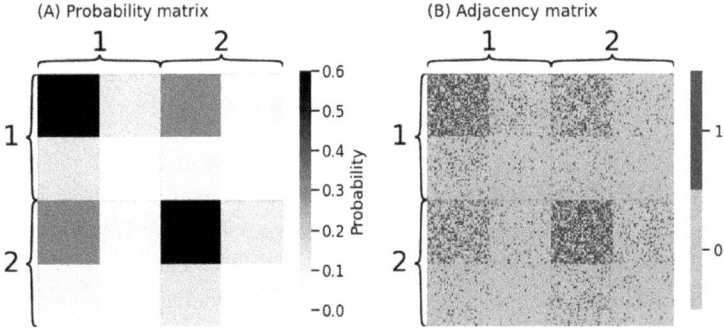

Figure 9.2.8 (**A**) The probability matrix for our network, and (**B**) a realization of our network.

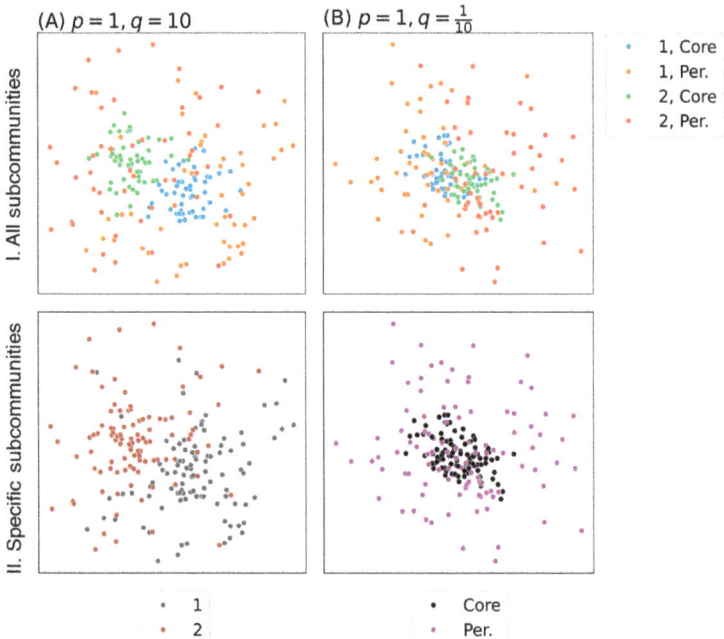

Figure 9.2.9 **(A)** A pairs plot of the node2vec embedding with $p = 1, q = \frac{1}{10}$, and **(B)** a pairs plot of the node2vec embedding with $p = 1, q = 10$. **(I)** All of the communities annotated, and **(II)** the specific communities annotated that the respective embedding settings tend to highlight.

```
return_hyperparameter=float(p),
    inout_hyperparameter=float(q),
  dimensions=d, num_walks=r, walk_length=T)
```

This is illustrated as a pairs plot of the first two dimensions in Figure 9.2.9(A) along with the true (unknown) community labels in Figure 9.2.9(A.I). The highest levels of node similarity are shared between the nodes in community 1 and 2, highlighted in Figure 9.2.9(A.II). Looking at the probability matrix for our network in Figure 9.2.8, subcommunities 1 and 2 tend to have comparatively high within subcommunity edge probabilities, but low between subcommunity edge probabilities. Therefore, local windows around a given node (the walks that we train the skip-gram network with) will tend to be in the same subcommunity 1 or 2, and our embedding will consequently favor differentiating the 1 and 2 subcommunities.

9.2.3.4   What Utility Is Added by a Second-Order Biased Random Walk?

The reason we leverage second-order biased random walks is that they give us flexibility. Since the node2vec procedure relies on the "corpus" of random walks, the behavior of these random walks will have a substantial influence on the resulting embedding. Let's see what happens to our embeddings as we tend to favor walking in a more depth-first type of manner, where $q = \frac{1}{10} < 1$:

> **Remark 9.2.4** Why are these methods called "diffusion methods"?
>
> Numerical analyses that use large sets of random walks are often referred to as diffusion methods. Diffusion is a process where particles spread out from an area of higher concentration to an area of lower concentration; consider, for instance, if you were to place a few drops of food coloring in a cup of water, the food coloring will diffuse throughout the water, rather than stay put.
>
> In many ways, the movement of a random walk throughout a network can be modelled as a diffusion process; in fact, many of the mathematical equations to describe particle diffusion can be adapted to networks. For this reason, random walks are often considered a subset of diffusion methods.

```
p=1; q=1/10; T=200; r=500
d = 4

np.random.seed(0)
Xhat2, _ = node2vec_embed(nx.from_numpy_array(A),
     return_hyperparameter=float(p), inout_hyperparameter=float(q),
            dimensions=d, num_walks=r, walk_length=T)
```

This is illustrated as a pairs plot in Figure 9.2.9(B.I) along with the true (unknown) community labels. This time, there are high similarities between the core nodes, but the periphery nodes tend to fall on the exterior, highlighted in Figure 9.2.9(B.II). Altering the hyperparameters for our random walks yield very different ways to represent the same network in Euclidean space.

9.2.4   Extending to Weighted or Directed Networks

It is easy to adapt the strategies we have developed so far to weighted or directed networks. If the network takes nonnegative weights, and the weights w_{ij} can be interpreted to indicate the "strength" of a connection between a node i and j, we can just let the transition probabilities p_{ij} be the weights normalized by the out-degree from node i; that is:

$$p_{ij} = \frac{w_{ij}}{d_i}$$

where the out-degree is the quantity $d_i = \sum_{j=1}^{n} w_{ij}$. The remainder of the strategies developed in this section can be directly applied with the transition probability matrix defined in this manner.

Bibliography

[1] Jumper J, Evans R, Pritzel A, Green T, Figurnov M, Ronneberger O, et al. Highly accurate protein structure prediction with AlphaFold. Nature. 2021 Aug.;596:583–589.

[2] Berman HM, Westbrook J, Feng Z, Gilliland G, Bhat TN, Weissig H, et al. The Protein Data Bank. Nucleic Acids Res. 2000 Jan.;28(1):235–242.

[3] Contributors to Wikimedia projects. Alexander Fleming – Wikipedia; 2023. [Online; accessed Feb. 4, 2023.]

[4] Weininger D. SMILES, a chemical language and information system. 1. Introduction to methodology and encoding rules. J. Chem. Inf. Comput. Sci. 1988 Feb.;28(1):31–36.

[5] Weininger D, Weininger A, Weininger JL. SMILES. 2. Algorithm for generation of unique SMILES notation. J. Chem. Inf. Comput. Sci. 1989 May;29(2):97–101.

[6] Weininger D. SMILES. 3. DEPICT. Graphical depiction of chemical structures. J. Chem. Inf. Comput. Sci. 1990 Aug.;30(3):237–243.

[7] Wu Z, Ramsundar B, Feinberg EN, Gomes J, Geniesse C, Pappu AS, et al. MoleculeNet: a benchmark for molecular machine learning. Chem. Sci. 2018 Jan.;9(2):513–530.

[8] Fey M, Lenssen JE. Fast graph representation learning with PyTorch Geometric. ArXiv e-prints. 2019 Mar.

[9] Paszke A, Gross S, Massa F, Lerer A, Bradbury J, Chanan G, et al. PyTorch: An imperative style, high-performance deep learning library. In: Advances in Neural Information Processing Systems 32. Curran Associates, Inc.; 2019, pp. 8024–8035.

[10] Novick PA, Ortiz OF, Poelman J, Abdulhay AY, Pande VS. SWEETLEAD: an in silico database of approved drugs, regulated chemicals, and herbal isolates for computer-aided drug discovery. PLoS One. 2013 Nov.;8(11):e79568.

[11] Landrum G. RDKit: Open-Source Cheminformatics Software. 2016.

[12] Géron A. Hands-On Machine Learning with Scikit-Learn and TensorFlow. Sebastopol, CA, USA: O'Reilly Media, Inc.; 2017.

[13] Prince SJ. Understanding Deep Learning. MIT Press; 2023.

[14] Scarselli F, Gori M, Tsoi AC, Hagenbuchner M, Monfardini G. Computational capabilities of graph neural networks. IEEE Trans. Neural Networks. 2008 Dec.;20(1):81–102.

[15] Sanchez-Lengeling B, Reif E, Pearce A, Wiltschko AB. A gentle introduction to graph neural networks. Distill. 2021 Sep.;6(9):e33.

[16] Labonne M. Hands-On Graph Neural Networks Using Python: Practical Techniques and Architectures for Building Powerful Graph and Deep Learning Apps with PyTorch. Packt Publishing; 2023.

[17] Bronstein MM, Bruna J, Cohen T, Veličković P. Geometric deep learning: Grids, groups, graphs, geodesics, and gauges. ArXiv e-prints. 2021 Apr.

[18] Isaacson DL, Madsen RW. Markov Chains: Theory and Applications. Hoboken, NJ, USA: Wiley; 1976.

[19] Mikolov T, Chen K, Corrado G, Dean J. Efficient estimation of word representations in vector space. arXiv. 2013 Jan.

[20] Mikolov T, Sutskever I, Chen K, Corrado G, Dean J. Distributed representations of words and phrases and their compositionality. arXiv. 2013 Oct.

[21] Grover A, Leskovec J. node2vec: Scalable Feature Learning for Networks. In: KDD '16: Proceedings of the 22nd ACM SIGKDD International Conference on Knowledge Discovery and Data Mining. New York, NY, USA: Association for Computing Machinery; 2016, pp. 855–864.

[22] Goodfellow I, Bengio Y, Courville A. Deep Learning. MIT Press; 2016.

Appendix A Network Model Theory

In this appendix, we dive into network modeling theory. Many strategies, such as the latent position testing and latent distribution testing in Section 7.1, become more digestible when we understand them as tests that assume slightly different statistical models than in the main text. In this appendix, we will learn the following:

1. Section A.1 introduces important mathematical and probability concepts for the remainder of the appendix,
2. Section A.2 gives the probabilistic foundations and motivations for graph models,
3. Section A.3 introduces the Erdös–Rényi network model,
4. Section A.4 introduces the stochastic block model,
5. Section A.5 introduces the degree-corrected stochastic block model,
6. Section A.6 introduces the random dot product graph, and
7. Section A.7 introduces the generalized random dot product graph.

Throughout this section, we make use of results from a variety of papers, which are largely captured by [2], [1], and [3].

A.1   Background

This section requires familiarity with all of the mathematical operations and concepts from probability and statistics explained in the Terminology. In this section, we standardize common notation that often differs across various probability and statistics texts.

A.1.1   Notation

1. *Extrapolatory ellipses*: We often summarize a sequence of natural numbers with ellipses; for example, $\{1, \ldots, n\}$. These ellipses indicate continuation of the indexing pattern up to the last index in the sequence. For instance, in the sequence above, the ellipses represent 4, 5, 6, ... up to $n - 1$. This interpretation applies to both vectors and matrices, where the numbering pattern continues upward.
2. *Shorthand for sequences of natural numbers*: The notation $[n]$ denotes a sequence of natural numbers from 1 to n. In set notation, $[n] = \{1, \ldots, n\}$.

3. *Useful numerical spaces*: Common numerical spaces are denoted by double-faced print. They are the natural numbers $\mathbb{N}$, the integers $\mathbb{Z}$, the nonnegative integers $\mathbb{Z}_{\geq 0}$, and the real numbers $\mathbb{R}$.

4. *Shorthand for arbitrary values from numerical spaces*: The notation $x \in S$ indicates that x (a scalar, a vector, or a matrix) has values from the numerical space S. For example:
   - $x \in \mathbb{R}$ means that x is an arbitrary real number.
   - $\vec{x} \in \mathbb{R}^d$ means that $\vec{x}$ is an arbitrary vector with d elements, where each element $x_i \in \mathbb{R}$ is an arbitrary real number.
   - $\vec{x} \in [K]^d$ or $\vec{x} \in \{1, \ldots, K\}^d$ indicates a vector where each element x_i is a natural number that is at most K.
   - $X \in \mathbb{R}^{r \times c}$ represents an arbitrary matrix with r rows, c columns, and real-valued elements.

5. *Vector in-line notation*: We sometimes describe a vector $\vec{x}$ using in-line notation to capture its dimensionality. The notation $\vec{x} = (x_i)_{i=1}^d$, for instance, represents:

$$\vec{x} = \begin{bmatrix} x_1 \\ x_2 \\ \vdots \\ x_d \end{bmatrix}.$$

This notation applies for both scalar and random vectors.

6. *Matrix in-line notation*: We describe a matrix X using in-line notation to capture its dimensions: $X = (x_{ij})_{i \in [r], j \in [c]}$ or $\left((x_{ij})_{j=1}^c \right)_{i=1}^r$. This notation "unrolls" X first across j from 1 to c, and then down i from 1 to r, representing a matrix with r rows and c columns:

$$X = \begin{bmatrix} x_{11} & \cdots & x_{1c} \\ \vdots & \ddots & \vdots \\ x_{r1} & \cdots & x_{rc} \end{bmatrix}.$$

A.1.2   Probability Distributions and Distribution Functions

1. *Distribution functions for random variables*: $\mathbf{x} \sim F$ indicates that the random variable $\mathbf{x}$ has the distribution F. For instance, $\mathbf{x} \sim Bern(p)$ denotes a Bernoulli random variable with probability p:

$$Pr(\mathbf{x} = x) = \begin{cases} p & x = 1 \\ 1 - p & x = 0 \end{cases}.$$

In this case, realizations of $\mathbf{x}$, denoted by x (no bold-face), resemble a coin flip: Heads ($x = 1$) occurs with probability p and tails ($x = 0$) with probability $1 - p$. This simplifies to:

$$Pr(\mathbf{x} = x) = p^x (1 - p)^{1-x}.$$

Familiarity with these common probability distributions enhances understanding of the material:

- Bernoulli distribution: $Bern(p)$, with probability parameter p,

- Categorical (Multinoulli) distribution: $Categorical(\vec{p})$, with probability vector $\vec{p}$,

- Normal distribution: $\mathcal{N}(\mu, \sigma^2)$ with mean μ and variance σ^2, and

- Uniform distribution: $Unif(a, b)$, with minimum a and maximum b.

We provide in-line descriptions of these distributions as needed throughout the text.

2. *Distribution functions for random vectors*: The notation $\vec{\mathbf{x}} \sim F$ indicates that the random vector $\vec{\mathbf{x}}$ has a distribution F. In general, we assume statistical independence (potentially conditional on other random variables), allowing us to describe the distribution of each element $\mathbf{x}_i$ individually rather than by conditioning on the entire vector $\vec{\mathbf{x}}$. This approach simplifies random vector distributions to more manageable random variable distributions. We sometimes use the term "dimensions" to describe vector elements. For a scalar vector $\vec{x}$, the ith dimension is simply the ith element, x_i. Similarly, for a random vector $\vec{\mathbf{x}}$, the ith dimension $\mathbf{x}_i$ is a random variable.

3. *Distribution functions for random matrices*: The notation $\mathbf{X} \sim F$ indicates that the random matrix $\mathbf{X}$ has distribution F. In general, we assume statistical independence (potentially conditional on other random variables) for elements of random matrices, allowing us to describe the distribution of each element $\mathbf{x}_{ij}$ individually rather than for the entire matrix $\mathbf{X}$. Thus, we can just look at the individual elements of $\mathbf{X}$, denoted $\mathbf{x}_{ij}$, as having distributions.

   - There is one important exception to this, which will arise for the a posteriori random dot product graph, which will use an *distribution on an inner product space*. In this case, instead of describing $\mathbf{X}$ itself or individual entries $\vec{\mathbf{x}}_i$, we will describe a family of distributions for random vectors, which are the rows of $\mathbf{X}$. We will try our best to explain these in an intuitive way without going outside of the scope of a graduate understanding of statistics.

4. *Parametrized functions*: A *parameter* in statistics is a number or set of numbers that uniquely define the behavior of a distribution. For parametrized random variables, such as $\mathbf{x} \sim Bern(p)$, $\mathbf{x}$ follows a Bernoulli distribution with parameter p. While p remains constant for a given $\mathbf{x}$, realizations of $\mathbf{x}$ (0s and 1s) vary. Probability statements about $\mathbf{x}$, like $Pr(\mathbf{x} = 0, p) = 1 - p$, depend on both p and the value $x = 0$ that $\mathbf{x}$ takes. To distinguish the static nature of p from the stochastic realizations of $\mathbf{x}$, we use subscript notation: $Pr_p(\mathbf{x} = x)$ instead of $Pr(\mathbf{x} = x, p)$. This notation clarifies that p is a distribution parameter for $\mathbf{x}$, not a variable changing with different realizations of $\mathbf{x}$. Alternatively, when we wish to emphasize the dependence of a probability on the parameter (such as for maximum likelihood estimation), we may write $Pr(\mathbf{x} = x; p)$, with the semicolon denoting that everything after the semicolon is a parameter.

5. *Arbitrary sets of parameters*: When describing random variables generally, we often use unrestrictive notation. A generic random variable $\mathbf{x}$ might follow a

Bernoulli distribution with parameter p, or a normal distribution with mean μ and variance σ^2. To accommodate these varying parameter sets, we use θ to denote an arbitrary set of parameters. For example, θ could represent $\{p\}$ for a Bernoulli distribution or $\{\mu, \sigma^2\}$ for a normal distribution. This notation allows us to describe $\mathbf{x}$ in terms of θ without specifying the exact parameter set each time. Note that θ can denote parameters for a random variable $\mathbf{x}$, a random vector $\vec{\mathbf{x}}$, or a random matrix $\mathbf{X}$.

A.1.3   Abuses of Notation

Statistical work often employs "abuses of notation," where a single notation takes on multiple meanings. We will use one such abuse regularly.

A random variable, random vector, or random matrix can be uniquely defined by its cumulative distribution function (CDF). Though CDFs are not distributions themselves, they uniquely specify distributions. For example, $\mathbf{x} \sim \mathcal{N}(\mu, \sigma^2)$ means that $\mathbf{x}$ follows a normal distribution with mean μ and variance σ^2. Equivalently, we might write $\mathbf{x} \sim F_{\mu, \sigma^2}$, where:

$$F_{\mu, \sigma^2}(x) = \int_{-\infty}^{x} f_{\mu, \sigma^2}(x) \mathrm{d}x.$$

Here, $f_{\mu, \sigma^2}(x)$ is the probability density function of the normal distribution. While F_{μ, σ^2} is not itself a distribution, it uniquely defines the normal distribution with parameters μ and σ^2.

This notation allows for generality. We can write $\mathbf{x} \sim F$ to indicate $\mathbf{x}$ follows an arbitrary distribution with CDF F, without specifying the distribution family or parameters. This notation is particularly useful when discussing distributions on inner product spaces.

A.2   Foundations of Random Network Models

To understand network models, it is crucial to understand the concept of a network as a random quantity, taking a probability distribution. We observe a realization A and consider it random: We assume that there existed a network-valued random variable $\mathbf{A}$ that generated our realization. Since $\mathbf{A}$ is a random variable, we can describe it using a probability distribution. This distribution, denoted by Pr, assigns probabilities to all possible configurations of $\mathbf{A}$. We express this relationship notationally as $\mathbf{A} \sim Pr$, meaning "the random network $\mathbf{A}$ is distributed according to Pr."

Our claim that Pr assigns probabilities to every possible realizations of $\mathbf{A}$ raises a question: How many possibilities exist for a network with n nodes? We focus on simple networks, where the network is unweighted (A is binary), undirected (A is symmetric), and loopless (A is hollow). Let $\mathcal{A}_n$ denote the set of all possible adjacency matrices A corresponding to simple networks with n nodes. Each $A \in \mathcal{A}_n$ is:

1. a *binary* or *unweighted* $n \times n$ matrix: $A \in \{0, 1\}^{n \times n}$, and $a_{ij} \in \{0, 1\}$,
2. a *symmetric* $n \times n$ matrix: $A = A^\top$, so $a_{ij} = a_{ji}$, and
3. a *hollow* $n \times n$ matrix: $diag(A) = 0$, or $a_{ii} = 0$ for all $i = 1, ..., n$)

We define $\mathcal{A}_n$ as:

$$\mathcal{A}_n = \{A: A \text{ is an } n \times n \text{ matrix which is binary, symmetric, and hollow}\}.$$

We express the concept that Pr assigns probabilities to all possible configurations of $\mathbf{A}$ as $Pr: \mathcal{A}_n \to [0, 1]$. For any $A \in \mathcal{A}_n$, a possible realization of random network $\mathbf{A}$, $Pr(\mathbf{A} = A)$ represents a probability between 0 and 1. When the context clearly defines $\mathbf{A}$, we may simplify $Pr(\mathbf{A} = A)$ to $Pr(A)$, indicating the probability that $\mathbf{A}$ takes the value A. Now, we turn to the question posed earlier: How many possible adjacency matrices exist in $\mathcal{A}_n$?

Consider a single $A \in \mathcal{A}_n$. An $n \times n$ matrix A has n^2 entries. However, $\mathbf{A}$ is simple and loopless, eliminating n possible self-loops. This leaves $n^2 - n = n(n-1)$ potential edges, ignoring diagonal entries a_{ii} for all $i \in [n]$. The undirected nature of simple networks implies $a_{ij} = a_{ji}$ for every pair i and j: Knowledge of an entry in the upper triangle of A (a_{ij} where $j > i$) determines the corresponding lower triangle entry. This symmetry halves the $n(n-1)$ nondiagonal entries, resulting in $\frac{1}{2}n(n-1) = \binom{n}{2}$ free entries in A. Each entry of A can be either 0 or 1, yielding two possible values for each randomly determined edge. To illustrate:

1. For a 2×2 matrix A, there is $\binom{2}{2} = 1$ unique entry, with two possible values. The two possible forms of A are:

$$\begin{bmatrix} 0 & 1 \\ 1 & 0 \end{bmatrix} \text{ or } \begin{bmatrix} 0 & 0 \\ 0 & 0 \end{bmatrix}. \tag{A.1}$$

2. For a 3×3 matrix A, there are $\binom{3}{2} = 3$ unique entries, each with two possible values. The $2^3 = 8$ possible forms of A are:

$$\begin{bmatrix} 0 & 1 & 1 \\ 1 & 0 & 1 \\ 1 & 1 & 0 \end{bmatrix} \text{ or } \begin{bmatrix} 0 & 1 & 0 \\ 1 & 0 & 1 \\ 0 & 1 & 0 \end{bmatrix} \text{ or } \begin{bmatrix} 0 & 0 & 1 \\ 0 & 0 & 1 \\ 1 & 1 & 0 \end{bmatrix} \text{ or} \tag{A.2}$$

$$\begin{bmatrix} 0 & 1 & 1 \\ 1 & 0 & 0 \\ 1 & 0 & 0 \end{bmatrix} \text{ or } \begin{bmatrix} 0 & 0 & 1 \\ 0 & 0 & 0 \\ 1 & 0 & 0 \end{bmatrix} \text{ or } \begin{bmatrix} 0 & 0 & 0 \\ 0 & 0 & 1 \\ 0 & 1 & 0 \end{bmatrix} \text{ or} \tag{A.3}$$

$$\begin{bmatrix} 0 & 1 & 0 \\ 1 & 0 & 0 \\ 0 & 0 & 0 \end{bmatrix} \text{ or } \begin{bmatrix} 0 & 0 & 0 \\ 0 & 0 & 0 \\ 0 & 0 & 0 \end{bmatrix}. \tag{A.4}$$

To generalize this for any n, we use combinatorics. For each of the $\binom{n}{2}$ entries in A that can take different values, we multiply the total number of possibilities by 2. With two choices for each of x items, we have 2^x possible adjacency matrices. Given our knowledge of the number of different elements in A, we can express the total number of unique adjacency matrices in $\mathcal{A}_n$, called its *set cardinality*, as $2^{\binom{n}{2}}$. The cardinality of $\mathcal{A}_n$ is denoted by $|\mathcal{A}_n|$. For $n = 15$, $|\mathcal{A}_{15}| = 2^{\binom{15}{2}} = 2^{105}$, which exceeds 10^{30} possible networks. As n increases, $|\mathcal{A}_n|$ grows rapidly. The following code demonstrates how $|\mathcal{A}_n| = 2^{\binom{n}{2}}$ changes with n:

```
import seaborn as sns
import numpy as np
from math import comb


n = np.arange(2, 51)
logAn = np.array([comb(ni, 2) for ni in n])*np.log10(2)
```

We have established probability distributions on networks and a set $\mathcal{A}_n$ of all adjacency matrices to which these distributions must assign probabilities. A network model, then, is a set $\mathcal{P}$ of probability distributions on $\mathcal{A}_n$:

$$\mathcal{P} \subseteq \{Pr : Pr \text{ is a probability distribution on } \mathcal{A}_n\}.$$

We simplify $\mathcal{P}$ through parametrization. Let Θ be the set of all possible parameters of the random network model, and $\theta \in \Theta$ a particular parameter choice governing a specific network-valued random variable $\mathbf{A}$. We can then express $\mathcal{P}$ as:

$$\mathcal{P}(\Theta) = \{Pr_\theta : \theta \in \Theta\}.$$

For a random network $\mathbf{A}$ following a network model, we write $\mathbf{A} \sim Pr_\theta$, where θ is an arbitrary set of parameters.

In traditional univariate or multivariate statistical modeling, a categorical model often serves as a natural choice for discrete sample spaces like $\mathcal{A}_n$. This approach would assign a single parameter to each possible configuration of an n-node network, resulting in $|\theta| = |\mathcal{A}_n| = 2^{\binom{n}{2}}$. However, this model presents two significant limitations:

1. Storage requirements: For $n = 15$, defining θ would require over 10^{30} bits of storage, exceeding 10^8 zetabytes – more than the world's total storage capacity.
2. Estimation challenges: Obtaining a reasonable estimate of $2^{\binom{n}{2}}$ parameters becomes infeasible for any nontrivial number of nodes n, even with multiple observed networks. For a single observed network A, the estimate $\hat{\theta}$ would have a 1 corresponding to the observed network and 0s elsewhere. This implies a deterministic network-valued random variable $\mathbf{A}$, even when this is not the case. With multiple observations, $\hat{\theta}$ would likely consist of point masses on observed networks and 0s elsewhere, failing to generalize to new observations.

More reasonable descriptions of $\mathcal{P}$ focus on the family of independent-edge random networks, which assume that the edges of the network are generated independently or independently conditional on particular variables, a property that simplifies modeling assumptions crucial for proper estimation and rigorous statistical inference.

A.2.1   Equivalence Classes

The concept of *probability equivalence classes* is central to the models we will explore. A probability function describes how effectively a random variable $\mathbf{A}$ with parameters $\mathbf{A} \sim Pr_\theta$ can model an observation A. It expresses the probability $Pr_\theta(\mathbf{A})$ of observing A given parameters θ.

An equivalence class $E \subseteq \mathcal{A}_n$ has the following properties, given fixed parameters θ:

1. For $A, A' \in E$, $Pr_\theta(A) = Pr_\theta(A')$.
2. For $A \in E$, and $A'' \in E'$, where E and E' are different equivalence classes, $Pr_\theta(A) \neq Pr_\theta(A'')$.
3. Different equivalence classes are therefore mutually disjoint: $E \cap E' = \varnothing$.
4. Given $\mathcal{A}_n$ and Pr_θ, we can partition the sample space into equivalence classes E_i, where $i \in \mathcal{I}$ is an arbitrary indexing set. This partition satisfies $\bigcup_{i \in \mathcal{I}} E_i = \mathcal{A}_n$.

The role of equivalence classes in network models and parameter estimation is useful background for network models in Chapter 4 and parameter estimation in Section 5.1.

In the following sections, different types of network models will provide us with the probability Pr_θ. Using this function, we effectively simplify the total number of possible networks (which as described above, is infeasibly large and would be impossible to fit given finite data) down to far simpler questions about the parameters that define these different equivalence classes. These equivalence classes (and the parameters that differentiate them) will typically be much simpler to analyze than it would be to analyze the $2^{\binom{n}{2}}$ possible networks that we defined above.

A.2.2   Independent-Edge Random Networks

The following models represent special families of *independent-edge random networks*, which are network-valued random variables in which all edges are independent. For every adjacency $\mathbf{a}_{ij}$ of the random variable $\mathbf{A}$, $\mathbf{a}_{ij}$ is independent of $\mathbf{a}_{i'j'}$ whenever $(i, j) \neq (i', j')$.

In simple networks, we can assume that each edge (i, j) exists with probability p_{ij}, which may differ for each edge. This model describes $\mathbf{a}_{ij}$ as having a $Bern(p_{ij})$ distribution for every $j > i$, independent of every other edges in $\mathbf{A}$. We consider only the entries where $j > i$, because our networks are simple, implying that $\mathbf{a}_{ji}$ is a deterministic function of $\mathbf{a}_{ij}$. The random network is loopless, so $\mathbf{a}_{ii} = 0$ for all i.

We define the *probability matrix* $P = (p_{ij})$ for the network-valued random variable $\mathbf{A}$. A random network with independent edges and edge probabilities given by P is an Inhomogeneous Erdös–Rényi random network, denoted $\mathbf{A} \sim IER_n(P)$. These are often known as independent-edge random networks. This model simplifies probability calculations for network realizations.

For *independent random variables* $\mathbf{x}$ and $\mathbf{y}$, recall that $Pr(\mathbf{x} = x, \mathbf{y} = y) = Pr(\mathbf{x} = x)Pr(\mathbf{y} = y)$. Using this independence property, we can express the probability of a network realization as:

$$Pr(\mathbf{A} = A) = Pr(\mathbf{a}_{11} = a_{11}, \mathbf{a}_{12} = a_{12}, \ldots, \mathbf{a}_{nn} = a_{nn})$$

$$= Pr(\mathbf{a}_{ij} = a_{ij} \text{ for all } j > i)$$

$$= \prod_{j>i} Pr(\mathbf{a}_{ij} = a_{ij}), \quad \text{independence assumption.} \qquad (A.5)$$

For a Bernoulli distributed $\mathbf{a}_{ij}$ with probability p_{ij}, since $Pr(\mathbf{a}_{ij} = a_{ij}) = p_{ij}^{a_{ij}}(1 - p_{ij})^{1-a_{ij}}$:

$$Pr_\theta(A) = \prod_{j>i} p_{ij}^{a_{ij}}(1 - p_{ij})^{1-a_{ij}}.$$

While this model is generalizable, estimating each p_{ij} individually presents challenges. Maximum likelihood estimation with a single realization A would yield $p_{ij} = a_{ij}$. Even with multiple realizations, this approach ignores potential structural insights into $\mathbf{A}$ and requires estimating numerous p_{ij} values.

Subsequent sections will introduce less restrictive assumptions about p_{ij}, allowing for more expressive random networks while maintaining analytical tractability.

A.3   Erdös–Rényi Random Networks

The Erdös–Rényi (ER) model simplifies the network generation process with a single parameter and an independent and identically distributed (iid) assumption, as follows.

Parameter	Space	Description
p	$[0, 1]$	Probability of an edge between any pair of nodes

In an Erdös–Rényi network, each node pair connects with probability p and remains unconnected with probability $1 - p$. For each edge $\mathbf{a}_{ij}$ where $j > i$, $\mathbf{a}_{ij}$ is sampled independently and identically from a Bernoulli distribution with probability p.

"Independent" means that the occurrence of one edge does not affect the others. "Identical" means that every edge exists with the same probability p. We assume that the networks are undirected, meaning an edge $\mathbf{a}_{ij}$ from node i to j implies an edge $\mathbf{a}_{ji}$ from node j to i. We also assume loopless networks, prohibiting self-connections (all $\mathbf{a}_{ii} = 0$).

For an adjacency matrix $\mathbf{A}$ of an Erdös–Rényi network with probability p, we write $\mathbf{A} \sim ER_n(p)$.

A.3.1   Probability

For Erdös–Rényi networks, the probability of realizations can be derived from the general form for independent-edge graphs:

$$Pr_\theta(A) = \prod_{j>i} Pr_\theta(\mathbf{a}_{ij} = a_{ij}).$$

Given the Erdös–Rényi model's assumption that the probability matrix $P = (p)$, or $p_{ij} = p$ for all i, j, we have:

$$Pr_\theta(A) = \prod_{j>i} p^{a_{ij}} (1 - p)^{1-a_{ij}}$$

$$= p^{\sum_{j>i} a_{ij}} \cdot (1 - p)^{\binom{n}{2} - \sum_{j>i} a_{ij}}$$

$$= p^m \cdot (1 - p)^{\binom{n}{2} - m}.$$

Here, $Pr_\theta(A)$ depends only on $m = \sum_{j>i} a_{ij}$, the number of edges in the network represented by adjacency matrix A. The equivalence classes for Erdös–Rényi networks are the sets:

$$E_i = \{A \in \mathcal{A}_n : m = i\}$$

where i ranges from 0 (minimum possible edges) to $\binom{n}{2}$ (maximum possible edges, for simple networks).

A.3.2   Relaxations for Nonsimple Networks

Our previous discussions focused on *simple networks*: binary/unweighted, loopless, and undirected networks. Simple networks have adjacency matrices containing only 0s and 1s, with a hollow diagonal and symmetry between the lower and upper triangles. However, real-world networks often deviate from these constraints. Let us consider how to adapt our models for such cases:

We maintain the assumption of binary networks. We will examine three possible "relaxations" of our current assumptions about simple networks. A *relaxation* is a loosening of a set of assumptions to more flexible situations. We present these relaxations separately to clearly demonstrate how each alters the generative model.

We will show how the generative setup changes by modifying the following text, which we used to describe a simple Erdös–Rényi network (unweighted, undirected, and loopless):

"In an Erdös–Rényi network, each node pair connects with probability p and remains unconnected with probability $1 - p$. For each edge $\mathbf{a}_{ij}$ where $j > i$, $\mathbf{a}_{ij}$ is sampled independently and identically from a Bernoulli distribution with probability p. We assume that the networks are undirected, meaning an edge $\mathbf{a}_{ij}$ from node i to j implies an edge $\mathbf{a}_{ji}$ from node j to i. We also assume loopless networks, prohibiting self-connections (all $\mathbf{a}_{ii} = 0$)."

A.3.2.1   Unweighted and Undirected Network with Loops
This relaxation removes the assumption of a loopless network. We now allow edges $\mathbf{a}_{ii}$ to exist, extending the Bernoulli distribution to cases where $j \geq i$, rather than just just $j > i$.

Our revised description of the Erdös–Rényi network is:

For each edge $\mathbf{a}_{ij}$ where $j \geq i$, $\mathbf{a}_{ij}$ is sampled independently and identically from a Bernoulli distribution with probability p. We assume that the networks are undirected, meaning an edge $\mathbf{a}_{ij}$ from node i to j implies an edge $\mathbf{a}_{ji}$ from node j to i. We also assume loopless networks, prohibiting self-connections (all $\mathbf{a}_{ii} = 0$).

A.3.2.2 Unweighted and Loopless Network with Directionality

This model removes the symmetry assumption of $\mathbf{A}$, allowing for directed networks. We make independent distributional assumptions for all adjacencies $\mathbf{a}_{ij}$ where $j \neq i$, rather than just $j > i$. We maintain $\mathbf{a}_{ii} = 0$, preserving the hollowness of $\mathbf{A}$ (and the looplessness of the network).

Our revised description of the Erdös–Rényi network is:

For each edge $\mathbf{a}_{ij}$ where $j \neq i$, $\mathbf{a}_{ij}$ is sampled independently and identically from a Bernoulli distribution with probability p. We assume that the networks are undirected, meaning an edge $\mathbf{a}_{ij}$ from node i to j implies an edge $\mathbf{a}_{ji}$ from node j to i. We assume the networks are loopless, prohibiting self-connections (all $\mathbf{a}_{ii} = 0$).

A.3.2.3 Unweighted Network with Loops and Directionality

This model allows for both loops and directed edges by removing the constraints on symmetry and self-connections.

Our revised description of the Erdös–Rényi network is:

For each edge $\mathbf{a}_{ij}$, for all possible combinations of nodes i and j, $\mathbf{a}_{ij}$ is sampled independently and identically from a Bernoulli distribution with probability p. We assume that the networks are undirected, meaning an edge $\mathbf{a}_{ij}$ from node i to j implies an edge $\mathbf{a}_{ji}$ from node j to i. We assume the networks are loopless, prohibiting self-connections (all $\mathbf{a}_{ii} = 0$).

A.4   Stochastic Block Models

A.4.1   A priori Stochastic Block Model

The *a priori SBM* assumes known community assignments for all nodes. We denote the number of communities by K. The order of community labels is arbitrary. The a priori SBM has two parameters, as follows.

Parameter	Space	Description
$\vec{z}$	$[K]^n$	The community assignment vector, assigning communities for each node
B	$[0,1]^{K \times K}$	The block matrix, assigning edge probabilities to pairs of communities

The *community assignment vector* $\vec{z}$ designates each node's community membership. This n-length vector contains one element for each node, with values ranging from 1 to K. Formally, $\vec{z} \in \{1, \dots, K\}^n$. Each element z_i represents the community assignment for the i(th) node.

For example, in a network with two communities ($K = 2$), where the first two nodes belong to community 1 and the last two to community 2:

$$\vec{z} = \begin{bmatrix} 1 & 1 & 2 & 2 \end{bmatrix}^{\top}.$$

The *block matrix* $B \in [0,1]^{K \times K}$ is a $K \times K$ matrix that defines edge probabilities between communities. For a pair of nodes i and j, we first use $\vec{z}$ to find their community memberships z_i and z_j. Then, $b_{z_i z_j}$ gives their edge probability. In undirected networks, B is symmetric, so $b_{kk'} = b_{k'k}$ for all pairs of communities k and k'.

The generative model for the a priori SBM defines edge probabilities based on community memberships. For nodes i and j in communities k and k' respectively, the probability of an edge between them is $b_{kk'}$, the (k, k') entry of the block matrix. Formally, given z_i and z_j, $\mathbf{a}_{ij}$ is sampled independently from a $Bern(b_{z_i z_j})$ distribution for all $j > i$. The adjacencies $\mathbf{a}_{ij}$ are not necessarily identically distributed, as their probabilites depend on the community of their nodes. We denote an a priori SBM network with block matrix B and node-assignment vector $\vec{z}$ as $\mathbf{A} \sim SBM_n(\vec{z}, B)$.

A.4.1.1   Probability

The probability calculation for the a priori SBM is straightforward, given that $\vec{z}$ is a parameter. With our independence assumption:

$$Pr_{\theta}(A) = Pr_{\theta}(\mathbf{A} = A)$$
$$= \prod_{j>i} Pr(\mathbf{a}_{ij} = a_{ij}; B, \vec{z}), \quad \text{Independence Assumption.}$$

In the a priori SBM, each edge $\mathbf{a}_{ij}$ depends solely on the community assignments of nodes i and j. Thus:

$$Pr_{\theta}(\mathbf{a}_{ij} = a_{ij}; B, \vec{z}) = Pr(\mathbf{a}_{ij} = a_{ij}; B, z_i, z_j).$$

The independence assumption ensures that community assignments of other nodes do not affect edge (i, j).

For the a priori SBM, the probability matrix $P = (p_{ij})$ reflects the block structure. Given z_i and z_j, each adjacency $\mathbf{a}_{ij}$ is sampled independently and identically from a $Bern(b_{z_i z_j})$ distribution, so $p_{ij} = b_{z_i z_j}$. The probability of observing adjacency matrix A is therefore:

$$Pr_{\theta}(A) = \prod_{j>i} b_{z_i z_j}^{a_{ij}} (1 - b_{z_i z_j})^{1-a_{ij}}.$$

This expression can be simplified heavily. For any node–node pairing (i, j) where $z_i = k'$ and $z_j = k$, p_{ij} is equal to the same value $b_{kk'}$. Therefore, we can instead take the product over all possible community–community pairings, and take a second product over all (i, j) node–node pairings that have the indicated community pairing, since each node–node pairing would only fall into a single community–community pairing. This gives:

$$Pr_{\theta}(A) = \prod_{k,k' \in [K]} \prod_{i,j: z_i = k', z_j = k} b_{k'k}^{a_{ij}} (1 - b_{k'k})^{1-a_{ij}}$$

$$= \prod_{k,k'\in[K]} b_{k'k}^{m_{k'k}} (1 - b_{k'k})^{n_{k'k}-m_{k'k}}. \tag{A.6}$$

Here, $n_{k'k}$ represents the number of possible edges between communities k' and k: $n_{k'k} = \sum_{j>i} 1_{z_i=k'} 1_{z_j=k}$.

And $m_{k'k}$ denotes the observed edges between these communities: $m_{k'k} = \sum_{j>i} 1_{z_i=k'} 1_{z_j=k} a_{ij}$.

The probability for a single (k',k) community pair resembles that of an Erdös–Rényi random variable.

The a priori SBM, like the ER model, exhibits equivalence classes in the sample space $\mathcal{A}_n$ based on their probability. For a two-community setting with given $\vec{z}$ and B, these equivalence classes are:

$$E_{a,b,c}(\vec{z}, B) = \{A \in \mathcal{A}_n : m_{11} = a, m_{21} = m_{12} = b, m_{22} = c\}.$$

Networks in the same equivalence class share identical community sizes. The number of possible equivalence classes increases with the number of communities and varies with the distribution of nodes across communities.

A.4.2   A Posteriori Stochastic Block Model

The *a posteriori SBM* treats community assignments as a random variable, unlike the a priori SBM. Understanding this model requires familiarity with the concept of a probability simplex.

We first define a vector $\vec{\pi} = (\pi_k)_{k\in[K]}, \pi_k \in [0,1]$ with K elements, where each π_k indicates the probability of a node's assignment to community k:

$$\pi_k = Pr(\mathbf{z}_i = k).$$

This vector requires two additional constraints to represent a valid probability distribution:

1. Nonnegativity: For all k, $\pi_k \geq 0$, as probabilities cannot be negative.
2. Unity sum: $\sum_{k=1}^{K} \pi_k = 1$, the law of total probability.

The K-probability simplex encompasses all possible probability vectors $\vec{\pi}$ for a categorical random variable with K possible outcomes. Formally:

$$\left\{ \vec{\pi} : \text{for all } k \; \pi_k \geq 0, \; \sum_{k=1}^{K} \pi_k = 1 \right\}.$$

For example:

1. For a fair coin, $\vec{\pi} = \left(\frac{1}{2}, \frac{1}{2}\right)$ and $\vec{\pi}' = \left(\frac{9}{10}, \frac{1}{10}\right)$ both belong to the 2-probability simplex.
2. For a fair die, $\vec{\pi} = \left(\frac{1}{6}, \frac{1}{6}, \frac{1}{6}, \frac{1}{6}, \frac{1}{6}, \frac{1}{6}\right)$ belongs to the 6-probability simplex.

In the a posteriori SBM, the K-probability simplex represents the space of probability vectors that could assign each node to one of the K-communities.

Table A.1. Parameters of the a posteriori SBM

Parameter	Space	Description
$\vec{\pi}$	The K-probability simplex	The probability of a node being assigned to community K
B	$[0,1]^{K \times K}$	The block matrix, which assigns edge probabilities for pairs of communities

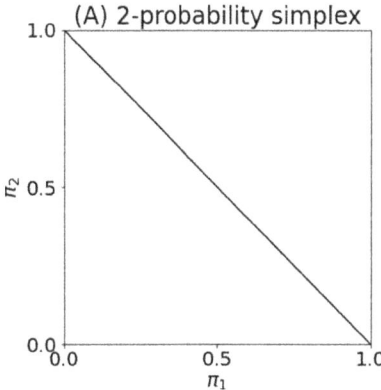

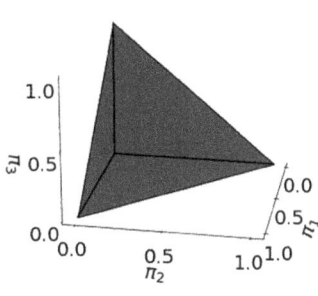

Figure A.4.1 **(A)** The 2-probability simplex, and **(B)** the 3-probability simplex.

Figure A.4.1(A) illustrates the 2-probability simplex as a diagonal line from $(0,1)$ to $(1,0)$, representing all possible π_1, π_2 pairs. Figure A.4.1(B) shows the 3-probability simplex as a triangular surface with vertices at $(1,0,0)$, $(0,1,0)$, and $(0,0,1)$, encompassing all possible (π_1, π_2, π_3) tuples. Table A.1 shows the two parameters of the a posteriori SBM.

The a posteriori SBM extends the a priori SBM by treating the node-assignment vector as unknown. This introduces $\vec{z}$ as a *latent variable*: unobserved but crucial for model description. Here, $\vec{z}$ takes values in $\{1, \ldots, K\}^n$, with each realization $\vec{z}$ assigning an integer between 1 and K to each of the n nodes, indicating community membership.

Statistically, each community assignment $\mathbf{z}_i$ is sampled independently and identically from $Categorical(\vec{\pi})$, where $\vec{\pi}$ specifies the probability π_k of assignment to each community k. Samples from $Categorical(\vec{\pi})$ are categorical values corresponding to the community assignment of each node i.

The block matrix B functions identically to its role in the a posteriori SBM. The generative model for the a posteriori SBM closely resembles that of the a priori SBM:

1. Given $z_i = k'$ and $z_j = k$, $\mathbf{a}_{ij}$ are independent $Bern(b_{k'k})$.
2. $\mathbf{z}_i$ are sampled independently and identically from $Categorical(\vec{\pi})$

For an a posteriori SBM network with adjacency matrix $\mathbf{A}$ and parameters $\vec{\pi}$ and B, we write $\mathbf{A} \sim SBM_n(\vec{\pi}, B)$.

A.4.2.1   Probability

For the a posteriori SBM, $\theta = \{\vec{\pi}, B\}$ are the model parameters. The probability of observing a particular adjacency matrix A generated by $\mathbf{A}$ is:

$$Pr_\theta(A) = Pr_\theta(\mathbf{A} = A).$$

By the law of total probability, we can express this as a summation over all possible realizations of the node assignment variable $\vec{\mathbf{z}}$. Let $\mathcal{Z} = [K]^n$ be the space of all possible realizations $\vec{\mathbf{z}}$:

$$Pr_\theta(A) = \sum_{\vec{z} \in \mathcal{Z}} Pr_\theta(\mathbf{A} = A, \vec{\mathbf{z}} = \vec{z}) \qquad (\text{A.7})$$

Using the definition of conditional probability, we can rewrite this as:

$$Pr_\theta(A) = \sum_{\vec{z} \in \mathcal{Z}} Pr_\theta(\vec{\mathbf{z}} = \vec{z}) Pr_\theta(\mathbf{A} = A \mid \vec{\mathbf{z}} = \vec{z}).$$

Each entry $\mathbf{z}_i$ in $\vec{\mathbf{z}}$ is sampled independently and identically from $Categorical(\vec{\pi})$. For a $Categorical(\vec{\pi})$-valued random variable, the probability mass function is $Pr(\mathbf{z}_i = z_i; \vec{\pi}) = \pi_{z_i}$; that is, each entry π_{z_i} denotes the probability that a given community assignment $\mathbf{z}_i$ is in community z_i.

When taking the product of n π_{z_i} terms, many values can be repeated. For example, if $\vec{z} = [1, 2, 1, 2, 1]^\top$, three z_is have a value of 1, and two z_is have a value of 2. Therefore, we will end up with three π_1 terms and two π_2 terms, regardless of their order. So, we only need track the count of each π term.

We can express this using the indicator function $\mathbb{1}_{\{z_i = k\}}$ and counter for community probability assignments π_k. Let $n_k = \sum_{i=1}^n \mathbb{1}_{\{z_i = k\}}$ denote the number of nodes in community k. This yields:

$$Pr_\theta(\vec{\mathbf{z}} = \vec{z}) = \prod_{i=1}^n Pr_\theta(\mathbf{z}_i = z_i), \quad \text{independence assumption of } z_i\text{s}$$

$$= \prod_{i=1}^n \pi_{z_i}, \quad \text{p.m.f. of a categorical R.V.}$$

For each node i, given a community assignment vector $\vec{z}$, each node will be assigned to exactly one (and only one) community. Therefore:

$$Pr_\theta(\vec{\mathbf{z}} = \vec{z}) = \prod_{k=1}^K \prod_{i : z_i = k} \pi_k$$

$$= \prod_{k=1}^K \pi_k^{n_k}.$$

Now we consider the conditional probability term $Pr_\theta(\mathbf{A} = A \mid \vec{\mathbf{z}} = \vec{z})$. Given $\vec{\mathbf{z}} = \vec{z}$, all entries are independent. This result matches the one we obtained for the a priori SBM in Equation (A.6):

$$Pr_\theta(\mathbf{A} = A \mid \vec{\mathbf{z}} = \vec{z}) = \prod_{k',k} b_{\ell k}^{m_{k'k}} (1 - b_{k'k})^{n_{k'k} - m_{k'k}}.$$

Combining these into the integrand gives:

$$Pr_\theta(A) = \sum_{\vec{z} \in \mathcal{Z}} Pr_\theta(\mathbf{A} = A \mid \vec{\mathbf{z}} = \vec{z}) Pr_\theta(\vec{\mathbf{z}} = \vec{z})$$

$$= \sum_{\vec{z} \in \mathcal{Z}} \prod_{k=1}^{K} \left[\pi_k^{n_k} \cdot \prod_{k'=1}^{K} b_{k'k}^{m_{k'k}} (1 - b_{k'k})^{n_{k'k} - m_{k'k}} \right].$$

This approach implies that the a priori SBM is similar to the a posteriori SBM but with the latent community assignment vector treated as known.

A.5   Degree-Corrected Stochastic Block Model (DCSBM)

The degree-corrected stochastic block model (DCSBM) addresses the degree-homogeneity limitation of SBMs detailed in Section 4.7.1. Like the stochastic block model, the DCSBM has both a priori and a posteriori variants.

A.5.1   A priori DCSBM

In the a priori DCSBM, community assignments are known in advance. Let K denote the number of communities. The a priori DCSBM has three parameters, as follows.

Parameter	Space	Description
$\vec{z}$	$[K]^n$	The community assignment vector, communities for each node
B	$[0,1]^{K \times K}$	The block matrix, which assigns edge probabilities for pairs of communities
$\vec{\theta}$	$\mathbb{R}_+^n$	The degree correction vector, which adjusts the degree for pairs of nodes

The latent community assignment vector $\vec{z}$ and block matrix B are identical to those in the a priori SBM.

The degree correction vector $\vec{\theta}$ consists of positive scalars θ_i. Each θ_i modifies the connectivity of node i, increasing or decreasing its edge probabilities.

In the generative model for the a priori DCSBM, given community assignments z_i and z_j, $\mathbf{a}_{ij}$ is sampled independently from a $Bern(\theta_i \theta_j b_{z_i z_j})$ distribution for all $j > i$. Here, θ_i "corrects" the edge probabilities for node i, adjusting them relative to the block probabilities $b_{\ell k}$.

For an a priori DCSBM network $\mathbf{A}$ with parameters $\vec{z}$, $\vec{\theta}$, and B, we write $\mathbf{A} \sim DCSBM_n(\vec{z}, \vec{\theta}, B)$.

A.5.1.1   Probability

The probability derivation for the a priori DCSBM follows that of the a priori SBM, with $p_{ij} = \theta_i \theta_j b_{k'k}$ replacing $b_{k'k}$ when $z_i = k'$ and $z_j = k$. This yields:

$$Pr_\theta(A) = \prod_{j>i} \left(\theta_i \theta_j b_{k'k}\right)^{a_{ij}} \left(1 - \theta_i \theta_j b_{k'k}\right)^{1-a_{ij}}.$$

Further simplification is limited because probabilities depend on specific i and j pairs through the degree-correction factors. Unlike the SBM, we cannot reduce this expression in terms of $n_{k'k}$ and $m_{k'k}$.

A.5.1.2   A posteriori DCSBM

The a posteriori DCSBM extends the a posteriori SBM in the same way that the a priori DCSBM extends the a priori SBM. The modifications are minor and follow directly from the preceding discussion on the a priori DCSBM.

A.6   Random Dot Product Graphs

A.6.1   A priori RDPG

The a priori random dot product graph (RDPG) assumes a known latent position matrix $X \in \mathbb{R}^{n \times d}$. The a priori RDPG has the following parameter.

Parameter	Space	Description
X	$\mathbb{R}^{n \times d}$	The matrix of latent positions for each node n

Each row $\vec{x}_i$ represents the *latent position* of a node i, a d-dimensional real-valued vector. The number of dimensions d is the *latent dimensionality*. X therefore looks like:

$$X = \begin{bmatrix} \vdash & \vec{x}_1^\top & \dashv \\ & \vdots & \\ \vdash & \vec{x}_n^\top & \dashv \end{bmatrix}.$$

The generative model for the a priori RDPG, given latent position matrix X, is as follows:

1. For all $j > i$, $\mathbf{a}_{ij} \sim Bern(\vec{x}_i^\top \vec{x}_j)$ independently.
2. The network is undirected, so $\mathbf{a}_{ji} = \mathbf{a}_{ij}$ for $i < j$.
3. The network is loopless, so $\mathbf{a}_{ii} = 0$.

We denote an a priori RDPG with parameter X as $\mathbf{A} \sim RDPG_n(X)$.

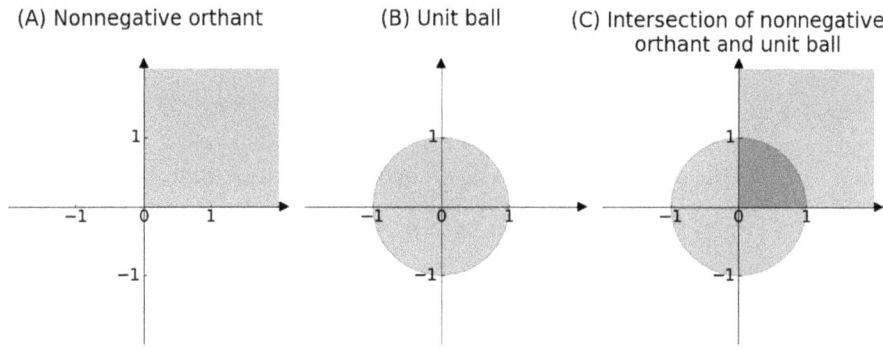

Figure A.6.1 (**A**) The nonnegative orthant, (**B**) the unit ball, and (**C**) their intersection.

A.6.1.1 Probability

The probability calculation for an RDPG, given X, is simplified by the independence assumption:

$$Pr_\theta(A) = \prod_{j>i} Pr(\mathbf{a}_{ij} = a_{ij}).$$

Using the probability mass function of a Bernoulli random variable and noting that the probability matrix $P = (\vec{x}_i^\top \vec{x}_j)_{ij}$ we derive:

$$Pr_\theta(A) = \prod_{j>i} \left(\vec{x}_i^\top \vec{x}_j\right)^{a_{ij}} \left(1 - \vec{x}_i^\top \vec{x}_j\right)^{1-a_{ij}}, \quad a_{ij} \sim Bern\left(\vec{x}_i^\top \vec{x}_j\right).$$

Probability equivalence classes exist for RDPGs, but their intuition is more complex than for ER and SBM models. We omit their explicit formulation here.

A.6.2 A Posteriori RDPG

The a posteriori RDPG introduces a new concept: the *intersection of the unit ball and the nonnegative orthant*. An orthant generalizes the concept of a two-dimensional quadrant to higher dimensions. The nonnegative orthant contains points where all of entries are nonnegative.

We define the d-dimensional *nonnegative orthant* as:

$$\left\{\vec{x} \in \mathbb{R}^d : x_i \geq 0 \text{ for all } i\right\}.$$

Figure A.6.1(A) shows the nonnegative orthant in two dimensions, corresponding to the upper right quadrant of the standard coordinate system.

The *Euclidean norm* for a point $\vec{x}$ with coordinates x_i for $i = 1, \ldots, d$ is defined as:

$$\|\vec{x}\|_2 = \sqrt{\sum_{i=1}^{d} x_i^2}.$$

The *closed Euclidean unit ball* is the set of points with Euclidean norm is at most 1:

$$\left\{ \vec{x} \in \mathbb{R}^d : \|\vec{x}\|_2 \le 1 \right\}.$$

Figure A.6.1(B) shows the two-dimensional unit ball.

The intersection of two sets A and B contains elements present in both sets:

$$A \cap B = \{x : x \in A, x \in B\}.$$

The intersection of the unit ball and the nonnegative orthant, denoted $\mathcal{X}_d$, is:

$$\mathcal{X}_d = \left\{ \vec{x} \in \mathbb{R}^d : \|\vec{x}\|_2 \le 1, x_k \ge 0 \text{ for all } k \right\}.$$

Figure A.6.1(C) illustrates $\mathcal{X}_d$ in dark grey. $\mathcal{X}_d$ has a crucial property: For any $\vec{x}$ and $\vec{y}$ in $\mathcal{X}_d$, their inner product $\langle \vec{x}, \vec{y} \rangle = \vec{x}^\top \vec{y}$ is bounded between 0 and 1. This property stems from the Cauchy–Schwartz inequality and the characteristics of $\mathcal{X}_d$.

The Cauchy–Schwartz inequality states that $\langle \vec{x}, \vec{y} \rangle$ can be at most the product of $\|\vec{x}\|_2$ and $\|\vec{y}\|_2$:

$$\langle \vec{x}, \vec{y} \rangle \le \|\vec{x}\|_2 \|\vec{y}\|_2.$$

Since vectors in $\mathcal{X}_d$ have norms at most 1, their inner product cannot exceed 1. Additionally, as $\mathcal{X}_d$ lies in the the nonnegative orthant, the inner product of its vectors can never be negative.

The a posteriori RDPG extends the a priori RDPG analogously to the relationship between the a posteriori SBM and the a priori SBM. Instead of knowing the latent position matrix X, we know the distribution characterizing individual latent positions. The parameter for the a posteriori RDPG is shown in the following table.

Parameter	Space	Description
F	Vector distribution	Distribution governing each latent position on $\mathcal{X}_d$

The parameter F is an *inner-product distribution* defined on $\mathcal{X}_d$. F has a key property: The inner product of any two of its vectors must be a probability. Formally, for any $\vec{x}_i, \vec{x}_j \in \mathcal{X}_d$, $0 \le \vec{x}_i^\top \vec{x}_j \le 1$. This property is crucial as $\vec{x}_i^\top \vec{x}_j$ represents the probability of an edge in the adjacency matrix.

In the a posteriori RDPG, the latent position matrix is a matrix-valued random variable. We denote the random latent position for node i as $\mathbf{x}_i$. Each $\mathbf{x}_i$ is sampled independently and identically from the inner-product distribution F. The random latent-position matrix $\mathbf{X}$ comprises these latent vectors $\mathbf{x}_i$ for all n nodes.

The edge model for the a posteriori RDPG is conditioned on this unobserved latent-position matrix:

1. For $j > i$, given $\mathbf{x}_i = \vec{x}$ and $\mathbf{x}_j = \vec{y}$, $\mathbf{a}_{ij}$ follows a $Bern(\vec{x}^\top \vec{y})$ distribution.
2. The network is undirected: $\mathbf{a}_{ji} = \mathbf{a}_{ij}$ for $i < j$.
3. The network is loopless: $\mathbf{a}_{ii} = 0$ for all i.

We denote an a posteriori RDPG with parameter F as $\mathbf{A} \sim RDPG_n(F)$.

A.6.2.1 Probability

The probability calculation for the a posteriori RDPG is complex due to the unobservable nature of the latent position matrix $\mathbf{X}$. We must use integration to derive an expression for the probability.

We consider realizations of $\mathbf{X}$, where each row is $\vec{\mathbf{x}}_i \sim F$ independently. For simplicity, we assume that F is a discrete distribution on $\mathcal{X}_d$. This assumption simplifies notation without loss of generality; for continuous distributions, sums would be replaced by multivariate integrals, and probability mass functions would be replaced by probability density functions.

Let p denote the probability mass function F. We first employ the independence assumption:

$$Pr_\theta(A) = Pr_\theta(\mathbf{A} = A) = \prod_{j>i} Pr(\mathbf{a}_{ij} = a_{ij}).$$

We then marginalize over the relevant rows of $\mathbf{X}$:

$$Pr(\mathbf{a}_{ij} = a_{ij}) = \sum_{\vec{x} \in \mathcal{X}_d} \sum_{\vec{y} \in \mathcal{X}_d} Pr(\mathbf{a}_{ij} = a_{ij}, \vec{\mathbf{x}}_i = \vec{x}, \vec{\mathbf{x}}_j = \vec{y}).$$

We can further simplify this expression using conditional probability and the independence of latent positions:

$$Pr(\mathbf{a}_{ij} = a_{ij}, \vec{\mathbf{x}}_i = \vec{x}, \vec{\mathbf{x}}_j = \vec{y}) = Pr(\mathbf{a}_{ij} = a_{ij}|\vec{\mathbf{x}}_i = \vec{x}, \vec{\mathbf{x}}_j = \vec{y})Pr(\vec{\mathbf{x}}_i = \vec{x}, \vec{\mathbf{x}}_j = \vec{y}).$$

Given the independence of $\vec{x}_i$ and $\vec{x}_j$:

$$Pr(\vec{\mathbf{x}}_i = \vec{x}, \vec{\mathbf{x}}_j = \vec{y}) = Pr(\vec{\mathbf{x}}_i = \vec{x})Pr(\vec{\mathbf{x}}_j = \vec{y}).$$

Therefore:

$$Pr(\mathbf{a}_{ij} = a_{ij}, \vec{\mathbf{x}}_i = \vec{x}, \vec{\mathbf{x}}_j = \vec{y}) = Pr(\mathbf{a}_{ij} = a_{ij}|\vec{\mathbf{x}}_i = \vec{x}, \vec{\mathbf{x}}_j = \vec{y})Pr(\vec{\mathbf{x}}_i = \vec{x})Pr(\vec{\mathbf{x}}_j = \vec{y}).$$

Conditional on $\vec{\mathbf{x}}_i = \vec{x}_i$ and $\vec{\mathbf{x}}_j = \vec{x}_j$, $\mathbf{a}_{ij}$ follows a $Bern(\vec{x}_i^\top \vec{x}_j)$ distribution. Therefore:

$$Pr(\mathbf{a}_{ij} = a_{ij}|\vec{\mathbf{x}}_i = \vec{x}, \vec{\mathbf{x}}_j = \vec{y}) = (\vec{x}^\top \vec{y})^{a_{ij}}(1 - \vec{x}^\top \vec{y})^{1-a_{ij}}.$$

Combining these results:

$$Pr(\mathbf{a}_{ij} = a_{ij}, \vec{\mathbf{x}}_i = \vec{x}, \vec{\mathbf{x}}_j = \vec{y}) = (\vec{x}^\top \vec{y})^{a_{ij}}(1 - \vec{x}^\top \vec{y})^{1-a_{ij}} Pr(\vec{\mathbf{x}}_i = \vec{x})Pr(\vec{\mathbf{x}}_j = \vec{y}).$$

So our complete expression for the probability is:

$$Pr_\theta(A) = \prod_{j>i} \sum_{\vec{x} \in \mathcal{X}_d} \sum_{\vec{y} \in \mathcal{X}_d} (\vec{x}^\top \vec{y})^{a_{ij}}(1 - \vec{x}^\top \vec{y})^{1-a_{ij}} Pr(\vec{\mathbf{x}}_i = \vec{x})Pr(\vec{\mathbf{x}}_j = \vec{y}).$$

A.7   Generalized Random Dot Product Graph (GRDPG)

The generalized random dot product graph (GRDPG) represents the most general random network model in this book. It addresses a key limitation of the RDPG model.

In the RDPG, the probability matrix $P = XX^\top$. As discussed in Section 4.5, this constrains P to be positive semidefinite, limiting the types of network structure that can be modeled. The GRDPG overcomes this restriction.

A.7.1   A priori GRDPG

The a priori GRDPG assumes known latent position matrix X and *signature* (p,q). Its parameters are as follows.

Parameter	Space	Description
X	$\mathbb{R}^{n \times d}$	The matrix of latent positions for each node n
p,q	$[d]$	The signature of the GRDPG

X is similar to that in the RDPG, with each row $\vec{x}_i$ representing the d-dimensional latent position of node i.

The *signature* (p,q) defines the matrix $I_{p,q}$, where $p + q = d$:

$$I_{p,q} = \begin{bmatrix} I_p & 0_{p \times q} \\ 0_{q \times p} & -I_q \end{bmatrix},$$

where I_n denotes the n-dimensional identity matrix. The generative model for the a priori GRDPG is:

1. For all $j \neq i$, $\mathbf{a}_{ij} \sim Bern(\vec{x}_i^\top I_{p,q} \vec{x}_j)$ independently.
2. For loopless networks, $\mathbf{a}_{ij} = 0$ for all i.

We denote an a priori GRDPG with latent positions X and signature (p,q) as $\mathbf{A} \sim GRDPG_n(X)$ with signature p and q.

A.7.2   A Posteriori GRDPG

The a posteriori GRDPG closely resembles the a posteriori RDPG, with two parameters, as follows.

Parameter	Space	Description
F	vector distribution	A distribution which governs each latent position defined on $\mathcal{X}_d$
p,q	$[d]$	The signature of the GRDPG

In this model, the latent position matrices are treated as latent variable matrices. The latent positions are sampled independently and identically from F.

The edge model for the a posteriori GRDPG is conditioned on the unobserved latent-position matrices:

1. For $j \neq i$, given $\vec{\mathbf{x}}_i = \vec{x}$ and $\vec{\mathbf{x}}_j = \vec{y}$, $\mathbf{a}_{ij}$ follows a $Bern(\vec{x}^\top I_{p,q} \vec{y})$ distribution independently.
2. Assuming a loopless network, $\mathbf{a}_{ii} = 0$ for all i.

We denote an a posteriori GRDPG with parameter F and signature (p, q) as $\mathbf{A} \sim GRDPG_n(F)$ with signature p and q.

A.8   Inhomogeneous Erdös–Rényi (IER)

Previous models characterized edge-existence probabilities using fewer than $\binom{n}{2}$ parameters. This simplification stems from the practical challenge of estimating $\binom{n}{2}$ different probabilities, especially for large networks. With a single network observation, estimating unique probabilities for each edge is infeasible. Furthermore, assuming edges share no common properties limits our ability to characterize underlying structures, such as the latent positions in RDPGs.

The inhomogeneous Erdös–Rényi (IER) represents the most general form of independent-edge random networks. An IER random network is defined by a single parameter:

Parameter	Space	Description
P	$[0, 1]^{n \times n}$	The edge probability matrix

The probability matrix P is an $n \times n$ matrix with entries p_{ij} between 0 and 1. For simple networks, P is symmetric. The generative model for IER networks resembles previous models:

1. For $j > i$, edges $\mathbf{a}_{ij}$ are independent $Bern(p_{ij})$ random variables.
2. $\mathbf{a}_{ii} = 0$ for all i (loopless network).
3. $\mathbf{a}_{ji} = \mathbf{a}_{ij}$ (undirected network).

We denote an IER network $\mathbf{A}$ with probability matrix P as $\mathbf{A} \sim IER_n(P)$.

All previously discussed models are special cases of the IER model. For instance, ER models use probability matrices with identical entries, while a priori RDPGs use probability matrices of the form $P = XX^\top$ for some $n \times d$ real matrix.

The IER random network represents the limit of stochastic block models as the number K of communities approaches the number of nodes n. An SBM where each node forms its own community is equivalent to an IER random network. In this case, the SBM block matrix B would have $n \times n$ unique entries. An SBM where each node forms its own community is exactly an IER, showing that the IER is a limiting case of SBMs.

A.8.0.1   Probability

The probability for an IER random network uses the independence assumption and the p.m.f. of a Bernoulli-distributed random variable $\mathbf{a}_{ij}$:

$$Pr_\theta(A) = Pr(\mathbf{A} = A)$$
$$= \prod_{j>i} p_{ij}^{a_{ij}}(1 - p_{ij})^{1-a_{ij}}.$$

Bibliography

[1] Athreya A, Fishkind DE, Tang M, Priebe CE, Park Y, Vogelstein JT, et al. Statistical inference on random dot product graphs: A survey. J. Mach. Learn. Res. 2017 Jan.;18(1): 8393–8484.

[2] Chung J, Bridgeford E, Arroyo J, Pedigo BD, Saad-Eldin A, Gopalakrishnan V, et al. Statistical connectomics. Ann. Rev. Stat. Appl. 2021 Mar.;8(1):463–492.

[3] Rubin-Delanchy P, Cape J, Tang M, Priebe CE. A statistical interpretation of spectral embedding: The generalised random dot product graph. J. R. Stat. Soc. Ser. B Stat. Methodol. 2022 Sep.;84(4):1446–1473.

Appendix B Learning Representations Theory

The network representation techniques introduced in the main text have substantial mathematical foundations. This appendix explores the theoretical underpinnings of these approaches. We cover:

1. Section B.1 presents the maximum likelihood estimation for ER and SBM models, and the limitations that necessitate spectral approaches for RDPGs (Section B.1).
2. Section B.2 discusses more advanced theoretical underpinnings of random dot product graphs and spectral embeddings for networks.
3. Section B.3 extends this advanced discussion to multiple network models and simultaneous spectral embeddings of multiple networks.

B.1   The Basics of Maximum Likelihood Estimation

This section introduces *maximum likelihood estimation* (MLE), a fundamental technique for estimating probability distributions given data. We explain why MLE provides desirable estimators for learning about random networks from network-valued datasets. For a thorough overview of statistical inference, see [1].

Random networks, $\mathbf{A}$, are distinct from their observations A. This limitation poses a challenge for network scientists: How can we make useful claims about an underlying property (characterized by $\mathbf{A}$) when we only observe one (or a few) samples of it (in the form of A)?

MLE addresses this challenge by estimating properties of random variables using only the available data. In network statistics, this often means working with a single sample assumed to be a realization of the random variable of interest. The properties we aim to learn are called estimands.

The most useful property from Chapter 4 is the independent-edge assumption. For independent-edge random network models, we assume edges are independent, so from Equation (A.5):

$$Pr_\theta(\mathbf{A} = A) = \prod_{j>i} Pr_\theta(\mathbf{a}_{ij} = a_{ij}).$$

To illustrate the concept of MLE, consider a simple example. Suppose we flipped a coin 10 times and observed 6 heads, and we did not know whether the coin had an equal probability of heads or tails, 0.5, ahead of time. Our best guess of the heads probability would be $\frac{6}{10}$. MLE provides a formal basis for this optimal guess.

B.1.1   The Method of Maximum Likelihood Estimation (MLE)

Consider the coin flip example. We define the outcome of the ith coin flip as the random variable x_i, which takes one of two possible values: heads (1) or tails (0). We observe 10 total coin flips, with realizations denoted by x_i, with possible i ranging from 1 to 10. Our question of interest is: How do we estimate the probability of the coin landing on heads, without knowing the true probability value p?

Since x_i takes the value 1 or 0 with probability 0.5, we describe it as a $Bern(0.5)$ random variable. Sets of random variables are *identically distributed* if their underlying distributions are the same. As all 10 of our x_i are identically distributed, they share the same $Bernoulli(0.5)$ distribution.

We also assume the outcomes of the coin flips are mutually independent. This means the probability of observing all n outcomes simultaneously is the product of observing each outcome individually:

$$Pr_\theta(\mathbf{x}_1 = x_1, \ldots, \mathbf{x}_n = x_n) = \prod_{i=1}^{n} Pr_\theta(\mathbf{x}_i = x_i).$$

For a single coin flip, the probability of observing outcome i is, by definition of the Bernoulli distribution:

$$Pr_\theta(\mathbf{x}_i = x_i) = p^{x_i}(1 - p)^{1-x_i}.$$

Because x_i is either 0 or 1, $Pr_\theta(\mathbf{x}_i = x_i)$ is either p or $(1 - p)$. The notation Pr_θ indicates that the probability is a function of the parameter set θ for the random variable $\mathbf{x}_i$. In this case, $\theta = p$, as p is the only parameter for each $\mathbf{x}_i$.

For n total outcomes, the probability is:

$$Pr_\theta(\mathbf{x}_1 = x_1, \ldots, \mathbf{x}_n = x_n) = \prod_{i=1}^{n} Pr(\mathbf{x}_i = x_i),$$

$$= \prod_{i=1}^{n} p^{x_i}(1 - p)^{1-x_i},$$

$$= p^{\sum_{i=1}^{n} x_i}(1 - p)^{n-\sum_{i=1}^{n} x_i}. \tag{B.1}$$

Consider the case of 10 coin flips and 6 heads. MLE provides a way to formalize that our guess of p, denoted $\hat{p}$, is 0.5. We define the *likelihood function* of our sequence $\mathcal{L}(p; x_1, \ldots, x_n)$ for a given value of the parameter p:

$$\mathcal{L}(p; x_1, \ldots, x_n) = Pr(\mathbf{x}_1 = x_1, \ldots, \mathbf{x}_n = x_n; p).$$

The term "; p" emphasizes that the probability of observing the data depends on the parameter p, which is equivalent to Equation (B.1) since the parameter $\theta = p$. The likelihood function reframes p as a variable, and our goal as how "likely" that variable is, given the observed data (which is fixed within the confines of our experiment). MLE finds the value of p that maximizes the likelihood. We can visualize the likelihood function for different values of p:

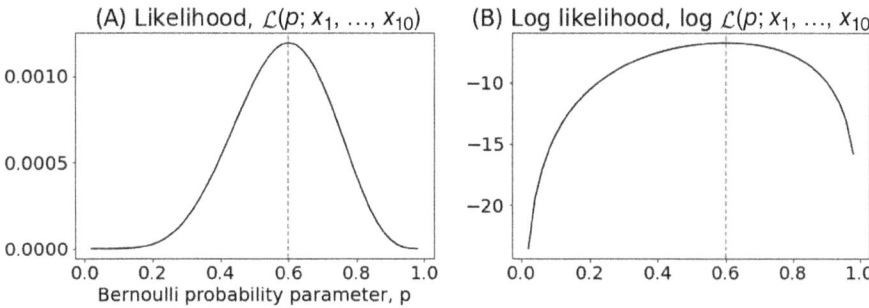

Figure B.1.1 (**A**) The likelihood for the coin flip example, with $p = 0.6$ in gray, and (**B**) the log likelihood for the coin flip example.

```
import numpy as np

p = np.linspace(.02, .98, num=49)
nflips = 10; nheads = 6
likelihood = p**(nheads)*(1 - p)**(nflips - nheads)
```

Figure B.1.1(A) illustrates the likelihood function for the coin flip example, with $p = 0.6$ highlighted in gray, and Figure B.1.1(B) shows its log likelihood. Our intuitive guess of $p = 0.6$ indeed corresponds to the MLE for the Bernoulli probability parameter p.

Maximizing the log likelihood often simplifies the problem. The log function is monotone, meaning if $x < y$, then $\log x < \log y$. Consequently, if p^* maximizes the likelihood, it also maximizes the log likelihood, as the monotonicity of the log function preserves critical points.

The log likelihood of Equation (B.1) (often abbreviated with ℓ instead of $\log \mathcal{L}$) is:

$$\ell(p; x_1, \ldots, x_n) = \log \mathcal{L}(p; x_1, \ldots, x_n) = \log \left[p^{\sum_{i=1}^{n} x_i} (1 - p)^{n - \sum_{i=1}^{n} x_i} \right],$$

$$= \sum_{i=1}^{n} x_i \log(p) + \left(n - \sum_{i=1}^{n} x_i \right) \log(1 - p).$$

We can compute the log likelihood in Python:

```
loglikelihood = nheads*np.log(p) + (nflips - nheads)*np.log(1 - p)
```

Figure B.1.1(B) illustrates the log likelihood. The maximizing probability (gray) is the same for both the likelihood and log likelihood, despite the dissimilar appearance of the two plots. At the maximum, the slope of the tangent line is 0, a critical point of the function.

To find the maximal point of the log likelihood function with respect to variable p:

1. Take the derivative of the log likelihood with respect to p.
2. Set it equal to 0 and solve for the critical point p^*.
3. Verify that the critical point p^* is indeed an estimate of a maximum, $\hat{p}$.

Using the result derived above, and the facts that $\frac{d}{du}\log(u) = \frac{1}{u}$ and $\frac{d}{du}\log(1-u) = -\frac{1}{1-u}$:

$$\frac{d}{dp}\ell(p;x_1,\ldots,x_n) = \frac{\sum_{i=1}^n x_i}{p} - \frac{n - \sum_{i=1}^n x_i}{1-p} = 0,$$

$$\Rightarrow \frac{\sum_{i=1}^n x_i}{p} = \frac{n - \sum_{i=1}^n x_i}{1-p},$$

$$\Rightarrow (1-p)\sum_{i=1}^n x_i = p\left(n - \sum_{i=1}^n x_i\right),$$

$$\sum_{i=1}^n x_i - p\sum_{i=1}^n x_i = pn - p\sum_{i=1}^n x_i,$$

$$\Rightarrow p^* = \frac{1}{n}\sum_{i=1}^n x_i.$$

To confirm p^* as an estimate of a maximum, we would take the second derivative and verify that it is negative at p^*. We omit this step here. For bounded parameters, we would also check the extreme values (0 and 1) to ensure they are not potential maximums. As p^* satisfies these conditions, it serves as our maximum likelihood estimate. By convention, we denote estimates with a hat, so this value becomes $\hat{p}$.

With 6 heads in 10 outcomes, the MLE is therefore:

$$p^* = \hat{p} = \frac{6}{10} = 0.6.$$

This result aligns with our intuition.

This simple example illustrates parameter estimation via MLE in its most basic form. As scenarios become more complex, particularly with network-valued data, effective parameter estimation becomes increasingly challenging.

B.1.2   MLE for ER

Section A.3 derived the probability (and likelihood) for network realizations A where $A \sim ER_n(p)$:

$$Pr_\theta(A) = p^m \cdot (1-p)^{\binom{n}{2}-m}.$$

Here, $m = \sum_{i<j} a_{ij}$ represents the total edge count in network A. Following our approach for the coin example and noting that $\mathcal{L}(\theta; A) = Pr_\theta(A)$:

$$\ell(\theta; A) = \log\left[p^m \cdot (1-p)^{\binom{n}{2}-m}\right],$$

$$= m\log p + \left(\binom{n}{2} - m\right)\log(1-p). \tag{B.2}$$

Taking the derivative with respect to p and setting it to zero yields:

$$\frac{d}{dp}\ell(\theta; A) = \frac{m}{p} - \frac{\binom{n}{2} - m}{1-p} = 0,$$

$$\Rightarrow p^* = \frac{m}{\binom{n}{2}}.$$

The second derivative at p^* is negative, confirming that p^* maximizes the likelihood. We denote this maximum likelihood estimate as $\hat{p}$:

$$\hat{p} = \frac{m}{\binom{n}{2}}.$$

This formula for computing an estimate from the data is called an *estimator*. The resulting quantity, when computed from actual data, is an *estimate*. An estimator may be a random quantity if the data are unknown, while an estimate is a specific realization of the estimator for a given network.

B.1.2.1   Studying Sampling Distributions of Estimators

To study an estimator such as the ones we obtain via MLE, we must make a significant assumption: The observed network A is a realization of a random network $\mathbf{A}$ with quantifiable properties. This leads to a typical statistical inference process:

1. Develop a plausible statistical model for the data. This is embodied as a model for $\mathbf{A}$ (e.g., $\mathbf{A} \sim ER_n(p)$).
2. Create an estimator for a relevant quantity (the *estimand*) within that model. The estimand will typically be a parameter (e.g., p for an ER network).
3. Analyze the estimator's properties within the assumed model's context for $\mathbf{A}$.

After understanding the estimator's behavior, we can apply it to the observed data to draw conclusions about our network.

When assessing estimator performance, we often use the notation $\hat{\boldsymbol{\theta}}_n$, where n denotes the sample size (in this case, the number of network nodes). For example, $\hat{\mathbf{p}}$ might be written as $\hat{\mathbf{p}}_n$ to highlight its dependence on node count. We are analyzing the estimator's properties within the context of the model for $\mathbf{A}$, a random variable. So, the estimator itself is also a random variable, since it is a function of a random variable (and therefore also bold-faced).

The difference between an estimator and a true underlying parameter is characterized by the estimator's sampling distribution. The *sampling distribution* of an estimator $\hat{\boldsymbol{\theta}}_n$ describes how estimates $\hat{\theta}_n$ vary across different realizations of the random network $\mathbf{A}$. The sampling distribution is fundamental to understanding estimator behavior.

B.1.2.2   Unbiasedness of the Estimator of the Probability Parameter for the ER Network

In an ideal scenario, repeating our experiment many times with new networks would yield probability estimates that, on average, equal the actual probability. In statistical theory, this concept is called estimator unbiasedness. An *unbiased estimator* for a parameter is expected to yield that parameter on average when estimating it using sample data. For an estimator $\hat{\boldsymbol{\theta}}_n$ and an underlying population parameter θ (the estimand), we express this as:

$$\mathbb{E}\left[\hat{\theta}_n\right] = \theta.$$

To clarify, unbiasedness does not imply that the estimate $\hat{p}_n$ equals the probability p. Generally, we do not expect our estimate to exactly match the true parameter. An unbiased estimator means that if we examined many realizations of $\mathbf{A}$, the average of the estimates would equal its true parameters.

When $\mathbf{A}$ is an $ER_n(p)$ random network, our estimate for its p parameter is:

$$\hat{p}_n = \frac{m}{\binom{n}{2}}$$

and the underlying estimator (which is a function of the random network $\mathbf{A}$) is:

$$\hat{\mathbf{p}}_n = \frac{m}{\binom{n}{2}}.$$

The number of edges in the random network, $\mathbf{m}$, is a function of the random variable $\mathbf{A}$.

To compute the expected value:

$$\mathbb{E}[\hat{\mathbf{p}}n] = \mathbb{E}\left[\frac{\mathbf{m}}{\binom{n}{2}}\right].$$

Since $\mathbf{A}$ has n nodes, $\frac{1}{\binom{n}{2}}$ is a constant, so we can factor it out:

$$\mathbb{E}[\hat{\mathbf{p}}n] = \frac{1}{\binom{n}{2}}\mathbb{E}[\mathbf{m}].$$

We defined m to be $\sum_{i<j} a_{ij}$, which also depends on our realization of $\mathbf{A}$, so it is random in the context of our estimator. Therefore:

$$\mathbb{E}[\mathbf{m}] = \mathbb{E}\left[\sum_{i<j} \mathbf{a}_{ij}\right].$$

Next, we use the linearity of expected value:

$$\mathbb{E}\left[\sum_{i<j} \mathbf{a}_{ij}\right] = \sum_{i<j}\mathbb{E}[\mathbf{a}_{ij}] = \sum_{i<j} p_{ij},$$

using the result from Section 4.6.2. Since we know that $p_{ij} = p$ for $ER_n(p)$ random networks:

$$\mathbb{E}[\mathbf{m}] = \binom{n}{2} p.$$

Putting this back together:

$$\mathbb{E}[\hat{\mathbf{p}}_n] = \frac{1}{\binom{n}{2}}\binom{n}{2} p = p.$$

Since $\mathbb{E}[\hat{\mathbf{p}}_n] = p$, our underlying estimand $\hat{\mathbf{p}}_n$ is unbiased for the underlying probability p.

Showing Unbiasedness with Simulations

We can demonstrate this property numerically using a parametric bootstrap, which allows us to examine the behavior of a function of a random variable when its distribution becomes complex. For example, consider two independent random variables $\mathbf{x}$ and $\mathbf{y}$, each following a standard normal distribution (mean 0, variance 1). While it may not be immediately apparent that $\mathbf{x}^2 + \mathbf{y}^2$ follows a χ-squared distribution with two degrees of freedom, we can use a parametric bootstrap to estimate properties of $\mathbf{x}^2 + \mathbf{y}^2$ through simulation. Let's simulate 1000 realizations of $\mathbf{x}$ and $\mathbf{y}$, then examine the behavior of their squares:

```python
import scipy as sp

# simulation of 1000 values from the N(0,1) distn
n = 1000
xs = np.random.normal(loc=0, scale=1, size=n)
ys = np.random.normal(loc=0, scale=1, size=n)
# compute the square
xssq = xs**2
yssq = ys**2
sum_xsq_ysq = xssq + yssq

# compute the centers for bin histograms from 0 to maxval in
# 30 even bins
nbins = 30
bincenters = np.linspace(start=0, stop=np.max(sum_xsq_ysq), num=nbins)

# compute the pdf of the chi-squared distribution for X^2 + Y^2, which
     when
# X, Y are N(0, 1), is Chi2(2), the chi-squared distn with 2 degrees
     of freedom
dof = 2
true_pdf = sp.stats.chi2.pdf(bincenters, dof)
```

Figure B.1.2(A) plots a normalized histogram of `sum_xsq_ysq` (black bars) against the true distribution of $\mathbf{x}^2 + \mathbf{y}^2$ (gray line). The histogram represents the approximate density of $\mathbf{x}^2 + \mathbf{y}^2$ estimated using the parametric bootstrap, while the gray line shows the exact density. These align almost perfectly.

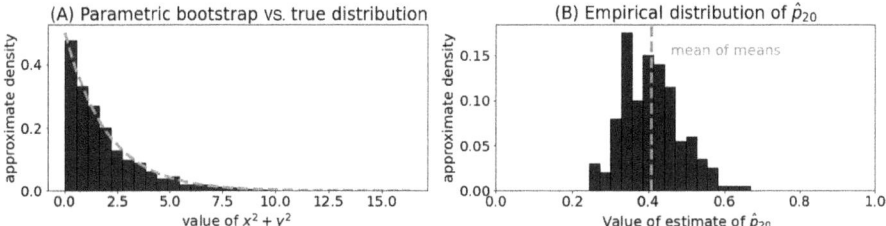

Figure B.1.2 **(A)** A comparison of the density from a parametric bootstrap (black) and the χ-squared distribution (gray), and **(B)** the distribution of $\hat{\mathbf{p}}_n$ computed via a parametric bootstrap (black) with the mean of the estimates (gray).

To compute the mean of $x^2 + y^2$, we can use the parametric bootstrap samples:

```
print("Approximate mean: {:2f}".format(np.mean(sum_xsq_ysq)))
# mean of chi-squared is just its degrees of freedom; here, 2
print("True mean: {:2f}".format(2))
```

This approach approximates the mean without requiring the complex derivation to prove that $x^2 + y^2$ follows a χ-squared distribution with two degrees of freedom.

Computing exact distributions for estimators becomes significantly more challenging when dealing with networks and functions of networks. Parametric bootstraps offer a straightforward visualization technique to verify intuition without extensive numerical derivation.

For a given n, we aim to obtain a distribution for the probability parameter, $\hat{\mathbf{p}}_n$. We simulate 100 network realizations of $\mathbf{A}$ following $ER_{20}(0.4)$ (20 nodes with edge probability 0.4). For each network j, we estimate the probability parameter $\hat{p}^{(j)}$. A histogram of these $\hat{p}^{(j)}$ values approximates the distribution of $\hat{\mathbf{p}}_{20}$:

```
import graspologic as gp

n = 10 # number of nodes
nsims = 200 # number of networks to simulate
p = 0.4

# realizations
As = [gp.simulations.er_np(n, p, directed=False, loops=False) for i in
    range(0, nsims)]
# fit ER models
fit_models = [gp.models.EREstimator(directed=False,
    loops=False).fit(A) for A in As]
hatps = [model.p_ for model in fit_models] # the probability parameters
```

Figure B.1.2(B) displays the distribution of $\hat{\mathbf{p}}_{20}$ as a histogram of `hatps`, along with the true probability parameter and the mean of `hatps`.

The mean of the estimates closely approximates the underlying probability for the random networks, $p = 0.4$. With more simulations, we expect this mean to converge even closer to $p = 0.4$. This empirical result demonstrates the unbiasedness property of $\hat{\mathbf{p}}_n$ that we proved rigorously earlier.

B.1.2.3   Consistency of the Estimator of the Probability Parameter in an ER Random Network

While unbiasedness is valuable, its statement is limited: It guarantees only that the average of repeated estimates over infinite experiments would equal the true probability. In practice, we often observe only one network. A more desirable property would be that our estimator $\hat{\mathbf{p}}_n$ of the underlying parameter p is reliable when we collect sufficient data.

This property is called *asymptotic consistency*, or simply consistency. An estimator is asymptotically consistent if it converges in probability to the true underlying parameter as the number of network nodes increases.

Mathematically, asymptotic consistency means that for any $\epsilon > 0$, $Pr(|\hat{\mathbf{p}}_n - p| > \epsilon) \to 0$ as the number of nodes approaches infinity. In other words, given a sufficiently large network, probability estimates will be arbitrarily close to the network's true probability p.

To prove this statement, we begin by computing the variance of $\hat{\mathbf{p}}_n$. Using the definition of $\hat{\mathbf{p}}_n$:

$$\mathrm{var}(\hat{\mathbf{p}}_n) = \mathrm{var}\left(\frac{\mathbf{m}}{\binom{n}{2}}\right).$$

Since the variance of a constant times a random quantity is that constant squared times the variance of the random quantity:

$$\mathrm{var}(\hat{\mathbf{p}}_n) = \frac{1}{\binom{n}{2}^2} \mathrm{var}(\mathbf{m}).$$

We need the variance of $\mathbf{m}$, where $\mathbf{m} = \sum_{i<j} \mathbf{a}_{ij}$. For independent-edge random networks, the $\mathbf{a}_{ij}$ are independent, so the variance of their sum is the sum of their variances:

$$\mathrm{var}(\hat{\mathbf{p}}_n) = \frac{1}{\binom{n}{2}^2} \sum_{i<j} \mathrm{var}(\mathbf{a}_{ij})$$

All edges have the same probability p and thus the same distribution, so their variances are identical. There are $\binom{n}{2}$ possible edges where $i < j$, so:

$$\mathrm{var}(\hat{\mathbf{p}}_n) = \frac{1}{\binom{n}{2}^2} \cdot \binom{n}{2} \mathrm{var}(\mathbf{a}_{ij})$$

$$= \frac{1}{\binom{n}{2}} \mathrm{var}(\mathbf{a}_{ij}). \tag{B.3}$$

Now we compute the variance of $\mathbf{a}_{ij}$. Recall that $\mathrm{var}(\mathbf{x}) = \mathbb{E}[(\mathbf{x} - \mathbb{E}[\mathbf{x}])^2]$:

$$\mathrm{var}(\mathbf{a}_{ij}) = \mathbb{E}[(\mathbf{a}_{ij} - \mathbb{E}[\mathbf{a}_{ij}])^2].$$

We know $\mathbb{E}[\mathbf{a}_{ij}] = p$, so:

$$\mathrm{var}(\mathbf{a}_{ij}) = \mathbb{E}[(\mathbf{a}_{ij} - p)^2] = \mathbb{E}[\mathbf{a}_{ij}^2 - 2p\mathbf{a}_{ij} + p^2].$$

Using linearity of expectation and that p^2 and $2p$ are constant:

$$\mathrm{var}(\mathbf{a}_{ij}) = \mathbb{E}[\mathbf{a}_{ij}^2] - 2p\mathbb{E}[\mathbf{a}_{ij}] + p^2 = \mathbb{E}[\mathbf{a}_{ij}^2] - 2p^2 + p^2, \quad \mathbb{E}[\mathbf{a}_{ij}] = p$$
$$= \mathbb{E}[\mathbf{a}_{ij}^2] - p^2.$$

We need the second moment of $\mathbf{a}_{ij}$. Using the law of total expectation:

$$\mathbb{E}[\mathbf{a}_{ij}^2] = \sum_{a \in 0, 1} a^2 \cdot Pr(\mathbf{a}_{ij} = a).$$

Since $\mathbf{a}_{ij}$ is 0 with probability $(1 - p)$ and 1 with probability p:

$$\mathbb{E}[\mathbf{a}_{ij}^2] = 1^2 \cdot p + 0^2 \cdot (1 - p) = p.$$

Therefore:

$$\text{var}(\mathbf{a}_{ij}) = p - p^2 = p \cdot (1 - p).$$

Combining this with Equation (B.3):

$$\text{var}(\hat{\mathbf{p}}_n) = \frac{1}{\binom{n}{2}} \cdot p(1 - p) = \frac{p(1 - p)}{\binom{n}{2}}. \tag{B.4}$$

We complete this proof using Chebyshev's inequality. For a random variable $\mathbf{x}$ with finite mean $\mathbb{E}[\mathbf{x}] = \mu$ and finite variance σ^2, *Chebyshev's inequality* states that for any $k > 0$:

$$Pr(|\mathbf{x} - \mu| \geq k\sigma) \leq \frac{1}{k^2}.$$

Chebyshev's inequality upper-bounds the probability that the difference between a random quantity and its mean μ exceeds $k\sigma$. For continuous random variables, the distinction between $\geq$ (from Chebyshev's inequality) and $>$ (from our original goal) is often negligible (see also Remark B.1.1).

Noting that σ is a constant parameter of $\hat{\mathbf{p}}_n$, and setting $k = \frac{\epsilon}{\sigma}$ with the mean of $\hat{\mathbf{p}}_n$ being p, we get:

$$Pr\left(|\hat{\mathbf{p}}_n - p| \geq \frac{\epsilon}{\sigma}\sigma\right) \leq \frac{1}{\left(\frac{\epsilon}{\sigma}\right)^2},$$

$$\leq \frac{\sigma^2}{\epsilon^2},$$

where σ^2 is the variance of $\hat{\mathbf{p}}_n$. Using the result from Equation (B.4) for σ^2:

$$Pr\left(|\hat{\mathbf{p}}_n - p| \geq \epsilon\right) \leq \frac{p(1 - p)}{\binom{n}{2}\epsilon^2},$$

$$\leq \frac{1}{\binom{n}{2}}\frac{p(1 - p)}{\epsilon^2},$$

where p and ϵ are constants. Recalling that $\binom{n}{2} = \frac{1}{2}n(n - 1)$:

$$Pr\left(|\hat{\mathbf{p}}_n - p| \geq \epsilon\right) \leq \frac{1}{n(n - 1)}\frac{2p(1 - p)}{\epsilon^2}.$$

As n grows, this upper-bound approaches zero. Because probabilities are non-negative and the probability is upper-bounded by something converging to zero, the probability itself must also approach zero. This is known as the "sandwich theorem," because the probability is "sandwiched" between an upper-bound and its natural lower bound of zero.

Therefore, $Pr(|\hat{\mathbf{p}}_n - p| \geq \epsilon) \to 0$ as n approaches infinity, demonstrating that $\hat{p}_n$ is asymptotically consistent.

> **Remark B.1.1** Finer points of $\geq$ and $>$ when illustrating asymptotic consistency
>
> The original statement for asymptotic consistency used $> \epsilon$, whereas our proof used $\geq \epsilon$. The distinction is negligible here due to the arbitrariness of ϵ and the continuity of $\hat{\mathbf{p}}_n$. For a detailed discussion, consult a probability theory textbook such as [2].

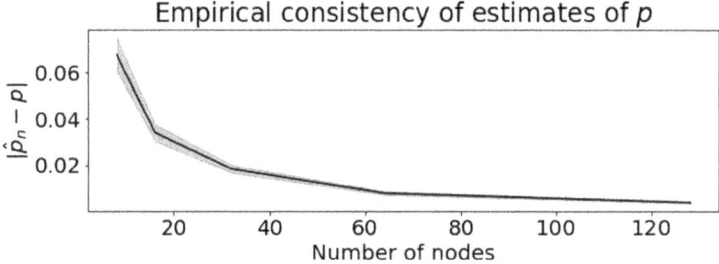

Figure B.1.3 A plot of the average difference $|\hat{p}_n - p|$ (solid black line), and the range in which 95 percent of the empirical samples fall (gray ribbon).

Showing Consistency with Simulations

Asymptotic consistency describes the limiting behavior of $\hat{\mathbf{p}}_n$ as n grows. We must consider multiple choices of n to demonstrate that the difference $|\hat{\mathbf{p}}_n - p|$ diminishes with high probability as n increases.

We select n as powers of 2 from $2^3 = 8$ to $2^7 = 128$. For each n, we perform 100 simulations, each yielding an estimate of the probability. This simulation may take several minutes:

```
from pandas import DataFrame
ns = [8, 16, 32, 64, 128]
nsims = 200
p = 0.4
results = []
for n in ns:
  for i in range(0, nsims):
    A = gp.simulations.er_np(n, p, directed=False, loops=False)
    phatni = gp.models.EREstimator(directed=False,
        loops=False).fit(A).p_
    results.append({"n": n, "i": i, "phat": phatni})
res_df = DataFrame(results)
res_df["diff"] = np.abs(res_df["phat"] - p)
```

Figure B.1.3 displays the results. The solid line represents the sample empirical average difference $|\hat{p}_n - p|$, estimating $\mathbb{E}[|\hat{\mathbf{p}}_n - p|]$. The gray ribbon encompasses the middle 95 percent of the empirical differences. As the number of nodes increases, the difference between $\hat{p}_n$ and p decreases, evident in both the decreasing average difference and the narrowing gray ribbon. This trend towards zero demonstrates that for any ϵ, we can find a sufficiently large n such that $|\hat{\mathbf{p}}_n - p|$ exceeds ϵ with very low probability, empirically supporting asymptotic consistency.

B.1.3   MLE for SBM

For a realization A of a random network $\mathbf{A} \sim SBM_n(\vec{z}, B)$ (an a priori SBM), we derived the probability:

$$Pr_\theta(A) = \prod_{k,k' \in [K]} b_{k'k}^{m_{k'k}} \cdot (1 - b_{k'k})^{n_{k'k} - m_{k'k}},$$

where $n_{k'k} = \sum_{i<j} \mathbb{1}_{z_i=k} \mathbb{1}_{z_j=k'}$ represents the number of possible edges between nodes in community k and k', and $m_{k'k} = \sum_{i<j} \mathbb{1}_{z_i=k} \mathbb{1}_{z_j=k'} a_{ij}$ represents the number of edges in the realization A between nodes within communities k and k'.

The log likelihood of $Pr_\theta(A)$, equal to the log of the probability above, is:

$$\ell(\theta; A) = \sum_{k,k' \in [K]} \left[m_{k'k} \log b_{k'k} + (n_{k'k} - m_{k'k}) \log(1 - b_{k'k}) \right].$$

Each block (between communities k and k') behaves similarly to an ER network; note the similarities between this expression and Equation (B.2). The a priori SBM resembles a collection of communities of ER networks. Taking the partial derivative of $\log Pr_\theta(A)$ with respect to any probability term $b_{l'l}$ reveals:

$$\frac{\partial}{\partial b_{l'l}} \ell(\theta; A) = \frac{\partial}{\partial b_{l'l}} \sum_{k,k' \in [K]} m_{k'k} \log b_{k'k} + (n_{k'k} - m_{k'k}) \log(1 - b_{k'k}),$$

$$= \sum_{k,k' \in [K]} \frac{\partial}{\partial b_{l'l}} \left[m_{k'k} \log b_{k'k} + (n_{k'k} - m_{k'k}) \log(1 - b_{k'k}) \right].$$

For summands where $k \neq l$ and $k' \neq l'$, the partial derivative with respect to $b_{l'l}$ is 0:

$$\frac{\partial}{\partial b_{l'l}} \left[m_{k'k} \log b_{k'k} + (n_{k'k} - m_{k'k}) \log(1 - b_{k'k}) \right] = 0,$$

as the quantity to the right of the partial derivative is not a function of $b_{l'l}$. Therefore:

$$\frac{\partial}{\partial b_{l'l}} \ell(\theta; A) = 0 + \frac{\partial}{\partial b_{l'l}} \left[m_{l'l} \log b_{l'l} + (n_{l'l} - m_{l'l}) \log(1 - b_{l'l}) \right]$$

$$= \frac{m_{l'l}}{b_{l'l}} - \frac{n_{l'l} - m_{l'l}}{1 - b_{l'l}} = 0,$$

$$\Rightarrow b_{l'l}^* = \frac{m_{l'l}}{n_{l'l}}.$$

Omitting the second derivative test and a test of the extremes of $\hat{b}_{l'l}$ (0 or 1), we conclude that the MLE of the block matrix B for an a priori SBM random network $\mathbf{A}$ is the matrix $\widehat{B}$ with entries:

$$\hat{b}l'l = \frac{ml'l}{n_{l'l}}.$$

B.1.3.1 Consistency and Unbiasedness of the Estimate for the Probability Parameter in an a priori SBM Network

The estimator of the probability parameter $\hat{b}l,l'$ is unbiased and consistent for the probability bl,l', similar to the argument made for the probability parameter $\hat{p}$ in an ER network. The key difference lies in the need for these statements to apply to each community in the SBM. The unbiasedness result for the a priori SBM closely resembles that of the ER random network.

B.1.4 MLEs for Other Flavors of Random Networks

The standard a priori SBM has several variations, such as the a priori degree-corrected SBM (DCSBM). The approaches described here apply to these SBM variants as well. While we do not provide explicit proofs to minimize mathematical complexity, readers are encouraged to consider how to obtain reasonable (unbiased and consistent) estimates for the parameters of these models. As a starting point, the MLE of the degree correction for a node i is:

$$\hat{\theta}_i = \frac{d_i}{m}$$

where d_i represents the node degree of node i, and m represents the total number of nodes in the network. This estimator would then be incorporated into the likelihood function for the DCSBM, facilitating the determination of the MLE for each block probability.

B.1.5 Limitations of MLE for a posteriori Models and Random Dot Product Graphs

The a posteriori SBM introduces additional complexity with its pair of parameters: the block matrix, B, and the community probability vector, $\vec{\pi}$. The log likelihood for an a posteriori SBM is:

$$\mathcal{L}(\theta; A) = \sum_{\vec{\tau} \in \mathcal{T}} \prod_{k=1}^{K} \left[\pi_k^{n_k} \cdot \prod_{k'=1}^{K} b_{k'k}^{m_{k'k}} (1 - b_{k'k})^{n_{k'k} - m_{k'k}} \right].$$

Taking the logarithm yields:

$$\ell(\theta; A) = \log \left(\sum_{\vec{\tau} \in \mathcal{T}} \prod_{k=1}^{K} \left[\pi_k^{n_k} \cdot \prod_{k'=1}^{K} b_{k'k}^{m_{k'k}} (1 - b_{k'k})^{n_{k'k} - m_{k'k}} \right] \right).$$

While the logarithm of a product simplifies to a sum of logarithms, no such simplification exists for the logarithm of a sum. Consequently, finding a closed-form expression for an MLE becomes extremely complex. Similar challenges arise when applying MLE to the RDPG or other sophisticated network models.

Approximation techniques, such as expectation maximization (EM), offer potential strategies for estimating the maximum likelihood. However, we opt instead for spectral methods, introduced in Chapter 5, which provide comparable performance with less computational complexity.

B.2   Theoretical Considerations for Spectral Embeddings

This section requires a firm understanding of linear algebra, matrix analysis, and multivariate probability theory. While we have introduced some concentration inequalities in Appendix B.1, readers should understand how these concepts extend to random vectors and matrices. We recommend reviewing the primer [3] on concentration inequalities before proceeding. For more detailed derivations, see [4].

Disclaimer about Classical Statistical Asymptotic Theory
Network analysis presents unique challenges for deriving large sample properties of estimators. The concept of sample size becomes ambiguous in network settings. In classical statistics, sample size typically refers to the number of independent observations, such as poll participants. Networks, however, consist of interdependent edges formed by interactions between nodes.

Nodes are often the sampled units in network analysis. Yet each additional node introduces a new set of interactions with existing nodes, often necessitating more parameters in the model. Recent literature has addressed some of these challenges for the models and estimators introduced in Chapter 5.

B.2.1   Adjacency Spectral Embedding

This section summarizes important results on spectral embeddings, focusing on the theoretical properties of the adjacency spectral embedding (ASE) introduced in Section 5.3. The utility of `ase` is clarified in the context of the RDPG model from Section 4.4. For a more formal treatment of RDPGs, refer to Appendix A.6. For a comprehensive review of these results, see [4] and [5].

Our analysis examines how effectively spectral embedding methods estimate the latent positions of a random network generated from the RDPG model. Ideally, these embeddings should closely approximate the true latent positions. The results presented here demonstrate that these estimates converge to the true positions as the network size increases. Furthermore, we characterize the limiting distribution of these estimates, analogous to classical central limit theorems in statistics.

Consider a random adjacency matrix $\mathbf{A} \sim RDPG_n(F)$, where the latent positions $\vec{\mathbf{x}}_i \overset{iid}{\sim} F$ for all nodes i. Recall from Appendix A.6 that F is a distribution supported on the intersection of the unit ball and the nonnegative orthant.

We express the latent position matrix as $\mathbf{X} = [\vec{\mathbf{x}}_1, \ldots, \vec{\mathbf{x}}_n]^\top$, where row i contains the vector $\vec{\mathbf{x}}_i \in \mathbb{R}^d$ representing the latent position of node i. The upper-triangular entries of $\mathbf{A}$ are independent with probability:

$$Pr(\mathbf{a}_{ij} = 1) = \vec{\mathbf{x}}_i^\top \vec{\mathbf{x}}_j, \qquad \text{for all } i < j.$$

We denote the d-dimensional adjacency spectral embedding of $\mathbf{A}$ as $\widehat{\mathbf{X}} = \mathtt{ase}(\mathbf{A}, d) \in \mathbb{R}^{n \times d}$.

B.2.1.1 Statistical Error of the Adjacency Spectral Embedding

Consistency

The latent position matrix $\mathbf{X}$ of network $\mathbf{A}$ encodes crucial node properties, such as community assignments and the latent geometry characterizing edge probabilities (as noted in Section 5.3). The proximity between true and estimated latent positions (obtained from $\mathtt{ase}$) depends on several factors.

Comparing estimated and true latent positions presents an unavoidable challenge: the nonidentifiability problem of random dot product graphs (see Concept 5.5.5). Given a matrix $\mathbf{X}$, we can find another matrix $\mathbf{Y} \in \mathbb{R}^{n \times d}$ producing the same edge probability matrix:

$$\mathbf{P} = \mathbf{X}\mathbf{X}^\top = \mathbf{Y}\mathbf{Y}^\top.$$

Generally, if the columns of $\mathbf{X}$ are linearly independent, all matrices $\mathbf{Y}$ satisfying this relation are equal up to a linear transformation by an orthogonal matrix. Specifically, there exists a matrix $\mathbf{W}$ of size $d \times d$ such that $\mathbf{Y} = \mathbf{X}\mathbf{W}$, where $\mathbf{W}$ satisfies $\mathbf{W}^\top \mathbf{W} = \mathbf{I}$. These transformations include rotations in $\mathbb{R}^d$, reflections, or combinations thereof, all preserving inner products and maintaining relative distances between latent positions. For example, changing the signs of $\mathbf{X}$'s columns (reflection) does not alter the inner products of their rows, leaving matrix $\mathbf{P}$ unaffected.

To ensure the columns of $\mathbf{X}$ are linearly independent with high probability, we make a technical assumption: The second moment matrix $\Delta = \mathbb{E}[\vec{\mathbf{x}}_i \vec{\mathbf{x}}_i^\top] \in \mathbb{R}^{d \times d}$ has nonzero eigenvalues. This condition simplifies the types of nonidentifiabilities we may encounter, as the probability of having correlated columns in $\mathbf{X}$ becomes negligible for sufficiently large n.

The first result we examine concerns the error of the adjacency spectral embedding ($\mathtt{ase}$) method, which is the difference between $\mathbf{X}$ and the estimated latent position matrix $\widehat{\mathbf{X}}$. This estimator consistently estimates the latent positions: As the sample size (number of nodes) increases, the estimated latent positions converge to the true latent positions. We can quantify the typical distance between these matrices explicitly in terms of the sample size n, the dimension of the latent positions d, and a constant c that depends only on the distribution of the latent positions F.

Specifically, with probability approaching one as n approaches infinity, the largest distance between the true and estimated latent positions satisfies:

$$\max_{i \in [n]} \left| \widehat{\vec{\mathbf{x}}}_i - \mathbf{W}\vec{\mathbf{x}}_i \right| \leq \frac{c\sqrt{d} \log^2 n}{\sqrt{n}}.$$

Here, $\mathbf{W} \in \mathbb{R}^{d \times d}$ is an orthogonal matrix (dependent on $\widehat{\mathbf{X}}$ and $\mathbf{X}$) that accounts for the nonidentifiability of the latent positions. This equation demonstrates that the true and estimated latent positions (after an appropriate orthogonal transformation) are uniformly close to each other and converge as n increases. We use the term "uniformly close" because the constant c applies to all n nodes. Note that the error rate also depends on the model dimension d; as d increases, the parameter space expands, leading to increased estimation error.

Asymptotic Normality

A further result on the asymptotic properties of $\mathtt{ase}$ concerns the distribution of the estimation error – the difference between the estimated latent position $\widehat{\vec{\mathbf{x}}}_i$ (for a given node i) and the true parameter $\vec{\mathbf{x}}_i$. While consistency ensures this difference shrinks with n (after proper orthogonal transformation), more precise quantification of this difference is necessary for certain statistical tasks, such as hypothesis testing or confidence interval estimation, which require knowledge of the estimation error's distributional properties.

Distributional results for the rows of the adjacency spectral embedding demonstrate that the error in estimating true latent positions converges to a mixture of multivariate normal distributions as the network size grows. Specifically, the difference between $\widehat{\mathbf{X}}$ and $\mathbf{X}$, after a proper orthogonal transformation $\mathbf{W}_n \in R^{d \times d}$ converges to this mixture distribution.

We can express the multivariate cumulative distribution function for a given vector $\vec{z} \in \mathbb{R}^d$ as:

$$Pr\left(\sqrt{n}\left(\widehat{\vec{\mathbf{x}}}_i - \mathbf{W}_n \vec{\mathbf{x}}i\right) \leq \vec{z}\right) \xrightarrow[n \to \infty]{} \int \mathbb{R}^d \, \Phi_d\left(\vec{z}, \Sigma(\vec{\mathbf{x}})\right) \, dF(\vec{\mathbf{x}}),$$

where $\Phi_d(\cdot, \Sigma(\vec{\mathbf{x}}))$ is the cumulative distribution function of a d-dimensional multivariate normal distribution with zero mean and covariance matrix $\Sigma(\vec{\mathbf{x}}) \in \mathbb{R}^{d \times d}$. The integral on the right-hand side operates over all possible values of $\vec{\mathbf{x}} \in \mathbb{R}^d$, integrated with respect to the distribution of the latent positions, which are sampled independently from F. The covariance matrix $\Sigma(\vec{\mathbf{x}})$ depends on a specific latent position value $\vec{\mathbf{x}} \in \mathbb{R}^d$, and is given by:

$$\Sigma(\vec{\mathbf{x}}) = \Delta^{-1} \mathbb{E}\left[\vec{\mathbf{x}}_i \vec{\mathbf{x}}_i^\top \left(\vec{\mathbf{x}}^\top \vec{\mathbf{x}}_i - \left(\vec{\mathbf{x}}^\top \vec{\mathbf{x}}_i\right)^2\right)\right] \Delta^{-1}.$$

For certain distribution classes, this expression can be further simplified to yield a more specific form of the asymptotic distribution of $\widehat{\vec{\mathbf{x}}}_i$. For instance, in an a priori stochastic block model, $\widehat{\vec{\mathbf{x}}}_i$ can only take a finite number of different values, and the distribution F has mass points on these values, allowing for an explicit formula for the covariance matrix and asymptotic distribution.

The two results presented in this section establish the fundamental properties of adjacency spectral embedding under the RDPG model. However, these findings extend beyond this particular method and model. Researchers have developed extensions of these results to encompass a broader class of network models, including the GRDPG [6].

Similar results exist for other embedding methodologies. For example, the Laplacian spectral embedding (LSE, introduced in Section 5.4) exhibits properties analogous to $\mathtt{ase}$, namely consistent estimates with known asymptotic distributions. However, the precise formulation of these theorems for LSE is more complex.

A working example of spectral convergence concepts as they relates to Erdös–Rényi networks is provided in Online Appendix D.1.

B.2.2 Application: Two-Network Hypothesis Testing

The results previously discussed demonstrate that the true and estimated latent positions are close to each other, and in fact, their distance gets smaller as n increases. As such, ase provides an accurate estimator of the latent positions. This result justifies the use of $\widehat{X}$ in place of X for subsequent inference tasks, such as community detection, vertex nomination, or classification. The theoretical results for ase have multiple implications. One of them is that the estimated latent positions carry almost the same information as the true latent positions, and we can even quantify how different they are. This is particularly useful for performing statistical inference tasks about node properties. Here we consider one of these tasks: two-sample hypothesis testing [7].

Comparing the distribution of two populations is a frequent problem in statistics and across multiple domains. In classical statistics, a typical strategy to perform this task is to compare the mean of two populations by using an appropriate test statistic. Theoretical results on the distribution of this statistic (either exact or asymptotic) are then used to derive a measure of uncertainty for this problem (such as p-values or confidence intervals). Similarly, when comparing two observed networks, we may wonder whether they were generated by the same mechanism. The results discussed before have been used to develop valid statistical tests for two-network hypothesis testing questions.

A network hypothesis test for the equivalence between the latent positions of a pair of networks with aligned nodes can be constructed by using the estimates of the latent positions. Formally, let X, Y be the latent position matrices, and define $\mathbf{A} \sim RDPG(X)$, $\mathbf{B} \sim RDPG(Y)$ as independent random adjacency matrices. We can test whether the two networks have the same distribution by comparing their latent positions via a hypothesis test of the form:

$$H_0: X =_W Y \qquad \text{against} \qquad H_a: X \neq_W Y,$$

where $\mathbf{X} =_W Y$ denotes that X and Y are equivalent up to an orthogonal matrix $W \in \mathcal{O}_d$, where $\mathcal{O}_d$ is the set of $d \times d$ orthogonal matrices. Since we do not have access to the true latent positions, we can use the estimates $\widehat{X}$ and $\widehat{Y}$ to construct a test statistic. This test statistic is defined as

$$t = \frac{\min_{W \in \mathcal{O}_d} \|\widehat{X}W - \widehat{Y}\|_F}{\sqrt{d\gamma^{-1}(A)} + \sqrt{d\gamma^{-1}(B)}}.$$

Here, $\|\widehat{X}W - \widehat{Y}\|_F$ is the Frobenius distance between the estimated latent positions (after adjusting for the nonidentifiability). This distance compares how similar the two latent positions are. It is therefore natural to think that larger values of this distance will give more evidence against the null hypothesis.

The test statistic also incorporates a normalizing constant of the form $\sqrt{d\gamma^{-1}(A)} + \sqrt{d\gamma^{-1}(B)}$. Here $\sigma_1(A) \geq \cdots \geq \sigma_n(A) \geq 0$ denote the singular values of A (similarly for B), $\delta(A) = \max_{i \in [n]} \sum_{j=1}^{n} a_{ij}$ denotes the largest observed degree of the network, and

$$\gamma(A) = \frac{\sigma_d(A) - \sigma_{d+1}(A)}{\delta(A)}$$

is a constant that standardizes the test statistic. It can be shown under appropriate regularity conditions that, under the null hypothesis, this test statistic will remain bounded with high probability by a constant that depends on the significance level of the test, and will diverge with n for some specific alternatives. Thus, t provides a way to construct a consistent test for the hypothesis testing problem described above.

B.3   Theory for Multiple Network Models

Models for multiple network data often assume that there is a known one-to-one correspondence between the nodes of the networks. If this correspondence is unknown, an estimate can be obtained via graph matching (Section 7.3). Once the nodes are correctly matched, models for multiple networks exploit the shared structure across the networks to obtain accurate estimates. In this section we review theoretical challenges in these circumstances. Excellent academic survey papers such as [8; 9; 10] span this problem space.

Given a pair of network adjacency matrices $\mathbf{A}$ and $\mathbf{B}$ with n nodes each (but possibly permuted), the graph matching problem seeks to align the networks by identifying the correct correspondence between their nodes. This alignment can be achieved by finding a permutation matrix $\mathbf{P}$ of size $n \times n$ that makes the networks $\mathbf{A}$ and $\mathbf{P}^\top \mathbf{B} \mathbf{P}$ similar.

Many methods exist to perform graph matching. Here we focus on the following optimization problem (which is reviewed more thoroughly in Section 7.3):

$$\widehat{\mathbf{P}} = \mathrm{argmin}_{\mathbf{P}} \|\mathbf{A} - \mathbf{P}^\top \mathbf{B} \mathbf{P}\|_F^2.$$

The accuracy of node matching across networks depends on this estimated permutation matrix $\widehat{\mathbf{P}}$. We denote by $\mathbf{P}^*$ the true permutation matrix that aligns the two networks, which is the object we aim to estimate. In principle, if a unique solution exists that gives $\mathbf{A} = (\mathbf{P}^*)^\top \mathbf{B} \mathbf{P}^*$, the two networks are isomorphic (i.e., equal up to some permutation of the nodes), and matching the nodes across the networks is possible. However, in the presence of noise (which is typically the case), the networks are not isomorphic, and hence the solution to the optimization problem above becomes more relevant.

The literature has studied the feasibility of finding the correct matching under different random network models, including correlated Erdös–Rényi networks. This section reviews some of the results for the correlated Erdös–Rényi (ER) model described in 4.9.3 and developed in [11].

The correlated ER model has two parameters: the edge probability and the correlation across a pair of networks. These parameters are crucial in understanding the feasibility of solving the graph matching problem. The edge probability controls the amount of information present in each network. If it is close to zero, the information available to match the networks is low, making the problem harder. The correlation parameter controls the level of similarity across the networks. A large correlation value facilitates network matching, as the edges exhibit similar or exactly the same patterns in both networks. Formally, given parameters $q \in (0, 1)$ and $\rho \in [-1, 1]$, the $n \times n$ adjacency matrices $\mathbf{A}$ and $\mathbf{B}$ are distributed as correlated ER random networks if each network is marginally distributed as an ER of the form $\mathbf{A} \sim ER_n(q_n)$, $\mathbf{B} \sim ER_n(q_n)$, but the edge pairs satisfy $\mathrm{corr}(\mathbf{a}_{ij}, \mathbf{b}_{ij}) = \rho$. If $\rho = 0$, the networks are independent realizations of an ER network with no common structure between them. If $\rho = 1$, the networks are isomorphic. We denote the two networks as $\mathbf{A}, \mathbf{B} \sim \rho ER_n(q_n)$.

Having defined the model, we next consider whether the solution of the graph matching optimization problem (defined in Concept 7.3.4) recovers the correct solution. Under the correlated ER model, this recovery is possible when the correlation between the networks and the edge probability are sufficiently large.

Formally, if $\rho \geq c_1 \sqrt{\frac{\log n}{n}}$ and $q_n \geq c_2 \frac{\log n}{n}$, for two positive fixed constants c_1 and c_2, the solution of the graph matching problem is correct with high probability when the graphs are sufficiently large. These conditions ensure that the correlation across the networks is large enough to provide sufficient shared information, while the edge density is sufficiently above zero to ensure enough edges within each network. Stronger versions of this result have been developed to study sharp information thresholds for the exact recovery of the matching solution. While finding the solution of the graph matching optimization problem is NP-hard, many efficient algorithms with theoretical guarantees on exact recovery have been developed in recent years. These topics, however, are beyond the scope of this book [12].

B.3.1 Joint Spectral Embeddings

B.3.1.1 Omnibus Embedding (omni)

The omnibus embedding described in Section 5.5.4 jointly estimates the latent positions under the joint random dot product network (JRDPG) model, which is discussed in Section 4.9.1. Briefly, the model is $\{\mathbf{A}^{(1)}, \ldots, \mathbf{A}^{(M)}\} \sim JRDPG_{n,M}(\mathbf{X}_n)$, where the rows of $\mathbf{X}_n \in \mathbb{R}^{n \times d}$ are iid samples from some distribution F with realizations in $\mathbb{R}^d$. Let $\mathbf{O} \in \mathbb{R}^{Mn \times Mn}$ be the omnibus matrix of $\mathbf{A}^{(1)}, \ldots, \mathbf{A}^{(m)}$ and $\widehat{\mathbf{Z}}_n = \mathrm{ase}(\mathbf{O}, d) \in \mathbb{R}^{mn \times d}$.

Under this setting, it can be shown that the rows of $\widehat{\mathbf{Z}}_n$ are a consistent estimator of the latent positions of each individual network as $n \to \infty$, and that:

$$\max_{i \in [n], m \in [M]} \left\| (\widehat{\mathbf{Z}}_n)_{(m-1)n+i} - \mathbf{W}_n(\mathbf{X}_n)_i \right\| \leq \frac{c\sqrt{M} \log(Mn)}{\sqrt{n}} \tag{B.5}$$

for some constant c. In words, this illustrates that the estimated latent positions $(\mathbf{Z}_n)_{(m-1)n+i}$ (a vector) for a given network m and a given node i are uniformly close to the underlying latent position matrix $(\mathbf{X}_n)_i$, with respect to the same orthogonal transform $\mathbf{W}_n$ across all networks. The omnibus embeddings for each network are therefore "aligned" to one another (since they are all aligned to the underlying latent positions up to the same orthogonal transformation).

Furthermore, a central limit theorem for the rows of the omnibus embedding asserts that:

$$\lim_{n \to \infty} Pr\left\{\sqrt{n}\left(\mathbf{W}_n(\widehat{\mathbf{Z}}_n)_{(m-1)n+i} - (\mathbf{X}_n)_i\right) \leq \vec{z}\right\} = \int_{\mathbb{R}^d} \Phi\left(\vec{z}, \widehat{\Sigma}(\vec{\mathbf{x}})\right) dF(\vec{\mathbf{x}}), \quad \text{(B.6)}$$

for some covariance matrix $\widehat{\Sigma}(\mathbf{x})$. For more details, check out the original paper at [13].

B.3.1.2   Multiple Adjacency Spectral Embedding (mase)

The $COSIE$ model described in Section 4.9.2 gives a joint model that characterizes the distribution of multiple networks with expected probability matrices that share the same common invariant subspace. The mase algorithm in Section 5.5.3 is a consistent estimator for this common invariant subspace, and results in asymptotically normal estimators for the individual symmetric matrices. Specifically, let $\mathbf{S}_n \in \mathbb{R}^{n \times d}$ be a matrix with orthonormal columns (that is, $\mathbf{S}^\top \mathbf{S} = \mathbf{I}_d$) and $\mathbf{R}_n^{(1)}, \ldots, \mathbf{R}_n^{(M)} \in \mathbb{R}^{d \times d}$ score matrices such that $\mathbf{P}_n^{(l)} = \mathbf{S}_n \mathbf{R}_n^{(l)} \mathbf{S}_n^\top \in [0,1]^{n \times n}$, $(\mathbf{A}_n^{(1)}, \ldots, \mathbf{A}_n^{(M)}) \sim COSIE_{n,M}\left(\mathbf{S}_n; \mathbf{R}_n^{(1)}, \ldots, \mathbf{R}_n^{(M)}\right)$, and $\widehat{\mathbf{S}}_n, \widehat{\mathbf{R}}_n^{(1)}, \ldots, \widehat{\mathbf{R}}_n^{(1)}$ be the estimators obtained by mase. Under appropriate regularity conditions and sufficient enough signal on each network, the estimate for $\mathbf{S}_n$ is consistent as $n, M \to \infty$, and there exists some constant $c > 0$ such that:

$$\mathbb{E}\left[\min_{\mathbf{W} \in \mathcal{O}_d} \left\|\widehat{\mathbf{S}}_n - \mathbf{S}_n \mathbf{W}\right\|_F\right] \leq c\left(\sqrt{\frac{1}{Mn}} + \frac{1}{n}\right), \quad \text{(B.7)}$$

where $\mathcal{O}_d$ is the set of d-dimensional orthogonal matrices. In other words, the expected difference between the shared latent positions and the true latent positions (up to an optimal orthogonal transformation) shrinks as the number of nodes and number of networks increases.

In addition, the entries of $\widehat{\mathbf{R}}_n^{(m)}$, $m \in [M]$ are asymptotically normally distributed. Namely, there exists a sequence of orthogonal matrices $\mathbf{W}_n$ such that:

$$\frac{1}{\sigma_{m,j,k}}\left(\widehat{\mathbf{R}}_n^{(m)} - \mathbf{W}_n^\top \mathbf{R}_n^{(m)} \mathbf{W}_n + \mathbf{H}_M^{(m)}\right)_{jk} \xrightarrow{\mathcal{D}} \mathcal{N}(0,1),$$

as $n \to \infty$, where: $\mathbb{E}[\|\mathbf{H}_M^{(m)}\|] = \mathcal{O}\left(\frac{d}{\sqrt{M}}\right)$ and $\sigma_{m,j,k}^2 = \mathcal{O}(1)$. In other words, the entries of $\widehat{\mathbf{R}}_n^{(m)}$ are normally distributed about the underlying score matrices $\mathbf{R}_i^{(m)}$ when properly oriented by the orthogonal matrix $\mathbf{W}$, where this orthogonal transformation is the same across all networks. For more details about the mase algorithm, see [14].

Bibliography

[1] Casella G, Berger RL. Statistical Inference. Boston, MA, USA: Cengage Learning; 2001.

[2] Durrett R. Probability: Theory and Examples. 2nd ed. Belmont, CA: Duxbury Press; 1996.

[3] Vershynin R. High-Dimensional Probability: An Introduction with Applications in Data Science. Cambridge, England, UK: Cambridge University Press; 2018.

[4] Athreya A, Fishkind DE, Tang M, Priebe CE, Park Y, Vogelstein JT, et al. Statistical inference on random dot product graphs: A survey. J. Mach. Learn. Res. 2017 Jan.;18(1): 8393–8484.

[5] Sussman DL, Tang M, Fishkind DE, Priebe CE. A consistent adjacency spectral embedding for stochastic blockmodel graphs. J. Am. Stat. Assoc. 2012 Sep.;107(499): 1119–1128.

[6] Rubin-Delanchy P, Cape J, Tang M, Priebe CE. A statistical interpretation of spectral embedding: The generalised random dot product graph. J. R. Stat. Soc. Ser. B Stat. Methodol. 2022 Sep.;84(4):1446–1473.

[7] Tang M, Athreya A, Sussman DL, Lyzinski V, Park Y, Priebe CE. A semiparametric two-sample hypothesis testing problem for random graphs. J. Comput. Graph. Stat. 2017 Apr.;26(2):344–354.

[8] Conte D, Foggia P, Sansone C, Vento M. Thirty years of graph matching in pattern recognition. Int. J. Pattern Recognit. Artif. Intell. 2004 May;18(03):265–298.

[9] Foggia P, Percannella G, Vento M. Graph matching and learning in pattern recognition in the last 10 years. Int. J. Pattern Recognit. Artif. Intell. 2013 Oct.;28(01):1450001.

[10] Yan J, Yin XC, Lin W, Deng C, Zha H, Yang X. A Short Survey of Recent Advances in Graph Matching. In: ICMR '16: Proceedings of the 2016 ACM on International Conference on Multimedia Retrieval. New York, NY, USA: Association for Computing Machinery; 2016, pp. 167–174.

[11] Lyzinski V, Fishkind DE, Priebe CE. Seeded graph matching for correlated Erdös–Rényi graphs. J. Mach. Learn. Res. 2014 Jan.;15(1):3513–3540.

[12] Pedarsani P, Grossglauser M. On the privacy of anonymized networks. In: ACM Conferences. New York, NY, USA: Association for Computing Machinery; 2011, pp. 1235–1243.

[13] Levin K, Athreya A, Tang M, Lyzinski V, Priebe C. A Central Limit Theorem for an Omnibus Embedding of Multiple Random Dot Product Graphs. In: 2017 IEEE International Conference on Data Mining Workshops (ICDMW). 2017.

[14] Arroyo J, Athreya A, Cape J, Chen G, Priebe CE, Vogelstein JT. Inference for multiple heterogeneous networks with a common invariant subspace. J. Mach. Learn. Res. 2021;22(142):1–49.

Appendix C Overview of Machine Learning Techniques

This appendix contains useful intuition for machine learning techniques that are used without introduction in the main content of the book.

1. Section C.1 discusses details about the silhouette score.

C.1   The Silhouette Score and Unsupervised Clustering Quality

The silhouette score [1] provides a statistic for comparing clusterings with different numbers of clusters. At its core, the silhouette score measures how similar nodes in the same cluster are to nodes in other clusters. For a given number of clusters, spatially distinct groupings (neither too many clusters for a single group of points, nor too few clusters for multiple distinct groups) tend to yield higher silhouette scores. This statistic is particularly useful because it can be applied to any unsupervised learning technique without restrictive assumptions. In contrast, other popular techniques like the Bayesian information criterion (BIC) require specific assumptions about the underlying data being clustered.

To compute the silhouette score, we require several components:

1. Data points x_i for i from 1 to n, representing the estimated latent positions of the network nodes.
2. Predicted community labels z_i, assigning each node to one of K possible clusters.
3. The set C_k, containing the indices of nodes assigned to cluster k. For example, in a ten-node network with two clusters where the first five nodes belong to cluster 1 and the last five to cluster 2, $C_1 = 1, 2, 3, 4, 5$ and $C_2 = 6, 7, 8, 9, 10$.
4. The quantity n_k, representing the total number of nodes in community k.

We then calculate:

1. The dissimilarity of a node i from other nodes in its community:

$$a_i = \frac{1}{n_k - 1} \sum_{j \in C_k, i \neq j} \|\vec{x}_i - \vec{x}_j\|.$$

Here, $|\vec{x}_i - \vec{x}_j|$ is the Euclidean distance between vectors $\vec{x}_i$ and $\vec{x}_j$. We compute distances over all nodes in community k except node i, then average by dividing by $n_k - 1$.

2. The dissimilarity of a node i from nodes in a different community:

$$b_{il} = \frac{1}{n_l} \sum_{j \in C_l} \| \vec{x}_i - \vec{x}_j \|.$$

For a node i in community k, we calculate its average distance from all nodes in some other community l.

3. The most similar alternative community for node i:

$$d_i = \min_{l \text{ is a community}} b_{il}.$$

This represents the community with the smallest dissimilarity from node i, i.e., the best alternative cluster assignment for i.

The silhouette score of node i in community k is then defined as:

$$s_i = \begin{cases} \frac{d_i - a_i}{\max(a_i, d_i)} & n_k > 1 \\ 0 & n_k = 1. \end{cases}$$

A silhouette value s_i near 1 indicates that node i is much more similar to points in its own cluster than to those in the best alternative cluster. Conversely, a value near -1 suggests that node i is more similar to points in a neighboring cluster than to those in its assigned cluster.

The overall silhouette score for K clusters is the average of the node-wise silhouettes:

$$\texttt{silhouette score}_K = \frac{1}{n} \sum_{i=1}^{n} s_i.$$

Bibliography

[1] Rousseeuw PJ. Silhouettes: A graphical aid to the interpretation and validation of cluster analysis. J. Comput. Appl. Math. 1987 Nov.;20:53–65.

Index

For EU product safety concerns, contact us at Calle de José Abascal, 56–1°,
28003 Madrid, Spain or eugpsr@cambridge.org.

www.ingramcontent.com/pod-product-compliance
Ingram Content Group UK Ltd.
Pitfield, Milton Keynes, MK11 3LW, UK
UKHW051542181225
466164UK00005B/204